Integrations of Clinical
and Social Psychology

Integrations of Clinical and Social Psychology

Edited by
GIFFORD WEARY
HERBERT L. MIRELS

Ohio State University

New York   Oxford
OXFORD UNIVERSITY PRESS
1982

Copyright © 1982 by Oxford University Press, Inc.

LIBRARY OF CONGRESS CATALOGING IN PUBLICATION DATA
Main entry under title:

Integrations of clinical and social psychology.

   Bibliography: p.
   Includes index.
   1. Psychology, pathological—Social aspects.
2. Psychotherapy—Social aspects.   3. Clinical
psychology—Social aspects.   I. Weary, Gifford,
1951–   .   II. Mirels, Herbert L., 1937–
RC455.I52   616.89   81–16896
ISBN 978-0-19-503051-8   AACR2

Printed in the United States of America

To our parents,
and to Ann and Aviva

PREFACE

> One achieves mental health to the extent that one becomes aware of one's interpersonal relations.
>
> Harry Stack Sullivan

The recognition that dysfunctional behaviors necessarily must be viewed within their social context has existed for many years. However, this concern with social contextual factors was more of a general philosophy than a "working" theoretical formulation that could be directly applied to the conceptualization of particular problems and treatments. More recently, a number of scholars (e.g., Brehm, 1976; Goldstein, Heller, & Sechrest, 1966) have begun to emphasize how specific theoretical perspectives and bodies of research findings in social psychology may be valuable to clinicians in therapeutic enterprises. In general, these writers have relied largely upon extrapolation from basic social psychological research to suggest hypotheses relevant to a variety of psychotherapeutic variables.

The present volume was undertaken because of the growing amount of work being done on social psychological factors involved not only in treatment activities, but also in attribution, development, and maintenance of maladaptive behavior patterns. We have attempted to bring together a collection of works which provide a broad sample of current research that bridges the areas of clinical and social psychology. We could not hope to represent the many individual strands of such integrative research and, consequently, have had to be somewhat selective. Each chapter deals with the application of various social psychological principles to clinical concerns. For example, how do beliefs about the nature of mental disorders influence such matters as who becomes a mental patient and how patients are treated? Do self-schemata of depressed and nondepressed people differ? Are there possible differences in depressives' and nondepressives' processing of personal information about others? Are symptoms forms of impression management? How are self-evaluative attitudes related to dysfunctional behavior and affective reactions? These and other questions are discussed in the following chapters.

The organization of the book is somewhat arbitrary. We begin with a discussion of methodological issues and possibilities in clinical-social research. The subsequent chapters, which are concerned with theoretical and empirical issues, have been organized into three main sections dealing with social psychological processes involved in clinical judgments, the development of maladaptive behaviors, and treatment. The volume concludes with an examination of the current status and possible future directions of integrative clinical-social research.

A number of people have contributed valuable assistance in the planning and execution of this project. At the volume's inception, John H. Harvey and several of the contributors to the book provided helpful advice. Marcus Boggs' counsel and encouragement were invaluable during the preparation and organization of the manuscripts. Patti Watson, Jami Christopher, and Sheryl Solomon provided a major contribution in the form of typing and technical assistance. We also would like to express our gratitude to the Department of Psychology at Ohio State University and to our faculty colleagues for various forms of assistance during the project.

Columbus, Ohio   G. W.
January 1982   H. L. M.

CONTENTS

Introduction: The Value of a Social Psychological Approach to Clinical Issues   3

ELLEN J. LANGER

one
DEVELOPING THE INTEGRATION OF CLINICAL AND SOCIAL PSYCHOLOGY   7

1. The Application of Social Psychology to Clinical Practice: A Range of Possibilities   9

   SHARON S. BREHM AND TIMOTHY W. SMITH

two
SOCIAL PSYCHOLOGICAL PROCESSES IN CLINICAL JUDGMENT   25

2. "Everyday" versus Normative Models of Clinical and Social Judgment   27

   NANCY CANTOR

3. Beliefs About Mental Disorders: Findings and Implications   48

   AMERIGO FARINA AND JEFFREY D. FISHER

4. Commentary: Social Psychological Processes in Clinical Judgment   72

   JERRY S. WIGGINS

three
SOCIAL PSYCHOLOGICAL PROCESSES IN THE DEVELOPMENT OF MALADAPTIVE BEHAVIORS   77

5. Self-reference and Person Perception in Depression: A Social Cognition Perspective   79

   NICHOLAS A. KUIPER, PAUL A. DERRY, AND MICHAEL R. MACDONALD

6. Symptoms as Self-handicapping Strategies: The Virtues of Old Wine in a New Bottle   104

   C. R. SNYDER AND TIMOTHY W. SMITH

7. Selection and Processing of Self-Evaluative Information: Experimental Evidence and Clinical Implications   128

   J. SIDNEY SHRAUGER

8. Depression and Deviance   154

   DAN COATES AND BARBARA A. PETERSON

9. Commentary: Social Psychological Processes in the Development of Maladaptive Behaviors   171

   STEVEN A. KOPEL

four
SOCIAL PSYCHOLOGICAL APPROACHES TO CLINICAL INTERVENTION STRATEGIES   179

10. Emerging Integrations of Clinical and Social Psychology: A Clinician's Perspective   181

    STANLEY R. STRONG

11. Effort Justification in Psychotherapy   214

    JOEL COOPER AND DANNY AXSOM

12. A Social Psychological Approach to Hypnotic Behavior   231

    NICHOLAS P. SPANOS

13. Social Support, Adjustment and the Elderly Spinal Cord Injured: A Social Psychological Analysis   272

    RICHARD SCHULZ AND SUSAN DECKER

14. Commentary: The Social Psychology of Clinical Intervention: Applied Precision or Useful Perspectives?   287

    PHILIP R. COSTANZO

five
CONCLUSION 295

15. The Integrations of Clinical and Social Psychology: Current Status and Future Directions   297

    GIFFORD WEARY, HERBERT L. MIRELS, AND JOHN S. JORDAN

Index   303

Integrations of Clinical
and Social Psychology

Introduction

THE VALUE OF A SOCIAL PSYCHOLOGICAL APPROACH TO CLINICAL ISSUES

ELLEN J. LANGER
HARVARD UNIVERSITY

One cannot understand the individual without knowing the group. One cannot appreciate the boundaries of the group without knowing the deviations of its individual members. To the extent that this proposition is true, it is surprising that clinical and social psychology have not been as inextricably bound in practice as they would seem to be in theory. While there is clearly reliance of each field on the other, this book deals primarily with ways in which clinical psychology is dependent upon social psychology.

The etiology of all psychopathology is necessarily social in nature. One cannot judge what is deviant in behavior (physiological or overt motor behavior), cognitions, or emotions without an appreciation of what the larger group is doing, thinking, or feeling. To deviate obviously means to deviate from something, and it implicitly is the clinician's job to assess what that something is. If everyone in the client's culture is turning to the right and the client is turning to the left, that seemingly trivial deviation may indicate extreme pathology. Similarly, the seemingly most extreme negative behavior would not indicate pathology if the entire culture were performing it. The group from which the client comes, then, is crucial to the understanding of which behaviors are maladaptive and need changing and which are not and therefore may remain unchanged. But often explicit reference to this group is ignored. Instead, assumptions about this group are implicitly made and are part of the clinician's valuable intuitions that help in his or her diagnosis. When the client comes from the same subculture as the therapist, this process presents no problem and implicit assumptions will work. When he or she does not, it may be quite another story.

Assume, for example, that a potential patient, an elderly woman, enters a clinician's office and complains that people, including her own children, are "out to get me and are driving me crazy!" She may instantiate and say, for example, that her daughter is trying to freeze her out of their home—"Every time I turn the thermostat up, she turns it down!"—and that once a week her son-in-law tries to poison her. Without knowledge about the (immediately relevant) group from which this individual comes, an accurate assessment is almost precluded. The evaluation will not be improved by contrasting this person's behavior with that of other patients of the clinician's (unless they are part of the same group from which she derives her identity) nor by comparing this person with the clinician's nonpatient associates and friends.

What is needed are an appreciation of the psychological context of the behavior and an understanding of the accepted limitations, values, and goals of the group with whom the behaver identifies. Behavior originates with reference to a particular social milieu. However, often the external environment changes so that the behavior seems no longer to be demanded by the situation. When this pronounced change occurs, quite normative behavior may appear strangely atypical. It is for this reason that it would behoove the therapist to question *explicitly* the client's reference groups and first try to make sense out of the behavior before labeling it maladaptive.

Clearly, therapists already do something like this, regardless of their particular theoretical bent. For example, if the elderly woman in our example were Catholic and her son-in-law were Jewish, the therapist, no doubt, would understand why she thought his attempts to have her eat meat instead of fish on Friday felt to her as though the son-in-law were trying to kill her. But even after this was cleared up, it would seem that she had serious problems—after all, there was that issue with her daughter.

There are several reasonable ways a therapist could deal with this issue. But what form would a social psychological approach take? While that surely would vary from psychologist to psychologist, all probably would begin by gathering information about the client's group and by asking how this behavior (being "excessively" cold) may be normal. By first taking the behavior at face value, one would soon learn that with age there *typically* comes a heightened sensitivity to temperature. The solution to the problem, then, becomes rather straightforward: The elderly mother should either dress more heavily or the daughter should dress more lightly. Now real problems that may have nothing to do with paranoia may be therapeutically addressed.

Thus, cultural considerations may be of paramount importance in arriving at appropriate diagnoses. In light of this influence, one may ask why the therapist cannot question the client about her or his culture/subculture during the intake interview so that these cultural considerations may be gotten out of the way early, before they cloud important personal issues. Regrettably, even if the therapist asks, the individual will rarely know the answer. That which is pervasive in a culture is often taken for granted by the individual group members. That which is known is known usually because outgroups have made it known. Therefore, it is not very likely that the individual will reveal a stereotype that the therapist does not already know.

Knowledge of the groups from which the client comes is only the start of a social psychological analysis. Such an analysis must include consideration of the possibility that the behavior in question is situation-determined even—or perhaps especially—when it is characteristic of the group as a whole. Behavior that is situational in origin is amenable to change. And, as many of the chapters in the present volume illustrate, the key to change lies in social variables, such as normal expectations, attributions, and social comparisons, attitudes, and values.

All of the theories of social psychology are relevant to clinical issues. Many of them

INTRODUCTION

are discussed in this fine book. For example, Cantor (Chapter 2) reviews the considerable literature concerned with models of social judgment processes and presents evidence suggesting that the processes underlying social and clinical judgments are analogous. In addition, chapters by Snyder and Smith, Farina and Fisher, Strong, and Schulz and Decker reveal the importance of attributional processes in the development, maintenance, and treatment of deviant behaviors. Research by Cooper and Axsom (Chapter 11) indicates the importance of dissonance arousal and reduction in psychotherapy. In fact, if we put the clinical implications aside, this book could stand by itself as a very updated text in applied social psychology. Given that and the persuasive way the clinical issues are worked into the individual chapters, all that is left to accomplish is that this social theory find its way into clinical practice.

one

DEVELOPING THE INTEGRATION OF CLINICAL AND SOCIAL PSYCHOLOGY

The chapter in this section presents a range of possible methodological approaches that could be used to investigate the application of social psychological principles to clinical practice. As Brehm and Smith point out, most of the previous discussions of the application of social psychology to clinical endeavors have focused on the implications for clinical work that could be derived from existing social psychological laboratory research. While believing that laboratory research may well remain the best methodological strategy for testing specific theoretical issues drawn from social psychology, Brehm and Smith note that the findings of such research may or may not generalize to real-world clinical problems and settings. Accordingly, they describe and present examples of a number of alternative strategies that may be useful in evaluating the validity of laboratory research and in the application of social psychology to clinical practice.

1

THE APPLICATION OF SOCIAL PSYCHOLOGY TO CLINICAL PRACTICE: A RANGE OF POSSIBILITIES

SHARON S. BREHM
TIMOTHY W. SMITH
UNIVERSITY OF KANSAS

The notion that social psychological theory and research could be applied to clinical practice and thereby increase our clinical effectiveness has been with us for a long time. The "father of social psychology," Kurt Lewin, addressed the dynamics of various clinical states (e.g., mental retardation and children's emotional disturbance). Numerous other writers since (e.g., Brehm, 1976; Carson, 1969; Frank, 1961, 1973; Goldstein, Heller, & Sechrest, 1966; Sheras & Worchel, 1979; Winett, 1970) have proposed the utility of this application, and both editions (1971 and 1978) of the *Handbook of Psychotherapy and Behavior Change* have included a chapter on social psychological approaches. This plethora of suggestions has not, however, translated very much into actual usage. As any examination of what clinicians actually do can show us, the amount of talk about social psychological applications has far exceeded implementation of these ideas.

It is likely that this failure on the part of clinicians to apply social psychological theory and research stems in large part from the way in which social psychological findings have been communicated. Basic theoretical work in social psychology is, of course, usually published in social psychological journals, and these journals are not widely read by practicing clinicians. Furthermore, most suggestions for the application of social psychology to clinical endeavors have taken basic laboratory findings and pointed out how these findings could be relevant in the clinical enterprise. It has been quite rare for social psychological research to be conducted with clinical populations or in clinical settings. Beyond the issue of where one publishes, then, this approach has raised a serious issue about the validity of such applications. That is, is it reasonable to generalize from the "normal" college-age subjects who participate in the vast majority of social psychological studies to the clinical populations and problems of interest to clinicians?

In regard to the latter issue, Kazdin (1978) has provided a lucid and helpful discussion of the role of analogue research in the investigation of clinical issues. Pointing out that the problem of generalization is quite complex, Kazdin notes that the laboratory setting differs in many ways from clinical settings, e.g., subject (client) characteristics, type of behavior addressed, and type of assessment used. Moreover, Kazdin points out that these differences may differentially mediate generalization. For example, clinical populations typically have more severe problems (or need more extensive behavioral change) than the problems or behavior change that one is likely to encounter or elicit in the laboratory. In this sense, it will presumably be harder to get an effect in the real world than in the laboratory. On the other hand, Kazdin points out that clients are usually motivated to change, whereas college freshmen in an experiment have no such underlying motivation. In this sense, it may be easier to get an effect in the real world than in the laboratory. Thus, while the laboratory and real clinical work are clearly different, how likely it is that any finding from the laboratory will generalize to the clinic is a more complex issue than it may at first appear.

Furthermore, as Kazdin notes, we really have little choice but to continue analogue research of some type. Methodologically adequate studies of the effects of actual therapy with actual clients and experienced clinicians are exceedingly expensive and difficult; they are, therefore, rare. Moreover, when such studies are done, they are usually restricted to relatively global comparisons of treatment strategies (e.g., psychodynamic vs. behavior therapy as in Sloane, Staples, Cristol, Yorkston, & Whipple, 1975).

The implications of the above considerations for the application of social psychology to clinical practice seem reasonably clear. First, if social psychological applications are to be taken seriously, then these applications must be investigated with populations and in settings closer to those of clinical interest. Second, this does not mean, however, that only some idealized pitting of social psychological therapy against behavior therapy and psychodynamic therapy would be of benefit. Instead, it suggests that there is a range of methodological strategies that could be used to investigate social psychological application, and that use of this full range would allow both for a more adequate examination of generalization and for a more compelling case to be made to clinicians.

In what follows, some examples will be given of this range of methodological approaches. This account should in no way be taken as all-inclusive, but it should point up the range that exists and highlight some of the points along the way. Figure 1.1 illustrates the various kinds of methodological strategies that we shall describe. For each type of strategy, we shall either discuss relatively recent empirical work carried out under the rubric of interest or allude to well-known or readily available (i.e., included in the present volume) exemplars. Our purpose in this chapter is to give specific demonstrations of the rich variety of methodological strategies available to investigators interested in the application of social psychological principles to clinical practice.

Basic laboratory research

There is, of course, an enormous amount of social psychological research that has been conducted in the laboratory. As noted above, most of the discussions of the application of social psychology to clinical practice have focused on the implications for clinical work that could be derived from existing laboratory research, and previous writings (e.g., Brehm, 1976) contain extensive examples of this approach. We believe that laboratory research will remain the best methodological approach for testing specific and finely drawn theoretical issues in social psychology. Laboratory research and the theoretical models examined therein should also remain primary sources for hypotheses that possibly can be applied to clinical issues. The value of these hypotheses in understanding clinical phenomena and processes can then be evaluated through the alternative methodological strategies to be described in the rest of this chapter.

Role-playing clinical situations

Role playing has a long and conflictual history in psychology. While some investigators

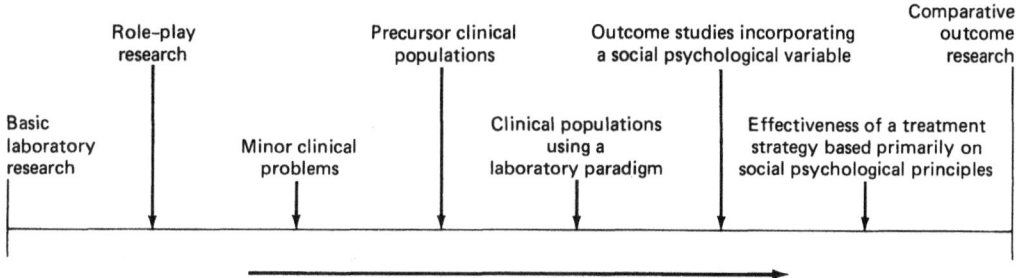

Figure 1.1. A continuum of research strategies for the application of social psychology to clinical psychology.

advocate its use, many researchers (both basic and applied) are not particularly enamored of it. Recognizing that "role playing" is just that—i.e., hypothetical and not real behavior—we still would maintain that role-play research can perform a useful function of initial hypothesis testing. Moreover, such research would seem to provide a bridge between basic research and more applied, clinical research: Role-play experiments can be constructed so as to bear more resemblance to the clinical setting of interest than most traditional laboratory studies, but they allow for more experimental precision and control than most field studies. If role-play studies are to serve a useful function in explicating the application of social psychology to clinical practice, it would seem critically important that reasonably active forms of role playing be employed and, thereby, that subjects become as involved as possible in the role-play scenario.

An example of this kind of research is found in a study conducted by Stivers and Brehm (1980). They derived the hypotheses for this study from reactance theory (Brehm & Brehm, in press) as applied to the clinical setting. It was assumed that all clients come into therapy with freedoms that are important to them. One type of freedom that might have particular relevance to therapy is the client's belief that he or she has the freedom *to try* to exert personal control *and* the freedom *not to try* to exert personal control over any specific problem. Notice that the emphasis here is on *trying* to exert control. Many (and maybe, most) clients would not perceive themselves to have the freedom not to have a problem. Indeed, it is usually the perceived lack of control over problems that sends clients into therapy. Stivers and Brehm believed, however, that most clients would feel that they do have the freedom to try to resolve a given problem by exerting personal control over that problem and, as well, the freedom not to try to do this.

Depending on the circumstances, these freedoms may be differentially important. For some problems and some individuals, the freedom to try to exert personal control will be very important. For other problems and individuals, the freedom not to try to exert personal control will be the more important. While any number of factors may serve to enhance the importance of either freedom, such factors as the direct impact of the problem on the person's life and expectations of being able to resolve the problem through exerting personal control may increase the importance of the freedom to try to exert personal control. On the other hand, less direct impact, lower expectations of being able to resolve the problem by exerting personal control, and contemplation of unpleasant events while trying may all enhance the importance of not trying to resolve a problem through exerting personal control.

The importance of exerting personal control may also differ among therapists. One of the major distinctions among different theories of therapy concerns their emphases on different sources of control over the outcomes of events. Thus, any of several different attributions of control could be conveyed to the client by a therapist. Since a client may value more the freedom to try to exert personal control *or* the freedom not to try to exert personal control, a therapist's attribution of control may be either compatible or incompatible with the more important freedom. Stivers and Brehm hypothesized that where the therapist's communication was incompatible, this would represent a threat to the client's freedom and psychological reactance would be aroused. Reactance was expected to be expressed in opposition to the therapist communication and, perhaps, in lowered evaluation of the therapist.

In this study, female undergraduates participated in a role-play analogue of a therapeutic interaction. Each subject was met at the door of an experimental room that was arranged to resemble an office, and she was seated facing a desk with a tape recorder on it. The experimenter explained that she was interested in studying counselor-client interactions and that, because of the difficulties of studying actual therapeutic sessions, a role-play simulation had been created to examine those aspects of counselor-client interactions that were of interest.

Each subject was asked to role play a client going to see a counselor at a university counseling center for the first time. She was given a written description of one of two client situations and asked to take her time reading it over and to imagine herself in this person's place. One of the situations, a conflict about whether to stay in a troubled romantic relationship, was designed to increase the importance of trying to exert personal control over the outcome of the situation. The other, a conflict about whether to stay in a friendship with a close friend who was severely depressed and try to help that friend work out the depression, was designed to increase the importance of the freedom not to try to exert personal control.

When the subject reported herself ready to identify with the role of the client, she was asked to imagine that she had just presented the problem to the counselor. She then heard a tape that presented stereotypical views from either a behavioristic, a psychodynamic, or a client-centered perspective. The behavioristic tape emphasized rewards and punishments in the environment as determinants of problem outcomes. The psychodynamic tape stressed deeply rooted personality traits as determinants, and the client-centered tape emphasized the client's own decisions and deliberate actions as key determinants. Thus, the first two tapes emphasized determination of the outcome of the situation by something outside the client's personal control, whereas the third emphasized client responsibility for the outcome. After the subjects had listened to the tape, the experimenter (who had left the room during the tape and was blind to all experimental conditions) interviewed the subject about her reaction to the supposed counselor. Subjects responded to all interview questions by giving ratings on a scale from 1 to 10. From information gathered during the debriefing, it would appear that subjects became highly involved in this role-play study. Many of them spontaneously commented on how easy it had been for them to identify with their problem, how they had had similar problems themselves, and how interesting they had found the study to be.

Two measures are of major interest for our present discussion. Heightened reactance arousal was expected to lead to both motivational and attitudinal effects. As a measure of motivation, subjects were asked how much they intended to exert control over the outcome of their presenting problem. A significant interaction between Freedom Made Important (the freedom to try to exert personal control vs. the freedom *not* to exert personal control) and Counselor Communication (behavioristic vs. psychodynamic vs. client-centered) was obtained. Planned individual comparisons within each level of Freedom Made Important were then performed to see if the means for the behavioristic and psychodynamic conditions were, as they were expected

Table 1.1. Mean Ratings for Evaluation Index and for Subjects' Intention To Exert Personal Control (Stivers & Brehm, 1980)

	Behavioristic	Psychodynamic	Behavioristic and Psychodynamic Combined[1]	Client-Centered
High Importance of the Freedom To Try To Exert Personal Control				
Intention[2] (pretest = 8.13)	8.20	9.40	—	8.20
Evaluation index[3]	3.43	2.90	3.17	8.05
High Importance of the Freedom Not To Try To Exert Personal Control				
Intention[2] (pretest = 5.13)	5.20	5.10	5.15	4.10
Evaluation index[3]	6.55	5.45	—	3.88

[1] Conditions combined only when statistically equivalent.
[2] The greater the number, the greater the intention to exert personal control.
[3] The greater the number, the more positive the evaluation.

to be, equivalent. For the Freedom Not To Try condition, this was the case (Table 1.1). The combined mean of these two conditions was then compared with the mean for the client-centered condition. As had been predicted, motivation to exert personal control was significantly lower for those subjects who heard the counselor communication that emphasized that problem outcomes were determined by one's own actions. Thus, for subjects who valued the freedom not to try to exert personal control, the communication emphasizing one's possession of control reduced the motivation to try.

Within the Freedom To Try condition, the means for the behavioristic versus psychodynamic communications were significantly different. In light of this unexpected difference, each mean was then compared individually with the client-centered condition. For subjects who had heard the psychodynamic tape, motivation to try was significantly greater than for subjects who had heard the client-centered tape, whereas subjects in the behavioristic and client-centered conditions did not differ in reported intention to try to exert personal control. The former result was in accordance with theoretical predictions; the latter was not. Thus, opposition to the counselor's emphasis on personal control was obtained in only one of the two conditions in which the subject's more important freedom was incongruent with the communication.

Subjects were also asked to evaluate the counselor on a number of measures (i.e., agreement with the counselor, perceptions of counselor helpfulness, desire to see the same counselor again, and desire to see a different counselor). These measures were combined in an overall evaluation index, and a significant interaction between Freedom Made Important and Counselor Communication was obtained. Using the same set of planned comparisons described above for the motivation measure, it was found that, although the means for the behavioristic and psychodynamic communications were significantly different for subjects who had read the problem designed to enhance the importance of the freedom not to try to exert personal control, each differed significantly from the mean for the client-centered subjects. As had been predicted, client-centered subjects were less favorable toward the counselor than subjects in the other two conditions. For subjects who had read the problem designed to increase the importance of the freedom to try to exert personal control, the behavioristic and psychodynamic conditions were statistically equivalent and the combined mean from these two conditions differed significantly from that of the client-centered communication. Among these conditions, client-centered subjects were, as had been predicted, more favorable toward the counselor.

Some other data are helpful in interpreting these findings. First, it should be noted that problem-consistent communications (i.e., those communications that emphasized the degree of personal control that was consistent with the important freedom created by the presenting problem) did not appear to affect reported motivation. The means for an independent sample of pretest subjects who had simply read one of the two problem descriptions and responded to the question, "How much do you feel that your decisions and actions control the outcome of this situation?" are given in Table 1.1. It can be seen from these data that the average intentions to exert personal control reported by subjects who heard problem-consistent communications were highly similar to pretest means. Oppositional intentions, on the other hand, were induced in two of the three conditions in which subjects heard freedom-inconsistent communications. In this study, then, freedom-consistent communications did not appear to affect motivation; inconsistent communications, however, did appear to induce motivational change.

Second, subjects' anticipated outcome for the problem they had assumed in the role play did not differ as a function of experimental condition and, indeed, was relatively positive (overall mean = 6.58, where 10 indicated the most positive outcome). Differential expectations about the outcomes of the two problems cannot, therefore, explain the obtained interactions between Freedom Made Important and Counselor Communication.

The results of this study suggest that in situations where therapist communications about personal control are inconsistent with the client's perceived freedom regarding his or her efforts to exert personal control, opposition to the therapist and derogation of the therapist's efforts may occur. A few caveats, however, are in order. This was a role-play study, and these results can provide only hypotheses about what might happen in an actual clinical setting. Moreover, even within the controlled laboratory setting, one important unpredicted effect was obtained. Subjects in the Freedom To Try condition who heard the behavioristic tape reported intentions to exert personal control that did not differ from the intentions expressed by subjects who heard the freedom-consistent client-centered communication. It should be noted, however, that subjects in this condition did evaluate the therapist in accordance with a priori predictions.

These findings suggest the possibility that at least some therapeutic messages about environmental control may lead to conflicting interpretations in relationship to one's desired personal control. Perhaps such messages may be interpreted *either* as implying an individual's lack of control—by emphasizing a source of control outside the individual—or as implying the individual's possession of personal control by suggesting an ability to influence the environment. Such a possibility suggests that therapists who emphasize the power of environmental contingencies might be well advised to assess the way in which their clients are interpreting the personal-control implications of such an emphasis.

It should also be noted that there is another way to look at the implications for clinical practice that stem from the results of the Stivers and Brehm study. While this study assumed that motivated opposition to the therapist as well as derogation of the therapist would reduce therapeutic effectiveness, there is the possibility that reactance arousal could be used to facilitate desired therapeutic outcomes. Various writers (in particular, Haley, 1963, and Rosen, 1953; for reviews, see Raskin & Klein, 1976; Tennen, Rohrbaugh, Press, & White, in press) have suggested that telling the client to do the opposite of that which is desired to happen in therapy can be an effective way to elicit the desired behavior. The data from the Stivers and Brehm study could be turned about in just such a "paradoxical" fashion. If, for instance, one wished to motivate a client who valued the freedom to try to exert personal control to try even harder to exert such control, the present results suggest that one way to do this is to deliver feedback that unambiguously opposes this notion of personal control. Similarly, if the therapeutic goal is to lower the motivation to exert personal control with a client who values the freedom not to try to exert personal control, opposing this belief may be a more effective way of obtaining this decrement than supporting the original valued freedom.

It is important to point out, however, that the apparent effectiveness of paradoxical, or oppositional, techniques may in some cases be offset by damage done to the interpersonal relationship between the therapist and client. In the Stivers and Brehm study, oppositional motivation was accompanied by derogation of the therapist who was being opposed. Presumably whether any given therapist is willing to pay this interpersonal price will depend on a number of factors, such as the perceived resiliency of the present therapeutic relationship and the likelihood of success with paradoxical, in contrast to more traditional, therapeutic techniques. The Stivers and Brehm data may, we suspect, be most usefully interpreted not as indicating that damage to the therapeutic relationship makes paradoxical techniques too risky to use, but more simply as pointing out that such damage may occur and should be taken into consideration prior to the using of such techniques.

Minor clinical problems

The treatment of minor clinical problems has been extensively utilized in research on behavior therapy and, in recent years (e.g., Cochran & Sobol, 1976; Kazdin, 1978), has become the focus of considerable controversy. Typical subject populations are composed of college undergraduates who report having animal phobias, test anxiety, or social anxiety. The argument against this approach is obvious. Does anyone know of a single practicing clinician who has ever had a client come into therapy because of a snake phobia? There are, however, at least two arguments in favor of continuing research of this sort. The first point is that it is *not* clear that we cannot make any generalizations from these minor problems to more major ones. Indeed, the success of systematic desensitization in actual clinical as well as experimental analogue situations suggests that some generalization may be quite feasible. Second, while no one dies of these types of problems, people who experience these states do suffer from them, and, in this sense, these problems may be minor but they are also clinical. Various evaluative anxieties (e.g., test, speech, and social anxiety), for example, are related to reduced performance abilities and can obviously be the source of considerable discomfort. Moreover, from a strictly practical point of view, the availability of these problem groups in college populations makes them good candidates for programmatic research. Research efforts with such populations can be aimed at investigating social psychological variables involved in the etiology and maintenance of these problems (see Chapter 6 by Snyder and Smith) as well as in the treatment process.

In regard to the latter, we might point out that social psychological concepts have been seen as relevant to behavior therapy approaches to these minor clinical problems. For example, Goldfried and Davison (1976) have suggested that issues of reactance arousal (Brehm & Brehm, in press) are important in therapies designed to alter clients' maladaptive beliefs (i.e., systematic rational restructuring as in Goldfried, Decenteceo, & Weinberg, 1974). From a more general perspective, Craighead and Craighead (1980) have pointed out the implications of the extensive social psychological literature on persuasive communications for behavior therapies involving the modification of self-statements.

Precursor clinical populations

As noted, one of the advantages of conducting research with college students having minor clinical problems is the ready access that academic researchers have to this population. The same advantage accrues when working with precursor clinical populations. The basic reasoning behind this latter approach is that we may be able to identify some individuals in the college population that are at high risk for developing significant psychological or psychophysiological problems in later life. Research with these individuals may be directly relevant for providing information on the developmental course of the problem of interest and on possible strategies for reducing younger people's risk for developing the problem. More indirectly, research with precursor populations may have implications for the treatment of older individuals actually experiencing the problem.

This kind of methodological approach is of relatively recent origin and, thus far, is quite restricted in its utility. Perhaps the best current example of this approach is found in work on the Type A coronary-prone behavior pattern. One can measure Type A behavior in college students as well as in middle-aged people. While no direct link has yet been established between being a Type A personality in one's twenties and coronary proneness in middle-age, Type A students do display the behavioral and autonomic features associated with middle-aged Type A persons. By inference, then, college-age Type A persons are at high risk for later displaying Type A behavior and for running the associated high risk for coronary disturbance.

Most of the previous research on the dimensions of the Type A coronary-prone behavior pattern has focused on behavioral and physiological correlates of this individual difference classification. In our research (Smith & Brehm, in press, 1981), we have begun to examine the cognitive processes associated with the behavior pattern. While both studies have some potential implications for intervention strategies with Type A individuals, we shall restrict our discussion here to the former study.

In this study, we examined the correlations between the student version of the Jenkins Activity Scale (Glass, 1977) and Jones's (1969) measure of Ellis's (1962) irrational beliefs. Since the student version of the JAS is used with college students, it has not been used to predict actual incidence of heart disease. It has, however, been found to correlate reliably with measures of the Type A behavior pattern (i.e., adult JAS, interview method) that have been found predictive of coronary heart disease (MacDougall, Dembroski, & Musante, 1979). Jones's Irrational Beliefs Test generates ten scale scores (ten items each) corresponding to Ellis's specific irrational beliefs, as well as an overall score for general irrational thinking. The ten scales and their correlations with the full-scale JAS scores are displayed in Table 1.2.

This research addressed two major questions. First, we were interested in seeing whether or not increasing "Type-Aness" was associated with increasing endorsement of any of Ellis's irrational beliefs. If such an association was found, this would suggest that one could work directly with these cognitions. Such work would be based not necessarily on the belief that the cognitions cause the behavior pattern, but at least on the supposition that any such cognitive structures may facilitate the maintenance of the behavior pattern. Second, we wanted to determine whether or not there were any sex differences in the correlational pattern obtained. Most of the previous research in this area has been conducted with male subjects and some of the research that involved females (e.g., Carver, in press) has obtained rather confusing results.

The data obtained from the 77 female and 72 male subjects participating in the study are displayed in Table 1.2. It can be seen that in both males and females, increasing Type-Aness was associated with the subject's disagreeing with the idea that it is easier to avoid problems than to face them (e.g., "It is easier to avoid than to face certain life difficulties and self-responsibilities"). In addition to this general finding, there were some rather intriguing sex differences. Male subjects showed, in addition to the negative correlation with problem avoidance, a positive correlation between the Type A pattern and high self-standards of achievement (e.g., "One should be thoroughly competent and achieving in all possible respects if one is to consider oneself worthwhile"). Females, on the other hand, did not show a significant positive correlation with high achievement standards. Instead, in-

Table 1.2. Correlations of Pattern A and Cognitive Measures (Smith & Brehm, in press)

	Type A (JAS)		
	Full Sample	Males	Females
Demand for approval	−.16[2]	−.16	−.16
High achievement	.11	.24[2]	.01
Blame proneness	.17[2]	.15	.19[1]
Frustration reactivity	.12	−.02	.24[2]
Emotional irresponsibility	−.14[1]	−.07	−.20[1]
Anxious overconcern	.18[2]	.05	.31[3]
Problem avoidance	−.41[4]	−.51[4]	−.32[3]
Dependency	−.15[1]	−.15	−.14
Fatalism	.12	.06	.16
Perfectionism	.03	.13	−.04
IBt Total	.01	−.05	.01

[1] $\leq .10$
[2] $\leq .05$
[3] $\leq .01$
[4] $\leq .001$

creasing Type-Aness for females was associated with anxious overconcern (e.g., "If the possibility of dangerous or unfortunate events occurring in the future exists at all, one should be terribly concerned about it") and with frustration reactivity (e.g., "It is catastrophic when things are not the way one would like them to be").

Thus, the most consistent and strongest relationship between the Type A behavior pattern and Ellis's irrational beliefs was found for problem avoidance. Type A individuals tended to disagree with this belief and, instead, tended to endorse a belief in an active-mastery style of coping. Such a belief is highly consistent with the behaviors associated with the Type A pattern (i.e., time urgency, impatience, achievement striving, etc.).

While sharing the belief in active mastery, male and female Type A's differed in other cognitive correlates. As mentioned above, Male Type A's tended to endorse a belief in high achievement standards. It is obvious how Type A behaviors such as competitiveness, job involvement, and achievement striving could reflect this belief. For females, the Type A pattern was associated with a more diffuse set of correlates, especially anxious overconcern and frustration reactivity. This particular set of beliefs is consistent with Glass's notion that the Type A pattern reflects an attempt to maintain control over environmental demands and requirements. These sex differences raise the possibility that different motivational factors may underlie similar Type A behaviors in males and females. These differences could also have implications for the situations most likely to elicit Type A behavior from males and females.

Taken as a whole, these findings, in which were obtained cognitive correlates (i.e., irrational beliefs) of the Type A pattern that are consistent with behavioral components of the pattern, suggest that cognitive variables may be a useful target for attempts to alter the behavior pattern. Cognitive restructuring interventions have been demonstrated to be effective in working with other target populations (e.g., test anxiety: Meichenbaum, 1972; anger: Novaco, 1976). Recent research also has indicated that cognitive restructuring is effective in reducing self-reported Type A behavior (Jenni & Wollersheim, 1979), and this type of intervention might be useful in modifying the overt behavioral and autonomic aspects of the Type A pattern as well. Moreover, it may be crucially important in any such interventions to tailor them differentially for males and females.

It seems reasonable that cognitive intervention techniques should be based on a thorough assessment of the relevant cognitions exhibited by Type A individuals. Although the correlational nature of the present study and the restriction of its subject population to young adults dictate some caution in interpreting these results, findings from this study may be viewed as offering a useful beginning to this kind of assessment.

Clinical populations in laboratory research paradigms

Laboratory paradigms have been widely used in clinical research, especially in the study of specific processes involved in presumed clinical entities such as schizophrenia (e.g., Chapman & Chapman, 1973; Shakow, 1963) and depression (e.g., Donnelly, Waldman, Murphy, Wyatt, & Goodwin, 1980). Applications of social psychological principles to clinical practice, however, have seldom utilized such an approach. We consider this to be unfortunate since, as we shall try to demonstrate in our description of the following study, the use of laboratory research paradigms with clinical populations would seem to offer a useful way to examine possible applications of social psychological theory to the clinical endeavor.

Self-confrontation of clients in psychotherapy through the use of audio- and videotape playbacks of their behavior has become an increasingly popular therapeutic device. Since self-confrontation inherently involves self-focused attention, objective self-awareness theory (Duval & Wicklund, 1972) provides a theoretical framework and an associated data base for generating predictions about the effects of self-focused attention in clinical populations. Given concerns about the effectiveness of self-confrontation (see Gur & Sackeim, 1978, for a review) and the absence of a theoretical model of the self-confrontation process, Gibbons, Smith, Brehm, and Schroeder (1980) used objective self-awareness theory and research in evaluating three hypotheses concerning the effects of self-focused attention in a clinical population. Past research with normal subjects has indicated that self-focused attention (a) amplifies affective experience (Scheier, 1976; Scheier, Carver & Gibbons, in press), (b) makes self-reports of behavior more accurate (Pryor, Gibbons, Wicklund, Fazio, & Hood, 1977), and (c) may lead to greater acceptance of responsibility for one's actions (Duval & Wicklund, 1973; but see Federoff and Harvey, 1976, in which self-focused attention reduced self-attributed responsibility for outcomes that threatened self-esteem). These three effects have obvious implications for psychotherapy in general and self-confrontation in particular.

To determine whether or not these effects of self-focused attention would occur in clinical populations, Gibbons et al. asked a sample of alcoholic patients and general psychiatric patients at a veterans' hospital to fill out a series of questionnaires in either the presence or the absence of a self-focusing stimulus (i.e., a mirror). The first questionnaire pertained to the subject's perceptions of the seriousness of his problem, the role of luck in determining it, and his responsibility for the onset and treatment of the problem. Subjects also responded to an affect questionnaire and to questions about the length of time they had had their problem and how many times they had been hospitalized for it.

Results of this study indicated that self-awareness did not increase patients' acceptance of responsibility for their problems. There was some indication, however, that self-focused attention increased accuracy of self-reports concerning hospitalization. Moreover, self-focused attention clearly increased the self-reported *negative* affect of general psychiatric patients. In general then, this study indicated little in the way of beneficial effects of self-focused attention. The suggested increase in accuracy of self-reports about hospitalization seems a relatively small gain in contrast to the increase in negative mood evidenced by the general psychiatric patients and the failure to find any increase in acceptance of responsibility as a function of self-focus. Obviously there are large differences between self-focused attention as operationalized in this study and as it occurs in self-confrontation therapy. However, the Gibbons et al. study provides some initial data and perhaps outlines an avenue for the application of the theory of objective self-awareness and previous research on self-awareness with normal subjects to attempts to understand the role of self-focused attention in psychotherapy.

Outcome studies incorporating social psychological variables

While many outcome studies may have inadvertently included variables that would be deemed important by social psychological theory, there have been few such studies that have undertaken the direct and specific examination of such variables. One exception to this can be found in the research conducted on the role of choice in facilitating treatment effectiveness. There are a variety of social psychological theories (e.g., cognitive dissonance, reactance, self-perception) that converge (for reviews of this convergence, see Brehm, 1976 and Brehm & McAllister, 1980) on the prediction that greater client choice in the therapy process should lead to greater effectiveness of the treatment.

While the theoretical prediction is thus quite clear, most of the research in this area has suffered from a number of methodological and substantive problems. For example, analogue studies by Devine and Fernald (1973), Gordon (1976), and Kanfer and Grimm (1978) have all appeared to demonstrate a positive effect of subjects' choosing their own treatment from among a set of at least two treatment alternatives. Unfortunately, however, close inspection of the data from these studies reveals that none of them determined whether there was a positive effect of choice *or* a negative effect of depriving subjects of expected treatment choice (or perhaps both). In addition, all of these studies used subject populations with either minor clinical problems (Devine & Fernald: fear of snakes) or unassessed need for the treatments offered (Gordon: relaxation; Kanfer & Grimm: reading skills improvement). (More detailed discussion of these studies and their methodological problems can be found in Brehm & Brehm, in press and Harris & Harvey, 1978.)

There is, then, a strong need for research on the effects of choice that provides better baseline data such that the directionality of effect can be assessed and that uses actual clinical populations. Chapter 11 in this volume, by Cooper and Axsom, reports on a series of studies that, taken as a whole, appears to provide the most compelling evidence now available on the role of choice in promoting treatment effectiveness (see also Langer & Rodin, 1976, and Schulz, 1976, briefly described below).

Therapeutic strategies based wholly (or primarily) on social psychological theory

As one might expect from the preceding discussion, the conduct of an actual treatment program based wholly (or primarily) on social psychological theory is quite rare. Two investigators have reported such social psychological treatments in their research on factors that influence the well-being of institutionalized aged populations. Langer and Rodin (1976) found that increasing the sense of personal choice and control in the daily activities of an institutionalized elderly population produced positive changes in self-reported activity and alertness as well as improved ratings by residence staff and greater participation in residence activities. Schulz (1976) demonstrated that giving an institutionalized aged population either cognitive or decisional control over the timing of visits by college students resulted in improved physical and psychological well-being as well as increased activity levels. Follow-up data from the Langer and Rodin study (Rodin & Langer, 1977) taken 18 months following the treatment indicated that the positive results persisted. Follow-up data from the Schulz study (Schulz & Hanusa, 1978), however, indicated sharp declines after treatment termination in the adjustment of subjects receiving the previously beneficial treatments and even a somewhat higher mortality rate among these groups. These findings underscore the need for follow-up data in all clinical treatment studies.

One of the most interesting and provocative examples of therapeutic strategies based on social psychological theory that we know of is found in a paper by Ayllon, Allison, and Kandel (1980). These investigators made use of a treatment for oppositional behavior based on Varela's (1971) "persuasion by successive approximation using reactance." The initial component of this technique is the formulation of a hierarchy of statements relevant to the desired behavior that range from the most likely to be accepted by the client to the least likely. The therapist then tries to persuade the client of the opposite of each statement, attempting thereby to create psychological reactance and motivate the client to publically commit herself or himself to the desired statement. The therapist progresses up through the hierarchy until the client has committed herself or himself to all the desired statements. Typically, the last statement(s) concerns a behavioral intention on the part of the client that, if carried through, would ameliorate the problem behavior.

Ayllon et al. report two interventions with four normal children who were classified by their teacher as the most disruptive in the class. All were males from 11 to 13 years of age, and all were performing poorly in their academic subjects as well as being disruptive. The teacher considered all four boys as capable of at least average work, and repeated efforts by the teacher to discourage the disruptive behavior as well as conferences with the parents had failed to improve the children's classroom behavior.

After a baseline of the children's disruptive behavior and academic performance had been established, each of the four children was counseled successively by one of two therapists. The therapist (presumably in consultation with the teacher and the parents) drew up the hierarchy of statements that the therapist wished each child to agree with. The following is a condensed version of that hierarchy.

1. What I will say will be the truth.
2. I am not working too hard in school right now.
3. I care about school.
4. When I'm disruptive, it is on my own volition.
5. I can change on my own volition.
6. I can do academic work on my own volition.
7. I will commit myself to doing my schoolwork.

Ayllon et al. provide a condensed transcript of the dialogue between one of the students and his therapist. A few excerpts from this transcript are given below.

T. Before we even start talking, I must admit I'm not sure whether we should even bother. I have found that a lot of students don't even tell the truth and can't keep their word. You probably won't tell the truth either.
S. I'll tell the truth to you.
T. Well, that's good to hear; we won't be wasting our time talking then. I guess you must really be working hard in school these days.
S. Myself, I'm not. I'm really just kind of loafin' around. The other kids are workin' hard. You know, the ones who get good grades. . . . .
T. I guess it's hopeless then. You wouldn't even consider trying it the other way around—work first, play later.
S. No. Well, I could try. *I* know what you're trying to do—you're trying to get me to do my work in school, aren't you?
T. I'm not trying to get you to do anything— I can't make you do anything you don't want to do.
S. But you and Mrs. Q would like me to do my work, right?

T. I would like it if you would like it. But I know you aren't willing to even give it a try.
S. I would give it a try.
. . . .
T. Would you write something for me?
S. Like what?
T. Like what you have told me you are going to do.
S. You write it. I don't like to write. You write it and I'll sign it.
T. You dictate it to me, okay? I, (student's name)
S. I, (student's name), give my word that I will get my seat work done and handed in by Mrs. Q's deadline. I will do this until the end of the school. (Student then signs the statement immediately.)
T. (Student's name), are you sure you want to do this until the end of school? We could make it for just a couple of days instead.
S. No. I'll work until the end of school.

For three of the children in this study, the successive persuasion technique was quite successful. Disruptive behavior was reduced from a mean of 47 percent to a mean of 19 percent; academic performance in math increased from 22 percent correct to 83 percent correct. Ayllon et al. report that these children's behavior improved dramatically on the first day after "behavioral persuasion" and that the desired changes were maintained for the rest of the study (an average of 12 days for each child).

For the fourth child, success was only temporarily achieved. While the first day after the intervention showed impressive improvement in both behavior and math performance, these improvements vanished on the following day. Ayllon et al. decided to repeat the behavioral persuasion session with this child, but this time with the school principal, the teacher, and the child's father in attendance. After this session, this child's disruptive behavior decreased from a mean of 50 percent to a mean of 30 percent and his math performance increased from 11 percent correct to 73 percent; the improvement figures are averages of the six days after the second treatment session during which this student's behavior was monitored.

It would be inappropriate to generalize too much from these findings. A very small sample of subjects was used, and these subjects (relative to other noncompliant children seen clinically) were exhibiting only a moderate level of problem behaviors. Nevertheless, Ayllon et al.'s findings are extremely interesting and suggest the possibility that the reactance techniques developed by Varela and used by him with adults can be effectively applied across a considerable age span.

Conclusions and future directions

The range of methodological strategies for building a data base for the application of social psychology to clinical practice outlined above provides a clear set of guidelines as to *how* this potentially useful integration of these fields can take place. The question remains as to *what* general topics in this integration offer the greatest possibilities for the further understanding and more effective treatment of maladaptive behavior.

Perhaps the most intriguing but largely neglected area of useful integration is the social psychology of clinical services. Goffman (1961) and Braginsky, Braginsky, and Ring (1969) have offered interesting perspectives on mental institutions. Recent work has also begun to investigate the clinician's causal attributions concerning client problems (Batson, 1975; Shenkel, Snyder, Batson, & Clark, 1979; Snyder, 1977; Snyder, Shenkel, & Schmidt, 1976). The study by Stivers and Brehm (1980) reported above investigated the effects of clinicians' communications on reactance arousal in clients. Chapter 2 by Cantor and Chapter 3 by Farina and Fisher discuss social psychological factors in clinical judgment. The utility of these efforts and of the approach that they outline lies in their potential for elucidating cognitive and interpersonal processes in the typical delivery of clinical services. The result of the continued development and eventual use of this body of knowledge could include the elimination of undesirable effects inherent in typical clinical service delivery and enhancement of inherent strengths.

The most active area of integration to date is that concerning the development and maintenance of maladaptive behaviors. The work of Smith and Brehm (in press, 1981) on cognitive processes in the Type A pattern, recent research on attribution processes in depression (e.g., Seligman, Abramson, Semmel, & von Baeyer, 1979), and research on interpersonal behavior in depression (Hokanson, Sacco, Blumberg, & Landrum, 1980) are representative of some possibilities in this area of integration, as are the chapters by Kuiper, Derry, and MacDonald; Snyder and Smith; Shruger; and Coates and Peterson that appear in this volume. This work indicates that social psychology has much to offer to the understanding of maladaptive behavior. Continued research efforts based on social psychological research and theory and employing clinically relevant populations promise to be continually useful.

Finally, the most difficult, costly, and challenging area for integration is the application of social psychology to clinical interventions. The utility of this potential integration must eventually be demonstrated through the use of treatments based on social psychological concepts and evaluated in research designs that include appropriate controls and use actual clinical populations. The Gibbons et al. (1980) study indicates that social psychological concepts can guide investigations of processes within psychotherapy techniques. Controlled-treatment studies incorporating social psychological variables are also necessary. The work by Cooper and Axsom on dissonance in psychotherapy (Chapter 11 in this volume) and the treatment studies described in the present chapter offer some indication that these efforts may be fruitful. Traditional data-based clinical procedures (e.g., systematic desensitization, assertiveness training, modeling), however, have received empirical support from a far greater number of research efforts. By comparison, techniques based on social psychology are interesting but as yet unproven. For the suggested integration of social and clinical psychology to affect the day-to-day delivery of clinical services, broader empirical support must be obtained. Within that considerable task lies the challenge to those who advocate the integration of these two disciplines.

References

Ayllon, T., Allison, M. G., & Kandel, H. J. *Changing behavior through systematic verbal persuasion.* Unpublished manuscript, Georgia State University, 1980.

Batson, C. D. Attribution as a mediator of bias in helping. *Journal of Personality and Social Psychology*, 1975, *32*, 455–466.

Bergin, A. E., & Garfield, S. L. (Eds.). *Handbook of psychotherapy and behavior change.* New York: Wiley, 1971.

Braginsky, B., Braginsky, D., & Ring, K. *Methods of madness: The mental hospital as a last resort.* New York: Holt, Rinehart, & Winston, 1969.

Brehm, S. S. *The application of social psychology to clinical practice.* Washington, D.C.: Hemisphere, 1976.

Brehm, S. S., & Brehm, J. W. *Psychological reactance: A theory of freedom and control.* New York: Academic Press, in press.

Brehm, S. S., & McAllister, D. A. A social psychological perspective on the maintenance of therapeutic change. In P. Karoly & J. J. Steffen (Eds.), *Improving the long-term effects of psychotherapy.* New York: Gardner Press, 1980.

Carson, R. C. *Interaction concepts of personality.* Chicago: Aldine, 1969.

Carver, C. J. Perceived coercion, resistance to persuasion, and the Type A behavior pattern. *Journal of Research in Personality*, in press.

Chapman, L. J., & Chapman, J. P. *Disordered thought in schizophrenia.* Englewood Cliffs, N. J.: Prentice-Hall, 1973.

Cochrane, R., & Sobol, M. P. Myth and methodology in behavioral therapy research. In M. P. Feldman and A. Broadhurst (Eds.), *Theoretical and experimental bases of the behavior therapies.* New York: Wiley, 1976.

Craighead, L., & Craighead, W. E. Implications of persuasive communication research for the modification of self-statements. *Cognitive Therapy and Research*, 1980, *4*, 117–134.

Devine, D. A., & Fernald, P. S. Outcome effects of receiving a preferred, randomly assigned, or nonpreferred therapy. *Journal of Consulting and Clinical Psychology*, 1973, *41*, 104–107.

Donnelly, E. F., Waldman, I. N., Murphy, D. L., Wyatt, R. J., & Goodwin, F. K. Primary affective disorder: Thought disorder in depression. *Journal of Abnormal Psychology*, 1980, *89*, 315–319.

Duval, S., & Wicklund, R. *A theory of objective self-awareness*. New York: Academic Press, 1972.

Duval, S., & Wicklund, R. A. Effects of objective self-awareness on attribution of causality. *Journal of Experimental Social Psychology*, 1973, *9*, 17–31.

Ellis, A. *Reason and emotion in psychotherapy*. New York: Lyle Stuart Press, 1962.

Federoff, N., & Harvey, J. Focus of attention, self-esteem, and the attribution of causality. *Journal of Research in Personality*, 1976, *10*, 336–345.

Frank, J. D. *Persuasion and healing* (Rev. ed.). Baltimore: The Johns Hopkin University Press, 1973.

Garfield, S. L., & Bergin, A. E. (Eds.). *Handbook of psychotherapy and behavior change* (2nd ed.). New York: Wiley, 1978.

Gibbons, F. X., Smith, T. W., Brehm, S. S., & Schroeder, D. J. *Self-awareness and self-confrontation: The role of focus of attention in the process of psychotherapy*. Unpublished manuscript, University of Kansas, 1980.

Glass, D. C. *Behavior patterns, stress, and coronary disease*. New York: Lawrence Erlbaum Associates, 1977.

Goffman, E. *Asylums*. New York: Doubleday, 1961.

Goldfried, M. R., & Davison, G. C. *Clinical behavior therapy*. New York: Holt, Rinehart, & Winston, 1976.

Goldfried, M. R., Decenteceo, E. T., & Weinberg, L. Systematic rational restructuring as a self-control technique. *Behavior Therapy*, 1974, *5*, 247–254.

Goldstein, A. P., Heller, K., & Sechrest, L. B. *Psychotherapy and the psychology of behavior change*. New York: Wiley, 1966.

Gordon, R. M. Effects of volunteering and responsibility on perceived value and effectiveness of a clinical treatment. *Journal of Consulting and Clinical Psychology*, 1976, *44*, 799–801.

Gur, R. C., & Sackeim, H. A. Self-confrontation and psychotherapy: A reply to Sanborn, Pyke, and Sanborn. *Psychotherapy: Theory, Research, and Practice*, 1978, *15*, 258–265.

Haley, J. *Strategies of psychotherapy*. New York: Grune and Stratton, 1963.

Harris, B., & Harvey, J. Social psychological concepts applied to clinical processes: On the need for precision. *Journal of Consulting and Clinical Psychology*, 1978, *46*, 326–328.

Hokanson, J. E., Sacco, W. P., Blumberg, S. R., & Landrum, G. C. Interpersonal behavior of depressive individuals in a mixed motive game. *Journal of Abnormal Psychology*, 1980, *89*, 320–332.

Jenni, M., & Wollersheim, J. Cognitive therapy, stress management training, and the Type A behavior pattern. *Cognitive Therapy and Research*, 1979, *3*, 61–73.

Jones, R. G. *The Irrational Beliefs Test*. Wichita, Kan.: Test Systems, 1969.

Kanfer, F. H., & Grimm, L. G. Freedom of choice and behavioral change. *Journal of Consulting and Clinical Psychology*, 1978, *46*, 873–878.

Kazdin, A. E. Evaluating the generality of findings in analogue therapy research. *Journal of Consulting and Clinical Psychology*, 1978, *46*, 673–686.

Langer, E., & Rodin, J. The effects of choice and enhanced personal responsibility for the aged: A field experiment in an institutional setting. *Journal of Personality and Social Psychology*, 1976, *34*, 191–198.

MacDougall, J., Dembroski, T., & Musante, L. The structural interview and questionnaire methods of assessing coronary prone behavior in male and female college students. *Journal of Behavioral Medicine*, 1979, *2*(1), 71–83.

Meichenbaum, D. Cognitive modification of test anxious college students. *Journal of Consulting and Clinical Psychology*, 1972, *39*, 370–380.

Novaco, R. Treatment of chronic anger through cognitive and relaxation controls. *Journal of Consulting and Clinical Psychology*, 1976, *44*, 681.

Pryor, J. B., Gibbons, F. X., Wicklund, R. A., Fazio, R., & Hood, R. Self-focused attention and self-report validity. *Journal of Personality*, 1977, *45*, 513–527.

Raskin, D. E., & Klein, Z. E. Losing a symptom through keeping it: A review of paradoxical treatment techniques and rationale. *Archives of General Psychiatry*, 1976, *33*, 548–555.

Rodin, J., & Langer, E. Long term effects of a control relevant intervention with the institutionalized aged. *Journal of Personality and Social Psychology*, 1977, *85*, 897–902.

Rosen, J. *Direct psychoanalysis*. New York: Grune and Stratton, 1953.

Scheier, M. F. Self-awareness, self-consciousness and angry aggression. *Journal of Personality*, 1976, *44*, 627–644.

Scheier, M. F., Carver, C. S., & Gibbons, F. X. Self-focused attention and reactions to fear. *Journal of Research in Personality*, in press.

Schulz, R. The effects of control and predictability on the psychologial and physical well-being of the institutionalized aged. *Journal of Personality and Social Psychology*, 1976, *33*, 563–573.

Schulz, R., & Hanusa, B. H. Long-term effects of control and predictability-enhancing interventions: Findings and ethical issues. *Journal of Personality and Social Psychology*, 1978, *36*, 1194–1201.

Seligman, M.E.P., Abramson, L. Y., Semmel, A., & von Baeyer, C. Depressive attributional style. *Journal of Abnormal Psychology*, 1979, *88*, 242–247.

Shakow, D. Psychological deficit in schizophrenia. *Behavioral Science*, 1963, *8*, 275–305.

Shenkel, R. J., Snyder, C. R., Batson, C. D., & Clark, G. M. Effects of prior diagnostic information on clinicians' causal attributions of a client's problems. *Journal of Consulting and Clinical Psychology*, 1979, *47*, 404–406.

Sheras, P. L., & Worchel, S. *Clinical psychology: A social psychological approach*. New York: Van Nostrand, 1979.

Sloane, R. B., Staples, F. R., Cristol, A. H., Yorkston, N. J., & Whipple, K. *Psychotherapy versus behavior therapy*. Cambridge, Mass.: Harvard University Press, 1975.

Smith, T. W., & Brehm, S. S. Cognitive correlates of the Type A coronary-prone behavior pattern. *Motivation and Emotion*, in press.

Smith, T. W., & Brehm, S. S. Person perception and the Type A coronary-prone behavior pattern. *Journal of Personality and Social Psychology*, 1981, *40*, 1137–1149.

Snyder, C. R. "A patient by any other name" revisited: Maladjustment or attributional locus of problem? *Journal of Consulting and Clinical Psychology*, 1977, *45*, 101–103.

Snyder, C. R., Shenkel, R. J., & Schmidt, A. Effects of role perspective and client psychiatric history on locus of problem. *Journal of Consulting and Clinical Psychology*, 1976, *44*, 467–472.

Stivers, M., & Brehm, S. S. *The influence of perceived personal control on responses to communications concerning sources of control*. Unpublished manuscript, University of Kansas, 1980.

Tennen, H., Rohrbaugh, M., Press, S., & White, M. D. Reactance theory and therapeutic paradox: A compliance-defiance model. *Psychotherapy: Theory, Research, and Practice*, in press.

Varela, J. A. *Psychological solutions to social problems*. New York: Academic Press, 1971.

Winett, R. A. Attribution of attitude and behavior change and its relevance to behavior therapy. *The Psychological Record*, 1970, *20*, 17–32.

two

SOCIAL PSYCHOLOGICAL PROCESSES IN CLINICAL JUDGMENT

Practicing clinicians frequently are called upon to make a variety of judgments and decisions in connection with their professional activities. They may be asked, for example, to judge whether an individual's behavior is pathological, what may have caused the dysfunctional behavior pattern, what diagnosis should be made, should hospitalization be recommended, or whether the individual is suicidal. In the first chapter of this section, Cantor argues that processes involved in making clinical judgments are similar to those involved in "everyday" social judgments. Specifically, she argues that three components of the clinical judgment process—categorization, hypothesis testing, and decision making—have analogies in everyday social judgment. Cantor notes that performance on those component tasks historically has been evaluated from the perspective of rather rigid normative models developed to describe performance in other domains. Recent studies indicate that these normative models are not descriptively accurate. Accordingly, Cantor suggests that everyday models—the prototype model of categorization, the theory-driven model of hypothesis testing, and the independent-decision models of decision making—may do a better job of description in both clinical and social domains.

Farina and Fisher, in Chapter 3, examine historical and contemporary beliefs about the causes of mental disorders. These authors present research evidence indicating that such beliefs are poorly organized and lack coherence and, as a result, are quite malleable. Farina and Fisher also examine the role of beliefs about mental disorders in the mental health field. In particular, they focus on "medical model" and "social learning" beliefs about the causes of mental disorders and the consequences of such beliefs for the clinician, patient, and general public. The implications of the issues raised by Farina and Fisher are profound and far-reaching.

Finally in this section, Wiggins comments on the contributions provided by Cantor and by Farina and Fisher. In addition to highlighting the important similarities and differences in the two papers, Wiggins extends the discussion of the nature of clinical judgment and social perception processes.

2

"EVERYDAY" VERSUS NORMATIVE MODELS OF CLINICAL AND SOCIAL JUDGMENT

NANCY CANTOR
PRINCETON UNIVERSITY

Three components of clinical and social judgment

The present chapter is concerned with three components of the clinical judgment process—categorization, hypothesis testing, and decision making—for which analogies exist in everyday social judgment. First, underlying any diagnosis is the body of declarative knowledge about different psychiatric syndromes, their associated clinical features, and rules of thumb for recognizing patients belonging to a diagnostic category. A clinician has a mental dictionary-encyclopedia of diagnostic categories, compiled through direct experience with patients and through information acquired indirectly from diagnostic manuals. Such is the set of knowledge that permits a psychiatrist to describe a "schizophrenic in the abstract" and the rules of thumb enabling the recognition of a "schizophrenic in the concrete." This component of clinical categorical knowledge has an "everyday" analogy in the extensive knowledge that the social perceiver draws on to label and sort common objects, people, and social situations.

The second component, the clinician's procedural knowledge for testing hypotheses and hunches about patients, includes a collection of information-gathering techniques (primarily centered around clinical interviews), as well as procedures for informally evaluating the validity and reliability of the observed data. Consider the private practitioner conducting an interview with a patient who claims to be extremely depressed. Again, an everyday analogy exists in the conversations and observations engaged in by social perceivers to "test" impressions and hunches about other people, friends, and acquaintances. Third, the clinician may also draw on another set of procedural knowledge, strategies for pooling qualitatively different sets of

---

This research and the preparation of this manuscript were supported in part by National Science Foundation Grant BNS 80-22253 to Nancy Cantor. I would like to thank George Miller, Edward E. Smith, Rita French, Juan Mezzich, Mark Snyder, Marilyn Shaw, and Janet Riggs for collaboration on the work reported in this chapter. Also, I wish to thank Jonathan Baron for comments relevant to this work.

information and making a binary decision about a single patient. For example, the veterans hospital clinician may need to integrate a diagnostic profile, a drug-responsiveness record, and a home situation report in order to decide whether or not to release a particular patient. To find an everyday analogy to the clinical decision-making task, simply imagine yourself about to buy a car and trying to combine bits of data from *Consumer Reports*, a next-door neighbor, and your own test drives of various makes—the decision is a risky one, based on qualitatively diverse information and requiring a simple accept/reject outcome.

Historically, performance on these component clinical judgment tasks has been evaluated from the perspective of normative models of categorization and decision making derived from biological taxonomic work, experimental methods of hypothesis testing, and statistical decision theory. The untrained psychologist also performs many of the same categorization and decision-making tasks as the trained clinician. As intuitive psychologist, friends, employers, consumers, and parents/spouses have to categorize, interview, and search for evidence to test impressions and make decisions under uncertainty. Not surprisingly, these everyday social cognition tasks have also been studied by analogy to a rational-person model of impression formation, attributions, and choice—the everyday thinker is expected to test impressions and form attributions by performing analysis of variance (Kelley, 1973), make consumer choices so as to maximize the expected value of gambles (Slovic, Fischhoff, & Lichtenstein, 1977) and be a true Bayesian, taking account of the prior probabilities of events, revising predictions in light of counterexamples, and remaining cautious in the light of small samples of surprising evidence (Nisbett & Ross, 1980). As Table 2.1 summarizes, these normative models of categorization, hypothesis testing, and choice have been popular as baseline comparisons in both the clinical and the everyday judgment literature.

Evidence gathered over the past 15 years, in both of these domains, suggests that while such normative models may be appropriate *prescriptive* models, they are not wholly accurate *descriptive* models of social judgments. Neither trained nor untrained psychologists create or use well-defined categorical systems, or follow the canons of scientific hypothesis testing and statistical decision theory very well. The violations of the normative models have led to important attempts to formulate more accurate *descriptive*, or "everyday," models of categorization (Rosch, 1978), hypothesis testing (Snyder, 1981), and decision making (Tversky & Kahneman, 1980). Substantial progress has been made in formulating a better descriptive model of everyday judgments. Quite a bit is known about the ways in which people categorize common objects like tables and chairs, gather information about others in interviews and discussions, and make decisions about cars to buy, secretaries to hire, or schools to attend. These reformulated descriptive models (of categorization, information search, decision making) are very relevant and appropriate for the clinical domain as well. It is time that attention be switched from verifying the standard normative models (which are more often falsified than verified) to verifying these more appropriate descriptive models. The links between clinical judgment and these everyday models (Table 2.1) need to be forged more concertedly. This is so in particular because there may be value to everyday models in a prescriptive, as well as in a descriptive, sense. It is not without rationality to suggest that the "fuzzy" models of categorization are better suited to the stimuli available in the social world for categorization, that scientific hypothesis testing cannot proceed without a theory to guide the search for data, and that the heuristics used in everyday decision making have cognitive computational benefits without actually sacrificing much. In other words, clinical diagnosis and judgment may not look as "messy" when compared with descriptive models developed in the social cognition domain; there may also be important functional aspects to these everyday-heuristic (as compared with scientific-normative) rules of diagnosis and judgment. Much more work

Table 2.1. Normative and Everyday Models of Social Cognitive and Clinical Judgment

Component Task	Normative Model	Everyday Model
Categorization	Well-defined categories and all-or-none categorization, as in biological taxonomic work	Fuzzy categories and probabilistic categorization
Hypothesis testing	Scientific hypothesis testing with equal-opportunity searches	Theory-driven hypothesis testing with confirmation searches
Decision making	Information integration and Bayesian revision, as in statistical decision theory	Categorical integration and risk aversion

is needed before it can be known what aspects of social life would be disrupted if people adhered to the normative model of rationality rather than to the heuristic model (Miller & Cantor, 1981). Finally, as Table 2.1 also suggests, there is precedent these days for thinking that we have come full circle—historians of science are suggesting that hypothesis testing has never been theory-free (Kuhn, 1962), the medical profession is informally proposing that its diagnostic process may *not* be well defined or pure, and decision theorists are beginning to test the "optimality" of expected utility theory (Shaw, 1981; Simon, 1978). Soon it may be necessary to draw the line of comparison the other way—that is, from the scientific-normative models to the everyday-heuristic ones.

The purpose of the present chapter is to suggest that there are orderly everyday models of categorization, hypothesis testing, and decision making which are *descriptively* more accurate, with regard to both clinical and social judgment, than the normative models typically used to evaluate clinical judgment. In addition, it is possible to speculate that with the appropriate safeguards, these heuristic models can be *prescriptively* useful as well—suggesting ways to design functional and realistic diagnostic, interview, and decision-making procedures. To support this line of argument, I shall consider each component in turn, presenting brief descriptions of the normative and everyday models, data relevant to their descriptive accuracy from either the clinical or the social judgment domain, and speculations about the prescriptive implications of acknowledging these everyday-heuristic models. First, I shall consider psychiatric diagnosis and models of categorization.

Categorization—fuzzy categories and prototype matching

An important component in the clinical judgment process is the body of categorical knowledge about psychiatric syndromes and the rules of thumb for making diagnoses that a clinician develops over the course of training and practice. Such is the declarative knowledge that aids the clinician in describing a prototypical schizophrenic in the abstract and in recognizing a schizophrenic patient in the concrete.

The normative model, promoted by the American Psychiatric Association (1968, 1978), for characterizing psychiatric syndromes combines an emphasis on syndromes as *diseases* (an analogy to medical diagnosis) with a classical model of disease categories (an analogy to biological taxonomies). According to this classical model there is a set of identifiable, nonoverlapping psychiatric syndromes, each associated with a small set of necessary and sufficient defining characteristics (Cantor, Smith, French, & Mezzich, 1980). Any member of the diagnostic category should possess all of these critical features, and any one possessing these features is a member of that category. The boundaries between diagnostic categories should be distinct, with few or no borderline cases, and interjudge and intrajudge reliability in categorization should be maximized. Cantor et al.

described the implications of this classical model of categories for a diagnostic category such as schizophrenia as follows:

Schizophrenia should have a set of defining features, like "withdrawal from interpersonal relations" and "associative disturbance," and only if clinicians determine the presence of these features (or signs) in a patient should they diagnose the patient as schizophrenic. Further, assuming that the features stay constant, the same clinician should diagnose the patient as schizophrenic on two different occasions; and assuming that two different clinicians are equally adept at detecting the critical features in a patient, both should reach the diagnosis of schizophrenia. Lastly, all patients diagnosed as schizophrenic should be relatively homogeneous in that they should all manifest withdrawal from interpersonal relations and associative disturbances.

The striving for a classical model of psychiatric diagnosis also was revealed recently in a piece on schizophrenia in the *Science Times* (*New York Times*, Feb. 17, 1981); Dava Sobel, abstracting from the February issue of *Archives of General Psychiatry*, says:

The word schizophrenia has been loosely used in popular accounts and scientific literature alike to cover everything from the ravings of the insane to the creative insights of genius. Even historical figures such as Sir Isaac Newton, Gregor Mendel and Charles Darwin have been called schizophrenic.

But *true* schizophrenia, research reveals, is a debilitating *illness* that may be transmitted through families and has *specific behavioral features*. Scientists believe that the more carefully they define the syndrome and the characteristics of those affected, the more likely they will be to come to understand it and cure it. To that end, *a rigorous new definition of schizophrenia* was fashioned for the *Diagnostic and Statistical Manual of Mental Disorders, Third Edition*, or "DSM-III," which was published by the American Psychiatric Association in 1980.

Supporters of this new precision in diagnosis are concerned about the persistent public misunderstanding of madness, particularly as it is spread by popular books such as *I Never Promised You a Rose Garden*. [Italics added for emphasis]

Apparently, despite claims that the new diagnostic manuals (DSM-III) would better reflect the way diagnoses are actually performed, the intent behind the revision is still to adhere to the basic canons of a classical model of categorization (for more thorough descriptions of the classical model, see Bruner, Goodnow, & Austin, 1956; Vygotsky, 1965; and Smith & Medin, 1979).

Unfortunately, psychiatric diagnosis has looked very messy by comparison to this idealized classical model:

Thus, few would want to claim that there are widely agreed-upon defining features for diagnostic categories like chronic undifferentiated schizophrenia or schizoaffective disorder. Similarly, every clinician knows that certain patients are borderline cases with respect to diagnosis. Further, patients within the same diagnostic category, even a relatively specific one like schizoaffective schizophrenia, can be quite heterogeneous when it comes to clinical features. (Cantor et al., 1980)

However, psychiatric diagnosis is not the only set of categorical knowledge and categorization rules that pale by comparison to the canons of the classical model. Recent evidence suggests that even the most mundane common object categories like tables and chairs (Rosch, 1978), not to mention more complex social categories like parties and extraverts (Cantor & Mischel, 1979), are not easily described by sets of critical features, overlap considerably in membership, and contain a heterogeneous collection of category members. Natural language categories, as used by both trained and untrained psychologists, do not conform to the scientific-normative models of categorization very well. Work in the domain of natural language categorization has made substantial progress toward deriving an alternative, more realistic model of categories that better describes how they are really used everyday. This descriptive model—which shall be referred to as the *prototype* model—provides a reasonable alternative to the classical one and, as will be shown generalizes quite well from the domain of common objects and everyday person perception to the domain of psychiatric syndromes.

According to the prototype model, categories are characterized by a (larger) set of *correlated* features, rather than the (small) set

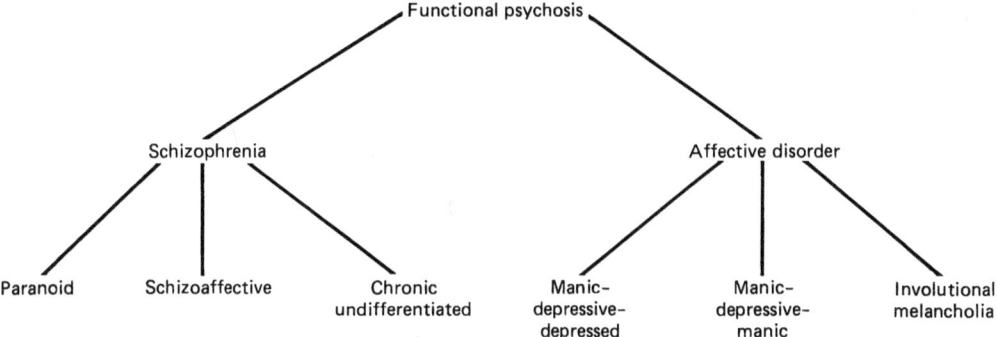

Figure 2.1. Nine psychiatric categories from DSM-II.

of necessary and sufficient *defining* features. The larger and looser set of correlated features—each of which is associated with some category members and not with others—makes up a *prototype* for the category. Simply loosening the defining features assumption of the classical model resolves a number of the problems that plagued that view:

First, the assumption does not require categories to have defining features, so the failure to specify defining features is no longer a problem. Second, prototypes are consistent with the existence of borderline cases. An item can be a borderline case if it fails to have many of the correlated features of a prototype, the way a tomato fails to have the correlated features of fruit. Third, prototypes permit extensive heterogeneity of category instances. Thus, one instance may contain most of the correlated features of the prototype and another may contain hardly any at all. (Cantor et al., 1980)

This alternative model of categorical knowledge has been very useful in describing the categories that people form about social situations (Cantor, Mischel, & Schwartz, in press) and different types of people (Cantor & Mischel, 1979). It also turns out that psychiatric diagnostic knowledge conforms much better to the fuzzy prototype description than to the classical descriptions provided in the diagnostic manuals (DSM-II or III). Consider data from a study performed by Cantor et al. (1980) to test the assumptions about categories derived from the prototype view.

Working with the taxonomy of diagnostic categories illustrated in Figure 2.1 (following DSM-II) we asked 13 experienced psychiatrists to list the clinical features of the prototypical patient from each of these nine diagnostic categories. To check for the presence of defining or only correlated features, the 13 lists generated for each category were compared for interpsychiatrist consensus. If defining features characterize these diagnostic categories, then one would expect full agreement on at least some features across the (experience of the) 13 clinicians for each category. Instead, all nine categories exhibited a similar pattern of correlated features: many unique features (a feature listed by only one clinician), a substantial number of features listed by two to four clinicians, and very few, if any, features listed by most of the 13 clinicians.

Further evidence consistent with the correlated features assumption of the prototype view was provided when consensual prototype lists (those containing features listed by three or more clinicians) for each category were scored for overlap with the defining feature sets of the DSM-II manual. First, many of the features in these prototypes were not in the DSM-II lists (e.g., 13 out of the 16 features in the affective disorders prototype were not in DSM-II for that category). Second, when some of the features did overlap across the prototype and manual lists for a given category, these were rarely features for which there had been full (or even close to full)

Table 2.2. Sample Measures of Intercategory Prototype Overlap

Category Pairs (A,B)	Number of Common Features	Number of Distinctive Features	
		(A–B)	(B–A)
(S, PS)	11	6	7
(S, CU)	12	5	3
(S, A)	1	16	15
(PS, CU)	8	7	10
(CU, IM)	2	13	17
(IM, MDD)	10	10	9
(MDM, MDD)	2	24	18
(PS, MDM)	6	12	20

Note. FP = *functional psychosis;* S = *schizophrenia;* A = *affective disorder;* MDD = *manic-depressive-depressed;* MDM = *manic-depressive-manic;* IM = *involutional melancholia;* PS = *paranoid schizophrenia;* CU = *chronic undifferentiated schizophrenia;* SA = *schizoaffective schizophrenia.*

consensus among the 13 clinicians. If these features had been operating as defining features for these clinicians for these categories, then such consensus should have been exhibited (see Smith & Medin, 1979, for further discussion of this issue).

Another dimension on which the prototype and classical models differ is with regard to predictions about intercategory similarity in a taxonomy. According to the classical model, the defining features of a category should also be true of all categories that are subsets of that category within the taxonomy (e.g., schizophrenia and paranoid schizophrenia). The looser assumption of the prototype model simply asserts that categories close in a taxonomy (e.g., schizophrenia and paranoid schizophrenia are in the same branch of the DSM-II taxonomy) will share proportionally more features in their prototypes than with categories more distant in the taxonomy (e.g., schizophrenia and manic-depression-depressed, which are in different branches of the DSM-II taxonomy). Our data on psychiatric prototypes were consistent with this view of statistical orderliness, without perfect feature nesting as required in a classical model. Additionally, there were violations of expectations about prototype overlap—for example, as the samples in Table 2.2 illustrate, the prototypes for paranoid schizophrenia and manic-depressive-manic shared more features than did those for manic-depressive-manic and manic-depressive depressed. These violations are expected in the context of a prototype model (see discussion on categorization below), but again do not fit with the assumptions of a classical model.

These data suggest that, as in the domains of common objects and personality and situation categories, psychiatric syndromes can be characterized by an orderly, but not classical, categorical system. The prototype model would appear to be a better *descriptive* one in this domain than the traditionally used classical model. In this regard, it is interesting to note that at least some changes in the DSM-III bring it closer to a fuzzy categorical system, whereas DSM-II remained loyal to the classical view: (1) DSM-III has eliminated many redundant category distinctions; (2) diagnostic categories are defined in DSM-III by larger sets of correlated features as compared with the earlier select, defining sets; (3) intercategory similarity and overlap are acknowledged and described rather than viewed as a detraction from the rigor of the system (as in DSM-II). This trend toward embracing an alternative model of psychiatric categories can only be applauded; however, the claims, echoed in the *Science Times* report mentioned above, that a new level of precision in definition has been reached in DSM-III suggest that the authors may have simply stumbled onto a prototype model without accepting its tenets.

The claim that the prototype model provides an alternative description of the categorical knowledge underlying psychiatric diagnosis also generalizes to principles of categorization itself. According to the classical model, categorization is simply a matter of presence or absence of all of the defining features of a category. By contrast, the prototype model characterizes categorization as a probabilistic process of assessing degree of similarity of a particular target to each of the prototypes for a set of relevant categories—categorization is a matter of degree. Categorization is made easy when a target shares a number of features with one prototype and is quite distinct from the others. It is more difficult when a target either shares many features with more than one prototype or is borderline (sharing few features) with regard to the relevant categories. These later cases are the instances, in the prototype view, when judgments should be unstable—changing over time and across judges—and made with low confidence.

Clinicians have frequently been criticized for providing unreliable diagnoses both in terms of the stability of a single clinician's judgments over time and in terms of the agreement across clinicians at any given time. But, how messy does clinical diagnosis look when the assumptions of an alternative to the classical normative model are tested? Cantor et al. (1980) also performed a second study to show that diagnostic behavior could be orderly if viewed from the perspective of the predictions of the prototype model. For this purpose, we asked a second group of nine psychiatrists to provide diagnoses and confidence ratings (for these diagnoses) for 12 patients. The psychiatrists read unedited case histories of 12 patients from the Palo Alto Veterans Administration Psychiatric Unit. The patients had been diagnosed in the hospital as belonging to one of four standard diagnostic categories: chronic undifferentiated schizophrenia, paranoid schizophrenia, manic-depressive-depressed, and manic-depressive-manic. There were three patients from each of the four categories. For each category there was one prototypical patient, one moderately prototypical patient, and one untypical patient. These typicality assignments had been made by scoring each case history for the number of clinical features in the history which had also been listed in the prototype for that diagnostic category by the 13 clinicians in our initial study. Prototypical patients shared many features (8 to 13 features) with the prototype, and untypical patients shared few features (four features) with the prototype for the diagnostic category to which the patient had been assigned in the hospital. The clinicians were asked to decide which of the four categories best fit each case and to provide a confidence rating (from 1 to 7 on a scale where high numbers indicate high confidence). The diagnostic judgment data from this study are shown here in Table 2.3. The table gives the diagnosis and associated confidence ratings for each clinician for the high, moderate, and low typical patient from each of the four diagnostic categories.

The prototype model makes specific assumptions about the effects of typicality on categorization: The greater the overlap in features between an instance and the category prototype, the more accurately and more confidently the instance can be classified. No such assumption is involved in the classical model because all members of a category share the necessary defining features and are thus equally "categorizable." The other relevant assumption of the prototype model concerns intercategory confusions: When the prototypes for two categories share many features, the categorizer may have difficulty distinguishing between members (even typical ones) of these categories. Again, the classical model does not make predictions about the form of intercategory confusion errors because an instance is categorized exclusively and conclusively on the basis of defining features. Cantor et al. used the diagnostic data illustrated in Table 2.3 to test these assumptions about categorization.

Table 2.3. Diagnoses and Confidence Ratings

Psychiatrist-Subject No.	Patient Typicality					
	High		Medium		Low	
	Diagnosis	Rating	Diagnosis	Rating	Diagnosis	Rating
Paranoid Schizophrenia						
1	PS	7	PS	7	CUS	6
2	CUS	4	PS	5	CUS	5
3	PS	5	PS	5	PS	2
4	PS	5	PS	7	PS	6
5	MDM	6	PS	5	PS	3
6	MDM	4	PS	5	PS	4
7	PS	4	PS	5	PS	5
8	PS	3	PS	5	CUS	5
9	MDM	5	PS	6	CUS	5
Sum rating for correct minus rating for incorrect	5		50		−1	
Chronic Undifferentiated Schizophrenia						
1	CUS	6	MDM	6	CUS	4
2	CUS	6	CUS	3	CUS	3
3	CUS	3	CUS	5	CUS	3
4	CUS	6	PS	2	PS	5
5	PS	4	CUS	2	CUS	2
6	CUS	5	CUS	5	CUS	5
7	CUS	6	CUS	3	PS	3
8	CUS	5	CUS	6	CUS	5
9	CUS	5	CUS	6	CUS	3
Sum rating for correct minus rating for incorrect	38		22		17	
Manic-Depressive-Depressed						
1	MDD	1	MDD	1	CUS	6
2	MDD	1	MDD	4	PS	5
3	MDD	1	MDD	6	PS	2
4	MDD	1	MDD	5	MDD	3
5	None		MDD	3	PS	2
6	MDD	3	MDD	3	CUS	4
7	MDD	2	MDD	3	CUS	6
8	MDD	1	MDD	6	MDD	3
9	MDD	1	MDD	1	MDD	3
Sum rating for correct minus rating for incorrect	11		32		−16	
Manic-Depressive-Manic						
1	MDM	5	MDM	4	MDM	1
2	MDM	5	MDM	6	MDM	3
3	MDM	7	MDM	5	PS	2
4	MDM	7	MDM	6	MDD	4
5	MDM	6	MDM	6	MDM	1
6	MDM	6	MDM	6	MDD	3
7	MDM	3	MDM	6	MDD	2
8	MDM	3	MDM	6	MDM	3
9	MDM	7	MDM	6	MDM	2
Sum rating for correct minus rating for incorrect	49		51		−3	

Note. From Cantor et al., 1980, PS = paranoid schizophrenia; CUS = chronic undifferentiated schizophrenia; MDD = manic-depressive-depressed; MDM = manic-depressive-manic. The confidence ratings were made using a 7-point scale with 1 = patient fits poorly in the category and 7 = patient fits well in the category.

As predicted from the prototype model (though not from the classical one), typicality had a clear effect on accuracy (match with hospital diagnosis) and confidence of diagnosis ($f(2,16) = 46.18$, $p < .001$). Specifically, untypical patients were diagnosed less accurately (mean number of correct diagnoses per category equals 4.75) and less confidently (mean confidence rating for correct diagnosis = 3.32) than were highly or moderately typical patients (mean accuracy = 8.00 and mean confidence = 4.52). While these clinicians were clearly more accurate and confident about highly and moderately typical patients than about untypical ones, the highly typical patients were not always diagnosed as easily and accurately as the moderate ones. In particular, for the manic-depressive and paranoid schizophrenic categories, contrary to expectations, the highly typical patients were diagnosed less accurately and confidently than the moderately typical ones. Inspection of these two highly typical case histories revealed two very interesting, though admittedly post hoc, explanations for these anomalies in diagnosis. First, the case history for the highly typical manic-depressive explicitly stated that many of the patient's symptoms were in remission. It should be noted that all of the clinicians correctly diagnosed this patient; they simply gave low confidence ratings for their diagnosis. Second, and more relevant to the prototype model, three of the four errors in diagnosis of the highly typical paranoid schizophrenic case were diagnoses using the manic-depressive-manic category. The reader may recall that in our initial study, the prototypes for these two categories shared unusually large numbers of features (see Table 2.2 and text on p. 32). In other words, it is not surprising that the clinicians would have trouble with this highly typical paranoid schizophrenic patient—many of the features in this case also appear in the prototype for another relevant category, manic-depressive-manic. According to the prototype model, accuracy and confidence of diagnosis should be a function of both patient typicality and intercategory similarity (measured by overlap in prototypes) among the set of relevant or possible diagnostic categories.[1]

There are a number of points worth noting about these data on diagnostic behavior. First, they clearly are described better by the prototype than by the classical model. Second, despite the fact that clinicians have been heavily criticized for errors and instability in clinical diagnoses, their diagnoses here were as *orderly* as would be expected in the context of a prototype model—they had trouble with untypical, borderline cases and with highly typical cases which overlapped with multiple categories in the set. In fact, similar categorization behavior and errors have been demonstrated in as simple a domain as that of common object categories like tables and cars (McCloskey & Glucksberg, 1978). Third, the descriptive and predictive accuracy of the prototype model in this study is particularly striking given that the scoring of patient typicality and intercategory similarity was based on prototypes generated by a different group of clinicians than those engaging in the actual diagnostic task. (And, a replication of these diagnostic results was also later obtained with clinicians in a totally new geographic setting.)

The prototype model of categories and categorization appears to provide a better, more accurate description of how categories are used in the psychiatric, as well as everyday social cognition, domain (see also Cantor & Mischel, 1979). However, it remains to be seen whether this approach will stimulate as clear a set of *prescriptive* principles as did the classical normative model. To speculate on this matter for a moment, consider the implications of adopting the fuzzy stimuli, fuzzy categories, and fuzzy categorization view in the domain of diagnosis. A diagnostic manual written in that style should represent diagnostic categories by *correlated feature sets* (i.e., listing large sets of features, perhaps with different weights for degree of association to the category), *fuzzy boundaries* (i.e., listing confusion categories which share similar prototypes), and *heterogeneity* of patient exemplars (i.e., listing multiple prototypical and unprototypical feature configurations for each category to give a flavor of the range and variety of membership). As to diagnosis and treatment, flexibility and variety are the keys—any given diagnosis is only a statement about degree of membership in a category and should be made as such, without the implications of pigeonholing a patient in *one* category or course of treatment. Multiple possible diagnoses should be kept in mind; confidence ratings for any given diagnosis should be salient when treatment decisions are made. The goal of diagnosis-treatment should not be to find the *one right* category and remain fixed in that diagnosis; rather, the possibility of multiple simultaneously and equivalently "right" diagnoses should be acknowledged. Change in diagnosis and treatment over time, rather than stability, should be the norm. Certainly, at both the manual and the diagnostic end, this is a less pure, clear, or fixed system than the one suggested by the classical view of categories. However, its flexibility and fuzziness do not *necessarily* imply that a system built on the prototype lines would be disorderly or excessively cumbersome to manage. In any case, given that prototype categorization appears to better describe and predict clinicians' behavior, it is at least worth developing the full implications of such a view. The new diagnostic manual of APA (DSM-III) is a start in this direction; however, it is crucial that the aim not be to get closer to rigid, pure, and stable *diagnoses* by loosening up the diagnostic definitions—a prototype model of categories works best with a prototype model of categorization.

Information gathering and hypothesis testing

Another way in which the clinician and the intuitive psychologist have been likened to a scientist is in the role of hypothesis tester and data gatherer. Both trained clinicians and untrained social perceivers have preconceptions about others and attempt to gather information in the service of "testing" these informal social hypotheses, or hunches, about others. Consider the clinician in private practice whose client's presenting complaint is "I'm a depressed person," or imagine yourself in an interaction with a person whom you have never met before but who is rumored to be a real "operator" type. In either case, there is a social hypothesis in mind (this person is depressive, an operator) and a more or less formal question-answer procedure (the clinical interview or a social conversation) through which to gather information to confirm or disconfirm the hypothesis. Moreover, as Table 2.1 suggests, the normative model is assumed to be the scientific hypothesis testing one derived by analogy to the experimental method.

As to information search, the clinician-as-scientist is supposed to set up the environment such as to allow all relevant (hypothesis-confirming and hypothesis-disconfirming) evidence to surface. The depressed patient should be asked about the times when he or she was ecstatically happy, as well as about those occasions when misery and loneliness hit. At the information-evaluation end, the clinician-as-scientist should be able to evaluate each piece of evidence in the light of the environment in which it was produced. Biases in the data sampling procedure should be taken into account, the size and reliability of the data sample evaluated, comparisons made to no-treatment controls, etc. For example, the clinician might consider whether a nondepressed patient or even the clinician herself or himself would or could have given the same set of responses. The clinician-as-scientist should, then, search for and receive all sorts of data, but should also be prepared to evaluate and reject unreliable evidence, as well as determine whether apparently hypothesis-confirming evidence could have surfaced either by chance or for hypothesis-irrelevant reasons. Hypothesis testing should involve "equal-opportunity" searches relevant to multiple different hypotheses. Hypotheses should be assumed to be wrong until reliable evidence to the contrary is found (the null-hypothesis approach). Such is the normative model of scientific hypothesis testing.

Recent work in the clinical and everyday social cognition domains suggest that, once again, this particular normative model is not descriptively accurate. It does not seem to capture the ways in which people interview each other or search memory to test an impression of someone or the manner in which data are evaluated to make a prediction about a person or social event (see Nisbett & Ross, 1980, for a full review of this literature). In particular, according to the normative model, the scientist begins the search and evaluation procedure committed only to the null hypothesis, ready to conduct an equal-opportunity search for data. Instead, the alternative everyday model of hypothesis testing can be characterized as theory-anchored and confirmation-biased—the lay scientist is more likely than not to confirm and conserve initial hypotheses than disconfirm or review them. This alternative model—a theory-anchored rather than a null-hypothesis-anchored one—surfaces in at least three ways in the hypothesis-testing chain: (1) the lay scientist usually operates with a single hypothesis in mind and conducts confirmation-skewed searches of memory or interviews (Snyder, 1981); (2) the lay scientist is overly impressed by data that fit a prior belief regardless of sampling biases and reliability issues (Tversky & Kahneman, 1980); (3) the lay scientist fails to take account of her or his role in shaping and eliciting theory-confirming data (Nisbett & Ross, 1980) and almost never compares treatment and no-treatment cells (Einhorn & Hogarth, 1978). In other words, whereas the hypothesis tester in the normative model is unobtrusive, objective, and open to all evidence, the everyday hypothesis tester is *reactive* and *interactive* in data gathering and *anchored* and *biased toward confirmation* in data evaluation.

Two points need to be made about this alternative everyday model: First, it is descriptively more accurate (than the idealized scientific one) both for everyday interview and evaluation encounters and for the clinical interview. Second, it does not simply describe a failure to meet the rational standards of scientific hypothesis testing—it is a true alternative model of hypothesis testing with prescriptive implications as well. It was noted earlier that the fuzzy categories model both better describes natural categorization and can provide the basis for an orderly, functional categorization system (in both the lay and the clinical domain). Similarly, the anchored and interactive hypothesis-testing model may both better describe clinical and other interviewing procedures (as they occur) and also, once acknowledged as such, form the basis for a functional, even rational, system.

As to the claim that the anchored and interactive model is descriptively more accurate than the equal-opportunity and objective one, illustrations can be found when people are asked to test impressions of others or simply to get acquainted with another person. Though these particular illustrations are not chosen from the clinical interview setting itself, similar examples can be found in the clinical literature (Bandura, Lipsher, & Miller, 1960; Frank, 1974; Oskamp, 1965; Welkowitz, Cohen, & Ortmeyer, 1967; Whitman, Kramer, & Baldridge, 1963). Fairly straightforward generalizations seem appropriate from the social cognition domain to the clinical domain.

Consider, as one example, a series of studies conducted by Snyder and Cantor (1979) to investigate the processes by which people test a social hypothesis based on information learned at an earlier date about another individual. Specifically, we are interested in the information that people would retrieve from memory to test a particular hypothesis—would this information be biased toward confirmation of the anchoring hypothesis being tested? Additionally, we were interested in the decisions about the hypothesis that people would make based on the retrieved information—would people take account of any sampling biases in their retrieval processes or would their decisions also be biased toward confirmation? To this end, we presented undergraduates at Stanford University and the University of Minnesota with a story about "a week in the life of Jane." They read about Jane's activities alone and with others, interacting with strangers and with friends, at work and in social situations, etc. The story contained equal amounts of instances of Jane behaving in an extraverted and an introverted fashion in different situations and at different times. Two days later the subjects returned and were told that Jane was applying for a job either as a research librarian (introvert-hypothesis condition) or as a real estate salesperson (extravert-hypothesis condition). They were asked to retrieve from memory any information they believed was relevant to "deciding Jane's suitability for this job." (This information was coded as hypothesis-confirming—extravert in real estate and introvert in librarian conditions—or -disconfirming by independent judges.) Then all participants were asked to judge Jane's suitability for both the (extravert) job of real estate salesperson and the (introvert) job of research librarian. According to the normative equal-opportunity model, one would expect that subjects in both conditions would retrieve as much introvert as extravert material about Jane. However, the data (shown for one of the studies in Table 2.4) supported the hypothesis-anchored model instead—subjects in the librarian condition retrieved more introvert than extravert material, and those with an extravert hypothesis to test (real estate condition) retrieved more extravert than introvert material. Moreover, their job suitability ratings were not adjusted to take account of these sampling biases; in the librarian hypothesis condition, Jane was rated as more suitable for that job than for the other job, whereas she was rated as better for a real estate than a librarian job in the real estate hypothesis condition. Furthermore, to the extent that participants reported relatively more confirming than disconfirming evidence, they regarded Jane as better suited for the job under consideration than for the other job ($r = .78$). These data, on social hypothesis testing from memory, are clearly more consistent with a theory-anchored, confirmation-skewed model than with the normative equal-opportunity, null-hypothesis one. At both the information-search and hypothesis-evaluation stages, people do not adjust their behavior to avoid the channeling effects introduced by having a single hypothesis clearly in mind.

It might be suspected that asking people to test hypotheses from memory increases the likelihood of confirmation-biased strategies being observed. However, it should be noted here that Snyder and Swann (1978) observed similar effects when people interviewed each other to test impressions about extraversion or introversion. Riggs and Cantor (1980) asked undergraduates to pick questions to ask a partner prior to engaging in a bargaining game. The bargaining game required "coolheadedness" under pressure, as well as particular card-game skills. The list of questions included anxiety-related questions, card-game skills questions, and neutral questions. Subjects who, in a pretest questionnaire, had reported *themselves* to be extreme on anxiety tended to ask their partners *more* anxiety-related questions than did nonanxious subjects. Moreover, the anxious subjects received in return a picture of a more anxious partner (as rated by naive judges) than did less anxious subjects. Again, both the information-search and the data-evaluation procedure were skewed toward confirming an initial hypothesis—though, in this case, the hypothesis was actually about the subject himself or herself. The bias in this instance is a bit like the flip of the "looking-glass self": instead of "seeing the self as others see you," our subjects came to treat the partner much as they saw themselves (see Markus & Smith, 1981, and Kuiper & Derry, 1981, for similar findings). And, as in the case of the hypothesis testing from memory studies, these subjects did not adjust their evaluations of their partners to take account of their own role in eliciting more/less anxiety-confirming (-disconfirming) material from the partner. (It should be noted that a clinical analogue for the effect of self-concept on information search about others does exist. Consider, for example, the importance of a clinician's own life experience in terms of reactions to a client's description of events and behavior. Moreover, a clinician's "theories" about etiology-behavior-situation relations clearly influence choice of questions to ask and evaluations of a patient's condition; see Langer & Abelson, 1974, as a related example.)

These data on theory-anchored information-search procedures are bolstered by other

Table 2.4. Differential Reporting of Evidence and Differential Suitability Judgments

	Extravert Hypothesis	Introvert Hypothesis
Type of Evidence		
Hypothesis-confirming	4.03	2.56
Hypothesis-disconfirming	1.00	1.28
Differential reporting	+3.03	+1.28
Job Suitability Judgments		
Job tested[1]	4.41	5.00
Job not tested[2]	3.29	2.50
Differential judgment	+1.12	+2.50

Note. From Snyder & Cantor, 1979, Experiment 2.
[1] Real estate salesperson for extravert hypothesis condition; research librarian for introvert hypothesis condition.
[2] Research librarian for extravert hypothesis condition; real estate salesperson for introvert hypothesis condition.

data in the social cognition literature. People are not likely to evaluate the validity or reliability of theory-confirming evidence (Tversky & Kahneman, 1980; Nisbett & Ross, 1980) and are rarely seen to compare such data with those from a no-treatment control group (Einhorn & Hogarth, 1978). For example, it is unlikely that subjects in the Riggs and Cantor (1980) experiment actually considered the fact that practically anyone could appear very anxious if asked a set of questions such as the following biased sample: Describe the last time that you felt anxious in meeting a stranger; describe an incident when you suffered from test anxiety. Or, did the subjects evaluating Jane's suitability for the extravert job of real estate salesperson consider the fact that even naturally introverted types could be described, on some occasions, as behaving in an extraverted fashion? Similarly, it is difficult to imagine a clinician who hears a collection of sad tales from a "depressed" client trying to evaluate the likelihood of hearing the same stories from an ostensibly "happy" person. Implicit in the hypothesis-testing and interview situation are a number of relevant comparison groups—for example, one might consider the likelihood of getting the same answers from people who are known to fit with alternative categories or the likelihood that the same person, if asked a different set of questions, would appear in a totally different light. However, there is little to suggest that either the clinician or the social perceiver makes use of these comparisons in hypothesis testing.

These data suggest that the model of hypothesis testing derived from experimental method does not accurately describe the procedures commonly used in everyday interchanges to test impressions about others. People do not seem to easily keep multiple hypotheses in mind, follow equal-opportunity searches (asking mixtures of confirming and disconfirming questions), or evaluate the fairness of the data sample and compare it for consistency with alternative hypotheses. Instead, it is more common to find an interview centered on a single hypothesis, with questions skewed toward confirmation of that hypothesis, and to find the interviewer accepting the hypothesis as long as a sufficient number of consistent bits of data are found. In a word, the norm is theory-driven hypothesis testing, not null-hypothesis testing.

In the best of all possible worlds, it might be nice to conduct equal-opportunity hypothesis-*testing* (vs. theory-anchored hypothesis-*confirming*) interviews. However, it is important to note the tremendous cognitive savings in effort and time associated with the anchored strategies more commonly employed. In informal conversation and clinical interviews, a premium is placed on quick responsiveness and free-wheeling interchange—in that context, it would be nonproductive and cumbersome to conduct equal-opportunity searches. Moreover, if one were to accept the theory-anchored quality of social hypothesis testing, it might be possible to safeguard such procedures against obvious biases and problems. For example, while it is difficult to *simultaneously* keep in mind multiple plausible hypotheses, it is less problematic to follow different lines of inquiry *sequentially*. Similarly, with one hypothesis in mind, it is less difficult to ask first a series of hypothesis-consistent questions and then a series of hypothesis-inconsistent questions than to try to mix one's approach.

Many safeguards can also be built in at the data-evaluation end, when there is frequently more time and fewer demands for responses (i.e., between sessions with a client, rather than during any particular session). At that time, the "fairness" of the sample of *questions* asked (not answers given) can be reevaluated and the set of answers given can be, at least implicitly, compared with other reference groups. Self-consciousness about data evaluation—about the role played by question selection in shaping the impression provided by the client or target person—can lead the interviewer to devise a totally new line of inquiry for the same interviewee to answer at a future time.

Also, given the luxury of repeated exposures, there is the possibility of building on feedback and getting a progressively wider and fairer sample of data about a particular person over time. In fact, I would argue that when there is the luxury of continual hypothesis-testing interactions (as in private clinical interviews), then theory-anchored searches are probably optimal—they are quick and easy and coherent and, when performed in the context of multiple sequential lines of inquiry, probably give a good picture of the many sides of a target person's behavior and characteristics (see Hogarth, 1981, for a similar argument). Clearly the danger is that the interviewer, after one exposure to a coherent set of answers confirming *one* hypothesis, settles into thinking that a *test* has been performed and all the data are already in. Instead, a self-conscious attitude on this issue would prompt the interviewer first to imagine all of the alternative hypotheses that those initial data are also consistent with and then to ask another, perhaps contrasting, set of questions on the next occasion in an attempt to elicit contrary data from the same target person. The interviewer needs to think of it as a continuous process—somewhat like an election—and not to jump to hasty conclusions based on early returns. Or, rather, maybe it is useful to each stage to operate with a conclusion in mind (even a hasty one), as long as one is self-consciously trying to get other data and to remain open to change. There is nothing wrong with *theory*-driven processing per se. It is wrong only when the processor thinks that a *fixed truth* has been found. Much as in the case of fuzzy categorization, the key element to clinicians' making this a functional system seems to be flexibility. At any given moment in the process, a hypothesis has been only more or less confirmed or suggestively supported, and probably at no point in the social impression testing process would it be wise to view the current hypothesis as "correct" or "verified." People are categorizable only to degrees, anyway, and the hypothesis tester can operate only with a "best guess" strategy.

Pooling information and making decisions

Clinicians are sometimes faced with the task of accepting or rejecting a particular option for a patient on the basis of multiple pieces of qualitatively different information. For example, consider the clinician who needs to decide whether to release a patient from an institution on the basis of information about the patient's record of responsiveness to a particular drug treatment, a behavioral profile or diagnosis, and a set of observations about the home situation. Note, first of all, that *uncertainty* pervades this choice problem. There is uncertainty about the relation between each bit of information and the eventual outcome—at best these are only imperfect predictors of the patient's outcome, and at worse they are unrelated to that uncertain outcome. Additionally, there is uncertainty even in the interpretation and coding of the data upon which the choice rests—the observations of reactions to drugs, ward behavior, and home situation all have room for error. In fact, this clinical scenario has all of the characteristics of the classic problems of choice under uncertainty studied by decision theorists in more mundane domains, such as consumer behavior and choice of gambles. As such, normative models of decision making under risk have provided a baseline of comparison for clinical decision making (Einhorn & Schacht, 1977, and Table 2.1).

Normative considerations, in this situation, arise at two levels: First, the uncertainty in the information and in the information-gathering procedures requires sensitivity and attention to problems of sampling, reliability, missing observations, treatment effects, etc. (These issues were considered, at least in brief, in the earlier discussion.) Uncertain data need to be treated gingerly, and as such the decision maker should avoid extreme predictions or decisions. Second, and more central at the moment, the decision maker needs to develop a strategy for pooling and integrating qualitatively different information in order to make as *optimal* an accept/reject decision as possible. In this second pooling task, the most widely used normative model is a linear combination rule in which the decision maker creates a single decision variable (based on a weighted integration of the multiple data points) about the option and accepts the option if and only if the value of this decision variable is above some criterion of acceptability. (This class of linear models includes expected utility models and Anderson's weighted integration models.) In the clinical example, this would involve assigning some numerical value to the patient's standing on each input dimension—a value representing responsiveness to the drug, severity of behavior, and severity of home situation—and then, perhaps, taking the average of these independent values to form a single impression of the patient's "situation." If the value on this decision variable was suffi-

ciently optimistic, then the patient could be released. Application of such a linear decision rule is "optimal" in that it will maximize the likelihood of a correct decision (i.e., "good" patients released and "poor" patients kept) over the long run. Moreover, such a combination rule is convenient because it provides for a single value for each option (i.e., an overall impression of the patient's prognosis), and this reduces a great deal of information to one nice package.

While this linear combination rule is clearly optimal in some respects (Slovic et al., 1977), recent evidence from the social cognition (Nisbett & Ross, 1980) and the clinical (Einhorn & Schacht, 1977) literature suggests that this normative model may not be *descriptively accurate* with regard to human decision-making capabilities or proclivities. For example, Nisbett and Ross describe the difficulties that people seem to have accurately and comprehensively characterizing data samples, assigning weights to individual data sources, attending to and integrating information about different attributes of a single target item or option, and resisting the sway of one particularly salient data point. For example, they report the following anecdote:

Our first anecdote concerns the cousin of one of the authors who expressed astonishment when the author happened to remark that Chicago was one of his favorite cities and that he visited it every chance he got. "I don't see how you could like Chicago," the cousin said. "Oh, you don't like it?" the author asked. "No," said the cousin, "I saw all those ugly tenements and factories from the freeway when I was driving here to visit you."

The reader undoubtedly knows enough both about sampling theory and about the variegated nature of American cities to be immune to any tendency to judge a city on so small a sample of its attributes. (p. 80)

As Nisbett and Ross point out, this anecdote illustrates the trouble that people seem to have following the canons of statistical decision theory and integrating across a variety of data samples, attributes, or dimensions to arrive at a single decision variable representing the target option. Instead, people seem to fix on a few salient data points, somehow categorically coding the option as acceptable or unacceptable on those dimensions separately, rather than integrating over dimensions. The city is unacceptable if it "could be that bad" on the "view from the freeway" dimension—an *extreme* value on one dimension is not outweighed by the collection of good or moderate values on other dimensions.

There are numerous examples now in the literature of apparent violations of the axioms of expected utility theory in human decision making (Kahneman & Tversky, 1973, 1979). However, as was the case with categorization and hypothesis testing, alternative everyday decision-making models descriptively more accurate and, perhaps, even prescriptively valuable have also emerged. For example, Hogarth (1981) recently suggested that the rules of thumb or heuristics, which the everyday decision maker seems to use (rather than applying complex integration strategies) may actually be functional because they save a great deal of cognitive energy. And, given the opportunity for corrective feedback in most (continuous) decision tasks, the errors caused by such "seat-of-the-pants" reactions may cost relatively little. Similarly, Shaw and Cantor (1981) recently suggested that the social decision maker may want to optimize other criteria, besides or in addition to expected value of the outcome, and consequently there may be more adequate decision rules than the linear combination one for these purposes.

Consider, for example, a decision rule of the following form: Instead of pooling the information into one decision variable, the decision maker could categorically code each different piece of information as indicating that the option is acceptable or unacceptable. After making a separate decision on each dimension, the decision maker is in a position to combine these independent decisions to form a final judgment. For example, the option could be accepted only if all of the independent decisions on each dimension are positive; conversely, the option could be rejected only if all the dimension-wise decisions are negative. A more complicated "swing-factor" rule would say that the decision maker relies on a favorite dimension when the option is clearly acceptable on that dimension. However, if the option is ambiguous or neutral on that favored dimension, she or he will check the other dimensions and accept the option only if its value on other dimensions is acceptable. Returning to the clinician's decision about whether to release an institutionalized patient or not—according to the independent decisions rule, the clinician will first separately code the reports on drug responsiveness, behavioral profile, and home situation as acceptable/unacceptable. Then, and only then, an overall decision to release might be made if, for example, all three reports indicated an acceptable situation. Or, the clinician might be most concerned with drug responsiveness and release the patient because the symptoms were clearly under control, regardless of the home situation.

The independent decisions rules have a number of advantages over the linear combination rules from the perspective of the everyday decision maker: First, they are simply easier from a calculation point of view; weights do not need to be assigned to the different information sources and qualitatively different information does not need to be equivalently scaled for combination. The clinician, for example, does not need to assign numerical values to the drug responsiveness, behavioral profiles, and home situation reports; rather he or she can simply code each as acceptable or not. (Of course, the drawback of the independent decisions rule is that it does not reduce the information load to a single overall value for each option, as does a linear combination rule.) A second, and more fundamental, advantage to these rules (over the more traditional linear ones) is that decision criteria other than the expected value of the outcome can be maximized. For example, suppose that individuals are very *risk averse* and simply do not want to accept an option if it has an extremely poor value on a particular dimension. According to a linear combination model, an option with a very extreme negative value on one dimension might still be accepted if, in the overall integration, this value was balanced by an extremely good value on another dimension. By contrast, because the independent decisions rule focuses attention on the independent acceptability of the option on each dimension, extreme disasters can be avoided easily through the use of the independent decisions rule. The clinician, as one example, could reject any option that involved releasing a patient to an unacceptable home situation, regardless of clear improvement in behavior and good responsiveness to drugs. Or, in the Nisbett and Ross Chicago example, using the independent decisions rule the cousin could be perfectly rational in rejecting Chicago as a place to live because on the "view from the highway" dimension it looks miserable, regardless of Chicago's other virtues as a city.

As a result of the ease and flexibility of the independent decisions rule, Shaw and Cantor (1981) suggested that it might provide a more accurate description of the strategies used in everyday decision making than the traditional linear combination rules. To test this hypothesis, we presented subjects with three standard decision problems—buying a car, hiring a secretary, and choosing a city to vacation in—and analyzed the strategies used by these subjects to combine information about an option and make a binary accept/reject decision about each option. The experiment was conducted as follows: There were three sessions for each subject; during a particular session a subject made repeated decisions about one of the problems. On each trial, subjects received two sets of information about a particular option and were asked to either accept or reject that option based on those data. To illustrate concretely, suppose this were the "buying a car" session. Then you, as subject, would be asked to make 100 decisions (after 200 practice trials) about 100 different makes of cars. On each trial you would be presented with car make X and two pieces of information about that option: (1) a probability estimate of the chances of that make of car having a good repair record in the first three years of life and (2) a probability estimate of the chances of finding an honest dealer for that make of car.[2] The decision on each trial would be whether to buy or not buy that make of car, given those two pieces of information. On each trial, then, the subject has to combine two pieces of information about a particular option and make an accept/reject decision about that option. This procedure provides us with a matrix of yes/no responses for each subject for each decision problem, which can be evaluated to determine the criteria used by that subject for such decisions. For example, for each subject performing the car decisions, we have the matrix of 100 decisions (yes/no decisions) for the 100 combinations of estimates about repair record and honest dealer availability. These matrices can be examined for evidence of use of the linear combination rule or any of the three variants of the independent decisions rule (as described on p. 42). Figure 2.2 presents schematic diagrams of the patterns of yes/no responses (on the car problem) that would characterize each of these different combination strategies. Without going into detail, suffice it to say that not one of our subjects, on any of the three decision problems, used a linear combination strategy. Instead, subjects used all three of the independent decisions strategies, often switching from one combination rule to the next across the three problems (see Shaw & Cantor, 1981, for a more detailed report).

Clearly more work is needed to determine when and if subjects do sometimes use linear combination rules in these everyday decision problems (e.g., if memory load were at issue). However, the excellent fit of these data to an independent decision strategy suggests that alternate combination rules are readily available, frequently used, and perhaps even more commonly used. These alternative decision rules are easy to use (e.g., categorical codes vs. the assigning of weights); they allow the decision maker to easily avoid a disastrous outcome on a particular dimension (e.g., the car has a likelihood of a horrible repair record) or, in the case of the swing factor model, generally to rely on a favorite dimension and consult other information only in ambiguous cases. These would seem to be very handy decision rules and may be better suited to some decision goals (e.g., avoiding extreme disasters) than are the normative

Car problem

Information sources
X_1 = Likelihood of finding honest dealer
X_2 = Likelihood of good repair record

(1) Independent decisions rule—negative

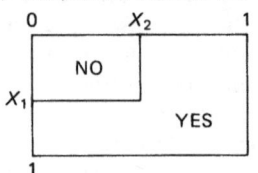

Subject says yes if the make of car has honest dealer availability estimate greater than or equal to criterion (X_1) *or* repair record estimate greater than or equal to criterion (X_2).

(2) Independent decisions rule—positive

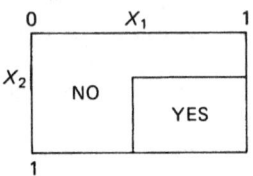

Subject says yes only if both honest dealer availability estimate is greater than or equal to criterion (X_1) *and* repair record estimate is greater than or equal to criterion (X_2).

(3) Independent decisions rule—swing factor

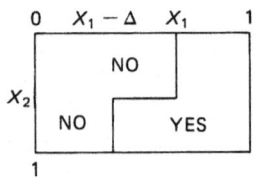

Subject says yes either if dealer availability estimate is greater than or equal to criterion (X_1) *or* if honest dealer availability estimate is ambiguous (between $X_1 - \Delta$ and X_1) and repair record is greater than or equal to criterion (X_2).

(4) Linear combination rule

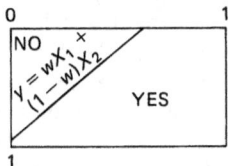

Subject forms a single one decision variable, $y = wX_1 + (1 - w)X_2$, by taking a weighted integration of the two estimates and then says yes if that decision variable is above criterion ($y \geq \beta$).

Figure 2.2. Schematic examples of response matrix for three forms of independent decisions rule and linear combination rule for the car problem.

rules derived from statistical decision theory (e.g., expected utility models).

Once again, as in the case of categorization and hypothesis testing, it is not clear that the standard models used to evaluate clinical and social judgment performance are really descriptively accurate in capturing the gist of what people are trying to do in decision-making situations. Moreover, as in those other cases, there are data to suggest *orderly* alternative (everyday) models of decision making. And, as before, I would like to suggest that the alternative strategies (in this case, the independent decision strategies) may be quite functional, fulfilling requirements of computational efficiency and most easily maximizing some important social goals (e.g., avoiding disastrous outcomes). (See Miller & Cantor, 1981, for more on this topic.) For example, the clinician in a hospital setting may firmly believe that patients should never be released into an unacceptable home situation, regardless of behavioral progress. If this is the goal (i.e., avoid the disastrous impact of the home situation at all costs), then an independent decisions strategy is both a more efficient and more direct way of maximizing such a goal than is use of the more complicated linear combination rules.

Given the impreciseness of the data on which a clinician relies in such choice situations, the optimal strategy may be the one that reduces the information the least, gives clear indication of impending disasters, and best reminds the clinician that such decision making is really only a progressive estimation process. The independent decisions strategy seems better suited for convincing a clinician to view the decision process as a continuous one, incorporating corrective feedback over time. Since the linear decisions rule provides the decision maker with a single, unified impression of the option (patient), it may promote (if only symbolically) a feeling of finality in the decision-making process. By contrast, the independent decisions rule preserves more of the original, separate bits of information about the option (patient) and, consequently, may promote flexibility and openness to revisions in future decision making. Also, because the independent decisions strategy also has alternative combination rules (Figure 2.2), it may again suggest to the decision maker that there are multiple ways to view a single option. The independent decisions rules, with the preservation of separate information and alternative combination rules, seem most in keeping with the noisy and uncertain data base and outcomes with which a clinical decision maker is typically concerned.

Everyday models and prescriptive implications

The present chapter has concentrated on three components of the clinical and social judgment process—categorization, hypothesis testing, and decision making. These components processes share at least two aspects: (1) they are processes for which strong similarities exist between the clinical and social domains and (2) performance on these tasks has typically been evaluated by comparisons to rather "rigid" normative models developed to describe performance in other domains. Clinical and social categorization has appeared messy by comparison with categorization in the biological sciences domain (Zigler & Phillips, 1961). Clinical and social hypothesis testing has appeared biased and error-prone by comparison with standards of scientific hypothesis testing (Nisbett & Ross, 1980; Snyder, 1981). And clinical and social decision making has appeared irrational and nonoptimal by comparison with statistical decision theories (Kahneman & Tversky, 1979; Nisbett & Ross, 1980). While these normative models have always been the basis for comparison, recent studies summarized here suggest that they are simply not descriptively accurate with regard to clinical or social categorization, hypothesis testing, or decision making. The standard normative models (listed in Table 2.1) may provide rules for how people *should* behave, but they do not seem to describe how people *do* behave across a wide variety of social cognition tasks (see Miller & Cantor, 1981, for a discussion of criteria for rationality in social cognition).

The standard normative models do not do a good job of describing everyday social cognition. But there are alternative perspectives on categorization, hypothesis testing, and decision making. In fact, the prototype model of categorization (Rosch, 1978), theory-driven model of hypothesis testing (Snyder, 1981), and independent decisions models of decision making (Shaw, 1981; Shaw & Cantor, 1981) seem to do a better job of description in both the clinical and the social domain. Despite the pervasive desire to use and fit behavior to the normative models, behavior that is consistent with these everyday models does not necessarily have to be characterized as either messy or suboptimal. As the studies summarized here suggest, fuzzy categorization, theory-driven hypothesis testing, and risk-averse decision making can be *orderly* if viewed within context and not through a mirror colored by expectations derived from the normative models. For example, using a prototype model it is possible to anticipate conditions under which clinicians will have particular trouble in diagnosis (Cantor et al., 1980, and text p. 33). And, having acknowledged that people use these alternate rules, it is possible to see the safeguards that might "improve" diagnosis and hypothesis testing. Sample safeguards were suggested here for the clinical hypothesis-testing interview and data evaluation process (see text p. 40). Moreover, behavior in accord with these everyday models need not be viewed as irrational or suboptimal. In particular, the fuzziness, instability, and uncertainty so pervasive in social stimuli and social events make the prescriptions of the normative models simply unrealistic for clinical or social judgments. A more realistic view of these social cognition tasks would encourage cognitive rules which are as flexible, fuzzy, and malleable as the social world upon which they operate. The everyday models (listed in Table 2.1 and described above) are actually better tuned to the continuous estimation and revision process that needs to be encouraged in social cognition. Well-defined categorical systems, scientific hypothesis testing, and optimal decision theories seem to encourage, though not always intentionally, the belief that there is a "right" answer—a true categorization, a correct hypothesis, and a best decision. This attitude may not be conducive to orderly, fair behavior in the clinical and social domains. Judgments in those domains require quick thinking about very complex and unstable stimuli and events. The requirements of cognition in social interaction are speed and decisive action. But decisions made under pressure are often poor and thoughtless. Given those conditions (fuzzy stimuli and pressures for hasty cognition), most optimal decision rules are those that encourage flexibility and continuous revisions. The everyday models seem to be better candidates for creation of this self-conscious attitude in social cognition than the standard normative models.

Notes

1. These results were replicated with a group of 14 pyschiatrists at the Western Psychiatric Institute at the University of Pittsburgh School of Medicine.

2. The stimuli on each trial consisted of two probability estimates; for example, in the car-decision problem the two estimates dealt with likelihood of a good repair record and honest dealer availability. For each estimate, the stimulus value on each trial was generated by sampling from one of two distributions: a "signal" distribution (e.g., good repair records, good availability) with a mean estimate of .7 and a "noise" distribution (e.g., poor repair records, poor availability) with a mean estimate for good record of .25. Half of the trials for each estimate were sampled from the "signal" distribution. Subjects were trained to expect variability, e.g., a good estimate could occur for a make of car with a "poor" record and a poor estimate occur for one sampled from the "good" record distribution. They also were told the prior probability of good record (.5) and the average estimate of likelihood of a good record given that the car actually had a good record ($\bar{X} = .7$) and given that it actually had a poor record ($\bar{X} = .25$). After making a decision on each trial, subjects received feedback as to the actual repair record (good or poor) and honest dealer availability (good or poor) for that make of car.

References

American Psychiatric Association. *Diagnostic and statistical manual of mental disorders* (2nd ed.). Washington, D.C.: Author, 1968.

American Psychiatric Association. *Diagnostic and statistical manual of mental disorders* (3rd ed., draft version of Jan. 15, 1978). (Available from the Task Force on Nomenclature and Statistics, American Psychiatric Association, 722 West 168th Street, New York, NY 10023.)

Bandura, A., Lipsher, D. H., & Miller, P. E. Psychotherapists' approach-avoidance reactions to patients' expressions of hostility. *Journal of Consulting Psychology*, 1960, 24, 1–8.

Bruner, J. S., Goodnow, J. J., & Austin, G. *A study of thinking*. New York: Wiley, 1956.

Cantor, N., & Mischel, W. Prototypes in person perception. In L. Berkowitz (Ed.), *Advances in experimental social psychology* (Vol. 12). New York: Academic Press, 1979.

Cantor, N., Mischel, W., & Schwartz, J. A prototype analysis of a naive psychology of situations. *Cognitive Psychology*, 1981, in press.

Cantor, N., Smith, E., French, R., & Mezzich, J. Psychiatric diagnosis as prototype categorization. *Journal of Abnormal Psychology*, 1980, *89* (2), 181-193.

Einhorn, H. J., & Hogarth, R. M. Confidence in judgment: Persistence of the illusion of validity. *Psychological Review*, 1978, *85*, 395-416.

Einhorn, H. J., & Schacht, S. Decisions based on fallible clinical judgment. *Human judgment and decision processes in applied settings*. New York: Academic Press, 1977.

Frank J. D. *Persuasion and healing*. New York: Schocken Books, 1974.

Hogarth, R. M. Beyond discrete biases: Functional and dysfunctional aspects of judgmental heuristics. *Psychological Bulletin*, 1981, in press.

Kahneman, D., & Tversky, A. On the psychology of prediction. *Psychological Review*, 1973, *80*, 251-273.

Kahneman, D., & Tversky, A. Prospect theory: An analysis of decision under risk. *Econometrica*, 1979, *47*, 263-291.

Kelley, H. H. The process of causal attribution. *American Psychologist*, 1973, *28*, 107-128.

Kuhn, T. S. *The structure of scientific revolutions*. Chicago: University of Chicago Press, 1962.

Kuiper, N., & Derry, P. The self as a cognitive prototype: An application to person perception and depression. In N. Cantor & J. Kihlstrom (Eds.), *Personality, cognition, and social interaction*. Hillsdale, N.J.: Erlbaum, 1981.

Langer, E., & Abelson, R. A patient by any other name . . . : Clinician group differences in labeling bias. *Journal of Consulting and Clinical Psychology*, 1974, *42*, 4-9.

Markus, H., & Smith, J. The influence of self-schemata on the perception of others. In N. Cantor & J. Kihlstrom (Eds.), *Personality, cognition, and social interaction*. Hillsdale, N.J.: Erlbaum, 1981.

McCloskey, M. E., & Glucksberg, S. Natural categories: Well-defined or fuzzy sets? *Memory & Cognition*, 1978, *614*, 462-472.

Miller, G., & Cantor, N. A critical review of R. Nisbett & L. Ross. *Human inference: Strategies and shortcomings of social judgment. Social Cognition*, 1982.

Nisbett, R. E., & Ross, L. *Human inference: Strategies and shortcomings of social judgment*. Englewood Cliffs, N.J.: Prentice-Hall, 1980.

Oskamp, S. Overconfidence in case-study judgments. *Journal of Consulting Psychology*, 1965, *29*, 261-265.

Riggs, J., & Cantor, N. Structural models in social interaction. Unpublished manuscript, Princeton University, 1980.

Rosch, E. Principles of categorization. In E. Rosch & B. B. Lloyd (Eds.), *Cognition and categorization*. Hillsdale, N.J.: Erlbaum, 1978.

Shaw, M. Attending to multiple sources of information. *Cognitive Psychology*, 1981, in press.

Shaw, M., & Cantor, N. Social decision-making. Manuscript in preparation, Princeton University, 1981.

Simon, H. A. Rationality as process and as product of thought. *American Economic Review*, 1978, *68*, 1-16.

Slovic, P., Fischhoff, B., & Lichtenstein, S. Behavioral decision theory. *Annual Review of Psychology*, 1977, *28*, 1-39.

Smith, E., & Medin, D. *Representation and processing of lexical concepts*. Paper presented at Sloan Conference, University of California, San Diego, March 1979.

Snyder, M. Seek, and ye shall find: Testing hypotheses about other people. In E. T. Higgins, C. P. Herman, & M. Zanna (Eds.), *Social cognition: The Ontario symposium*. Hillsdale, N.J.: Erlbaum, 1981.

Snyder, M., & Cantor, N. Testing hypotheses about other people: The use of historical knowledge. *Journal of Experimental Social Psychology*, 1979, *15*, 330-342.

Snyder, M., & Swann, W. Hypothesis-testing process in social interaction. *Journal of Personality and Social Psychology*, 1978, *36*, 1202-1212.

Tversky, A., & Kahneman, D. Casual schemas in judgments under uncertainty. In M. Fishbein (Ed.), *Progress in social psychology* (Vol. 1). Hillsdale, N.J.: Erlbaum, 1980.

Vygotsky, L. S. *Thought and language*. Cambridge, Mass.: MIT Press, 1965.

Welkowitz, J., Cohen, J., & Ortmeyer, D. Value system similarity: Investigation of patient-therapist dyads. *Journal of Consulting Psychology*, 1967, *31*, 48-55.

Whitman, R. M., Kramer, M., & Baldridge, B. Which dream does the patient tell? *Archives of General Psychiatry*, 1963, *8*, 277-282.

Zigler, E., & Phillips, L. Psychiatric diagnosis: A critique. *Journal of Abnormal and Social Psychology*, 1961, *63*, 607-618.

3

BELIEFS ABOUT MENTAL DISORDERS: FINDINGS AND IMPLICATIONS

AMERIGO FARINA
JEFFREY D. FISHER
UNIVERSITY OF CONNECTICUT

In the present chapter we shall examine the role of beliefs about mental disorders in the field of mental health. The term "field of mental health" refers to that broad array of institutions, individuals, and processes involved with the entire spectrum of mental disorders. Clearly this means persons suffering from mental problems, whether they are recognized as psychiatric patients or not, as well as practitioners (e.g., psychiatrists, aides, social service personnel) whose job it is to care for afflicted people. However, it is also important to consider the effect of different views of mental disorders on various segments of the general public, and we shall do this as well.

There are compelling reasons why we must consider the public, as well as patients and mental health workers, when we try to understand the role of beliefs about mental disorders. What all three groups believe to be the nature of mental disorders will influence such matters as who becomes a mental patient and how patients are treated. Consider that if mental disorders are believed to be totally genetically determined, it makes little sense to treat those afflicted by means of psychotherapy. Such an effort would be very much like trying to talk blue-eyed people into having brown eyes. On the other hand, eugenics, the removal of the responsible faulty genes from the population pool by such means as sterilization of the carriers, would be quite effective. This example is no invention of ours, presented as a dramatic illustration of what beliefs can theoretically do. Exactly this view has been forcefully advocated by prominent mental health professionals (e.g., Kallmann, 1959), and at least two states, North Carolina and Virginia, have, in the recent past, had and sometimes enforced laws which

---

We would like to thank the University of Connecticut Research Foundation for the support they provided, which made some of the research reported herein possible. This chapter was, in part, written while one of us (A.F.) had the privilege of being a Fellow of the Center for Advanced Study in the Behavioral Sciences during the year 1980–1981. We would like to express our appreciation for the support provided by the National Institute of Mental Health (Grant 5-T32-MH14581–05) and by the John D. and Catherine T. MacArthur Foundation. Work on this chapter was supported, in part, by a grant from the United States–Israel Binational Science Foundation.

made schizophrenic patients subject to sterilization.

In what follows, we shall review the role that various beliefs about mental disorders have played in the past and then consider the many consequences these beliefs have at present. Their effects will be considered separately for all three parties involved in the area of mental health: the public, the patient, and the mental health professional. In a more speculative vein, we shall consider the breadth of impact of some particular beliefs which we feel are of crucial importance in determining outcomes in the field of mental health (namely, a generalized disease view of mental disorders in comparison with generalized learning conceptions). We shall additionally be concerned with the effect of these "social learning" and "medical model" beliefs on conditions other than mental disorders, such as alcoholism and old age. Some constructs in the area of clinical psychology (e.g., locus of control, learned helplessness) which are pertinent to these particular beliefs will also be considered. Finally, we shall review some data which indicate areas of uncertainty about this class of beliefs and shall point out where caution is in order.

The central concept in our chapter is belief, and we shall begin by defining it. We shall use this term interchangeably with others, such as knowledge or information, and it will refer to assertions that are objectively verifiable. The statement "More men than women are alcoholic" expresses a belief, and, in principle, we can determine its truth or falsity. For example, we can find out the sex of all alcoholics in a given area. We want to distinguish beliefs from *attitudes*, which we shall use as interchangeable with terms such as "feelings" or "values," and regarding which truth and falsity have a totally different meaning than when referring to beliefs. "I don't like mental patients" expresses an attitude. It is subjective and not refutable by empirical evidence external to the speaker.

Attitudes and beliefs about mental disorders have very different properties, as Nunnally (1961) demonstrated many years ago. For example, Nunnally (p. 47) found marked differences in the beliefs of older and younger people about mental disorders and in the beliefs of less educated and more educated people. In contrast, all of these groups had very similar (uniformly unfavorable) attitudes. Also, attitudes toward mental aberrations have been remarkably stable over the course of eons in Western culture as well as other cultures (Farina, in press). However, beliefs have shown radical changes over relatively short periods of time.

But perhaps the most telling reason for differentiating these two classes of variables is their role in helping us to understand human behavior in the area of mental health and illness. As Rabkin's (1972) review makes clear, there is a rather weak and complex relationship between someone's attitudes toward mental disorders and the way she or he behaves. Some studies have found that people who express favorable attitudes toward mental patients will not necessarily behave more favorably toward them than will those whose attitudes are negative. Indeed, just the opposite results have sometimes been obtained. In contrast, studies of the relationship between beliefs about mental disorders and behaviors toward those afflicted seem to be much more comprehensible, useful, and promising, as will be seen.

Beliefs about mental disorders
Historical background

A consideration of past beliefs about the nature of mental disorders can be most helpful in understanding psychopathology at the present time. There are two major patterns which we believe should be noted. First, as suggested earlier, there have been dramatic changes over time in beliefs about mental disorders. The earliest beliefs of which we have records suggest that people thought mental problems were a supernatural phenomenon (e.g., the mentally deranged were viewed as possessed by demons or actually in league with the devil). This set of beliefs prevailed for a longer period than any other conception. A very different view came to be widely held both in Europe and in America about the middle of the nineteenth century (Deutsch, 1965). The afflicted were believed to have something quite natural and rather simple—perhaps even minor—wrong with them. It was thought they could easily be cured if they were brought to one of the many mental hospitals that were then being built. Then, in the early twentieth century, there emerged the belief that at least some mental disorders were genetically determined. Like someone's height or skin color, these disorders were practically unalterable. Later still, many people, both lay persons and mental health professionals, held the conviction that environmental conditions encountered during life determined if someone would or would not develop psychopathology.

These marked shifts in what mental disorders are thought to be suggest that such beliefs are fluid and malleable. Evidently, the understanding a society has of the basic nature of the phenomenon of psychopathology is quite unstable and changeable over time. This inconstancy is also indicated by the fact that at any given time beliefs vary from place to place. Thus, differences can be shown to exist for any selected period of time if we compare our society with other groups of people. Canadian Indian tribes have believed that some mental aberrations foretold the victim's change into a cannibal (Farina, 1976, p. 137). But even Europeans and Americans, whose cultures are certainly very similar, have different conceptions of mental disorders. Italians are much more inclined to see such conditions as genetically caused than Americans (Farina, 1976, p. 75).

The second pattern we must note is that the beliefs held by a society have very important consequences. How a society treats those stricken, and perhaps also how the sufferer behaves, depend on what is believed about the nature of mental disorders. When demons were thought to cause mental problems, theology was closely tied to the treatment of mental disorders. Priests, monks, and holy men were the psychiatrists and psychologists of that era and administered the equivalent of psychotherapy and tranquilizers. They exorcised demons, obtained confessions from those in league with the devil, and duly noted their activities. For example, some clerics in Vienna reported in 1583 that during that year they had cast out 12,652 living devils (Deutsch, 1965, p. 17). Even burning someone at the stake, a particularly common practice in the sixteenth century, is a reasonable procedure if it is truly believed that the corruptible body is possessed by a demon and that fire brings purification.

A later, more "natural" view of insanity was that blood was responsible for the malady. For example, the "father of American psychiatry," Benjamin Rush, who practiced at the end of the eighteenth and in the nineteenth century, wrote that the basic cause of mental disorders was an "overcharge" of blood (Deutsch, p. 78). Bleeding as a treatment for mental problems became extremely common, and the sufferer not infrequently died as a result of the treatment (Zilboorg & Henry, 1941, pp. 261–262). Finally, a very specific belief about insanity provides a particularly clear example of the practical consequences of such beliefs. In the nineteenth century in America, it was widely thought that "lunatics" were totally insensitive to cold (Deutsch, p. 159). Consequently, they were at times housed in quarters devoid of heat, even in winter and in cold climates. The discovery of that practice, in fact, was an important factor leading Dorothea Dix to devote her life to reforming the procedures for the care of the mentally disturbed.

The present

Contemporary beliefs about mental disorders are very unstructured, vague, and hesitantly held. People in our society are confused and uncertain about what mental disorders really are. Nunnally (1961, pp. 21–22) administered 240 statements about causes, symptoms, prognosis, treatments, and social significance of mental health problems to a sample of 349 persons. Subjects were asked to indicate their beliefs about the truth or falsity of each statement. When responses were factor-analyzed, only very weak item clusters were found. The first ten factors accounted for only 25 percent of the total variance. Items that would logically appear to go together were, in fact, found not to be consistent. For example, a given subject might answer as true both a statement that women have more nervous breakdowns than men and an item asserting that men and women are comparable in frequency of emotional problems. We did a similar study using a belief questionnaire composed of items selected by a panel of clinical psychologists for their clear portrayal of mental disorders as diseases or as end products of past learning (Farina, Fisher, Getter, & Fischer, 1978). Even with these rather homogeneous items, a factor analysis revealed very weak factors accounting for little variance. Thus, it seems that at present people's beliefs regarding mental disorders are decidedly not cohesive, poorly organized, and held tentatively and with little conviction.

Perhaps it is because people have such confused and uncertain views about the nature of mental disorders that beliefs can be so easily changed. At any rate, beliefs *are* very easily changed. Nunnally (1961), basing his conclusions on the numerous studies he carried out, states that "it is very easy to get people to accept new facts about mental health problems. People will gobble up any seemingly factual and authoritative-sounding information" (p. 237). Attending a class where mental health disorders are discussed (Costin & Kerr, 1962; Fisher & Farina, 1979), or merely being exposed to people with a well-defined set of beliefs (Manis, Houts, & Blake, 1963) has been shown to induce changes. Even a few sentences differing in content which are embedded in otherwise identical messages about mental health have been found to significantly alter beliefs in three separate experiments (Farina et al., 1978). Too, studies have shown that psychiatric patients alter their ideas about the nature of mental afflictions as a function of hospitalization (Harrow, Fox, & Detre, 1969; Manis et al., 1963; Smith, 1969). And volunteers, trainees, or paid workers who interact with mental patients often change their beliefs about mental disorders as a consequence of the interaction (Beckman, 1972; Gelfand & Ullman, 1961; Holzberg, Gewirtz, & Ebner, 1964; Paul & McInnis, 1974; Smith, 1969).

Beliefs may be changed in other settings as well. In a number of studies by Morrison and his colleagues, the attempt was made to openly alter beliefs by a procedure much like a seminar. Samples of community residents (Morrison & Teta, 1977), mental health professionals (Morrison & Becker, 1975), family caretakers (Morrison & Nevid, 1976a), and psychiatric outpatients (Morrison, 1976, 1977; Morrison & Nevid, 1976b) have all had their beliefs significantly shifted in the desired direction when compared with control subjects. These effects were still present when measured eight months after the manipulation. Beliefs about mental disorders have even been changed by very indirect procedures that merely *imply* that subjects should alter their ideas. That was demonstrated by Whitman and Duffey (1961) in a study that is important to our model. They measured the beliefs of mental patients before and after the patients were treated exclusively with drugs. We believe that being given drugs implies to the patient that his or her problem is somatic and biochemically caused. In accord with that implication of the treatment, patients significantly shifted their beliefs toward viewing their condition as a physical malady after their drug therapy.

Beliefs about mental disorders, then, are unstable, multifaceted, and highly complex. In addition to being easily changed, they vary concerning whether mental disorders are acute and sudden in onset or develop slowly and insidiously. Beliefs also differ as to whether there is assumed to be just one basic mental disorder and the variations we see are quantitative, or whether various mental afflictions are qualitatively different entities. In this chapter we shall confine ourselves mainly to one set (or cluster) of beliefs which we shall conceptualize as falling along a simple dimension. At one extreme, mental problems are construed as bodily diseases, as is, for example, pneumonia. A pathological process has developed as a result of internal or external causes, and the ensuing symptoms are as inevitable as fever when one has pneumonia.

At the other end of the continuum, more weight is assigned to learning experiences as the basic causes of mental problems. Mental disorders are viewed as resulting from faulty learning and from fear- and anxiety-provoking experiences, and psychiatric patients are thought to be somatically and biochemically like anyone else.[1]

Of course, most people's ideas will not be neatly coherent and unambiguously located at a specific point on this continuum. As the research reviewed earlier suggests, people's beliefs are often inconsistent and scattered along any dimension. In many cases, however, there will be a greater or lesser predominance of medical model or social learning beliefs. Also, it is theoretically possible for someone's ideas to be highly consistent and to fall in a restricted range of the continuum. In fact, this often happens as a result of systematic learning experiences (e.g., Fisher & Farina, 1979) or of media campaigns to change beliefs about mental disorders, or as a function of experimental manipulation.

The disease-to-social-learning continuum

There are a number of compelling reasons for our focusing on the medical model–social learning continuum of beliefs. A major reason why these beliefs particularly require attention is that they seem to play a central role in the overall domain of orientations toward mental disorders. People who are convinced that mental disorders are the ultimate outcome of particular learning histories are also likely to believe that such disorders are chronic and not acute and unpredictable in onset and that those not exposed to the pathogenic experience will not develop morbidity. Individuals who believe mental disorders are learned probably also consider them to be fundamentally similar, since they all result from one basic cause. On the other hand, if mental disorders are viewed as diseases, people bearing different diagnoses may be thought to be suffering from qualitatively different conditions, such as genetically caused biochemical errors in some cases and infectious processes in others. In addition to the centrality of beliefs along a medical model–social learning continuum, a second reason for our present focus is that more research has apparently been done on these beliefs than on any others in the field of mental health. We shall review much of that research in the present chapter.

A third reason why we should be concerned with medical model and social learning beliefs is the nationwide effort to change the public's orientation toward mental disorders and alcoholism being made by groups such as mental health associations and Alcoholics Anonymous. Such groups are attempting by various means (e.g., press releases, public service messages by television stations) to achieve nothing less than a wholesale modification in the beliefs of Americans. Clearly the intent is to shift beliefs toward viewing alcoholics and mental patients as victims of disease. We are told we should no more blame them for their comportment than we blame a person with a cold for sneezing. For example, an article that appeared recently in a major Connecticut newspaper discussed the orientation of the Glastonbury Mental Health Group. The group's president is quoted as saying, "Mental illness is not something to be ashamed of. It's really no different from, say, an attack of appendicitis or other illnesses" (*The Hartford Courant*, January 21, 1979). We have already reviewed data which indicate that these messages do accomplish the desired purpose, i.e., shift people's opinions in the direction of the message.

We have no quarrel with the certainly benign intent of this propaganda. Those responsible want society to give a more favorable and less stigmatizing reception to mental patients and alcoholics. The propagandists seem to think this will happen if such generally stigmatized people are viewed as sick and thus not responsible for their failures. Under these conditions it is presumed that the afflicted will not be viewed as weak, incompetent, and flawed. We are not arguing that there are no beneficial consequences of such messages. For example, it may be more comforting for alcoholics to think of themselves as sick than to believe their personality is the basis of their difficulty, although this remains to be demonstrated. But we will demonstrate that *some* consequences of this propaganda can be very unfavorable and that its continuation without additional research is of doubtful wisdom.

In addition to intentional attempts to change beliefs about mental disorders, there are more subtle ways which produce changes. The field of mental health is dominated by the medical profession, which determines how patients are cared for and treated. This clearly serves as an indirect source of information to people about the nature of mental disorders. Mental institutions are usually managed by physicians, and medical procedures, such as blood pressure measurement and X-rays, are used routinely. Less severe and more prevalent adjustment difficulties are likely to lead to contact with a medically trained person, and prescriptions for tranquilizers are so common it is a cause for alarm. We have already suggested that taking medication for emotional problems can lead to medical model views, and there are a large number of Americans doing just this. Valium is the most frequently prescribed drug in America (CBS "Sixty Minutes," July 30, 1978); a total of 44 million prescriptions for it were filled during a recent year in America alone ("CBS Evening News," September 10, 1979). And Valium is just a single brand of tranquilizer in one of a number of classes of them. Nonprescription calmatives are also selling well. Americans spent a total of 3.8 billion dollars for these preparations in a recent year ("CBS Evening News," May 22, 1979).

We believe the medical-chemical preeminence in mental health affects beliefs by swaying the general public as well as those with emotional difficulties to view adjustment problems as basically medical and somatic ailments. Anyone who observes adjustment difficulties being treated by a medical specialist and by means of drugs is likely to conclude that the problem is physical. After all, if the problem were due to deficiencies in social learning and in developing satisfactory interpersonal relationships, would not the corrective steps be quite different? A person experiencing such difficulties might then be talked to about social behavior or coached in relating to others. But the sufferer is being treated by a specialist who knows brain functioning, hormones, and biochemistry and whose curative tools are basically drugs. Hence, it appears likely that these practices will influence people to conclude that problems in adjustment are a kind of disease.

We also believe that a medical orientation influences the mental health field in another and quite different way. Beliefs held about medical disorders have come to *encompass* mental disorders. Consider, for example, the central medical tenet that the earlier morbid processes are discovered and treated, the better off the sufferer. In accordance with this doctrine, people are advised by such authoritative agents as mental health associations, experts, and textbooks to scrutinize themselves to see if symptoms of mental problems exist. If signs of morbidity (e.g., anxiety) are detected, people are further counseled to seek professional help quickly. Unfortunately, nearly everybody can discover such "symptoms" in the form of anxiety, depression, insomnia, and engagement in "shameful pleasures." The many behaviors that can be interpreted as reflecting mental disorders, and the tendency to view these as harbingers of worse things to come, may have a variety of negative consequences. They may lead us to overestimate our probability of developing a mental problem and to a widespread and wholly unjustified fear of mental disorders.

For instance, Gurin, Veroff, and Feld (1960) interviewed over 2,000 Americans and asked them if they ever felt they were going to have a nervous breakdown. Two of every ten subjects answered yes. Similar results were obtained by Terry (1971), who interviewed 175 college students and asked them to estimate their chances of going to a mental hospital in the future. Of these, 23 percent estimated their chance to be 50 percent or greater. This is not surprising, since the "symptoms" we come to view as reflecting mental disorders must be expected as a facet of life as inevitable as moments of joy, disappointments, or breathing. Our use of these to identify problems in ourselves is unfortunate, since it seems clear that symptoms of difficulty in adjustment (e.g., anxiety) are an entirely different matter from early signs of a disease such as cancer. But our medically oriented belief that they are "early warning signs" of problems, coupled with fear of mental disorders and a readiness to treat them at the earliest possible time, may well be important causes of the present-day stampede to mental health practitioners and druggists. In a great many instances people who notice such occurrences would be better served by trying to improve conditions themselves rather than by rushing off for guidance and help.

But clearly many people do rush off to professionals with doubts about their mental status. Those who do are apt to encounter another consequence, and a decidedly negative one, of medical beliefs about diseases in the field of mental health: Individuals who consult a physician or a psychiatrist are quite likely to have their fears substantiated. Scheff (1973) has provided unequivocal evidence indicating that the healing profession works on the assumption that people are sick unless proved healthy beyond a reasonable doubt. He reports a study by Bakwin that concerned a condition surely more objective than mental disorder—problems with tonsils. Bakwin began with 1,000 school children and found that 611 had had their tonsils removed. The rest (389) were examined by physicians, and 174 were selected for tonsillectomies. Another group of physicians examined the 215 remaining children, whose tonsils had just been judged healthy, and declared that 99 of them needed to have their tonsils extricated. Still another group of doctors examined the 116 children whose tonsils had been judged sound in all previous examinations and recommended tonsillectomies for about half of them.

For medical problems it may well be that this strategy is, all things considered, often a beneficial one for those who are afflicted. While there must be a great many people who have had healthy tonsils removed or who have endured other needless medical procedures, there are also probably many others whose lives were spared or prolonged by this practice. And generally no great harm appears to be done when a doctor acts on the false assumption that a medical disorder is present. But declaring someone to be mentally disordered is an entirely different matter. All kinds of negative consequences attend the individual known to be a mental patient (Farina, in press).

First of all, the mental patients' (or ex-mental patients') personal feelings and actual behaviors suffer simply as a function of knowing that others view them as such. They believe they are disliked, and their task performance deteriorates. There are also negative behaviors and evaluations from others. Generally, mental patients are quite severely stigmatized (e.g., they are perceived as incompetent and unpredictable, people do not want to associate with them, and mothers would even prefer an ex-prisoner as a babysitter to an ex-mental patient). Patients are less likely to be given jobs or even to be rented a room, and there are extreme legal sanctions for those declared insane. Although the situation is improving for patients, even according to recent laws such individuals can be forcibly locked up in a mental hospital or deprived of a driver's license, and control of their money can be taken away from them. These things do not happen to someone who has pneumonia or cancer. Thus, medical practices that seem to be beneficial when applied to medical disorders may be harmful when applied to mental problems.

Specific consequences of medical model and social learning beliefs

We have seen thus far that beliefs about the basic nature of mental disorder held in society are rather easily changed and have quite clear and important consequences. In what follows, we shall focus mainly on the array of beliefs of central interest in this chapter (i.e., the basic nature of mental disorders as a disease or the end result of particular environmental experiences). The knowledge which has accumulated over the years will be reviewed and the implications of these findings for the field of mental health discussed. The consequences of these beliefs will be considered separately for the public, for the victim of the mental problem, and for the mental health practitioner.

Research on consequences of beliefs for the public

Research indicates rather convincingly that someone afflicted with mental problems is evaluated more favorably by the public if the difficulty is presented as an interpersonal problem rather than as an illness. For example, a group of hospitalized mental patients was coached by Rothaus, Hanson, Cleveland, and Johnson (1963) to present themselves to different employment interviewers in one of two ways. On one occasion they described their hospitalization as due to an *illness*. They accomplished this by saying that they had suffered a nervous breakdown and were now being treated for a nervous condition and that treatment consisted of their being given tranquilizers and other drugs. To another employment interviewer they explained their hospitalization as due to *social problems*. On that occasion each patient described his own personality problems (e.g., revealing that he was shy and avoided people or tended to be antagonistic toward others) and reported receiving treatment in how to solve interpersonal problems. Employment interviewers judged the same patients, who otherwise behaved comparably in the two conditions, as more likely to be given a job in the social problems than in the illness condition.

Another study using very different procedures and done in a different country (Norway) strongly supports the finding of Rothaus *et al.* Ommundsen and Ekeland (1978) told their subjects, who were students of both sexes averaging 18 years of age, that they were participating in research on traffic accidents. After the subjects were divided into three groups, all received the same detailed description of a driver losing control of his car and running into a tree beside the road. However, for one group the driver was reported to have been hospitalized for an appendectomy, whereas for the other two groups he was described as having been a psychiatric patient. In addition, for one of the two latter groups the psychiatric condition was presented as an *illness* by quoting the ex-patient as saying, "Yes, I got ill . . . trouble with my nerves . . . it's a bad disease . . . but got medicines that helped. . . ." For the final group the psychiatric condition was attributed to social problems, with the patient quoted as saying, "Yes, I had troubles on the job . . . and economic problems . . . I guess there were more stress [sic] than I could cope with. . . ." The subjects were then asked to indicate how important 16 factors were in causing the accident. Eight of the factors placed the blame on the driver (e.g., driver thinking about other things), and the rest attributed the responsibility to circumstances (e.g., rainy weather). When the psychiatric disorder was presented as an illness, the driver was blamed significantly more for causing the accident than in the control (appendectomy) condition. There was no difference in blame between the control group and the condition where the psychiatric disorder was presented as due to social problems, and the difference between the two psychiatric conditions was not reliable.

Other research suggests that a mental patient whose condition is viewed as an illness is thought to have less self-control and to be more at the mercy of the morbid process than one whose condition is viewed as due to social and interpersonal factors. Farina et al. (1978) and Fisher and Farina (1979) did three studies on this issue, and the findings are depicted in Table 3.1. In the first study, male and female students were randomly divided into two groups. One group was induced to believe mental disorders were essentially social problems, and the other was led to believe they were a type of illness. The manipulation was accomplished in the context of describing the services of the student mental health clinic. As will be seen, this led to a variety of secondary beliefs with important implications for the field of mental health. For example, the group that was informed that mental disorders are manifestations of social problems thought the afflicted have more control over

Table 3.1. Belief Expressed by Subjects About Degree of Personal Control Over the Disorder

	Social Learning	Illness	$p<$
Study 1	3.25[1]	2.76	.02
Study 2	3.51	3.15	.02
Study 3	3.98	3.43	.02

Adapted from Farina et al. (1978) and Fisher and Farina (1979).
[1]The higher the number, the greater the extent of control believed to exist.

their difficulties than the group who looked upon psychiatric disorders as illnesses. Study 2 is an exact replication of Study 1 and had identical results. Study 3 was done quite differently. Here, the students in the social learning condition were enrolled in an abnormal psychology class taught by an instructor who described mental disorders as almost exclusively due to social learning. The students in the illness condition had an instructor who assigned an important role to genetic and somatic factors. Beliefs of the two groups of students were comparable on the first day of class, but by the end of the course they differed in many ways. The difference most relevant for the present discussion is that the social learning group, relative to the illness group, believed patients are better able to control their mental problems.

We previously indicated that a massive nationwide effort, though one without coordinated and central direction, is under way to change public beliefs toward viewing problems with alcohol consumption and difficulties in adjustment as illnesses. It seems that a major reason stimulating this effort is to reduce the public stigma of being a mental or alcoholic patient. But do people who are induced to view such problems as illnesses really become more favorably disposed toward the afflicted? An attempt to answer this question was made in the studies by Farina et al. (1978) and Fisher and Farina (1979), facets of which we just examined. In all three studies, subjects were asked how degrading they believed mental disorders to be. In none of the studies were there any significant differences between subjects who viewed disorders as illnesses and those who viewed them as interpersonal problems. Directional differences were the same in all three studies, with the social learning groups actually describing mental disorders as *less* degrading than the illness groups. These findings lend no support whatever to the assumption that if mental disorders are viewed as illnesses like any other, the afflicted will be less stigmatized by society. Possibly those who advocate an illness view of mental disorder think other benefits will ensue from such a shift in beliefs, such as an alleviation of the family's guilt and the promotion of greater self-respect on the part of the patient. But the failure to find support for the most central and seemingly reasonable assumption raises doubts about the existence of other possible benefits.

In all the studies reviewed thus far concerned with the public's role in mental disorders, random samples of subjects were selected and their beliefs were subsequently manipulated. Under these conditions, a shift in beliefs toward viewing mental problems as illnesses produces a less favorable reception and evaluation of the mentally afflicted. There is also evidence indicating that the same pattern of effects exists for subjects chosen for having preexisting beliefs that mental disorders are an illness, when compared with others who believe psychiatric conditions are learned. Golding, Becker, Sherman, and Rappaport (1975) developed a scale to measure traditional and nontraditional conceptions of mental disorders.[2] (Examples of items asserting the medical model and social learning points of view are, respectively, "Most mental patients are suffering from a chronic illness and are unlikely to improve" and "Mental illness is a learned way of coping with problems in life and can be unlearned as well.") The authors report that subjects with traditional conceptions of mental disorders rated deviant individuals as more disturbed than subjects with nontraditional views. They also indicated more reluctance to become friends with such individuals. In another study, Golding et al. showed videotapes of moderately deviant people to subjects with traditional and nontraditional views. The former subjects saw the patients as more deviant and expected greater difficulty in a social interaction with them than those with nontraditional views.

Clearly, Americans, and seemingly people of other nationalities as well, prefer an individual showing deviant behavior which is believed to be the result of learning and interpersonal problems to that which is thought to result from an illness. This suggests that people receiving treatment for a mental disorder would prefer to have their therapist view their problems as resulting from social learning rather than as an illness. Research fully substantiates this expectation. Colson (1970) presented two different explanations of behavior disorders to each of 56 graduate students of both sexes. One current professional view, subjects were told, was that such disorders were the result of an emotional illness "just like any other illness." The other view, they were informed, was that behavior disorders were the result of inappropriate or inadequate learning of coping skills. Subjects were asked if they themselves would rather be treated by a professional who would approach their problem from the former or the latter point of view. Of the 56 subjects, 49 preferred the professional with the social learning conception of mental problems.

Significance of public beliefs for the field of mental health

At the most general level, public beliefs about the basic nature of mental disorders importantly affect what happens to those who are afflicted. That conclusion seems inescapable when we examine what was believed at different times and the manner in which this affected the treatment of sufferers. A belief that demons were responsible for insanity was accompanied by the preeminence of theologians in curing these conditions, and the social treatment of the mentally disordered was as if they literally were not human. But the impact of beliefs is also quite apparent at the present time, when virtually all explanations are "rational" and "scientific." An illness, as opposed to a learning conception, leads to quite a different outlook and comportment toward mental patients. These contemporary conditions have both practical and theoretical significance, which we shall now consider.

A very critical matter for those of us involved in or even concerned about the mental health field is the social acceptance of people displaying deviant behaviors, particularly those perceived as afflicted with a mental disorder. The very ambitious goal of deinstitutionalization of mental patients, or even the very modest objective of returning some patients to the community, is dependent upon the reception society accords them. When patients leave the institution they obviously must stay somewhere. Many mental health workers believe that the community must accept not only the individual ex-mental patient, but facilities such as regional mental health centers as well if discharge from the hospital is to be successful. But neither ex-mental patients nor facilities for their care are wanted by society. People do not want ex-patients nearby, and former patients are refused jobs and housing just because they have been mentally disturbed. Some communities have even passed laws banning their presence (Farina, in press).

The research we have reviewed indicates that things can be done to change the situation and to make society more receptive. We have seen that societal beliefs about mental disorders can be readily changed and that such changes can produce beneficial consequences for the former patient. Unfortunately, the changes that are being wrought at present would seem to lead to a less favorable social reception. People are being told that mental disorders and alcoholism are illnesses like any other illness. We have seen what follows when such messages are internalized. The afflicted are rejected, evaluated less favorably, and perceived as less in control of the disorder. The idea that they are less able to control their affliction may contribute to the belief that mental patients are unpredictable, a characteristic which is perhaps the most salient hallmark of mental patients in the eyes of the public (Nunnally, 1961, p. 46).

The effort by well-intentioned people to place mental disorders in the category of illnesses should be reconsidered. The evidence we currently have clearly suggests that mental patients would be more welcomed by the community and better treated if their condition was seen to result from learning and interpersonal conflict. Perhaps that is the sort of message we should be conveying to people. Of course, as we have suggested, it is possible that some people under some conditions may benefit as a result of the public's belief that behavioral aberrations are illnesses. Families of mental patients may feel less guilty, and alcoholics may be enabled to retain more self-respect. However, whereas such benefits remain to be demonstrated, the negative consequences of these beliefs are quite apparent. We feel this state of affairs requires some second thoughts about whether we should induce people to believe that mental disorders are illnesses.

Unfortunately, we as individuals (mental health workers or not), are generally not in a position to influence public beliefs and in that way improve the lot of mental patients. We do not control the various media used to disseminate relevant messages. But there are ways by which we, even acting singly, may be able to have a meaningful effect. In accordance with research findings, we can teach ex-mental patients and others publicly identified as having mental problems (e.g., those treated in outpatient facilities) how to receive a more favorable reception from others. Individuals can be taught to present themselves to family, friends, and neighbors as having undergone stress and having been unable to effectively contend with it. Particularly in the very important matter of finding a job, they should emphasize the social-environmental nature of their difficulties. It would also appear helpful to have ex-patients indicate they are now relying on themselves for problem solution and that they are able to exercise considerable self-control. Concerning the professional treatment they have received, they should stress learning to cope with personal problems competently. These generalizations may also apply to alcoholics, but this has not yet been demonstrated.

The final issue we would like to consider in examining the role of society is *why* there seems to be a more unfavorable reaction to those with mental disorders which are viewed as an illness rather than as a product of experience and learning. We must necessarily speculate, but two explanations, which are not mutually exclusive and which may be related, appear worth pursuing. One is that the illness conception does not really clarify anything in the eyes of the public and, indeed, appears to make mental disorders more enigmatic and unfathomable. People see certain members of society who act in deviant and unaccountable ways and who are therefore identified as mentally disordered, insane, or crazy. The illness explanation tells them those people are afflicted by an illness like any other illness. But even moderately close attention reveals that what they have observed is like no illness with which they are acquainted. For example, there is no *physical* evidence of a morbid process, such as fever. And while some mental health practitioners advocate treating mental problems with procedures that are used with other illnesses (e.g., drugs), others employ totally different treatments (e.g., psychotherapy). What other illness receives this kind of treatment? Are cancer, hepatitis, or lumbago patients ever merely spoken with (as is done in psychotherapy) to cure their illnesses? And if the illness explanation seems vague and unintelligible to at least some mental health workers, how much clarity does it have for the public in terms of explaining the phenomenon of mental disorders?

We think it possible that the net consequences of assuring the public that a mental disorder is an illness is to make such conditions all the more mysterious, unfathomable, and perhaps frightening. And the less understandable mental disorders are, the less favorable public attitudes toward them seem to be. At least under some conditions, it has been shown that increasing degrees of uncertainty associated with such disorders lead to less favorable attitudes toward them. On the other hand, decreasing levels of uncertainty elicit more positive reactions (Nunnally, 1961).

A second explanation for the more negative public reaction to patients described as having an illness than to others whose problems are due to social learning revolves on some beneficial aspects of the latter orientation. A social learning view makes mental patients appear not as strange and different creatures, but as people like ourselves, and as such they may become more liked and accepted. If they have shown strange behavior under stressful conditions, we can understand this since we all have behaved irrationally in such situations. Also, if they have learned odd patterns of behavior and have accepted unusual beliefs, this, too, can be understood. All of us know about strikingly different practices learned by people in other societies, as well as by those in our own circle of acquaintances. When we have a social learning outlook we can identify with and thus understand such individuals, which may be a crucial matter permitting acceptance of another.

Research provides suggestive support for the hypothesis that identification may be responsible for the favorable treatment of deviant individuals whose condition we view as learned. In his obedience experiments, Milgram (1965) showed that when the teacher felt more similar to the victims, there was a decreased willingness to give shocks to them and a decrease in the intensity of the shock administered. And Ring and Farina (1969) had subjects administer an electric shock to someone they believed to be a mental patient after they had been informed about how well or poorly adjusted tests showed them, the subjects, to be. The more similar to a mental patient's a subject's adjustment was described as, the more favorably the patient was treated.

These findings suggest that another's strange behavior may be more tolerable to us if we think it is due to processes which, albeit in less extreme forms, we also recognize in ourselves (i.e., a social learning process).[3] On the other hand, disturbed behavior may be more threatening and unacceptable when we understand it to stem from factors which are not perceived to be present in most people (i.e., an illness).

Research on consequences of beliefs for the patient

In addition to affecting the behavior of the general public, medical model and social learning beliefs have profound effects on a patient's actions. First, it appears that patients perceive themselves as having more control over their condition if they believe it to be a result of social learning than if it is perceived as an illness. Morrison, Bushell, Hanson, Fentiman, and Holdridge-Crane (1977) observed that the more psychiatric outpatients believed mental disorders were illnesses, the more dependent they felt upon mental health professionals.[4] (Recall that in discussing the role of the public's beliefs on their behavior, we similarly found that a medical model orientation was associated with views that patients could not control their own behavior.) It does seem logical that the more patients think their difficulties are due to an illness, rather than to inept and inappropriate decisions and behavior, the more they should believe medical experts are needed to cure them and the less they should do to help themselves. Consequently, it may be that patients holding somatic views actually do less to improve their social and interpersonal functioning and are therefore more likely to become socially isolated and chronic cases. This interpretation is consistent with the findings of another study by Morrison (1976), in which one group of psychiatric outpatients had their views of mental disorders shifted in a social learning direction and another group served as a control. Six months after the manipulation, psychiatric hospitalization was less frequent in the experimental groups (one hospitalization among 13 subjects) than in the control group (four hospitalizations among 13 subjects).

The possibility that mental patients who believe they are stricken by an illness will torpidly accept their fate becomes more alarming when the previously cited study by Whitman and Duffey (1961) is considered. In that study, newly admitted patients were treated exclusively with drugs and the treatment was found to markedly shift their beliefs toward conceiving of their mental problems as illnesses. The authors conclude that "chemotherapy can result in strong denial of interpersonal difficulties and functional reasons for hospitalization" (p. 292). Since millions of people with mental problems are treated with drugs, there is the possibility of a vicious cycle affecting many of them. Individuals who are unable to cope with personal and interpersonal problems visit a mental health expert seeking help with those problems. They then receive drugs, which causes them to believe they are suffering from an illness, and thereafter cope with their problems in a less satisfactory way than before. Their worsened problems and increased dependence on the mental health expert make them continue as patients, in consequence of which they receive more drugs, and so on.[5]

Apparently it is not just individuals who are or have been psychiatric patients who feel there is little they can do to help themselves if they view mental disorders as a disease. On the contrary, research shows the same process takes place for average people with quite ordinary and mundane problems in adjustment. In the study by Fisher and Farina (1979), it will be recalled that two comparable groups of students had their beliefs shifted, one toward viewing mental disorders as learned and the other toward conceiving of them as illnesses. The latter group, relative to the former, also came to believe that medically based treatments were more likely to cure mental disorders, that it was of less value for them to identify the causes and solutions for their emotional problems, and that "standing on one's own feet and helping oneself" were of less value. They also reported using more drugs and/or alcohol to relieve emotional problems during the semester. What these findings suggest, then, is that a shift toward believing mental disorders are illnesses has a broad and logical effect on quite normal people which is similar to that observed in mental patients.

The dependent measures in the Fisher and Farina study were questionnaire responses, and we cannot be certain that the subjects really felt and behaved as they indicated. However, the results are closely supported by another study that used more behavioral measures. This study, in addition, provides clear information about the relationship between beliefs about mental disorders and behavior (Farina et al., 1978). Female college students were recruited to receive a psychotherapy session which, they were told, was intended to help them with their own personal problems. Half were then induced to view mental disorders as illnesses, and the rest were induced to view them as social and interpersonal problems. Following the therapy, they were asked to note in a journal during the subsequent week each time they thought about a personal problem such as was discussed in therapy. It was found that the social learning group thought about personal problems significantly more frequently than the disease group. Evidently people with an illness conception of mental disorders (patients and nonpatients alike) not only believe there is little they can do about their adjustment problems, but actually do little to improve or cope with their condition.

Further support for our suggestion that a medical model view will lead to less effective coping than a social learning orientation comes from studies done in another context.[6] Davison, Tsujimoto, and Glaros (1973) and Davison and Valins (1969) did research to determine if beneficial coping abilities attributed to medical causes are maintained for less time than those attributed to the self. In one study, subjects first received shocks and then were given a drug which they believed helped them cope with the pain of subsequent shocks. Subjects who were eventually told that the drug had been a placebo (i.e., that *they* were responsible for their ability to withstand the shocks) coped more effectively with later shocks than a group who attributed their earlier success to a medical cause. The same procedure was followed in a second study done with subjects with problems falling asleep, who were given drugs to help them with this difficulty. Half were later made to think the drugs were ineffective, so that *they* were really responsible for their success in falling asleep. The rest believed the drug had put them to sleep. Subsequently, the former subjects were better able to fall asleep than the latter.

These experiments indicate that when people feel responsible for solving a problem, they may respond more favorably than when they think solving the problem is beyond their control.[7] This is because the former conditions elicit perceptions of personal responsibility and the belief one has control. There are several reasons why these facilitate efforts to deal with a problem. First, perceived, as well as actual, control has been found to have numerous beneficial consequences (Garber & Seligman, 1980). In addition to engendering greater feelings of security, it elicits active attempts to exercise control over the environment. Second, when people believe their present situation has improved because of *their* efforts (as in the studies by Davison and his colleagues), they believe they have acquired the necessary skills to cope with it, and, in fact, in many cases they have. Because of this, such people are more likely to do something to cope with future difficulties rather than to passively accept the situation.

Significance of patient beliefs for the field of mental health

The above research has important implications for the field of mental health. If we expect individuals with psychiatric problems to do something to improve their situation, they must be made to feel they are capable of making such improvements. It seems to us that a very important matter in producing these feelings of control is the patient's belief about the nature of her or his condition. In many cases, it would be effective for practitioners to communicate to clients that they *do not* have a disease, but rather that their problems are due to difficult environmental and interpersonal problems which can be improved by thinking about them, understanding them better, and making changes in behavior. Concerning messages addressed to the general public for dealing with problems in adjustment, these should not be unqualified recommendations to find professional help. At present, the information given to people with such problems typically not only advocates obtaining professional help, but often advises urgent action.

Consider the Ann Landers column, which is carried by newspapers throughout the country. On a recent date, the final paragraph of the answer to one letter was as follows: "I urge you not to give up. Hang in there until you find someone [a psychotherapist] who fills the bill. It's worth the effort." Part of the answer to a second letter on the same day was, "There are many excellent mental health facilities in your city. I urge you to make an appointment at once. . . . Please get going. You are a sick girl" (*The Peninsula Times Tribune*, October 13, 1980). We believe such messages are often interpreted to mean mental health problems are understandable and modifiable only by highly trained professionals. They make mental difficulties seem like engine trouble in a car, only more complicated and with no owner's manual available to provide understanding. Furthermore, to carry the automobile analogy a bit further, the messages warn that additional driving without expert attention will bring disaster. Messages to the public by mental health associations, experts, and other agents should convey the information that we all have difficulty in adjustment and that people can think about their behavior and make some improvements by changing on their own.

The myriad drugs used in the mental health field represent a very special problem. We feel the crucial issue here is what the patient is told about the role drugs play in the treatment of mental disorders. It must not be said or implied that they play the same role in mental problems as penicillin plays in pneumonia, i.e., the drug cures the condition. Rather, patients should be led to view drugs as aids in the basic process of changing behaviors. Rather than analogous to penicillin given for pneumonia, drugs should be presented to patients as analogous to codeine given to endure the pain following an operation. The drug is an aid to the healing process, but it does not have a direct curative effect. Of course, there are people in the mental health field who believe that drugs work on mental disorders much as they do on pneumonia. But we are not aware of any convincing evidence supporting this view. Moreover, we believe at least some mental disorders are due to failures of the patient to mature, to develop the social skills necessary to interact with people, and to learn to enjoy social relationships. We do not see what drugs could do to directly change these basic problems. As someone is reported to have said, there is no drug which can be taken in order to play Beethoven on the violin.

Research on consequences of beliefs for the mental health worker

The beliefs mental health workers have about the nature of mental disorders have a clear effect on how they behave and, specifically, on how they treat patients. Moreover, we are able to discern from these findings that when mental health workers believe mental disorders are illnesses, the consequences are again negative, as they are for the public and patient components of the field of mental health. Two relevant studies have used a psychometrically refined general index, which is called the opinions about mental illness (OMI) questionnaire, to assess these beliefs (Cohen & Struening, 1962). While some items composing this questionnaire seem to assess attitudes, most pertain to beliefs, as these two variables were defined earlier. One of the studies entailed giving the OMI to representative samples of mental health workers at each of 12 mental hospitals (Cohen & Struening, 1964). The investigators wanted to see if the length of time patients spent in the community during the first year following admission could be predicted from OMI responses of staff members. In hospitals where the predominant staff belief was that mental patients have a specific type of illness, ex-patients spent fewer days in the community than those from hospitals where the staff held more of a social learning view. The researchers demonstrated that these results could not be attributed to differences across hospitals in degree of emotional disturbance of patients.

Ellsworth (1965) obtained results consistent with those of Cohen and Struening, although the relationship of his findings to the disease–social learning continuum of beliefs is unclear. The OMI and another questionnaire were given to nurses and aides, and hospitalized psychiatric patients under their care were asked to describe them. Staff members were perceived by the patients to behave just as their self-reported beliefs implied. Nurses and aides who thought psychiatric patients are dangerous and need limitations placed on their behavior were described as behaving in a controlling and restrictive way. Evidently the beliefs of mental health workers about the nature of mental disorders do have important consequences. They certainly appear to play a role in the treatment and care psychiatric patients receive.

Langer and Abelson (1974) were specifically concerned with beliefs that psychiatric problems are learned or are manifestations of a disease. Their subjects were two groups of mental health professionals; one group believed mental disorders were exclusively products of social learning, and the other group apparently thought biological factors played an important role. All were shown the same videotaped interview, but half of the subjects in each group were told the interviewee was a job applicant and the rest were informed he was a mental patient. The learning-oriented professionals described the interviewee comparably in the two conditions, but those with an illness view described the "patient" as significantly more disturbed than the "job applicant." Once again we see that a disease conception of mental disorders has an unfavorable effect, and in this instance both the professionals and the mental patients suffer. The patients are perceived as displaying disturbed behavior that is non-existent and may encounter unneeded restriction and treatment as a result. And the mental health workers' perception of reality is distorted, which may constitute a handicap to the satisfactory performance of their job.

These negative consequences may be engendered by the very procedures used to train our mental health "gatekeepers," according to a study by Morrison, Madrazo-Peterson, and Simons (1977). The term "gatekeepers" refers to those whose professional position gives them the power to decide whether someone will or will not go to an institution such as a mental hospital. The researchers measured the beliefs regarding mental disorders of physicians, who may exercise the legal power to commit someone to a mental hospital, and of lawyers, who can be in a position of defending someone threatened with commitment. They also assessed the views of medical and law students in an effort to determine what happens to people's beliefs as they become practicing lawyers or physicians. Both lawyers and physicians were reliably more likely to view mental disorders as illnesses than were the students. While this study does not tell us what the consequences of this shift are for potential mental patients, the other research reviewed suggests they will be negative. For example, potential patients will more likely be regarded as people afflicted with a disease and in need of hospitalization rather than as people who need to better learn how to get along with others.

Significance of mental health workers' beliefs to the field of mental health

The broad implications of the currently available research are that perhaps changes should be made in the view of mental disorders held by mental health workers, particularly professionals. Greater success might be achieved by placing in the major decision-making roles individuals having more of a social learning orientation rather than professionals with a disease conception of mental problems. This could be accomplished by giving greater emphasis to the role of learning in mental disorders in training mental health workers, especially medical specialists. This is already being done in some training institutions through the inclusion of courses or lectures by psychologists or sociologists. It has been shown that even practicing mental health professionals can have their beliefs changed by such procedures (Morrison & Becker, 1975).

Social learning and disease views: How generally applicable?

Up to this point, we have focused on the effects of disease and social learning views primarily as they relate to mental disorders. It has been shown that their effects can be quite pervasive, having consequences for the general public, the mental health practitioner, and the patient. Moreover, it seems that those with relatively severe adjustment difficulties, as well as anyone who has stress in day-to-day life, are affected in their actions by their views about the fundamental nature of emotional disorders. We feel that it is also quite probable that, in addition to affecting behavior regarding emotional disorders, beliefs along a disease–social learning continuum also have consequences for one's handling of many additional types of life problems which are more or less serious in nature. The discussion of this which follows will be highly speculative and clearly in need of corroboration by future research. However, it suggests that disease and social learning orientations may characterize our thoughts about a broad array of human problems and that the same lines of reasoning and patterns of findings reviewed earlier may apply here as well.

Alcoholism

As with mental disorders, a massive effort has been undertaken to convince the general public that alcoholism is a disease and should be treated medically. The National Institute of Alcohol Abuse, an arm of the federal government, has mounted a major campaign along just these lines. Also espousing related beliefs is Alcoholics Anonymous, an organization which has long been quite successful in changing public views about alcoholism.[8] In Alcoholics Anonymous publicity, prominent national figures reveal having this problem and, rather than being viewed as depraved, are admired for overcoming their "disease." One result of a disease view is that the states are establishing detoxification centers to replace the former "drunk tanks" in jails. And there are other benefits, at least for alcoholics, which accrue from their viewing a drinking problem as a disease rather than a result of personal shortcomings. Certainly people can be happier with themselves harboring the thought of being sick rather than thinking that they are failures and perhaps degenerates.

But consideration suggests that this wholesale change of beliefs may not be entirely good for either society or the person with the drinking problem. If beliefs operate for alcoholism as they do for mental problems which do not involve drinking, then this propaganda may produce some unwanted results. As with mental problems, the issue of self-responsibility and belief in the efficacy of personal action in changing a situation may be a central one. Consider what may occur if people with drinking problems believe that alcoholism is a disease. If they accept that view, they will likely feel that they need medical help. There is little that the individuals can do by themselves either to prevent their becoming an alcoholic or to deal with an existing problem. To resist the urge to drink, even enormous personal effort is not enough. What is needed is medication, medical guidance, and, often, hospitalization. Such beliefs leave people with few coping skills and may even contribute to their becoming alcoholics rather than coming to grips with the problem by making changes in their behavior or environment.

We should take special note of a related aspect of the medical and Alcoholics Anonymous views. Especially in the case of the latter, once one becomes an alcoholic, one is always an alcoholic. Although one may stop drinking, alcoholism, like a trick knee, is always there and ready to reemerge under certain conditions. These beliefs are akin to the well-known assertion that if ex-alcoholics have even one drink, they are lost, and seem to be particularly virulent ones for people with drinking problems. If someone who is convinced he or she is a victim of a disease with these characteristics does have a drink, he or she may think it futile to struggle and hence proceed to prolonged binges.

At the other extreme of beliefs, the alcoholic may not consider himself or herself any different from anyone else, except for drinking too much. This may be thought to result from learning inappropriate coping strategies, placing oneself in the wrong environment, or surrounding oneself with the wrong friends. The responsibility for the problem and its resolution may then seem to depend much more on personal action. Because of this, social learning and disease views of alcoholism may lead to different consequences. Individuals who see their condition as a social learning problem may be more likely to drink, but in moderate amounts. They may also be able to cope more effectively when they initially perceive alcohol consumption as becoming a problem. In contrast, people having a disease conception of alcoholism may resist the first drink but, once started, continue drinking. The results of studies on mental disorders suggest that these possibilities should be explored, especially in view of the extensive and evidently successful efforts to change beliefs of both the public and the afflicted about alcoholism.

One's beliefs about the nature of alcohol abuse also have important implications within the therapy context. If a person is taught that alcoholism is a disease, he or she may expect an external medical cure (e.g., effective drug therapy) and will view personal effort as relatively unimportant in resolving the problem. To the best of our knowledge, an effective medical cure for alcoholism does not yet exist, and it *is* very important for the afflicted individual to play an active, committed role in treatment. Thus, the changing of beliefs toward alcoholism to be more medical in orientation may be creating a generation of patients who are very difficult to treat and manage.

Another question involves recurrence of an alcoholism problem once one has "successfully" terminated treatment. In line with the studies cited earlier which suggest that people are more effective in dealing with problems (e.g., insomnia) if they come to believe that they personally are the cause of the cure, we would expect individuals with disease views of alcoholism to have higher recurrence rates than those treated with more of a social learning orientation (Davison et al., 1973; Davison & Valins, 1969). Colleti and Kopel (1979) and Colleti and Stern (1980) have reported results for abstention from smoking which support this possibility. After completing a program to stop smoking, subjects were asked to indicate how much they thought quitting had been due to their own efforts as opposed to factors such as luck and fate. It was found that at both one and two years after treatment, those who had felt more personally responsible were significantly more likely to be abstinent than those who had felt less personally responsible for stopping smoking. Evidently, those individuals who think that they themselves have caused the change feel they have learned the requisite skills to cope with their problem (and probably have), and they may be more successful in preventing reoccurrence.

This line of reasoning suggests some potential problems with the use of antabuse, for example. Use of this substance may (a) contribute a medical model view of alcohol abuse and (b) cause individuals to attribute success to the drug rather than to their abilities to cope, thus opening them to problems once the drug is withdrawn.[9]

Drug abuse

The line of reasoning suggested for alcohol abuse holds as well for drug abuse. To the extent that one views such a problem as a disease rather than a social learning difficulty, it is likely that one will feel less control over the condition, will exercise less control, and will be more dependent on external, medically oriented sources for a cure. If these sources were highly efficacious, such views would not be so problematic—but again, it seems evident that elements of personal control and a strong personal commitment are important to overcome these problems. Thus, drug addicts with a medical orientation may be led to assume a dependent role in therapy, which does not optimally promote progress. We also feel that "recovery" as a result of such a program, since it does not cause people to believe they have control (or teach them the necessary social-environmental skills to cope in the future), may be less likely to be permanent. When substances like methadone are used, these (like antabuse) may contribute to the patients' belief in a medical type of cause and cure for drug abuse and predispose them to future problems.

Also, we feel that medically oriented beliefs may actually contribute to the problem of drug abuse. We have grown up in a society which holds medical science and modern drugs in awe, and it is not difficult in our age to come to the conclusion that the body is a chemical system which merely has to be properly regulated in order to perform optimally. Such a view could clearly predispose one to take "uppers" when they seem necessary, "downers" when they seem appropriate, and so forth. As we indicated earlier, such a general medical orientation toward the body may predispose people to excessive dependence on medication even when this is unnecessary, as well as to drink.

Adjustment in old age

We feel that important matters pertaining to the aging process and adjustment in old age may also be affected by beliefs that fall along a continuum analogous to the one we have been speaking of thus far. On the one hand, many individuals and practitioners view problems experienced by aged individuals as reflecting nonoptimal responses by the person or society to the changes that occur with advanced age (e.g., illness, death of a spouse, retirement). Such responses are due to a faulty social learning process. In this view, the major obstacle to a rewarding and productive old age is not poor health, but attitudes and behaviors on the part of the aged individuals and society which are self-defeating (Butler, 1979). The individual can learn more constructive responses to life change events that will mitigate many of the negative effects traditionally associated with aging.[10] Generally, a social learning view attributes some importance to the effect of biological and physiological changes on problems in aging, but much less than the disease orientation, to be described below.

In terms of that set of beliefs, most difficulties associated with aging *are* due to medical or biological factors associated with advanced age (e.g., alterations in the human cell, biochemical changes in the body) rather than to personal and societal views and practices, which could be changed to improve matters by an appropriate social learning process (Butler, 1979). In this sense, there is a strong similarity between the aging process and a long-term disease, which over time results in complete deterioration of an individual's functioning. A part of these beliefs seems to be that the best way to ensure a rewarding and productive old age, and also to delay the aging process, is through proper medical care, research in the neurosciences, investigations in the immune and endocrine systems, and so on.

We feel that people differ in terms of which views they hold about the aging process and that these views will have important implications for how aged people behave and also for how practitioners, family members, and others treat aged individuals. Clearly, these two sets of beliefs differ markedly in terms of the amount of control the aged individual can be expected to have over her or his functioning and general fate, and lack of control is often associated with helplessness (Seligman, 1965) and depression. In several studies, imparting feelings of control to people in old-age homes has been found to lead to better health and functioning, and residents in a condition that fostered control were even more likely to be alive one year later (Langer & Rodin, 1976; Rodin & Langer, 1977).

Thus, it may be (a) that disease-oriented beliefs by aged individuals and practitioners may not be associated with optimal outcomes and (b) that changing these beliefs toward the social learning end of the continuum may foster positive outcomes. In line with past research, it would be anticipated that changes in perceived and actual control which would accrue from social learning beliefs could affect general feelings of hope, mood, mobility, self-help efforts, dependency, and overall health. It could even lead to more discharges to homelike settings and to fewer people dying in old-age homes.

Other implications

We have speculated about the implications of disease models and social learning beliefs for trivial and more serious problems in emotional adjustment, alcohol and drug use, and difficulties associated with advanced age. Since space limitations preclude a complete consideration of all the other areas where we feel our line of reasoning may apply, we shall suggest just two more: programs aimed at stopping people from smoking and weight loss programs. In both of these areas, it is felt that a social learning view of the problem will facilitate the development of coping skills necessary to accomplish the goal and will avoid relapse to former problems more than will disease beliefs. Indeed, the studies by Colleti and Kopel (1979) and Colleti and Stern (1980) provide empirical support for our view. Disease-oriented beliefs in these settings can be internalized in people through the general orientations held by society and the views of practitioners, as well as through the use of medically oriented treatments (e.g., diet pills, medical apparatus to stop smoking). Social learning orientations would have to be fostered through verbal means, suggesting to people that their problem is due to improper learning (e.g., learning to consider food as a reward; to associate cigarettes with relaxation) and environmental conditions (e.g., having favored snacks in one's house). The "cure," then, would come from learning alternative associations, unlearning old ones, and removing from one's environment substances which have harmful effects.

Generalizability to other psychological constructs

We have argued that beliefs along a disease–social learning continuum may have broad applicability to attempts to cope with a variety of life problems. It is also felt, as we have foreshadowed in our discussions up to this point, that these beliefs relate to two major content areas in clinical psychology: *learned helplessness* (Seligman, 1965) and *locus of control* (Rotter, 1954). This is because a major variable, perhaps the major difference between disease and social learning beliefs, concerns expectations of control. This is true at a conceptual level, and it has been demonstrated empirically in several of our studies (Table 3.1). It may be then that disease beliefs constitute a form of learned helplessness training, leading people to expect no contingency between their efforts to alleviate their problems and the outcomes. The types of outcomes associated with learned helplessness and lack of control in work by Seligman and his colleagues certainly parallel those we have observed in our research (e.g., Farina et al., 1978) as well as our speculations in areas where we have not yet done research. Similarly, the effects of disease views may be analogous to the imparting of an external locus of control, at least insofar as certain specific types of problems (e.g., emotional disorders) are concerned. Again, the types of effects we have observed and hypothesized for those with disease orientations parallel those found for externals in past research by Rotter and his associates, and the data and hypotheses for those with social learning views parallel those observed for internals.

Relationship to other models of the helping process

Our conceptualization of the effects of medical model and social learning beliefs in the mental health field interfaces well with several other models of the helping process. Here we shall focus briefly on two which seem especially relevant: the Fisher, Nadler, and Whitcher (1980) "threat to self-esteem" conceptualization of recipient reactions to aid (discussed also in Fisher, DePaulo, & Nadler, 1981) and the model of helping proposed by Brickman, Rabinowitz, Coates, Cohn, Kidder, and Karuza (1979).

Fisher et al. (1980) suggest that when aid is highly supportive to self-concept, recipients will tend to remain dependent on helpers and will exercise relatively few self-help efforts. On the other hand, when aid is relatively self-threatening, recipients will strive toward future independence and engage in a high level of self-help. This line of reasoning has been corroborated by past research on various dependency relationships (e.g., Fisher & Nadler, 1976). It is also in line with the data and theorizing presented herein for help when problems are described as medical model or social learning in origin. Clearly, a receipt of aid for a disorder which is believed to be medically caused is much less threatening than help when these problems are due to one's own failure in learning appropriate ways to deal with others, to cope with stress, etc. In the former case, one had no control over the circumstances which caused the problem and no ability to effect a cure; therefore help should not tend to be threatening. In the latter case, one is responsible for the problem and is assumed to have control over a cure, so that aid reflects a threatening failure to perform adequately in the past and perhaps also at present. In accord with the Fisher et al. (1980) model, when subjects in our studies were given aid in a medical model context (which is relatively supportive) they were highly dependent on the helpers and engaged in little self-help. Recipients of help that was believed to be due to a failure in social learning (which is relatively more threatening) exhibited less dependency and greater self-help.

The Brickman et al. (1979) model is also relevant to our present prediction of differential reactions to aid by those who believe their problems are due to medical causes rather than to social learning. Brickman et al. specify four types of helping processes, each reflecting a different combination of beliefs about the cause of the recipients' need state (themselves or external factors) and the locus of effective help (the needy individuals or others). Each leads to a different type of characteristic aid and to different sorts of responses by the needy. People assumed to have problems caused by external factors, for which it is believed effective help can be administered only by others, correspond to our medical model. Indeed, Brickman et al. label this condition the medical model and describe its theoretical effects as similar to those we have reported in our research. Our social learning type of help corresponds to Brickman et al.'s moral model of assistance, which occurs when the problem is self-caused and must be solved by the individual, and/or their compensatory model, which occurs when the problem is caused by factors outside the individual but must be solved by them. In both of these latter models, Brickman et al. assume that people will exert significantly greater efforts to improve their situation than when assistance is given in line with medical model beliefs about the origin of the problem and its cure. This agrees well with our description and experimental observations of the differential behavior of individuals with medical model and social learning beliefs. Thus, the Brickman et al. conceptualization of the helping process, as well as past research and theorizing by Fisher et al. (1980), parallels the conceptual approach we have taken in this paper.

Some cautions and limitations

Our program of research to this point has included two types of studies: (a) those attempting to change and/or establish disease or social learning beliefs and measure their effects, and (b) those attempting to measure preexisting orientations along a disease–social learning continuum and to correlate these with behaviors.[11] The first line of research has supported our hypotheses with considerable consistency. Essentially, it has shown that beliefs are easily changed by authoritative communications and that the hypothesized effects of disease and social learning orientations occur across a diverse array of behavioral and nonbehavioral (self-report) dependent measures. The second line of research, that attempting to relate preexisting orientations to self-reports and behavior, has been less consistent, for reasons which we shall detail below.

Our attempts to relate preexisting orientation along a belief continuum to a person's relevant thoughts and behaviors concerning emotional disorders have employed a single instrument to measure beliefs (described briefly in Farina et al., 1978). This instrument has not shown consistent relationships between beliefs and behavior for several reasons. First, as mentioned earlier, people's preexisting beliefs about mental disorders are often highly confused (i.e., they endorse conflicting elements of both social learning and disease views). Second, the instrument was written in too jargonistic a fashion and failed to communicate at a level which the general population could incorporate into their realm of experience.

The first problem, conflicting preexisting views about emotional problems, provides an important commentary on the current state of popular beliefs about mental disorders and some insights concerning why the general population may not be dealing well with such problems. We found that many people who took our instrument had beliefs which could appropriately be characterized as chaotic, and so it is not surprising that their beliefs did not predict their behavior. Some predominance of medical model or social learning beliefs, and some degree of coherence, would be necessary for the hypothesized relationships to be found. The inconsistency in many people's beliefs may also explain, in part, why we have found it so easy to change beliefs about emotional disorders in previous studies and to leave people with fairly consistent, coherent disease or social learning beliefs. When this is done, the types of behaviors we would expect seem to follow.

The second problem, that of constructing an instrument that people will be more readily able to relate to and understand, seems to be solved quite well at this point. We have developed a new measure, which we have now pilot-tested, that appears to have good psychometric properties and should prove to be quite useful in the future. The factor structure that we find is relatively clear, and it seems that inconsistencies which emerge likely reflect true inconsistencies in beliefs rather than failures to understand and/or interpret the instrument. It is hoped that this measure will be a useful tool in relating beliefs about mental disorders to behavior, in measuring initial dispositions and changes in beliefs, etc., and that it may be adapted in the future to assess beliefs about alcohol and drug abuse, the process of aging, and other relevant processes and states.

Notes

1. Undoubtedly, our present conceptualization of this dimension is overly simple and will have to be refined as more is learned. However, we feel that even with its present degree of elaboration, it makes a useful contribution to understanding the effects of beliefs about mental disorders on behavior.

2. The "traditional" conception is similar to the illness view, and the "nontraditional" orientation is more like a social learning belief.

3. There are studies which suggest that being made to feel similar to mental patients leads to an unfavorable, rather than a favorable, response (e.g., Novak & Lerner, 1968). The effect of assumed similarity is surely complex, and whether those apparently discrepant results are due to the use of different measures (i.e., behavior vs. questionnaire) or to other variables remains to be established.

4. Wehler (1979) replicated this study with psychiatric in-patients and also found that the more patients saw mental disorders as biological, the more dependent they felt upon mental health workers. The relationship was not statistically significant, however.

5. We want to emphasize we are not advocating total discontinuance of all drugs in the treatment of mental disorders. This issue will be discussed further at a later point in this chapter.

6. Our view has some similarity to other formulations, particularly Seligman's learned helplessness theory and Rotter's theory of locus of control. These are not being considered here since they are discussed in a later section.

7. Grimm's (1980) criticism of the studies by Davison and his colleagues does not appear to change this particular conclusion.

8. The Alcoholics Anonymous organization does not emphasize medical treatment per se, but does demand admission from alcoholics that they suffer from an illness. The organization also believes that more than a personal effort is necessary to deal with the problem (e.g., social and other forms of support are needed from reformed alcoholics, as well as the aid of God). The individuals' own actions, in and of themselves, are viewed as absolutely insufficient to effect a cure, since it is beyond their ability to control the problem.

9. While our assumption that there will be greater success in treating alcoholics and drug abusers (see below) if practitioners and/or clients have a social learning orientation has been relatively untested, strong supportive anecdotal evidence is offered by Cummings (1979).

10. The social learning view also assumes that problems associated with aging can also be due to a nonoptimal environment (e.g., an understimulating, restrictive, old-age home) and that improvements in one's condition can result from changes in one's environment.

11. Dana Christensen and Michael Pisano have collaborated with us in some of our yet unpublished research, and we wish to acknowledge their contribution.

References

Beckman, L. Locus of control and attitudes toward mental illness among mental health volunteers. *Journal of Consulting and Clinical Psychology*, 1972, *38*, 84–89.

Brickman, P., Rabinowitz, V. C., Coates, D., Cohn, E., Kidder, L., & Karuza, J. Helping. Unpublished manuscript, University of Michigan, 1979.

Butler, R. Cited in R. M. Henig, Ageism's angry critic. *Human Behavior*, 1979, *8*, 43–46.

Cohen, J., & Struening, E. L. Opinions about mental illness in the personnel of two large mental hospitals. *Journal of Abnormal and Social Psychology*, 1962, *64*, 349–360.

Cohen, J., & Struening, E. L. Opinions about mental illness: Hospital social atmosphere profiles and their relevance to effectiveness. *Journal of Consulting Psychology*, 1964, *28*, 292–298.

Colleti, G., & Kopel, S. A. Maintaining behavior change: An investigation of three maintenance strategies and the relationship of self-attribution to the long-term reduction of cigarette smoking. *Journal of Consulting and Clinical Psychology*, 1979, *47*, 614–617.

Colleti, G., & Stern, L. Two-year follow-up of nonaversive treatment for cigarette smoking. *Journal of Consulting and Clinical Psychology*, 1980, *48*, 292–293.

Colson, C. E. Effects of different explanations of disordered behavior on treatment referrals. *Journal of Consulting and Clinical Psychology*, 1970, *34*, 432–435.

Costin, F., & Kerr, W. D. Effects of an abnormal psychology course on students' attitudes toward mental illness. *Journal of Educational Psychology*, 1962, *53*, 214–218.

Cummings, N. Turning bread into stones. *American Psychologist*, 1979, *34*, 1119–1129.

Davison, G. C., Tsujimoto, R. N., & Glaros, A. G. Attribution and maintenance of behavior change in falling asleep. *Journal of Abnormal Psychology*, 1973, *82*, 124–133.

Davison, G. C., & Valins, S. Maintenance of self-attributed and drug-attributed behavior change. *Journal of Personality and Social Psychology*, 1969, *11*, 25–33.

Deutsch, A. *The mentally ill in America* (2nd ed.). New York: Columbia University Press, 1965.

Ellsworth, R. A behavioral study of staff attitudes toward mental illness. *Journal of Abnormal Psychology*, 1965, *70*, 194–200.

Farina, A. *Abnormal psychology*. Englewood Cliffs, N.J.: Prentice-Hall, 1976.

Farina, A. The stigma of mental disorders. In A. G. Miller (Ed.), *In the eye of the beholder*. New York: Holt, Rinehart and Winston, in press.

Farina, A., Fisher, J. D., Getter, H., & Fischer, E. H. Some consequences of changing people's views regarding the nature of mental illness. *Journal of Abnormal Psychology*, 1978, *87*, 272–279.

Fisher, J. D., DePaulo, B. M., & Nadler, A. Extending altruism beyond the altruistic act: The mixed effects of aid on the help recipient. In J. P. Rushton & R. M. Sorrentino (Eds.), *Altruism and helping behavior*. Hillsdale, N.J.: Erlbaum, 1981.

Fisher, J. D., & Farina, A. Consequences of beliefs about the nature of mental disorders. *Journal of Abnormal Psychology*, 1979, *88*, 320–327.

Fisher, J. D., & Nadler, A. Effect of donor resources on recipient self-esteem and self-help. *Journal of Experimental Social Psychology*, 1976, *12*, 129–150.

Fisher, J. D., Nadler, A., & Whitcher, S. J. Recipient reactions to aid: A conceptual review. Unpublished manuscript, University of Connecticut, 1980.

Garber, J., & Seligman, M.E.P. (Eds.). *Human helplessness: Theory and applications*. New York: Academic Press, 1980.

Gelfand, S., & Ullmann, L. P. Change in attitudes about mental illness associated with psychiatric clerkship training. *International Journal of Social Psychiatry*, 1961, *7*, 292–298.

Golding, S. L., Becker, E., Sherman, S., & Rappaport, J. The behavioral expectations scale: Assessment of expectations for interaction with the mentally ill. *Journal of Consulting and Clinical Psychology*, 1975, *43*, 109.

Grimm, L. G. The maintenance of self- and drug-attributed behavior change: A critique. *Journal of Abnormal Psychology*, 1980, *89*, 282–285.

Gurin, G., Veroff, J., & Feld, S. *Americans view their mental health*. New York: Basic Books, 1960.

Harrow, M., Fox, D. A., & Detre, T. Self-concept of the married psychiatric patient and his mate's perception of him. *Journal of Consulting and Clinical Psychology*, 1969, *33*, 235–239.

Holzberg, J. D., Gewirtz, H., & Ebner, E. Changes in moral judgment and self-acceptance in college students as a function of companionship with hospitalized mental patients. *Journal of Consulting Psychology*, 1964, *28*, 299–303.

Kallmann, F. J. The genetics of mental illness. In S. Arieti (Ed.). *American handbook of psychiatry* (Vol. I). New York: Basic Books, 1959.

Langer, E. J., & Abelson, R. P. A patient by any other name . . . : Clinician group difference in labeling bias. *Journal of Consulting and Clinical Psychology*, 1974, *42*, 4–9.

Langer, E. J., & Rodin, J. The effects of choice and enhanced personal responsibility for the aged: A field experiment in an institutional setting. *Journal of Personality and Social Psychology*, 1976, *34*, 191–198.

Manis, M., Houts, P. S., & Blake, J. B. Beliefs about mental illness as a function of psychiatric status and psychiatric hospitalization. *Journal of Abnormal Psychology*, 1963, *67*, 226–233.

Milgram, S. Some conditions of obedience and disobedience to authority. In I. Steiner & M. Fishbein (Eds.), *Current studies in social psychology*. New York: Holt, Rinehart and Winston, 1965.

Morrison, J. K. Demythologizing mental patients' attitudes toward mental illness: An empirical study. *Journal of Community Psychology*, 1976, *4*, 181–185.

Morrison, J. K. Changing negative attributions of mental patients by means of demythologizing seminars. *Journal of Clinical Psychology*, 1977, *33*, 549–551.

Morrison, J. K., & Becker, R. E. Seminar-induced change in a community psychiatric team's reported attitude toward mental illness. *Journal of Community Psychology*, 1975, *3*, 281–284.

Morrison, J. K., Bushell, J. D., Hanson, G. D., Fentiman, J. R., & Holdridge-Crane, S. Relationship between psychiatric patients' attitudes toward mental illness and attitudes of dependence. *Psychological Reports*, 1977, *41*, 1194.

Morrison, J. K., Madrazo-Peterson, R., & Simons, P. Attitudes toward mental illness: A conflict between students and professionals. *Psychological Reports*, 1977, *41*, 1013–1014.

Morrison, J. K., & Nevid, J. S. Demythologizing the attitudes of family caretakers about "mental illness." *Journal of Family Counseling*, 1976, *4*, 43–49. (a)

Morrison, J. K., & Nevid, J. S. Demythologizing the service expectancies of psychiatric patients in the community. *Psychology*, 1976, *13*, 26–29. (b)

Morrison, J. K., & Teta, D. C. Increase of positive self-attributions by means of demythologizing seminars. *Journal of Clinical Psychology*, 1977, *33*, 1128–1131.

Novak, D. W., & Lerner, M. J. Rejection as a consequence of perceived similarity. *Journal of Personality and Social Psychology*, 1968, *9*, 147–152.

Nunnally, J. C., Jr. *Popular conceptions of mental health*. New York: Holt, Rinehart and Winston, 1961.

Ommundsen, R., & Ekeland, T. J. Psychiatric labeling and social perception. *Scandinavian Journal of Psychology*, 1978, *19*, 193–197.

Paul, G. L., & McInnis, T. L. Attitudinal change associated with two approaches to training mental health technicians in milieu and social learning programs. *Journal of Consulting and Clinical Psychology*, 1974, *42*, 21–33.

Rabkin, J. G. Opinions about mental illness: A review of the literature. *Psychological Bulletin*, 1972, *77*, 153–171.

Ring, K., & Farina, A. Personal adjustment as a determinant of aggressive behavior toward the mentally ill. *Journal of Consulting and Clinical Psychology*, 1969, *33*, 683–690.

Rodin, J., & Langer, E. J. Long-term effects of a control-relevant intervention with the institutionalized aged. *Journal of Personality and Social Psychology*, 1977, *35*, 897–902.

Rothaus, P., Hanson, P. G., Cleveland, S. E., & Johnson, D. L. Describing psychiatric hospitalization: A dilemma. *American Psychologist*, 1963, *18*, 85–89.

Rotter, J. B. *Social learning and clinical psychology*. Englewood Cliffs, N.J.: Prentice-Hall, 1954.

Scheff, T. J. Decision rules, types of error, and their consequences in medical diagnosis. In R. H. Price & B. Denner (Eds.), *The Making of a mental patient*. New York: Holt, Rinehart and Winston, 1973.

Seligman, M.E.P. *Helplessness*. San Francisco: Freeman, 1965.

Smith, J. J. Psychiatric hospital experience and attitudes toward "mental illness." *Journal of Consulting and Clinical Psychology*, 1969, *33*, 302–306.

Terry, S. Felt vulnerability to mental illness by college students. Unpublished manuscript, University of Connecticut, 1971.

Wehler, R. Attitudes toward mental illness and dependency among hospitalized psychiatric patients. *Psychological Reports*, 1979, *44*, 283–286.

Whitman, J. R., & Duffey, R. F. The relationship between type of therapy received and a patient's perception of his illness. *Journal of Nervous and Mental Disorders*, 1961, *113*, 288–292.

Zilboorg, S., & Henry, G. W. *A history of medical psychology*. New York: Norton, 1941.

4

COMMENTARY: SOCIAL PSYCHOLOGICAL PROCESSES IN CLINICAL JUDGMENT

JERRY S. WIGGINS
UNIVERSITY OF BRITISH COLUMBIA

For many years, those who have concerned themselves with what Meehl (1960) referred to as "the cognitive activity of the clinician" have been operating under a tacit assumption that no longer appears tenable—namely, that there is something *special* about the clinician's cognitive activity, or about the tasks toward which it is directed, that sets it apart from "everyday" social judgment and decision making. As a consequence, the judgmental biases and shortcomings that have been demonstrated in studies employing clinicians as subjects have often been viewed as endemic to professionals. That these same biases and shortcomings had also been demonstrated in analogue studies of college students did not seem to affect the attitude that clinicians were a special breed, or at least that they *should* be.

In different ways, the two chapters in this section emphasize the similarities between everyday social judgment and the more specialized judgments made by clinicians. Farina and Fisher maintain that certain beliefs about the nature of mental disorders can determine the fate of psychiatric patients, whether these beliefs are held by the patients themselves, by persons in general (the public), or by mental health professionals (clinicians). That clinical judgment is influenced by beliefs about mental illness is suggested by studies such as that of Langer and Abelson (1974), which demonstrated that clinicians who subscribe to a biological interpretation of mental disorder tend to overdiagnose psychopathology as compared to clinicians who favor a social learning interpretation. To the extent that clinicians and laypersons share a common set of cultural beliefs about psychiatric patients, their categorizations of patients will be affected in similar ways. Farina and Fisher focus on the general implications of shared cultural beliefs for the field of mental health, and the conclusions they draw are most sobering. The material they review provides dramatic examples of the relevance of social psychology to clinical psychology.

Cantor's theoretical integration of the fields of clinical and social judgment emphasizes the similarities between clinicians and laypersons. In so doing, it raises, implicitly, the issue of reflexivity in psychological theorizing. A truly reflexive theory should apply equally to psychologists and to the persons they study; otherwise, qualitatively different processes would have to be invoked to account for the cognitive activities of professionals and those of laypersons. Kelly (1955) achieved reflexivity by postulating that all persons were, in effect, scientists who followed the canons of the hypothetico-deductive method in carrying out the business of their everyday lives (Little, 1972). Nisbett and Ross's (1980) notion of the intuitive scientist is a qualified version of this view. Cantor marshalls evidence for a radically reversed version of Kelly's postulate: all scientists (and clinicians) are persons. This is close to the ultimate reflexivity of Sullivan, that we are all "much more simply human than otherwise." And it sets the stage for a fresh (and refreshing) look at some well-traveled territory in the domain of clinical judgment.

Categorization

The prototype-matching interpretation of psychiatric categorization has implications that extend beyond attempts to model human judgment. The Roschian perspective focuses on the schemas we employ to impart meaning to objects and events and thereby emphasizes the constructed and relativistic nature of our concepts (Kelly, 1955). The concept of prototype is a "convenient grammatical fiction," and it is not assumed that prototypes exist in nature (Rosch, 1978). Although this assumption is easily granted with respect to natural categories, such as *bird* and *vegetable*, it may be more difficult to accept with respect to psychiatric patients. It has long been accepted that "textbook cases" (i.e., prototypes) of psychiatric disorder do not exist in nature, but the traditional view of mental disorders as disease *entities* deemphasizes the interpretive (constructive) nature of psychiatric diagnosis.

Neisser (1979) has provided an analysis of the concept of intelligence that would seem to apply with equal force to the concepts of descriptive psychiatry. Intelligence is the judged degree of resemblance between a real person and a prototype. The prototype of intelligence contains not a small set of necessary and sufficient defining features, but rather a large number of correlated features that are distributed in varying ways among intelligent persons. It is possible for two persons to be judged as highly intelligent even though they have few features in common, if they resemble the prototype in different ways:

> Thus, there is no such quality as *intelligence*, any more than there is such a thing as *chairness*—resemblance is an external fact and not an internal essence. (Neisser, 1979, p. 223)

If the concept of, for example, schizophrenia is the judged degree of resemblance between a patient and prototype, it may be more profitable to study the judgmental process involved in prototype matching than to grant existential status to the quality or essence of schizophrenia. This is not to say that we should study psychiatrists rather than patients. But it is meant to suggest that the field of social cognition can contribute, on a basic level, to a clarification of the subject matter of descriptive psychiatry.

Cantor's work suggests that the categories of psychiatric diagnosis are based on schemas that are organized according to the same (Roschian) principles as are categories of person perception. From hindsight, this is not surprising if one grants the obvious differences that arise when a highly selected population (patients) is observed by a highly specialized group (psychiatrists). But the specialized terminology of descriptive psychiatry tends to obscure the many similarities that exist between person perception and patient perception. For example, within the realm of person perception, it has been known for some time that the schemas we employ to impart meaning to interpersonal behavior may be represented structurally as a two-dimensional circular organization of categories based on the dimensions of dominance and affiliation (e.g., Carson, 1969; Foa & Foa, 1974; Leary, 1957). It has not been as widely recognized that the categories of psychiatric diagnosis display the same orderly two-dimensional structure (Plutchik, 1967; Plutchik & Platman, 1977). In fact, attributions of interpersonal traits, affects, and psychiatric diagnoses may all be accommodated within a common two-dimensional circular space (Schaefer & Plutchik, 1966). That psychiatric diagnostic categories are organized in terms of interpersonal schemas is not surprising in view of the fact that the majority of problems presented by patients are interpersonal in nature (Horowitz, 1979). The behaviors at issue are more extreme and less adaptive than those observed in normal populations, but they are encoded along common continua (Leary, 1957; Millon, 1969). The similarities in schema structure between person perception and patient perception may be considered as additional evidence for the existence of conceptual universals in interpersonal language (White, 1980).

Cantor notes that the shift from the traditional view of psychiatric categories to the prototype view may have prescriptive implications for such issues as the preparation of diagnostic manuals and the process and goals of diagnosis itself. A particularly well-taken point is that a flexible, probabilistic-based prototype system of diagnosis need not be unmanageable. The two-dimensional, circular representation of diagnostic categories just mentioned facilitates the interpretation of borderline cases and encourages the view of class membership as continuous rather than discrete. In fact, as the structural relations between diagnostic categories become better understood, it may be possible to develop relatively precise ways of applying categories which are themselves imprecise. A promising theoretical framework for this already exists for the second axis of DSM-III (Millon, 1981).

Data collection

Cantor also builds a convincing case for considering the prescriptive implications of the fact that clinicians gather data in theory-driven, confirmation-biased ways that tend to violate the canons of scientific hypothesis testing. One would certainly hope to preserve these features of data collection, and perhaps improve upon them, since they constitute the essence of clinical inquiry and since data gathered from such procedures, *when properly combined with more "objective" data*, yield increments in predictive accuracy (Sawyer, 1966). To maintain perspective here, we must distinguish between the contexts of discovery and justification and not prejudge the usefulness of data gathered under the heuristics of clinical inquiry.

The literatures of both social and clinical judgment are replete with examples of errors associated with theory-driven data processing. From these examples it is easy to gain the impression that a theory—any theory—will subvert the goal of accurate prediction. Yet, strangely, little attention has been paid to the issue of what theories clinicians actually adhere to—or for that matter to what might constitute a theory in this context. For these reasons, it is understandable that there has been little concern with the relationships (or lack of same) between the criterion target, the information available, and the constructs of the clinician in concrete assessment situations. A notable voice in the wilderness here is that of Jackson (1979), who has enumerated the minimal preconditions that must be met for valid clinical judgment and social perception. One of these preconditions is that the information given to (or presumably gathered by) the judge must be *theoretically* related to the behavior to be predicted and that the constructs involved should show evidence of construct validity. For a variety of reasons, Jackson feels that the constructs implicit in everyday normative schemas for organizing social stimuli ("trait-inferential networks") are among the most promising contenders for valid social inference. But first these constructs should be explicated with respect to the substantive, structural, and external considerations of construct validity (Loevinger, 1957). And these constructs are, more than likely, the same everyday categories of which Cantor writes.

Data combination

Cantor suggests that it may now be appropriate to question the "optimalness" of such time-honored models of data combination as the expected utility model, given that clinicians and other people often depart markedly from such models in arriving at decisions. There would seem to be two rather separate issues here. The first concerns the flexibility with which we consider alternative models in a given decision-making situation. It is certainly the case that the classical model of *weighted* linear combinations of input data has lost a great deal of its prescriptive appeal in light of recent evidence that the use of predictor weights "don't make no nevermind" (Wainer, 1976). And it is also true that there may be situations in which a noncompensatory, multiple-cutoff approach is required to ensure a minimal standard on one or more predictor variables. There is nothing sacred about any particular version of the expected utility model, and such models should serve the clinician rather than the converse.

The second, perhaps more basic, issue in Cantor's argument relates to the wisdom of employing expected utility theory as an overriding prescriptive framework for clinical decision making, in light of clinicians' strong intuitions to the contrary. Cantor's earlier arguments for challenging the conventional wisdom regarding categorization and data collection are most persuasive, and it is tempting to approach the topic of data combination in the same spirit of rebelliousness. But I find myself dragging my feet here. In the context of discovery, it seemed only proper to keep an open mind about the ultimate empirical worth of the material gathered by the clinician in his or her role as (theory-driven) data collector. Once we have entered the context of justification, however, it is difficult to ignore the substantial body of literature which suggests that the clinician has little in the way of credentials for being in the data-combination business. As a consequence, I am sympathetic to Cantor's suggestion that we should become more aware of alternative outcomes that clinicians may wish to maximize, but I remain skeptical about the accuracy with which they may accomplish this.

The evidence for the uniform superiority of statistical methods of data combination over intuitive methods loses much of its import when it is recognized that there are very few clinical situations in which the use of actuarial methods is practical or even possible. Clinical decision making is here to stay, and our challenge is to improve it rather than to derogate it. The normative-prescriptive model that requires mathematically optimal methods of maximizing the utilities of preferred outcomes may not represent an ultimate truth, but it seems to be the best game plan presently available. As a consequence, clinicians should be encouraged to learn to operate within the "system" and be willing to forego their intuitions for the common good, when necessary.

Perhaps the major contribution of the field of social cognition to clinical psychology has been the discovery that the judgmental biases and shortcomings of clinical decision makers often reflect systematic and efficient heuristics for dealing with complex social stimuli, rather than random departures from normative procedures. The recognition of the validity of everyday intuitions has created an atmosphere in which issues of the accuracy of clinical judgment can be considered constructively and profitably. Cantor's chapter provides a splendid example of this new atmosphere, and she makes one of the strongest cases for taking intuitions seriously. A strong case can be made for normative procedures in the realm of decision making, however, and other writers have emphasized ways in which intuitions can be brought more in line with normative canons. Nisbett and Ross (1980) discuss "debiasing" procedures that capitalize on intuitive biases in teaching people about their judgmental shortcomings. Arkes (1981) analyzes the major impediments to accurate judgment among clinicians and offers recommendations for minimizing their effects. Kahneman and Tversky (1979) describe a procedure in which normative principles can be integrated with the intuitions of judges. All of these procedures have in common a respect for the intuitions of human judges and a desire to help them make more accurate decisions.

References

Arkes, H. R. Impediments to accurate clinical judgment and possible ways to minimize their impact. *Journal of Consulting and Clinical Psychology*, 1981, *49*, 323–330.

Carson, R. C. *Interaction concepts of personality.* Chicago: Aldine, 1969.

Foa, U. G., & Foa, E. B. *Societal structures of the mind.* Springfield, Ill.: Charles C Thomas, 1974.

Horowitz, L. M. On the cognitive structure of interpersonal problems treated in psychotherapy. *Journal of Consulting and Clinical Psychology*, 1979, *47*, 5–15.

Jackson, D. N. *Some preconditions for valid clinical judgment and social perception.* Invited paper read at the Second Ontario Symposium on Social and Personality Psychology, University of Waterloo, October 1979.

Kahneman, D. & Tversky, A. Intuitive prediction: Biases and corrective procedures. *TIMS Studies in the Management Sciences*, 1979, *12*, 313–327.

Kelly, G. A. *The psychology of personal constructs* (Vols. 1 and 2). New York: Norton, 1955.

Langer, E. J., & Abelson, R. P. A patient by any other name . . . : Clinician group difference in labeling bias. *Journal of Consulting and Clinical Psychology*, 1974, *42*, 4–9.

Leary, T. *Interpersonal diagnosis of personality.* New York: Ronald Press, 1957.

Little, B. R. Psychological man as scientist, humanist and specialist. *Journal of Experimental Research in Personality*, 1972, *6*, 95–118.

Loevinger, J. Objective tests as instruments of psychological theory. *Psychological Reports*, 1957, *3*, 635–694. (Mongraph 9)

Meehl, P. E. The cognitive activity of the clinician. *American Psychologist*, 1960, *15*, 19–27.

Millon, T. *Modern psychopathology.* Philadelphia: W. B. Saunders, 1969.

Millon, T. *Disorders of personality: DSM III, Axis II.* New York: Wiley-Interscience, 1981.

Neisser, U. The concept of intelligence. *Intelligence*, 1979, *3*, 217–227.

Nisbett, R., & Ross, L. *Human inference: Strategies and shortcomings of social judgment.* Englewood Cliffs, N.J.: Prentice-Hall, 1980.

Plutchik, R. The affective differential: Emotion profiles implied by diagnostic concepts. *Psychological Reports*, 1967, *20*, 19–25.

Plutchik, R., & Platman, S. R. Personality connotations of psychiatric diagnoses: Implications for a similarity model. *Journal of Nervous and Mental Disease*, 1977, *165*, 418–422.

Rosch, E. Principles of categorization. In E. Rosch and B. B. Lloyd (Eds.), *Cognition and categorization.* Hillsdale, N.J.: Erlbaum, 1978.

Sawyer, J. Measurement *and* prediction: Clinical and statistical. *Psychological Bulletin*, 1966, *66*, 178–200.

Schaefer, E. S., & Plutchik, R. Interrelationships of emotions, traits, and diagnostic constructs. *Psychological Reports*, 1966, *18*, 399–410.

Wainer, H. Estimating coefficients in linear models: It don't make no nevermind. *Psychological Bulletin*, 1976, *83*, 213–217.

White, G. M. Conceptual universals in interpersonal language. *American Anthropologist*, 1980, *82*, 759–781.

three

SOCIAL PSYCHOLOGICAL PROCESSES IN THE DEVELOPMENT OF MALADAPTIVE BEHAVIORS

Within the last decade, there has been an increasing tendency for theorists and researchers to acknowledge the importance of social-cognitive processes in the pathogenesis, maintenance, and therapeutic treatment of a variety of dysfunctional behaviors. In the first chapter of this section, Kuiper, Derry, and MacDonald examine possible differences in the processing of information about the self and others in depressed and nondepressed individuals. Their work is based on a view of the self as a cognitive schema involved in the processing of personal and social information. These authors present a model that traces changes in self-schema processing along a continuum ranging from nondepression through increasing levels of severity to the realm of clinical depression. Specifically, they report findings indicating that the major difference between nondepressives and clinical depressives lies in the content of information schematically represented. This self-schema model represents the convergence of several different theoretical perspectives and may prove useful in the assessment and understanding of depression.

In the next chapter, Snyder and Smith present an historical account of the clinical literature that emphasizes the notion of symptoms as self-protective strategies. Snyder and Smith extend their account to the social psychological literature on self-handicapping. They suggest that self-handicapping can be viewed as a type of defense mechanism whereby the individual reduces a threat to self-esteem by actively seeking or creating additional causal explanations for her or his potential failure. Snyder and Smith review evidence relevant to the view of symptoms as self-handicapping strategies and suggest that the self-protective function of symptoms may be an important factor in the etiology and maintenance of maladaptive behaviors.

A lack of confidence or poor self-esteem is a common symptom of psychological difficulties. The third chapter in this section, by Shrauger, focuses on a number of self-regulatory processes which are related to individuals' general sense of self-confidence or self-esteem. In particular, Shrauger argues that the characteristic evaluative attitudes that individuals hold about themselves are the result of selective exposure and deployment of attention to self-relevant information. The importance of selective information processing for the development, maintenance, and modification of clinically significant problems is examined.

In the final chapter of this section on development and maintenance of maladaptive behaviors, Coates and Peterson highlight the importance of social norms in the maintenance and exacerbation of depression. These authors argue that our culture is particularly intolerant of depressive behavior and that expressions of sadness or depression are often met with disapproval. Coates and Peterson contend that, as a result of the negative sanctions against dysphoric behaviors, depressed people develop self-perceptions of being deviant and these self-perceptions, in turn, may complicate and exacerbate the original depression. These authors offer empirical support for their general "depression as deviance" perspective and consider its implications for the treatment of depression.

In his commentary, Kopel provides an historical context in which to view integrative research concerned with social psychological processes in the development of maladaptive behavior patterns. He argues that earlier research in this area proved to be noble but somewhat naive attempts to integrate clinical and social psychology and that current efforts, as exemplified by the chapters in this section, represent dramatic improvements. Kopel does, however, identify several empirical "traps" that researchers will need to address in future work. He concludes his commentary by describing two clinical cases that illustrate the potential importance of the various conceptualizations of maladaptive behavior and treatment recommendations provided in the chapters of this section.

5

SELF-REFERENCE AND PERSON PERCEPTION IN DEPRESSION: A SOCIAL COGNITION PERSPECTIVE

NICHOLAS A. KUIPER
PAUL A. DERRY
MICHAEL R. MACDONALD*
THE UNIVERSITY OF WESTERN ONTARIO

The present chapter documents a current research program focusing on the self-concept of depressives. This work stems directly from a series of social cognition experiments investigating the self-schema as an important component of the human information-processing system (Kuiper & Derry, 1981). The present approach represents a preliminary step in integrating this self-reference work with cognitive theorizing and research in the domain of depression. Within this domain, Beck and his colleagues have provided a clinically based model of the role of cognitive factors in depression (Beck, Rush, Shaw, & Emery, 1979). As such, Beck's model is utilized as a general theoretical framework for guiding this social cognition and clinical integration.

The overall goals of this research program are twofold. The first is to examine the potential existence and function of a self-schema in depressed individuals. This aspect of the program delineates possible content differences in the self-schemata of depressed and nondepressed people. In addition, it evaluates further parameters associated with a self-schema, including the efficiency, or speed, with which personal information is processed. In doing so, it maps out some of the important elements in self-reference and depression, particularly the dimension of severity. A second goal of our program is to explore possible differences in depressives' and nondepressives' processing of personal information about others. To date, relatively little research has focused on the implicit theories of personality or psychopathology held by pathological groups (Chan & Jackson, 1979). The current program addresses this limitation by documenting other-referent processing distinctions relating to depression.

Self-reference in nonpathological populations

Contemporary research in social cognition has increasingly emphasized a cognitive model of the self (Kuiper & Derry, 1981). In this model, the self is viewed as a cognitive pro-

---

*The research reported in this chapter was supported by an Ontario Mental Health Foundation Research Grant to the first and second authors.

totype, or schema, involved in the processing of personal and social information about one's self and others. As a hypothetical construct, a schema is said to consist of an organized cluster of stored knowledge, beliefs, and assumptions regarding aspects of the individual and his or her world. The content within each schema is built up and organized from an individual's day-to-day experiences and can be considered a framework, or "organized setting," against which the person bases perceptions and judgments concerning relevant information.

The present approach to the self is based on a view presented by Rogers, Kuiper, and Kirker (1977). They consider the self to be a cognitive structure which can be defined both in terms of its structure and in terms of its process. In terms of structure, the self-schema represents a hierarchically organized body of knowledge, stored in long-term memory. In terms of process, the self-schema has been shown to impart both facilitative and biasing effects on the processing of personally relevant information (Markus, 1977; Rogers et al., 1977).

The content of the self-schema can further be described as a list of features, or terms, characteristic of the individual, which have been "derived from a lifetime of experience with personal data" (Rogers et al., 1977). On the one hand, these features could be quite general and traitlike, similar to what Markus has referred to as "schemata." Examples include schemata such as independence-dependence and dominance-submissiveness. On the other hand, the self can be considered to also include more specific components, such as situation-specific behavioral examplars (Rogers et al., 1977).

Several lines of recent work have provided converging evidence for the notion of the self as a cognitive schema. For example, Rogers et al. (1977) had subjects make one of four ratings on individually presented adjectives (e.g., loyal, persistent). Included among the rating tasks were structural ("Is this word written in big letters?"), phonemic ("Does this word rhyme with a given word?"), semantic ("Does this word mean the same as a given word?"), and self-reference ("Does this word describe you?") cue questions. When all yes/no response ratings were completed, an unexpected free recall task was required, where subjects were requested to recall as many of the target adjectives as possible. Consistent with predictions generated from the depth of processing position (Craik & Tulving, 1975), the results showed that words rated under the self-referent task were associated with the greatest frequency of recall. As such, the self-referent task was concluded to have yielded the most elaborate spread of analysis and encoding in memory, leading to the most durable memory trace. These findings were interpreted as demonstrative of subjects' use of a self-schema as an interpretive frame for the encoding of personal data. When one encounters personal information, this structure is activated and becomes an important part of the information-processing system.

This social cognition approach to the self has received additional empirical support. For example, Rogers, Rogers, and Kuiper (1979) found that the number of adjectives falsely identified as being presented during the study phase of a recognition memory test increased as these adjectives became more self-referent or prototypical. This biasing "false alarms effect" has traditionally been considered one property of the operation of a cognitive prototype (Cantor & Mischel, 1979). Finally, it has also been demonstrated that rating times for self-referent personality judgments yield an "inverted-U RT effect" when plotted as a function of their degree (high, medium, low) of self-reference (Kuiper, 1981). This inverted-U effect is another property associated with the operation of a prototype.

The above model's attempt to strengthen the self-reference data-theory bridge may serve to overcome some of the shortcomings listed in Wylie's (1974) critique of self research and theorizing. One such criticism was the lack of clear empirical referents for many of the theoretical constructs employed. Contemporary research differs, in that a fundamental tenet of this approach is the establishment of a comprehensive empirical foundation for the proposed model of self. A potential benefit of this approach is that it provides a model which can be readily applied to other relevant areas of psychology, including the domain of depression.

Beck's cognitive model of depression

Currently, the most comprehensive account of information processing in depression is the description and theory provided by Beck, and his colleagues (1979). Based on clinical observation and research, Beck asserts that thought disturbance is the preeminent depressive phenomenon. In his descriptive accounts, Beck discusses the thematic content of depressive cognitions as a "negative cognitive triad," which consists of a negative, demeaning view of one's self, one's world, and one's future. The content of depressive cognitions seems to be predominantly blameful and derogatory in nature and self-referential in direction. Moreover, clinical observation suggests that as an individual becomes increasingly more depressed, information previously seen as neutral tends to take on more of a personalized meaning. This in turn results in more information concerning the world and the future being processed as self-referent and hence becoming negative and pessimistic in quality.

Beck discusses personalization, or self-reference, as one of the most prevalent distortions in the pattern of depressive thought. This cognitive distortion refers to situations in which egocentric interpretations dominate over more objective evaluations. As Beck has defined it, personalization "refers to the patient's proclivity to relate external events to himself when there is no basis for making such a connection" (Beck et al., 1979). In depressed individuals, this subjective bias may influence the perception and evaluation of events. People talking in the distance, for example, may be seen as self-directed. Once viewed as self-referential, these events may be further biased and judged as being negative and devaluative. It would not be unusual for the depressed person to interpret her or his experience of the world with thoughts of being thwarted, deprived, and depreciated.

As a complement to descriptions of depressed patients' thought patterns, Beck has also outlined a theoretical framework within which such descriptions can be incorporated. In this framework, Beck discusses cognitive structure and process in depression as a function of a depressive schema. The schema in Beck's model is similar to the schemata defined above and, as such, consists of an organized cluster of stored knowledge regarding aspects of the individual and his or her world. The ideational content of the depressive schema, inferred from self-report and from studies of depressed patients' dreams in psychotherapy, seems to involve themes characterizing the patient as a loser. It is this depressive schema, according to Beck, that is responsible for the systematic biases, negative distortions, and evaluative ruminations reported for depressives.

Negative self-reference in depression

Various empirical approaches have been used to investigate the negative self-perceptions posited by Beck. Both Laxer (1964) and Lunghi (1977) found that depressed patients rated themselves poorer on several self-rating scales than nondepressed controls. Similarly, Lishman (1972) revealed that depressed patients recalled much more negatively toned personal information about themselves than did nondepressed controls. Other studies on selective recall also relate to the depressed person's poor self-evaluation and perception of her or his own capabilities. For example, DeMonbreun and Craighead (1977) have demonstrated that depressed psychiatric patients, when asked to recall previous performance, typically underestimated the amount of reward they had received. Nelson and Craighead (1977) have shown that as well as underestimating reward, depressed patients also recall more punishment than do nondepressed patients. Overall, these studies indicate that depressives typically underestimate the positive information they actually receive and overestimate the negative.

Several studies have investigated the bias toward negative self-evaluations by attempting to clarify depressives' attributions for task outcomes. In a study where success and failure were experimentally controlled (Rizley, 1978), depressives and nondepressives were asked to judge how responsible luck, effort, and task difficulty were in determining outcome. Depressed college student subjects primarily made internal attributions for failure. This self-blame tendency was also found by Kuiper (1978) in a study employing mildly depressed female university students.

Summary and limitations of Beck's approach

The studies cited above combine to suggest that Beck's model has merit and that it is worthy of further empirical study. In particular, his basic assumptions regarding the functional role of cognitions in affecting mood and behavior have received some independent verification by other researchers (Brewer, Doughtie, & Lubin, 1980). Fundamental assumptions, such as the depressives' propensity to negatively bias personal information, have also received data-based confirmation (Kuiper, 1978; Lobitz & Post, 1979). Moreover, the therapeutic derivative of Beck's theory has proved effective relative to various controls (Beck et al., 1979; Shaw, 1977). Of note, however, is that several of the studies reviewed above involved depressed college students, and it is important that the findings also be assessed in clinically depressed patients. As such, our research program will focus on similarities and differences across these levels of depression.

More important, however, is that one critical aspect of Beck's theory has received very little direct experimental attention. As part of their broad cognitive view of depression, Beck et al. (1979) posited the operation of schemata leading to faulty information processing as central postulates of their theory. To integratively account for a host of depressive cognitions, Kovacs and Beck (1978) advanced that

silent assumptions or premises, bits of information, and conclusions provide the content of a cognitive schema. A schema is a relatively enduring structure that functions like a template. It actively screens, codes, categorizes, and evaluates information. By definition, it also represents some relevant prior experience.

The application of a schema-like concept to depression is appealing because it provides an integrative, heuristic framework in which observed depressive cognitions can be placed. Yet, in the form stated by Kovacs and Beck, discussion of these schemata is not sufficiently rigorous or operationalized to readily lend itself to empirical evaluation. Consequently, this critical component of the model has received little direct empirical attention. Thus, the very foundation of the schema theory—the storage and organization of personal experience by depressives—has received almost no empirical study. In this respect, our current research program represents a preliminary attempt to examine this central component of a schema model of depression and to assess its potential role in the development and maintenance of this disorder.

A social cognition approach to depression

One of the major objectives of our research program is to focus specifically on how personal information about the self and others is processed by depressed individuals. In general, this focus entailed a research strategy whereby depressed and nondepressed individuals made personality ratings about themselves (describes you?) and/or various others (best friends, people in general). These ratings concerned depressed and nondepressed content personal adjectives and were followed by a recall period in which subjects were required to recall as many of the adjectives as possible. Theoretical interest in this program focused on the nature of memory traces produced by the personality judgments. The empirical indicators of prime concern were recall performance and rating times for making the judgments. These measures were assessed according to both the target person involved (self, other) and the content of the personal adjectives (depressed, nondepressed). As such, one of the first steps in this program was to establish a suitable list of depressed and nondepressed content adjectives.

Acquiring depressed and nondepressed content personal adjectives

An important issue in depressive self-schema investigation involves the *content* of the construct under investigation. Rogers et al. (1977) conceptualized the self as a cognitive representation of hierarchically ordered features which can be modified through the accumulation of experience. In terms of the depressed individual, one implication is that the content embodied in the purported self-schema may alter as the person becomes increasingly depressed. Specifically, the content may change to become more aligned with depressive self-perceptions and experiences, producing a "content-specific" depressive self-schema.

The above notion of content specificity forms one of the major theoretical issues investigated in our research program. However, a prerequisite to this investigation is a set of personal adjectives which can be readily differentiated on the basis of their depressed or nondepressed content. This content requirement necessitated an initial normative study. Here, a wide variety of potentially "depressed" and "nondepressed" adjectives were rated in terms of their depressed or nondepressed content (Derry & Kuiper, 1979). This normative study formed the cornerstone for our research program and will be briefly outlined prior to a more complete examination of the content-specificity issue in depression.

NORMATIVE RATINGS FOR PERSONAL ADJECTIVES. The paradigm whereby subjects make self-reference (describes you?) judgments on personality adjectives has been extensively utilized with nonpathological groups. However, caution must be exercised in its application to pathological samples, such as depressives. One area of prime concern is the pathological versus nonpathological nature of the target adjectives employed. In studying the self-schema of depressives, one would logically wish to present both depressed and nondepressed content personal adjectives. As of yet, this has not been done (Davis, 1979). However, it would seem to be of extreme importance to conceptually match the stimulus materials to the construct under investigation (Kihlstrom & Nashby, 1980). Therefore, the existence of a purported negative self-schema in depression should be assessed by presentation of appropriately matched stimulus information (e.g., depressed content adjectives).

The intent of an initial study conducted by Derry and Kuiper (1979) was to obtain normative ratings on a long list of personal adjectives. These ratings would then be employed to generate a final sample of 30 depressed and 30 nondepressed personal adjectives, for use in subsequent research. To this end, two types of ratings were performed by a group of 72 university students: content (depressed vs. nondepressed) and imagery values. The content ratings were necessary to reliably distinguish groups of depressed and nondepressed adjectives. These ratings required a judgment regarding whether a depressed person would rate the adjective as self-descriptive. The imagery ratings were also important within the present context of an incidental recall paradigm, as Paivio (1971) has demonstrated that recall may vary as a function of stimulus imagery value. The instructions for this condition were to rate the ease with which each word aroused a mental image (Paivio, 1971).

In this study, several relevant sources in the existing personality and depression literature were scanned to provide the original pool of personal adjectives. Adjectives presumed to be nondepressed were obtained from scale descriptions of Jackson's (1967) Personality Research Form (PRF) and were viewed as representative of a broad range of normal characteristics. Those assumed to be depressed were obtained from Lubin's (1965) Depression Adjective Checklists (Forms A and B), and Beck's (1967) descriptions of the depressed individual. Of the 121 adjectives, 67 were of a depressive nature. Individual ratings were made along 7-point scales and were presented in random sequences for rating.

In selecting the 30 depressed and 30 non-

Table 5.1. The Derry & Kuiper Set of Nondepressed and Depressed Content Adjectives

	Nondepressed	Depressed	
	Achieving	Bleak	
	Amiable	Blue	
	Assertive	Criticized	
	Capable	Defeated	
	Consistent	Destroyed	
	Courteous	Dismal	
	Curious	Downcast	
	Durable	Downhearted	
	Forceful	Dull	
	Free	Empty	
	Gracious	Failure	
	Hasty	Forlorn	
	Helpful	Glum	
	Inquiring	Guilty	
	Jovial	Heartsick	
	Loyal	Helpless	
	Maternal	Hopeless	
	Neat	Inadequate	
	Neighbourly	Inferior	
	Orderly	Listless	
	Organized	Loser	
	Playful	Lost	
	Polite	Melancholy	
	Proper	Oppressed	
	Pushy	Solemn	
	Rational	Troubled	
	Rebellious	Unlucky	
	Sociable	Unwanted	
	Sturdy	Weak	
	Tidy	Weary	
Mean Ratings			t *Values*
Content[1]	1.95	5.51	$t = 39.65, p < .007$
Imagery[2]	4.55	4.33	$t = 1.54$, ns
Kucera-Francis frequency	25.50	26.90	$t = 0.11$, ns
Word length	7.20	7.03	$t = 0.43$, ns

[1]Lower numbers indicate adjectives descriptive of a depressed person.
[2]Lower numbers indicate lower imagery values.

depressed adjectives which would constitute the final set, the ratings of content and imagery plus word frequency (Kucera & Francis, 1967) and word length (number of letters per word) were considered and controlled for. First, the adjectives were selected on the basis of their extremity on content ratings. There was no overlap for content ratings, with all nondepressed adjectives having a rating greater than 4.75 and all depressed words falling below 2.85. In addition, adjectives were matched on imagery ratings, with values for all adjectives ranging between 3.50 and 4.70. The final set of depressed and nondepressed adjectives, along with their mean ratings and t values, are presented in Table 5.1.

Overall, two distinct groups of words emerged from the Derry and Kuiper (1979) normative study, being clearly distinguished on the basis of depressed versus nondepressed content. In addition, the two sets of adjectives were found to be equivalent on the basis of imagery values, word length, and word frequency. Given these sets, it becomes possible to pursue the specific issue of how the self may be involved in the processing of personal information in depressives.

Parameters of self-reference in depression: Content specificity and efficiency

CONTENT SPECIFICITY. Among the first studies to investigate self-reference in clinically depressed patients was that of Davis (1979). Using a paradigm similar to that used by Rogers et al. (1977), both clinically depressed and nondepressed subjects were asked to make self-referent (describes you?) and semantic decisions for 48 normal, nondepressed content adjectives. The results from Davis's study replicated earlier findings of enhanced recall for self-referent decisions in the nondepressed group of subjects, but not in the clinically depressed group. Davis found no self-reference enhancement and thus argued that a "self-schema is not an active agent in the encoding of personal information in depression" and that "depression involved non-schema-based responding."

However, an equally plausible interpretation of Davis's findings can be formulated in terms of a content-specificity notion (Kuiper & Derry, 1981). For clinically depressed individuals, given their documented negative self-image, the appropriate test for schema-based processing would be a test that used adjectives with depressed content. If content is important, then the nonpathological nature of the target stimuli employed by Davis may have been inappropriate for tapping the potential existence of a *depressive* self-schema in clinical depressives. Thus, the possibility remains that these depressives may have an integrated self-schema, but for different content than nondepressives. By incorporating depressive content in the personal adjectives, evidence for a depressive self-schema may be revealed.

A recent clinical study conducted by Derry and Kuiper (1980) offered a first step toward the resolution of the above issue through manipulation of the content (depressed vs. nondepressed) of the personal adjectives presented to clinically depressed patients, nondepressed psychiatric control patients, and normal nondepressed individuals. This study employed the individual testing procedure of the depth of processing paradigm (Craik & Tulving, 1975; Rogers et al., 1977, exp. 2), whereby individuals rated the previously normed depressed and nondepressed personal adjectives for structural, semantic, and self-referent attributes. Rating times were monitored for each of these judgments, with the ratings followed by an incidental recall period.

Actual group characteristics are shown in Table 5.2. As expected, separate analyses of variance for both the Beck Depression Inven-

Table 5.2. Group Characteristics for the Derry & Kuiper Clinical Study

Group[1]	BDI[2]	HRSD[3]	Wechsler Memory Scale	Age
Normal nondepressives ($n = 16$)	1.50	5.75	117.75	23.00
Nondepressed psychiatric controls ($n = 16$)	5.00	14.50	113.63	31.31
Clinical depressives ($n = 16$)	22.13	43.86	110.13	32.13

[1]All subjects were female volunteers. Normal nondepressed subjects were hospital staff and student nurses. The predominant diagnosis in the nondepressed psychiatric group was personality disorder, followed by anxiety and marital dysfunction.
[2]Beck Depression Inventory, range 0 to 63, with a score of 13 or above indicating clinical depression (Loeb, Beck, & Diggory, 1971).
[3]Hamilton Rating Scale for Depression, range 0 to 72, with a combined score of 28 or above indicating clinical depression (Hamilton, 1960).

Table 5.3. Rating Tasks and Cue Questions Used in the Derry & Kuiper Clinical Study

Task[1]	Cue Question[2]	Manipulation[3]
Structural	Small letters?	The adjective was presented in either the same type (upper case) as the question or in lower case.
Semantic	Means same as XXXX?	XXXX was either a synonym or a word unrelated to the target adjective.
Self-reference	Describes you?	Subject responded yes or no to indicate self-reference quality of the target adjective.

[1] Each subject rated ten depressed and ten nondepressed adjectives for each task.
[2] All questions were answered yes or no by subjects.
[3] Several different orders of word lists were generated to ensure that the adjectives (depressed and nondepressed content) were completely counterbalanced across the three rating tasks.

tory (Beck, Ward, Mendelson, Mock, & Erbaugh, 1961) and Hamilton Rating Scale for Depression (Hamilton, 1960) indicated that clinical depressives were significantly more depressed than either psychiatric controls or normals. In addition, further analyses revealed that the normal controls obtained higher scores on the Wechsler Memory Scale than either of the two patient groups. Finally, it was also found that the two patient groups were older, on the average, than the individuals in the normal, nondepressed group.[1]

In general, each subject in this experiment was exposed to the following sequence of events. First, the subject was required to make a series of ratings (structural, semantic, self-referent) on the 30 depressed and 30 nondepressed content personality adjectives. A cue question, followed by a target adjective, was shown via a two-field tachistoscope. For each question and adjective pair, the subject responded either yes or no. The structural, semantic, and self-referent rating tasks used in this experiment, along with their respective cue questions and manipulations, are shown in Table 5.3.

In the second part of this study, three minutes were allowed for the incidental recall of the rated adjectives. Finally, each subject made depressed versus nondepressed content ratings on the entire set of 60 adjectives, followed by a simple rating time task.

INCIDENTAL RECALL AND CONTENT SPECIFICITY. A number of content specificity predictions were generated for incidental recall performance in the Derry and Kuiper (1980) study. The first of these pertained to the clinically depressed group. It was suggested that these individuals possess an integrated self-schema, specific for depressive content. In this case, it was predicted that the usual recall superiority for self-referent encodings (relative to semantic ratings) would obtain only for *depressed* content adjectives, for clinical depressives. This type of finding would offer strong empirical support for Beck's contention that a negative self-schema exists for depression. On the other hand, Davis's (1979) conclusion that clinical depressives fail to process any personal information via a self-schema has different implications. Davis's view would predict poor self-referent recall, relative to semantic recall, for *both* depressed and nondepressed content personal adjectives, for these subjects.

Incidental recall predictions were also generated for the nondepressed subjects. In this respect, another purpose of the study was to provide evidence regarding self-reference recall patterns for *pathological* adjectives in normal, nondepressed individuals. The earlier review of self-reference effects indicated an enhancement in recall when the stimuli were normal personality adjectives. It is not known, however, whether this enhancement effect would extend to pathological material. The notion of content specificity suggested that this would not be the case and predicted that normal, nondepressed subjects would exhibit self-referent enhanced recall only for nondepressed content.

INCIDENTAL RECALL PERFORMANCE. In scoring the recall protocols for each subject, Derry and Kuiper employed a proportion-correct score to ensure that different numbers of yes and no ratings were not affecting recall scores. This adjusted recall score reflected the general findings that yes-rated words are better recalled than no-rated words (Craik & Tulving, 1975). The subject-specific proportion score adjusts for different numbers of yes and no responses. Thus, each subject's recall of yes-rated words under a given rating task, for a given type of content, was divided by the total number of yes ratings for that content and task. Consequently, the adjustment represented the proportion of recalled words each person rated yes for each task and type of content. A similar procedure was employed for no-rated words (see Rogers et al., 1977, for greater details).

The mean adjusted recall scores for all three groups in the Derry and Kuiper study are presented in Table 5.4. An analysis of variance of these data demonstrated a significant four-way interaction between groups, content, rating task, and rating (yes/no).[2] In this interaction, content-specific self-reference enhancement was apparent only for adjectives receiving a yes rating. As predicted, the depressed group showed recall superiority only for depressed adjectives receiving a self-reference yes rating. An appropriate post hoc analysis indicated that this mean was significantly greater than any means across remaining task conditions for the depressed group. Furthermore, within the depressed content self-reference yes condition, the post hoc analysis also showed that the depressed group's recall was superior to that of either nondepressed group. Conversely, but again consistent with the content-specificity predictions, the two nondepressed groups (normals and psychiatric controls) each revealed significantly higher self-referent yes recall for nondepressed content, when compared with depressives. Means for the two nondepressed groups in this condition were also significantly greater than any other means in the rating task conditions. Finally, there were no statistically significant differences when only the no-rated adjectives were considered.

Overall, the recall findings obtained by Derry and Kuiper replicated the basic depth of processing self-reference effect and extended into the domain of clinical depression. These findings suggest that clinical depressives employ a self-schema for personal information processing, but one which differs in terms of content from that of nondepressives. Specifically, these data support the notion that clinical depressives utilize a negative self-schema for the processing of personal data. This cognitive structure seems selective for the interpretation and encoding of negative personal material.

The prominence and centrality of depressed

Table 5.4. Mean Adjusted Recall for Depressives, Psychiatric Controls, and Normals as a Function of Content, Rating (Yes/No), and Rating Task

Group	Yes Ratings			No Ratings		
	Structural	Semantic	Self-Referent	Structural	Semantic	Self-Referent
DEPRESSED CONTENT						
Depressed	.00[1]	.10	.41	.01	.07	.11
Psychiatric controls	.01	.12	.18	.00	.02	.12
Normals	.01	.05	.08	.01	.04	.07
NONDEPRESSED CONTENT						
Depressed	.07	.05	.16	.02	.07	.15
Psychiatric controls	.03	.22	.36	.03	.08	.15
Normals	.05	.13	.43	.02	.17	.12

[1]Recall values can range from 0 to 1, with higher numbers denoting greater recall.

content in the self-schema of clinical depressives is theoretically consistent with Beck's (1967) model of depression. These findings are in contrast to those of Davis (1979), who studied a similar population of clinically depressed patients. Perhaps accounting for Davis's nonschema findings was his failure to appropriately assess the content of the self-schema. Conceptually, it seems inconsistent that a negative self-schema would facilitate the retention of nonpathological content. Again, this issue highlights the importance of matching the stimulus materials in the experimental paradigm to the construct under investigation (Kihlstrom & Nashby, 1980).

Further empirical support for the content-specificity notion resides in the Derry and Kuiper (1980) recall findings for the nondepressed psychiatric group. This group showed recall patterns reflecting nondepressed schematic content. In turn, this pattern suggests that the recall findings for clinical depressives are unique and specific to this disorder and cannot be attributed to psychopathology in general.

Final support for the content-specificity hypothesis comes from an examination of the Derry and Kuiper (1980) recall findings for normal nondepressives. As was the case with the nondepressed psychiatric controls, self-reference enhancement for this group was found to be limited to yes-rated nondepressed adjectives. This pattern corroborated earlier findings for nonpathological personal adjectives (Kuiper & Rogers, 1979) and also offered strong support for the content-specificity notion in normals. The failure to obtain elevated recall for depressed content clearly indicates that the act of making a self-referent judgment *alone* is insufficient to bolster recall. It is only when this judgment is made in conjunction with the content already embodied in the self-schema that superior recall results. This finding for nondepressed adjectives highlights the crucial interactive nature of the self-schema, in which the elaboration and increased retention of new input require the prior representation of compatible content in the self-schema.

POSITIVE AND NEGATIVE RECALL SCORES. An alternative means of conceptualizing the Derry and Kuiper (1980) findings would be to classify the adjectives in terms of positive and negative content. This conceptualization would be in accord with previous research on depression which used an idiographic approach to determine the positive and negative nature of personality information (Lloyd & Lishman, 1975). For the Derry and Kuiper data, the classification of adjective content was determined *idiographically* for each subject through the use of individual patterns of yes/no responses to the self-reference ratings. Positive personality information was defined as nondepressed (i.e., nonpathological) content endorsed with a yes rating and depressed or pathological content given a no rating. Both are positive in the sense that a given subject judges himself or herself to possess certain nonpathological normal characteristics, but *not* to possess pathological, depressed attributes. In further keeping with this rationale, negative personality information was defined as depressed content that received a yes rating and nondepressed content that received a no rating.

Using this technique, the original recall protocols were rescored to generate both a positive and a negative personality score for each subject for the self-reference task. The overall mean proportion recall scores for this analysis are presented in Table 5.5. An analysis of variance of these data demonstrated a significant interaction between groups and personality information. As expected from the content-specificity notion, it was found that both groups of nondepressives recalled significantly more positive information about themselves than negative. Also as expected, it was found that clinical depressives recalled significantly more negative information about themselves than positive.

RATING TIMES AND EFFICIENCY. In addition to addressing content effects on recall, a second objective of the Derry and Kuiper (1980) study was to focus on the efficiency, or processing parameter, of the self-schema. This was done via an analysis of rating time data

Table 5.5. Recall of Positive and Negative Personality Information for the Self-reference Task in the Derry & Kuiper Clinical Study

Personality Information	Clinical Depressives	Nondepressed Psychiatric	Normal Nondepressed
Positive[1]	.15[2]	.32	.25
Negative[3]	.25	.14	.07

[1] Positive recall = $\dfrac{\text{Nondepressed content yes recall} + \text{depressed content no recall}}{\text{Total nondepressed content yes} + \text{depressed content no ratings}}$

[2] Recall values can range from 0 to 1.0, with higher numbers denoting greater recall.

[3] Negative recall = $\dfrac{\text{Nondepressed content no recall} + \text{depressed content yes recall}}{\text{Total nondepressed content no} + \text{depressed content yes ratings}}$

for self-referent judgments. While the recall data revealed a bias for retention of schema-consistent information for both depressives and nondepressives, it did not indicate how *efficiently* this information may have been processed. The assumption underlying a schema interpretation is its assistance and facilitation in the processing of personal information. As such, the amount of time taken for self-referent personality judgments was used by Derry and Kuiper as an index of processing efficiency. Short response latencies in this paradigm would seem to indicate the use of a well-organized and efficient cognitive schema to assist in the quick processing of information (Kuiper & Rogers, 1979). Thus, if depressives also employ a well-organized and efficient self-schema to assist in self-referent judgments (albeit for different content than nondepressives), it was predicted by Derry and Kuiper that their overall rating times for the self-referent task would not be significantly longer than those of normal nondepressives.

In assessing this prediction, rating time was defined as the interval between the initial presentation of the adjective via the t-scope and the subject's yes or no response. As was the case with the adjusted recall data, the resulting rating time means were categorized as a function of group (depressed, psychiatric, normal), rating task (structural, semantic, self-referent), rating (yes, no), and content (depressed, nondepressed). When these data were subject to an analysis of variance, it was found that two of the three-way interactions were significant. Table 5.6 presents the most relevant portion of these data. Specifically, it plots the *self-referent* rating time means for the three groups as a function of yes/no ratings. A post hoc analysis of these means indicated there were no significant rating time differences between any of the groups for self-referent judgments that received a yes rating. With respect to no ratings, it was found that clinical depressives were not significantly slower in making self-reference judgments than the normal controls. The psy-

Table 5.6. Self-Referent Rating Times (msec) for Groups in the Derry & Kuiper Clinical Study

	Depressed	Psychiatric Controls	Normals
Yes	3.770	3.825	3.271
No	3.478	4.049	2.608

chiatric controls, however, did take significantly longer for these judgments than the normals.[3]

Overall, this pattern of rating time results provides important information bearing on the ease, or efficiency, with which clinical depressives process personal information. With no meaningful differences between depressives and normals in the time they took to make self-referent decisions, it seems clear that the depressive's self-schema is organized for the same degree of efficient processing for schema-consistent personal data as witnessed in normals.

This may not be the situation for the nondepressed psychiatric controls, however, whose self-reference no ratings were significantly longer than those of the normals. This pattern may represent a degree of uncertainty and disorganization concerning one's self-concept related to the forms of psychopathology found within this group. However, this disorganization would appear to be relatively mild, since this group's loss of processing efficiency was restricted to no ratings and did not produce a decrement for yes-rated self-reference recall. Further work would certainly be necessary to clarify the above interpretation and findings for this group. Yet it does suggest an important caveat for researchers, namely, that not all self-schemata necessarily function with equal efficiency. Hence, investigators seeking evidence of schematic processing for personal information need to evaluate not only content but also efficiency. Drawing conclusions based on fewer variables than these would appear to provide an incomplete perspective on the overall content and process of the self.

Further issues in depressives' processing of personal information

The data from the clinical study addressed the self-reference parameters of content specificity and efficiency. While this study provided information concerning the role of these parameters in clinical depressives, it still left several important social cognition factors unexplored. One such issue concerns the effects of depth, or severity, of depression on self-reference. In other words, how might mildly depressed individuals differ from clinical depressives, both in terms of the content of their self-schema and in terms of the efficiency with which they process various types of information about themselves? The study of mild depressives would serve to clarify the nature of such changes and also would aid in the formulation of a more complete model of self-reference in depression.

A second issue left unexplored in the clinical study relates to depressives' processing of social and personal information about *others*. The clinical study indicated that depressives exhibited specific content biases when processing information about themselves. However, it is also possible that depressed individuals may demonstrate systematic biases in their processing and recall of personal information about others. Our knowledge of these distinctions may again serve to facilitate our understanding of social cognition factors involved in depression. Moreover, this work would serve to bridge research on social and interpersonal aspects of depression (Lewinsohn, Mischel, Chaplin, & Barton, 1980; Youngren & Lewinsohn, 1980) with contemporary literature suggesting that the self-schema may also function to organize information about others in memory (Kuiper & Derry, 1981). This information could then be used to determine how depressed and nondepressed self-schemata may relate to generalized conceptions of psychopathology (Chan & Jackson, 1979).

Keeping in mind these two issues, the second phase of our research program was directed toward a more detailed examination of both severity and other-referent questions (Kuiper & MacDonald, 1980). This phase of the program utilized a modified version of the paradigm employed by Derry and Kuiper (1980). Instead of clinical depressives, the emphasis was on less severe levels of depression. Thus, mildly depressed university students (BDI mean of 13.33) were employed in this study, along with a control group consisting of nondepressed students (BDI mean of 3.65). In addition, the rating tasks were changed slightly. While the self-referent (describes you?) task was retained, the structural and semantic tasks were eliminated. In their place, subjects made other-referent ratings about someone they knew well (describes him/her?) and about people in general or the average person (describes others?). The remaining aspects of the Kuiper and MacDonald study were similar to the clinical study. Subjects rated the three target persons on the set of adjectives derived from the initial norming study (Derry & Kuiper, 1979). Again, we monitored rating times for these judgments and required subjects to recall as many of the adjectives as possible.

It is important to note that the Kuiper and MacDonald study should not be viewed as merely an analogue study of clinical depression. Instead, the intentional selection of mildly depressed individuals afforded the opportunity to investigate the content and efficiency parameters of the self-schema within this particular range and severity of depression.

In sum, theoretical interest in this phase of the program focused on the positive versus negative nature of the personality information processed for each target person. Our first concern was to establish the effects of mild depression on positive and negative self-referent processing. Our second was to map out any distinctions between mild depressives and normals in their positive and negative processing of personal information about others.

Negative self-reference and depth of depression

As indicated earlier, a large body of literature has converged on the notion that depressives display a bias toward the enhancement of negative self-referent material (DeMonbreun & Craighead, 1977; Laxer, 1964; Lunghi, 1977). However, one aspect of this research which has received only limited investigation is the exact relationship between severity of depression and use of idiosyncratic cognitive structures. On the one hand, it is possible that the content and efficiency parameters associated with a depressive self-schema may be responsive to variations in depression level. Content may be less negative for mild depressives, and the efficiency with which they process various types of personal information may differ markedly from that of either normals or more severely depressed individuals. On the other hand, it is possible that the self-schema of mild depressives may be indistinguishable from the self-schema of clinical depressives. In other words, severity per se may not play a role in determining either the content or the efficiency component of a depressive self-schema. This latter view would contend that *all* depressives, regardless of level, utilize the same type of idiosyncratic self-schema to process personal information about themselves.

The resolution of the above issue is theoretically important, as it would help to clarify the role of social cognition factors in the etiology, maintenance, and reoccurrence of this disorder. For example, Beck and his colleagues have proposed that depressive or negative content is "an enduring characteristic of the cognitive organization, present in the depression prone individual, even when he is not feeling depressed" (Weintraub, Segal, & Beck, 1974). It is the enduring nature of these negative schemata which is thought to predispose the individual to depression and play a primary role in the occurrence and reoccurrence of other depressive symptoms (Beck et al., 1979). Thus, Beck's theoretical stance would argue for the existence of negative self-referent information in individuals at all levels of depression, including individuals presently in remission.

Empirical evidence consistent with Beck's proposal comes from several remission studies. For example, Wittenborn and his associates (Altman & Wittenborn, 1980; Cofer & Wittenborn, 1980) have examined the personality characteristics of formerly depressed women. In contrast to women who have never been depressed, these former depressives still evidenced lower self-esteem, lower confidence, more helplessness, and an unhappier outlook toward life. These negative views toward the self and interpersonal relationships have also been found by other researchers investigating the cognitive and personality attributes of former depressives (Lunghi, 1977; Weintraub et al., 1974).

A problem with the literature just cited is that it does not clarify the extent to which remission features are *equivalent* to those displayed by currently depressed individuals. In this respect, further work hints at a possible relationship between level of depression and actual degree of negative information processing. For example, Buchwald (1977) found greater underestimates of positive performance feedback for more severe depressives. In a similar fashion, Lloyd and Lishman (1975) report a diminishing ratio between speed of recall of pleasant versus unpleasant memories as a function of increasing depth of depression. Using an idiographic procedure to determine the pleasantness of each memory for each subject, these researchers found that unpleasant memories were recalled faster in the most depressed subjects, relative to their recall of pleasant memories. This relationship was reversed for the nondepressed individuals.

Based on this literature, Kuiper and MacDonald (1980) predicted that the mild depressives in their study would recall as much positive information about themselves as negative. This finding would be conceptually consistent with the Lloyd and Lishman ratio for moderate depressives, which demonstrated equivalent speed of recall for pleasant and unpleasant thoughts.

Further predictions were also generated for the nondepressed sample in the Kuiper and MacDonald study. In contrast to depressives, research evidence generally indicates a positive bias in nondepressives' processing of personal information. For example, nondepressed university students in the Nelson and Craighead (1977) study recalled more positive and less negative feedback than depressives. In addition, Lloyd and Lishman found that pleasant memories were recalled more quickly than unpleasant memories among nondepressed control patients. This latter finding hints that nondepressives may employ an efficient self-schema to facilitate the processing of positive personal information. Converging support for this self-schema notion comes from the self-referent studies outlined previously (e.g., Derry & Kuiper, 1980; Markus, 1977; Rogers et al., 1977).

Further support for a positive bias in nondepressives was obtained in a recent study by Lewinsohn et al. (1980). Findings indicated that the normals in this study rated themselves much more positively on a number of social skills attributes than did outside observers trained to rate the competence of their social interactions. Lewinsohn et al. posited an "illusory warm glow" to account for these findings. Namely, they suggested that normals are characterized by a somewhat unrealistic self-enhancement bias, in which they perceive themselves more positively than others see them. In combination with the content-specificity notion, the Lewinsohn et al. illusory warm glow hypothesis suggests that normals' self-referent incidental recall should be significantly higher for positive relative to negative personal information.

RECALL PERFORMANCE. Following the alternative categorization scheme used in the clinical study, Kuiper and MacDonald calculated both a positive and a negative recall score for each target person in their study. As was the case in the Derry and Kuiper experiment, this was done idiographically for each subject.

The overall mean proportion recall scores for this categorization scheme are presented in Table 5.7. An analysis of variance of these data demonstrated a significant three-way interaction between groups, target persons and personality information.

Considering only the *self-referent* condition, a post hoc test indicated that nondepressives recalled significantly more positive information about themselves than negative. This finding was consistent with the self-referent prediction generated by Kuiper and MacDonald. Furthermore, these results for normals corroborate earlier findings with nondepressives and offer an independent replication of the content-specific nondepressive recall pattern documented by Derry and Kuiper. All of these studies support the notion of a

Table 5.7. Recall of Positive and Negative Personality Information for the Various Target Persons in the Kuiper & MacDonald Study

Personality Information	Target Person		
	Self-Reference	Generalized Other	Well-known Other
NONDEPRESSED GROUP			
Positive	.20[1]	.16	.11
Negative	.05	.34	.29
MILDLY DEPRESSED GROUP			
Positive	.22	.14	.13
Negative	.19	.11	.15

[1]Recall values can range from 0 to 1, with higher numbers denoting greater recall.

positive bias, or illusory warm glow, for normals' processing of personal information about themselves.

The self-referent recall findings for mild depressives in the Kuiper and MacDonald study were also in line with predictions. As expected, individuals at a mild level of depression recalled equal amounts of positive and negative personality information about themselves. This is in contrast to the findings for the more severe depressives in the clinical study, who displayed a clear content bias for negative information recall. Furthermore, mild depressives in this study recalled significantly more negative information about themselves than normals. This finding suggests that the only content difference between the self-schema of normals and mild depressives is the inclusion in the latter of negative self-referent material.

EFFICIENCY AND SELF-REFERENT RATING TIMES. An additional aim of the Kuiper and MacDonald study was to assess how efficiently positive and negative self-referent information is processed by various individuals. In this respect, the ratio derived by Lloyd and Lishman (1975) might be considered one measure of schematic processing efficiency. As suggested previously, short rating time latencies in this type of paradigm indicate the use of a well-organized and efficient cognitive schema, responsible for the greater accessibility of schema-consistent personal information. As such, the Lloyd and Lishman ratio hints that severely depressed individuals might employ an efficient self-schema to facilitate their processing of personal information. This suggestion received empirical support in the Derry and Kuiper clinical study.

The type of efficiency documented for clinical depressives may not, however, be evident at milder levels of depression. Instead, Kuiper and MacDonald reasoned that *both* negative and positive personal information may be processed less efficiently by these individuals. This lack of efficiency may stem from the mild depressive's uncertainty concerning applicable self-referent attributes. Perhaps the depression level of mild depressives may not be severe enough to warrant the full development and use of a negative self-schema. In turn, this uncertainty would increase the latency, or response time, for self-referent judgments concerning *negative* information. It is also possible that individuals at this level of depression may be uncertain of the status of positive material in their self-schema. If so, this would function to hinder the efficient processing of positive information. In short, Kuiper and MacDonald postulated that the self-schema of mild depressives may be in a state of flux, or transition, in which it is neither exclusively depressed nor exclusively nondepressed in content. Thus, the self-schema of individuals at this level of depression may incorporate elements of both types of content, but at the expense of efficient processing for either.

RATING TIME PERFORMANCE. In a fashion similar to that used in the clinical study, rating time was defined as the time period between the original presentation of the adjective on the television monitor until a yes or no response. Again, an idiographic procedure was used to calculate each subject's mean positive and negative rating time values. For each target, a subject's positive rating time score consisted of the mean rating time for all yes-rated nondepressed adjectives and no-rated depressed adjectives. Similarly, a negative score consisted of the mean rating time for no-rated nondepressed words and yes-rated depressed words.

The overall means for this classification procedure are shown in Table 5.8. The three-way interaction between these classification variables was significant, prompting a closer inspection of the rating time for the *self-referent* condition.

For nondepressives, Kuiper and MacDonald had predicted that schema-compatible information would be processed more quickly and efficiently than incompatible material. This proved to be the case, as the normals' rating time for positive information was found to be significantly faster than their judgment latency for negative material. This pattern converges on Lloyd and Lishman's rating time ratio for nondepressed individuals. In addition, it supports the notion that the self-schema in normals is oriented toward the efficient processing of positive personality information. Schema-compatible information is processed quickly via this cognitive structure, but without any decrement in positive recall performance (Table 5.7).

The Kuiper and MacDonald rating time findings for mild depressives were also as predicted. Table 5.8 indicates that these subjects did not display a significant rating time difference in their processing of self-referent positive versus negative information. In addition, their rating times for positive information were significantly longer than those of the nondepressives for the same condition. Taken together, these findings suggest a general lack of efficiency in self-referent processing at this particular level of depression. Furthermore, they support the notion that milder levels of depression might be marked by a period of uncertainty and confusion surrounding one's view of self. While the person may have already begun to experience some of the symptoms relating to depression, the mild nature of these symptoms may have prohibited their positive and precise identification. This potential difficulty in labeling nonsevere depression related experiences and phenomena may then contribute to a state of uncertainty and disorganization concerning one's self-schema. This diffuse state might even generalize to include formerly stable positive content, producing longer rating times for this condition as well.

At a more general level, it should be noted that the self-schema of mild depressives differs from that of clinical depressives, both in terms of the content and in terms of efficiency parameters. Not only do mild depressives incorporate both types of content, but they process this information in a less efficient manner. These distinctions will be elaborated on more fully following a consideration of mild depressives' processing of information about others.

Processing personal information about others

Some preliminary issues

A second concern in the Kuiper and MacDonald study was to systematically investigate the manner in which depressed individuals perceive various categories of other people. To this end, subjects made personality judgments about both the "average" person and someone they knew quite well. The former type of judgment was included to assess the possible magnitude of other-referent biases, unhampered by actual knowledge about a particular person. The inclusion of this target

Table 5.8. Rating Times for Positive and Negative Personality Information for the Various Target Persons in the Kuiper & MacDonald Study

Personality Information	Target Person		
	Self-Reference	Generalized Other	Well-known Other
	NONDEPRESSED GROUP		
Positive	2.28[1]	3.24	2.28
Negative	3.23	3.55	3.51
	MILDLY DEPRESSED GROUP		
Positive	3.49	3.30	3.19
Negative	3.71	4.31	3.23

[1] Rating times were measured in hundredths of a second.

allowed a measure of generalized conceptions of personality, including pathological, or negative, components. This measure was deemed important because the implicit theories of psychopathology held by depressed individuals may differ substantially from those held by nondepressives. As such conceptualizations can have an effect on subsequent social interactions and relationships (Darley & Fazio, 1980), their initial investigation and documentation were felt to be of primary concern.

The second type of other-referent judgment pertained to an actual person. Each subject in the Kuiper and MacDonald study was required to select and then rate the person they knew best. Several factors prompted the inclusion of this target. First, the person perception literature has hinted that there may be fundamental differences in the way we process and retain information about real people, compared with hypothetical, or fictitious, targets (Fiske & Cox, 1979). Our concern was to document the role of such a distinction in the domain of depression. This could be done via a comparison of rating time and recall performance for generalized versus well-known others. Second, further work in social cognition has suggested that degree of familiarity with the target may have a potent effect on the processing and organization of information about the person (Kuiper & Derry, 1981). This work suggests that a careful consideration of familiarity level is an important prerequisite to any social cognition research incorporating real targets.

Accordingly, a stringent set of criteria was employed by Kuiper and MacDonald to assist each subject in her or his selection of a well-known other. A three-stage nomination procedure was used to define each target. In the first stage, each subject was given the following instructions:

Write down the names of at least five people that you know very well, and are currently important in your life. These people can be family members, best friends, or anyone else that you feel you know quite well. Please do not include anyone in the list that you have known for less than three months.

In the second stage, subjects estimated how much time per week, over the past three months, has been spent with each of these persons. In the final step, subjects in this study made 7-point familiarity ratings for each person. Based on this procedure, the person with the highest familiarity rating was chosen as the well-known other to be rated. If any ties occurred, the second selection criterion of estimated hours per week was also employed, with the well-known other being the individual with the highest familiarity rating and the highest hours per week. Overall, these criteria ensured that all of the targets in this study were from within a narrow and prescribed range of familiarity.

OTHER-REFERENT PROCESSING IN DEPRESSIVES. A major objective of the Kuiper and MacDonald study was to investigate the manner in which depressive schemata may influence other-referent processing. This objective reflects the potential importance of other-referent perceptions, both for the depressives' view of self and for their ensuing interpersonal contacts with others. For example, one means whereby depressives may perpetuate (or even exacerbate) their negative view of self is via an other-referent contrast effect. Specifically, depressives may accentuate their negative self-image even further by perceiving others in highly unrealistic positive terms.

Consistent with the foregoing proposal, Lunghi (1977) found that depressives generally evaluated their own social relationships with a wide variety of others as poorer than normals. This negative perception was most pronounced for a generalized other and least evident in the case of a well-known, liked other. In a different paradigm, Lobitz and Post (1979) found that depressives evaluated the performance of hypothetical other patients on a word-association task as significantly better than their own performance. Subsequently, they also rewarded these generalized others more than themselves. Paradoxically, however, these positive perceptions of others may be quite negative for the depressed person when considered in light of a contrast-effect hypothesis. By artificially elevating positive attributes about others, this comparison process may serve to initiate and/or further highlight the depressive's negative view of self.

Based on the contrast-effect hypothesis, Kuiper and MacDonald formulated several incidental-recall predictions for the mild depressives in their study. The first of these concerned the recall of positive personality information. Here, it was suggested that depressives would recall more positive material about the other-referent targets than about themselves. Such a pattern would offer support for the positive component of a contrast effect in depressives. However, it is also possible that aspects of the contrast effect may emerge for negative personality information. Specifically, depressives may also underestimate the negative characteristics associated with others, when compared with normals or nondepressives. In turn, this component predicts poor other-referent recall for negative information by depressives, when compared with nondepressives.

OTHER-REFERENT PROCESSING IN NONDEPRESSIVES. The pattern of other-referent recall to be expected of nondepressives in the Kuiper and MacDonald study was more difficult to formulate. On the one hand, Lewinsohn et al. (1980) have suggested that the illusory warm glow for nondepressives may extend to the perception and evaluation of others. This suggestion, although not backed by data, favors a consistency hypothesis. Basically, this hypothesis suggests that individuals process information about others with the same biases used to process information about themselves. In turn, this consistency position would predict a positive personality information bias in normals' recall for other-referent targets. On the other hand, Lobitz and Post (1979) report that nondepressed patients expected higher performance for themselves on a word-association task than for unnamed other patients. While also very tentative, these data hint at a contrast effect whereby others are generally viewed by nondepressives in an unflatteringly negative fashion. Perhaps one process whereby normals promote their own self-enhancement (or warm glow) is via a degradation of personality attributes possessed by others. This contrast-effect position would predict a negative personality information bias in normals' recall of other-referent information. As in the case of depressives, it is possible that either of the preceding patterns (consistency or contrast) would be most pronounced for a hypothetical generalized other, as such views are unfettered by the constraints of actual knowledge about a real person.

OTHER-REFERENT RECALL AND RATING TIME PERFORMANCE. Turning first to the incidental recall data, an examination of the other-referent conditions in Table 5.7 suggests the existence of a contrast effect for nondepressives.

Specifically, a preliminary scanning of the normals' data shows a strong bias toward the retention of negative information about others. This bias was confirmed by a series of post hoc tests revealing that only normals recalled significantly more negative information about both other-referent targets than about themselves. Furthermore, it was only these individuals who displayed a pattern of recalling significantly more negative than positive information about others.[4] Taken together, these other-referent recall findings are at odds with a consistency interpretation. Rather than extending the illusory warm glow to others, normals appear to contrast themselves to a marked degree.

The contrast effect for normals was further reflected in their other-referent rating time data, as shown in Table 5.8. In the case of a generalized other, it was found that the nondepressives' positive information rating time was significantly longer than their rating time for either remaining target (self or well-known other). One possible interpretation of this pattern is that normals may be uncertain concerning the degree to which positive information applies to people in general. This uncertainty would then be reflected in longer rating times for this condition. In other words, a further component of the contrast effect in normals may be a hesitancy in responding when encountering positive information about others. Rather than automatically assuming that this information may pertain to people in general (a generalized illusory warm glow), normals may use a more cautious and critical evaluation process, which is suggested by the delayed response.

An important consideration in the rating time component of the contrast effect is that it was evident only for a generalized other. When required to make judgments about a well-known other, the nondepressives in the Kuiper and MacDonald study did not delay their positive responses. This suggests that actual knowledge about a specific person functioned to attenuate the rating time component of the normals' contrast effect. In general, this distinction reinforces the person perception proposal that the processing of personal information about others may be critically dependent upon the real or hypothetical nature of the target.

The incidental recall data obtained for mild depressives offered only partial support for a contrast-effect proposal. As indicated in Table 5.7, it was found that mild depressives did not recall more positive information about others than about themselves. In fact, several post hoc tests revealed that individuals at this mild level of depression still recalled more self- than other-referent positive material. This pattern parallels the positive recall findings for normals and, as such, does not offer empirical support for the positive component of a contrast effect in depressives. Instead, it appears that this effect is restricted to recall for negative personality judgments. Table 5.7 reveals that mild depressives recalled far less negative information about both other-referent targets than did nondepressives, with this difference being highly significant for the generalized other condition.

The negative component of a depressive contrast effect also emerged in the rating time data (Table 5.8). For a generalized other, mild depressives took significantly longer to process negative information than positive. It is possible that this delay may reflect some hesitancy or uncertainty in judging negative characteristics with respect to people in general. This uncertainty would be consistent with an unrealistically positive "halo effect" for generalized others. Hence, depressives may carefully deliberate over the applicability of negative attributes for this target.

Summary and implications of the other-referent findings

The other-referent results for nondepressives were fairly clear and pointed to a contrast-effect interpretation. This was demonstrated both in the higher recall for negative information about others and in the longer rating times for positive information in the case of a generalized other. Overall, this portion of the data lends little credence to the notion that a self-referent illusory warm glow extend to the perception of others.

The findings for mild depressives were slightly more complex, with a contrast effect evident only for negative information processing. The failure to obtain a contrast effect for positive material may relate to the mild level of depression tapped in this study. Thus, a critical next step would be the assessment of other-referent processing in more severe clinical depressives. Such an investigation would reveal the extent to which depression level interacts with both the positive and the negative components of a contrast effect.

Several other aspects of the present findings might also be explored in future research. Perhaps one of the more important avenues of exploration concerns the potential role of other-referent perceptions in formulating and guiding subsequent social interactions. The present findings indicate that the obtained contrast effects were most pronounced for a generalized other. Extrapolating to a social interaction setting, this condition might be most akin to meeting an unfamiliar person. Here, the perceiver might maximize the use of implicit theories of personality to form an expectation of the target person (Darley & Fazio, 1980). In turn, these expectations may help to shape the course of further social behaviors. Indeed, Cantor and Mischel (1979, p. 6) have proposed that such expectations may "constrain the subsequent behavior of the perceived as well as biasing the perceptions and actions of the perceiver." With respect to depression, these types of expectation effects may account, in part, for the social skills deficits prominently displayed by depressives (Youngren & Lewinsohn, 1980), as well as the general reluctance of normals to interact with depressives in various social settings (Coyne, 1976). Overall, then, these perceptions are worthy of further study, as they may act to exert a powerful influence on the social milieu experienced by depressives.

A self-schema model for depression

Presented in Table 5.9 is a conceptual overview of a self-schema model for depression. A major tenet of this model is that depth of depression is a critical factor in determining both content and efficiency parameters of the self-schema. The model casts schematic self-referent processing along a continuum ranging from the absence of depression through mild depression to clinical depression. In general, the model proposes (a) clear evidence for an efficient self-schema for nonpathological information in nondepressives, (b) a state of relative inefficiency in which both types of content are represented in the self-schema of mild depressives, and, finally, (c) a return to an efficient form of schematic processing in clinical depressives, but for depressed content. The evidence in support of these parameters is examined below.

Content parameter

At the nondepressed end of the continuum, convergent empirical support has emerged for a content-specific nonpathological self-schema. That is, nondepressed subjects in both the Derry and Kuiper and the Kuiper and MacDonald study revealed the highest levels of recall for nondepressed, or positive, content adjectives processed via the self-referent task. These findings extend previous related studies (e.g., Markus, 1977; Rogers et al., 1977) which have repeatedly documented the self as an important aspect of personal information processing. The notion that this structure operates to efficiently organize, store, and retrieve information that is consistent with one's view of self has thus received further empirical verification in our research program. In sum, for nondepressives, or normals, self-referent recall enhancement is obtained only when schema-consistent information is processed via the self-schema.

It would appear that mild levels of depression are accompanied by a disruption in one's organized and consistent view of self. For this group of depressives in the Kuiper and MacDonald study, the self appeared to contain both positive and negative information components. This suggests that these subjects have begun to view themselves with depressed, or negative, content in their self-schema, although positive information has not yet been displaced.

Table 5.9. A Self-Schema Model for Depression

Depth of Depression	Parameters of the Self-Schema	
	Content[1]	Efficiency[2]
Nondepressed	Nondepressed (positive)	Efficient
Mildly depressed	Both positive and negative	Inefficient
Clinically depressed	Depressed (negative)	Efficient

[1]Empirically measured by incidental recall for self-referent judgments.
[2]Empirically measured by rating times for self-referent judgments.

Finally, clear evidence of content-specific self-schema processing was obtained at the depressed end of the continuum. The clinical depressives in the Derry and Kuiper experiment revealed that any shift in the content of the self which may have occurred at mild levels of depression has become complete for depressed patients. The self-schema in clinical depressives is organized to facilitate the processing and output of depressive, or negative, information. This was seen in the elevated self-reference recall levels for depressed content adjectives. This prominence, or centrality, of depressed content, specific and unique to clinical depressives, empirically supports Beck's theoretical formulation of schemata in depression.

Efficiency parameter

Rating times were collected in both of our main experiments. Thus, evidence bearing on the efficiency parameter of the self-schema was obtained for several points along the depressive continuum. In the case of both clinical depressives and nondepressives, content-specific personal information was processed in an efficient manner. Previous research has consistently revealed that the self-schema in normals is highly efficient. In this respect, the clinical depressives in the Derry and Kuiper study were not significantly slower than normals in making self-referent decisions. In short, not only does the self-schema model describe an organizational breakdown and subsequent return to effective processing of schema-consistent information, but it also postulates a return to efficient processing for clinically depressed patients.

Overall, this model traces changes in self-schema processing along a continuum ranging from nondepression through increasing levels of severity to the realm of clinical depression. Both extremes of the depressive continuum are characterized by highly efficient, content-specific schematic processing of personal information. The only substantial difference between nondepressives and clinical depressives resides in the actual *content* of information schematically represented. The development of depressive symptoms at the midranges of the model's continuum seems to be accompanied by a disrupted and disorganized self-structure which no longer facilitates the efficient processing of either positive or negative personal information. As the depression level becomes more severe, the shift from nondepressed to depressed self-schema content becomes complete and limits the content of personal data which may be efficiently processed via self-reference.

Benefits of the model

RESEARCH ISSUES. One benefit of the proposed model may lie in its ability to serve as an organizing framework for drawing together and clarifying some of the cognitive literature pertaining to depression. In addition to providing an explanation for the results reported in our research program and those of others (Lloyd & Lishman, 1975), the model may also account for the "non-schema" results reported by Davis (1979). His general failure to find self-reference effects for nondepressed content in severe depressives points to the possibility that depressed content (which was not assessed) may have displaced nonpathological content in the self-schema of these individuals. Based on the model, one would not anticipate enhanced self-reference recall for schema-incompatible content in clinical depressives.[5]

A second contribution of the model is the importance and emphasis it places on the issue of severity, or depth, of depression. A long-standing debate in the depression literature has concerned the validity of generalizing results from analogue studies of mildly depressed college students to the population of clinical depressives (Depue & Monroe, 1978). Our findings imply a large degree of caution for researchers who attempt to make such extensions. With data suggesting that depressives exhibit significantly different patterns of self-perceptions as their depression level becomes more severe, the present line of investigation reveals that mildly depressed students are qualitatively distinct from their clinical counterparts. Thus, a *simple* extrapolation of the findings from the mildly depressed group would be inappropriate and misleading.

Finally, it should be noted that our present line of research is cross-sectional rather than longitudinal in nature. As such, changes *within* a given person regarding schematic processing cannot be assessed. The present findings permit conclusions regarding between-groups differences. Yet it is conceivable that intraindividual changes in the content and efficiency parameters of self-reference may also occur concomitant with the course of a depressive episode. Thus, another important line of investigation following from the current program is the longitudinal study of depressives over time. At present, we are undertaking such a study. This involves the assessment of the self-schema during a depressive episode (in clinical depressives) and again when the symptoms have been judged improved. We are hopeful that this study will reveal critical information regarding the stability of the depressives' self-schema.

CLINICAL ISSUES. The self-referent findings from the present studies would appear to hold some potential in terms of applied work in psychopathology. This extension would seem most apparent when assessment procedures in clinical practice are considered. Kihlstrom and Nashby (1980) have outlined in some detail the strategies whereby laboratory-based procedures from the study of social cognition could be employed in the general understanding and evaluation of individuals. In considering the nature of schemata and their effects on social cognition, these researchers highlight the need for special assessment techniques capable of revealing these structures in individuals who, by themselves, are unable to articulate their existence. An essential element of the Kihlstrom and Nashby argument is that procedures developed in the cognitive laboratory can be adapted for use in the clinic. One example is the use of desk-top microcomputers. Following the paradigm and rationale embodied in the present research, the client would be asked to make dichotomous yes/no self-reference decisions about standard items in a list of personality traits or moods. Relatively inexpensive hardware could record decision times for each item. Furthermore, the apparatus could be programmed to extract items from several levels of response (e.g., fast and slow negative, fast and slow positive) and present them for study under intentional learning conditions. False recognition items (Rogers et al., 1979) could be combined with other data to make quick, but empirically grounded, assumptions regarding the client's self-concept. Procedures such as these could assist the clinician in assessing the content of the client's self-schema toward a clearer understanding of his or her depth of depression.

The present self-referent findings also hold potential in terms of extensions to other areas of psychopathology. The paranoid personality, for example, makes consistent errors in self-referent processing. Such a client perceives many situations and events as personally threatening and interprets information in such a way as to be suspicious and mistrustful of others. With the appropriately normed set of personal adjectives, empirical investigation of the self-schema of paranoid individuals could proceed. Similar experimental strategies might also include extensions to obsessive-compulsive personality disorders and to hypochondriasis. Work in other laboratories is currently in progress, attempting to clarify the nature of self-schematic processing in such conditions as obesity (Markus & Smith, 1981) and bipolar affective illness (Myers, 1981). In short, the investigation of the content and efficiency implications of the self-schema holds considerable potential for increased understanding of a number of conditions and disorders. Both the student of psychopathology and the clinician would appear to benefit from such efforts.

Notes

1. Subsequent analysis of covariance indicated that these group differences in age and Wechsler Memory Scale scores did not have a significant impact on either recall or rating time performance.

2. A series of check analyses converged on the reliable and robust nature of this recall pattern. For example, the critical four-way interaction remained significant after both logarithmic and square-root transformations of the data. In addition, the removal of any mathematically undefined adjusted recall scores of 0/0 (1.3 percent of all data points) still resulted in a significant four-way interaction. Finally, an analysis of content ratings indicated that the content manipulation was equally meaningful for depressives and nondepressives. This eliminated this factor as a potential confound in the interpretation of recall data.

3. Logarithmic and square-root transformations of these rating time data produced the same pattern of results as reported. Furthermore, the results from the simple reaction time task ruled out the possibility of psychomotor retardation within either of the psychiatric groups. The nonsignificant group differences in simple rating time (overall $x = 620$ milliseconds) suggested that the longer self-reference rating times for the psychiatric controls reflected specific difficulties in schema-relevant processing, rather than a general response deficit.

4. A possible confound in interpreting both the recall and the rating time data is that depressives selected substantially different well-known others than nondepressives. However, responses to a "familiarity" questionnaire indicated that the well-known others selected by mild depressives and normals were comparable on a number of attributes. For example, a series of statistical comparisons revealed that the well-known others in each group were equivalent in terms of familiarity ratings, age, number of years known, and hours per week spent with. Also, in both groups there were approximately equal numbers of relatives and nonrelatives and of males and females. This equivalence suggests that alternative interpretations of these data, based on a different selection hypothesis, are probably not tenable.

5. More recent work by Davis and Unruh (1981) has utilized the same set of nonpathological personal adjectives as Davis (1979). Employing a multi-trial free recall paradigm, it was found that depressed subjects displayed lower degrees of subjective organization for their self-referent recall than nondepressives. Based on these findings, Davis and Unruh (1981, pp. 125–126) have again argued that "some depressives show nonschema based self-reference." However, this conclusion seems quite inappropriate and potentially misleading, given the failure to properly assess depressed content.

References

Altman, J. H., & Wittenborn, J. R. Depression-prone personality in women. *Journal of Abnormal Psychology*, 1980, *89*, 303–308.

Beck, A. T. *Depression: Clinical, experimental, and theoretical aspects*. New York: Harper & Row, 1967.

Beck, A. T., Rush, A. J., Shaw, B. F., & Emery, G. *Cognitive therapy of depression*. New York: Guilford Press, 1979.

Beck, A. T., Ward, C. H., Mendelson, M., Mock, J., & Erbaugh, J. An inventory for measuring depression. *Archives of General Psychiatry*, 1961, *4*, 561–571.

Brewer, D., Doughtie, E. B., & Lubin, B. Induction of mood and mood shift. *Journal of Clinical Psychology*, 1980, *36*, 215–226.

Buchwald, A. M. Depressive mood and estimates of reinforcement frequency. *Journal of Abnormal Psychology*, 1977, *86*, 443–446.

Cantor, N., & Mischel, W. Prototypes in person perception. In L. Berkowitz (Ed.), *Advances in experimental social psychology* (Vol. 12). New York: Academic Press, 1979.

Chan, D. W., & Jackson, D. N. Implicit theory of psychopathology. *Multivariate Behavioral Research*, 1979, *14*, 3–19.

Cofer, D. H., & Wittenborn, J. R. Personality characteristics of formerly depressed women. *Journal of Abnormal Psychology*, 1980, *89*, 309–314.

Coyne, J. C. Depression and the response of others. *Journal of Abnormal Psychology*, 1976, *85*, 186–193.

Craik, F.I.M., & Tulving, E. Depth of processing and the retention of words in episodic memory. *Journal of Experimental Psychology: General*, 1975, *104*, 268–294.

Darley, J. M., & Fazio, R. H. Expectancy confirmation processes arising in the social interaction sequence. *American Psychologist*, 1980, *35*, 867–881.

Davis, H. Self-reference and the encoding of personal information in depression. *Cognitive Therapy & Research*, 1979, *3*(1), 97–110.

Davis, H., & Unruh, W. R. The development of the self-schema in adult depression. *Journal of Abnormal Psychology*, 1981, *90*, 125–133.

DeMonbreun, B. G., & Craighead, W. E. Distortion of perception and recall of positive and neutral feedback in depression. *Cognitive Therapy and Research*, 1977, *1*, 311–329.

Depue, R. A., & Monroe, S. M. Learned helplessness in the perspective of the depressive disorders: Conceptual and definitional issues. *Journal of Abnormal Psychology*, 1978, *87*, 3–20.

Derry, P. A., & Kuiper, N. A. Content, imagery, social desirability, and emotionality ratings for depressed and nondepressed personal adjectives. Unpublished manuscript, University of Western Ontario, 1979.

Derry, P. A., & Kuiper, N. A. Schematic processing and self-reference in clinical depression. Unpublished manuscript, University of Western Ontario, 1980.

Fiske, S. T., & Cox, M. G. The effect of target familiarity and descriptive purpose on the process of describing others. *Journal of Personality*, 1979, *47*, 136–161.

Hamilton, M. A rating scale for depression. *Journal of Neurology, Neurosurgery, and Psychiatry*, 1960, *23*, 56–62.

Jackson, D. N. *A manual for the Personality Research Form*. Port Huron, Mich.: Research Psychologists Press, 1967.

Kihlstrom, J. F., & Nashby, W. Cognitive tasks in clinical assessment: An exercise in applied psychology. In P. C. Kendall & S. I. Hollen (Eds.), *Cognitive behavioral interventions: Assessment methods*. New York: Academic Press, 1980.

Kovacs, M., & Beck, A. T. Maladaptive cognitive structures in depression. *American Journal of Psychiatry*, 1978, *135*, 525–533.

Kucera, H., & Francis, W. N. *Computational analysis of present-day American English*. Providence, R. I.: Brown University Press, 1967.

Kuiper, N. A. Depression and causal attributions for success and failure. *Journal of Personality and Social Psychology*, 1978, *36*, 236–246.

Kuiper, N. A., & Derry, P. A. The self as a cognitive prototype: An application to person perception and depression. In N. Cantor & J. Kihlstrom (Eds.), *Personality, social interaction, and cognition*. Hillsdale, N.J.: Erlbaum, 1981.

Kuiper, N. A., & MacDonald, M. R. Self-reference and person perception in depression. Unpublished manuscript, University of Western Ontario, 1980.

Kuiper, N. A., & Rogers, T. B. Encoding of personal information: Self-other differences. *Journal of Personality and Social Psychology*, 1979, *37*, 499–514.

Kuiper, N. A., & Rogers, T. B. Convergent evidence for the self as a prototype: The "inverted-U RT effect" for self and other judgments. *Personality and Social Psychology Bulletin*, 1981, *7*, 438–443.

Laxer, R. M. Self-concept changes of depressive patients in general hospital treatment. *Journal of Consulting Psychology*, 1964, *28*, 214–219.

Lewinsohn, P. M., Mischel, W., Chaplin, W., & Barton, R. Social competence and depression: The role of illusory self-perceptions. *Journal of Abnormal Psychology*, 1980, *89*, 203–212.

Lishman, W. A. Selective factors in memory: Part 2, Affective disorder. *Psychological Medicine*, 1972, *2*, 248–253.

Lloyd, C. G., & Lishman, W. A. Effect of depression on the speed of recall of pleasant and unpleasant experiences. *Psychological Medicine*, 1975, *5*, 173–180.

Lobitz, W. C., & Post, R. D. Parameters of self-reinforcement and depression. *Journal of Abnormal Psychology*, 1979, *88*, 33–41.

Loeb, A., Beck, A. T., & Diggory, J. Differential effects of success and failure on depressed and nondepressed patients. *The Journal of Nervous and Mental Disease*, 1971, *152*, 106–114.

Lubin, B. Adjective checklists for measurement of depression. *Archives of General Psychiatry*, 1965, *12*, 57–62.

Lunghi, M. E. The stability of mood and social perception measures in a sample of depressive in-patients. *British Journal of Psychiatry*, 1977, *130*, 598–604.

Markus, H. Self-schemata and processing of information about the self. *Journal of Personality and Social Psychology*, 1977, *35*, 63–78.

Markus, H., & Smith, J. The influence of self-schemata on the perception of others. In N. Cantor & J. Kihlstrom (Eds.), *Personality, Social Interaction, and Cognition*. Hillsdale, N.J.: Erlbaum, 1981.

Myers, J. Self-reference and the encoding of personal information during affective episodes and remission. Unpublished doctoral dissertation, University of Calgary, 1981.

Nelson, R. E., & Craighead, W. E. Selective recall of positive and negative feedback, self-control behaviors, and depression. *Journal of Abnormal Psychology*, 1977, *86*, 379–388.

Paivio, A. U. *Imagery and verbal processes*. New York: Holt, 1971.

Rizley, R. C. Depression and distortion in the attribution of causality. *Journal of Abnormal Psychology*, 1978, *87*, 32–48.

Rogers, T. B., Kuiper, N. A., & Kirker, W. S. Self-reference and the encoding of personal information. *Journal of Personality and Social Psychology*, 1977, *35*, 677–688.

Rogers, T. B., Rogers, P. J., & Kuiper, N. A. Evidence for the self as a cognitive prototype: The "false alarms effect." *Personality and Social Psychology Bulletin*, 1979, *5*, 53–56.

Shaw, B. F. Comparison of cognitive therapy and behavior therapy in the treatment of depression. *Journal of Consulting and Clinical Psychology*, 1977, *45*, 543–551.

Weintraub, M., Segal, R. M., & Beck, A. T. An investigation of cognition and affect in depressive experiences of normal men. *Journal of Consulting and Clinical Psychology*, 1974, *42*, 911.

Wylie, R. C. *The self-concept: A review of methodological considerations and measuring instruments* (Vol. 1). Lincoln: University of Nebraska Press, 1974.

Youngren, M. A., & Lewinsohn, P. M. The functional relation between depression and problematic interpersonal behavior. *Journal of Abnormal Psychology*, 1980, *89*, 333–341.

6

SYMPTOMS AS SELF-HANDICAPPING STRATEGIES: THE VIRTUES OF OLD WINE IN A NEW BOTTLE

C. R. SNYDER
TIMOTHY W. SMITH
UNIVERSITY OF KANSAS, LAWRENCE

Once I was crazy and my ace in the hole
Was that I knew that I was crazy
So I never lost my self-control
I'd just walk in the middle of the road
I'd sleep in the middle of the bed
I'd stop in the middle of a sentence
And the voice in the middle of my head said
Hey, Junior, where you been so long
Don't you know me
I'm your ace in the hole. . . .

Ace in the hole
Lean on me
Don't you know me
I'm your guarantee
   From "Ace in the Hole"
   Paul Simon, 1979

History of symptoms as self-protective strategies

Alibis and Adler

The patient declares that he is unable to solve his task "on account of the symptoms, and only on account of these." He expects from the others the solution of his problems, and the excuse from all demands, or, at least, the granting of "extenuating circumstances." When he has his extenuating alibi, he feels that his prestige is protected. His line of success, embedded into the life process, can remain uninterrupted—by paying the price. (Adler, 1913, p. 42)

As this quote illustrates, the notion of symptoms[1] serving as a self-protective strategy is not a new one. In fact, this idea can be traced through the evolution of psychology in the twentieth century. In this vein, it is important to acknowledge the central role that Alfred Adler played in introducing and clarifying the self-protective, or safeguarding, role of symptoms. It was Adler who first asserted that symptoms may provide safeguards for self-esteem in both normal and clinical populations. The safeguarding role of symptoms emerged throughout Adler's writing (see Adler, 1913, 1914, 1929, 1931, 1933, 1936 a & b) and subsequently influenced the definition

---

The authors gratefully acknowledge the useful input of the following reviewers on the present manuscript: Benjamin Braginsky, Sharon S. Brehm, Alan F. Fontana, Raymond L. Higgins, B. Kent Houston, Edward E. Jones, Herbert L. Mirels, Rita J. Stucky, Gifford Weary, and Beatrice A. Wright.

of one of the most widely used psychological terms—*defense mechanisms.*

Adler and Freud disagree on symptoms as "defenses"

Freud utilized the concept of "defense" in his early writings, e.g., "The defence of neuropsychoses," written in 1894; and "Further remarks on the defence Neuro-Psychoses," written in 1896 (S. Freud, 1953), but did not use this term again until some 30 years later (Munroe, 1955). During this interim period, Freud employed the idea of "repression" to describe the mechanism that controlled instinctual desires. Accordingly, repression was conceptualized as the driving force behind symptoms. Whereas Freud saw symptoms as an unconsciously evoked protection against awareness of unacceptable thoughts and feelings, Adler regarded symptoms as excuses for past and future failures which threaten self-esteem. This latter view was unacceptable to Freud, who in 1910 felt that it was heretical to emphasize the importance of self, or ego, forces (A. Freud, 1948). In fact, Freud's view of symptoms represented a principal point of disagreement with Adler, and in 1911 this issue fueled the split between teacher and student (Colby, 1951).

By the mid-1920's, Freud had readopted the term defense and had changed his views such that he conceptualized repression as only one of many defenses and all symptoms as a form of defense. These two major points reflect accommodations that Freud made to Adlerian theory (Ansbacher & Ansbacher, 1967). However, although Freud revised his concept of defense mechanisms to more closely approximate Adler's safeguarding symptoms, it should be emphasized that an underlying difference in theory remained. Freud's defense mechanisms served to protect the ego from instinctual drives; Adler's safeguarding symptoms protected the individual's sense of self-esteem from environmental threats. Thus, Freud retained his emphasis on biological determinants, and Adler embraced a more social-environmental emphasis.

As a concept, "defense mechanism" has had an enormous impact on the field of psychology. Although this term is usually associated with Freud, *definitionally* it has taken on more of an Adlerian flavor. That is, defense mechanisms are often depicted as cognitive strategies that are used to reduce anxiety caused by threatening *external situations* with which the individual cannot otherwise adequately cope. The move in this direction was undoubtedly given impetus when Anna Freud acknowledged in 1936 that defenses ward off not only internal dangers, but external threats as well (A. Freud, 1948). In this vein, Adler's notion of symptoms as safeguards, or self-protective strategies, is most similar to the defense mechanism typically labeled "rationalization," which is one of several specific defense mechanisms (e.g., denial, reaction formation, projection) outlined by Anna Freud as she expanded the defense mechanism concept.

The view of symptoms as impression management

Symptoms as a self-protective strategy were generally subsumed under the defense mechanism rubric until the 1960's. At this point, several theorists began to explicitly note the purposive use of symptoms as a means of obtaining desirable personal outcomes. For the most part, however, these writers did not draw the comparison between their ideas and the early or evolved defense mechanism notions. (The negative connotations of the older psychoanalytic term may account for this fact.)

Although the writers of this period did not necessarily conceptualize their ideas under this label, their work had as a common core the idea of "impression management." Impression management, as introduced by Erving Goffman in 1959, reflects a process whereby persons control their publicly observable behavior so as to influence the impression others form of them. In fact, the idea that patients in mental hospitals may purposefully control their appearance or symptoms became the thrust of several important papers during the late 1950's and early 1960's (Artiss, 1959; Belknap, 1956; Dunham & Weinberg, 1960; Szasz, 1961). A defining characteristic of the symptom was its potential for allowing the person to deny responsibility for behavior (Haley, 1963). Noteworthy in this period was Eric Berne's popular book *Games People Play* (1964), in which the use of symptoms in the "wooden leg" game was described. Here, the protagonist is heard to exclaim, "What do you expect from a man with a wooden leg!" The symptom is seen as a way of lowering expectations, externalizing the cause of negative outcomes, and generally maximizing positive attributions.

In the mid-1960's, empirical evidence in support of impression management in clinical samples began to appear. In a series of well-designed studies by two sets of investigators, Benjamin Braginsky and his colleagues (Braginsky & Braginsky, 1967; Braginsky, Braginsky, & Ring, 1969; Braginsky, Grosse, & Ring, 1966; Braginsky, Holzberg, Ridley, & Braginsky, 1968) and Alan Fontana and his colleagues (Fontana & Gessner, 1969; Fontana, Klein, Lewis, & Levine, 1968), empirical evidence was provided to show that patients in mental hospitals purposefully vary the presentation of their symptoms in order to maximize personal benefits.

The introduction of the "self-handicapping" term

In 1978, the social psychologists E. E. Jones and Steven Berglas introduced the term "self-handicapping" (Berglas & E. E. Jones, 1978; E. E. Jones & Berglas, 1978). Conceptually, this term is similar to such previous notions as impression management, defense mechanisms, and safeguarding. Indeed, Jones and Berglas acknowledge the link to the earlier concepts by noting,

Therapists have long been aware of the appeal of the "sick" role to those who temporarily wish to drop out of life's competition. This is a form of self-handicapping where the body is seen as outside the system of personal responsibility. Many clinicians have noted that even the roles of "neurotic" and "mental" patients may be partly strategic in nature.

To quote these authors further, "The self-handicapper, we are suggesting, reaches out for impediments, exaggerates handicaps, and embraces any factor reducing personal responsibility for mediocrity and enhancing personal responsibility for success." Thus, the individual who employs a self-handicap may utilize Kelley's (1971) discounting and augmentation principles. In the case of poor performances, the role of the individual's ability or competence as a causal factor is discounted as a result of the addition of another possible causal factor, the impediment. In the case of success, the role of the individual's ability or competence is augmented since the success occurred in spite of the impediment.

While this self-handicapping notion coexists nicely with the aforementioned clinical literature, Jones and Berglas note that the underlying premise differs from that held by two major social psychological theories—social comparison theory (Festinger, 1954) and attribution theory (Heider, 1958; Kelley, 1971). Unlike these previous social psychological theories which suggest that people constantly seek situations where they may receive accurate information about themselves, self-handicapping presupposes that at times people *avoid* accurate information when their self-esteem is threatened. By adopting a symptom, the person increases the ambiguity as to the "real" underlying reason for a possible failure. Interestingly, the pursuit of attribute ambiguity phenomenon has received increasing theoretical and empirical support recently in social psychology (see, for review, Melvin L. Snyder & Wicklund, in press). Behind the veil of ambiguity supposedly generated by symptoms, the self-handicapper therefore is able to nurture a fantasy of self-esteem and competence.

Within the previously discussed historical context, Jones and Berglas's concept of self-handicapping can be viewed as a type of defense mechanism whereby the individual reduces a threat to self-esteem by actively seeking or creating an additional causal explanation for potential failure. The handicap, or impediment, involved is, in Adler's words, a safeguard (i.e., it protects self-esteem). It is noteworthy that the provision of additional causes for poor performance has been found to reduce anxiety associated with a threat to self-esteem (Burish & Houston, 1979). To the extent that the individual who self-handicaps is attempting to control the attributions made by others concerning his or her performance, the employment of a self-handicap has components of impression management. The impression others have of the actor (e.g., "sick," "mentally ill") would obviously influence the attributions they form.

In the next section, we shall expand on the Jones and Berglas definition of self-handicapping and provide examples for the reader. We offer the subsequent amplification of self-handicapping as a means of better understanding the role of symptoms as a self-protective strategy.

Definition and examples of the self-handicapping process

Updating the self-handicapping concept

The Jones and Berglas formulation of the self-handicapping process provides a valuable tool in applying empirical support to the older models of the strategic use of symptoms. Its usefulness can be increased, however, by further delineating the concept. In this regard, it should be noted that symptoms can be used in at least three ways to protect self-esteem and competence. First, as Jones and Berglas suggest, symptoms provide additional causes for potential failures and thereby diffuse the impact of negative feedback. Second, symptoms can also be strategically used to avoid the evaluative situation altogether (Kaplan, 1972, 1980). Third, symptoms can be employed to secure tangible rewards that may also bolster the person's sense of self-esteem and competence. In defining this process, it should be emphasized that the impediments found or created in self-handicapping are indeed handicaps. The obstacles invoked are socially viewed as negative characteristics or behaviors. However, by appeal to the negative, peripheral characteristic or behavior, the individual avoids the implications of performance for more central, highly valued dimensions.

With these concerns in mind, the following definition of self-handicapping is offered:

Self-handicapping may be understood as a process wherein a person, in response to an anticipated loss of self-esteem resulting from the possibility of inadequate performance in a domain where performance clearly implicates ability or competence, adopts characteristics or behaviors that superficially constitute admission of a problem, weakness, or deficit, but assist the individual in (1) controlling attributions (made by oneself or others) concerning performance so as to discount the self-relevant implications of poor performance and augment the self-relevant implications of success, (2) avoiding the threatening evaluative situation entirely, or (3) maintaining existing environmental conditions that maximize positive self-relevant feedback and minimize negative self-relevant feedback.

Along with this definition, it should be emphasized that self-handicapping results because of threats to self-esteem and competency on important, self-relevant dimensions.[2,3] Individuals who are not threatened on such a central dimension have no need to do so. What the individual gains in this process is the protection of perceived self-esteem.[4] The individual may gain tangible rewards (e.g., money, privileges), but these are viewed as relevant in the present formulation only insofar as they serve to foster an underlying sense of self-esteem and competence. It also should be noted that self-esteem and competency-linked dimensions are protected both in the handicapper's eyes and in the eyes of others. Both public and private issues can be present in the threat. Finally, what the individual incurs is an admission of a problem weakness, or deficit; moreover, it is presumed that what is lost in such an admission is not as highly valued as what is protected.

Arenas, options, and examples

Self-handicapping is most likely to occur in any arena where performance is subjectively related to the individual's sense of self-esteem or competence and where the individual is threatened with the possibility of poor performance. The student with an exaggerated investment in her or his intellectual competence may be especially prone to self-handicap in academic performance settings. For individuals who endorse athletic prowess as an important characteristic, self-handicapping may occur in conjunction with athletic competition. Interpersonal activities (e.g., "a good social life," "good relationships") may be valued to the extent that failure is a very threatening possibility. As such, this area also is ripe for the creation of impediments to successful performance. Finally, for those who place elevated importance on vocational achievement, self-handicaps may be invoked in looking for work, facing a potential promotion, or just facing daily tasks that include the possibility of poor performance.

Just as there are many arenas in which to handicap, there are many ways as well. Handicaps vary along two important dimensions: their duration and the extent to which they are self-evident versus requiring the self-handicapper's avowal. Individuals can find or erect lasting obstacles a long time before facing the evaluative setting or may wait until just prior to the evaluative setting to cite or plant the "hurdles." These cases identify the dimension of duration of the handicap. Similarly, the self-handicapper may simply cite (to self or others) an impediment to performance or may overtly perform actions that inhibit or reduce the probability of success. The former instances are corroborated only by the individual's testimony, and the latter are publicly observable.

To help clarify the process of self-handicapping, the arenas in which it occurs, and the dimensions along which it varies, the following examples are presented. Consider first the business executive who has become a chronic abuser of alcohol. Simultaneously being unsure of his or her ability to continue advancing within the corporate structure (or even fearful of being replaced by younger, better trained new employees) and placing much importance on such achievements, the individual faces a significant threat to self-esteem. As Jones and Berglas (1978) have suggested, the abuse of alcohol provides a ready explanation for marginal performance. Thereby the individual may discount personal ability as a cause for failure (e.g., not being promoted or given a raise) by making an attribution to his or her drinking problem. Because of the alcohol problem, the executive may be excluded from competing with peers for new, higher positions, thus avoiding future evaluative situations. Finally, if the alcohol abuser is a member of an alcohol abusing peer group, social interaction in that group may provide alternate self-esteem bolstering feedback. The explicit, overt nature of this handicap requires no other testimony on the part of the handicapper, and it is obviously of long duration.

Various evaluative anxieties may function as self-handicapping strategies. For example, the student who exhibits an exaggerated investment in intellectual competence and who faces several years of regular, difficult examinations obviously incurs a substantial threat to self-esteem. Complaints of severe test anxiety (e.g., "I get so nervous in tests that I forget what I know") can serve as a strategy for discounting the self-relevant implications of poor performance on past and future examinations. If the reported anxiety becomes debilitating enough, examinations may be avoided entirely. This particular handicap is based largely on the avowal of the handicapper and, if incorporated into the individual's self-concept (e.g., "I'm a test-anxious person" or "I have a problem with test anxiety"), could be of long duration.

Many individuals place extreme importance on receiving the approval or liking of others (Ellis, 1962). For these individuals, social activities can carry a salient threat to self-esteem. The adolescent boy who spends no effort to groom his personal appearance on the night of his first date with an attractive girl can be seen as adopting an obvious (i.e., requiring little avowal) handicap of short duration. By looking less than "sharp," he can attribute any upcoming rejection to his easily changeable appearance rather than to more enduring personality or physical characteristics. If continued, this strategy could also ensure the avoidance of other, future social evaluative situations.

For the serious athlete, competitive performances are closely linked to self-esteem. Marginal performances reflect marginal ability, and athletic ability is closely intertwined with the athlete's sense of self-worth. The sprinter who complains of a muscle pull a few days prior to a prestigious track meet may be adopting a self-handicapping strategy. Perhaps reacting to an actual sensation of pain or tightness in the muscle, the sprinter reports a temporary hindrance to optimal performance. Known to others only by the athlete's testimony, this probably short-lived handicap provides an alternate explanation for any failure in the upcoming race; moreover, it provides a source of augmentation of ability in case of success and may alternately function as a reason for entirely avoiding the evaluative situation (e.g., "the 'real' champion was injured and couldn't run").

From these examples it can be seen that self-handicapping occurs in response to a threat to self-esteem in a variety of arenas. Furthermore, it should be evident that the handicapper can use obstacles to obscure the true meaning of performance both from the self and from others. Likewise, it may be apparent to clinicians that some clients exhibit more than one handicap in anticipation of the next evaluative situation. Whatever the number of self-handicaps, however, they typically can be analyzed in terms of the duration and self-evidence avowal dimensions described in this section.

Motivational determinants of self-handicapping

Threat to self-esteem and competency in uncertain success feedback situations

Recent theory and research under the general label of "self-concept" trade on a common underlying idea—people are motivated to maintain their sense of self-esteem and competency (see, for review, Bowerman, 1978; Melvin L. Snyder, Stephan, & Rosenfield, 1978; Weary, 1979; and Wylie, 1979). Consistent with these theories, it can be hypothesized that the protection of self-esteem and competence is especially mobilized in those evaluative feedback arenas where the individual anticipates a precarious sense of success. The protective maneuver of self-handicapping is one strategy that allows the individual to preserve a sense of self-esteem and competence in such threatening situations.

Some amplification on the nature of the threatening situation that should elicit self-handicapping is warranted at this point. In anticipation of a situation where a person feels totally capable of achieving success, there is very little threat and therefore no real necessity for self-handicapping. In anticipation of a situation where the individual feels totally incapable of achieving success, it may also be the case that there is relatively little threat because the individual openly acknowledges the improbability of her or his (or perhaps, for that matter, anyone's) succeeding in that situation. In an attributional sense, therefore, the person facing an evaluative situation with a very low probability of success will acknowledge the correspondent inference (E. E. Jones & Davis, 1965) that no one could be expected to succeed in such a situation. Under this inferential set, self-handicapping should not result because failure can be externalized to the difficult task without any implications for a particular person's ability.[5] This leaves a vast arena of anticipated situations where the individual is uncertain as to personal capability of achieving success, and it is in these tenuous circumstances that self-handicapping may be invoked to shield a person's sense of self-esteem and competence. Simply put, there is no need to invoke self-handicapping in arenas where the probability of success is either very high or very low, but rather it is the threat inherent in the anticipation of an uncertain success feedback situation that necessitates the adoption of self-handicapping. If the reader reflects on the examples of self-handicapping illustrated in the previous section, he or she will discern that a shared theme is the protagonist's anticipation of an uncertain success feedback evaluation where failure clearly implicates ability or the competence image.

Self-handicapping in the service of self-esteem and competency: Empirical studies

Having recast the idea of the strategic use of symptoms under the explanatory label "self-handicapping" (E. E. Jones & Berglas, 1978), Berglas and Jones (1978) provided an empirical test of their conceptualization. A first experiment sought to demonstrate that people will adopt a self-handicapping strategy to protect their sense of self-esteem and competency when they (1) have experienced noncontingent success feedback rather than contingent success feedback and (2) are anticipating another subsequent feedback situation. More specifically, participants were recruited to an experiment that supposedly evaluated the effect of two specific drugs on intellectual performance. Half of the participants completed easily solved problems, and the other half completed insoluble problems. Both groups were then given feedback that they had done very well on the first test. Thus, the first condition represented contingent success and the second condition represented noncontingent success. Prior to taking a second test, participants were allowed to select to take either a drug that would facilitate their performance on the subsequent test ("Actavil") or a drug that would interfere with their performance on the subsequent test ("Pandocrin"). In order to make the potential effects of the drugs credible, the subjects were shown graphs illustrating how performance on the second test had improved for previous research participants who took Actavil and how performance had deteriorated for previous participants who took Pandocrin. Also, research participants were shown a "preliminary" *Physicians Desk Reference* report suggesting that Actavil facilitated and Pandocrin disrupted intellectual performance. As predicted, there was a significant effect of success feedback condition, with 60 percent of the noncontingent success group selecting the handicapping drug, Pandocrin, and only 19 percent of the contingent success group selecting Pandocrin. This overall effect was principally due to the fact that 70 percent of the males in the noncontingent success group selected Pandocrin and 13 percent of the males in the contingent success group selected Pandocrin; the results for the females were in the same direction although not as strong: 40 percent selected Pandocrin in the noncontingent success condition and 26 percent selected Pandocrin in the contingent success condition.

In a second study, Berglas and Jones replicated and refined their first study. In a similar experiment, participants took either a soluble or an insoluble first test and then were given either success feedback or no feedback about their performance. Then, prior to a second test, the participants could select whether they wished to take Actavil or Pandocrin. This second experiment was conducted to rule out an alternative explanation for the results of the first study, i.e., that the failure associated with the insolubility of the problems rather than the noncontingent sense of success could have caused the self-handicapping preference for Pandocrin. In support of the importance of a noncontingent sense of success, results showed that the insoluble problem success feedback group chose Pandocrin 50 percent of the time and the insoluble problem group, who had not been given any feedback and therefore did not have a sense of contingent success, chose Pandocrin 15 percent of the time; the remaining two experimental groups selected Pandocrin 17 percent and 18 percent of the time. Again, it was the male rather than female participants who contributed to this significant effect. (We shall defer a discussion of the differences in self-handicapping for males and females to a later section in the chapter.)

In both of these studies, we see that males who anticipate an uncertain success feedback situation are seduced by the self-handicapping drug. The second study suggests that a sense of failure in a first situation may not necessarily induce a threat in a subsequent situation because the second situation may remain unambiguous in that it also will result in failure.

It is under the influence of anticipating an *uncertain* subsequent situation, in which we perceive that we may or may not succeed, that self-esteem and competence are truly threatened. Self-handicapping should flourish in this set, and the Berglas and Jones results related to the elevated Pandocrin preferences of noncontingent success male subjects support this theory.

Recently, Weidner (in press) replicated the Berglas and Jones self-handicapping by drug choice finding in a study that included the Type A coronary-prone behavior pattern (Friedman & Rosenman, 1959) as an individual difference variable. Using a male undergraduate population, Weidner selected extreme Type A's and Type B's and exposed them to either contingent success feedback or noncontingent failure feedback on the first half of a mental task. As in the Berglas and Jones study, subjects were allowed to choose a performance-facilitating drug (Actavil) or a performance-inhibiting drug (Pandocrin) before beginning the second part of the task. Results showed that Type A's who had experienced failure feedback were significantly more likely to choose the performance-inhibiting drug than Type A's exposed to success feedback or Type B's exposed to either success or failure feedback. The latter three groups did not differ in their drug choices. Thus, Type A's exposed to failure and threatened with further evaluation chose to self-handicap. These findings are consistent with other research indicating that Type A's exhibit exaggerated achievement striving (Burnam, Pennebaker, & Glass, 1975; Carver, Coleman, & Glass, 1976) and greater fear of failure (Gastorf & Teevan, 1980). The Type A's self-esteem is more likely to be threatened by failure, and thus the Type A is more likely to engage in self-handicapping.

It is interesting to note that the Berglas and Jones and Weidner results indicating that drug use can serve as a self-handicap parallel the results of two studies investigating the factors which elicit alcohol consumption among heavy social drinkers. While operating from a different theoretical framework (viz., a tension-reduction model of alcohol consumption), the results of two studies indirectly support the notion that alcohol consumption increases when it serves as a viable explanation for poor performance in evaluative settings. Higgins and Marlatt (1973) found that threat of shock did not increase the alcohol consumption of social drinkers, and Higgins and Marlatt (1975) demonstrated that a social evaluative threat (viz., being evaluated on social desirability by a group of individuals of the opposite sex) did lead to increased alcohol consumption. While the authors did not interpret their results within an attributional framework, it may be that threat leads to increased drinking only when alcohol consumption can serve as an excuse for poor performance that would otherwise implicate important self-relevant dimensions.

Smith, Snyder, and Handelsman (in press) reasoned that test-anxious individuals may utilize their test-anxiety symptoms in a self-handicapping manner. As a test of this proposition, highly test-anxious female college students were recruited for an experiment. Students in the evaluative conditions were told that local norms were being developed for a widely used group intelligence test and that they would be taking this test in two parts. They were also told that they would be given feedback on their score at the completion of the entire test.[6] Students in a nonevaluative condition were told that they would be taking a test in two parts and that the test was merely one the researchers were developing and thus wanted to see what people felt about the test items. Further, they were told that they would not be given feedback about how they had done on the entire test. All students then completed the first half of a test on which they achieved some correct and some incorrect answers (this established the anticipation set of uncertain success for the second part of the test). For students in the evaluative set, three different instructions were delivered regarding the effects of test anxiety on the overall performance on the test. The explicit self-handicapping condition students were told that anxiety interferes with performance on the test. In a second evaluative condition, students were told that anxiety seemed to have no effect at all on test performance. In a third evaluative condition, students were given no information about the influence of anxiety on test performance.

Before taking the second part of the test, students reported their level of state anxiety, which served as the major dependent variable in this study. Results showed that the students in the nonevaluative condition reported lower anxiety than students in all three evaluative conditions. In terms of self-handicapping, this result follows because these individuals were not anticipating any feedback and thus there was not the threat to their sense of self-esteem and competence that was inherent in the evaluative experimental set. Within the evaluative conditions, results showed that the explicit self-handicapping condition students and the no information condition students reported higher anxiety than the "anxiety has no effect" (non-self-handicapping) condition students. Thus, highly test-anxious students in anticipation of an ambiguous evaluative set reported elevated levels of anxiety whether or not the "inhibiting" effect of anxiety was explicitly noted, but lessened their reported anxiety when this anxiety was portrayed as not influencing performance. Based on these results, therefore, one inference is that in intellectually evaluative situations where eventual success feedback is uncertain, highly test-anxious people may naturally employ their anxiety symptoms as a self-handicapping strategy.

In a similar study, Smith, Snyder, and Perkins (1981) suggested that hypochondriacal individuals may use the symptoms of physical illness as a self-handicapping strategy. In order to test this hypothesis, female undergraduates scoring high on a measure of hypochondriasis (MMPI hypochondriasis scale) were recruited for an experiment. As in the Smith, Snyder, and Handelsman test-anxiety study, students in two evaluative conditions were told that they would be taking a widely used diagnostic test, in this case a measure of "social intelligence." The first part of the test was a pencil and paper social perception test, the second part a role-play test of their responses to various social situations. After completing the first part of the test (which was quite difficult, thus creating the anticipation of uncertain success) and while anticipating the role-play test, subjects in the evaluative conditions received one of two different instructions about the effects of symptoms (in this case, symptoms of physical illness) on performance used in the test-anxiety study (symptoms have no effect, no instructions). Subjects then completed a questionnaire about their health over the last year (i.e., trait health) and the number and degree of physical symptoms they had experienced in the last 24 hours (i.e., state or current health). As in the test-anxiety study, hypochondriacal subjects tended to report their symptoms in a manner that reflected self-handicapping. Hypochondriacal subjects in the "illness has no effect" condition and subjects in the nonevaluative condition reported fewer state and trait health problems than subjects given no instructions about the effect of health on performance. Evaluative threat and instructions about the effect of symptoms had no effect on the symptom reporting of nonhypochondriacal subjects. Thus the results supported the notion that, in anticipation of an evaluation of social skills where success is uncertain, hypochondriacal individuals may employ health problems as a self-handicapping strategy.

Self-handicapping in the service of tangible gains or self-esteem and competency: Empirical studies

In the mid-1960's, a series of empirical studies appeared that confirmed the idea that mental patients may control their behavior in order to achieve tangible *and* psychological gains. As noted earlier, these studies are conceptualized under the rubric of impression management. What is germane for the present topic is the finding that mental patients may simultaneously employ their symptoms to their advantage in obtaining tangible rewards and in maintaining their sense of self-esteem. Before addressing the motivational underpinning of this behavior, it would be useful to provide a few experimental examples that emphasize the material gains that may accompany the exhibition of psychological symptoms.

Braginsky and his colleagues have performed a series of studies demonstrating impression management on the part of mental patients (see, for review, Braginsky et al., 1969). For example, using a paper and pencil "mental status" test, patients who wanted to remain in the hospital (chronics) reported themselves as being sick whereas patients who wanted to be discharged (first admissions) reported themselves as being healthy (Braginsky et al., 1966). A second study amplified these findings (Braginsky & Braginsky, 1967). Male patients who were diagnosed as schizophrenics were interviewed under the belief that they were being (1) considered for discharge, (2) considered for open-ward status, or (3) given a mental status exam (a periodic psychological "checkup"). Psychiatrists then rated the tape-recorded interviews, and results revealed that the patients in the discharge and mental status conditions were seen as having significantly higher degree of psychopathology and as being more in need of hospital control than the patients in the open-ward condition.

Fontana and his colleagues have also empirically demonstrated impression management tactics by mental patients (see, for review, Fontana et al., 1968). In one particularly noteworthy study, Fontana and Klein (1968) showed that the notorious schizophrenic "deficit" (Shakow, 1962) in psychomotor coordination may in part be a presentational phenomenon. Schizophrenic in-patients were divided into two groups: one group consisting of subjects who were seen as motivated to appear competent (healthy presenters) and the second of subjects seen as motivated to appear incompetent (sick presenters). Patients were given a psychomotor reaction time task under the anticipatory set that the task was either evaluative or nonevaluative. The evaluative set emphasized that the person would be told how he was doing in relation to other people who had taken the reaction time psychomotor task, and the nonevaluative set did not mention any such comparative information. Going from the nonevaluative to the evaluative set, the deficit in psychomotor performance for healthy presenters decreased, but for sick presenters it increased. This finding, along with the Braginsky results, suggests that patients may *verbally* and *behaviorally* manifest their symptoms in uncertain evaluative settings in order to achieve personal needs and goals.

The aforementioned impression management studies imply that the goal of the symptom presentation is rather tangible in nature, i.e., to keep the patient in the hospital (with its accompanying food and shelter). In applying the self-handicapping theory to these data, however, we would hypothesize that the presentation of symptoms eventuates in *psychological* self-esteem payoffs as well as the more material benefits emphasized in this research. By remaining in the hospital, for example, the patient maintains a controlled and safe environment where he or she knows how to succeed. To quote Adler (1931) again:

To some degree or other, every neurotic restricts his sphere of action, his contacts with the whole situation. He tries to keep at a distance the real confronting problems of life and confines himself to circumstances in which he feels able to dominate. In this way he builds for himself a narrow stable, closes the door, and spends his life away from the wind, the sunlight, and the fresh air. (p. 53)

In this protected environment the patient may thus maintain a semblance of self-esteem or competency. In this sense, the in-patient's storyline of "what do you expect out of me, I'm a chronic schizophrenic" (Fontana, 1980) captures the essence of self-esteem maintenance through self-handicapping. In fact, the protection of the psychological self-esteem needs may be just as important motivationally as the material rewards that accompany symptom manifestation. Even if the symptom manifestation does not result in tangible rewards related to maintaining one's in-patient status, the patient who is discharged "sick" can still invoke the self-esteem maintenance associated with self-handicapping. For example, if one is discharged from the hospital as sick and then fails, the self-esteem is maintained because the sickness caused the failure (Kelley's discounting principle); conversely, if one is discharged from the hospital as sick and succeeds, the self-esteem is given a boost because one succeeded in spite of the sickness impediment (Kelley's augmentation principle).

Self-esteem and competency for whom: Oneself or an audience?

The individual utilizing self-handicapping may do so to maintain a sense of self-esteem and competence in his or her own eyes and in the eyes of others. Related to this issue, a manipulation was performed to establish a public versus private self-handicapping set in the previously mentioned Berglas and Jones (1978) study on drug choice. In the public condition, the experimenter knew how well the person had done on the first test and presumably therefore how well the person should do on the second test; in the private condition, the experimenter did not know how well the person had done on the first test and presumably therefore could not guess how well the person should do on the second test. Results showed that differential self-handicapping did *not* occur in the public as compared to private conditions. Although it is tenuous to make inferences based on the "confirmation" of the null hypothesis, one interpretation of these results is that private self-esteem and competency motives may not be distinguishable from public motives.[7] Berglas and Jones aptly summarize these findings in particular and the issue in general by noting:

> The notion of a strategy may suggest that self-handicapping is directed only to a public effect, that we are talking essentially about the self-presentational control of *others'* attributions concerning our basic, underlying competence. Although the possible effects on an audience, including an experimenter or test administrator, may augment the tendency to choose performance settings that obscure the drawing of correspondent inferences about competence (cf. Jones & Davis, 1965), we propose that the basic purpose behind such strategic choices is the control of the actor's *self*-attributions of competence and control. The choice of self-handicapping settings should occur, therefore, even if the susceptible person were being tested under conditions of total privacy. (p. 407)

Normal versus pathological self-handicapping

Self-handicapping and everyday life

From the examples discussed earlier, it is obvious that self-handicapping can be viewed as a common occurrence. Indeed, it is probably a rare individual who could honestly admit to never having indulged in this process. However, self-handicapping strategies vary in their severity. In their milder forms, such strategies are undoubtedly somewhat adaptive. Without the occasional appeal to handicaps, life would consist of far too frequent and unpleasant confrontations with one's limitations. While there is no clear demarcation between normal, adaptive self-handicapping and its pathological, or self-defeating, forms, overly frequent and extreme use of such strategies is indeed a problem. Thus, the clearly normal and the clearly pathological forms of self-handicapping employ the same dynamics in achieving similar ends. However, the more extreme degrees of this process are likely to be seen as (1) being socially disturbing, (2) indirectly and over time creating as much if not more personal distress than they avoid,[8] and (3) limiting the individual's range of available responses to the demands of everyday life. Some tentative suggestions for attempting to delineate normal and maladaptive self-handicapping are offered in this section.

Distinguishing dimensions

PERCEPTION OF THREAT. One factor that is helpful in contrasting normal and pathological self-handicapping is the extent to which individuals perceive threat in uncertain success feedback situations. Extreme self-handicappers may have a greater sensitivity to threat and/or a lower tolerance for threat (i.e., they may respond defensively to lower levels of threat). More severe strategies can be viewed as a reflection of the magnification of perceived threat in uncertain success arenas; moreover, severe strategies probably involve several uncertain success feedback arenas. In regard to intensification of threat, for example, the student who drinks before every exam including minor ones is behaving more pathologically than is the student who drinks only before finals. The former is employing his or her strategy in response to lower "objective" levels of threat because each test is phenomenologically experienced as *very* threatening. Furthermore, the greater the number of perceived uncertain success feedback arenas (e.g., academics, vocational pursuits, interpersonal relationships) that are closely tied to self-esteem and competency, the greater the possibility for the development of more severe self-protective styles. If an individual feels compelled to guard her or his self-esteem across a wide variety of uncertain success feedback situations, it is likely that self-protective responses will become more severe. Overall, the perceptual distortion of threat and the number of uncertain success feedback situations that are perceived as central to the person combine to influence the frequency with which the individual invokes self-handicapping strategies.

INTENSITY AND PERVASIVENESS OF THE IMPEDIMENT. Normal, adaptive handicapping strategies tend to be both less extreme and less extensive than their more pathological counterparts. They involve relatively mild, limited, unintrusive behaviors or characteristics that are viewed as affecting a small range of activities. For example, the softball pitcher's failure to practice the week before an important game has little impact on or relevance to academic, vocational, or interpersonal concerns and is hardly an extreme behavior. In more problematic forms of self-handicapping, however, the impediment has a much wider range of convenience and is much more pronounced. Thus, the chronic alcoholic's drinking is quite likely to interfere with performance in almost all aspects of life and is certainly an extreme form of behavior.

REVERSIBILITY AND STABILITY OF THE IMPEDIMENT. Minor handicaps tend to be more temporary than their more pathological counterparts. They also tend to be more reversible. A strategically employed "reactive" depression is not as maladaptive as a more chronic, intractable strategically used depression. The life span of impediments ranges from the very brief (e.g., "I got so anxious I forgot my lines") to the nearly indefinite (e.g., chronic psychiatric patients). In addition, impediments range from the easily reversible to the nearly permanent. For example, it is much easier to become a chronic alcoholic than to stop being one.

COST OF THE IMPEDIMENT. Pathological self-handicaps tend to be much more costly than milder strategies. Their cost can be assessed along two dimensions: (1) the value of what is lost directly in admission of the weakness, problem, or deficit and (2) the value in what is lost indirectly by the limitations imposed by the handicap. For example, the person who claims acute social anxiety in order to diffuse or avoid the negative self-esteem and competency implications of social rejection incurs the cost of being viewed as weak or overly emotional and mildly deviant. In addition, such a person incurs the indirect cost of a consequently reduced range of available friends, recreational activities, and possibly even vocational opportunities. The severe agorophobic who employs his or her symptoms as a way of avoiding evaluation in a variety of settings suffers even greater costs in both areas. The severe agorophobic's opportunities to move about freely are sacrificed, and society may subsequently label this as deviant. Consequently, the agorophobic may experience a reduction in available options in almost all arenas.

Coyne (1976) has illustrated how the strategic use of a symptom (viz., depression) can exact an increasingly dear price. Coyne suggests that following a stressful event individuals require reassurance and support, perhaps in the interest of maintaining self-esteem.[9] Without the social skills to elicit such social support directly, the individual progressively exaggerates depressive symptoms in order to elicit support. While such ploys may initially provide desired results, further use of depressive symptoms becomes aversive to the members of the individual's social network and they eventually withdraw. This withdrawal of friends causes the depressive to further exaggerate his or her symptoms in an effort to regain social support, and the exaggeration, being increasingly aversive to others, leads to even more withdrawal. The impending cycle of mutually exacerbating withdrawal and depressive behavior in Coyne's analysis is an excellent illustration of how strategically employed symptoms can outlive their cost-effectiveness and place the individual in a somewhat intractable and unfortunate situation.

The maintenance of self-handicapping

Self-reinforcing properties: From alternative explanations to avoidance

As described in an earlier section, symptoms may be employed in at least two interrelated reinforcing ways to protect a person's sense of self-esteem and competence. First, the symptom provides an alternative face-saving explanation for potential failure[10] (e.g., "It's better to be test-anxious than dumb"). Second, the symptom serves as a reason to avoid the potential evaluative situation (e.g., "I was so uptight about the test that I skipped the class"). Alternative explanation or avoidance thus represents rewarding self-protective verbal and overt behavioral scripts whose underlying theme suggests "I really am competent." Consider the hypothetically seductive and self-perpetuating *intraperson* alternative explanation and avoidance properties of the following clinical examples.

ANXIETY PATTERNS. Performance-related anxieties (e.g., speech anxiety, test anxiety, social anxiety) can serve effectively as alternative explanations because of their acknowledged debilitating effects on task performance. In more extreme forms, these anxiety patterns may serve as reasons to avoid uncertain success feedback situations entirely.

DEPRESSION. The low levels of energy, interest, and effort associated with depression may serve as an alternative cause for poor performance and provide a reason to avoid evaluative situations.

ANGER AND HOSTILITY. A poorly controlled temper can serve as a possible alternative cause for poor performance, particularly in interpersonal situations. The successful completion of an interpersonal interaction can be easily disrupted by an angry outburst.

SUBSTANCE ABUSE. By far the most directly strategic use of substance abuse lies in its role as an alternative cause for poor performance. Alcohol, marijuana, and many other drugs can be readily employed in this manner because of their disruptive effects on performance. Likewise, substance abuse patterns can serve as vehicles for avoiding anticipated uncertain evaluative settings.

PSYCHOTIC BEHAVIOR. The psychotic individual faces an uncertain feedback situation armed with the alternative explanation that uncontrollable forces (i.e., the mental illness) really account for his or her performance. For the most part, however, the psychotic individual need not be overly dependent on the alternative explanation mechanism because in point of fact he or she is "excused" from almost all uncertain feedback evaluative settings. Further, many psychotic individuals find interpersonal responsibility distressing, and the psychotic role inherently includes the reduction of such requirements (Fontana, 1980).

Societal reinforcing properties

The previous section indicates that self-handicapping may be maintained by the individual because of its intrinsic rewards. Beyond these internal rewards, however, there are extrinsic

DO PROFESSIONALS BELIEVE SELF-HANDICAPPERS? The impression management studies suggest that the answer to this question is yes. Recall the Braginsky and Braginsky (1967) study. Patients underwent an interview under the belief that they were being considered for discharge or that their open-ward status was being questioned. In the former set, where their residency status was in jeopardy, patients convincingly presented themselves as "sick." Three psychiatrists rated these discharge condition patients as having a higher degree of psychopathology and as being in greater need of hospital control than patients in the open-ward condition. Interestingly, however, no differences in the amount of disturbed behavior in the actual interviews was observed by the psychiatrists in this study. In other words, the professionals' judgments of psychopathology and need for control must have been based *more on the patients' reported symptoms than on the symptoms manifested*. It was not how sick they appeared, but how sick the patients said they were that influenced the psychiatrists. Not only are professionals prone to agree with the strategic self-handicapping, therefore, but they evidently may make their judgments based on the patients' verbalization of the reality of the symptom.

Applied and experimental research has rather consistently revealed that professionals have a bias in attributing the source of a client's problem to dispositional rather than situational factors (Batson, 1975; Carkhuff, 1969; C. R. Snyder, 1977; C. R. Snyder, Shenkel, & Schmidt, 1976). If this is the case, then the self-handicapping strategy may be solidified even further. The person who on occasion consumes too much liquor, for example, is diagnosed as an alcoholic; the individual with some problems in sleeping becomes the insomniac; and so forth. The symptom is not only acknowledged by the professional, but it expands to become a person-based label for the entire individual (see Schur, 1971, for related discussion on labeling theory; also see R. A. Jones, 1977, for a related discussion on clinical diagnosis and the effects of the resulting labeling of emotional disorders).

THE MENTAL HOSPITAL: SHELTER, FOOD, AND REDUCED RESPONSIBILITY. The seductive end to the self-handicapping journey may be the mental institution. By admitting to a severe problem, the person may find that she or he is offered the tangible benefits of a place to live and ample food. Likewise, there are certainly reduced responsibility demands within the mental institution. In fact, after an examination of admission records to a mental institution, Braginsky et al. (1967) suggest that a resort metaphor is in order:

a relatively large portion of admissions to the hospital are indeed friends who enter the hospital together, not because they simultaneously "caught" schizophrenia but simply because they wanted to enjoy together the resort potentials of the mental hospital. Entrance to the hospital, therefore, does not necessarily reflect deficiency, helplessness, or social rejection. . . . We do not mean to imply that mental patients, without a care in the world, are holding hands and frolicking merrily across the hospital grounds. This is neither typical behavior at resorts nor is it typical at the mental hospital. The findings suggest, rather, that a close parallel exists between the mental hospital and the resort, but that merriment is not a salient dimension. The similarities between these seemingly disparate social settings, instead, take the following forms: both social settings impose minimal external demands; offer their residents similar physical settings with corresponding social activities (such as swimming pools, movie theatres, lounges, and so on); do not expect their residents to be productive; maximize the residents' opportunity for choosing their desired life style; are explicitly service installations designed to refresh and refurbish their residents. (pp. 156–157)

THE LEGAL SYSTEM. While a full discussion of the potential rewards associated with the adoption of a particular symptom in legal settings is beyond the scope of the present section, one example should illustrate the point. Consider the legal treatment of "crimes of passion" (e.g., anger, fear, jealousy). By advocating that one was under the influence of these strong emotions, a defendant may lessen or sometimes nullify the prescribed punishment for a full range of criminal acts, including homicide. In this vein, the legal system represents a microcosm in which we can see the formalized excuse value linked to emotions (Averill, 1976). Thus the legal system reflects an underlying societal viewpoint. As Averill, DeWitt, and Zimmer (1978) put it, "being 'gripped' by anger, 'seized' by fear, 'torn' by guilt, 'overcome' by grief, . . . these expressions suggest . . . a lack of personal control and, consequently, an abnegation of responsibility for the consequences of one's action" (p. 325).

The self-handicapping cycle

The previous discussion suggests a scenario of events in which self-handicapping should be tenaciously maintained. Initially, the budding self-handicapper may acknowledge a symptom prior to a particularly uncertain feedback situation. Sheltered by the alternative explanation offered by the symptom, the person nurtures an image of self-esteem and competence. Friends may even provide a sympathetic ear (for they, too, may invoke an occasional handicap). Fueled by this turn of events, the person employs the handicap again in future evaluative situations. In fact, the person may utilize the symptom as a "legitimate" reason to avoid the evaluative situation entirely. If the self-handicapper eventually seeks the help of a mental health professional, he or she may find that the professional agrees that the symptom is the problem. Furthermore, the professional may employ a dispositional label to characterize the individual's symptom. With the dispositional "diagnosis" in mind, the professional may selectively elicit responses from the person which tend to confirm the tentative assessment (Mark Snyder & Swann, 1978). The resulting increase in the clinician's confidence in his or her assessment further bolsters the case for a dispositional label. After the label is endorsed by the professional, the person may embrace it in further arenas. Thus, a self-fulfilling prophecy (Darley & Fazio, 1980; Rosenthal & Jacobson, 1968; Rosenthal & Rubin, 1978) may evolve in which the person progressively conforms to the label implied by the particular handicap (e.g., depressed, anxious, disturbed, alcoholic). For the self-handicapping individual who ends up in an institution of some sort, tangible rewards such as shelter and food are garnered. Likewise, a reduced set of expectations on the part of relatives, peers, and professional helpers enables the person to maintain some semblance of self-esteem and competence. In this hypothetical sequence of events, the intrinsic self-reinforcing properties mesh well with the extrinsic, societal rewards for self-handicapping. The cycle turns easily.

Therapeutic interventions for self-handicapping

As shown in the previous section, there are many factors that sustain self-handicapping strategies. Not too surprisingly, therefore, by the time the self-handicapping individual reaches the mental health professional, many of the associated self-perpetuating intrinsic and extrinsic reward patterns are well established. The helper and the handicapper thus face a stern task. The following suggestions, derived from the authors' therapeutic experiences as well as from an analysis of the theoretical bases of self-handicapping, are offered for the reader's consideration.

Identify the self-handicapping

At this point, there are no published research data or diagnostic instruments that specifically address the issue of assessing self-handicapping. This diagnosis issue is further complicated by the fact that self-handicapping probably often represents only one of several factors contributing to a maladaptive behavior. Given these caveats, however, there are nevertheless certain signs that suggest the possible existence of self-handicapping. First, clients who emphasize the importance of evaluative arenas on their sense of self-esteem may be especially susceptible to self-handicapping strategies. This overemphasis of the evaluative–self-esteem link is obviously a necessary precondition that underlies many defensive coping strategies. Second, clients who explicitly or implicitly evidence a symptom or excuse in conjunction with a particular evaluative situation (or situations) may be utilizing self-handicapping. Again, the symptom manifestation along with evaluative situations is characteristic of other defensive coping strategies. Third, clients who are manifesting self-handicapping will admit that they have a weakness or a deficit (e.g., test anxiety, alcoholism). This varies somewhat from other defensive strategies in that such strategies may not convey any deficiency on the part of the person.

Given the lack of definitive information on the ability to arrive at a differential diagnosis of self-handicapping, a useful therapeutic tact may be to routinely consider the self-handicapping properties for almost all maladaptive behavior patterns. Accordingly, the therapist may be advised to regard self-handicapping as one hypothesis, or explanatory dynamic, that may guide subsequent treatment interventions for a variety of clients.

Modify attributional referents: From dispositions to situations

Self-handicapping persons are aware of their symptom(s) before they seek professional help. Furthermore, it has been suggested that rather than ascribing the symptoms to situational factors, the eventual help-seeking person may arrive at a dispositional self-diagnosis of the symptoms (Storms & McCaul, 1976; Valins & Nisbett, 1971). For example, instead of attributing a halting speech pattern to the situational factors associated with talking in front of a large group, the person develops a dispositional label that she or he is a stutterer. Related research also suggests that individuals in the professional helper role tend to see clients as being relatively more influenced by person factors than by situation factors (Batson, 1975; Batson & Marz, 1978; Bradley & Harvey, 1977; C. R. Snyder, 1977; C. R. Snyder et al., 1976). This latter finding has unfortunate implications because the professional's dispositional label may serve to entrench the person further in the self-handicapping pattern. Furthermore, if the professional recommends institutionalization for the person, this reinforces the self-handicapping dispositional label *and* provides further tangible and psychological rewards.

In order to facilitate the change in the self-handicapping pattern, the professional should help the person to modify his or her dispositional self-diagnosis so that more external, situational causes are accepted (Davison, 1966). This has the advantage of stopping the subsequent intrinsic and extrinsic rewards that may flow from a dispositional attribution. Through the adoption of a situational explanation, the stability of the self-handicapping pattern is lessened, i.e., it is more temporary in nature since it is linked to a particular situation. The aforementioned analysis of providing situational specificity to the self-handicapping strategy is analogous to behavioral interventions whereby the person with diffusely located problems (e.g., "I'm always anxious") is taught to pinpoint the exact antecedents of the problem (e.g., "I begin to get anxious when I try to prepare for an exam"). Once the situational antecedents are identified, then behavior-oriented therapists are better able to "shape" the person's maladaptive pattern of responding. In the case of self-handicapping, it would be especially important to continue therapeutic interventions once the self-handicapping strategy has been moved from a dispositional to a situational context. Otherwise, the therapist may be merely reinforcing the self-handicapping pattern in a particular situational context. Thus, once the situational context of the self-handicapping is discovered, the therapist should employ a variety of techniques (mentioned below) to alleviate the evaluative threat associated with the particular situational context. By framing the self-handicapping symptom in a specific situational context, the therapist has a greater ability to treat the underlying threat to self-esteem and competence.

Directly lessen evaluative threat of uncertain success feedback arenas

There are two interrelated issues that characterize the self-handicapping individual's perception of anticipated uncertain success feedback situations. First, the self-handicapping person is overly sensitive to potential uncertain evaluative situations. Thus, the self-handicapping person phenomenologically may accentuate the threat inherent in such situations. Second, the self-handicapper may often perceive several important arenas as containing the possibility of uncertain feedback. Therapeutically, therefore, the first goal is to decrease the intensity of the perceived threatening nature of these situations and to facilitate the individual's spending less time anticipating uncertain evaluative settings. A second therapeutic goal is to decrease the number of arenas that elicit the threatening evaluative concerns.

Once the particularly threatening feedback arena or arenas have been identified, a variety of techniques may be employed to diminish the associated elevated emotionality. Whether desensitization, implosive, gestalt, role-playing, or a variety of other techniques are employed, they all share the goal of lessening the catastrophizing emotionality that is linked to the anticipated uncertain success feedback situation. The self-handicapping person can also be encouraged to redefine the threatening situations. In this vein, one potentially useful therapeutic intervention would be to encourage self-handicapping persons to accept their limitations and to simultaneously bring their ideal selves into line with their real selves. This process, if successful, would diminish the number of situations in which the person felt the need to self-handicap. Perhaps it may be helpful to the client to redefine uncertain success feedback situations as "challenges" where sometimes one fails and sometimes one succeeds. Or, the self-handicapper could be encouraged to develop cognitive explanations as to why the anticipated situation will not be so bad after all (see Bennett & Holmes, 1975, and Burish & Houston, 1979, for experimental support for the threat-reducing effects of cognitive redefinition). The use of realistic reevaluation of perceived threats is a basic premise of rational emotive therapy (RET; Ellis, 1962). RET and a coping skill behavior therapy technique based on Ellis's work, systematic rational restructuring (Goldfried, Decenteceo, & Weinberg, 1974), are particularly suited for changing self-handicapping behavior by altering the appraisal of threat. These techniques have been found effective in reducing a variety of symptomatic complaints (e.g., Goldfried, Linehan, & Smith, 1978; Kanter & Goldfried, 1979; Trexler & Karst, 1972).

In the aforementioned sequence of treatment, the self-handicapping individual should be able successively to delimit the exact nature of the threatening aspects of the particular uncertain success feedback situation, as well as to reduce the perceived threat by realistic reevaluation. In this way, the overgeneralization of self-handicapping to many situations may be curtailed.

Reinforce existing and build new success feedback arenas

The driving force behind self-handicapping is the protection of the person's sense of self-esteem and competency. The self-handicapping symptoms are hypothesized to occur in those feedback arenas where the person anticipates uncertain feedback. One means of decreasing the overall impact of or overemphasis on self-handicapping is to recognize the already existing success arenas in a particular person's life. In this way, increased value and importance could be attached to what the person already does well. Another way to delimit self-handicapping is to help people develop other important areas in their lives where they can achieve a sense of success feedback for their activities. If people can nurture one or more avenues through which they can be rather certain of attaining success, then, at least sometimes, a sense of self-esteem and competency can be sustained without their having to resort to self-handicapping. These latter therapeutic suggestions regarding the reinforcement of existing success feedback arenas and the building of new success feedback arenas, like the other suggested interventions, are obviously not meant to apply only to self-handicapping individuals. Rather, as most clinicians would probably attest, these interventions may have applicability to a range of other symptom patterns.

Future research directions
Individual differences moderating variables

There are several individual differences variables that may have some impact on the self-handicapping phenomenon. Although there is little or no direct empirical evidence pertaining to individual differences and self-handicapping, there are plausible and intriguing leads to consider. The following examples are not intended to provide an exhaustive list of individual differences factors that may influence self-handicapping, but they serve to illustrate our point.

SEX DIFFERENCES. As noted earlier, self-handicapping should occur in those arenas that are especially linked to a person's sense of self-esteem. One emerging viewpoint of sex role differences is that females derive a sense of esteem from person-oriented activities and males derive a sense of esteem from task-oriented activities (Maccoby & Jacklin, 1974; Minton & Schneider, 1980). Perhaps, for example, the underlying reason for the self-handicapping drug preferences of males and not females in the Berglas and Jones (1978) study was that the intellectual task was seen as "masculine." Or, the use of drugs may be an outlet that is seen as societally appropriate for males. In this vein, it may be productive to ascertain whether females are prone to self-handicap in person-oriented situations.[11]

AGE DIFFERENCES. Society often bestows rather unfavorable stereotypes on older people. Among the negative stereotypes, the symptoms of grouchiness, tiredness, mental slowness, forgetfulness, illness, sexual disinterest, and rigidity are often cited (Harris, 1975; McTavish, 1971). Not only are many of these "agism" stereotypes inaccurate, but unfortunately they also may provide ready-made self-handicaps. To the extent to which older people become seduced by their stereotypical age self-handicaps, society loses the contributions of an important group of people who could use their considerable talents to maintain a sense of self-esteem and competency. For these reasons, an exploration of self-handicapping symptoms in individuals of different ages is warranted.

PERSONALITY DIFFERENCES: LOCUS OF CONTROL AS AN EXAMPLE. Individuals who have an external as compared to an internal locus of control as measured by Rotter's (1966) I-E scale tend to emphasize factors such as chance, fate, and luck as determining their anticipation of success in a variety of evaluative arenas (see, for reviews, Joe, 1971; Lefcourt, 1972; Phares, 1976). It follows, therefore, that external locus of control individuals should perceive their outcomes in evaluative feedback arenas as being especially uncertain. This external stance should, in turn, predispose the individual toward self-handicapping strategies. Although no reported study has tested this hypothesis, the literature is suggestive. For example, after receiving failure feedback on intellectual tasks, externals devalue the task and blame the experimental environment more so than do internals (Davis & Davis, 1972; Phares, 1971; Phares, Wilson, & Klyver, 1971). Furthermore, Phares and Lamiell (1974) have demonstrated that externals "choose to perform on tasks that allow them, before the fact, to escape responsibility for any anticipated failure." In this latter experiment, higher external locus of control people exhibited a greater preference for taking IQ tests that had built-in rationalizations than for taking tests that had no such rationalizations for poor performance.

Self-handicapping populations

Further investigations into clinical populations that employ self-handicapping strategies are needed. Some populations are obvious targets because there has already been some analysis of their self-handicapping potential. Jones and Berglas (1978), for example, have made a theoretical case for the link between alcoholism and self-handicapping. An empirical test of this proposition has not yet been carried out. Likewise, Berglas and Jones (1978) have noted that normal people may employ drug usage in a self-handicapping fashion. An empirical test of the self-handicapping behavior of drug abusers has yet to be made. Other populations are logical targets for study simply because they may be easily linked to self-handicapping on an intuitive basis. As a case in point, investigations into the self-handicapping properties of hypochondriacs' behavior should prove fascinating (Smith, C. R. Snyder, & Perkins, 1981). To expand our potential search, perhaps the DSM-III manual may represent a catalog of populations whose defining symptoms may be examined for their self-handicapping content.

Beyond the exploration of self-handicapping with intact clinical populations, it may also prove useful to develop and validate an individual differences self-report scale that taps the propensity to self-handicap. With such a scale, one could measure the person's disposition to self-handicap regardless of whether or not the person was a member of a previously defined clinical population. This potential scale would be theoretically useful in unraveling how dispositional differences in self-handicapping may interact with situational factors. Moreover, this scale might prove useful in a clinical sense. That is, a clinician could employ it as a means of establishing a treatment plan.[12] Or, if a state form of the scale were available, changes in self-handicapping as a function of therapy could also be examined.

Therapy outcome studies

A natural progression from the identification of populations or individuals who engage in excessive self-handicapping is the search for effective therapeutic interventions. So far, however, there have been no reported studies in which self-handicapping was the therapeutic outcome focus. Research is needed to pinpoint which particular intervention techniques are most effective in reducing the self-handicapping behavior of treatment groups relative to waiting-list controls.

In an earlier section on therapeutic interventions, we speculated about certain interventions that may prove effective. One obvious study, for example, would compare the decreased self-handicapping of three treatment groups relative to a waiting-list control group. The first treatment group could be given interventions aimed at lessening the evaluative threat inherent in the anticipated uncertain feedback arenas. The second treatment group could be given interventions geared to change the attributional basis of the self-handicapping from a dispositional to a situational context. The third treatment group could be given interventions designed to foster arenas where the self-handicapping person may be relatively assured of garnering success feedback. If one of the three treatment approaches is particularly effective in lessening the self-handicapping pattern, then further replication and refinement of this approach would be warranted. Or, perhaps a package treatment composed of one or more of the aforementioned (or any other new) techniques may be developed. Likewise, one of the methodological refinements in such studies would be to develop self-report and observational techniques for measuring self-handicapping.

The virtue of a new bottle for old wine

Although we have argued in the present chapter that symptoms may be employed in a self-protective fashion, we do not wish to assert that symptoms are "nothing but" a self-protective device. Rather, the self-protective function of symptoms is probably one of several factors that are involved in the etiology and maintenance of maladaptive behavior.

While symptoms are undoubtedly determined by a variety of factors, the available data suggest that this self-protective role of symptoms may be an important one. Previous theories positing the self-protective functions of symptoms (e.g., defense mechanisms) have been criticized for lacking empirical support. Simultaneously, however, such theories have seemed consistent with clinical observation. In order to provide empirical support for the long-held clinical beliefs concerning the self-protective functioning of symptoms, self-handicapping and related social psychological theory and methods appear to be promising. Along these lines, self-handicapping has two key ingredients of a useful theory: It allows for the derivation of testable hypotheses, and, equally as important, it can be applied to real clinical phenomena.

In closing, we acknowledge that we stand in a long line of psychoanalysts, clinical psychologists, and social psychologists who have worked to refine the role of symptoms as self-protective strategies. As such, the present ideas on self-handicapping reflect a new vessel for encapsulating an old notion. As we contemplate this "new bottle," therefore, it is appropriate to savor the "old wine":

The patient selects certain symptoms and develops them until they impress him as real obstacles. Behind his barricade of symptoms the patient feels hidden and secure. To the question, "What use are you making of your talents?" he answers, "This thing stops me; I cannot go ahead," and points to his self-erected barricade. *We must never neglect the patient's own use of his symptoms.* (italics added, Adler, 1929, p. 13)

Notes

1. Traditionally, psychological symptoms have been viewed as verbal complaints or directly observable behaviors that indicate the presence of an underlying or more general disorder. More recent formulations have deemphasized the notion of underlying or more general disorders and have focused on symptoms as simply indicating distress, discomfort, or maladaptive patterns of behavior.

2. A related point has been made in the area of attributional egotism, where it has been argued that the motivation to deny responsibility for explicit failure feedback is activated most strongly on dimensions related to self-esteem (Miller, 1976; Nichols, 1975). It should be emphasized, however, that self-handicapping differs somewhat from what has been called "attributional egotism" (see Melvin L. Snyder, Stephan, & Rosenfield, 1978). In attributional egotism, the individual totally externalizes the blame for failure and no sense of personal responsibility is admitted. In self-handicapping, however, the individual acknowledges a weakness (e.g., "I choked" or "I drank too much") in order to preserve a more central sense of self-esteem and competency.

3. The self-handicapping process may be, in many cases, a quite conscious, active process. At times, however, individuals may be unwilling to explicitly acknowledge the strategic use of symptoms. In order for the self-protective strategy to function optimally, individuals may have to avoid full awareness of their ploy. This state of affairs can be viewed as what Gur and Sackeim (1979) have labeled "self-deception." Individuals may reap the instrumental effects of their tactic while actively avoiding attending to its purposeful nature.

4. Self-esteem in the present discussion refers to the individuals' (positive) evaluation of their abilities, competency, and characteristics. The sense of competency (i.e., the degree to which the individual can secure desired outcomes on effects) is occasionally specifically singled out in the discussion because of its importance in determining an individual's level of self-esteem.

5. One exception to this scenario may occur in a situation where persons privately believe that they have no possible chance of succeeding in a subsequent situation, but they perceive that others *expect them* to.

6. This method underscores the importance of two components in establishing a potential self-handicapping set. First, an initial test should be perceived as being high in "diagnosticity," or the ability to validly and accurately predict how a person may do on a subsequent evaluative test. Second, the subsequent anticipated test needs to be perceived as an important evaluative task, also high in "diagnosticity," about which the person is truly concerned.

7. This lack of differentiation between public and private self-esteem has also been suggested in the general area of attributional egotism, or self-serving attributions (Weary, 1979; Weary & Arkin, 1980).

8. The question may be asked as to why such patterns would continue if the costs outweigh the benefits. As with many forms of maladaptive behavior, the self-defeating results may accrue slowly over time and the contingencies between the self-handicapping and the negative effects may not be directly apparent to the individual. Finally, the

short-term reduction in anxiety due to reduction of threat to self-esteem may continue to be sufficiently reinforcing to maintain the behavior in the presence of more long-term aversive consequences.

9. Although Coyne focuses primarily on interpersonal gains, we would argue that the end result of social support and reassurance is the maintenance of the individual's sense of worth.

10. Within an attributional egotism paradigm, some support for the self-esteem protective character of providing alternative explanations has been shown. For example, Burish and Houston (1979) report that people feel better when they are provided with an alternative explanation for their poor cognitive performance as compared with when they are provided with no such alternative explanation.

11. Some support for this speculation is found in an attributional egotism study in which females were egocentric in an alleged "feminine" task (Rosenfield & Stephan, 1978).

12. One difficulty with the development of a self-handicapping scale is that it then may be employed merely to label potential clients as self-handicappers. Optimally, an individual differences scale serves as a means of (1) developing hypotheses about a particular client and (2) providing a clue as to what therapeutic interventions to attempt. In reality, however, individual differences scales have often served to perpetuate an unfortunate labeling process.

References

Adler, A. Individual psychologische behandlung der neurosen. In D. Sarason (Ed.), *Jahreskurse für ärztliche fortbildung.* Munich: Lehmann, 1913.

Adler, A. Das problem der "distanz": Über einen grandcharakter der neurose und psychose. *Internationale Zeitschrift für Individualpsychologie,* 1914, *1*, 8–16.

Adler, A. *Problems of neuroses: A book of casehistories.* London: Kegan Paul, Trench, Truebner, 1929.

Adler, A. *What life should mean to you.* Boston: Little, Brown, 1931.

Adler, A. *Der sinn des lebens.* Vienna, Leipzig: Rolf Passer, 1933.

Adler, A. Das todes problem in der neurose. *Internationale Zeitschrift für Individualpsychologie,* 1936, *14*, 1–6. (a)

Adler, A. The neurotic's picture of the world. *International Journal of Individual Psychology,* 1936, *2*, 3–13. (b)

Ansbacher, H. L., & Ansbacher, R. R. *The individual psychology of Alfred Adler.* New York: Harper & Row, 1967.

Artiss, K. *The symptom as communication in schizophrenia.* New York: Grune & Stratton, 1959.

Averill, J. R. Emotion and anxiety: Sociocultural, biological, and psychological determinants. In M. Zuckerman & C. D. Spielberger (Eds.), *Emotion and anxiety: New concepts, methods and applications.* New York: Erlbaum-Wiley, 1976.

Averill, J. R., DeWitt, G. W., & Zimmer, M. The self-attribution of emotion as a function of success and failure. *Journal of Personality,* 1978, *46,* 323–347.

Batson, C. D. Attribution as a mediator of bias in helping. *Journal of Personality and Social Psychology,* 1975, *32,* 455–466.

Batson, C. D., & Marz, B. Effects of professional and nonprofessional role orientation on perception of clients' needs. Unpublished manuscript, University of Kansas, 1978.

Belknap, I. *Human problems of a state mental hospital.* New York: McGraw-Hill, 1956.

Bennett, D. H., & Holmes, D. S. Influence of denial (situational redefinition) and projection on anxiety associated with threat to self-esteem. *Journal of Personality and Social Psychology,* 1975, *32,* 915–921.

Berglas, S., & Jones, E. E. Drug choice as a self-handicapping strategy in response to noncontingent success. *Journal of Personality and Social Psychology,* 1978, *36,* 405–417.

Berne, E. *Games people play.* New York: Grove Press, 1964.

Bowerman, W. R. Subjective competence: The structure, process and function of self-referent causal attributions. *Journal for the Theory of Social Behavior,* 1978, *8,* 45–75.

Bradley, G. W., & Harvey, J. H. Effects of attributed freedom to seek therapy and severity of disturbance on perceived locus of problem. Paper presented at the Southeastern Psychological Association, 1977.

Braginsky, B., & Braginsky, D. Schizophrenic patients in the psychiatric interview: An experimental study of their effectiveness at manipulation. *Journal of Consulting Psychology,* 1967, *31,* 546–551.

Braginsky, B., Braginsky, D., & Ring, K. *Methods of madness: The mental hospital as a last resort.* New York: Holt, Rinehart and Winston, 1969.

Braginsky, B., Grosse, M., & Ring, K. Controlling outcomes through impression management: An experimental study of the manipulative tactics of mental patients. *Journal of Consulting Psychology*, 1966, *30*, 295–300.

Braginsky, B., Holzberg, J., Ridley, D., & Braginsky, D. Patient styles of adaptation to a mental hospital. *Journal of Personality*, 1968, *36*, 283–298.

Burish, T. G., & Houston, B. K. Causal projection, similarity projection, and coping with threat to self-esteem. *Journal of Personality*, 1979, *47*, 57–70.

Burnam, M., Pennebaker, J., & Glass, D. Time consciousness, achievement striving, and the Type A coronary-prone behavior pattern. *Journal of Abnormal Psychology*, 1975, *84*, 76–79.

Carkhuff, R. R. *Helping and human relations*, Vol. 1. New York: Holt, Rinehart and Winston, 1969.

Carver, C., Coleman, A., & Glass, D. The coronary-prone behavior pattern and the suppression of fatigue on a treadmill test. *Journal of Personality and Social Psychology*, 1976, *33*, 460–466.

Colby, K. M. On the disagreement between Freud and Adler. *American Imago*, 1951, *8*, 229–238.

Coyne, J. Toward an interactional description of depression. *Psychiatry*, 1976, *39*, 28–40.

Darley, J., & Fazio, R. Expectancy confirmation processes arising in the social interaction sequence. *American Psychologist*, 1980, *35*, 867–881.

Davis, W. L., & Davis, D. E. Internal-external control and attribution of responsibility for success and failure. *Journal of Personality*, 1972, *40*, 123–136.

Davison, G. C. Differential relaxation and cognitive restructuring in therapy with a "paranoid schizophrenic" or "paranoic state." *Proceedings of the American Psychological Association*, 1966, 177–178.

Dunham, H. W., & Weinberg, S. K. *The culture of the state mental hospital*. Detroit: Wayne State University Press, 1960.

Ellis, A. *Reason and emotion in psychotherapy*. New York: Lyle Stuart, 1962.

Festinger, L. A theory of social comparison processes. *Human Relations*, 1954, *7*, 117–140.

Fontana, A. Personal communication, 1980.

Fontana, A. F., & Gessner, T. Patients' goals and the manifestation of psychopathology. *Journal of Consulting and Clinical Psychology*, 1969, *33*, 247–253.

Fontana, A. F., & Klein, E. B. Self-presentation and the schizophrenic "deficit." *Journal of Consulting and Clinical Psychology*, 1968, *32*, 250–256.

Fontana, A. F., Klein, E. B., Lewis, E., & Levine, L. Presentation of self in mental illness. *Journal of Consulting and Clinical Psychology*, 1968, *32*, 110–119.

Freud, A. *The ego and the mechanisms of defense*. London: Hogarth Press, 1948.

Freud, S. *Sigmund Freud: Collected Papers* (Vol. I). London: Hogarth Press, 1953.

Friedman, M., & Rosenman, R. Association of specific overt pattern with blood and cardiovascular findings: Blood clotting time, incidence of arcus sinilis, and clinical coronary artery disease. *Journal of the American Medical Association*, 1959, *169*, 286.

Gastorf, J., & Teevan, R. Type A coronary-prone behavior pattern and fear of failure. *Motivation and Emotion*, 1980, *4*, 71–76.

Goffman, E. *The presentation of self in everyday life*. New York: Doubleday, 1959.

Goldfried, M., Decenteceo, E., & Weinberg, L. Systematic rational restructuring as a self-control technique. *Behavior Therapy*, 1974, *5*, 247–254.

Goldfried, M., Linehan, M., & Smith, J. Reduction of test anxiety through cognitive restructuring. *Journal of Consulting and Clinical Psychology*, 1978, *46*, 32–39.

Gur, R., & Sackeim, H. Self-deception: A concept in search of phenomenon. *Journal of Personality and Social Psychology*, 1979, *37*, 147–169.

Haley, J. *Strategies of psychotherapy*. New York: Grune & Stratton, 1963.

Harris, L. *The myth and reality of aging in America*. New York: National Council on the Aging, 1975.

Heider, F. *The psychology of interpersonal relations*. New York: Wiley, 1958.

Higgins, R., & Marlatt, A. Effects of anxiety arousal on the consumption of alcohol by alcoholics and social drinkers. *Journal of Consulting and Clinical Psychology*, 1973, *41*, 426–433.

Higgins, R., & Marlatt, A. Fear of interpersonal evaluation or a determinant of alcohol consumption in male social drinkers. *Journal of Abnormal Psychology*, 1975, *84*, 644–651.

Joe, V. C. A review of the internal-external control

construct as a personality variable. *Psychological Reports*, 1971, *28*, 619–640.

Jones, E. E., & Berglas, S. Control of attributions about the self through self-handicapping strategies: The appeal of alcohol and the role of underachievement. *Personality and Social Psychology Bulletin*, 1978, *4*, 200–206.

Jones. E. E., & Davis, K. E. From acts to dispositions: The attributional process in person perception. In L. Berkowitz (Ed.), *Advances in experimental social psychology* (Vol. 2). New York: Academic Press, 1965.

Jones. R. A. *Self-fulfilling prophecies: Social, psychological, and physiological effects of expectancies*. Hillsdale, N.J.: Erlbaum, 1977.

Kanter, N., & Goldfried, M. Relative effectiveness of rational restructuring and self-control desensitization in the reduction of interpersonal anxiety. *Behavior Therapy*, 1979, *10*, 472–490.

Kaplan, H. B. Toward a general theory of psychosocial deviance: The case of aggressive behavior. *Social Science and Medicine*, 1972, *6*, 593–617.

Kaplan, H. B. *Deviant behavior in defense of self*. New York: Academic Press, 1980.

Kelley, H. H. *Attributions in social interaction*. Morristown, N.J.: General Learning Press, 1971.

Lefcourt, H. M. Recent developments in the study of locus of control. In B. A. Maher (Ed.), *Progress in experimental personality research* (Vol. 6). New York: Academic Press, 1972.

Maccoby, E. E., & Jacklin, C. N. *The psychology of sex differences*. Stanford, Calif.: Stanford University Press, 1974.

McTavish, D. G. Perceptions of old people: A review of research methodologies and findings. *The Gerontologist*, 1971, *11*, 90–102.

Miller, D. T. Ego involvement and attributions for success and failure. *Journal of Personality and Social Psychology*, 1976, *34*, 901–906.

Minton, H. L. & Schneider, F. W. *Differential psychology*. Monterey, Calif.: Brooks/Cole, 1980.

Munroe, R. L. *Schools of psychoanalytic thought*. New York: Dryden Press, 1955.

Nichols, J. G. Causal attributions and other achievement-related cognitions: Effects of task outcome, attainment value and sex. *Journal of Personality and Social Psychology*, 1975, *31*, 379–389.

Phares, E. J. *Locus of control in personality*. Morristown, N.J.: General Learning Press, 1976.

Phares, E. J. Internal-external control and the reduction of reinforcement value after failure. *Journal of Consulting and Clinical Psychology*, 1974, *42*, 872–878.

Phares, E. J., Wilson, K. G., & Klyver, N. W. Internal-external control and the attribution of blame under neutral and distractive conditions. *Journal of Personality and Social Psychology*, 1971, *18*, 285–288.

Rosenfield, D., & Stephan, W. G. Sex differences in attributions for sex-typed tasks. *Journal of Personality*, 1978, *46*, 244–259.

Rosenthal, R., & Jacobson, L. *Pygmalion in the classroom*. New York: Holt, Rinehart and Winston, 1968.

Rosenthal, R., & Rubin, D. B. Interpersonal expectancy effects: The first 345 studies. *The Behavioral and Brain Sciences*, 1978, *3*, 377–415.

Rotter, J. B. Generalized expectancies for internal versus external control of reinforcement. *Psychological Monographs*, 1966, *80*, (1, Whole No. 609).

Schur, E. M. *Labelling deviant behavior*. New York: Harper & Row, 1971.

Shakow, D. Segmental set: A theory of the formal psychological deficit in schizophrenia. *Archives of General Psychiatry*, 1962, *6*, 1–17.

Smith, T. W., Snyder, C. R., & Handelsman, M. M. On the self-serving function of an academic wooden leg: Test anxiety as a self-handicapping strategy. *Journal of Personality and Social Psychology*, in press.

Smith, T. W., Snyder, C. R., & Perkins, S. On the self-serving function of hypochondria: Physical symptoms as self-handicapping strategies. Unpublished manuscript, University of Kansas, 1981.

Snyder, C. R. "A patient by any other name" revisited: Maladjustment or attributional locus of problem. *Journal of Consulting and Clinical Psychology*, 1977, *45*, 101–103.

Snyder, C. R., Shenkel, R. J., & Schmidt, A. Effects of role perspective and psychiatric history on diagnostic locus of problem. *Journal of Consulting and Clinical Psychology*, 1976, *44*, 467–472.

Snyder, Mark, & Swann, W. Hypothesis testing processes in social interaction. *Journal of Personality and Social Psychology*, 1978, *36*, 1202–1212.

Snyder, Melvin L., Stephan, W. G., & Rosenfield, D. Attributional egotism. In J. H. Harvey, W. J. Ickes, & R. Kidd (Eds.), *New directions in attribution research* (Vol. 2). Hillsdale, N.J.: Erlbaum, 1978.

Snyder, Melvin L., & Wicklund, R. Attribute ambiguity. In J. H. Harvey, W. J. Ickes, & R. F. Kidd (Eds.), *New directions in attribution research* (Vol. 3). Hillsdale, N.J.: Erlbaum, in press.

Storms, M. D., & McCaul, K. D. Attribution process and emotional exacerbation of dysfunctional behavior. In J. H. Harvey, W. J. Ickes, & R. F. Kidd (Eds.), *New directions in attribution research* (Vol. 1). Hillsdale, N.J.: Erlbaum, 1976.

Szasz, T. *The myth of mental illness*. New York: Paul B. Hoeber, 1961.

Trexler, L., & Karst, T. Rational-emotive therapy, placebo, and no treatment effects on public speaking anxiety. *Journal of Abnormal Psychology*, 1972, 79, 60–67.

Valins, S., & Nisbett, R. E. *Attribution processes in the development and treatment of emotional disorders*. Morristown, N.J.: General Learning Press, 1971.

Weary, G. Self-serving attributional biases: Perceptual or response distortions? *Journal of Personality and Social Psychology*, 1979, 8, 1418–1420.

Weary, G., & Arkin, R. M. Attributional self-presentation. In J. H. Harvey, W. J. Ickes, & R. F. Kidd (Eds.), *New directions in attribution research* (Vol. 3). Hillsdale, N.J.: Erlbaum, in press.

Weidner, G. Self-handicapping following learned helplessness treatment and the Type A coronary-prone behavior pattern. *Journal of Psychosomatic Research*, in press.

Wylie, R. C. *The self-concept* (Vol. 2). Lincoln: University of Nebraska Press, 1979.

7

SELECTION AND PROCESSING OF SELF-EVALUATIVE INFORMATION: EXPERIMENTAL EVIDENCE AND CLINICAL IMPLICATIONS

J. SIDNEY SHRAUGER
STATE UNIVERSITY OF NEW YORK AT BUFFALO

Perhaps the most distinctive development in both social and clinical psychology during the 1970's was a shift in our collective concern away from motivational and affective variables and toward cognitive processes. The way we store, retrieve, remember, forget, combine, and generalize from information has become a preoccupation of the field. Particularly notable has been the increasing interest in cognitions about the self and the role of self-relevant attitudes in behavior. The concept of self has surfaced from the murky backwaters of psychological theory to gain a level of attention and legitimacy that had largely been denied it for several preceding decades. Within both clinical and social psychology, the self has served a dual role as an object for appraisal and as a set of hierarchical constructs which provide an organizational structure for the encoding and processing of one's experience (Epstein, 1973; Greenwald, 1980; Mancuso & Ceely, 1980; Markus, 1977). Information about the self is special. A growing array of evidence suggests that we encode self-relevant information more readily (Rogers, Kuiper, & Kirker, 1977), recall it better (Bower & Gilligan, 1979; Ross & Sicoly, 1979), and may evaluate it differently (Shrauger & Terbovic, 1976) than we do information about others or information not directly related to the self.

Of the many aspects of self-relevant attitudes that have been explored, none has received more attention than the evaluative dimension of self-appraisal. The favorability of self-evaluation seems important intuitively because of its apparent relationship to individuals' emotional reactions and its implications for behavior. A sense of self-worth or self-esteem is assumed to be essential to the maintenance of positive emotional reactions, and a negative self-image is viewed as an important component of major clinical syndromes such as depression (Beck, 1967). Similarly, a sense of self-confidence, competence, or efficacy (Bandura, 1977) is also seen as essential to one's engaging in activities which may be difficult or threatening. Anxiety

---

The author is grateful to Normal Mandel, Timothy Osberg, Tom Schoeneman, and Robert Kelly for their comments on an earlier draft of this manuscript.

and systematic avoidance of certain situations are assumed to be due to the absence of a sense of personal competence. Whether it is with reference to morality or capability, how "good" or "bad" one is must be perceived as having important emotional and behavioral implications.

This chapter focuses on self-regulatory processes which are related to individuals' general sense of self-confidence or self-esteem.[1] It is interesting that although the psychiatric diagnostic system provides no categories specifically for problems in self-evaluation, such problems are commonly perceived by clients as important components of their psychological difficulties. In a recent survey of 100 clients coming to an outpatient psychiatric setting, 13 percent chose lack of self-confidence from a list of 16 common presenting complaints as their most important problem (Shrauger & Turner, 1981). Another 31 percent saw it as one of their three most important concerns. Lack of self-confidence was the most frequently mentioned complaint in a list which included such common symptoms as anxiety, depression, and marital difficulties. An additional 10 percent listed self-dissatisfaction as their most important problem, and 23 percent listed it as one of their three most significant concerns. In nonclinical populations, concerns about self-evaluation are also common. The author has found, for example, that in a sample of undergraduates, 23 percent of males and 34 percent of females indicated that they were generally lacking in self-confidence. Thus, concerns about one's personal competence and capabilities are widespread in both clinical and nonclinical populations, and the factors involved in their maintenance seemingly merit attention on practical as well as conceptual grounds.

Investigations of self-evaluative attitudes within the social and clinical fields have developed quite independently of one another and with little apparent attention to work in the other field. The theoretical and empirical perspectives taken have also reflected differences in the approach to research that is generally characteristic of each field. Clinical research has focused on how cognitions are related to dysfunctional behavior and affective reactions. This work has been undertaken primarily within the framework of that loosely integrated set of concepts and intervention techniques that has become known as cognitive behavior therapy. People's cognitions about themselves have been seen as relatively stable and consistent across time and often across situations. Some theorists, such as Ellis (1962), argue that there is also consistency across individuals in the basic beliefs which underlie dysfunctional behavior. Research strategies have mainly relied on individual differences paradigms in which the self-relevant cognitions of people differing along some clinically significant dimension, such as level of depression, are compared. It is assumed that there is a causal relationship between the dysfunctional self-relevant statements of various clinical groups and their behavioral or emotional difficulties. This assumption of causality is more directly evident in the other major class of clinical studies, which has involved intervention techniques. These investigations are based on the assumption that clinical symptoms can be ameliorated by the clinician's helping people modify their thoughts about themselves and their experiences, usually through the identification and rehearsal of adaptive statements about themselves and the situations they encounter. It is implied that by having people focus on or repeat certain favorable self-relevant cognitions they will attend to and come to believe these cognitions and will modify their feelings and behavior to make them more consistent with the content of these verbal statements.

Examinations of self-relevant attitudes within the traditions of social psychology have focused more on the situational determinants of cognitions, emphasizing individual differences less and focusing more on how people attempt to maintain favorable self-relevant attitudes as well as the conditions which may lead to negative self-appraisal (Duval & Wicklund, 1972). Within social psychology, much emphasis has been placed on the self-deluding tendency of most people to see themselves in more flattering terms than reality might justify (e.g., Bradley, 1978). Thus, whereas investigations within the social psychological framework have attempted to describe more conventional and typical patterns of behavior, they have usually not emphasized the utility of these mechanisms of self-evaluation, either in terms of their emotional consequences for the individual or in terms of their facilitation of accurate self-appraisal. The social psychological tradition has focused more on the ways that people protect themselves from unfavorable evaluation and on the conditions which facilitate or hamper such self-evaluative processes.

Although the specific interests and methods of inquiry in clinical and social psychology have differed, a common assumption of both areas is that the extent and degree of self-relevant attention will have an important effect on stable self-relevant attitudes and on one's behavior. The major aim of this paper is to examine the roles that the selection and processing of self-relevant information play in determining the general favorability of people's attitudes toward themselves. Particular attention will be given to the relationship between individual differences in self-confidence and self-esteem and the appraisal of self-relevant information. It is contended that the characteristic evaluative attitudes which people hold about themselves are a product of selective exposure and deployment of attention to self-relevant information and that the development of optimal methods for modification of these processes involves the awareness and examination of these processes of attention deployment and interpretation.

Attention will first be given to the extent to which self-relevant attitudes are a function of objective feedback about one's capabilities, since selective attention would not be so relevant if external indexes of competence or capability were isomorphic with one's self-perceptions. Then different aspects of selective exposure and attention to self-relevant information will be distinguished and the available evidence on each surveyed. The implications of these findings will then be examined in terms of the way that attention is directed toward the self in psychotherapy, and some potential hazards of the therapy process will be delineated. Finally, some implications of the research evidence on selective exposure and attention will be examined and suggestions offered for directing self-relevant attention in psychotherapy.

External evidence and subjective competence
Self-perceptions versus actual performance

As Schultz's Snoopy has aptly put it, "It doesn't matter whether you win or lose—until you lose." There is little doubt that winning, or being successful, for most people most of the time brings a spurt of positive emotion, a sense of pleasure, well-being, competence, and, frequently, money in the bank. There is also little doubt that losing seldom has the same results. What is more at issue, however, is how people decide whether or not they are successful, what criteria for competence they employ, and to what extent their sense of their own capabilities actually matches objective indexes of their skill.

This section examines the extent to which people's actual performance in situations relates to their subjective perceptions of how they will perform or have performed. Objective indexes of performance are considered to be concrete and externally defined criteria for evaluating the adequacy of one's behavior. They include such things as school grades, behavior in a social situation, or number of items correct on a problem-solving task. Subjective appraisals, or self-perceptions, of competence involve people's own assessments of their capabilities or personal qualities. These assessments may be reflected in expectations regarding future performance or evaluations of previous or current behavior. Subjective appraisals may include people's judgments of rather narrow or concrete behaviors, such as how many items they got correct on a particular task, or they may involve more global or affectively toned appraisals of how good they are at some activity, how competent they are relative to others, or how worthy or desirable they are as individuals.

In examining the relationship between objective evidence and subjective appraisals, consideration will first be given to how people's self-perceptions regarding specific attributes correspond with objective, external measures of these attributes. Then the relationship between more global self-evaluations, such as self-esteem measures and external indexes of competence in specific activities, will be examined.

The accuracy of self-perceived competence has probably been most extensively examined with regard to perceptions of intellectual or cognitive tasks, which may not be surprising given the importance of these activities and the extent to which formal means for assessing them have been developed. There is extensive evidence indicating that people quite accurately perceive the adequacy of their performance on specific intellectual tasks. For example, individuals who show greater initial confidence about their skill at anagrams and reasoning problems are more likely to be successful at them (Lefcourt, Hogg, Struthers, & Holmes, 1975; Lorge & Solomon, 1960). Several studies have indicated that people's judgments of their subsequent academic performance are likely to be at least as predictive of their actual performance as are standard aptitude test data (Biggs & Tinsley, 1970; Binder, Jones, & Strowig, 1970; Holland & Nichols, 1964; Keefer, 1969).

Not only do people's perceptions of their intellectual competence correspond with their typical performance, but they can also assess variations from their typical behavior. Linsenmeier and Brickman (1980) have marshalled considerable evidence that is consistent with the notion that people can predict how their performance on a given occasion will differ from their typical behavior in similar situations. They find that for a given level of ability at a task, a person's performance level will increase as the person's level of expectation for favorable performance increases. This occurs not only for cognitive tasks but for more exotic activities, such as handling snakes (Bandura, Adams, & Beyer, 1977).

One cannot determine here, of course, whether the accuracy of these judgments was a function of sensitivity to a change in one's performance level that was about to take place or was due to the fact that, having made a commitment to a certain level of functioning, one felt constrained to try to achieve it.

In judging competence in areas other than academic abilities, relationships between one's appraisal of one's abilities and objective indexes of these abilities have been less evident. With regard to social skills, for instance, some evidence indicates that perceived and actual social facility are sometimes related (Mandel & Shrauger, 1980). The more typical observation, however, has been that people who differ in their level of comfort and perceived competence are difficult to distinguish from one another on objective indexes of competence in social situations (Arkowitz, Lichtenstein, McGovern, & Hines, 1975; Borkovec, Stone, O'Brien, & Kaloupek, 1974; Glasgow & Arkowitz, 1975).

There are several reasons why self-appraisals of social competence might agree less with external criteria than do appraisals of attributes such as intellectual competence, and these may provide some more general insight into the conditions under which self-evaluations of specific capabilities are likely to match external criteria of those attributes. One possibility is that the criteria by which people evaluate both their own and other people's social behavior are less clearly agreed upon than are those for areas such as academic ability. People's judgments about what constitutes social skill may depend a great deal on their preferences, personal styles, and values. A second possibility is that the cross-situational generality of some attributes, e.g., social skills, may be modest. The studies evaluating the relationship between self-perceived social skill and actual skill have often assessed social behavior in high-demand laboratory settings, which may not reflect people's characteristic interpersonal behavior. Related to the issue of a lack of specific and widely held criteria for judging social skill is the possibility that people may not receive as extensive and systematic feedback in social skills as they do in such areas as intellectual, musical, or athletic ability. Certainly there are no final exams, formal auditions, or all-star teams in these and some other important areas of functioning. Feedback may be less extensive if there are no formal procedures for communicating it and fewer clearly specified criteria. Furthermore, those evaluations that are received may often be implicit and ambiguous, with greater latitude for idiosyncratic interpretation. Thus, in evaluating the extent to which people can perceive their own capabilities accurately, it seems important to note several things about the attributes being assessed: how explicit and widely agreed upon the criteria for assessing the dimension are; how consistently people behave with regard to that dimension across different situations; and how frequently and readily evaluations on that dimension are communicated.

We have seen that objective indexes of performance in a specific area such as school achievement may relate to people's self-perceptions of how they have performed or are likely to perform in the future. One might also ask whether or not these objective measures of performance in a specific area relate more to affectively toned judgments of that particular ability or more to global evaluations of one's competence or desirability as an individual. Do people who have higher grade averages, for example, perceive themselves to be "smarter" or more "competent individuals" or more "worthwhile people" than individuals with lower averages? These issues are important because one would intuitively expect that more generalized self-relevant concepts would have a greater impact on people's typical affective tone and behavior than would more concrete and discrete appraisals. Unfortunately, however, this assumption has not been tested.

A number of investigations have examined the relationship between objective performance in specific areas and more global self-perceptions, such as self-confidence or self-esteem. Once again, however, these have mainly involved indexes of intellectual ability. There is considerable evidence that better academic performance is related to more favorable self-evaluation (see Purkey, 1970, for review). In addition people with higher levels of general self-esteem sometimes perform better on specific intellectual tasks such as work manipulation (Hechler & Weiner, 1974) and digit symbols (Shrauger & Rosenberg, 1970), although other investigations have shown no significant differences in the problem-solving skills of individuals with different levels of self-esteem (Shrauger & Osberg, 1980; Shrauger & Terbovic, 1976).

Evidence in areas other than intellectual competence suggests that the development of a specific skill can enhance self-esteem. Koocher (1971) found that boys in a YMCA program who learned to swim showed a greater decrease in self–ideal-self discrepancy than did those who either failed to learn or already knew how. These same data suggest, however, that the learning of a specific skill may have a relatively transient effect on self-esteem, since pretreatment levels of self–ideal-self discrepancy were the same for those who knew how to swim and those who did not. Other investigations have also indicated that giving people feedback that they have greater competence in one area than they had originally perceived does not appreciably enhance their self-assessments in other areas, and those changes which do occur tend to dissipate over time (Haas & Maehr, 1965; Maehr, Mensing, & Natzger, 1962).

The bulk of research relating general self-evaluations to competence in specific performance areas had been geared not toward predicting cross-situational performance differences as a function of confidence or esteem but toward situational parameters which either minimize or enhance the differential performance of high and low self-esteem individuals. A number of studies have indicated that the performance of high and low self-esteem individuals differs primarily in either anxiety-provoking situations or situations in which attention is drawn to their behavior. Thus, low self-esteem individuals who have failed at a previous task perform more poorly on subsequent tasks than do those with high self-esteem, whereas the two groups typically do not differ if they have previously been successful (Feather, 1968; Schalon, 1968; Shrauger & Sorman, 1977; Stotland, Thorley, Thomas, Cohen, & Zander, 1957). Directing attention toward oneself has shown effects similar to those of failure. For example, Brockner (1979a; 1979b) and Brockner and Hulton (1978) have found that low self-esteem individuals perform less favorably under conditions in which either situational or characterological self-consciousness is high. Also, when performance takes place in front of an audience, low self-esteem individuals perform more poorly than those with high self-esteem, although the two groups perform comparably with no audience (Shrauger, 1972).

On the one hand, these studies suggest many instances in which differences in general self-evaluation are not matched by differences in performance on specific intellectual tasks. Even though performance differences are not frequently, or even typically, present, a person's self-assessment may still be influenced by those situations in which performance differences do occur. The situations in which performance differences have occurred, such as after failure or when attention is directed to oneself, may be particularly important for the assessment of the attribute in question and also for one's general sense of competence or worth.

To summarize the findings regarding the relationship between self-perceived and objective indexes of performance, it appears that although perceived competence on a specific attribute is sometimes highly related to objective competence, this is not always the case. Perceived and actual competence may be more comparable when the attribute assessed has clear and widely accepted performance criteria which are frequently either observed by the performers or communicated to them. The extent to which a person's specific abilities or skills are reflected in a more global sense of competence or self-worth is less clear. Intellectual performance is the only specific ability which has been examined, and in this area relationships with competence depend on situational factors. Perhaps it seems obvious that one's general sense of competence should be based substantially on some aggregation of one's objective skills and capabilities, but this has not been well demonstrated. It may be that, in large measure, individuals' self-confidence and self-esteem are independent of objective indexes of their capability.

Evaluative feedback from others

Another source of evaluative information which is related to one's objective competence but also separable from it is the nature of feedback that one receives from others. Perhaps self-confidence is determined not so much by selective attention or processing of information as by one's receiving different evaluative input from others. It is commonly assumed that our self-perceptions are determined substantially, if not primarily, by others' impressions of us, or at least by our perceptions of those impressions. This intuitive observation forms the conceptual base for the social psychological theory of symbolic interactionism, which most forcefully emphasizes the role of others' perceptions in self-evaluations (Cooley, 1902; Mead, 1934). Cooley developed the notion of the looking-glass self, in which people's self-perceptions are reflections of the way that they think they are viewed by others. He said, "A self idea of this sort seems to have three principal elements: The imagination of our appearance to the other person; the imagination of his judgments of that appearance, and some sort of self-feeling such as pride or mortification" (p. 152). A critical question within this perspective is how much our perceptions of others' view of us really mirror their actual impressions or how much they are autogenic creations which reflect primarily our own appraisals, which we assume are also shared by others.

Recent examination of the experimental and naturalistic evidence relevant to the symbolic interactionist concept of self-perception suggests that the importance of others' judgments as determinants of self-perceptions is not well established (Shrauger & Schoeneman, 1979). The experimental studies have typically employed a paradigm involving first the obtaining of self-assessments, then the presenting of feedback discrepant with initial self-judgments, and finally the obtaining of self-appraisals again. Although changes in self-perceptions are typically reported, the actual significance of these changes is unclear, mainly because of the importance of situational demands and the limited duration of demonstrated effects. Naturalistic studies of the relationship between others' assessments and changes in self-assessments have had design limitations which made it impossible to determine the extent to which changes in self-perceptions are actually influenced by others' evaluations. Changes in self-attitudes may have resulted as much from subjects' own observations of changes in behavior as from others' perceptions.

When one analyzes the steps that are required before the perceptions of others can have an impact upon one's self-judgments, it is not surprising that their importance is problematic. Once others have perceived and evaluated an individual's behavior, they must then be willing to communicate their opinions to the individual. However, people frequently are unwilling to express their views about others directly, or even indirectly, particularly when those views are negative (Blumberg, 1972). Although norms regarding the evaluation of other people's behavior probably vary widely across different subcultures and situations, good manners, charity, and fear may all combine to minimize the communication of unfavorable appraisals. Evaluative inhibition may not be confined to casual relationships. Goffman (1955) noted this "not-even-your-best-friend-will-tell-you" phenomenon when he pointed out that unfavorable evaluations of close associates are typically given only when directly solicited and then only when people have made their own negative self-appraisals.

Even if people are willing to express their views, these can only change one's self-perceptions if they are discrepant with those self-perceptions. If others express opinions similar to one's own, the opinions will likely function only to strengthen initial self-perceptions. Also, any ambiguity or subtlety in others' opinions may allow one to interpret these opinions as being more congruent in favorability with one's own self-perceptions than they actually are (Jacobs, Berscheid, & Walster, 1971).

Finally, for data from others to have an impact on one's self-perceptions, these data must be viewed as having sufficient credibility for one to modify one's self-perceptions, perceptions which may have been established over extensive periods of self-observation. The issue of the credibility of the evaluation then becomes important, with several facets of credibility likely to contribute to one's judgment of the value of the information. Evaluators' expertise may be important, either in terms of their knowledge of attributes being judged, such as musical or athletic ability, or in terms of their knowledge of the person judged on the dimensions being evaluated. The acceptance of negative feedback has been found to be dependent upon the extent to which the evaluator is perceived as an authority on the attribute being assessed (Halperin, Snyder, Shenkel, & Houston, 1976). The evaluator's motivation for making his or her judgments is also a factor in assessing credibility. If the evaluation seems ingratiating, pointedly demeaning, engendered by sympathy, or otherwise strategically motivated, its validity may be negated. For these reasons, the evaluation of others may not always be seen as credible even when it is communicated and accurately perceived.

Given the tortuous road that others' judgments must travel before they have an impact on self-perceptions, their significance in everyday life may well be modest. The frequency and intensity of favorable and unfavorable assessments from others might have little bearing on the favorability of one's self-evaluations. Before reaching such a conclusion, however, it is important to recognize limitations in the available data which make this conclusion premature. First, there has been little investigation of how evaluations are communicated in ongoing social interactions. People may act to determine how many and what type of evaluations they receive from others. How frequently they interact socially, what type of evaluative situations they expose themselves to, and how often they elicit evaluations either directly or subtly all may affect the information they receive. Moreover, these factors may operate independently of one's objective level of competence or skill and could, therefore, provide a distinctive influence on people's judgments of themselves.

In one of the few investigations of the relationship between self-evaluations and evaluations from others in ongoing life situations, Schoeneman (1979) asked undergraduate students to report the bases for their knowledge about several personality attributes and to monitor the evaluations that they received from others over a ten-day period. After selecting a series of attributes which described them, the students answered open-ended questions indicating the sources of their knowledge regarding these attributes. These responses were categorized into three sources of knowledge: self-observation, feedback from others, and social comparison (observations of differences between one's own behavior and that of other people). It was expected that others' observations would be at least as important a determinant of these attributes as self-observations and social comparison. By contrast, however, in two separate subject samples using somewhat different assessment procedures, there was an almost identical pattern of findings, with self-observations mentioned 70 percent of the time, feedback from others 20 percent, and social comparison 10 percent. Rankings of the three sources of information showed the same order of importance, and similar results have recently been obtained with a different sample of college students (Schoeneman & Nash, 1981) and with preschool and grade-school children (Schoeneman, Tabor, & Nash, 1981). This does not necessarily mean that evaluations from others are a less important source of information than self-observation, but it does indicate that they are at least less salient and/or less readily reported.

Schoeneman also found that subjects high and low in self-esteem did not differ in the favorability of the evaluative feedback they reported receiving from others. The only difference between the groups in reported evaluations was a tendency, particularly among males, for low self-esteem subjects to perceive a greater number of people as evaluators of their behavior than did high self-esteem subjects. Although support for the null hypothesis does not arouse great confidence, it does seem that any response biases or self-presentational differences between high and low self-esteem subjects would favor the high self-esteem individuals' reporting more favorable evaluations, and therefore the lack of any such effects might be notable.

Overall, there is little conclusive evidence that evaluations from other people provide an important determinant of people's self-appraisal that is clearly distinguishable from objective data on which people might develop their own independent self-appraisals. Whether this situation reflects the actual lack of such effects or merely the paucity of conclusive evidence generated to date is still unclear. What is evident, however, is that despite the intuitive appeal of the notion that self-evaluations are influenced by overt appraisal from others, the evidence regarding their impact has yet to be demonstrated.

Selective exposure and attention to information

One implicit assumption running through much of the research on the influence of others' judgments in self-evaluation is the idea that people are rather passive recipients of others' appraisals. Yet the individual may actively influence the nature of the information that he or she encounters and attends to and may process it in ways which either enhance or minimize its impact on self-evaluation. In examining these processes, we shall begin with ways in which individuals actively shape the nature of the feedback they receive by choosing the activities that they will engage in and the information to which they will attend. Then we shall move toward the examination of processes which seem to be determined less by the environment in which people find themselves and more by their autonomous generation of information from previous experience to which they might attend. Six different stages in the selection and processing of self-relevant information are delineated: selection of activities to engage in, selective attention to standard data, labeling of self-relevant behavior, appraisal of the credibility of evaluative information, selective retention of evaluative information, and spontaneous generation of evaluative information. These roughly follow a sequential ordering of different stages in the course of attention and information processing at which information could have an effect on one's self-evaluation. Thus, if one does not expose oneself to a situation, information from that situation may not be attended to or its credibility evaluated. If the credibility of the information is seriously questioned, then it will not matter whether it is spontaneously retrieved. At the same time, processing of information at one stage might influence the evaluation of subsequent information at some earlier stage. For example, the readiness with which one recalls playing well against a particular tennis opponent may influence the likelihood that one will seek a rematch with that opponent. The way one labels an ambiguous evaluation from another person may depend on what information one spontaneously generates about other interactions with that person or similar individuals. Thus, over time, one's behavior at one stage of information processing may affect behavior at other stages.

Selection of activities to engage in

In everyday life, the nature of the evaluative information on which people may judge themselves is shaped in large measure by the type of situations to which they expose themselves. Most people have considerable control over the type of interpersonal interactions, work situations, and recreational activities that they are involved in. As Epstein (1979, 1980) recently observed, choice regarding one's activities may considerably enhance the stability and consistency of people's behavior beyond that which might be inferred from assessment in controlled laboratory situations. It may also enhance the consistency of their experience and the manner in which they come characteristically to view their own behavior. With regard to self-evaluation, individuals may substantially influence their level of self-appraisal by choosing to engage in activities about which they feel either more or less confident. If a sense of competence or efficacy is an important motive, as is frequently assumed (Bandura, 1977; White, 1959), one might expect that individuals would typically choose to engage in activities about which they feel more confident.

At the same time, the strength of this general tendency might also be influenced by an individual's general level of self-confidence. Following a need-reduction or self-enhancement model (S. C. Jones, 1973; Shrauger, 1975), one might assume that individuals who had low levels of general self-confidence would have a stronger tendency to choose activities on which they had greater confidence than would individuals with high levels of self-confidence. High-confidence individuals might be more likely to choose activities based on factors other than their confidence. From a different perspective, it might be argued that high levels of self-confidence are more likely to be achieved if people selectively expose themselves to situations on which they feel highly confident and avoid those on which they feel less confident.

The foregoing propositions regarding confidence and choice of activity were tested in a recent study in which subjects were asked to choose which types of psychological experiment they would participate in (Shrauger & Mathios, 1981). Subject selection was based on responses to the Personal Evaluation Inventory (Shrauger, 1981), a self-report measure of both general self-confidence and confidence in those specific areas of functioning which students had indicated to be more important in determining their confidence in themselves. Levels of confidence in two areas—meeting new people and intellectual activities—were considered in selecting subjects. Two subject groups were selected whose confidence in one area was higher than that in the other (high-meeting–low-intellectual and high-intellectual–low-meeting). These subjects were contacted by telephone and asked to take part in an experiment for credit toward their introductory psychology course requirement. Those who agreed to meet at the designated time constituted the experimental sample. After agreeing, they were told that there were actually two experiments being run and that they could choose either one which involved an intellectual task or one in which they would meet and interact with new people. As expected, people chose to take part more often in the experiment involving the area in which they felt greater confidence, $X^2 = 7.15; p < .01$. This was the case for both the high-intellectual–low-meeting and high-meeting–low-intellectual groups. Subjects who chose the meeting people task had higher scores on the meeting people subscale than those who did not, $F(1.65) = 17.23, p < .001$, and those who chose the intellectual task had higher scores on the intellectual subscale, $F(1.65) = 19.05, p < .001$.

Differences in general self-confidence were compared for those subjects who chose the task on which they had greater confidence and those who chose the task on which they had less confidence. Subjects who chose the experimental task in which they had higher confidence had lower overall scores on the self-confidence scale than did those who chose the task on which they were less confident, $F(1.65) = 4.13; p < .05$. One possible reason for this might have been that subjects low in general self-confidence had larger discrepancies between their level of confidence in meeting people and in intellectual activities. This was not, however, the case. There was, as one might expect, a tendency for high general confidence people to be more confident in both their high- and low-confidence areas. It may be that if people hold a certain minimal level of confidence, whether generally or in a specific area of functioning, factors aside from their perceived competence are likely to determine their choice of activities. This suggests that, although there is a general tendency for people to move away from activities in which they feel less confidence, people with higher confidence do not necessarily develop it by avoiding activities about which they have relatively less assurance. There has been very little examination of the role of confidence in determining people's choice of activities in everyday life situations and of the effects of such choices on subsequent emotion and self-appraisals. These are topics, however, which would certainly seem to merit exploration.

Selective attention to standard data

Sometimes people may not be able to choose the activities they will engage in, but they may still be able to exercise control over the evaluative input they receive if both positive and negative data are available within the same context. Such "mixed reviews" afford the perceivers some latitude in deciding what information to either attend to or ignore and how much time to spend in exposing themselves to certain feedback.

Mischel, Ebbesen, and Zeiss (1973) explored the tendency of people to selectively attend to self-relevant information as a function of their initial manipulated self-perceptions and the favorability of the information received. Subjects who had previously been given a success experience on an abilities test spent more time examining personality test results describing their assets and less time examining results describing their liabilities than did those who failed or were in a control group. Swann and Read (1981) examined a similar phenomenon using self-generated rather than manipulated self-evaluations. Based on their initial self-descriptions, subjects were divided into self-likable and self-dislikable groups. They then received evaluations from a partner in the study which they were lead to believe would be either favorable or unfavorable. Self-likable subjects spent more time reading evaluations they expected to be favorable than those they expected to be unfavorable, whereas self-dislikable subjects did the opposite.

Similar findings are also reported with depressed subjects. Studies with subjects who differ in their level of depression are sometimes reported here because negative self-evaluations are seen as an important component of depressive mood (Hollon & Kendall, 1980) and clinical depression (e.g., Beck, Rush, Shaw, & Emery, 1979). Studying clinically depressed and nondepressed VA psychiatric patients, Roth and Rehm (1980) had subjects make predictions about common word associations and then gave them the opportunity to study items on which they had allegedly succeeded or failed. Depressed patients chose much more frequently to see those items on which they had failed than did the nondepressed subjects. Since the depressed subjects had previously described themselves more unfavorably than the nondepressed patients, it appears that they were attending more to that information which was consistent with their initial self-evaluations.

These studies indicate that people are more prone to attend to information about themselves which is consistent with their initial level of self-evaluation, whether that self-evaluation has been induced or is relatively stable. The generality of this tendency is, of course, problematic. It may reflect a more specific instance of a pattern reported by Snyder and Swann (1978) in which people elect to receive that information which they feel will likely confirm their initially held self-perceptions. It should be noted, however, that the dominant motivation for seeking information about one's competence may vary widely across situations. Some information may be valuable primarily because it provides accurate data about one's capabilities which can help one plan subsequent behavior and modify one's actions adaptively. In other instances, particularly when people perceive themselves as being unable to change the behavior in question, disconfirming information may only be stress-producing and may therefore be avoided.

The relevance of the type of information that people attend to would be greatest in situations in which they either do not have the opportunity to examine all of the available self-relevant data or can effectively ignore the information. If the information cannot be totally avoided, then its overall impact will be a function mainly of the significance that is ascribed to it and the readiness with which it is recalled.

Labeling of self-relevant behavior

In the section above entitled "Self-perceptions versus actual performance," it was pointed out that, although people can judge certain aspects of their performance quite well, there are other areas of functioning in which objective indexes of competence are unrelated to either specific self-evaluations or general self-esteem. This would suggest that people with different levels of self-evaluation would each ascribe different evaluative labels to their own behavior even when the behaviors of all the individuals involved were objectively comparable. There is evidence, for example, that people's level of self-esteem relates to the favorability of their ongoing self-evaluation. Vasta and Brockner (1979) had subjects high and low in general self-esteem monitor their frequency of making positive and negative self-evaluations during standard periods of their daily activity. They found that subjects high in self-esteem reported fewer negative self-evaluations than those with low self-esteem. Although this finding is useful in suggesting how self-esteem relates to evaluative behavior outside the laboratory, the study affords no control over the objective adequacy of the behavior subjects were observing.

In another investigation, high and low self-esteem subjects evaluated their performance on a cognitive task on which it was possible to appraise their actual competence (Shrauger & Terbovic, 1976). In an initial session, subjects performed a series of concept-formation tasks. They returned one week later and were shown a videotape of their performance and asked to evaluate its adequacy. Half of the subjects were told the videotape was of their own performance, and the other half were told it was someone else's performance, although it was actually another person performing the task in the same way that they had. Although high and low self-esteem subjects actually performed comparably, high self-esteem subjects evaluated their performance more favorably than low self-esteem individuals. Low self-esteem subjects also rated their performance lower when it was ascribed to themselves than when it was ascribed to someone else.

A similar tendency toward differential labeling has been evidenced in clinical investigations of depressed and nondepressed patients (Roth & Rehm, 1980). This procedure, which also used videotape recording, involved subjects' observing tapes of their behavior in a role-playing situation and recording the frequency of certain behaviors which had been labeled by the examiner as positive or negative. Analyses controlling for differences in the actual frequencies of the behaviors indicated that depressive clients reported fewer positive behaviors and more negative behaviors than nondepressed clients.

These findings indicate that even when reporting concrete and specific behaviors under directed attention and high demands for accuracy, individuals differing on self-esteem or affective level may evaluate their own comparable behavior differently. One might expect that under conditions of less restraint, such as those which might be found in many everyday situations, the prospect for differential evaluations of one's behavior would, if anything, be greater.

Appraisal of the credibility of evaluative information

Once information has been attended to and labeled as having some evaluative significance, its potential influence on the individual depends upon the credibility that is ascribed to it. Is the information seen as valid and accurate and therefore presumably worthy of serious consideration?

The evaluative tone of the information one receives has been widely demonstrated to be related to the credibility which is typically ascribed to it (Snyder, Shenkel, & Lowery, 1977). Not surprisingly, people are generally more accepting of positive information than negative, although in most investigations this might be due to a predominance of positive attitudes in individuals' self-concepts and their readier acceptance of information consistent with their own attitudes. As one might expect, the acceptance of favorable or unfavorable information depends upon the consistency of that information with one's general level of self-evaluation (Korman, 1968). People are certainly more likely to find evidence that concurs with their initial self-evaluations to be more credible than that which refutes them. Of greater interest, however, is the question of whether general levels of self-evaluation influence the acceptance of favorable and unfavorable information when people's initial levels of agreement with that information are comparable. Some relevant evidence comes from a study in which feedback about their performance on a social sensitivity task was given to subjects who differed in their general self-esteem but were comparable in their self-perceived social sensitivity (Shrauger & Rosenberg, 1970). Surreptitious assessment of changes in perceived social sensitivity revealed that high self-esteem subjects raised their self-ratings of social sensitivity following positive feedback, whereas low self-esteem subjects lowered theirs following negative feedback. The self-ratings of high self-esteem subjects given negative feedback and low self-esteem subjects given positive feedback did not change.

In a more recent investigation, undergraduate students in the subject pool who scored in the upper and lower quartiles of the Self-Confidence Scale were asked to take part in a study on the usefulness of personality assessment techniques (Shrauger & Kelly, 1981). Subjects received a computerized sheet which contained 12 descriptive statements that were purportedly generated about them from actuarial analyses of personality test data they had completed at the beginning of the semester. Each subject received a distinct set of statements, all of which were drawn from items of the Self-Confidence Scale. The items for each subject were selected so that the subject had agreed and disagreed with half of both the positive and the negative statements. Statements were selected so that they covered a range of content areas and did not directly contradict one another. Subjects were allowed to look at the items for 90 seconds, and, following an interpolated task, they were given a list of the feedback statements along with 12 standard filler statements and asked to indicate their degree of agreement with each. It was emphasized that these ratings were designed to evaluate subjects' perceptions of the validity of the personality assessment measure, and the effort was made to indicate skepticism about the measure and to minimize demands that the statements be accepted. Analyses of agreement ratings for the feedback items indicated that high self-confidence subjects agreed more with positive statements than did low self-confidence subjects, whereas low-confidence subjects agree more with negative statements, $F (1.29) = 6.33, p = .019$. Efforts had been made to control the initial level of subjects' agreement with all statements by using only statements to which subjects had answered either agree or disagree. This was not possible in a few instances, however, and therefore differences in initial and final agreement scores were analyzed. These also indicated that high-confidence subjects showed relatively more agreement with positive statements and low-confidence subjects showed more agreement with negative statements.

These data suggest that individuals with high general levels of self-evaluation, relative to those with low self-evaluations, give greater credence to favorable evaluative input and less to negative evaluative input, and that this occurs even when the initial feedback has been judged to be comparably valid. The mechanisms underlying these phenomena are unclear, although it is possible that the evaluative component of the information is focused on more strongly than the specific content and that when the evaluative component matches existing self-relevant attitudes that information is then given greater credence than statements whose evaluative tone disagrees with the dominant level of self-evaluations.

Selective retention of evaluative information

The impact of any information on one's self-evaluation would likely depend not only on how it is attended to and processed when it is initially received but also on the readiness with which it can subsequently be retrieved. There is indication that people tend to recall more accurately information which is consistent with their own initial self-perceptions than that which is inconsistent (Suinn, Osborne, & Page, 1962). This would suggest that people with positive self-evaluations would recall more favorable information about themselves than those with negative self-evaluations and that people with negative self-evaluations would remember more unfavorable information. To examine this assumption, some investigations have looked at recall of situations in which one had performed either successfully or unsuccessfully. Silverman (1964) gave subjects a current events test, had them score it, and then presented false norms to induce success or failure. He found that high self-esteem subjects given success feedback more accurately recalled their responses than those given failure feedback. The reverse was true for low self-esteem subjects. In a similar vein, Crary (1966) found that when subjects were asked to recall the names of items they had done, high self-esteem subjects remembered more names accurately when they had outperformed their partner and low self-esteem subjects had better recall when their partner had outperformed them. One assumes from these data that when people recall aspects of an event associated with success or failure they are also recalling the success and failure experience and their own competence or lack of competence.

Swann and Read (1981) recently examined the recall of favorable and unfavorable information more directly. Subjects who had previously described themselves relatively favorably or unfavorably were led to expect positive or negative information from others. All subjects received both positive and negative feedback and were later asked to recall the statements they had received. Subjects tended to recall statements that were consistent in favorability with their initial self-descriptions. Also, subjects who were led to expect favorable information recalled more favorable than unfavorable statements, and those who expected to receive unfavorable evaluations tended to recall more unfavorable evaluations.

Selective recall of success and failure experience has also been examined in populations differing in their scores on depression scales. Typically, subjects have been given either bogus or accurate feedback with regard to their performance on a series of ambiguous perceptual or cognitive tasks and have later been asked to estimate the frequency of reinforcements or punishments they received. Wener & Rehm (1975) gave female students 20 percent and 80 percent positive reinforcement on a word-association task and found that those with higher depression scores estimated that they had received fewer reinforcements than those with lower depression scores. Buchwald (1977) examined recall of correct responses on a learning task and found that, with actual correct responses partialed out, subjects with higher depressive mood tended to underestimate their number of correct responses and subjects with lower depression scores tended to underestimate less or to overestimate. This tendency was significant, however, only for females. In another investigation, which apparently used both male and female students, different recall levels of standardized feedback as a function of reported level of depression occurred only under some reinforcement conditions (Nelson & Craighead, 1977). Using a similar task, but testing VA outpatients instead of students, DeMonbreun and Craighead (1977) found that patients who were depressed (based on scores in the Beck Depression Inventory) estimated that they had received less favorable feedback than nondepressed psychiatric patients and, in some instances, than nonpsychiatric controls.

Although there are consistent differences in recall as a function of initial level of self-evaluation, it should be pointed out that all of the recall tasks reported here involved very short time periods, and it is not certain that the same differences among groups would obtain over longer recall intervals. Also, in most of the studies one had to recall the frequency of repeated and similar reinforcements, whereas in everyday life it is likely the recall of distinct, individual events that is the most important for determining one's self-perceptions. Perhaps most significant is the fact that in all of these studies subjects are specifically asked to recall things as accurately as they can, and thus one is obtaining an index of maximal rather than typical recall, so that it is impossible to know whether these patterns are characteristic of an individual's usual recollection of previous experiences.

Spontaneous generation of evaluative information

As important as it is to know how well people are able to recall evaluative information when it is specifically requested, it seems at least as important to evaluate the nature of their characteristic thinking patterns, particularly the type of evaluative information which they generate spontaneously. It was expected that an individual's general level of self-confidence would be related to the nature of spontaneously generated evaluative statements. If relatively stable self-evaluations are a function of people's typical thinking patterns, then these self-evaluations should be related to the readiness with which favorable and unfavorable evaluative statements are generated. In the same evaluative situation, individuals with high levels of self-confidence would be expected to generate more favorable cognitions than would individuals with low self-confidence. These differences in evaluative statements generated could be the result of several factors, such as differential attention to or labeling of one's behavior or the generation of a different set of memories or associations following some initial situationally relevant cognition.

There has been little examination of the relationship between characteristic levels of self-evaluation and the type of cognitions that people report generating in different situations. To examine this relationship, the cognitions reported by subjects in the upper and lower quartiles of the Self-Confidence Scale were obtained in a performance situation which was likely to elicit a high frequency of evaluative judgments (Shrauger & Mathios,

1981). Along with the impact of general confidence levels, the importance of perceived competence in the general area on which performance was being evaluated was also considered. Subjects were asked to take part in a study involving their intellectual problem-solving skills. The 31 male and 30 female undergraduates who were tested individually were given the instructions for a concept-formation task (Shrauger, 1972) and were then left alone for two minutes before the experiment began, purportedly so the examiner could check some materials. When the examiner returned, subjects were given three minutes to write down whatever they had been thinking about while they were alone. They were encouraged to report all the thoughts that had occurred to them, however relevant or irrelevant they might be. This task was justified as an effort to examine the relationship between cognitive activity and performance styles. Subjects were then given one minute each to solve eight concept-formation problems, at the end of which time they waited another two minutes for the next part of the study to begin. They then recorded their thoughts during the waiting period, first using a free-response format and then completing a thought-listing form in which they checked from a list of 22 thoughts as many as they had experienced during that time.

Thoughts listed on the free-response measure were placed independently by the judges in one of seven categories: positive, negative, or neutral self-relevant statements (I know I don't do well at this sort of thing); positive, negative, or neutral task-relevant statements (There are five dimensions that can be part of my concept); or extraneous statements (I have to stop at the grocery store on the way home). The two judges agreed on their categorization of 78 percent of the statements, but analyses were done separately for each rater to evaluate the consistency of the findings across judges. The statements in the thought-listing inventory were also divided into the same seven categories. Analyses of variance for the frequency of different types of thoughts indicated that subjects high in general self-confidence checked more positive thoughts on the thought-listing form and fewer negative thoughts than did subjects low in general self-confidence. They did not differ consistently, however, in their free-response indexes of positive and negative thoughts. Specific self-confidence was related to the frequency of free-response thoughts, with negative self-relevant statements being given more by subjects low in specific self-confidence, particularly after they had performed the task. Significant interactions between general and specific self-confidence indicated, however, that specific self-confidence was important mainly for subjects high in general self-confidence. This finding underscores the importance of examining both individuals' general confidence and their situation-specific confidence when predicting responses to performance situations (Shrauger, 1972; Shrauger & Osberg, 1980). Specific self-confidence groups differed in the frequency of their positive thoughts on the thought-listing form but not on the free-response form, with more positive self-relevant and task-relevant thoughts tending to be given by subjects high in specific confidence. Differences in the frequency of positive and negative statements were not a function of differences between the specific self-confidence groups' actual performance. These results suggest that in performance situations the spontaneous generation of positive and negative evaluative statements is a function of both one's general level of confidence and one's confidence regarding the specific attribute that is being evaluated. In the present situation, negative statements both about oneself and about the task were minimized only when the individual was high in both general and situation-specific confidence. This may have been because the task seemed relatively difficult, but it does suggest that at least in some situations the cognitions of individuals high in general confidence vary more as a function of their perceived competence in the area on which they are performing than do those of low-confidence individuals.

In perhaps the only published study investigating the relationship between stable self-relevant attitudes and the evaluative tone of cognitions in a specific situation, male undergraduates scoring high and low in heterosocial anxiety recorded their thoughts prior to interacting with a young woman (Cacioppo, Glass, & Merluzzi, 1979). Subjects high in social anxiety generated more negative self-relevant statements. Also those who generated more negative statements also described themselves more negatively on a semantic differential scale completed immediately after they had listed their statements.

The nature of the cognitions that individuals typically generate when confronted with various situations may be one of the most important areas for further investigation. This is true not only because it has been explored only minimally but also because it may come closest to the kind of ongoing cognitive activity that is usually targeted for modification in clinical contexts.

Implications of research evidence for psychotherapy

Limits of generalization

To what extent do the research data on information processing and self-evaluation have implications for clinical populations and for the process of psychotherapy? Several issues must be considered in deciding how appropriately one can extrapolate from the laboratory findings discussed here to clinical contexts. Some of the most important of these are addressed here.

The therapeutic utility of directing people's attention toward themselves rests on the assumption that differences in stable self-relevant attributes are actually caused by selective processing of self-relevant information. Almost all of the data cited thus far on the relationship between self-confidence and information processing are correlational, and they provide no definitive evidence that changes in self-confidence are produced by different patterns of information processing. It is quite possible, for example, that both self-confidence scores and information-processing differences reflect variations in factors such as self-presentational style or willingness to acknowledge negative attributes rather than differences in genuine self-perceptions. One cannot rule out such factors definitively, of course, although the modest correlations between the Self Confidence Scale and the Marlowe-Crowne Scale, $r(140) = .21; p < .01$, suggests that self-confidence is quite distinct from the need for social approval or a strategic style of self-presentation.

Furthermore, some experimental evidence indicates that when individuals are asked to focus on specific self-evaluative statements, their levels of reported self-confidence and affect are modified in the direction of the self-evaluative statements. Wilson and Krane (1980), for example, gave subjects some self-esteem and mood scales and three weeks later had them attend to a series of positive, negative, or neutral self-relevant statements and then retake the scales. Subjects who focused on positive statements had higher self-confidence and lower depression scores than those who focused on either neutral or negative statements. Other studies have shown similar changes in reported affect as a function of attention to favorable or unfavorable self-relevant statements (Coleman, 1975; Velten, 1968).

Although these findings provide more direct evidence that focusing attention on aspects of oneself can influence more stable self-perceptions, they also have limitations. For example, self-evaluations were obtained immediately following exposure to the self-statements, and so it is unclear how long-lasting the effects of such exposure would be. At the same time, one might argue that if people are continuously exposing themselves selectively to new information, the process may have substantial cumulative impact even if one instance of selective attention has only a short-term effect. Demand characteristics of the situation might also contribute substantially to the effects of selective attention despite the fact that efforts are often made to control for them (Polivy & Doyle, 1980). In evaluating demand factors, however, one must distinguish between behavioral changes which are the result of a desire to conform to the wishes or expectations of the assessor and those which occur because the procedures seem reasonable and efficacious to the subjects themselves. Changes based on an effort to conform to others' expectations would likely be transient and of little practical value, but those based on subjects' perceptions of the plausibility of the procedures might well be stable and significant. In the therapy situation, in fact, there may be built-in expectancies for change which would enhance the impact of selective exposure processes over those that have been demonstrated in experimental studies.

With regard to the issue of causality, then, one must acknowledge that most of the data are correlational, and studies which have manipulated self-statements have confounding factors which are difficult to eliminate. The efficacy of therapeutic interventions involving the manipulation of self-statements might support a causal connection, although it is always difficult to determine the active ingredients in any treatment program.

Since most of the research reported, including that on depression, has been done using nonclinical populations, another obvious consideration in generalizing to clinical contexts is whether the subject populations are comparable to clients in the nature of their self-evaluations or their level of dysfunction. If abnormal populations are notably more deviant and distressed than the experimental subjects, then the role of self-evaluative processes in the etiology and maintenance of their difficulties could be inferred with less assuredness. To obtain some evidence on this issue, scores on the Self-Confidence Scale obtained by experimental subjects in the low-confidence groups were compared with those of a group of clients who had referred themselves for treatment of problems centered around negative self-perceptions and who took the scale as part of their initial clinical evaluation. Their scores were comparable to those of experimental subjects in low-confidence groups, which suggests that clients might tend to show patterns of processing self-relevant information similar to those of subjects in the studies reviewed. Although some studies of depression have used clinical populations (DeMonbreun & Craighead, 1977; Roth & Rehm, 1980), studies with nonclinical groups often use considerably less stringent criteria than those employed in diagnosing clinical depression (e.g., Nelson & Craighead, 1977). Generalizations from nonclinical populations of depressives should be made with particular caution because of the heterogeneity regarding depressive disorders and their potential etiology (Depue & Monroe, 1978). Our appraisal of the clinical applicability of selective attention studies will be enhanced as the use of clinical subject samples increases and as there is more attention in clinical assessment to the formal evaluation of problems in self-perception.

Another concern regarding the therapeutic implications of the research findings discussed here is whether the dependent measures that were obtained involve behaviors which are important in ongoing life experiences. Tasks such as deciding which of two types of experiments to participate in or remembering words associated with successfully or unsuccessfully completed activities are unlikely to find their way into many people's lives in just the way they were presented in experimental studies. Yet the process of choosing activities in which to take part or recalling self-relevant information certainly occurs frequently, and perhaps with more potential for variation in individual responses in everyday life situations than in experimental studies. Experimental studies may in fact minimize the importance of some of the processes examined because in an experimental context people may be constrained to be as accurate, unbiased, and socially appropriate as they can and more characteristic but idiosyncratic aspects of their attending to, and processing of, information may be minimized. The greatest limitation of the experimental data may be that studies often assess subjects' maximal, or optimal, behavior rather than their typical behavior.

Discussion of selective information processing for the development, maintenance, and modification of clinically significant problems involving self-evaluations must proceed with an acknowledgement that the subject samples and behaviors assessed may not be wholly comparable to those that are

Typical focus in psychotherapy

Having considered some of the ways that the selection and processing of information are related to the favorability of subjects' self-evaluations, it may be instructive to examine the therapeutic process in terms of how attention is usually focused on the self during therapy. When one considers the usual nature of psychotherapy interactions, it appears that there are at least three factors which may work to direct the clients' attention more toward negative aspects of themselves. Most types of psychotherapy, no matter how exotic, involve directing of clients' attention to their own behavior and feelings. Clients become objects of appraisal and evaluation in that their behavior, emotions, and motivation are scrutinized by themselves and their therapists. This situation would seem to optimize the condition that Duval and Wicklund (1972) have labeled "objective self-awareness," which is attention to oneself as an object of appraisal and assessment. A quasitherapeutic set has not been used to induce objective self-awareness, but such a set would certainly seem to be as powerful an impetus for inducing that state as the typical induction procedures that are used, such as seating people in front of a mirror. The usual impact of inducing objective self-awareness has been to make individuals feel more negative toward themselves in most situations, presumably because they have a heightened awareness of the discrepancy between their actual behavior and their idealized standards for behavior. Empirical investigations have usually confirmed the assumption that objective self-awareness enhances negative affect except when the individual is in a very positive mood, in which case positive feelings are enhanced (Wicklund, 1975). Therefore, one might expect that the psychotherapy situation might have an inherent tendency to reduce the level of clients' satisfaction with their behavior and to enhance the salience of their shortcomings.

The likelihood of this outcome is increased when one considers the usual content of therapy sessions. One striking feature of psychotherapy is that the therapist and client typically focus on personal concerns, difficulties, and inadequacies of the client. If one is to facilitate change, it must first be determined what is "wrong" with clients, what aspects of their behavior they and/or the therapist feel should be changed. To be sure, the emphasis on shortcomings and maladaptive aspects of behavior may vary with different clients, theoretical perspectives, and stages of treatment. Yet, the focus is clearly on problems. If the favorability of people's self-evaluations is related to the self-relevant information they attend to, however, prolonged selective exposure to the most troublesome and disturbing aspects of their experience could conceivably make them feel worse about themselves and could be hazardous to their mental health. Although people usually come to therapy to feel better about themselves rather than worse, clients often report not liking to come to treatment because they are constantly reminded of their difficulties. Such feelings may well be spurred by a concentration on the person's inadequacies and shortcomings.

Therapists' perceptions of their clients may also encourage clients to focus on their difficulties. Wills (1978) recently reviewed research comparing therapists' perceptions of their clients with other peoples' perceptions and with clients' self-perceptions. He concludes

that helpers' perceptions of a given target are consistently less favorable than lay person's perceptions, irrespective of whether the target person is normal or psychologically impaired. . . . [H]elpers rate clients substantially less favorably than they rate themselves, for dimensions including general evaluation as well as problem-solving capability.

With some populations, such as alcoholics, the differences may be dramatic (Reinehr, 1969). Hill (1974) presents data on the categorization of psychotherapy interactions by independent observers in which he indicates that therapists were six times more likely to convey to clients that they had seen themselves too favorably than they were to indicate that clients had seen themselves too negatively. In the previous section on evaluations from others, questions were raised regarding the actual impact of others' comparisons on self-evaluations. The nature of the therapy situation, however, may enhance the potential influence of therapists' judgments. First, the therapists' perceived expertise may make their evaluations unusually potent. They may be seen as authorities with regard to the judgment of attributes like motives and emotions, for which criteria other than the clients' own self-appraisal are minimal. Furthermore, since the clients may talk more candidly to therapists than to almost anyone else in their environment, therapists may be seen as having a unique fund of information on which to base their appraisals. Some evidence suggests that the acceptance of negative as opposed to positive feedback from others is more dependent on credibility of the information source (Halperin et al., 1976). Although therapists' roles may inhibit them from making certain observations about clients, therapists may also feel freer than other people to convey impressions about clients' conflicts and nonnormative motives. It is also possible that clients are particularly susceptible to influence from others because they may be experiencing confusion and self-doubt at the time they enter therapy.

To the extent that the therapists' judgments are conveyed either directly or indirectly to clients, they may not only focus on clients' attention selectively on the most negative aspects of their functioning but also communicate expectancies regarding clients' capacities to change their behavior or to deal with the difficulties they are experiencing. Concepts such as "resistance" and "masochism" can be seen as theoretical formulations of the expectation that people frequently have great difficulty in changing behaviors that seemingly have negative consequences for them. Again, therapists' perceived expertise may give their expectations added weight. The author is reminded of a client who was otherwise functioning comfortably and effectively but who became quite anxious whenever she considered discontinuing a pharmacologically insignificant dose of a tranquilizer she was taking. Although she claimed she could function effectively without the drug, she indicated that a former therapist had told her she would fall apart if she discontinued the drug, and she was understandably apprehensive about this prospect. Conceivably, the therapist's expectation was a convenient excuse for her, but her eventual successful withdrawal seemed to have been substantially postponed by it.

A variety of factors may contribute to the relatively negative judgments therapists make of clients. Wills (1978) suggests that this may be caused by therapists' negative reactions to clients' resistance to influence, by their dissimilarity in factors such as socioeconomic level, or by a strong need to account for clients' maladaptive behavior. Other possibilities are "defensive" self-descriptions on the part of clients or differences stemming from the therapists' vantage point as an observer trying to account for clients' behavior and clients' position as actors trying to understand their own actions. Jones and Nisbett (1971) have offered the widely supported contention that we tend to account for our own behavior in terms of parameters of the situation in which we are behaving, whereas we account for the behavior of others in terms of their stable personal characteristics. Since therapy focuses mainly on clients' shortcomings and maladaptive behavior and these are primarily what the therapist must account for, it is likely that the therapist will be drawn to perceiving them as reflecting stable generalized deficiencies in the client rather than as the result of situational factors.

The consequences of helpers' more negative perceptions of clients may depend a good deal on the accuracy of their views. Is the greater skepticism of the helper in some sense justified objectively and therefore useful to convey to clients? Although there are many investigations of differences in the perceptions of clients and therapists, there have been few investigations of how valid these differences are when measured against some specified criterion. Investigations which have been done have focused primarily on the prediction of the outcome of psychotherapy treatment. Most of the investigations have shown self-predictions to be as good predictors of psychotherapy outcome as therapist predictions or ratings of clients (Goldstein & Shipman, 1961; Saltzman, Leutgert, Roth, Creaser, & Howard, 1976; Uhlenhuth & Duncan, 1968), and the only instance in which therapists' ratings were clearly better was one in which clients were unaware of the type of treatment they would receive (Martin & Sterne, 1975). Thus, there is little basis for assuming that clients' judgments are appreciably less valid than those of therapists.

Regardless of the accuracy of differential judgments, there remains the question of whether it is therapeutically more beneficial to focus clients primarily on their strengths and favorable attributes or on areas of vulnerability and deficit. Posed in such a global way, the question is not readily answerable. Obviously clients differ both from one to another and within different areas of their own functioning with regard to the type of self-relevant information they select, attend to, and ignore. Yet the extent to which therapists focus on personal strengths and areas of competence as opposed to ferreting out areas of inadequacy and incompetence is a potentially significant parameter of psychotherapy outcome which has not been extensively examined. It would be overly simplistic and reductionistic to consider psychotherapy merely in terms of attention to favorable and unfavorable self-relevant attributes, and this is not suggested. At the same time, it seems dangerously short-sighted in evaluating the therapy process not to consider the frequency and readiness with which strengths and assets of clients are attuned to as opposed to shortcomings and limitations.

Using selective information processing in psychotherapy

Although psychotherapy may typically direct individuals' attention away from their strengths and favorable attributes, there are a number of ways in which therapy might serve to redirect clients' attention toward these qualities when that seems appropriate. Cognitive behavior therapy is perhaps the only widely used and professionally recognized intervention procedure in which the systematic redirection of clients' attention toward more favorable aspects of themselves is an explicit and frequently used component. This redirection has been achieved primarily by attempting to modify the individual's spontaneous generation of negative thoughts and increase the frequency of positive thoughts. There are additional ways in which this process may be facilitated. The distinctions between different phases of information processing that have been outlined here suggest some other ways of attending to and evaluating self-relevant information which might be employed in therapy.

Looking first at the selection of interaction situations, although some cognitive behavior therapists are grounded in the behavioral notion of the importance of external reinforcements, cognitive approaches have not typically focused on the idea that people might enhance their probabilities of favorable self-assessment by selecting to engage in activities and interact in environments in which they might likely behave competently and experience success. Ellis (1962), for example, seems pointedly to minimize the relevance of external reinforcements, deliberately asking clients to do things which may lead to negative external consequences but which the clients may then counter with their own internally generated positive cognitions. The merits of this approach in contrast to one which attempts to maximize the prospects of positive external outcomes have not been examined empirically, but intuitively it seems that if one engaged in objectively competent behavior, this might increase the likelihood that one could maintain a focus on favorable self-relevant attitudes, particularly if this was unusually difficult for one. There are obviously limitations in the extent to which people can be directed toward situations that induce favorable outcomes, but efforts in this respect may be useful when clients needlessly and repetitiously expose themselves to situations in which they consistently perform ineffectively or receive unfavorable evaluations.

With regard to selective attention, therapists will typically not have the chance to observe directly how much their clients selectively attend to negative information when it is received or ignore positive information. Neither can one always tell exactly how much ambiguous evaluative information is likely to be viewed as unfavorable. Clients must at least have attended sufficiently to the information to recall it without significant distortion. When this happens, it may be possible to bring out instances of selective attention or distorted recall by having the clients reconstruct in detail the nature of recent events which they had interpreted negatively. It may also be possible on occasion to do this for events going on in the therapy session by eliciting clients' interpretations of therapists' comments which might have appeared to be negative.

Perhaps the most effective method for dealing with selective attention and distorted labeling of evaluative information is to verbally innoculate clients regarding the probability of this behavior's occurrence and have them record it when they felt it might be going on. Although every such instance of this behavior will not be identified, particularly if the pattern has become habitual, clients typically report many such occurrences. Specifically, it may be useful to ask clients to list the favorable aspects of any mixed evaluative appraisal and to examine any alternative interpretations that might be possible regarding ambiguous events or evaluations that occurred in their everyday life.

Several investigations cited previously have pointed to the importance of people's expectancies regarding future outcomes as being particularly important determinants of their receptivity to evaluative information. Expectancies have been found to be important determinants of both the amount of time spent in attention to information (Swann & Read, 1981) and of the recall of such information (Mischel et al., 1976; Swann & Read, 1981). In some of these investigations, it appears that manipulation of expectancies about future outcomes may mitigate the effects of previous success and failure experiences in determining selective attention to evaluative information. Since subsequent expectations may typically be inferred from previous performance, it is likely that in many naturally occurring situations previous performance may influence the processing of future information primarily by determining the individual's expectancies about the favorability of that information. This suggests that it may be particularly useful in therapy to examine with clients the nature of their expectations about future events, and to try to work with them on the modification of negative expections. Not only may this minimize tendencies to selectively focus on information which is negative but it may also help the person to resist engaging in behavior which confirms negative expectancies.

In experimental studies, initial expectancies have been particularly important in appraising the credibility of the evaluative input that one receives. Therapists may well want to be alert to ways in which clients differentially evaluate the credibility of favorable and unfavorable evaluations, particularly the tendency to undercut the validity of favorable input. It is often useful in this regard to require clients to challenge their own reasoning when they question the validity of a positive evaluation or give strong credence to a negative one.

The interventions discussed thus far have involved encouraging clients to adapt more balanced or valid patterns of attending to and interpreting information about themselves. It is assumed that enhancing the accuracy of clients' perceptions will facilitate a reduction in their symptoms. This may well be the case, but at the same time considerable evidence suggests that people who have the most accurate self-perceptions are not necessarily the most psychologically well adjusted. For example, depressed patients' self-perceptions of their positive attributes were quite congruent with those of observers, whereas normal controls and nondepressed psychiatric patients judge themselves significantly more positively than observers judged them to be (Lewinsohn, Mischel, Chaplin, & Barton, 1980). Alloy and Abramson (1979) found that students scoring high on the Beck Depression Inventory made accurate estimates of the degree of contingency between their responses on a problem-solving task and the outcomes they received. Nondepressed subjects, however, tended to overestimate the degree of contingency for desired outcomes and to underestimate it for undesired outcomes. Studies on the recall of previous reinforcement which were cited above indicate that depressed students recall their previous reinforcement patterns most accurately than do nondepressed students, who recall these reinforcement contingencies overly favorably (Buchwald, 1977; DeMonbreun & Craighead, 1977; Nelson & Craighead, 1977; Wener & Rehm, 1975). Accuracy as a function of self-esteem has shown a similar pattern, with low self-esteem subjects evaluating their previous performance fairly accurately and high self-esteem subjects overestimating theirs (Shrauger & Terbovic, 1976).

The predisposition toward overly charitable self-evaluations is not confined to subjects who are unusually high in self-confidence or low in depressive affect. Rather they are widespread and are reflected in diverse behavior patterns, such as overestimating one's own contribution to group outcomes (Johnston, 1967), or predicting that favorable future events are more likely to occur to oneself than to the average person (Weinstein, 1980). On the one hand, a consistent pattern of self-delusion in people's appraisals of themselves would seemingly lead to difficulties when they were confronted with the inaccuracy of their perceptions. We may all recall examples of such confrontations and the distress they can produce. However, these situations may not present so much discomfort as that experienced by individuals who constantly face the cold and sometimes unflattering truth about themselves. Overly favorable self-perceptions may not be all that harmful simply because people are not that frequently confronted with direct and unambiguous evidence about the quality of their behavior and therefore their inappropriately favorable appraisals may not be challenged. If this is the case, then the most important function of many self-evaluations may be not to give people a realistic view of themselves but rather to govern their affective reactions. The primary, or even the exclusive, consequences of how they choose to see themselves may be for their emotional state. In such circumstances, the observation of Hazlitt that "life is the art of being well deceived" may ring particularly true. It may be useful to point out to clients that objective appraisals about the nature of their functioning are unlikely, and possibly even unattainable. In such circumstances, it would seem reasonable to emphasize that they have the choice of holding either favorable or unfavorable impressions about the adequacy of their behavior and that they might as well choose to perceive themselves favorably even if that belief is a judiciously charitable self-deception.

Note

1. Self-confidence refers to individuals' sense of competence or skill in areas of performance where ability can be evaluated. Self-esteem refers to the general level of favorability, respect, and regard which individuals hold toward themselves. It may include a sense of morality or desirability as a person as well as a competence or skill.

References

Alloy, L. B., & Abramson, L. Y. Judgment of contingency in depressed and nondepressed students: Sadder but wiser? *Journal of Experimental Psychology: General*, 1979, *108*, 441–485.

Arkowitz, H., Lichtenstein, E., McGovern, K., & Hines, P. The behavioral assessment of social competence in males. *Behavior Therapy*, 1975, *6*, 3–13.

Bandura, A. Self-efficacy: Toward a unifying theory of behavioral change. *Psychological Review*, 1977, *84*, 191–215.

Bandura, A., Adams, N. E. & Beyer, J. Cognitive processes mediating behavioral changes. *Journal of Personality and Social Psychology*, 1977, *35*, 125–139.

Beck, A. T. *Depression: Clinical, experimental, and theoretical aspects*. New York: Harper & Row, 1967.

Beck, A. T., Rush, A. J., Shaw, B. F., & Emery, G. *Cognitive therapy of depression: A treatment manual*. New York: Guilford Press, 1979.

Biggs, D. A., & Tinsley, D. J. Student-made academic predictions. *Journal of Educational Research*, 1970, *63*, 195–197.

Binder, D. M., Jones, J. G., & Strowig, R. W. Non-intellective self-report variables as predictors of scholastic achievement. *Journal of Educational Research*, 1970, *63*, 364–366.

Blumberg, H. H. Communication of interpersonal evaluations. *Journal of Personality and Social Psychology*, 1972, *23*, 157–162.

Borkovec, T. D., Stone, N., O'Brien, G., & Kaloupek, D. Identification and measurement of a clinically relevant target behavior for analog research. *Behavior Therapy*, 1974, *5*, 503–514.

Bower, G. H., & Gilligan, S. G. Remembering information related to one's self. *Journal of Research in Personality*, 1979, *13*, 420–432.

Bradley, G. W. Self-serving biases in the attribution process: A reexamination of the fact or fiction question. *Journal of Personality and Social Psychology*, 1978, *36*, 56–71.

Brockner, J. Self-esteem, self-consciousness, and task performance: Replications, extensions, and possible explanations. *Journal of Personality and Social Psychology*, 1979, *37*, 447–461. (a)

Brockner, J. The effects of self-esteem, success-failure, and self-consciousness on task performance. *Journal of Personality and Social Psychology*, 1979, *37*, 1732–1741. (b)

Brockner, J., & Hulton, A.J.B. How to reverse the vicious cycle of low self-esteem: The importance of attentional focus. *Journal of Experimental Social Psychology*, 1978, *14*, 564–578.

Buchwald, A. M. Depressive mood and estimates of reinforcement frequency. *Journal of Abnormal Psychology*, 1977, *86*, 443–446.

Cacioppo, J. T., Glass, C. R., & Merluzzi, T. V. Self-statements and self-evaluations: A cognitive-response analysis of heterosocial anxiety. *Cognitive Therapy and Research*, 1979, *3*, 249–262.

Coleman, R. E. Manipulation of self-esteem as a determinant of mood of elated and depressed women. *Journal of Abnormal Psychology*, 1975, *84*, 693–700.

Cooley, C. H. *Human nature and the social order*. New York: Scribner's, 1902.

Crary, W. G. Reactions to incongruent self-experiences. *Journal of Consulting Psychology*, 1966, *30*, 246–252.

DeMonbreun, B. G. & Craighead, W. E. Perception and recall of evaluative feedback by depressed and nondepressed persons. *Cognitive Therapy and Research*, 1977, *1*, 311–329.

Depue, R. A., & Monroe, S. M. The unipolar-bipolar distinction in the depressive disorders. *Psychological Bulletin*, 1978, *85*, 1001–1029.

Duval, S., & Wicklund, R. A. *A theory of objective self awareness*. New York: Academic Press, 1972.

Ellis, A. *Reason and emotion in psychotherapy*. New York: Lyle Stuart; Citadel Press, 1962.

Epstein, S. The self-concept revisited: Or a theory of a theory. *American Psychologist*, 1973, *28*, 404–416.

Epstein, S. The stability of behavior: I. On predicting most of the people much of the time. *Journal of Personality and Social Psychology*, 1979, *37*, 1097–1126.

Epstein, S. The stability of behavior: II. Implications for psychological research. *American Psychologist*, 1980, *35*, 790–806.

Feather, N. T. Change in confidence following success or failure as a predictor of subsequent performance. *Journal of Personality and Social Psychology*, 1968, *9*, 38–46.

Glasgow, R., & Arkowitz, H. The behavioral assessment of social competence in dyadic heterosexual interaction. *Behavior Therapy*, 1975, *6*, 488–498.

Goffman, E. On face-work: An analysis of ritual elements in social interaction. *Psychiatry: Journal for the Study of Interpersonal Processes*, 1955, *18*, 213–231.

Goldstein, A. P., & Shipman, W. B. Patient expectancies, symptom reduction and aspects of the initial psychotherapeutic interview. *Journal of Clinical Psychology*, 1961, *17*, 129–133.

Greenwald, A. G. The totalitarian ego: Fabrication and revision of personal history. *American Psychologist*, 1980, *35*, 603–618.

Haas, H. I. & Maehr, M. L. Two experiments on the concept of self and the reaction of others. *Journal of Personality and Social Psychology*, 1965, *1*, 100–105.

Halperin, K., Snyder, C. R., Shenkel, R. J., & Houston, B. K. Effects of source status and message favorability on acceptance of personality feedback. *Journal of Applied Psychology*, 1976, *61*, 85–88.

Hechler, P. D. & Weiner, Y. Chronic self-esteem as a moderator of performance consequences of expected pay. *Organizational Behavior and Human Performance*, 1974, *11*, 97–105.

Hill, C. E. A comparison of the perceptions of a therapy session by clients, therapists, and objective judges. *Journal of Social and Abnormal Science, Catalog of Selected Documents in Psychology*, 1974, *4*, 16 (Ms. No. 564).

Holland, J. L., & Nichols, R. C. Prediction of academic and extracurricular achievement in college. *Journal of Educational Psychology*, 1964, *55*, 55–65.

Hollon, S. D., & Kendall, P. C. Cognitive self-statements in depression: Development of an automatic thoughts questionnaire. *Cognitive Therapy and Research*, 1980, *4*, 383–395.

Jacobs, L., Berscheid, E., & Walster, E. Self-esteem and attraction. *Journal of Personality and Social Psychology*, 1971, *17*, 84–91.

Johnston, W. A. Individual performance and self-evaluation in a simulated team. *Organizational Behavior and Human Performance*, 1967, *2*, 309–328.

Jones, E. E., & Nisbett, R. E. *The actor and the observer: Divergent perceptions in the causes of behavior.* New York: General Learning Press, 1971.

Jones, S. C. Self and interpersonal evaluations: Esteem theories versus consistency theories. *Psychological Bulletin*, 1973, *79*, 185–199.

Keefer, K. E. Self-prediction of academic achievement by college students. *Journal of Educational Research*, 1969, *63*, 53–56.

Koocher, G. P. Swimming, competence and personality change. *Journal of Personality and Social Psychology*, 1971, *18*, 275–278.

Korman, A. K. Task success, task popularity and self-esteem as influences on task liking. *Journal of Applied Psychology*, 1968, *52*, 484–490.

Lefcourt, H. M., Hogg, E., Struthers, S., & Holmes, C. Causal attributions as a function of locus of control, initial confidence, and performance outcomes. *Journal of Personality and Social Psychology*, 1975, *32*, 391–397.

Lewinsohn, P. M., Mischel, W., Chaplin, W., & Barton, R. Social competence and depression: The role of illusory self-perceptions. *Journal of Abnormal Psychology*, 1980, *89*, 203–212.

Linsenmeier, J.A.W., & Brickman, P. Expectations, performance, and satisfaction. Unpublished manuscript, 1980.

Lorge, I., & Solomon, H. Group and individual performance in problem solving related to previous exposure to problem, level of aspiration and group size. *Behavioral Science*, 1960, *5*, 28–38.

Maehr, M. L., Mensing, J., & Natzger, S. Concept of self and the reactions of others. *Sociometry*, 1962, *25*, 353–357.

Mancuso, J. C., & Ceely, S. G. The self as memory processing. *Cognitive Therapy and Research*, 1980, *4*, 1–25.

Mandel, N. M., & Shrauger, J. S. The effects of self-evaluative statements on heterosocial approach in shy and nonshy males. *Cognitive Therapy and Research*, 1980, *4*, 369–381.

Markus, H. Self-schemata and processing information about the self. *Journal of Personality and Social Psychology*, 1977, *35*, 63–78.

Martin, P. J., & Sterne, A. L. Prognostic expectations and treatment outcome. *Journal of Consulting and Clinical Psychology*, 1975, *73*, 572–576.

Mead, G. H. *Mind, self and society.* Chicago: University of Chicago Press, 1934.

Mischel, W., Ebbesen, E. B., & Zeiss, A. R. Selective attention to the self: Situational and dispositional determinants. *Journal of Personality and Social Psychology*, 1973, *27*, 129–142.

Mischel, W., Ebbesen, E. B., & Zeiss, A. M. Determinants of selective memory about the self. *Journal of Consulting and Clinical Psychology*, 1976, *44*, 92–103.

Nelson, R. E., & Craighead, W. E. Selective recall of positive and negative feedback, self-control behavior and depression. *Journal of Abnormal Psychology*, 1977, *86*, 379–388.

Polivy, J., & Doyle C. Laboratory induction of mood states through the reading of self-referent mood statements: Affective changes or demand characteristics? *Journal of Abnormal Psychology*, 1980, *89*, 286–290.

Purkey, W. W. *Self-concept and school achievement.* Englewood Cliffs, N.J.: Prentice-Hall, 1970.

Reinehr, R. C. Therapist and patient perceptions of hospitalized alcoholics. *Journal of Clinical Psychology*, 1969, *25*, 443–445.

Rogers, T. B., Kuiper, N. A. & Kirker, W. S. Self-reference and the encoding of personal information. *Journal of Personality and Social Psychology*, 1977, *35*, 677–688.

Ross, M., & Sicoly, F. Egocentric biases in availability and attribution. *Journal of Personality and Social Psychology*, 1979, *37*, 322–336.

Roth, D., & Rehm, L. P. Relationships among self monitoring processes, memory, and depression. *Cognitive Therapy and Research*, 1980, *4*, 149–157.

Saltzman, C., Leutgert, M. J., Roth, C. H., Creaser, J., & Howard, L. Formation of a therapeutic relationship: Experiences during the initial phase of psychotherapy as predictors of treatment duration and outcome. *Journal of Consulting and Clinical Psychology*, 1976, *44*, 546–555.

Schalon, C. L. Effect of self-esteem upon performance following failure stress. *Journal of Consulting and Clinical Psychology*, 1968, *32*, 497.

Schoeneman, T. J. Two studies of the validation of self theories. Unpublished Doctoral Dissertation. State University of New York at Buffalo, 1979.

Schoeneman, T. J., & Nash, D. L. The sources of self-knowledge. Unpublished manuscript, 1981.

Schoeneman, T. J., Tabor, L. E., & Nash, D. L. Children's perceptions of the sources of self-knowledge. Unpublished manuscript, 1981.

Shrauger, J. S. Self-esteem and relations to being observed by others. *Journal of Personality and Social Psychology*, 1972, *23*, 192–200.

Shrauger, J. S. Responses to evaluation as a function of initial self-perceptions. *Psychological Bulletin*, 1975, *82*, 581–596.

Shrauger, J. S. Development and validation of a self-confidence scale. Unpublished manuscript, 1981.

Shrauger, J. S., & Kelly, R. J. Self-confidence and endorsement of external evaluations. Unpublished manuscript, 1981.

Shrauger, J. S., & Mathios, A. D. General and specific self-confidence and the generation of self-evaluative statements. Unpublished manuscript, 1981.

Shrauger, J. S., & Osberg, T. M. The relationship of time investment and task outcome to casual attributions and self-esteem. *Journal of Personality*, 1980, *48*, 360–378.

Shrauger, J. S. & Rosenberg, S. E. Self-esteem and the effects of success and failure feedback on performance. *Journal of Personality*, 1970, *38*, 404–417.

Shrauger, J. S. & Schoeneman, T. J. Symbolic interactionist view of self-concept: Through the looking glass darkly. *Psychological Bulletin*, 1979, *86*, 549–572.

Shrauger, J. S., & Sorman, P. B. Self-evaluations, initial success and failure, and improvement as determinants of persistence. *Journal of Consulting and Clinical Psychology*, 1977, *45*, 784–795.

Shrauger, J. S., & Terbovic, M. L. Self-evaluation and assessments of performance by self and others. *Journal of Consulting and Clinical Psychology*, 1976, *44*, 564–572.

Shrauger, J. S., & Turner, L. Clients' presenting complaints and expectations for treatment. Unpublished manuscript, 1981.

Silverman, I. Self-esteem and differential responsiveness to success and failure. *Journal of Abnormal and Social Psychology*, 1964, *69*, 115–119.

Snyder, C. R., Shenkel, R. J., & Lowery, C. R. Acceptance of personality interpretations: The "Barnum effect" and beyond. *Journal of Consulting and Clinical Psychology*, 1977, *45*, 104–114.

Snyder, M., & Swann, W. B. Hypothesis testing processes in social interaction. *Journal of Personality and Social Psychology*, 1978, *36*, 1202–1212.

Stotland, E., Thorley, S., Thomas, E., Cohen, A. R., & Zander, A. The effects of group expectations and self-esteem upon self-evaluation. *Journal of Abnormal and Social Psychology*, 1957, *54*, 55–63.

Suinn, R. M., Osborne, D., & Page, W. The self-concept and accuracy of recall of inconsistent self-reported information. *Journal of Clinical Psychology*, 1962, *18*, 473–474.

Swann, W. B., & Read, S. J. Self-verification processes: How we strain our self-conceptions. *Journal of Experimental Social Psychology*, 1981, *17*, 351–372.

Uhlenhuth, E. H., & Duncan, D. B. Subjective change with medical student therapists: I. Course of relief in psychoneurotic outpatients. *Archives of General Psychiatry*, 1968, *18*, 428–438.

Vasta, R., & Brockner, J. Self-esteem and self-evaluative covert statements. *Journal of Consulting and Clinical Psychology*, 1979, *47*, 776–777.

Velten, E. A laboratory task for induction of mood states. *Behaviour Research and Therapy*, 1968, *6*, 473–482.

Weinstein, N. D. Unrealistic optimism about future life events. *Journal of Personality and Social Psychology*, 1980, *39*, 806–820.

Wener, A., & Rehm, L. P. Depressive affect: A test of behavioral hypotheses. *Journal of Abnormal Psychology*, 1975, *84*, 221–227.

White, R. W. Motivation reconsidered: The concept of competence. *Psychological Review*, 1959, *66*, 297–333.

Wicklund, R. A. Objective self-awareness. In L.

Berkowitz (Ed.), *Advances in experimental social psychology* (Vol. 8). New York: Academic Press, 1975.

Wills, T. A. Perceptions of clients by professional helpers. *Psychological Bulletin*, 1978, *85*, 968–1000.

Wilson, A. R., & Krane, R. V. Changes in self-esteem and its effects on symptoms of depression. *Cognitive Therapy and Research*, 1980, *4*, 419–421.

8

DEPRESSION AND DEVIANCE

DAN COATES
BARBARA A. PETERSON
UNIVERSITY OF WISCONSIN—MADISON

Cultures vary widely in their acceptance of depressive behavior (Stainbrook, 1954), and ours is apparently particularly intolerant (Bart, 1974). We dislike others who seem sad or unhappy and often expect people to recover rapidly from critical disruptions in their lives. Victimized individuals may frequently find that their experience does not match up to these arbitrary pro-happiness norms; they feel more depressed and disturbed, and feel that way for a longer period of time than social standards say they should. As a result, their initial sadness may be complicated and increased by additional negative feelings, such as guilt for failing to cope adequately or fear that their "deviant" unhappiness signals a deeper psychopathology. If so, providing the depressed with convincing evidence that their negative feelings are not so unusual or deviant may help to ease their depression.

In this chapter, we begin by discussing the victim's need to validate the appropriateness of her or his reactions, some of the social obstacles preventing validation, and the negative consequences of those obstacles for the afflicted individual. We then present research exploring the extent to which depressed people feel deviant and how reducing their feelings of deviance may affect their depression. Finally, we consider the implications of our results for treating depression.

Seeking validation

In some ways at least, most of us want to feel that we are "normal," like other people. Social psychologists have repeatedly shown that many people will conform their behavior to the actions of others, even when doing so means acting inconsistently with their true perceptions and beliefs (Asch, 1951; Hollander & Willis, 1967; Sherif, 1935). We may even distort reality in order to maintain our sense of normalcy, for example, by overesti-

---

Research reported in this manuscript was supported by grants to the first author from the Biomedical Committee of the University of Wisconsin at Madison. The authors would like to thank Nancy Franzen, David Lloyd, and Malin Goodman for their help in conducting the research. Special thanks go to Tina Winston for her assistance in running subjects, analyzing the data, and preparing the manuscript.

mating the extent to which others will act as we do (Ross, 1977; Ross, Green, & House, 1977). Perhaps one area where it is especially important for us to feel normal is in the domain of emotional experience, particularly negative emotional experience. After all, if we have unpleasant affective states which are markedly different from the experience of others, the implication is that we are not coping as well as we should and perhaps that we are seriously emotionally disturbed. Unfortunately, the way we treat victims in our society may often make it difficult for them to see their emotional reactions or themselves as normal.

Research in social psychology indicates that people do try to determine whether their responses to negative events are normal. Some years ago, Schachter (1959) investigated how stress affected people's interest in being with others. He brought college students to his laboratory, showed them a frightening array of sparking, threatening electrical equipment, and told them they would receive painful electric shocks in a few minutes. In some experiments, he then gave subjects a choice among waiting alone in a comfortable room with some magazines, waiting with others who were not in the experiment, and waiting with others who would also be shocked. Most of the subjects chose to wait with others who were facing the same unpleasant prospects as they were. These results, and a series of other studies, led Schachter to conclude that novel, arousing situations elicit a drive for self-evaluation in humans. We seek out similarly afflicted others, at least in part, because we want to know if our emotional reactions to the situation are appropriate ones, and often the only way we have to find out is by comparing our responses and feelings with those of others who are encountering similar stress. Subsequent studies provide further support for this argument (Wrightsman, 1960; see also Cottrell & Epley, 1977, for a review).

As Coates and Wortman (1980) suggest, if fairly mild outcomes, such as electric shock, elicit a drive to validate our feelings and reactions, it might be expected that such a drive would be even stronger when we encounter more serious negative events, such as the death of a loved one or serious illness. The fact that we can agree with labeling certain life events "negative" indicates that there is sufficient consensus concerning these events to suggest that some dysphoria is an appropriate response. But there is a wide range of other questions about reactions to such events for which the answers are not so clear. How intense should the negative affect be? How long should it last? Are other symptoms, such as sleeplessness or lack of appetite, supposed to occur along with the dysphoria? Discussions with others who are dealing with similar problems could provide some resolution of these issues. But, outside of the laboratory, similarly afflicted others simply may not be available. If they are encountered at all, it may often be in rather public settings, such as hospital waiting rooms, where anything more than superficial conversations are unlikely to occur (Wortman & Dunkel-Schetter, 1979). Therefore, people trying to cope with some negative life event may often have to turn to social norms and unafflicted others in their attempts to evaluate the appropriateness of their responses.

In our society, standards defining what constitutes an appropriate response to negative life events are fairly vague. Even mental health professionals do not agree on how to distinguish between normal sadness and pathological depression (Kendell, 1977; Lewinsohn, 1974). However, within this ambiguous context, there seems to be a definite bias toward condemnation of any more than minimal dysphoria. Our intolerance of depression, and our belief that people should rapidly recover from severe loss, are evidenced in the way we treat the bereaved. People who have lost a loved one, an inextricable and significant part of their life for years, are typically given a short time off for the funeral and then are expected to return to full functioning at the job and in their lives (Aries, 1974; Kastenbaum, 1977). In other cultures, such loss is expected to result in a lengthier period of withdrawal from day-to-day responsibilities as the bereaved are allowed and encouraged to work through their grief and reestablish their place in the social network (Habenstein & Lamers, 1963; Krupp & Kligfeld, 1962; Mathison, 1970; Rosenblatt, Walsh, & Jackson, 1976). Our social standards requiring that the bereaved rapidly return to normal functioning may often be unrealistically harsh. As Gorer (1965, p. 131) put it, in our society, "mourning is treated as if it were a weakness, a self-indulgence, a reprehensible bad habit, instead of a psychological necessity."

If such antidepression norms do exist, we would expect them to be adopted and enforced in day-to-day social interactions, and there is some evidence that this occurs. Strangers derogate and dislike not only seriously depressed people they meet in experiments (Coyne, 1976a), but also others who seem just mildly distressed (Coates, Wortman, & Abbey, 1979; Gergen & Wishnov, 1965). Many people appear to overstate their own level of satisfaction and avoid giving any indication of unhappiness. In surveys, a majority of people say they are happier (Andrews & Withey, 1976) and have fewer problems (Best & Andreasen, 1977) than most other people, whereas very few say they are less satisfied than the average person. Since it is logically impossible for most people to actually be better off than most people, respondents in these surveys may be denying, at least publicly if not privately, some of their own troubles and sadness. Even when acquaintances rather than researchers ask "How are you?" the predominant response seems to be "Fine!" or some other positive self-description. So, among strangers or mere acquaintances, such as co-workers or fellow students, people who are not feeling so happy may get the impression that they are the only ones who feel that way and that others disapprove of their sadness.

We might expect that depressed people could find more comfort in their intimate relationships with friends and family members, but even here they may get the message that they are strange and unusual. While others may occasionally communicate to victims that it is appropriate and normal to feel upset and depressed, they are more likely to try to reduce or eliminate the depression rather than validate it. Silver and Wortman (1980), in an extensive review of the negative life events literature, describe several studies indicating that friends and relatives often expect much milder depressions and much quicker recoveries than the victims themselves actually experience. Members of the social environment make these expectations known to the victim, sometimes in a very direct and demanding way, but probably more often through well-intentioned acts of kindness. As Coates and Wortman (1980) point out, others initially respond to depressed persons with attempts to directly cheer them up, minimize their problem, or distract them from their worries. Several observers have noted that such attempts do not help the depressed and may even make them feel worse (see Coates & Wortman, 1980, for a review). By trying to eliminate the depression, members of the social environment inevitably also communicate that the depression is improper, unwarranted, or unnecessary. Thus, such reactions provide the victims with further evidence that their feelings are unusual and inappropriate and perhaps foster a painful feeling of deviance and isolation.

Of course, these attempts to reduce or eliminate the depression communicate more than just that the depression is inappropriate. They also communicate that people care about and want to help the depressed person. Many authors suggest that such expressions of concern are "secondary gains" that reinforce and maintain the depression (Burgess, 1969; Eastman, 1976; Liberman & Raskin, 1971). Perhaps, then, the depressed fail to show much improvement following such social feedback, not because these reactions make them feel deviant, but because these responses reward the depressed for acting unhappy.

However, the depressed may not find others' expressions of kindness to be very supportive or rewarding at all. Several authors (Coates & Wortman, 1980; Coyne, 1976b; Wortman & Dunkel-Schetter, 1979) have argued that the predominant social response to others who are hurt or depressed can best be described as ambivalent. Depressive symptoms, such as weeping and other expressions of abject misery, are powerful elicitors of help and concern from others (Burgess, 1969; Coyne, 1976b), but they are also very discomforting and unattractive to people (Coates et al., 1979; Coyne, 1976a; Gergen & Wishnov, 1965). While others are reluctant to directly express any negative feelings to someone who is already suffering (Hastorf, Northcraft, & Picciotto, 1979; Kleck, Ono, & Hastorf, 1966), these feelings do tend to come out in a number of ways. Supportive verbal statements may be combined with rather unfriendly nonverbal behaviors, such as fewer smiles and less eye contact (Davis, 1961; Hinchliffe, Hooper, & Roberts, 1978; Kleck et al., 1966) or increased general avoidance (Lewinsohn & Schaffer, 1971; Lewinsohn, Weinstein, & Shaw, 1969). Even direct verbal statements, while mostly supportive, may occasionally be punctuated with hostile or derogatory comments (Howes & Hokanson, 1979). Such conflicting communication will probably leave the depressed feeling more confused than liked and quite suspicious as to just how sincere others' kindness and support really are (Coates & Wortman, 1980). It may also provide the depressed with further evidence that they are indeed strange, since they elicit such disturbed responses from others.

So it seems that broad social standards, strangers, and even intimates all reinforce the message that sadness is peculiar and unusual. This message could have a number of negative consequences for depressed people. First of all, they are likely to feel deviant and unlike other people, which would probably increase their loneliness and isolation (Dubrey & Terrill, 1975; Lewinsohn, 1974; Peplau, Russell, & Heim, 1979). They may also feel guilty. Watzlawick, Weakland, and Fisch (1974) specifically argue that depressed people feel like failures because they cannot experience the positive emotions that everyone around them tells them to have. Bart (1974, p. 140) writes, "When people are unhappy, they suffer not only from the affect of sadness itself, but from experiencing guilt about the feeling. Whatever the cause of the original depression, they are unhappy because they are depressed. . . . Since depression is not believed to be a natural state, there must be something wrong with the individual who is unhappy." Finally, people who are sad may begin to doubt their own sanity. Nisbett, Borgida, Crandall, and Reed (1976) report that insomniacs often worry that their sleeplessness is indicative of a more general and serious psychopathology, and these authors suggest that depressed people make similar inferences about their negative affect. Interview studies with victim groups, such as widows (Glick, Weiss, & Parkes, 1974; Marris, 1958; see also Silver & Wortman, 1980, for a review), indicate that the discrepancy between their actual grief and their socially conditioned expectations frequently results in fears of "going crazy." Clearly, the pro-happiness norms in our society could play an important role in changing someone who is merely sad into someone with the added guilt, loneliness, and anxiety that are characteristic of more serious, clinical depression.

If there are antidepression norms in our society which exacerbate the condition of depressed people, we would expect, first of all, that depressed people will show a greater sense of deviance than nondepressed people. We might also expect that, unlike nondepressed people, the depressed will enjoy an opportunity to meet and talk with others who also seem problem-ridden and unhappy. Finally, it would seem that depressed people will feel better if they realize that others also have negative reactions like theirs and that they are not so unusual or strange. In the following sections of the chapter, we present the results of a few pilot projects aimed at testing these expectations.

Depression and the false consensus bias

There is some evidence indicating that most of us see ourselves as less deviant than others might. Ross and his colleagues (Ross, 1977; Ross et al., 1977) have argued that we are generally susceptible to a "false consensus bias." The term refers to people's tendency to see their own choices, characteristics, and behaviors as relatively common while viewing alternative responses as relatively unusual. The word "relative" has a specific meaning in this definition. The operation of a false consensus bias does not necessarily lead us to consider ourselves as being among the majority in all ways. We will probably realize, for example, that very few people are born with 11 toes, even if we are among this minority. But, if we were born with 11 toes, we would be inclined to believe that this characteristic is more widespread among the population than would someone born with ten toes. That is, we tend to see our traits and responses as more common than people who have different characteristics see them.

In their research, Ross et al. asked college students to choose between hypothetical or actual alternatives and to estimate how many of their peers would choose each alternative. Their results support the existence of a false consensus bias. Compared with people who do not decide as they do, students overestimate the percentage of others who would agree with their selections. Other studies show that students are similarly biased in estimating how common their personal characteristics and preferences are (Ross et al., 1977, Study 3) and how much social support exists for their opinions on a number of issues (Goethals, Allison, & Frost, 1979). Apparently, most of us like to believe that there are a significant number of others who think, feel, and act as we do.

However, if pro-happiness social norms lead the depressed to feel deviant, we might expect them to see their own characteristics and preferences as less common than nondepressed people do. In a very simple attempt to determine the relationship between false consensus and depression, we administered the Beck (1967) Depression Inventory and a questionnaire similar to that employed by Ross et al. to 432 introductory psychology students. The false consensus measure consisted of six hypothetical choice situations, such as buying either broccoli or asparagus when both are on sale. People were also asked to indicate whether they would allow a recording of their comments to be used in a television commercial, spend a free evening at a play or movie, watch a child abuse special or variety show on television, purchase a book or record album, and choose an elective course in literature or philosophy. Students checked off the alternatives they preferred and then filled in the percentage of peers they believed would choose each selection. Percentages were added across questions for each subject, and the mean percentage of agreement was correlated with the Beck scores. The result was a small but significant correlation coefficient ($r = -.26, p < .001$), indicating that depressed people are more inclined to see themselves as unusual and unlike others.

Obviously, the size of the correlation coefficient is not overwhelming, but we thought it was nonetheless encouraging to our general argument of depression as deviance for a number of reasons. First of all, our population consisted of fairly functional college students and, as such, probably included few very seriously depressed people. Thus we may have had a rather restricted range of depression scores, which would, of course, limit the correlation coefficient. Second, people seem to like being unique in socially approved ways (Snyder & Shenkel, 1976). It might be expected, then, that there would be some people who have a low false consensus bias but feel quite good about being different. Despite this opposing tendency, we still find a significant negative relationship between false consensus and depression. Finally, while it may not be surprising to find that the depressed would feel peculiar in some ways, it is striking that they would feel that way even about such personal characteristics as preferences for vegetables or types of recreation. The finding that depressed people feel even slightly more unusual in the mundane and unemotional choices we asked about suggests that many may have a fairly generalized view of themselves as deviants.

Our findings here suggest a potentially interesting direction for future research on depression and cognitive processes. Despite the traditional view of the depressed as very prone to information distortion and biased interpretation (Beck, 1974), there is growing evidence that they are more accurate in some types of judgments and perceptions than the nondepressed are (Abramson & Alloy, 1980; Alloy & Abramson, 1979; Lewinsohn, Mischel, Chaplin, & Barton, 1980). If the consensus estimates of the nondepressed are inflated (Ross, 1977), perhaps the lower estimates of the depressed reflect a more realistic view. Of course, it is also possible that the depressed are just as biased as the nondepressed in their consensus judgments, but in the opposite direction.

Unfortunately, the accuracy of our subjects' consensus estimates cannot be determined from the present results. Borrowing from Ross et al. (1977), we asked each student to guess "what percentage of your peers, people like you" would choose each alternative. We do not know what groups subjects may have considered to be peers, so it is obviously impossible to determine the actual percentage of choices in those populations. By asking for consensus estimates that are tied to more specific reference groups, future studies may be able to determine whether the lower estimates of the depressed represent a distorted or accurate assessment.

Clearly, depression is not maintained solely by feelings of being different, but the results here suggest that self-perceived deviance may play at least some part in exacerbating this condition. If so, it would follow that reducing the depressed's sense of deviance could also reduce their negative affect and related symptoms. We explore this possibility in the next section.

Reducing depression by increasing consensus

Drawing from research on the potential therapeutic effects of misattribution (see Storms, Denney, McCaul, & Lowery, 1979, for a review), Nisbett, et al. (1976) reasoned that depressed people would feel better if they were informed that dysphoria and distress were common reactions among others in their situation. Given this information, the researchers expected people to attribute their unhappiness to external causes rather than to their own maladjustment and thereby experience some relief. They contacted groups of students who regularly "had the blues," students who considered themselves chronically depressed, and highly stressed first-year professors. Subjects were either provided with scientifically based reports explaining that their negative reactions were very common or simply told they would be participating in a study on stress and moods. This attempt at consensus therapy failed. People who were led to believe that many of their peers were also unhappy showed no more reduction in their depression than the people who had been told only that they were in a study.

These results indicate that there is little therapeutic value in merely informing depressed people that their negative reactions are statistically common. However, it is still possible that depressed people could be helped by other types of consensus information. Nisbett et al. argue that their manipulation failed because the subjects were not convinced by the reports they were given. In a society where sadness is denied and disapproved of, people are inclined to present themselves as fairly happy. Abstract information indicating that depression is widespread may seem rather incredible when contrasted with concrete, day-to-day interactions suggesting that others are feeling fine. If the depressed groups had been provided with more concrete evidence of consensus, they might have been more persuaded by it and perhaps would have felt less deviant and depressed as a result.

While Nisbett et al. did not explore this possibility with depressed people, they did find that budding psychology majors are more convinced by concrete than abstract information. Students who were in the process of deciding on future classes were given written statistical summaries of the ratings made by all students who had previously taken the courses along with the personal, oral recommendations of a small panel of advanced psychology majors. Despite the greater reliability and validity of the statistical summaries, students were more inclined to make their selections according to the panel's suggestions (see also Nisbett & Borgida, 1975). Apparently, people find others' accounts of their personal experiences more compelling than scientific data. Perhaps, then, depressed people would feel less unusual and unhappy if they could actually talk to one of their peers who also appears problem-ridden and dissatisfied.

Even if the depressed do not feel relieved by meeting unhappy others, it might be expected that they would at least enjoy the interaction. To the extent that sad people seek self-validation, we would predict that, like the subjects in Schachter's (1959) experiment, they would prefer the company of similarly afflicted others. Such company may be all the more dear in a society where negative emotions are not ordinarily expressed or discussed. While most of us apparently prefer others who are in a positive mood (Coates et al., 1979; Coyne, 1976a; Gergen & Wishnov, 1965), there are some indications that depressed people are more attracted to troubled individuals. In an experiment dealing with cognitive distortions, Hammen and Krantz (1976) gave depressed and nondepressed college students a bogus test supposedly measuring their abilities as therapists. The researchers were surprised to find that the depressed subjects were more interested in careers as therapists than the nondepressed subjects. Perhaps this greater interest reflects the depressed's desire to meet similarly afflicted others. Golin, Hartman, Klatt, Munz, and Wolfgang (1977) showed films of people crying to depressed and nondepressed students. The depressed people reported greater empathy for the tearful models, suggesting they also may have liked them more. While neither of these studies offer very direct support, the findings are consistent with the prediction of mutual affinity among the depressed.

Will the depressed feel relieved by concrete evidence that they are not alone in their troubles? Will they, unlike the nondepressed, enjoy meeting others who are dissatisfied with their lives? To investigate these issues, we conducted a pilot study on the reaction of depressed and nondepressed people to others' expressed mood (Coates & Lloyd, 1980). The procedures and findings from this study are detailed below.

Method

The study had a 2 × 3 between subjects design. Depressed and nondepressed subjects spoke with other students who had been instructed to present themselves as either cheerful, complaining, or like a typical student. The subjects then filled out ratings on their impressions of the other person and their reactions to the conversation.

We identified depressed and nondepressed subjects by administering the Beck Depression Inventory in introductory psychology classes. We contacted both depressed and nondepressed students to participate in the study, using a score of 9 as our cutoff point. Of the 66 subjects who were finally included in the experiment, half were considered depressed and had a mean BDI score of 13.42. The 33 nondepressed subjects had a mean BDI score of 3.23.

A few weeks after they filled out the depression scales, subjects were contacted and asked to participate in a study on first impressions. Arrangements were made with each subject to be at home and ready to receive a phone call at a certain time. Then members of a separate group of nondepressed students were contacted and asked to come individually to our laboratory. These students were our stimulus persons who phoned the subjects.

When they got to the laboratory, the callers were met by an experimenter. The experimenter explained that the study was about first impressions and told the callers that they would talk briefly with another student over the phone. The experimenter gave the callers three typed questions to discuss with their partners, concerning school and school-related experiences. The callers were also given written and oral instructions about the type of statements they should make during the conversation. In the *cheerful condition*, callers were basically requested to keep the conversation positive, discussing only courses they enjoyed and school experiences they found rewarding. In the *problem-oriented condition*, the students were instructed to look upon the conversation as an opportunity to complain about anything that bothered them with school. They were asked to focus on courses they disliked and on any academic problems they might be having, and not to mention good classes or other features of school that they enjoyed. Finally, callers in the *control condition* were simply asked to discuss the questions with their partners as they would with any student they had just met. All the callers were asked not to reveal to the subject the fact that they had received special instructions.

Once the instructions had been given, the experimenter called the subject at home, made sure he or she was ready and available, and then turned the phone over to the caller. The students were left alone during their conversations, but after ten minutes a second experimenter entered the room. This second experimenter was blind to the instructions the caller had received. The caller was directed to another room, and then the second experimenter asked the subject on the phone to answer some questions, our dependent measures. Finally, the at-home subjects were carefully questioned about any suspicions concerning the nature of the experiment. All of the subjects believed the experiment was concerned with first impressions and were not aware that callers had received special instructions.

Results

Our dependent measures included manipulation checks and questions about the subjects' impressions of how likable their partner was, how enjoyable and helpful the conversation had been, and how happy they felt at the moment. Subjects answered four separate items about each of these areas[1] by using 9-point scales anchored "not at all" and "very much." Scores on the four separate questions in each category were summed to form an overall measure of the effectiveness of the manipulation and each general dependent variable. A 2 (depressed vs. not depressed) × 3 (type of instruction) analysis of variance was then performed on these combined scores.

The manipulation checks basically asked how positive and optimistic the caller seemed to be. Callers in the cheerful condition were rated as most positive (mean = 28.42), control callers were rated as moderately positive (mean = 25.28), and problem-oriented callers were rated as least positive (mean = 24.22). There is a significant difference between these means $F(2,60) = 3.24, p < .04$, indicating that our expressed mood manipulation was generally effective. However, it should be pointed out that the difference between ratings of caller satisfaction in the problem-oriented and control conditions is quite small. In a society where depression is taboo, it might be expected that people would be more adept at appearing cheerful than they would be at enacting a sad role.

The ratings of partner attractiveness and enjoyment of the conversation were highly intercorrelated and show a similar pattern of results. We had expected that nondepressed people would find interactions with cheerful others to be most rewarding and that depressed people would prefer problem-oriented others. This is apparently what occurred. There was a significant depression level by instruction interaction on ratings of enjoyment with the conversation, $F(2,60) = 7.00, p < .002$, and a nearly significant interaction on ratings of caller attractiveness, $F(2,60) = 2.98, p < .06$. The means are presented in Table 8.1. As the means show, the depressed subjects were most pleased by conversations with problem-oriented others and least pleased with cheerful others. The nondepressed subjects displayed just the opposite pattern, rating their talks with cheerful partners as most enjoyable and their interactions with complaining partners as least enjoyable.

We had also expected that depressed people would find conversations with unhappy others more helpful and feel better after meeting another person who appeared to share their dissatisfaction. However, there were no significant differences between the conditions on

Table 8.1. Level of Depression by Type of Instruction Interactions

Dependent Variable	Level of Depression	Type of Instruction		
		Cheerful	Control	Problem-Oriented
Combined enjoyment ratings	Depressed	28.82	30.67	33.08
	Nondepressed	32.83	31.40	27.25
Combined attraction ratings	Depressed	27.22	29.40	30.15
	Nondepressed	30.50	29.56	24.83

ratings of the helpfulness of the conversation and only one main effect for the mood ratings. No matter what type of caller they spoke with, the depressed subjects rated their mood lower (mean = 23.42) than the nondepressed subjects did [mean = 30.58, $F(1,60) = 3.92$, $p < .03$]. There is no evidence, then, that the depressed found any of the conversations particularly useful or uplifting.

Discussion

The findings from our study are consistent with the general depression as deviance argument and may have some interesting implications for understanding the social situation and social desires of the depressed. Unfortunately, though, the results tell us little about the effects of different types of interactions on depressed mood. As such, they leave open the possibility that socializing with similarly afflicted others could actually be detrimental for the depressed. In this section, we shall discuss both the social and the personal implications of our findings for depressed people.

In our study, nondepressed subjects were most displeased by their conversations with problem-oriented others. This finding is consistent with past research showing that we typically dislike others who are sad or victimized (Coates & Wortman, 1980; Coates et al., 1979; Coyne, 1976a; Gergen & Wishnov, 1965; Lerner & Simmons, 1966). We may prefer to think of ourselves as sympathetic to others in misery. We may even try to behave toward them in a sympathetic way. But mounting research evidence indicates that feelings of disapproval frequently accompany our expressions of care and support for the depressed. These negative reactions are most likely communicated to people who are unhappy and obviously do not help them to feel any better (Coates & Wortman, 1980). But, to the extent that sadness violates social norms, we would expect it to elicit negative social sanctions.

We also found that, unlike their more jovial counterparts, the depressed subjects most enjoyed talking with people who admitted having problems and difficulties. Previous research has shown that subjects who are anxiously awaiting noxious outcomes in the laboratory prefer to be with others in a similar state (Cottrell & Epley, 1977; Schachter, 1959). The results here extend this past work by demonstrating that depressed people also seem to prefer the company of others who share, at least to some extent, their dissatisfaction and unhappiness. This finding may have important implications for the way people typically respond to others who are sad. Several observers have noted that members of the social environment frequently react to the depressed by pointing out benefits and other positive aspects of their existence (Coates & Wortman, 1980; Watzlawick et al., 1974). But in our study, cheerful chatter was less gratifying for the depressed than the open acknowledgement that life has its pitfalls and problems. The depressed may be more appreciative, therefore, of others who try to validate rather than change their negative feelings.

While our findings have clear practical ramifications for people who interact with depressed others, a theoretical explanation for why these results occurred is not so clear. We predicted that the depressed would prefer troubled others because such others provide concrete evidence that sadness is not so unusual after all. But there could be other factors or processes that might account for the depressed's interpersonal preferences. For example, it has been repeatedly demonstrated that people like others whose opinions and beliefs are similar to their own (Byrne, 1971). The depressed may have been drawn to the problem-oriented callers because of shared beliefs while still feeling that their own emotional reactions were peculiar and deviant. We did not include any direct measure of self-perceived deviance, such as the false consensus questionnaire, because we felt that such measures would be very difficult to administer over the phone. However, since the pilot data were generally encouraging, we are currently planning a follow-up study to more carefully investigate the extent to which conversations with mildly troubled strangers affect feelings of deviance among the depressed.

While the depressed subjects did enjoy meeting the problem-oriented callers, they apparently did not feel any better after speaking with them. There were no differences in reported mood between depressed subjects who spoke with cheerful, problem-oriented, or control callers. However, there were a number of features in our study which may have minimized our chances of finding any differences in mood. First of all, our manipulation was rather weak. Even with extensive therapy, it can be difficult to lighten depressive dysphoria (Beck, 1967). It is perhaps unreasonable to expect a ten-minute conversation to have much impact on such an intransient condition. In addition, our callers were instructed to discuss only school and school-related experiences. It is quite possible that many of our depressed subjects were most concerned with problems outside of academia. As a result, their feelings of deviance may have remained relatively stable, and so they experienced no increase in positive affect. Finally, our mood measures were quite limited. Researchers typically employ more extended scales to measure mood (e.g., Coyne, 1976a), but since we were questioning people over the phone, we deliberately tried to minimize the number of items we asked. Because of all these problems, our study may have been an inadequate test of the hypothesis that concrete evidence of shared sadness will promote more positive affect among the depressed.

Clearly, a better test of the hypothesis would be provided by a study which included both more extensive and sensitive measures and a group of depressed people who discuss common problems on a prolonged or regular basis. But there are some serious ethical concerns in conducting such a study. The results from our pilot experiment indicate that depressed people may well enjoy such discussions. But the findings also leave open the possibility that meetings of this type could prove ultimately detrimental to the depressed's condition. Indeed, several authors have suggested that depressed people may be harmed by associating with others who share their affliction. Golin et al. (1977) speculate that an affinity for distressed others could lead the depressed to use sad people as models, thereby maintaining or even increasing their symptomatic behaviors and negative affect. Nisbett et al. (1976) point out that if depressed people believe that others in their situation are also miserable, they may conclude that their problems are even more insurmountable than they had previously realized and consequently feel even worse. Wortman and Dunkel-Schetter (1979) also express concern about the possible negative impact similarly afflicted individuals could have on one another.

While we very much wanted to test the effectiveness of a stronger version of consensus therapy, we did not want to do so at the emotional expense of our participants. We settled on a compromise pilot study, which is not nearly as informative as we would like it

Peer support groups and depression

The question of whether interactions with similarly afflicted others are helpful or harmful is not just an issue of theoretical interest. It is also a very practical concern. There has been in recent years a growing proliferation of peer support or self-help groups for many different types of victims (Gussow & Tracy, 1976; Hurvitz, 1976; Katz & Bender, 1976; Wexler, 1977). While these peer support groups vary widely in their specific structure and program, Levy (1976) points out that the groups are almost always composed of people with common problems who regularly meet to discuss their difficulties and ways of coping with them. Mental health professionals are usually not included in such groups and if present serve only in an ancillary role. If interactions with similarly afflicted others are potentially harmful, these groups might be precipitating crises and depressions which their nonprofessional members will not likely be able to relieve.

Much has been written about the self-help movement, and most of it is decidedly favorable (Borkman, 1976; Hays & Danieli, 1976; Lieberman & Borman, 1979; Steinman & Traunstein, 1976; Tracy & Gussow, 1976). However, there has been little done by way of evaluating such groups, and what work is available is based only on impressionistic, unsystematic data (e.g., Antze, 1976; Glaser, 1976; Sheldon, 1978). Several authors have pointed out that more rigorous outcome evaluation studies of peer support groups simply do not exist (Levy, 1978; Lieberman & Borman, 1976). We conducted several computer searches through the literature and were unable to find any study which specifically assessed the effects of peer support groups on depression among members. Apparently, the question of whether peer support groups promote or reduce depression remains unexplored.

A careful evaluation study of peer support groups would include, as a minimum, one set of people who actually participate in the group and a waiting-list control group. To test questions of theoretical importance, we would also want to shape the group discussions and to add additional control groups. But given the arguments for the potential destructiveness of peer support groups (Golin et al., 1977; Nisbett et al., 1976; Wortman & Dunkel-Schetter, 1979) and the lack of reliable information about the impact of such groups on depression, such a study seems risky at best. It is difficult to justify exposing people to potentially harmful treatments or, even worse, making them wait for a potentially harmful treatment simply for research purposes (see Schulz, 1978, for further discussion of these ethical issues). However, these peer support groups are being conducted whether we study them or not. To the extent that we investigate only existing self-help groups, without interfering with their procedures or programs, we are not exposing people to any danger they are not already risking by themselves.

This is the approach we chose to take. We were able to gain access to a self-help program for women who considered themselves to have serious eating or weight problems. This was a typical peer support group. It included a nonprofessional facilitator and the members themselves, all of whom met for a few hours once a week to discuss their common eating problems and ways of dealing with them. Unfortunately, since we were working with an existing program, we did not have as much leeway in conducting the research as we would have liked. The organizers of the program were convinced of its effectiveness and refused to make some women wait to join in order to provide a control group. As a result, we were limited to taking before and after measures.

Simple pretest and posttest studies of therapeutic effectiveness are notoriously uninformative. If the people who receive the treatment show improvement, there is always a plethora of alternative explanations for the results. Depression tends to dissipate with time anyway, and without the benefit of a waiting-list control group it is impossible to determine whether any reduction in depression is due to the treatment itself or merely to the passing of time. Since the problem-ridden people who join such groups are likely to be high in depression, any evident reduction could be an artificial result of statistical regression to the mean. However, all of the most obvious alternative explanations for before and after comparisons seem to apply primarily to a finding of improvement. It is more difficult to think of alternative explanations for the finding that people get more depressed as they continue to participate in the group. So, if such groups are harmful, a before and after study could potentially reveal this.

As part of a more general questionnaire about eating problems and group goals, we gave the Zung (1965) Depression Scale to the women in these groups at their first meeting and again after they had attended at least four group meetings. In all, 18 women came to the first group session. Of these, 16 filled out and returned our pretest. Two of these women failed to attend at least four sessions, and another four women failed to return our posttest questionnaire. Thus we have complete before and after data for ten of the women who participated in the groups.

These ten women showed a marked decrease in their depression scores. Their pretest mean was 54.72, and their posttest mean was 42.54 ($T = 3.41, d.f. = 9, p < .008$). As we have pointed out, the interpretation of these results is necessarily quite limited. But they do indicate that the groups were not harmful, at least not harmful enough to leave the women more depressed afterward than they had been when they joined the groups.

These findings help to ease our concerns about the impact of peer support groups on depression and open the way for more carefully structured and controlled studies. We currently have one such study under way. We should note that the results are also consistent with our earlier arguments about the potential value of intensive consensus therapy. Obviously, there are so many competing explanations for why the women were less depressed after attending the group sessions that we cannot be at all certain that their improvement was due to a reduced sense of deviance. But, after all, the results could have turned out more negatively, which would clearly raise problems for the consensus therapy notion. Our findings here do not prove there is any value in getting similarly afflicted people together, but they do indicate that this is a fairly safe and potentially fruitful area for further investigation.

Conclusions and implications

The depression as deviance argument which we have been expounding in this chapter has three basic premises. First of all, we maintain that in our society, expressions of even mild unhappiness are disapproved by others. In our phone study, we found that nondepressed subjects tend to dislike others who talk about their problems. The second premise is that, as a result of the negative social sanctions against sadness, depressed people come to feel that they are deviants. In support of this notion, we found that depressed people tend to view even trivial and mundane choices they make as more unusual than nondepressed people do. Finally, we argued that these feelings of deviance could complicate and exacerbate the depression, so that depressed people might feel better if they could be convinced that their dysphoria was not so unusual after all. Consistent with this premise, we found that depressed subjects most enjoyed conversations with troubled callers and were less depressed after attending a support group of similarly afflicted others. While each of our separate attempts at data collection has certain problems and weaknesses, the overall pattern of results is supportive of the general depression as deviance argument. Since there is at least some empirical support for this perspective on depression, it seems worthwhile to consider its implications for both the paraprofessionals and the professionals who try to help depressed people.

While the results from our phone study have practical implications for anyone who interacts with depressed people, they may seem most directly applicable to the paraprofessionals who work on crisis lines or suicide prevention call-in programs. The results suggest that people who phone into such programs may be more pleased by counselors who reveal their own problems than by those who try to cheer up the caller. Indeed, some authors have proposed such a tack as a way of dealing with clinical patients more generally (Jourard, 1964). However, it is important to point out some limitations of this recommendation. In our experiment, the depressed subjects were not calling for help; in fact, they were not even aware that the study had anything to do with depression. While the depressed may feel validated by meeting someone who happens to have problems, they could resent someone who appears to be trying to help them by discussing his or her own difficulties. Such an approach, in a helping context, might well seem patronizing or even unsympathetic. Obviously, a study in which the conversations of actual phone counselors are varied would help to establish the extent to which a problem-disclosing approach would be advisable for these paraprofessionals.

Professional therapists and researchers should perhaps be aware of the extent to which they have contributed to antidepression norms in our society. For example, some clinicians (e.g., Ellis, 1962, 1973) stress that while we may not be able to control what happens to us, we can control how we feel about it. The obvious implication of this statement for depressed people is that they are not doing a very good job of controlling their emotions, despite the fact that depressive reactions frequently may be involuntary responses (Silver & Wortman, 1980). Similarly, Lindemann (1944) distinguished between "normal" and "morbid" grief, and bereaved individuals continue to be categorized in this way by researchers and therapists (Schulz, 1978). Perhaps the most important differences between these two types of grief is that the morbidly bereaved are sadder and stay that way for a longer time. This distinction reflects an intolerance of prolonged unhappiness and an insensitivity to the experience of bereaved individuals. Rather than simply accepting that some people take longer to overcome such a loss or considering that some people may have cared more, relied more, or otherwise lost more than others, mental health professionals tend to apply pejorative labels which connote some type of psychopathology. Such labels could ultimately be more destructive than the prolonged sadness (Farina, Fisher, Getter, & Fischer, 1978; Scheff, 1966).

Mental health professionals may also want to consider increasing their use of peer support groups. In a survey of counselors and therapists conducted by Levy (1978), few of the respondents had ever referred clients to self-help groups and a considerable minority indicated that they never would. Such groups cannot provide the expertise and experience of professionals, but they may be able to fulfill certain functions that the professionals cannot. For example, a counselor may be able to explain to a widow or a cancer patient that depression is a very common and appropriate response. But, as Silver and Wortman (1980) point out, such information is like the abstract consensus data that Nisbett et al. (1976) found to be ineffective in altering depression. Peer support groups, on the other hand, can provide concrete evidence of consensus, and our results at least suggest that such evidence can be helpful for the depressed. Professionals may well find, therefore, that such groups can be very usefully combined with therapy.

Perhaps the most important implication of our depression as deviance argument is the realization that norms of appropriate affect or recovery speed are arbitrary social inventions. People who are considered morbid grievers in our culture could well be seen as well-adjusted in another (Rosenblatt et al., 1976). These norms reflect the values and preferences of our society, but by no means constitute guidelines for determining who is or is not psychologically maladjusted. While we may all know that our judgments and interpretations are culture bound, counselors, therapists, and depressed people themselves may often forget this point when they attempt to evaluate the appropriateness of emotional reactions.

Note

1. The specific questions employed were as follows. (1) *As manipulation checks*, "How cheerful was the person you talked with? How sad do you think the person you talked with is? To what extent did the other person discuss pleasant things, things they liked or enjoyed? To what extent did the other person discuss problems, things they disliked or found bothersome?" These manipulation checks were asked last, to avoid possibly sensitizing subjects to hypotheses in the study. (2) *As measures of liking*, "Do you like the person you talked with? Would you like to spend more time talking with the other person? Did you find the other person attractive or appealing in any way? Would you want to get to know the other person better?" (3) *As measures of enjoyment with the conversation*, "Did you find the conversation with the other person pleasant? How much did you enjoy talking with the other person? Did you feel uncomfortable during the conversation? Did you find the conversation with the other person upsetting in any way?" (4) *As measures of the helpfulness of the conversation*, "Did you find the conversation with the other person at all helpful? Do you think the conversation you had was useful to you in any way? To what extent do you feel that the conversation you just had was a waste of time? Do you feel you learned anything of value from your talk with the other person?" (5) *As measures of subjects' mood*, "How happy do you feel right now? Would you say you were in a good mood right now? To what extent are you experiencing negative feelings or emotions right now? How pleasant do you feel right now?"

References

Abramson, L. Y., & Alloy, L. B. Judgment of contingency: Errors and their implications. In A. Baum and J. E. Singer (Eds.), *Advances in environmental psychology: Applications of personal control* (Vol. 2). Hillsdale, N.J.: Erlbaum, 1980.

Alloy, L. B. & Abramson, L. Y. Judgment of contingency in depressed and nondepressed students: Sadder but wiser? *Journal of Experimental Psychology: General*, 1979, *108*, 441–485.

Andrews, F. M., & Withey, S. B. *Social indicators of well-being*. New York: Plenum Press, 1976.

Antze, P. The role of ideologies in peer psychotherapy organizations: Some theoretical considerations and three case studies. *Journal of Applied Behavioral Science*, 1976, *12*(3), 323–346.

Aries, P. The reversal of death: Changes in attitudes toward death in western societies. In D. E. Stannard (Ed.), *Death in America*. Philadelphia: University of Pennsylvania Press, 1974.

Asch, S. E. Effects of group pressure upon the modification and distortion of judgments. In H. Guetzkow (Ed.), *Groups, leadership, and men*. Pittsburgh: Carnegie Press, 1951.

Bart, P. B. The sociology of depression. In P. Roman and H. Trice (Eds.), *Explorations in psychiatric sociology*. Philadelphia: Davis, 1974.

Beck, A. T. *Depression: Causes and treatment*. Philadelphia: University of Pennsylvania Press, 1967.

Beck, A. T. The development of depression: A cognitive model. In R. J. Friedman and M. M. Katz (Eds.), *The psychology of depression: Contemporary theory and research*. Washington, D.C.: Winston-Wiley, 1974.

Best, A. & Andreasen, A. R. Consumer response to unsatisfactory purchases: A survey of perceiving defects, voicing complaints, and obtaining redress. *Law and Society Review*, 1977, *11*, 701–742.

Borkman, T. Experiential knowledge. A new concept for the analysis of self-help groups. *Social Services Review*, 1976, *50*(3), 445–456.

Burgess, E. P. The modification of depressive behaviors. In R. D. Rubin and C. M. Franks (Eds.), *Advances in behavior therapy*. New York: Academic Press, 1969.

Byrne, D. *The attraction paradigm*. New York: Academic, 1971.

Coates, D., & Lloyd, D. L. *Depressed and nondepressed reactions to others' expressed mood*. Unpublished manuscript, University of Wisconsin–Madison, 1980.

Coates, D., & Wortman, C. B. Depression maintenance and interpersonal control. In A. Baum and J. E. Singer (Eds.), *Advances in environmental psychology: Applications of personal control* (Vol. 2). Hillsdale, N.J.: Erlbaum, 1980.

Coates, D., Wortman, C. B. & Abbey, A. Reactions to victims. In I. H. Frieze, D. Bar-Tal, and J. S. Carroll (Eds.), *New approaches to social problems*. San Francisco: Jossey-Bass, 1979.

Cottrell, N. B. & Epley, S. W. Affiliation, social comparison, and socially mediated stress reduction. In J. M. Suls and R. L. Miller

(Eds.), *Social comparison processes*. Washington, D.C.: Hemisphere Publishing, 1977.

Coyne, J. C. Depression and the response of others. *Journal of Abnormal Psychology*, 1976, *85*(2), 186–193. (a)

Coyne, J. C. Toward an interactional description of depression. *Psychiatry*, 1976, *39*, 28–40. (b)

Davis, F. Deviance disavowal: The management of strained interaction by the visibly handicapped. *Social Problems*, 1961, *9*, 120–132.

Dubrey, R. J., & Terrill, L. A. The loneliness of the dying person: An exploratory study. *Omega*, 1975, *6*(4), 357–371.

Eastman, C. Behavioral formulations of depression. *Psychological Review*, 1976, *83*, 277–291.

Ellis, A. *Reason and emotion in psychotherapy*. New York: Stuart, 1962.

Ellis, A. *Humanistic psychotherapy: The rational-emotive approach*. E. Sagarin (Ed.), New York: McGraw-Hill, 1973.

Farina, A., Fisher, J. D., Getter, H., & Fischer, E. H. Some consequences of changing people's views regarding the nature of mental illness. *Journal of Abnormal Psychology*, 1978, *87*(2), 272–279.

Gergen, K. J., & Wishnov, B. Others' self-evaluations and interaction anticipation as determinants of self-presentation. *Journal of Personality*, 1965, *2*(3), 348–358.

Glaser, K. Women's self-help groups as an alternative to therapy. *Psychotherapy: Theory, Research and Practice*, 1976, *13*(1), 77–81.

Glick, I. O., Weiss, R. S., & Parkes, C. M. *The first year of bereavement*. New York: Wiley, 1974.

Goethals, G. R., Allison, A. S., & Frost, M. Perceptions of the magnitude and diversity of social support. *Journal of Experimental Social Psychology*, 1979, *15*, 570–581.

Golin, S., Hartman, S. A., Klatt, E. N., Munz, K., & Wolfgang, G. L. Effects of self-esteem manipulation on arousal and reactions to sad models in depressed and nondepressed college students. *Journal of Abnormal Psychology*, 1977, *86*(4), 435–439.

Gorer, G. *Death, grief, and mourning*. New York: Anchor Books, 1965.

Gussow, Z., & Tracy, G. S. The role of self-help clubs in adaptation to chronic illness and disability. *Social Science and Medicine*, 1976, *10*, 407–414.

Habenstein, R. W., & Lamers, W. M. *Funeral customs the world over*. Milwaukee: Bulfin Printers, 1963.

Hammen, C. L., & Krantz, S. Effect of success and failure on depressive cognitions. *Journal of Abnormal Psychology*, 1976, *85*, 577–586.

Hastorf, A. H., Northcraft, G. B., & Picciotto, S. R. Helping the handicapped: How realistic is the performance feedback received by the physically handicapped. *Personality and Social Psychology Bulletin*, 1979, *5*(3), 373–376.

Hays, D., & Danieli, Y. Intentional groups with a specific problem orientation focus. In M. Rosenbaum and A. Snadowsky (Eds.), *The intensive group experience*. New York: The Free Press–Macmillan, 1976.

Hinchliffe, M. K., Hooper, D., & Roberts, J. F. *The melancholy marriage: Depression in marriage and psychosocial approaches to therapy*. New York: Wiley, 1978.

Hollander, E. P., & Willis, R. H. Some current issues in the psychology of conformity and nonconformity. *Psychological Bulletin*, 1967, *68*, 62–76.

Howes, M. J., & Hokanson. J. E. Conversational and social responses to depressive interpersonal behavior. *Journal of Abnormal Psychology*, 1979, *88*(6), 625–634.

Hurvitz, N. The origins of the peer self-help psychotherapy group movement. *Journal of Applied Behavioral Science*, 1976, *12*(3), 283–294.

Jourard, S. M. *The transparent self*. Princeton, N.J.: Van Nostrand, 1964.

Kastenbaum, R. J. *Death, society, and human experience*. Saint Louis: Mosby, 1977.

Katz, A. H., & Bender, E. I. *The strength in us: Self-help groups in the modern world*. New York: Franklin-Watts, 1976.

Kendell, R. E. The classification of depressions: A review of contemporary confusion. In G. D. Burrows (Ed.), *Handbook of studies in depression*. New York: Excerpta Medica, 1977.

Kleck, R., Ono, H., & Hastorf, A. H. The effects of physical deviance upon face-to-face interaction. *Human Relations*, 1966, *19*, 425–436.

Krupp, G. R., & Kligfeld, B. The bereavement reaction. *Journal of Religion and Health*, 1962, *1*, 222–246.

Lerner, M. J., & Simmons, C. H. Observers' reactions to the "innocent victim": Compassion or rejection? *Journal of Personality and Social Psychology*, 1966, *4*(2), 203–210.

Levy, L. H. Self-help groups: Types and psychological processes. *Journal of Applied Behavioral Science*, 1976, *12*(3), 310–322.

Levy, L. H. Self-help groups viewed by mental health professionals: A survey and comments. *American Journal of Community Psychology*, 1978, *6*(4), 305–313.

Lewinsohn, P. M. Clinical and theoretical aspects of depression. In K. S. Calhoun, H. E. Adams, and K. M. Mitchell (Eds.), *Innovative treatment methods in psychopathology*. New York: Wiley, 1974.

Lewinsohn, P. M., Mischel, W., Chaplin, W., & Barton, R. Social competence and depression: The role of illusory self-perceptions. *Journal of Abnormal Psychology*, 1980, *89*, 203–212.

Lewinsohn, P. M., & Schaffer, M. Use of home observations as an integral part of the treatment of depression: Preliminary report and case studies. *Journal of Consulting and Clinical Psychology*, 1971, *37*, 87–94.

Lewinsohn, P. M., Weinstein, M. S., & Shaw, D. A. Depression: A clinical research approach. In R. D. Rubin and C. M. Franks (Eds.), *Advances in behavior therapy*. New York: Academic Press, 1969.

Liberman, R. P., & Raskin, D. E. Depression: A behavioral formulation. *Archives of General Psychiatry*, 1971, *24*, 515–523.

Lieberman, M. A., & Borman. L. D. Self-help and social research. *Journal of Applied Behavioral Science*, 1976, *12*(3), 455–463.

Lieberman, M. A., & Borman, L. D. *Self-help groups for coping with crisis*. San Francisco: Jossey-Bass, 1979.

Lindemann, E. Symptomatology and management of acute grief. *American Journal of Psychiatry*, 1944, *101*, 141–148.

Marris, R. *Widows and their families*. London: Routledge & Kegan Paul, 1958.

Mathison, J. A cross-cultural view of widowhood. *Omega*, 1970, *1*, 201–219.

Nisbett, R. E., & Borgida, E. Attribution and the psychology of prediction. *Journal of Personality and Social Psychology*, 1975, *32*, 932–943.

Nisbett, R. E., Borgida, E., Crandall, R., & Reed, H. Popular induction: Information is not necessarily informative. In J. S. Carroll and J. W. Payne (Eds.), *Cognition and Social Behavior*. Hillsdale, N.J.: Erlbaum, 1976.

Peplau, L. A., Russell, D., & Heim, M. The experience of loneliness. In I. H. Frieze, D. Bar-Tal, and J.S. Carroll (Eds.), *New approaches to social problems*. San Francisco: Jossey-Bass, 1979.

Rosenblatt, P. C., Walsh, R. P., & Jackson, D. A. *Grief and mourning in cross-cultural perspective*. New York: Human Relations Area File Press, 1976.

Ross, L. The intuitive psychologist and his shortcomings: Distortions in the attribution process. In L. Berkowitz (Ed.), *Advances in Experimental Social Psychology* (Vol. 10). New York: Academic Press, 1977.

Ross, L., Green, D., & House, P. The "false consensus effect": An egocentric bias in social perception and attribution processes. *Journal of Experimental Social Psychology*, 1977, *13*, 279–301.

Schachter, S. *The psychology of affiliation*. Stanford, Calif.: Stanford University Press, 1959.

Scheff, T. J. *Being mentally ill: A sociological theory*. Chicago: Aldine, 1966.

Schulz, R. *The psychology of death, dying and bereavement*. Reading, Mass.: Addison-Wesley, 1978.

Sheldon, D. M. Self-help in mental health? *Journal of the Maine Medical Association*, 1978, *69*(7), 193–194, 198.

Sherif, M. A. A study of some social factors in perception. *Archives of Psychology*, 1935, *27*(187), 1–60.

Silver, R. L., & Wortman, C. B. Coping with undesirable life events. In J. Garber and M.E.P. Seligman (Eds.), *Human helplessness: Theory and application*. New York: Academic Press, 1980.

Snyder, C. R., & Shenkel, R. J. Effects of "favorability," modality, and relevance on acceptance of general personality interpretations prior to and after receiving diagnostic feedback. *Journal of Consulting and Clinical Psychology*, 1976, *44*(1), 34–41.

Stainbrook, E. Cross-cultural evaluation of depressive reactions. In P. H. Hock and J. Zubin (Eds.), *Depression*. New York: Grune and Stratton, 1954.

Steinman, R., & Traunstein, D. M. Redefining deviance: The self-help challenge to the human services. *Journal of Applied Behavioral Science*, 1976, *12*(3), 347–361.

Storms, M. D., Denney, D. R., McCaul, K. D., & Lowery, C. R. Treating insomnia. In I. H. Frieze, D. Bar-Tal, and J. S. Carroll (Eds.), *New approaches to social problems*. San Francisco: Jossey-Bass, 1979.

Tracy, G. S., & Gussow, Z. Self-help groups: A

grass-roots response to a need for services. *Journal of Applied Behavioral Science*, 1976, *12*(3), 381–396.

Watzlawick, P., Weakland, J., & Fisch, R. *Change: Principles of problem formation and problem resolution*. New York: Norton, 1974.

Wexler, P. Peer self-help groups. *Psychiatric Quarterly*, 1977, *49*(2), 153–155.

Wortman, C. B., & Dunkel-Schetter, C. Interpersonal relationships and cancer: A theoretical analysis. *Journal of Social Issues*, 1979, *35*(1), 120–155.

Wrightsman, L. S. Effects of waiting with others on changes in level of felt anxiety. *Journal of Abnormal and Social Psychology*, 1960, *61*, 216–222.

Zung, W.W.K. A self-rating depression scale. *Archives of General Psychiatry*, 1965, *12*, 63–70.

9

COMMENTARY: SOCIAL PSYCHOLOGICAL PROCESSES IN THE DEVELOPMENT OF MALADAPTIVE BEHAVIORS

STEVEN A. KOPEL
CMDNJ RUTGERS MEDICAL SCHOOL and RUTGERS UNIVERSITY

Empirically based psychological principles from areas other than clinical psychology have for some time now clearly contributed to the understanding and treatment of maladaptive behaviors. Perhaps the most systematic, comprehensive, and well-known of these extrapolations is the application of learning theory and principles in the behavioral approach (e.g., Ullmann & Krasner, 1969). Here, the medical/disease model was rejected. The notion that "normal" learning processes underlie the development and maintenance of maladaptive, as well as adaptive, behaviors opened the door for the nonclinical researcher and theorist to contribute to the clinical arena. The early extrapolations were narrowly focused on overt motor behaviors and limited to principles of operant and classical conditioning (e.g., Ullmann & Krasner, 1965). A more sophisticated base developed with the expansion to *social* learning theory (e.g., Bandura, 1969; Kanfer & Phillips, 1970) and more recently to a formal recognition of cognitive behavior therapy (e.g., Beck, 1976; Meichenbaum, 1977). This evolution has led to more broadly defined concepts of behavior and environment (Keefe, Kopel, & Gordon, 1978). Behavior is no longer limited to overt motor responses, but rather includes cognitive and physiological responses which are observable to and measurable by the individual and/or others. Thus, the client's own cognitions and self-instructions have achieved a legitimate status in behavior therapy.

It is important to note that the early "resistance" on the part of the behavioral approach to the acceptance of cognitive factors rested, in large part, in the traditional clinical link of these factors with hypothetical constructs of intrapsychic processes which lacked empirical validation. The true strength of the clinical behavioral approach is its firm commitment to empiricism. The acceptance of the role of specific cognitive factors has been contingent upon empirical evidence of validity and clinical utility. In this spirit, this commentary on the four chapters in this section will review and evaluate the integration of social psychological research and theory with clinical psychology. Specifically, I shall examine both the social psychological research itself to evaluate the empirical *base* for the extrapolations and the evidence for validity and utility in the clinical arena. Also, I shall offer some of my own conceptualizations and clinical suggestions based upon my relevant research and clinical practices.

In evaluating the empirical base presented in this section, an historical context is useful. In the late 1960's and early 1970's, social psychologists began to note the relevance of major lines of social psychological research to clinical psychology. Much of this work stemmed from attribution theory (Heider, 1958; Kelley, 1967), Schachter's (1964) theory of emotionality, and Bem's (1967, 1972) self-perception theory. In fact, Valins and Nisbett's (1971) contribution is directly relevant to the topic of concern. Some of the major problems with these earlier extrapolations were that the research often (1) found statistically significant but clinically meaningless effects, (2) employed dependent variables of questionable relevance to the clinical area, (3) used nonclinical college student populations, (4) employed deceptive procedures which preclude clinical applications for ethical and practical reasons, and (5) prematurely suggested clinical applications prior to direct empirical testing of the hypotheses in the clinical arena.

These problems have, in general, been more than adequately dealt with in the chapters in this section. The authors have cited many clinical studies as evidence for their conclusions. Furthermore, the limitations in the research have for the most part been made explicit, and hypotheses which are in need of further investigation have been delineated. Clearly, the current efforts to integrate social and clinical psychology in this section represent a dramatic improvement from the earlier noble but rather naive work (cf. Kopel, 1975). In the interest of fairness, it is obviously clear that these earlier attempts have proved quite heuristic (as evidenced by the chapters in this book) and that an appraisal of naiveness ten years later is not necessarily a criticism as much as an indication of the progress of the field.

In turning attention to the chapters of this section, there are some empirical "traps" that can be identified. A central notion in all the chapters is that individuals are processing information and arriving at cognitions and self-inferences which have effects on their adaptive and maladaptive behaviors and affective states. In some cases where research has been cited as support for the conclusions reached, it is not clear that the purported cognitive processes had actually occurred and mediated the effects on the dependent measures. For example, Snyder and Smith assume that test-anxious individuals' self-esteem may be less threatened by the acknowledgement of being test-anxious than the acknowledgement of poor academic performance. Their research findings in this area (Smith, Snyder, & Handelsman, 1980) are consistent with that interpretation, but there is no direct evidence of this evaluative process. In general, it appears that researchers who investigate any cognitive mediating process should provide direct measures or checks on the effects of the experimental manipulations on these cognitive variables to support their theoretical explanations of their results. Otherwise, we are merely collecting data consistent with but not evidence of our explanations. This problem has been a major pitfall in cognitive research. In my own research (Kopel, 1972), I was initially bewildered when I directly assessed the attributional cognitions of subjects following a manipulation to decrease external attribution and increase self-attribution of a "drug"-induced behavior change. External attribution decreased as evidenced by rating scales; however, self-attribution remained unchanged, contrary to the theoretical model underlying this research. One important result of this finding was my realization that self-external attributions are not unidimensional, that is, they can vary independently. In another study (Kopel & Arkowitz, 1974) on role playing as a source of self-observation (self-perception) and behavior change, explanations of the results were discussed in terms of self-observed cues and inferences drawn from them. This particular study and the interpretations were strengthened by the fact that we actually checked on the role-play manipulation by measuring changes in several types of self-observed cues and showed consistent, large correlations with the dependent measures. Thus, in addition to the predicted group differences on the dependent measures, we were able to provide evidence that changes in the dependent measures were significantly and strongly associated with the variables we considered in our explanation of the results. Although this research strategy is not frequently seen in the published literature, I believe it should be viewed as a basic requirement, particularly in the area of cognitive research.

To complicate matters, it should be pointed out that in studies which do assess cognitions directly there is the problem of reactive effects. In fact, we may actually in some cases *impose* the assumed cognitive process merely as an artifact of our assessment. For example, Shrauger, in his chapter on self-evaluation, describes a study in which the effects on positive and negative thoughts of high and low self-confidence subjects were different, depending upon whether the assessment was via a checklist or a free-response format. It is certainly reasonable to suspect that the checklist may have provided information which raised cognitions that were not present prior to that point. In general, if we ask people whether they had certain thoughts or to rate their attributions, self-evaluations, or self-inferences, we may in fact be suggesting that they think about their thinking in new ways which change their report of their prior cognitions. Now that we have identified the dilemma, are we destined to remain informed prisoners of the trap and merely acknowledge our paradox? Fortunately, the answer is no. Adopting the Solomon four-group design (see Campbell & Stanley, 1966) to this research area provides us with a research strategy that not only will allow us to remove the reactive effects of our measurement of cognitions, but also will permit an assessment of those reactive effects. Basically, I am suggesting that for a random half of the subjects in each experimental condition we do not assess the mediating cognitions but rather only collect the behavioral measures.

The importance of directly assessing the proposed mediating cognitive processes in a cognition-behavior chain is crucial to the field. At times, it seems to me that the cognitive processes proposed by some researchers are so complex and inferential in nature that it is more parsimonious to assume they are more representative of the researcher's cognitive styles and intellectual abilities than those of the typical person. A good example is Storms and Nisbett's (1970) attributional explanation of their insomnia study.

Although the authors in this section have for the most part resisted the temptation of premature clinical suggestions, the reader should be cautious to any suggestions which have not been directly tested and replicated with the relevant clinical population in a clinical setting. A lesson can be learned from some of the earlier integrations. For example, the use of false heart rate feedback had been suggested as a therapeutic means of reducing maladaptive emotionality (Valins & Ray, 1967). Although this suggestion seemed to be based upon a large body of social psychological research and theory (e.g., Schachter & Singer, 1962; Valins, 1966), there were problems to the extrapolation. First, there was prior evidence that other cognitive manipulations, such as misattribution effects, may be moderated by anxiety level. Nisbett and Schachter (1966) found their misattribution manipulation from fear of shock to a "pill" worked for low-anxiety but not for high-anxiety conditions. Valins and Ray employed subjects with initially low fear levels. More important have been both the failures to replicate the false heart rate feedback effect with snake phobic subjects (Kent, Wilson, & Nelson, 1972; Rosen, Rosen, & Reid, 1972) and the supportive evidence from studies on public-speaking anxiety (Borkovec, Wall, & Stone, 1974) and test anxiety (Koenig, 1973). Borkovec and Glasgow (1973) suggested and demonstrated that the behavioral pretest was the moderating variable in these mixed results. The "cognitive desensitization" effects occurred if and only if the behavioral pretest was *not* employed. It appears that the actual autonomic arousal experienced and perceived during the pretest may override the false feedback manipulation in which the subjects are erroneously led to believe that they are not physiologically responding to the phobic stimulus. Since phobic clients typically have had many past experiences perceiving the real physiological impact, the clinical relevance of the false heart rate feedback strategy appears severely limited.

A further problem in generalizing the social psychological research on misattribution and false physiological feedback to the clinical arena is the obvious ethical issues raised by deceptive procedures, as well as the effect on trust in the client-therapist relationship. It seems that this important issue had been ignored by the early "extrapolators," in major part, because these researchers were social psychologists rather than clinical psychologists and thus perhaps less exposed and sensitive to these particular issues. As more clinical researchers and practitioners became familiar with and contributory to the integrations, the concerns about deception surfaced and the focus shifted to applications of principles rather than adoption of the deceptive procedures per se (e.g., Kopel & Arkowitz, 1975).

The concerns regarding the generalizability of social psychological research to the clinical area should diminish to the extent that the researchers in both areas communicate and collaborate with each other. The hypotheses generated by one field can be tested by the researchers in the other, either independently or in collaborative efforts. In fact, these interrelationships may be the basic defining characteristic of the notion of "Integrations of Clinical and Social Psychology." The integrations should not merely be limited to shared content, but should extend to the process of gaining knowledge.

The clinical implications and recommendations provided by the authors in this section are clearly consistent with a broad-based social learning theory view of "psychopathology." In essence, the maladaptive behavioral and/or affective pattern is seen as arising from the same processes that are responsible for the etiology and maintenance of "normal" behavior.

One common thread that runs through all the chapters of this section is the importance placed upon the *evaluative* situation and the individual's style of reacting to performance feedback, including competency as well as the drawing of self-inferences which influence self-esteem and self-concept. The notion of *consistency* appears in many different forms throughout these chapters. For example, the negative biasing style of the self-evaluation of depressed individuals can be viewed as a primary factor in the maintenance and perhaps etiology of clinical depression.

The source of this consistency and self-fulfilling process, I believe, is the pervasive training and reinforcement we all receive throughout our lives in the *trait model* of personality. The model is so widely accepted and implicit in people's thinking about themselves and others that it is used for the most part without awareness and automatically. It is useful to examine the assumptions of the trait model (e.g., Allport, 1966) to understand how people typically think about themselves and others and to understand how this process can "get them in trouble." The trait model assumes that an individual acts in certain ways because she or he has a particular trait or personality characteristic (e.g., dependency, aggressiveness, honesty). These traits are viewed for the most part as *consistent* across situations, *stable* over time, and general *causes* of behavior. Behaviors are seen as direct *signs* of the personality trait. The strength of the trait is related to the number of the signs—an additive model. "Importantly, the trait label is considered not merely a descriptor, but rather is seen as an underlying personality characteristic that *causes* the observable behaviors [signs]" (Keefe et al., 1978).

Unfortunately, the consequences of employing an implicit trait model of personality can be devastating and vicious to the individual who adopts negative self-trait labels. The most common questions I encounter in a clinical intake session involve the clients' asking whether they are "crazy," "sick," or "abnormal." These clients talk about their depression or their anxiety as if these are real entities that cause their problems. They view themselves as depressed, anxious, unassertive, dependent, or weak people and then, what is most important, they explain and at times excuse the difficulties on the basis of these personality traits.

In general, I almost always work on two interrelated tracks with these clients. First, I teach them the "explanatory fiction" of their trait model and the negative results of the use of that model. Furthermore, I teach them to use a social learning model and in so doing to "normalize" the explanations of their problems. I also stress that it is normal to have problems in life and the real problem lies in how they are attempting to deal with these difficulties. I point out the vicious cycle of being upset, depressed or anxious about their anxiety or depression and how this *secondary "upsetness"* feeds into their problem. The second track involves teaching the actual skills needed for adequate problem solving and employing various clinical procedures and techniques that lead to therapeutic change. This clinical problem-solving approach and the teaching of the social learning model of personality lie in direct contrast to traditional therapeutic approaches and theories of psychopathology.

In reading the general clinical recommendations provided in this section, I was pleased to see how frequently I have already adopted these strategies in my own clinical practice. There are several clinical cases that are worthy of detailed description as specific illustrations of these strategies so that the reader may better see how the clinician translates strategy into procedure.

Several years ago a young woman entered therapy with the presenting complaint of chronic depression. Following a comprehensive assessment phase, it became clear that this woman was in fact quite competent and was experiencing a relatively high level of positive reinforcing events. Her major problem seemed to be her overly negative style of self-evaluating. She focused on and magnified almost any negative event and deemphasized, qualified, or otherwise diminished the importance or relevance of positive events. She frequently used what I call the "yes, but" style of acknowledging a positive event or performance and then qualifying in such a manner as to undermine the potential positive effects on self-esteem or future expectations of ability or performance. Following discussions about her self-evaluation, she seemed to understand the process but the pattern did not change. I then instructed her to carry out the following daily assignment. She was to select two relatively positive and two relatively negative events that occurred each day. For these four events, she was to make a self-evaluation on a rating scale using her own evaluatory labels. In addition to the self-evaluation, I asked her to rate each event a second time, using as the evaluator, not herself, but a hypothetical person who was totally objective and totally informed about the events. The instructions included a caution to make genuine self-evaluations based upon her real feelings and thoughts. The purpose of the objective other ratings was described in terms of a comparison from which to learn how she biased her self-evaluations. It was emphasized that she should not purposely alter the self-evaluations but rather learn a more accurate, fairer frame of reference. As expected, her self-evaluations during the first week for both positive and negative events were consistently more negative than the objective other ratings. In the therapy session, we reviewed these events, making explicit her reasoning behind both sets of evaluations. Over the subsequent weeks, the discrepancy between self and objective other ratings decreased, with a clear shift in self-evaluations in the positive direction. Finally, the two sets of evaluations appeared virtually identical and remained so during the remainder of therapy. The change seemed to reflect a basic shift in her style of self-evaluation and not merely a response to demand characteristics or instructions. Although other clinical procedures were simultaneously used and thus a clear interpretation of causality was precluded, it seemed clear that this evaluation change procedure contributed in a major way to the therapeutic alleviation of depression that occurred in this case.

The innovative clinical procedure employing the objective other evaluation ratings fits well into the conceptualizations and recommendations given in this section. The focus was clearly on the process of self-evaluation. The discussions in session contrasted the overly stringent self-evaluation criteria typically used with the more reasonable objective criteria. Perhaps most important, the contrast took place in the client's natural environment so that the learning, insight, new frame of reference for evaluation, and new style of evaluating occurred in the criterion situation itself rather than merely in the therapist's office. Other important breakthroughs in this case occurred when the client replaced her implicit trait model with the social learning model by rejecting her previous view that her depression *caused* her to feel and act in an unhappy manner. In her own words, "I finally realized that I am responsible for the depression by what I think, act, and feel." Clearly, her sense of being sick, weak, and deviant shifted. There were also prior signs of a self-handicapping process that seemed to drop out as she shifted her self-perceptions and gained control over her mood states.

One of the highest risk situations for individuals who are not typically vulnerable to emotional problems is the "crisis." The acute stress of a marital separation or divorce, for example, has been a common precipitating factor for many clients that I have seen. In general, the *secondary upset* has been a major contributor to the problem in these cases. That is, the clients are feeling anxious, depressed, or generally upset about their inability to handle their emotions and the situation adequately. Their competency in other spheres may be disrupted as well. Interference in work is often due to the high level of anxiety, inability to concentrate, or severe tiredness due to sleep disturbance. I commonly hear such complaints as "I'm falling apart," "I can't live like this," "I'm weak," "I'm too dependent," or "I can't cope." Implicit in these complaints is a sense of deviance, a sense that there is a basic personality flaw or weakness that underlies the adjustment problem. Teaching clients a situational attribution is critical in these cases. The objective is to teach them to acknowledge the very real difficulty of the situation they are in and the normalcy of the stress reaction, while at the same time providing them directly with additional coping skills to enhance their problem-solving ability and feeling of competency. Recently, I have developed the "Mark Spitz analogy" to help clients overcome the fatal flaw self-perception. Here, I make the point that no matter how strong or competent people are, they will still encounter problems if the situation is severe enough. I point out that even Mark Spitz would likely drown in the ocean during a storm. I also ask clients to describe how well they believe their peers would actually do if faced with the same situation. If need be, I supply objective feedback if their expectations of others' competency are unrealistic. In many of these cases, self-handicapping feeds into the problem. For example, the individuals give themselves permission not to be responsible in the work setting because of the stress they are experiencing in their relationship or readjustment. Initially, others at work will often accept these excuses, but if poor work performance persists, then additional stress may be the consequence.

A number of years ago, a 45-year-old woman whom I was seeing as an outpatient entered a session extremely upset and agitated (Kopel & Arkowitz, 1975). She had a chronic history of rehospitalizations with a schizophrenic diagnosis. She reported awakening in the middle of the night and seeing ghostlike figures floating around her room. Her immediate reaction was panic that she was having another "schizophrenic break" and would require rehospitalization once again, despite consistent clinical signs of steady improvement and stability over the previous months. After receiving the details of her experience, my major concern was the effect of her panic regarding a "break" and the self-fulfilling process that seemed to have already begun. I then offered her a normal explanation for her experience in terms of the retinal noise of spontaneous optic nerve firings which occur when there is minimal external visual stimuli. I also stressed her drowsy condition at the time of the occurrence. I asked her to close her eyes and to see the lights and shapes which this phenomenon causes, explaining that we all have this experience. I proposed an experiment in which she turn on the nightlight near the bed if the frightening experience were to reoccur. The expectation was that the light would interfere with the normal experience of retinal noise and the figures would disappear. At our next session, she entered with a sly smile and reported that the experience had occurred again. She had turned the light on and it had stopped. In fact, she had amusingly repeated this on-off control several times. The terrifying experience shifted to a fascination totally under her control without the prior negative implications and panic. There were no further reports of this problem occurring. I believe that a rehospitalization was avoided in this case, in spite of an hallucinatory experience, because the panic self-fulfilling process was short-circuited.

Both from my clinical experience and from my research (e.g., Kopel & Arkowitz, 1974), it seems to me that corrective information gained through "behavioral demonstration" (i.e., experiential learning) is much more powerful than comparable feedback given verbally, although the latter can certainly be used to reinforce and strengthen the former. The clinical strategies suggested by the authors in this section typically involve the verbal interchange between client and therapist. I would strongly urge that these interchanges be strengthened by procedures which provide a self-observed behavioral demonstration so that new positive self-inferences arise which enhance self-esteem, self-confidence, and a sense of competency.

Helping clients to abandon their trait model and to shift their style of self-evaluation and attribution may not be sufficient for long-term therapeutic success. Feelings and self-perceptions of deviance, incompetence, and uncertainty of success/failure feedback are likely to be resistant to change unless individuals actually have new experiences from which they can directly infer normalcy, competency, and expectations of success (see Bandura's 1977 notion of self-efficacy). Thus, the therapist need be *equally* concerned with problem-solving and coping skill training to increase the actual probability of successful outcome.

Traditional approaches to psychopathology and psychotherapy generally tend to ignore the importance of problem-solving and coping skills, and the behavioral approach has, in general, not done justice to the self-perception and cognitive factors. It is clear that both social psychological and clinical research consistently show the interaction of the cognitive-behavior chain link, with each component repeatedly affecting the other, typically in a spiraling manner. Unfortunately, those with vested interests in either the behavioral or the cognitive component have directed much attention to the issue of which is more important in explaining and treating psychological problems. I believe that the chapters in this section, as well as the overwhelming empirical evidence in general, show that they are *both* primary. The most powerful way to understand and treat maladaptive patterns is to acknowledge the inseparable interaction of behavior and cognitions and to intervene clinically on both factors. If we commit ourselves to this broad empirical base to derive clinical strategies, then we can focus our energy and our ingenuity on designing the specific innovative clinical procedures that most effectively translate empiricism into therapeutic benefit.

References

Allport, G. W. Traits revisited. *American Psychologist*, 1966, *21*, 1–10.

Bandura, A. *Principles of behavior modification*. New York: Holt, Rinehart and Winston, 1969.

Bandura. A. Self-efficacy: Toward a unifying theory of behavior change. *Psychological Review*, 1977, *84*, 191–215.

Beck, A. T. *Cognitive therapy and the emotional disorders*. New York: International Universities Press, 1976.

Bem, D. J. Self-perception: An alternative interpretation of cognitive dissonance phenomena. *Psychological Review*, 1967, *74*, 183–200.

Bem, D. J. Self-perception theory. In L. Berkowitz (Ed.), *Advances in experimental social psychology* (Vol. 6). New York: Academic Press, 1972.

Borkovec, T. D., & Glasgow, R. E. Boundary conditions of false heartrate feedback effects on avoidance behavior: A resolution of discrepant results. *Behavior Research and Therapy*, 1973, *11*, 171–177.

Borkovec, T. D., Wall, R. L., & Stone, N. M. False physiological feedback and the maintenance of speech anxiety. *Journal of Abnormal Psychology*, 1974, *83*, 164–168.

Campbell, D. T., & Stanley, J. C. *Experimental and quasi-experimental design for research.* Chicago: Rand McNally, 1966.

Heider, F. *The psychology of interpersonal relations.* New York: Wiley, 1958.

Kanfer, F. H., & Phillips, J. S. *Learning foundations of behavior therapy.* New York: Wiley, 1970.

Keefe, F. J., Kopel, S. A., & Gordon, S. B. *A practical guide to behavioral assessment.* New York: Springer, 1978.

Kelley, H. H. Attribution theory in social psychology. In D. Levine (Ed.), *Nebraska symposium on motivation, 1967.* Lincoln, Neb.: University of Nebraska Press, 1967.

Kent, R. N., Wilson, G. T., & Nelson, R. Effect of false heart rate feedback on avoidance behavior: An investigation of "cognitive desensitization." *Behavior Therapy*, 1972, *3*, 1–6.

Koenig, K. P. False emotional feedback and the modification of anxiety. *Behavior Therapy*, 1973, *4*, 193–202.

Kopel, S. A. Attribution theory, self-perception, and the maintenance of behavior change. Paper presented at the meeting of the Western Psychological Association, Portland, Ore., April 1972.

Kopel, S. A. Invited book review of H. S. London & R. E. Nisbett (Eds.), *Thought and feeling: Cognitive alteration of feeling states.* Chicago: Aldine, 1974. *Behavior Therapy*, 1975, *6*, 726–729.

Kopel, S. A., & Arkowitz, H. Role-playing as a source of self-observation and behavior change. *Journal of Personality and Social Psychology*, 1974, *29*, 677–686.

Kopel, S. A., & Arkowitz, H. The role of attribution and self-perception in behavior change: Implications for behavior therapy. *Genetic Psychology Monographs*, 1975, *92*, 175–212.

Meichenbaum, D. H. *Cognitive behavior modification.* New York: Plenum Press, 1977.

Nisbett, R. E., & Schachter, S. Cognitive manipulation of pain. *Journal of Experimental Social Psychology*, 1966, *2*, 227–236.

Rosen, G. M., Rosen, E., & Reid, J. Cognitive desensitization and avoidance behavior: A re-evaluation. *Journal of Abnormal Psychology*, 1972, *80*, 176–182.

Schachter, S. The interaction of cognitive and physiological determinants of emotional state. In L. Berkowitz (Ed.), *Advances in experimental social psychology* (Vol. 1). New York: Academic Press, 1964.

Schachter, S., & Singer, J. E. Cognitive, social and physiological determinants of emotional state. *Psychological Review*, 1962, *69*, 379–399.

Smith, T. W., Snyder, C. R., & Handelsman, M. M. On the self-serving function of an academic wooden leg: Test anxiety as a self-handicapping strategy. Unpublished manuscript, University of Kansas, 1980.

Storms, M. D., & Nisbett, R. E. Insomnia and the attribution process. *Journal of Personality and Social Psychology*, 1970, *16*, 319–328.

Ullmann, L. P., & Krasner, L. (Eds.), *Case studies in behavior modification.* New York: Holt, 1965.

Ullmann, L. P., & Krasner, L. *A psychological approach to abnormal behavior.* Englewood Cliffs, N.J.: Prentice-Hall, 1969.

Valins, S. Cognitive effects of false heart-rate feedback. *Journal of Personality and Social Psychology*, 1966, *4*, 400–408.

Valins, S., & Nisbett, R. E. *Attribution processes in the development and treatment of emotional disorders.* New York: General Learning Press, 1971.

Valins, S., & Ray, A. Effects of cognitive desensitization on avoidance behavior. *Journal of Personality and Social Psychology*, 1967, *7*, 345–350.

four

SOCIAL PSYCHOLOGICAL APPROACHES TO CLINICAL INTERVENTION STRATEGIES

In the preceding section, the authors of the various chapters presented several current areas of research that illustrate the importance of social-cognitive processes in the development and maintenance of dysfunctional behaviors. In addition, a number of therapeutic strategies were suggested. This section of the book will focus more directly on research concerned with social psychological processes relevant to treatment activities. In the first chapter, Strong describes his research attempts, which span two decades, to understand the principles of behavior change. His efforts have been aided by social psychological theory and research on social influence and attribution processes. Strong's research endeavors have led to the development of an interaction model based on the notion that people behave to control each other in interpersonal interactions. This model represents an ambitious integration of communication theory, systems theory, and social psychological principles.

Recently, clinicians have become increasingly interested in common strategies, or behavior change principles, that exist across the major psychotherapeutic approaches. In the second chapter of this section, Cooper and Axsom examine whether effort justification processes may be one such common, active ingredient in many therapies. More specifically, these authors propose that the extreme effort required of individuals in psychotherapy will, under certain conditions, create pressures toward therapeutic success through the arousal and subsequent reduction of cognitive dissonance. Cooper and Axsom report several recent experiments they have conducted using "effort therapies" to produce therapeutic changes in clinically relevant target behaviors.

Spanos, in the third chapter, presents a social psychological account of a widely used treatment approach—hypnosis. He argues that hypnotic behavior is, above all else, social behavior. Consequently, it can be understood only by taking into consideration subjects' motivations to respond in terms of role requirements specified by the hypnotic situation and subjects' interpretations concerning these requirements. Spanos further argues that subjects' interpretations of the role requirements may vary because a number of aspects of the hypnotic situation are ambiguous and therefore open to alternative interpretations. Spanos's intriguing formulation of hypnotic behavior as social behavior, then, stresses the intimate and dynamic interplay of social context and cognition.

A substantial body of literature has offered support for the notion that social support systems facilitate individuals' coping with stressful life events. In the final chapter, Schulz and Decker ask what it is about social interaction that facilitates coping and promotes life satisfaction in an elderly, physically disabled population. Specifically, these authors examine from the perspective of three social psychological theories—learned helplessness, social comparison, and exchange theories—the possible processes through which social support networks facilitate effective coping. Schulz and Decker suggest that these theories not only may help us understand the characteristics and functions of support networks, but also may provide a context within which social programs and individual interventions can be evaluated.

In his commentary, Costanzo argues that social psychology's major contribution to clinical issues lies in the provision of useful perspectives rather than of techniques directly transposable to clinical procedures. He sees the chapters in this section as sharing a desirable emphasis on subject/client active phenomenology and as regarding the factors influencing this phenomenology as key to effective clinical intervention. Costanzo concludes with the intriguing extraction of four propositions implied in the chapters. These propositions would appear to have wide generality and to have relevance to much of the current research at the interface of clinical and social psychology.

10

EMERGING INTEGRATIONS OF CLINICAL AND SOCIAL PSYCHOLOGY: A CLINICIAN'S PERSPECTIVE

STANLEY R. STRONG
VIRGINIA COMMONWEALTH UNIVERSITY

This chapter is a personal account of one clinician's efforts to understand the process of change in counseling and psychotherapy. The search began in graduate school in the early 1960's. Counseling then (even at the University of Minnesota!) was fully in the grips of Rogerian thinking. Unfortunately, I found I could not digest it. My professors and fellow students extolled the wonder of change through self-actualization and saw themselves as catalysts who were most effective when they impinged least on their clients. They did not influence clients. They did not impose their values and perceptions on clients, and when I confronted clients and gave advice and directives, they were horrified and ostracized me. I quietly conformed to their norm and attempted to exercise my natural directiveness only in the privacy of unsupervised sessions with clients. In the process of conforming, I had vague insights into a powerful process of influence of therapists on clients that was effective because it was overlooked and denied. The whole process felt dishonest as I began to perceive a paradox of powerful therapist influence on clients within a context of therapist denial of influence and heartfelt protestations of honesty and transparency.

My dissatisfaction with Rogerian and analytic approaches to counseling was offset by nascent behavior therapy. I became a Skinnerian evangelist. The applications of Skinnerian principles to psychological treatment (Lindsley, 1956) seemed highly promising and refreshingly straightforward. Provocative demonstrations of verbal conditioning in interview settings (Greenspoon, 1955) implied that therapy could be viewed and analyzed from the perspective of behavior principles as a special instance of more general phenomena of behavior control and modification. With enthusiasm and excitement, I poured over the studies of verbal conditioning and attempted to build a model of counseling processes based on reinforcement and extinction principles (Strong, 1964).

About this time, I had the good fortune of studying social psychology under Aronson. I was angered and repulsed by the Lawrence and Festinger (1962) studies that purported to show that rats experienced cognitive dissonance. In an effort to find the fatal flaw of

Festinger's whole approach, I read all of the dissonance studies I could find. To my surprise and regret, I could not find a fatal flaw and reluctantly had to accept the phenomenon as real. Shortly after that, Skinner came to visit Minnesota and, in a meeting with students and faculty, I asked him how counseling and psychotherapy could be understood. He replied that the application of his work on verbal behavior and the analysis of reinforcement, extinction, and stimulus discrimination would suffice. Aronson then asked him to account for dissonance effects. I was troubled when Skinner replied, "Who would want to?"

How to apply social psychological principles to the process of therapy eluded me until I began to study tne social psychology of organizations under Weick. As he applied social psychological principles and laboratory research methods to organizations (Weick, 1965), I realized that counseling and psychotherapy were simply two-person organizations. The applications Weick made could be translated to the two-person organization. About this time, Schofield published his book *Psychotherapy: The Purchase of Friendship* (1964), in which he introduced the common factors thesis of the effective ingredients of psychotherapy. Working from Frank's (1961) ideas, Schofield argued that therapeutic change in any approach to psychotherapy was a function of relationship, belief, and status differential factors. The common factors thesis gave form to the ideas I had latched onto, and I set about the task of analyzing the process of change in counseling and psychotherapy from a social psychological perspective.

Development of the social influence point of view

That psychotherapy was a process of social influence was far from evident in the 1960's. Not only was this view not widely accepted, it was widely unacceptable. Psychotherapy was a unique encounter that was sacred and not amenable to scientific analysis (Austin, 1961). The process was to be understood not in terms of what the therapist did, but in terms of the dynamic processes of personality.

While the therapist served as an artful catalytic agent, attention was focused on how the client's intrapersonal processes changed, how the personality restructured, or actualized, in the mystical and unique encounter between client and therapist. In retrospect, it is clear that the advent of behavior therapy was a harbinger of dramatic and revolutionary change in the conception of psychotherapy, a change fostered by the training of counseling and clinical psychologists in the Boulder model of scientist-practitioner.

Acceptance of the notion of interpersonal influence as a basic to psychotherapy seemed dependent on identifying a body of solid empirical facts that practitioners would see as relevant to therapy. The then active area of attitude and opinion change through communication seemed to hold promise. As I outlined in 1968:

In opinion-change research, a communicator attempts to influence his audience in a predetermined direction; in counseling, the counselor attempts to influence his client to attain the goals of counseling. Verbal communication is the main technique used by an opinion changer in influencing his audience; verbal communication is also the counselor's main means of influencing his client. For both, these communications present opinions or conceptions different than or discrepant from the opinions or conceptions of the audience or client. Finally, characteristics of the communicator as perceived by the audience, characteristics of the audience, and the characteristics of the communication affect the success of influence attempts. These characteristics have been given much attention in both fields.

The argument that counseling was an interpersonal influence process was molded around Festinger's (1957) dissonance formulation of the factors that facilitate opinion change as the mode of choice when a person receives a discrepant communication. It was argued that when people receive communications presenting positions different from their own opinions, they experience dissonance. The magnitude of dissonance experienced is a function of the magnitude of the perceived discrepancy. Communication recipients can resolve the dissonance by discrediting the communicator, devaluating the importance of the issue, changing the communicator's opinion, or seeking other support for their opinions. Alternatively, recipients can change their opinions. Perceived characteristics of the communicator, such as expertness, trustworthiness, and attractiveness, diminish the likelihood of discrediting the communication and counterpersuasion. Involvement in the issue diminishes the likelihood of devaluating the importance of the issue. The 1968 paper reviewed the extensive research findings that documented the effects of these factors in achieving opinion change with discrepant messages. Working from the notions of Raven (1965), Schofield (1964), and Frank (1961), I was able to identify the aspects of the counseling situation that manipulated the variables of expertness, attractiveness, trustworthiness, and involvement in counseling. The analysis emphasized reputational, contextual, and behavioral cues to expertness, trustworthiness, and attractiveness and therapy components that induce and maintain high client involvement in the process that are for the most part intrinsic aspects of the therapy process. Finally, it was argued that counseling and psychotherapy could be best viewed as two-stage processes. The first stage is devoted to the development of perceived therapist characteristics and client involvement, and the second stage is devoted to the presentation of discrepancies between behaviors and attitudes through interpretations, homework assignments, empathy, directives, and other therapeutic methods: "whatever is necessary to enable the client to achieve his goals" (Carkhuff, 1966).

A series of laboratory experiments demonstrating the impact of expertness, trustworthiness, and attractiveness on opinion change in an interview setting furthered the arguments that opinion change research was relevant to therapy and that therapy was an interpersonal influence process (Schmidt & Strong, 1970, 1971; Strong & Schmidt, 1970a, 1970b). The intent of the series of studies was to demonstrate the relevance of the concepts to counseling and psychotherapy in a situation that practitioners would see as more similar to therapy than the experiments in social psychology upon which the concepts rested. The experiments recruited students to participate in studies on the effectiveness of counseling procedures for helping students gain more accurate estimates of their levels of achievement motivation, a topic not uninvolving for college students. In 20-minute interviews, students interacted with counselors who used relatively standard interview methods to facilitate students' exploration of their level of achievement motivation. At the end of the interview, the counselor expressed his opinion about each student's level of achievement motivation, an opinion that was carefully set at a known discrepancy from the student's preinterview self-estimate. The independent variables in the studies were factors of introduction, context, and counselor interview behavior that were intended to manipulate students' perceptions of counselor expertness, trustworthiness, and attractiveness. The high levels of the independent variables used features similar to traditional counseling and psychotherapy practices. The treatments intended to induce perceptions of inexpertness, untrustworthiness, and unattractiveness were extreme and unlikely to be found in practice. Such treatments included introducing the counselor as a graduate student just beginning to study counseling, revealing personal and highly damaging facts about other students allegedly taking part in the study, and remaining deadpan, unresponsive, and inattentive in the interview. The objective of the series of studies was to demonstrate that expert, trust, and attractive factors in therapy significantly affect the ability of therapists to influence clients. This objective could be achieved only by comparing traditional aspects of therapy with conditions highly dissimilar to traditional aspects of therapy. Another objective of the series was to demonstrate the utility of controlled experiments in exploring the impact of therapy processes on outcome (Strong, 1971).

In retrospect, it is clear that the studies provided at best shaky evidence of the impact of counselor characteristics on influence and outcome. They nonetheless stimulated a great deal of interest, and over the decade of the

1970's the tenets of the effort were accepted: counseling and psychotherapy are interpersonal influence processes, are processes to which the theories and results of basic psychology are relevant, and are processes amenable to experimental study and analysis.

A recent monograph by Corrigan, Dell, Lewis, and Schmidt (1980) reviewed the research on factors that affect clients' perceptions of counselors' expertness, trustworthiness, and attractiveness and the impact of these perceptions on influence and change in counseling. They cite over 100 studies reported in the 1970's investigating these issues, clear evidence of a high level of acceptance of the assertions of the 1968 paper, a later effort with Matross (Strong & Matross, 1973), and the seminal work of Goldstein (1966) and Goldstein, Heller, and Sechrest (1966). The Corrigan et al. review documents a number of reputational, contextual, and behavioral cues that strongly affect client perception of expertness, attractiveness, and trustworthiness and supports, though in a qualified way and not as straightforwardly as originally asserted, the important influence of these factors in counseling and psychotherapy.

Applications of attribution theory to counseling and psychotherapy

The studies with Schmidt and those with Dixon (Strong & Dixon, 1971) strengthened my belief that clients were influenced greatly by the therapist in psychotherapy. After all, if students can be induced to change their self-ratings of achievement motivation in short 20-minute encounters with counselors, the influence of counselors on clients in longer encounters over several sessions must be great. However, a thorny problem began to emerge: What about clients is influenced in psychotherapy? A tentative groping toward an answer grew out of an experiment with Schmidt that failed. In an attempt to demonstrate the effect of trustworthiness on influence in counseling, Strong and Schmidt (1970b) conceived an untrustworthy condition that entailed a series of gross and obnoxious manipulations. Students who volunteered for the study were informed prior to the session that the interview they would have would be confidential; yet when they arrived for the interview, the interviewer informed them that he was videotaping the interview to show to his psychology classes. As the interview proceeded, the interviewer showed an overreaching interest in the student's descriptions of self-doubts and personal faults. In the middle of the interview, the interviewer leaned toward the hapless student and in essence said (in a highly confidential manner), "Jim Jones, with whom I just talked, really has some serious personal problems and I don't think he should be in school. I'm going to talk to the dean to see what can be done about him." The interviewer then completed the interview and the student returned to the reception area to fill out a form on which he indicated his perception of the interviewer and his self-rating of achievement motivation.

To our astonishment, students did not rate the interviewer as untrustworthy. While those receiving such bald-faced handling rated the interviewers lower on trustworthiness than did those whose interviewers behaved in a highly trustworthy manner, they did not rate the deviant interviewer as untrustworthy. In debriefing sessions, several students expressed perceptions that suggested the source of their unexpected behavior. They said that they had wondered about the interviewer's strange behavior but, as they looked about them and noted the one-way mirror and the video camera, had concluded that the interviewer was simply performing a role that had been assigned to him for the experiment. Instead of seeing him as untrustworthy, they marveled at the interviewer's skill in carrying out the role and concluded that he was a very likable person with a great deal of talent! Clearly, this was a phenomenon that my understanding of influence processes could not encompass.

The results of the study thrust me back into the library to pore over social psychological literature in search of concepts that would help explain the students' reactions. In the search, I found Bem's (1965) analysis of self-perception and, through Bem, Kelley's (1967) statement of attribution theory and the work of Jones and Davis (1965) and Heider (1958). It became clear to me that Schmidt and I had assumed that people make straight correspondent inferences from behavior to dispositions and that such an assumption was wrong. Rather, people search the information at their disposal and make liberal use of discounting principles in accounting for others' behaviors.

This discovery led to a theory of the role of causal attribution in counseling and psychotherapy (Strong, 1970). The paper was written before social psychologists filled the journals with studies on attribution processes and thus rested entirely on the theoretical notions of Heider, Kelley, Jones and Davis, and Bem. The model of counseling presented in the paper assumes that people do not have immediate access to knowledge about their intentions and dispositions but rather deduce them by analyzing what they do and the effects their actions achieve. The theory assumes that people seek counseling when they find that their attributional conclusions about their behavior are unstable or ineffective in guiding their actions or create personal discomfort by forcing them to assume personal responsibility for socially undesirable actions and effects. Therapists analyze the troubling events in the clients' lives and encourage reattribution by (1) introducing possible alternative actions with different effects that would change clients' perceptions of the intended effects of their actions, (2) presenting normative information about typical actions to change clients' beliefs about how typical or deviant their behavior is and thus which acts are appropriate for personal attribution, (3) presenting different philosophies of when people are responsible for their behavior, and (4) presenting nomenclatures for intentions and dispositions that account for behavior found to be personally caused. The theory proposes that therapists' attributional efforts are intended (1) to increase the accuracy of clients' attributions so that clients can better guide their own behavior and thus live more effectively and (2) to externalize socially undesirable behavior to diminish and eliminate intense emotional reactions to such behavior.

The model proposes that behavior change results from client compliance to therapist directives as a function of the therapist's social power over the client. However, the therapist leads the client to attribute behavior change to intrapsychic growth factors rather than to the therapist's power and directives to enhance the maintenance of behavior change. The model thus resolves the paradox of why therapists deny their influence on clients and casts the denial into the role of a necessary technique to achieve lasting therapeutic change.

Generating research to explore and demonstrate the tenets of the theory of the role of attribution in psychotherapy proved to be difficult. Gray was able to demonstrate the role of normative information on personal attribution in a study of female students' self-ratings of creativity (Strong & Gray, 1972). Students in groups of three (one student was a confederate) took tests of creativity and received feedback that they did better than, the same as, or more poorly than other students taking the test. In subsequent individual interviews, the students' scores were compared with test norms that showed that they did worse than, about the same as, or better than most other students taking the test. Gray found that for both manipulations, students changed their self-ratings of creativity to mirror their standing with respect to other students.

A key issue was whether clients' self-perceptions could be determined by counselors' presentations of information about action alternatives, behavior norms, dispositional labels, and consistency of achieved effects. Matross and I (Strong, Matross, & Danser, 1981) devised a complex study intended to explore this question. We reasoned that we could explore these attributional processes in the interview if we provided all subjects with the same experience and then varied the information available to them about the actions of others, the possible dispositional meanings of their actions, and events in their lives related to their actions. When students arrived for the experiment, presented as a study of the relationship of personal history to scores on personality tests, a receptionist informed them that the psychologist who would interview them had not yet arrived and asked them to wait in the interview room. While they waited, a graduate student happened by and asked them to take a test to help complete data collection for his master's thesis. Before they completed the test, the receptionist burst into the room, informed the students that the psychologist had arrived, and grabbed away the test. After a few moments, the interviewer entered the room and proceeded with the interview. The interviewer informed the student that the experience was part of the study and that the interview would be devoted to exploring why the student had surrendered the test to the receptionist. The interview was carefully scripted so that the interviewers varied attributional information according to the independent variables of interest. In the course of the interview, the interviewers told some of the students that, while they might have refused to give up the test, very few other students had done so (average condition). Other students learned that most of the other students had retained and completed the test (deviant condition). The interviewers told about half of the students that, to the interviewers' way of thinking, the students' behavior was explained by low assertiveness. The others were simply invited to speculate about possible causes of their behavior. Finally, for half of the students in the deviant low-assertive condition, the interviewers spent the last 20 minutes of the 40-minute interview exploring events in the students' lives that indicated low assertiveness. The other half of the students in the deviant low-assertive condition were left to talk into a taperecorder about experiences in their lives that might be related to their behavior in the incident.

The effects of the information conditions were assessed by comparing pre and post self-ratings of assertiveness and by the explanations students gave for their behavior in response to an incomplete sentence, "My response to the incident indicates that I am _____." The sentence completion responses were then categorized as "low assertive" or "other." The results for the self-ratings and the sentence completion were the same. None of the students who were invited to speculate about the causes of their behavior in the incident ascribed their behavior to low assertiveness regardless of whether their behavior was presented as like that of the others or deviant. Of those whom the interviewers told they believed the behavior indicated low assertiveness, more than half indicated low assertiveness as the explanation of their behavior. More students indicated low assertiveness when they were told that their behavior was deviant than when they were informed that their behavior was like that of most of the other students, but this result was not statistically significant. The greatest effect (but not statistically significant) was in the deviant low-assertive condition with the guided review of personal history information, where nine of the twelve students in the condition indicated low assertiveness as the cause of their behavior in the incident.

The results of the study were puzzling from the standpoint of attribution theory. Why did nearly half of the students who were told that their behavior stood with that of most of the others accept the low-assertiveness attribution? As we reflected on students' behavior in the interviews, we recalled that students showed an inordinate interest in the fact that any students had refused to comply and had completed the test. Perhaps simply being aware of action alternatives that even a few take has a destabilizing influence on external attribution. In all, however, the results seemed to confirm more than anything else that a psychologist's presentation of a discrepant opinion has a powerful effect on the recipient's self-evaluation. The major utility of the study has proved to be the development of elaborate scripting methods of controlling independent variables in relatively long and complex interviews. Parenthetically, I report with melancholy that my colleagues did not believe that the study was relevant to counseling and the report languished for a decade in my filing cabinet.

The study just described occasioned yet another broad search for more helpful and fundamental ways to conceptualize the nature of change in psychotherapy. The search focused on Lewin's early work (1935, 1936), general systems theory (Von Bertalanffy, 1968), and cybernetic modeling (Klir & Valach, 1967) and resulted in theoretical statements of the application of field theory and systematic causality to change in counseling (Strong, 1973a), a cybernetic model of behaving organisms (Strong, 1973b), and a short paper on pragmatic causal distortion (Strong, 1976). The pragmatic causal distortion paper proposes that the causal determinates of behavior are multiple and are most correctly conceptualized as force vectors acting on the person contemporaneously with the behavior. Therefore, identifying the causes of behavior as either environmental or personal are systematic distortions in the perception of causality, distortions that have pragmatic utility in helping clients change their behavior. Basically, three types of causal distortions have therapeutic utility in psychotherapy:

1. Attributing socially undesirable behavior to external causes relieves clients of personal responsibility and diminishes excessive emotional reactions such as anxiety and guilt.
2. Attributing distressing and ineffective psychological symptoms to external events in upbringing provides clients with understandable reasons for their behaving in personally defeating ways and relieves emotional distress that arises from their finding out that they are personally responsible for their self-defeating behaviors.
3. Attributing self-defeating behavior to personal and controllable causes operating contemporaneously with the behavior, such as irrational ideas and languishing effort, provides clients with causes they can act on to regain self-control and achieve more adaptive behavior.

The paper outlines a system of therapy that intertwines the three causal distortions in an evolving effort to free deviant behavior for change, decrease reactive emotional disturbance, and stimulate clients to change therapeutically. A key concept in the theory is the notion that clients are the active agents in the change process and counselors guide and stimulate client efforts by presenting attributional information in the interview.

In 1976, I was invited to contribute a chapter on the social psychological approach to psychotherapy research to the revision of the *Handbook of Pyschotherapy and Behavior Change*. I plunged into the social psychological journals once again and discovered the vast literature on causal attribution that had emerged since 1970. Pittman (1975), Dweck (1975), and Weiner and Kukla (1970) suggested a profound effect of causal attribution on behavior change. Pittman demonstrated that the misattribution of emotional arousal could profoundly affect attitude change. Dweck found that a systematic program of reattribution about the causes of failure with "helpless" schoolchildren eliminated their helplessness. Weiner and Kukla demonstrated with adults that information about the causes of failure and success profoundly affected subsequent efforts to achieve. These studies suggested that a key aspect of achieving therapeutic change was to lead clients to focus their causal attributions on factors they could control, namely, effort and cognitions. They reinforced the notion presented in the paper on pragmatic causal distortion (Strong, 1976) that clinicians' attributional analyses of past actions in therapy have the objective not of increasing the accuracy of clients' causal attributions, but of refocusing clients' attention and attributions on causes they can control and thus use to achieve therapeutic change.

The theory presented in the *Handbook* chapter (Strong, 1978) conceptualizes people as cybernetic self-control systems who scan the environment, focus on relevant information, process their observations (including making causal inferences), compare observations with internal standards, draw upon a repertoire of potential actions, and act on their environments with the intention of diminishing discrepancies between observed and desired states. The purpose of psychotherapy is to present information that will stimulate clients to change observational, processing, or action aspects of the self-control cycle to increase the clients' effectiveness in self-control. A major target of information in therapy

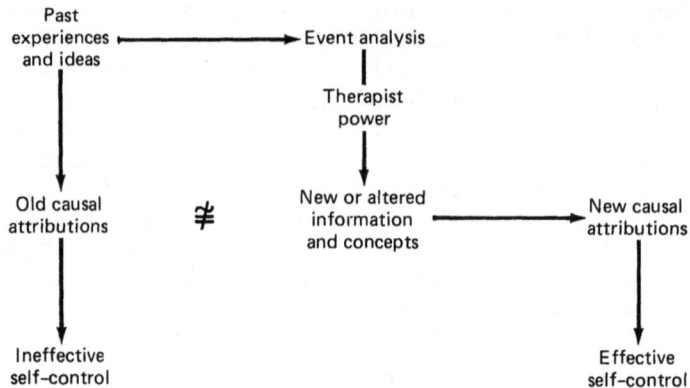

Figure 10.1 Psychotherapy change process model: New credible information from event analysis in psychotherapy which is incongruent with old causal attributions leads to changed attributions and effective self-control. (From Strong, 1978; reprinted by permission)

is clients' attributions about the causes of behaviors and situations that clients find troubling and wish to change. The theory keys on focusing attributions on personally controllable factors as critical to facilitating therapeutic change and assumes that controllable causes, such as effort, ideas, and attitudes, equip clients to act effectively in controlling their environments. The focus on controllable causal attributions is the major difference between the attribution concepts presented in the *Handbook* chapter and those presented in the 1970 attribution therapy paper. The earlier attribution theory keyed on the notion of helping clients achieve correct attributions, a concept that fell victim to the idea that all attributions are distortions of causality (Strong, 1976). Thus the pragmatic utility of attributions takes precedence over the notion of accuracy in the *Handbook* chapter.

The model of the process of therapeutic change presented in the *Handbook* chapter is illustrated in Figure 10.1. The model proposes that past experiences and ideas have led clients to attribute causes that lead to ineffective self-control. Through the process of analyzing clients' past experiences, therapists introduce new attributional information and concepts that are discrepant from clients' past conceptions. Clients accept the new information and concepts because of therapists' social power over clients. The new information and concepts, once accepted, lead clients to make new causal attributions about the nature of behaviors and events that in turn lead to effective self-control and therapeutic change. The basic change dynamic is clients' concern for psychological consistency. New discrepant information places clients in psychological inconsistency and thus stimulates clients to change to achieve consistency.

Much of the *Handbook* chapter is devoted to reviewing the vast social psychological literature on factors that control people's attributional conclusions about the causes of events and proposes that therapists should make purposive use of these principles in the process of event analysis in therapy. The principles of attributional information presentation are highly similar to those proposed in the 1970 causal attribution paper, except that in 1970 the notions rested entirely on theoretical constructs. By 1978, the principles were supported by extensive empirical findings.

An underlying theme of the *Handbook* chapter is that psychotherapy is a branch of applied social psychology:

Psychotherapy can be viewed as a branch of applied social psychology. Psychotherapy is a setting for interpersonal influence, an area of study in social psychology. The major targets for change in psychotherapy are client behaviors in social interactions. How clients feel about themselves (vis-a-vis others), how effective they are in controlling themselves (in social interaction), and how effectively they control their environments (mostly other people) are aspects of behavior in social interaction, which is the major focus of social psychology. (p. 101)

The paper ends with the observation:

Psychotherapy as a field of applied social psychology is newly born. Time and serious conceptual and research efforts will determine its fruitfulness and longevity. (p. 129)

In a study designed to test the assumption that the controllability of causes attributed for symptoms in therapy is crucial to equipping clients to change, Strong, Wambach, Lopez, and Cooper (1979) generated two causal frameworks for procrastination. A controllable framework identified the causes of procrastination to be avoidance of responsibility, lack of self-discipline, and lack of definition of goals. An uncontrollable framework identified the causes of procrastination to be repressed impulses stemming from unresolved conflicts with authority figures in the past. The subjects recruited for the study were students who said they were troubled with procrastination and wanted to do something about it. They were screened on a self-report procrastination log to eliminate those who identified themselves as procrastinators but did little procrastinating. The students identified for the study were randomly assigned to one of three treatment conditions—uncontrollable interpretation, controllable interpretation, and reflection—and a testing-only control group.

In the course of two interviews spaced one week apart, interviewers in the interpretation conditions delivered six interpretations, three in each interview, that emphasized the causes identified in the causal frameworks. The interviews were carefully scripted to control the flow of the interview, and interviewers had memorized the interpretations to be delivered and other aspects of the interviews, such as beginning statements, ending statements, and other interview transitions. The reflection interviews were the same as the interpretation interviews except that the interpretations were eliminated and the interviewers faithfully reflected the notions presented by students. Also varied was the nature of the homework assignments in each condition. In the controllable condition, students were assigned the task of establishing goals and accomplishing, between the interviews, two tasks agreed upon by the counselor and the client. Students in the uncontrollable, reflection and testing-only conditions were assigned the task of studying three TAT cards between the interviews. Students in the uncontrollable condition were to think about and write down for discussion in the second interview instances of conflict with authority figures, especially parents, that the pictures evoked. Students in the reflection condition and the testing-only condition were to study the pictures and write down anything the pictures reminded them of for discussion at the second interview. Students filled out a series of questionnaires over the course of the study, including a scale to assess the students' perceptions of the controllability of the causes of their procrastination and a procrastination self-rating form.

The most pertinent results of the study are students' scores on the procrastination self-rating scale presented in Figure 10.2 by testing time (pretest, after the first interview, after the second interview, and posttest, all spaced one week apart). The pattern of mean scores differed significantly in time between the interpretation conditions combined and the reflection condition, largely as a function of striking increases in ratings of procrastination after the first interview and strong decreases by the end of the second interview in the interpretation conditions. While self-ratings of procrastination behavior did not differ markedly between students in the controllable and uncontrollable conditions, students did differ on their responses at posttest to the question, "Has participating in this study had an effect on your procrastination during the past week or has participation had no effect?" Eight of the 12 students in the controllable condition reported that the study had led them to do

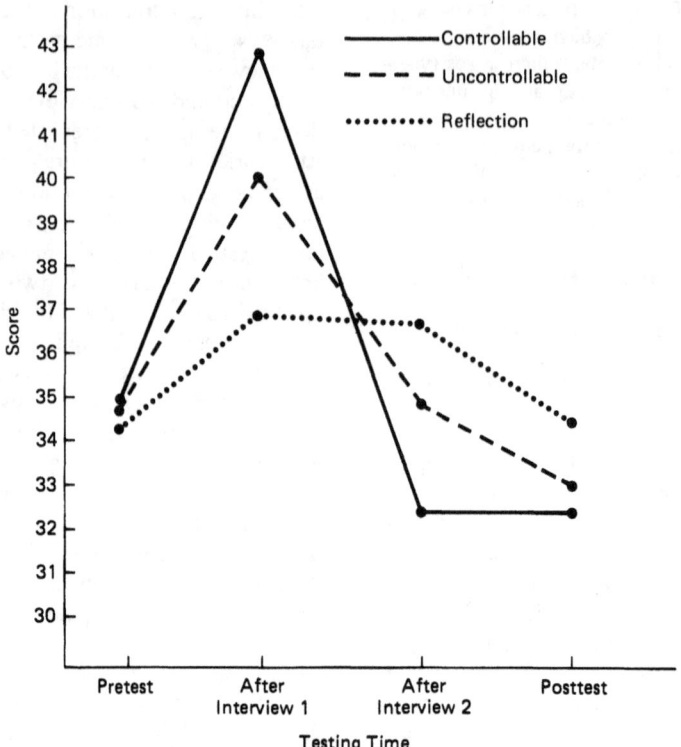

Figure 10.2. Means of procrastination scores for controllable interpretation, uncontrollable interpretation, and reflection conditions at the four testing times. (From Strong et al. 1979; reprinted by permission)

something about their procrastination as did seven of the 12 students in the reflection condition. Only three of the 12 students in the uncontrollable condition so reported.

The results suggested that the controllable interpretations encouraged more rapid and possibly greater decreases in procrastination than did the uncontrollable interpretations and thus lent support to the hypothesis of the effects of controllability on helping clients change. However, aspects of the results were disquieting about the validity of the controllability hypothesis. Overall, the controllable and uncontrollable interpretation effects on students' procrastination were more similar than different. Several students in the uncontrollable condition changed. For example, in a debriefing session, one student in the uncontrollable condition reported that he had decided that he was not going to be controlled any longer by the consequences of parental conflicts. He had sat down immediately, done his back homework, studied for an upcoming exam, and was now determined to keep abreast with his work. The reactions of this young man and others like him in the uncontrollable condition repudiated the controllability hypothesis. If the concept had been right, those receiving the uncontrollable interpretations should have been rendered helpless by lodging the causes of their behavior beyond their ability to do anything about it. Yet many of them changed. If both controllable and uncontrollable interpretations enable students to change, then therapeutic change must be a function of some factor more fundamen-

EMERGING INTEGRATIONS

tal than the controllability of causes identified in therapy.

The conclusion that the controllability of causes identified in psychotherapy was not a fundamental causal element in therapeutic change was based on a philosophy of the meaning of human behavior and the utility of research results for psychotherapy. I assume that all behavior is lawful and meaningful and can never be assigned meaningfully to statistical variation. Variation between individuals cannot be dismissed through group methods of statistical data analysis. This is especially important when the subject of interest is psychotherapy. A therapist works with one client and must apply behavior principles to an N of one. Group data have meaning to therapists only as replications over individuals, all of whom respond in the same way to a treatment. Using this criterion, any individual in the uncontrollable condition who reported that the interpretations aided her or him to change therapeutically discredited the controllability hypothesis.

Further evidence against the controllability hypothesis was obtained in a study by Claiborn, Ward, and Strong (1981) that replicated in essence the Strong et al. (1979) study. The Claiborn et al. study focused on another hypothesis, that the similarity of the content of an interpretation to client belief is a critical factor in the acceptance and thus effectiveness of an interpretation. The results of the study have been reconstituted in Figure 10.3 to allow a direct comparison of the effectiveness of controllable and uncontrollable interpretations. Students in both interpretation conditions significantly decreased their procrastination self-ratings over the four weeks of the study, and the decreases were essentially the same. Of course, without time controls it is not possible to make strong statements about

Figure 10.3. Means of procrastination scores for controllable and uncontrollable interpretation conditions at the four testing times. (From Claiborn et al., 1981; reprinted by permission)

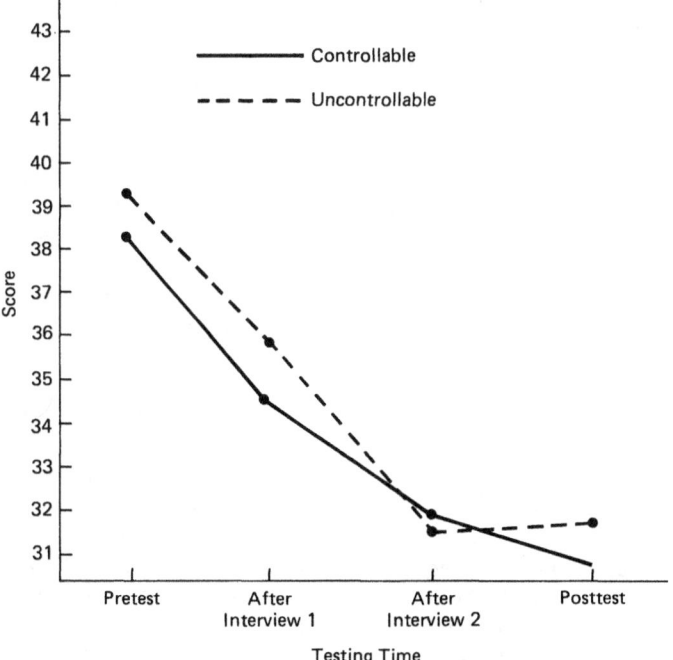

observed changes being a function of the interpretations or, for that matter, of the interviews, statements that can at best rest on a comparison of the results of the reflection condition of Strong et al. presented in Figure 10.2. It is clear, however, that differences in controllability between the treatments did not differentially affect therapeutic change.

The failure of the controllability hypothesis set off yet another broad search for ideas that could encompass the seeming paradox that controllable causes and self-control notions facilitate change and so do uncontrollable causal attributions. In the search, Lopez ran across the work of Watzlawick, Weakland, and Fisch (1974) and, through it, Watzlawick, Beavin, and Jackson (1967) and the Jackson volumes (1968a, 1968b). Their work proposes a dramatic shift in the analysis of therapeutic processes. To them, symptoms are strategies of interpersonal control intended to limit the response possibilities of those with whom clients interact, including therapists. Indeed, all human behavior is viewed in this same light, as strategies of interpersonal control emitted and maintained for the purpose of having an effect on the behavior of others. Interpersonal interactions are viewed as systems of behavior, systems that have laws and relationships of their own, and behavior in interaction is seen as largely controlled by the characteristics of the interaction system rather than by the internal characteristics of the interactants. Therapy is seen as an interaction system in which the client behaves symptomatically to control the therapist and the therapist behaves therapeutically to disrupt the client's symptomatic behavior and induce therapeutic change. In this framework, a primary function of interpretations is to disrupt the client's symptomatic patterns of relationship control.

Interaction theory

The discovery of communication theory began a two-year effort to integrate the insights of communication theorists about the nature of human interaction and change with social psychological and systems theory concepts and resulted in a theory of change through interaction (Strong & Claiborn, 1982). The theory assumes that people are proactive agents who seek their maintenance and growth through actively controlling others in interpersonal relationships. This in itself is a considerable departure from the usual views of people in scientific psychology. Learning theory and the early formulations of social psychologists, such as communication research and dissonance theory, suggest that people are pawns and responders to environmental control. People are faced with variations of reinforcement and other behavioral and environmental information and respond as best they can, conforming to powerful environmental constraints. With the advent of attribution theory, people were promoted to the status of information processors and analysts who deduce relationships and arrive at attributional conclusions using methods that often lead to false conclusions and misattributions (Kelley, 1967; Ross, 1977; Snyder, 1976). Interaction theory promotes people once again, this time to the role of causal foci of their own actions and creators of effects on the environment. People seek to control and manipulate the environment to render it to their own purposes. People are envisioned as open systems characterized by that elusive quality of being alive. People are maintained by incessant dynamic processes that convert materials and information from one state to another, processes that Von Bertalanffy (1968) labeled steady states. Even the dynamic processes of maintenance are not constant as people, through intrinsic and largely unknown processes, constantly change, grow, and increase in complexity and differentiation.

The most profound fact of human existence is that the environment people seek to control for their own ends is made up of other people who also seek to control for their own purposes. That humans are social animals is indisputable (Aronson, 1980). The implications of this indisputable fact, however, have been underappreciated by many psychologists. If human behavior is focused on control of others in interpersonal interaction, then human

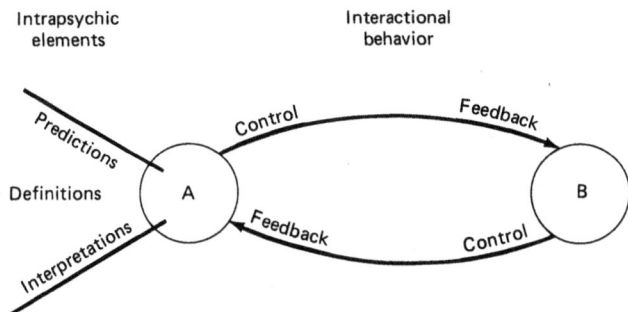

Figure 10.4. The interlocking interaction system of control and feedback between two people. (From Strong and Claiborn, 1982; reprinted by permission)

behavior can be understood best through the analysis of interaction variables and dynamics. Yet, most social and clinical theories focus on intrapersonal variables and dynamics for behavioral analysis (Kiesler, 1981). The notion that people behave to control each other in interactions is conceptualized in Figure 10.4, in which two persons, A and B, are interlocked in a system of interaction through their behaviors intended to control each other, depicted by the arrows connecting them. Each person's effort to control the other is also feedback to the other that informs the other about the success of his or her previous efforts to exert control. Feedback is processed by people and is conceptualized as processes of interpretation, definition, and prediction. Each person must decipher messages from the other, a process of interpretation. Then the feedback is compared with internal standards of the behavior the person desired to elicit from the other, conceptualized as the desired definition of the relationship. Finally, the person predicts what further control effort would likely stimulate the other to behave as desired, and the next exchange is launched. Each control effort is at once a cause of the other's next control effort and an effect of the other's previous control effort, giving rise to the phenomenon of circular causality. In any exchange, to identify one party's behavior as the cause of the other's behavior is to arbitrarily punctuate the flow of behavior (Watzlawick et al., 1967) and gives rise to the false notion of linear causality in interpersonal relations. Each control effort is at once the consequence of previous exchanges and the stimulant of the next exchange. Each behavioral event carries the history of the interaction between two people to the next exchange. As a result, person A's control effort is a consequence not only of B's last effort to control A but also of A's previous effort to control B. A control effort at time t responds to the impact of the control effort at time $t - 1$, and so on.

The intrapsychic elements of interpretation, definition, and prediction are consequences of previous interactions and the current state of the organism. Because intrapsychic processes are formed in past experiences, people behave as cybernetic systems. Their behavior is intended to conform the other's behavior to definitions drawn from past interactions, is based on interpretations and predictions formed in past interactions, and is drawn from behavioral repertoires formed in past interactions. Thus, people tend to establish present interaction patterns in the mold of past interactions.

While interactants intend to control the behavior of the other, the control exerted is only in the weak sense of inviting the other to conform to the intended pattern because the other is also intent on controlling the behavior of the person. People cannot be compelled by others to behave in any particular way but are vulnerable to others' efforts to influence them as a result of their incessant needs that must be met through interaction. Successful control of others involves inviting them to exert control using the behaviors desired by making the desired method of control too enticing to pass up and undesired methods of control too undesirable or punishing to emit.

An individual's need to control others makes the individual highly vulnerable to the control of others and leads to the observation that people appear to be controlled by their environments. The situation is illustrated by the control of a gunner's behavior exerted by a target he or she is intent on hitting. Because of the gunner's intent to hit the target, his or her behavior conforms to the vicissitudes of the target. However, when the gunner's interest turns to other matters, the target is stripped of its controlling effects.

Because people must control the behavior of others who are equally intent on controlling them, management of the impressions others have of one's personal characteristics and intentions take on primary importance in human behavior. Each party's behavior is guided by her or his perceptions of the other's intentions, needs, desired definition, strategies of control, interpretations of events, and vulnerabilities to control. Goffman (1959) expressed this situation thusly:

> Regardless of the particular objective which the individual has in mind, and of his motive for having this objective, it will be in his interest to control the conduct of others, especially their responsive treatment of him. This control is achieved largely by influencing the definition of the situation which the others come to formulate, and he can influence this definition by expressing himself in such a way as to give them the kind of impression that will lead them to act voluntarily in accordance with his own plan. (pp. 3-4).

The pervasiveness of impression management in interpersonal interaction has only recently come to the attention of social psychologists (Schlenker, 1980; Tedeschi, 1981; Tedeschi, Schlenker, & Bonoma, 1971). Impression management is usually identified with efforts to present a "good" impression. At a deeper level, impression management refers to the individual's efforts to lead others to conclusions about his or her personal characteristics that invite them to use the control behaviors he or she desires the others to emit. For example, a person presenting herself or himself as depressed does not wish to elicit an impression of capability and competence but of helplessness and pathetic neediness, an impression intended to elicit sympathy and helpfulness. In many interactions, people put their best foot forward to generate impressions of capability, morality, and attractiveness because these impressions result in enhanced ability to influence others in most interactions and thus enhance the probability of meeting needs in interactions (Tedeschi et al., 1971). The importance of impression management in social interaction can be appreciated by comparing the requirements for chopping down a tree with the requirements for persuading another to accept a date. A person about to chop down a tree need not be concerned about the tree's impressions of his or her personal characteristics and can proceed immediately to drive the axe home into the hapless tree. But a person seeking a date must achieve impressions of attractiveness and a witty and charming personality before she or he has any prospect of getting the date. Thus, a vast portion of human behavior is in service of creating impressions of personal characteristics that will lead the other to "act voluntarily in accordance with his own plan" (Goffman, 1959, p.4).

Psychological symptoms and persuasive asymmetry

Communication theorists (Bateson, 1972; Haley, 1963; Jackson, 1968a, 1968b; Palazzoli, Boscolo, Cecchin, & Prata, 1978; Watzlawick et al., 1967) assume that psychological symptoms are relationship control strategies that can be understood through the analysis of their impact in relationships. A similar point of view has emerged from clinicians following the seminal work of Sullivan (1953) and is repeatedly expressed in a recent book on interpersonal psychotherapy (Anchin & Kiesler, 1981). According to this way of thinking, therapists seek to identify the strategies and disrupt them by responding asocially or untypically to the client's behavior (Beier, 1966; Kiesler, 1979). Obviously, not all relationship control strategies are identified as symptomatic of psychological problems. Strategies identified as symptomatic are extreme, unusual, and dominant in interactions with others. People use many and varied strategies of control in interactions, and a person becomes identified as in need of help when one or a few strategies become his or her dominant method of coping with others. Symptomatic control strategies are marked by components that are personally destructive to the person, clearly the case with depression, hysteria, anxiety, helplessness, delusions, and withdrawal. Strategies classifiable as symptoms fail to maintain relationships because of their extreme nature and punishing impact on interactants. Symptomatic strategies often are presented as being beyond the control the actor. People identified as having psychological problems experience themselves as being unable to control their own behavior and thus are helpless to change or to be changed by others.

How control strategies marked by the above characteristics develop is suggested in a recent study by Orvis, Kelley, and Butler (1976). They wished to explore the attributional practices of couples in dealing with conflict. They asked members of heterosexual couples who had been living together for at least two years to identify several behaviors they or their partners performed that they or their partners did not like and to indicate how they accounted for the behaviors. Orvis et al. categorized the attributions and identified how frequently the members performing the behaviors (the actors) and their partners used the attributional categories. They found that actors and partners did not give the same causal explanations for undesirable behaviors. Actors attributed their undesirable behaviors to their preferences and beliefs, the enjoyment afforded by the activity, and circumstances and states of the environment. Partners attributed the actors' undesirable behaviors to the actors' negative personal characteristics and their negative attitudes toward the partner.

It is possible to interpret these results in terms of the highly replicated differences between actors and observers in accounting for actors' behaviors (Jones & Nisbett, 1971). A more dynamic interpretation is to view the attributions as central elements of the actors' and partners' efforts to exert control over each other with respect to the undesirable behavior. In discussing this possible interpretation of their data, Orvis et al. remark:

> We believe it will be necessary (from this perspective) to deal with perception and communication as inseparable processes and, particularly, to view them in the context of relationship-maintaining processes. (p. 365)

They suggest that a person's causal explanation of an interactant's behavior, though it must be constrained by conventions of plausibility and rationality, may not be rational, accurate, or complete in a scientific sense or even given to change the partner's mind about the particular incident, but rather is intended to change what the interactant will do or how she or he will view the behavior next time:

> At a more general level, as noted earlier, explanations acknowledge and reinstate the basic normative structure of the relationship regarding behavior. Thus, the discussion of causes, itself, acts as a causal influence on later behavior. (p. 381)

As conflict over undesirable behaviors intensifies, attributions may become more and more extreme and dominant in the relationship and become identifiable as psychological symptoms.

From the perspective of interaction control, actors' explanations of the causes of their behaviors are attributional strategies intended to resist their partners' attempts to stimulate them into changing their behaviors. Justifying undesirable behavior by attributing it to environmental circumstances and changing attitudes and beliefs to present undesirable behavior as the logical consequences of personal beliefs are the major strategies students use in studies of counterattitudinal forced compliance (Festinger & Carlsmith, 1959; Hoyt, Henley, & Collins, 1972; Schlenker, Forsyth,

Leary, & Miller, 1980; Verhaeghe, 1976). In these studies, students are induced by the social power of the experimenter and the demand characteristics of the experiment, to behave in socially undesirable ways that are contrary to their initial attitudes. The studies then explore the variables that determine whether the counterattitudinal performances will be followed by attitude change, or, more precisely, attitude moderation (Cialdini, Levy, Herman, & Evenbeck, 1973). The studies have shown that, when performance can be justified by lack of choice, monetary inducement, or revenge and when the acts do not have consequences for others, students do not moderate their opinions in line with the counterattitudinal behaviors. Attitude moderation occurs when recourse to the above tactics is cut off, for example, by the students' being led to believe that the experimenter (or others) believes that the students chose voluntarily to help the experimenter and that the act will have a negative impact on others. Under conditions such as these, performance of counterattitudinal socially undesirable acts leads to changes in personal preferences and beliefs consistent with the acts. Attitude moderation seems to have the function of averting the danger of appearing to have malevolently chosen to injure or lie to another.

The forced compliance literature and the Orvis et al. study show that people justify socially undesirable behavior by recourse to external justification when possible and to benign (but peculiar) personal preferences when external justification is not possible. These studies also suggest that, when such attributional tactics are not possible, people resort to attributing undesirable behavior to personal causes over which they have no control (Gaes, Kalle, & Tedeschi, 1978). In more readily recognizable clinical language, the three tactics of defense identified in these studies can be labeled justification, rationalization, and helplessness. These tactics occur as defenses against interactants' accusations of malevolent personal causes such as a lack of concern for the welfare of the interactants. The interactions of two people concerning undesirable behaviors, with one trying to stimulate the partner to abandon the undesirable behaviors by attacking the credibility of the partner and the other attempting to deflect such charges through justification, rationalization, and helplessness, form a persuasive asymmetry in interaction. The parties are engaged in persuasive efforts that counter one another. Their efforts are not the same or equivalent; they are asymmetric. Thus the label for the patterns of the interaction: persuasive asymmetry. Persuasive asymmetry must be pervasive in social interactions, especially between intimates. As undesired behaviors recur, interactants intensify the attack and the defense taking more and more extreme positions that become identifiable as psychological symptoms as derogation and defense become dominant forms of interaction behavior.

It seems possible that many psychological symptoms are extreme behaviors that interactants develop in their efforts to persuade one another to change and resist changing in persuasive asymmetry. Extensive recourse to derogation as a persuasion method probably is associated with negativism, pessimism, anger, and hostility, hardly qualities likely to promote healthy relationships and personal happiness. Extensive recourse to external justification is probably associated with feelings of a lack of personal control over behavior and hysterical denial of responsibility for one's behavior. Extensive use of rationalization is easily cast into the mold of pathological lying and hysterical denial of responsibility. Extensive denial of personal control over behavior due to uncontrollable impulses and deep-seated personality complexes should be associated with depression, conversion reactions, helplessness, and paralysis. While speculative, casting these research results into an interactional mold suggests possible origins and interpersonal functions of a number of psychological symptoms commonly seen in psychological treatment.

Orvis et al.'s data suggest that derogatory attacks on credibility are a common form of persuasion. In light of the importance of maintaining credible impressions in interactions, it makes sense that this persuasion tactic should be common. Most systems of psychotherapy rely on this same tactic to stimulate clients to change. In most systems of therapy, the recommended contents for interpretations imply incompetence and immorality to be the causes of symptomatic behavior. For example, interpretations that link symptoms to unresolved complexes from the past (Bordin, 1968), irrational thinking (Ellis, 1962), incomplete neurolinguistic structures (Bandler, Grinder, & Satir, 1976), and distorted experiencing (Rogers, 1951) imply incapability. Interpretations identifying irresponsibility as the cause of symptomatic behavior (Glasser, 1965; Strong, 1980) imply immorality.

Efforts to stimulate the abandonment of undesired behavior and efforts to resist change occur in the theater of the causal meanings of the behavior. Much effort in psychotherapy is aimed at arriving at causal explanations (meta-attributions) about clients' causal attributions for their behaviors. Therapist meta-attributions about clients' unhealthful attributions about problem behaviors are intended to stimulate clients to abandon symptomatic attributional strategies in interactions with others rather than to deduce "accurate" explanation and often take the form of persuasive attacks on clients' credibility. In speculating about the implications of their data to an interactional point of view, Orvis et al. (p. 381) comment:

Meta-attributions will figure importantly in the evaluation of persons. When a given explanation is not credible to its hearer, he is likely to wonder why it was given. This raises questions about the speaker's candor, perceptiveness, and rationality. To the extent that the inadequacies of explanations can be attributed to the properties of the explainer, serious doubt may be cast on the future of the given relationship. For how can one count on stable and productive interactions with a person who locates his behavior dishonestly or absurdly in the causal structure of the world: Hence, meta-attributions—explanations for explanations—will be a basic and important part of evaluation of individuals. Further, the issue of why a given attribution is made may often, itself, become a matter of open discussion and conflict between close associates.

Therapeutic change through relationship formation

Clinical and counseling psychologists commonly assume that therapeutic change becomes a possibility after a stable relationship is established with a client. From an interactional perspective, this order of events in psychotherapy is backwards. Rather, therapeutic change is generated in the process of forming the relationship. This concept of the relationship between therapeutic change and relationship formation stems from an interactional analysis of the process of relationship formation. When two people meet, they begin their encounter with notions of what their relationship should be like based on their respective desired definitions for the relationship. As they exchange behaviors, each attempts to channel the other's behavior to provide feedback that is consistent with his or her desired definition of the relationship. When both interpret the other's control strategies to be consistent with their desired definitions, the relationship can be said to be congruent and further behavior in the interaction will tend to maintain the structure and definition of the relationship. If either or both parties find interpreted feedback to be discrepant with their desired definitions, the relationship can be said to be incongruent and further behavior in the interaction will invite the other to change his or her control strategy to achieve greater congruence in the relationship. If both experience discrepancy between interpreted feedback and desired definition, both will maneuver to change the other's behaviors. When only one experiences discrepancy, that person will behave to invite the other to change and the other will attempt to counter and eliminate the person's efforts to stimulate change. In either case, behavior in incongruent relationships is characterized by efforts to stimulate the other to change. The outcome of the struggle to achieve congruence in the interaction can be changes in one or both parties' guiding notion of the desired definition of the relationship, termination of the relationship, or persistence of efforts to persuade and counterpersuade in a stable yet incongruent relationship characterized by incessant conflict and tenacious continuance.

Stability refers to the continuance of the relationship, and congruence refers to the mutuality of definitions of what the nature of the relationship should be. The concepts combine to create a fourfold classification of relationships.

[Members of] stable congruent relationships engage in mutually agreeable interaction patterns without the interruptions of discrepancy, change, [or discontinuance]. Unstable congruent relationships are charcterized by mutuality and . . . [discontinuance]. While the interaction is mutually agreeable, it is also prone to interruption . . . [due to] variations in the participants' needs for the relationship. Stable incongruent relationships are characterized by constant efforts to change and counterchange that stimulate and reinforce each other in patterns that cycle endlessly. Neither party will accept the other's proposals, and the relationship has mutuality only in the sense of the tacit acceptance of repeating patterns of disagreement and dogged determination to continue the relationship. Unstable incongruent relationships are at risk, and either one or both parties will change or the relationship will terminate. (Strong & Claiborn, 1982)

To generate therapeutic client change, psychotherapy must be an unstable incongruent relationship, characterized by efforts to induce change and counterchange, and is therapeutic when the outcome is the therapeutic change of the client. Successful psychotherapy evolves into an unstable congruent relationship. To have a therapeutic outcome, the therapist must prevent the relationship from being terminated before therapeutic change is achieved, prevent the unstable incongruent relationship from degenerating into a stable incongruent relationship that goes on indefinitely without achieving therapeutic change, and focus change on the client's behavior rather than the therapist's. Key dynamics of the therapeutic process are factors that prevent premature termination, prevent the emergence of stable incongruence, and determine who changes and how they change.

Variables that determine whether change or termination is the consequence of relationship incongruence are the dependence of the parties on the relationship and the magnitude of discrepancy experienced between interpreted feedback and desired relationship definition. Dependence of one person on another is a function both of the needs the person perceives himself or herself to have that are relevant to the relationship and of the resources he or she perceives to be available from the other through the relationship that are relevant to the needs. The extent to which a person is vulnerable to the persuasive efforts of another is a function of his or her dependence on the relationship with the other. The reciprocal of dependence is social power, which determines the extent that another can stimulate a person to change. The magnitude of an other's social power is identical to the person's dependence on the relationship with the other. Change is also a function of the psychological discrepancy between the relationship pattern that the person interprets the other's feedback to propose and the person's desired definition of the relationship. Discrepancy is the psychological cost that would be incurred by complying to the proposed change. Discrepancy and social power jointly determine the outcome of a persuasive message. The greater the discrepancy, the less likely a proposal to change will result in change; the greater the power, the more likely a proposal to change will result in change. The theoretical linear relationship between change and the interaction of the magnitudes of social power and discrepancy has seldom been upheld in research (Aronson, Turner, & Carlsmith, 1963; Bergin, 1962; Strong & Dixon, 1971) because the social power of one party on the other is never complete and thus the relationship breaks down with larger discrepancies. Client change in psychotherapy is a function of the client's dependence on the relationship with the therapist and the therapist's artful management of proposals for change such that they generate discrepancies for the client that are within the client's range of acceptance. Too much discrepancy will lead to rejection and client termination of the relationship.

The relationship of change to dependence

and discrepancy is complicated in interactions by the fact that both parties are dependent on each other. If both parties were not dependent on the relationship, it would never have come into being. The magnitude of the parties' dependencies and the discrepancies both experience are the determinants of whether the relationship terminates or continues. Because both parties are dependent on the relationship, each is never faced with the single alternative of conforming to the proposals of the other, but also has available the option of counterproposing change. Other things being equal, the person most dependent on the relationship will experience the most change as a result of relationship incongruence. As participants are more equal in dependence, the outcome is more likely to be a negotiated settlement with both parties giving and taking.

In psychotherapy, clients maneuver to gain therapists' acceptance of a relationship that entails the clients' symptoms while therapists maneuver to gain clients' acceptance of a relationship that entails clients' behaviors which therapists consider to be psychologically healthy. A major tenet of interpersonal psychotherapy is that clients attempt to control therapists with symptomatic behavior and, if they succeed, relationships with therapists will maintain rather than disrupt client symptoms (Kiesler, 1981). When a therapist unwittingly accepts a client's definition of their relationship, the relationship degenerates into stable incongruency and does not yield therapeutic change. A greater dependence of clients on therapists than of therapists on clients and a therapist strategy of discrepancy management that prevents premature termination and prevents the development of stable incongruency will result in the clients' experiencing change in the process of relationship formation.

The assumption that people are proactive and controlling suggests that change is a strategy intended to gain power in relationships. The notion of change as a power enhancement tactic is supported by results reported by Jones (1964), who found in hierarchical organizations that subordinates' conformity to organizational norms increased their ability to influence their superiors, and by Cialdini and his associates (Braver, Linder, Corwin, & Cialdini, 1977; Cialdini & Mirels, 1976), who found that change in beliefs in accord with the proposals of a communicator increased the communicator's perception of the intelligence and attractiveness of the compiler. The direction of change in interaction is a function of the needs of the more powerful party and the resources of the more dependent party. This follows from the assumption that the relationship definitions to which people attempt to gain others' compliance are the patterns of relationships that people believe will allow them to meet their needs. Thus, clients change in psychotherapy toward therapist needs that are operative in the therapeutic relationship. Unfortunately, very little is known about the needs therapists fulfill in therapeutic encounters with clients. One can speculate that the major therapist need operative in therapeutic relationships is the need to convert the client to the "truth" (Lowe, 1976). Therapists function as "secular priests" (Albee, 1977) and are committed to delivering suffering others to their versions of how life is most effectively lived. Therapists are committed to one or another therapeutic philosophy of healthful functioning, and their efforts to prove that their philosophy is correct reveal their desire to convert others to their views.

Therapists' needs to convert clients to their views of "the good life" provide clients with opportunities to gain power over therapists by accepting therapists' versions of the good life and in the process to experience therapeutic change (at least from the therapists' perspective). That such a client change yields power for the client with respect to the therapist follows from the formulation of social power. The client's adoption of the behaviors the therapist proposes provides the therapist with resources that meet the therapist's need to convert others to the behaviors she or he believes represents healthful functioning and thus increases the therapist's dependence on the client. Other therapist needs may be operative in the therapeutic interaction, such as needs to be seen as benevolent, needs to control, and needs for esteem, affection, and sex. These needs may reinforce therapeutic change or detract from it, depending on whether client strategies to capitalize on these needs entail psychologically healthy interaction behaviors.

Therapeutic change arises out of the process of client and therapist negotiation of a mutually acceptable definition for their relationship, and the outcome depends crucially on the relative dependencies of client and therapist on the relationship, the therapist's artful presentation of discrepancy to the client, the needs of the therapist operative in the relationship, and the resources available to the client that allow him or her to exploit the therapist's needs. As a client experiences therapeutic change, the power imbalance between client and therapist diminishes and the relationship evolves toward congruence based on the client's acceptance of the therapist's notion of healthy interaction behavior. But client therapeutic change diminishes the client's need for a relationship with the therapist, since the need arises from discomfort associated with symptomatic behavior. Thus, a successful therapeutic relationship becomes unstable and terminates as it achieves congruence.

Therapeutic change as spontaneous compliance

Therapeutic change is a result of client compliance to therapist demands for change. However, obtaining client behavior change during the process of relationship formation does not guarantee positive therapeutic outcome. Bandura (1978) identified three aspects of outcome to be considered in evaluating the effectiveness of psychological treatment: induction during treatment, generalization of change across situations and behavior modalities, and maintenance of change over time. Bandura comments:

Because psychological change involves different facets, each governed by diverse sets of determinants, investigators must differentiate the major subprocesses in their theorizing and experimentation. Separate programs of research are needed to identify the conditions that are best suited for creating psychological changes, those that promote generalization of changes across modalities and settings, and those that govern whether or not instated changes will endure. (pp. 97–98)

Attribution theory and research suggest that changes people attribute to stable aspects of their personalities, such as abilities, attitudes, and beliefs, generalize and endure; behavior changes attributed to environmental factors and changeable personal characteristics, such as effort to change, do not. The strongest and most provocative demonstrations of this principle are reported by Miller, Brickman, and Bolen (1975). In one of the studies they report, teachers attempted to get the children in their classrooms to pick up papers from the floor and keep the classrooms tidy. In a "persuasion" condition, teachers' interventions were of the form "How messy this room is!", "Pick up all these papers!", "How could you be so untidy!", and "You simply must be more tidy!" In an "attribution" condition, teachers attributed tidiness directly to students, using interventions such as "I am impressed by how tidy you are!" and "You are very ecologically minded and keep your classroom clean!" In both conditions, the interventions resulted in the rooms being tidy as long as the teachers maintained the "tidy room" campaign. However, as soon as the teachers stopped their treatment, classrooms receiving the persuasion treatment returned to their previous messy state. But classrooms that received the attribution interventions remained tidy long after the interventions were discontinued. Students in both conditions probably changed their behaviors in response to the social power of the teachers. But in the persuasion condition, students apparently attributed their tidiness to their teacher's insistence that they be tidy. In the attribution condition, children apparently attributed their tidiness to their own characteristics and thus maintained tidiness as a consequence of the continuing presence of the cause of their behavior, viz., their personal concern for tidiness. Such a change can be called spontaneous compliance, which is defined as behavior that is emitted in compliance to external factors but is attributed to personal causes.

The personal causes to which spontaneous compliance is attributed are spontaneous factors over which the person does not exert direct voluntary control, such as abilities, dispositions, attitudes and beliefs, personal growth, spirits acting within the person, or other more mysterious uncontrollable personal forces. Spontaneous compliance occurs when circumstances draw the person's attention away from the external pressures responsible for the behavior, draw the person's attention to internal nonvolitional causes, or make it to the person's advantage to avoid being held responsible for voluntarily choosing to emit the behavior. While the behavior is a function of the external factors to which the person complies, it is attributed to spontaneous cause forces working within the person over which the person does not have volitional control.

Research on counterattitudinal forced compliance demonstrates spontaneous compliance. In these studies, students are led to behave in ways that are socially undesirable by the social power of experimenters. The studies demonstrate that when students can attribute their actions to environmental circumstances, such as large financial payment, lack of choice, or revenge, compliance with the experimenters' wishes is of no consequence to the students' subsequent behavior. If attribution to external circumstances is cut off, students attribute their actions to internal causes, experience changes in attitudes and beliefs, and tenaciously maintain the changes (Gaes et al., 1978). Hoyt et al. (1972) summarized the implications of the forced compliance phenomenon for therapeutic practices:

Many change, growth, and therapy techniques often use social pressure to entice a participant to behave in a counterattitudinal (novel or healthy) way. The source of change often is, in fact, social pressure from the group, but every effort is made to conceal this fact and to lead the participant to believe that he, himself, is personally responsible for his independent and significant behaviors. Since most of us tend to deny the importance of social influence in determining our behavior, social pressure may be a special kind of *external* pressure for behavior change which leads the individual to (a) engage in the act and (b) infer that he is personally responsible for his actions. This internal attribution, whether correct or incorrect, will maximize the probability that the act will produce lasting personal change. (p. 209)

Spontaneous compliance occurs in situations that require that volitional control of one's own behavior be denied. Many psychological symptoms are this kind of behavior but are more aptly labeled spontaneous defiance. The victim resists others' attempts to persuade him or her to change by presenting the undesired behavior as caused by personal dispositions that are beyond his or her volitional control. For example, people who act depressed do so with the experience of a lack of volitional control over their behavior; the behavior is experienced as being caused by uncontrollable personal characteristics. Such behavior has the interactional impact of removing the possibility of counterpersuasion: people cannot be expected to exert control over behavior they do not voluntarily control. The person is doing the behavior but at the same time denies that he or she controls the behavior.

Dramatic examples of spontaneous compliance are responses in hypnosis, spiritual manifestations, and demon possession. In these situations, people respond to compliance pressures but perceive the behavior to be controlled by forces working in them, such as spirits or other perplexing and unidentified uncontrollable internal causes. Spontaneous compliance often involves emitting behaviors that are not considered volitional, such as analgesia, suggesting that spontaneous compliance can operate at a deeper level of behavior control than conscious self-control. Spontaneous compliance can transcend the limitations of effortful voluntary self-control and can lead to profound and persistent change that is experienced as change in basic personality structure.

Most theories of psychotherapy insist that

therapeutic change must be at the level of personality reorganization rather than at the level of simple symptom remission. Such a point of view expresses a concern for the issue of the maintenance of change and implicitly recognizes the power of spontaneous compliance. While change in therapy results from compliance pressures and demand characteristics, therapists go to great lengths to draw client attention away from these pressures and avoid providing explicit justifications for change in therapy. Therapeutic dictums that therapists never tell clients what to do, never give advice, and never directly tell clients to stop symptomatic behaviors avoid giving clients external justifications to account for induced change. The dictums function to allow personal attributions for change and thus help generate generalized and persistent therapeutic change.

Spontaneous compliance as therapeutic change is generated in psychotherapy through negation and affirmation paradoxes. The negation paradox induces the elimination of symptoms as a spontaneous event, and the affirmation paradox induces healthy interaction behaviors that are experienced as spontaneous expressions of changes in the deeper personality. The negation paradox is operationalized by therapist interventions that seem to encourage client symptomatic behaviors within a context that requires their elimination. Jackson and Haley (1968) have pointed out the importance to therapeutic outcome of the practice Freud introduced of being permissive and accepting of symptomatic behaviors. Therapist interest in the client's symptomatic behavior, shown in attending, reflecting, questioning, and commenting, encourages the client to use symptomatic control tactics in the interaction. However, the context of therapy is that its purpose is to eliminate symptoms, and other therapeutic interventions, such as interpretations and other means of responding asocially and untypically (Beier, 1966) to the client, serve to disrupt the controlling impact of symptomatic behaviors. Yet, as the disrupting and contextual aspects of therapy succeed in eliminating symptomatic behaviors, the elimination of the symptoms occurs in the face of the therapist's seeming encouragement of symptom expression. Thus, the elimination of the symptoms cannot be attributed to the therapist's demands that the symptoms cease and so the client necessarily attributes symptom remission to spontaneous causes.

More recently, therapeutic techniques have been introduced that are more explicit about encouraging symptom expression in the therapeutic interaction than are the more subtle attention and permissiveness techniques of traditional practices. Gestalt therapists direct clients to perform symptoms in extreme and exaggerated forms and at the same time refuse to respond to the symptoms with sympathy and rescue, responses that symptomatic behavior is typically expected to evoke in interactants (Eshbaugh, 1976). Jackson and his colleagues (Jackson, 1968a, 1968b; Watzlawick et al., 1967) have introduced the notion of symptom assignment where clients are directed to perform symptoms in intense and exaggerated forms in the interview and in homework between interviews. Palazzoli et al. (1978) and others (Haley, 1978; Minuchin, 1974) have introduced the notion of interpreting symptoms in positive terms and thus seemingly encouraging symptom continuance through reframing them as positive and healthful behaviors. These are explicit applications of the negation paradox, and clinical evidence attests to their effectiveness in stimulating the elimination of symptoms (L'Abate & Weeks, 1978). Such blatant tactics should generate attributions of therapeutic change to powerful personal factors and thus generate highly stable therapeutic change. They explicitly deny clients evidence of situational demands for the elimination of symptoms. Clients are faced with having changed in spite of the therapists' insistence that they not change. What conclusion remains but that the personal factors responsible for change are so powerful that they overrode compliance to the therapists' demands?

The effectiveness of explicit methods of presenting the negation paradox to generate therapeutic change has been assessed in a recent series of studies of brief psychotherapy

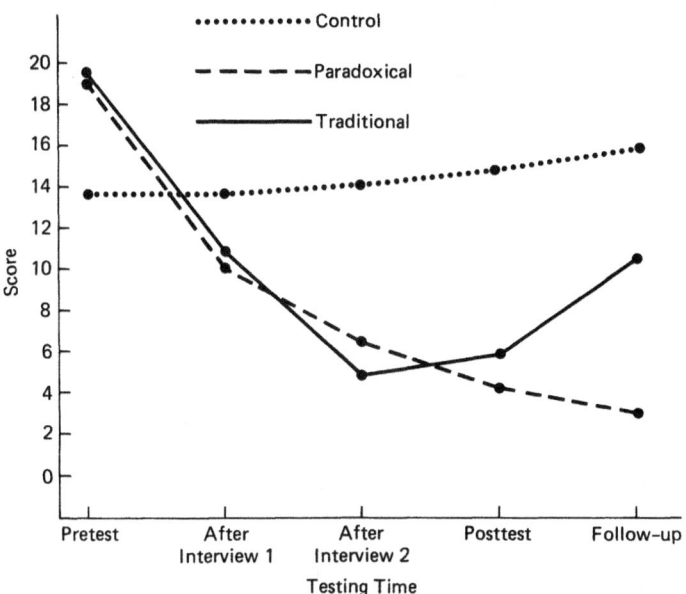

Figure 10.5. Means of scores on the Beck Depression Inventory for the paradoxical interpretation, traditional interpretation, and control conditions at the five testing times. (From Beck and Strong, 1981; reprinted by permission)

(Beck & Strong, 1981; Lopez & Wambach, in press; Wright & Strong, in press). In these studies, students who were moderately depressed (Beck & Strong) or were procrastinators (Lopez & Wambach; Wright & Strong) and wished to change were recruited for studies on the effectiveness of brief counseling and psychotherapy methods. Beck and Strong solicited student volunteers who were moderately depressed as measured on the Beck Depression Inventory. The students experience two 40-minute interviews spaced one week apart and were assessed on the BDI during treatment, one week after treatment, and one month later. The students were randomly assigned to one of three conditions: a testing-only control, a traditional interpretation treatment, and a paradoxical interpretation treatment. The interviews were carefully scripted and differed only in the interpretations the interviewers gave in the treatments. In the traditional interpretation treatment, interviewers interpreted depression symptoms as reflecting irrational and idiosyncratic thinking, basic avoidance and rejection of others, and passive-aggressive punishment of others. In the paradoxical treatments, interviewers interpreted depression symptoms as reflecting great tolerance for solitude, the good fortune of being aware of feelings, and a willingness to sacrifice for the sake of others. These students were seen as choosing to feel badly about themselves rather than to take their grievances out on others and thus as suffering personally rather than causing others to suffer.

The major results of the treatments are presented in Figure 10.5. Students in both interview treatment conditions strongly and significantly decreased their self-ratings of depression on the BDI during the treatment period. Of greatest significance was the impact of the treatments on the maintenance of change after treatment was discontinued. At a one-month follow-up, it was found that students who had received the traditional treatment had experienced considerable symptom relapse but students who had received the

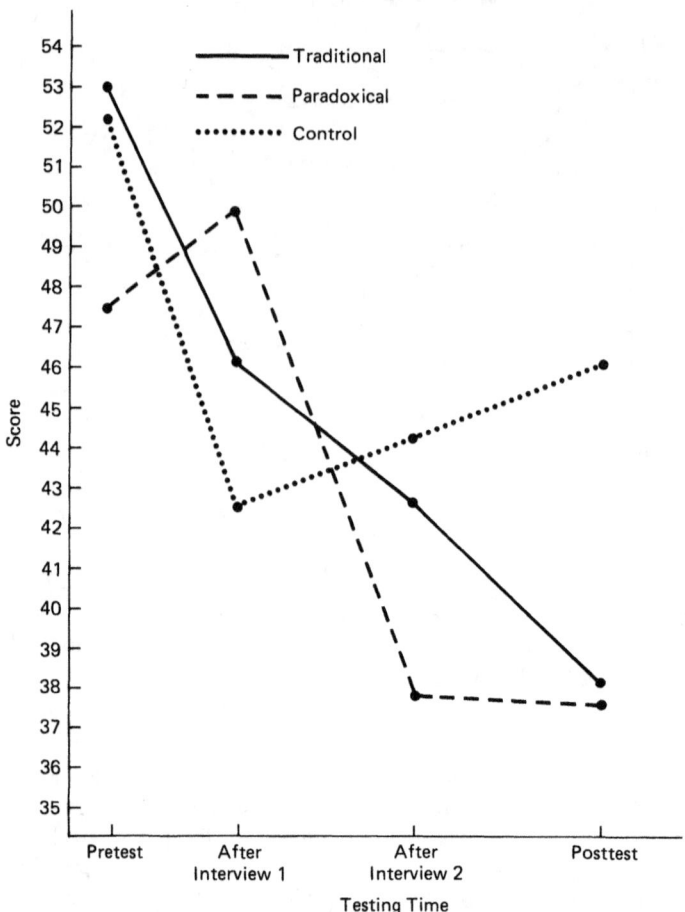

Figure 10.6. Means of procrastination scores for the traditional directive, paradoxical directive, and control conditions at the four testing times. (From Lopez & Wambach, 1982; reprinted by permission)

paradoxical treatment had continued to experience symptom remission.

Lopez and Wambach (in press) and Wright and Strong (in press) explored the effectiveness of directives to continue symptomatic behavior in facilitating the remission of symptoms in the context of two interview interventions with procrastinators. Lopez and Wambach randomly assigned students to three conditions, a testing-only control condition, a traditional directive condition, and a paradoxical directive condition. In the paradoxical directive condition, interviewers directed students to continue procrastinating by taking out their books and steadfastly not studying for 30 minutes each day between interviews. In the traditional directive conditions, students were directed to take out their books and study as much as possible each day between interviews.

The impact of the treatments on the students' self-ratings of procrastination is presented in Figure 10.6. Both the directive to stop procrastinating and that to continue procrastinating resulted in decreases in self-rated procrastination that were significantly greater than the decreases reported by students in the testing-only control condition. Lopez and Wambach included only a one-week-later posttest and thus did not directly test the maintenance hypothesis. A point possibly related to maintenance is that students in the traditional directive condition increased their ratings on a controllability scale between pretesting and posttesting but students in the paradoxical condition did not, suggesting that students in the traditional condition came to believe more strongly that they could willfully control their procrastination. Students in the paradoxical condition did not indicate that they experienced greater personal control of procrastination even though they decreased their procrastination. We can speculate that the students in the paradoxical condition were left without explanation for their decreased procrastination behavior and might have attributed the change to personal causes. If so, we would expect greater maintenance of decreased procrastination.

Wright and Strong compared the effects of two forms of paradoxical directives on procrastination behavior. The directives differed from those of Lopez and Wambach in that the interviewers first learned exactly how the students procrastinated and, at the end of each of the two interviews, assigned the students the task of maintaining these specific behaviors. The study had three conditions: a testing-only control and two directive conditions. In one directive condition, students were told to continue exactly the same procrastination behaviors that they reported in the interview. In the other directive condition, students were told to continue *some* of their procrastination behaviors, whichever ones they chose. The guiding hypothesis of the study was that the perception of choice would increase student compliance with the directive and thus lead to continuance of procrastination rather than defiance and discontinuance as expected with the "exactly the same" directive.

The results of the directives on procrastination behavior self-ratings are presented in Figure 10.7. Students in both directive conditions decreased their self-ratings of procrastination behavior over the period of the experiment significantly more than did students in the testing-only condition. While students in the "choice" condition decreased their procrastination somewhat less than those in the "exactly the same" condition, the difference was far from significant. Unfortunately, Wright and Strong did not include a longer-term follow-up (the last measure was one week after the second interview) and thus did not directly test the maintenance hypothesis. Student responses to questions at the posttest suggest that the "exactly" condition students might have experienced a stronger maintenance effect than the "choice" condition students in that the former tended to exclaim their astonishment at the disappearance of procrastination whereas the latter emphasized choice and effort as responsible for decreases in procrastination. For example, one student in the "exactly" condition wrote:

Amazingly I didn't have to work at it—I was told to observe and for some reason I had a very difficult time procrastinating. Especially the second time around—the study was a success.

Taken as a whole, the three studies document the effectiveness of explicit paradoxical techniques in operationalizing the negation paradox and stimulating symptom remission. Beck and Strong directly, and Lopez and Wambach and Wright and Strong indirectly, provide evidence that encouraging the continuance of symptomatic behavior increases the maintenance of symptom remission, possibly by removing identifiable situational cues that would allow the attribution of change to external and effortful causes and encouraging attribution of change to stable personal causes.

In the affirmation paradox, clients are induced to adopt healthy interaction behavior as a spontaneous expression of their deeper personalities. Adoption of healthy interactional behavior requires that therapists (1) present desired behavior and insist that the behavior be adapted as part of the definition of the relationship, (2) identify an internal process or agent responsible for change that acts beyond the client's volitional control, and (3) communicate that the change is a result of the internal process or agent. Desired behavior is

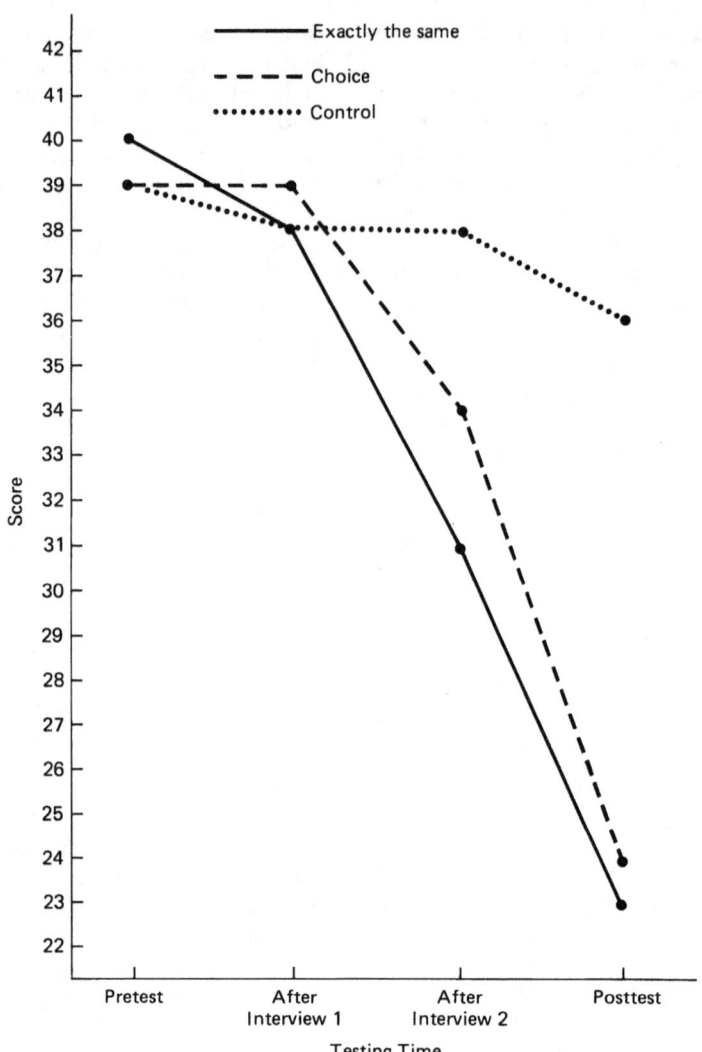

Figure 10.7. Means of procrastination scores for "exactly the same" directive, "choice" directive, and control conditions at the four testing times. (From Wright & Strong, 1982; reprinted by permission)

presented through interpretations, therapist self-disclosures, examples of others, metaphors, reflections, questions, verbal reinforcement, direct instruction about how the client should think and react in situations, and therapist's modeling of desired behaviors. The role of the therapist as a model is probably significant and powerful. How therapists react to clients, view events, and present themselves is a potent force in molding client behavior. The pattern of desired behavior adopted by the client is to a great extent idiosyncratic to each therapist, though ideas of desired behaviors are widely shared by therapists as a result of common allegiances to particular schools of therapy and general convergence among therapists on ideas about sound relationship behavior (Fiedler, 1950).

It is not enough for clients to adopt the behaviors desired by therapists. Generalization and maintenance require that clients be induced to adopt the desired behaviors as spontaneous expressions of their basic characteristics, and thus the source of change needs to be presented as some internal agent of change, such as the actualizing self, emerging rationality, released psychological energy from resolved complexes, basic responsibility, the spirit of God acting in the person, or magnetic forces. In systems of psychotherapy, the same agents are presented as responsible for both the removal of symptoms and the enstatement of desired behavior. Unfortunately, there is no research on the affirmation paradox.

The structure of psychotherapy

The therapist initiates the therapeutic encounter by inquiring about why the client has come to therapy. In the first few minutes, the basic structure of therapy is formed with clients' describing the problems in living that led them to seek therapy and therapists' listening and commenting to facilitate client descriptions. In the initial encounter, the therapist enters the client's system and accepts aspects of the client's definition of their relationship. Van Der Veen (1965) and others (Moos & MacIntosh, 1970; Ruzicka & Naun, 1976) have shown that, in the initial encounter, different therapists behave more similarly to one another in interacting with a particular client than do different clients in interacting with a particular therapist. Crowder (1972) documented the role difference between client and therapist in the encounter. He analyzed the interview transcripts of 25 therapist-client pairs over nine or more sessions and found that most client responses were support-seeking, passive-resistive, and hostile-competitive while very few were supportive-interpretative. In contrast, 90 percent of therapist responses were supportive-interpretative and none were support-seeking. The therapist directly and indirectly induces the client into the client role during the initial encounter. Lennard and Bernstein (1960), in a study of eight therapist-client pairs over long-term therapy, found that therapist behaviors characterized as "orientation" (asking for and giving repetitions, clarifications, and confirmations) accounted for nearly 70 percent of the therapists' propositions during the initial period of therapy and diminished in frequency as therapy continued.

An initial purpose in the encounter is to identify the clients' symptomatic interaction behaviors from descriptions of the troubling events in the clients' lives and by evoking the troubling behavior patterns in the here-and-now encounter. A major source of diagnosis is the therapists' awareness of the pattern of interaction behavior that the clients' behavior evokes from the therapists (Kiesler, 1979). Clients' symptomatic behaviors are intended to control interactants, and thus the behaviors therapists find themselves doing, thinking, and feeling are a rich source of information about clients' symptoms.

Therapy begins as a complementary relationship (Haley, 1968), with therapists overtly in charge and clients depending on therapists for directions and solutions. Therapists quickly convert their complementary control of their relationships with clients to meta-complementary control: Therapists place clients in overt charge of the encounter. Thus, in a relationship in which the therapist is clearly in charge, the therapist places the client in charge. The maneuver places the client's efforts to gain control of the therapist within the permissive authority of the therapist and eliminates the potential that the client will gain symmetry or equality with the therapist. If the client were to gain a symmetrical relationship with the therapist, the therapist's ability to gain client's compliance to the therapist's definition of the relationship would be seriously impaired and therapeutic change would not be likely to emerge from the encounter. The therapist's meta-complementary control of the relationship sets the stage for spontaneous compliance for, while the client is vulnerable to the therapist's insistence that the client adopt the therapist's definition of the relationship, such adoption occurs within the context of apparent client control of the relationship. Thus the client is rendered personally responsible for changing.

Therapist meta-complementary control eliminates the client's ability to comment on the therapist's behavior, that is, to meta-communicate about the therapist's statements. In carrying out the negation and affirmation paradoxes, therapist communications are contradictory in that they direct the client to spontaneously do as the therapist demands (Hodges & Brandt, 1978). Contradictory communications are successful in creating spontaneous compliance only when meta-communication about their contradictory nature is banned in the relationship. The structure of therapy is a double bind (Bateson, Jackson, Haley, & Weakland, 1968). The client is required to comply to the therapist's demands for change and to attribute the compliance to spontaneous personal causes, is prevented from breaking the bind by commenting on the therapist's contradictory communications, and is prevented from leaving the situation because of his or her dependence and the therapist's careful management of discrepancy. Lennard and Bernstein (1960) provide striking evidence of the development of an implicit ban on client meta-communication in the relationship. They found that, in the first session, comments on the therapist-client interchange were initiated by clients in one out of six occurrences. By the third month of therapy, clients initiated such meta-communications only once out of 33 occasions.

A probable consequence of the intense focus in the therapeutic relationship on client processes is the induction in the client of a heightened state of objective self-awareness. Duval and Wicklund (1972) introduced the notion of objective self-awareness and differentiated it from an alternative state, subjective self-awareness. In most circumstances, people focus their attention on their environment and are aware of themselves only subjectively as actors. However, when people turn their attention to themselves as the object of attention, they view their behavior much as do other observers (Jones & Nisbett, 1971) and as a consequence are inclined to attribute their actions to personal causes rather than external causes. Wicklund (1975) has reviewed research results that show that people in a state of objective self-awareness experience enhanced consistency between attitudes and actions and higher conformity to reference group standards. The structure of therapy probably generates objective self-awareness and thus enhances client susceptibility to therapist interventions and enhances generalization of therapeutic change across behavior modalities and situations.

Client's enhanced susceptibility to the evaluations of reference groups (and therapists are the most important point of reference in therapy) occurs in the context of an attributional set of the therapist's that assigns undesired client behavior to external causes, factors and desired behaviors to stable personal dispositions. Gould and Sigall (1977) found that observers instructed to empathize with an actor automatically adopted such an attributional pattern. Passer, Kelley, and Michela (1978) found that the single most important factor in determining the pattern of causal attribution observers use to account for the behavior of actors is their positive or negative feelings about the actor. At the positive pole of the affect dimension, observers attribute disliked behavior to external causes and liked behavior to the personal characteristics of the actor. The pattern of attribution is the opposite at the negative pole. The effect of observers' affective evaluations on the causes observers attribute for actors' desired and undesired behaviors has been demonstrated in laboratory experiments with students (Regan, Straus, & Fazio, 1974), marital pairs (Goffman, Notarius, Markman, Bank, & Yoppi, 1976), and adults in interactions with children (Messé, Stollak, Larson, & Michaels, 1979). The therapist's empathy set operationalizes the basic causal tenets of the negation and affirmation paradoxes in that undesired behavior is attributed (ultimately) to external factors and thus rendered vulnerable to change and desired behaviors are attributed to the client's personal dispositions and thus rendered likely to generalize and be maintained in the long run. Because the empathy set underlies all therapist communications, the basic attributional pattern necessary for therapeutic spontaneous compliance is relentlessly reinforced throughout the therapeutic encounter. The combination of the controlled structure of the interchange, the attention focus on the client, and the therapist's positive empathic attitude toward the client "create[s] client focus on self, client self-disclosure, and therapeutic behavior change, such as Rogers (1957) postulated it would" (Strong & Claiborn, 1982).

As therapists diagnose clients' symptomatic patterns of interaction, they initiate asocial interventions such as interpretations, directives, and instructions aimed at disrupting the symptom patterns. The asocial (untypical) interventions intensify the forces of change that are initiated by the basic therapeutic structural features of role, control, objective self-awareness, and empathy. The structural features continue throughout therapy and are the core facilitative factors in generating therapeutic change. The use of asocial therapeutic interventions requires artful management of discrepancy generation within clients' toleration for discrepancy based on their dependency on the relationship. These therapist interventions fully operationalize the negation and affirmation paradoxes; and therapeutic change is steadily nourished by the therapists' abiding need to convert clients to the truth.

As clients accept therapists' invitation to control the relationship with healthy interaction behavior, they steadily experience less discrepancy and gain increasing power over therapists. At the same time, therapist power over clients steadily diminishes as the needs for the relationship associated with the symptom pattern diminish. As the relative power of the two participants equalizes, the relationship becomes symmetric. As power equalizes, therapists begin to respond to clients with remarks about themselves rather than focusing their remarks on the clients, and thus therapists relinquish meta-complementary and complementary control of the relationship. As is typical of structured interactions between friends (Albert & Kessler, 1978), therapy is terminated with summaries of the learnings from the interaction by both parties, discussion of plans for possible future contact, exchange of warm appreciation, and parting thanks-giving (Bieber, Patton, & Fuhriman, 1977). The now unstable relationship terminates just as it achieves congruence.

Epilogue

In this chapter, I have described my journey over two decades in search of an understanding of therapeutic processes. The journey has been spurred continuously by the development in experimental social psychology of concepts that seem more applicable to therapeutic processes. The journey has been marked with repeated attempts to build a comprehensive model of therapeutic processes. Each model in turn has collapsed under the weight of the failure of experiments intended to demonstrate the truth of the main tenets of the model. The interaction model, representing the merger of communication theory, systems theory, and social psychological principles, seems to tap many of the processes of the therapeutic encounter, and I am encouraged to think that it has some glimmer of truth about it. Yet, I have no doubt that it, too, will fall victim to empirical test and its failure will stimulate yet another attempt to integrate the pieces into a comprehensive theory. There can be no other outcome for a restless scientist-practitioner thrashing about in the dark in search of truth.

References

Albee, G. W. The protestant ethic, sex, and psychotherapy. *American Psychologist*, 1977, *32*, 150–161.

Albert, S., & Kessler, S. Ending social encounters. *Journal of Experimental Social Psychology*, 1978, *14*, 541–553.

Anchin, J. C., & Kiesler, D. J. (Eds.). *Handbook of interpersonal psychotherapy*. New York: Pergamon, 1981.

Aronson, E. *The social animal* (3rd edn.). San Francisco: Freeman, 1980.

Aronson, E., Turner, J., & Carlsmith, J. M. Communicator credibility and communication discrepancy as determinants of opinion change. *Journal of Abnormal and Social Psychology*, 1963, *67*, 31–36.

Austin, A. W. The functional autonomy of psychotherapy. In J. R. Braun (Ed.), *Clinical psychology in transition*. Cleveland: Howard Allen, 1961.

Bandler, R., Grinder, J., & Satir, V. *Changing with families*. Palo Alto: Science and Behavior Books, 1976.

Bandura, A. On paradigms and recycled ideologies. *Cognitive Therapy and Research*, 1978, *2*, 79–103.

Bateson, G. *Steps to an ecology of mind*. New York: Ballantine Books, 1972.

Bateson, G., Jackson, D. D., Haley, J., & Weakland, J. H. Toward a theory of schizophrenia. In D. D. Jackson (Ed.), *Communication, family and marriage: Human communication* (Vol. 1). Palo Alto: Science and Behavior Books, 1968.

Beck, J. T., & Strong, S. R. *Positive Connotation: Stimulating therapeutic change with paradoxical interpretations*. Unpublished manuscript, Virginia Commonwealth University, 1981.

Beier, E. G. *The silent language of psychotherapy*. Chicago: Aldine, 1966.

Bem, D. J. An experimental analysis of self-persuasion. *Journal of Experimental Social Psychology*, 1965, *1*, 129–218.

Bergin, A. E. The effect of dissonant persuasive communications upon changes in a self-referring attitude. *Journal of Personality*, 1962, *30*, 423–438.

Bieber, M. R., Patton, M. J., & Fuhriman, A. J. A meta language analysis of counselor and client verb usage in counseling. *Journal of Counseling Psychology*, 1977, *24*, 264–271.

Bordin, E. S. *Psychological counseling* (2nd edn.). New York: Appleton-Century-Crofts, 1968.

Braver, S. L., Linder, D. E., Corwin, T. T., & Cialdini, R. B. Some conditions that affect admissions of attitude change. *Journal of Experimental Social Psychology*, 1977, *13*, 565–576.

Carkhuff, R. R. Counseling research, theory, and practice—1965. *Journal of Counseling Psychology*, 1966, *13*, 467–480.

Cialdini, R. B., Levy, A., Herman, C. R., & Evenbeck, C. Attitude politics: The strategy of moderation. *Journal of Personality and Social Psychology*, 1973, *25*, 100–108.

Cialdini, R. B., & Mirels, H. L. Sense of personal control and attributions about yielding and resisting persuasive targets. *Journal of Personality and Social Psychology*, 1976, *33*, 395–402.

Claiborn, C. D., Ward, S. R., & Strong, S. R. Effects of congruence between counselor interpretations and client beliefs. *Journal of Counseling Psychology*, 1981, *28*, 101–109.

Corrigan, J. B., Dell, D. M., Lewis, K. N., & Schmidt, L. D. Counseling as a social influence process: A review. *Journal of Counseling Psychology*, 1980, *27*, 395–441.

Crowder, J. E. Relationship between therapist and client interpersonal behaviors and psychotherapy outcome. *Journal of Counseling Psychology*, 1972, *19*, 68–75.

Duval, S., & Wicklund, R. A. *A theory of objective self-awareness*. New York: Academic Press, 1972.

Dweck, C. S. The role of expectations and attributions in the alleviation of learned helplessness. *Journal of Personality and Social Psychology*, 1975, *31*, 674–685.

Ellis, A. *Reason and emotion in psychotherapy*. New York: Lyle Stuart, 1962.

Eshbaugh, R. N. Frustration, fun and folly. In C. Hatcher & P. Himelstein (Eds.), *The Handbook of gestalt therapy*. New York: Jason Aronson, 1976.

Festinger, L. *A theory of cognitive dissonance*. Evanston, Ill.: Row, Peterson, 1957.

Festinger, L. A., & Carlsmith, J. M. Cognitive consequences of forced compliance. *Journal of Abnormal and Social Psychology* 1959, *58*, 203–210.

Fiedler, F. The concept of an ideal therapeutic relationship. *Journal of Consulting Psychology*, 1950, *14*, 239–245.

Frank, J. D. *Persuasion and healing*. Baltimore: Johns Hopkins, 1961.

Gaes, G. G., Kalle, R. J., & Tedeschi, J. T. Impression management in the forced compliance situation. *Journal of Experimental Social Psychology*, 1978, *14*, 439–510.

Glasser, W. *Reality therapy: A new approach to psychiatry*. New York: Harper & Row, 1965.

Goffman, E. *The presentation of self in everyday life*. Garden City, N.Y.: Doubleday, 1959.

Goffman, J., Notarius, C., Markman, H., Bank, S., Yoppi, B., & Rubin, M. E. Behavior exchange theory and marital decision making. *Journal of Personality and Social Psychology*, 1976, *34*, 14–23.

Goldstein, A. P. Psychotherapy research by extrapolation from social psychology. *Journal of Counseling Psychology*, 1966, *13*, 38–45.

Goldstein, A. P., Heller, K., & Sechrest, L. B. *Psychotherapy and the psychology of behavior change*. New York: Wiley, 1966.

Gould, R., & Sigall, H. The effects of empathy and outcome on attribution: An examination of the divergent perspectives hypothesis. *Journal of Experimental Social Psychology*, 1977, *13*, 480–491.

Greenspoon, J. The reinforcing effect of two spoken sounds on the frequency of two responses. *American Journal of Psychology*, 1955, *68*, 409–416.

Haley, J. *Strategies of psychotherapy*. New York: Grune & Stratton, 1963.

Haley, J. An interactional explanation of hypnosis. In D. Jackson (Ed.), *Therapy, communication, and change (Human communication*, Vol. 2). Palo Alto: Science and Behavior Books, 1968.

Haley, J. *Problem-solving therapy*. San Francisco: Jossey-Bass, 1978.

Heider, F. *The psychology of interpersonal relations*. New York: Wiley, 1958.

Hodges, K. K., & Brandt, D. Measurement of attribution of causality in counselor behavior. *Journal of Counseling Psychology*, 1978, *25*, 343–348.

Hoyt, M. F., Henley, M. D., & Collins, B. E. Studies in forced compliance: Confluence of choice and consequences on attitude change. *Journal of Personality and Social Psychology*, 1972, *23*, 205–210.

Jackson, D. D. (Ed.). *Communication, family and marriage*. Palo Alto: Science and Behavior Books, 1968. (a)

Jackson, D. D. *Therapy, communication, and change*. Palo Alto: Science and Behavior Books, 1968. (b)

Jackson, D. D., & Haley, J. Transference revisted. In D. Jackson (Ed.), *Therapy, communication, and change (Human communication*, Vol. 2). Palo Alto: Science and Behavior Books, 1968.

Jones, E. E. *Ingratiation: A social psychological analysis*. New York: Appleton-Century-Crofts, 1964.

Jones, E. E., & Davis, K. E. From acts to dispositions: The attribution process in person perception. In L. Berkowitz (Ed.), *Advances in experimental social psychology* (Vol. 2). New York: Academic Press, 1965.

Jones, E. E., & Nisbett, R. E. *The actor and the observer: Divergent perceptions of the causes of behavior*. Morristown, N.J.: General Learning Press, 1971.

Kelley, H. H. Attribution theory in social psychology. In D. Levine (Ed.), *Nebraska symposium on motivation, 1967*. Lincoln: University of Nebraska Press, 1967.

Kiesler, D. J. An interpersonal communication analysis of relationship in psychotherapy. *Psychiatry*, 1979, *42*, 299–311.

Kiesler, D. J. Interpersonal theory for personality and psychotherapy. In J. C. Anchin & D. J. Kiesler (Eds.), *Handbook of interpersonal psychotherapy*. New York: Pergamon, 1981.

Klir, G. J., & Valach, M. *Cybernetic modeling*. Princeton, N.J.: Van Nostrand, 1967.

L'Abate, L., & Weeks, G. A bibliography of paradoxical methods in psychotherapy of family systems. *Family Process*, 1978, *17*, 95–98.

Lawrence, D. H., & Festinger, L. *Deterrents and reinforcement: The psychology of insufficient reward*. Stanford, Calif.: Stanford University Press, 1962.

Lennard, H. L., & Bernstein, A. *The anatomy of psychotherapy: Systems of communication and expectation*. New York: Columbia University Press, 1960.

Lewin, K. *A dynamic theory of personality*. New York: McGraw-Hill, 1935.

Lewin, K. *Principles of topological psychology*. New York: McGraw-Hill, 1936.

Lindsley, O. R. Operant conditioning methods applied to research in chronic schizophrenia. *Psychiatric Research Reports*, 1956, *5*, 118–153.

Lopez, F. G., & Wambach, C. Effects of paradoxical and self-control directives in counseling. *Journal of Counseling Psychology*, in press.

Lowe, C. M. *Value orientations in counseling and psychotherapy: The meanings of mental health* (2nd edn.). Cranston, R.I.: Carroll Press, 1976.

Messé, L. A., Stollak, G. E., Larson, R. W., & Michaels, G. Y. Interpersonal consequences of person perception in two social contexts. *Journal of Personality and Social Psychology*, 1979, *37*, 369–379.

Miller, R. L., Brickman, P., & Bolen, D. Attribution versus persuasion as a means for modifying behavior. *Journal of Personality and Social Psychology*, 1975, *31*, 430–441.

Minuchin, S. *Families and family therapy*. Cambridge, Mass.: Harvard University Press, 1974.

Moos, R. H., & MacIntosh, S. Multivariate study

of the patient-therapist system: A replication and extension. *Journal of Consulting and Clinical Psychology*, 1970, *35*, 298–307.

Orvis, B. T., Kelley, H. H., & Butler, D. Attributional conflict in young couples. In J. H. Harvey, W. J. Ickes, & R. F. Kidd (Eds.), *New directions in attribution research* (Vol. 1). Hillsdale, N.J.: Erlbaum, 1976.

Palazzoli, M. S., Boscolo, L., Cecchin, G., & Prata, G. *Paradox and counterparadox*. New York: Jason Aronson, 1978.

Passer, M. W., Kelley, H. H., & Michela, J. L. Multidimensional scaling of the causes for negative interpersonal behavior. *Journal of Personality and Social Psychology*, 1978, *36*, 951–962.

Pittman, T. S. Attribution of arousal as a mediator in dissonance reduction. *Journal of Experimental Social Psychology*, 1975, *11*, 53–63.

Raven, B. H. Social influence and power. In J. D. Steiner & M. Fishbein (Eds.), *Current studies in social psychology*. New York: Holt, Rinehart and Winston, 1965.

Regan, D. T., Straus, E., & Fazio, R. Liking and the attribution process. *Journal of Experimental Social Psychology*, 1974, *10*, 385–397.

Rogers, C. R. *Client-centered therapy*. Boston: Houghton Mifflin, 1951.

Rogers, C. R. The necessary and sufficient conditions of therapeutic personality change. *Journal of Consulting Psychology*, 1957, *21*, 95–103.

Ross, L. The intuitive psychologist and his shortcomings: Distortions in the attribution process. In L. Berkowitz (Ed.), *Advances in experimental social psychology* (Vol. 10). New York: Academic Press, 1977.

Ruzicka, M. R., & Naun, R. Range of verbal behavior as a function of counselor philosophy and coached-client role behavior. *Journal of Counseling Psychology*, 1976, *23*, 283–285.

Schlenker, B. R. *Impression management*. Monterey, Calif.: Brooks/Cole, 1980.

Schlenker, B. R., Forsyth, D. R., Leary, M. R., & Miller, R. S. Self-presentational analysis of the effects of incentives on attitude change following counterattitudinal behavior. *Journal of Personality and Social Psychology*, 1980, *39*, 553–577.

Schmidt, L. D., & Strong, S. R. "Expert" and "inexpert" counselors. *Journal of Counseling Psychology*, 1970, *17*, 115–118.

Schmidt, L. D., & Strong, S. R. Attractiveness and influence in counseling. *Journal of Counseling Psychology*, 1971, *18*, 348–351.

Schofield, W. *Psychotherapy: The purchase of friendship*. Englewood Cliffs, N.J.: Prentice-Hall, 1964.

Snyder, M. Attribution and behavior: Social perception and social causation. In J. H. Harvey, W. J. Ickes, & R. F. Kidd (Eds.), *New directions in attribution research* (Vol. 1). Hillsdale, N.J.: Erlbaum, 1976.

Strong, S. R. Verbal conditioning and counseling research. *Personnel and Guidance Journal*, 1964, *42*, 660–669.

Strong, S. R. Counseling: An interpersonal influence process. *Journal of Counseling Psychology*, 1968, *15*, 215–224.

Strong, S. R. Causal attribution in counseling and psychotherapy. *Journal of Counseling Psychology*, 1970, *17*, 388–397.

Strong, S. R. Experimental laboratory research in counseling. *Journal of Counseling Psychology*, 1971, *18*, 106–110.

Strong, S. R. Systematic causality in counseling: Applications to theory, practice, and research. *Counseling and Values*, 1973, *17*, 143–151. (a)

Strong, S. R. A system model of behaving organisms and persons: Implications to behavior change in counseling. *Office for Student Affairs Research Bulletin*, University of Minnesota, 1973, *14* (1). (b)

Strong, S. R. Pragmatic causal distortion in counseling. *British Journal of Guidance and Counseling*, 1976, *4*, 59–65.

Strong, S. R. Social psychological approach to psychotherapy research. In S. L. Garfield & A. E. Bergin (Eds.), *Handbook of psychotherapy and behavioral change*. New York: Wiley, 1978.

Strong, S. R. Christian counseling with homosexuals. *Journal of Psychology and Theology*, 1980, *8*, 279–287.

Strong, S. R., & Claiborn, C. D. *Change through interaction: Social psychological processes of counseling and psychotherapy*. New York: Wiley-Interscience, 1982.

Strong, S. R., & Dixon, D. N. Expertness, attractiveness, and influence in counseling. *Journal of Counseling Psychology*, 1971, *18*, 562–570.

Strong, S. R., & Gray, B. L. Social comparison, self-evaluation, and influence in counseling. *Journal of Counseling Psychology*, 1972, *19*, 178–183.

Strong, S. R., & Matross, R. P. Change processes in counseling and psychotherapy. *Journal of Counseling Psychology*, 1973, *20*, 25–37.

Strong, S. R., Matross, R. P., & Danser, D. A study of attribution techniques in the interview. *Perceptual and Motor Skills*, 1981, *53*, 451–455.

Strong, S. R., & Schmidt, L. D. Expertness and influence in counseling. *Journal of Counseling Psychology*, 1970, *17*, 81–87. (a)

Strong, S. R., & Schmidt, L. D. Trustworthiness and influence in counseling. *Journal of Counseling Psychology*, 1970, *17*, 197–204. (b)

Strong, S. R., Wambach, C. A., Lopez, F. G., & Cooper, R. K. Motivational and equipping functions of interpretation in counseling. *Journal of Counseling Psychology*, 1979, *26*, 98–107.

Sullivan, H. S. *The interpersonal theory of psychiatry*. New York: Norton, 1953.

Tedeschi, J. T. (Ed.). *Impression management theory and social psychological research*. New York: Academic Press, 1981.

Tedeschi, J. T., Schlenker, B. R., & Bonoma, T. V. Cognitive dissonance: Private ratiocination or public spectacle? *American Psychologist*, 1971, *26*, 685–695.

Van Der Veen, F. Effects of the therapist and patient on each other's therapeutic behavior. *Journal of Consulting Psychology*, 1965, *29*, 19–26.

Verhaeghe, H. Mistreating other persons through simple discrepant role playing: Dissonance arousal or response contagion. *Journal of Personality and Social Psychology*, 1976, *34*, 125–137.

Von Bertalanffy, L. *General system theory: Foundations, development, applications*. New York: G. Braziller, 1968.

Watzlawick, P., Beavin, J., & Jackson, D. *Pragmatics of human communication*. New York: Norton, 1967.

Watzlawick, P., Weakland, J., & Fisch, R. *Change: Principles of problem formation and problem resolution*. New York: Norton, 1974.

Weick, K. E. Laboratory experimentation with organizations. In J. G. March (Ed.), *Handbook of organizations*. Chicago: Rand McNally, 1965.

Weiner, B., & Kukla, A. An attributional analysis of achievement motivation. *Journal of Personality and Social Psychology*, 1970, *15*, 1–20.

Wicklund, R. A. Objective self-awareness. In L. Berkowitz (Ed.), *Advances in experimental social psychology* (Vol. 8). New York: Academic Press, 1975.

Wright, R. M., & Strong, S. R. Stimulating therapeutic change with directives: An explorative study. *Journal of Counseling Psychology*, in press.

11

EFFORT JUSTIFICATION IN PSYCHOTHERAPY

JOEL COOPER
DANNY AXSOM
PRINCETON UNIVERSITY

Psychotherapy demands sacrifice. It requires money, time, concentration, and sweat. Few would deny that these attributes are common to all forms of therapy. All involve effort. We would like to focus on this variable—effort—and show how it may help all therapies to effect positive change in clients. More specifically, we propose that the extreme effort required of those in psychotherapy will, under certain conditions, create pressures toward therapeutic success through the arousal and subsequent reduction of cognitive dissonance. We shall detail this *effort justification process*, present evidence which suggests its applicability as a model of psychotherapy, and attempt to differentiate the process from alternative explanations.

The psychology of effort justification

Festinger (1961) captured the flavor of effort justification when he noted that frequently we learn to love what we suffer to achieve, and anyone who has encountered an over-zealous jogger should have an intuitive feel for this. The effort justification hypothesis is a part of Festinger's theory of cognitive dissonance.

Dissonance theory takes the view that, under the proper conditions, inconsistency among cognitions causes an uncomfortable psychological tension (Festinger, 1957). A person experiencing dissonance seeks to reduce the tension, often by altering one or more cognitions to bring about a greater degree of consistency. Participants in research on effort justification are requested to expend a high degree of either physical, cognitive, or emotional stress in order to achieve a particular goal. Dissonance is created between the cognition that a high degree of effort is being expended and the cognition that the goal is not sufficiently attractive to justify that effort. By changing their cognitions about the value of the goal that they are suffering to attain, the participants can *justify* their expenditure of effort and thereby reduce their psychological tension. And so they come to love what they suffer to achieve.

The classic demonstration of effort justification in social psychology was conducted by Aronson and Mills (1959). They recruited female students to participate in an ongoing discussion group on the psychology of sex. Upon arriving, subjects were asked to take a "screening test" to ensure that they would be able to contribute openly to discussions. This test constituted the effort manipulation. High-effort subjects read aloud a list of obscene words and two vivid descriptions of sexual activity from contemporary novels; low-effort subjects simply read a shorter list of sex-related but innocuous words, such as "prostitute." All subjects were told they had passed this screening. Subjects were then told that the discussion would take place over an intercom system to reduce possible embarrassment. It was added that since they had not done the week's assigned reading, they should just "listen in" for that session. What they heard was a standard recording of an exceedingly boring, rambling discussion about secondary sex behavior in lower animals. High-effort subjects had thus freely chosen to undergo an embarrassing "initiation" to become part of a group that, from first indications at least, was tedious and nonstimulating. As predicted, when compared to low-effort subjects and a control group that received no screening test, high-effort subjects rated both the discussion and its participants significantly more favorably. The goal—participating in the group—came to be rated more attractively to justify the effort expended.

One point needs to be clarified. The concept of effort as used within the effort justification paradigm is meant in its most generic sense. In psychotherapy, effort usually consists of many unpleasant events, including the expenditure of time and money and the experiencing of unpleasant emotions. In the research arena, effort has been operationalized with such diverse manipulations as physical exercise (Linder, Cooper, & Wicklund, 1968), delayed auditory feedback (Zimbardo, 1965), concentration (Cohen, 1959), electric shock (Gerard & Mathewson, 1966), and embarrassment (Aronson & Mills, 1959). All of the diverse variations of effort are not necessarily similar in the degree of kinetic energy expended, but all are psychologically effortful in the sense that something is being endured which is not pleasant. As a working definition, we shall consider an activity to be effortful for an individual if it is an activity that she or he would find more unpleasant than pleasant and therefore would not normally undertake.

Effort justification in psychotherapy

Consider a psychotherapy client faced with an intake, or initiation. This client has decided to seek help and as a first step has agreed to undergo a diagnostic interview. Prior to the interview, the client is likely to feel anxious. He or she may worry, "Will they find that I'm mentally ill? What will other people think?" This person is about to enter a strange situation in which he or she will publicly acknowledge problems to persons trained to delve into his or her deepest secrets and motivations. During the session, the client completes test form after test form—MMPI, Eysenck Personality Inventory, California Psychological Inventory, etc.—all of which take time and energy. He or she discusses personal problems in depth with a therapist, an experience likely to be embarrassing and emotionally painful. The whole intake, in fact, has now stretched to over five and a half hours. This client has clearly, by the end of the interview, made a substantial sacrifice and public commitment toward recovery. The similarity to Aronson and Mills's study is worth noting. We might expect that the *goal* of therapy would become more attractive, and hence, through processes initiated by effort justification, the client would be more likely to improve.

The intake described above was actually conducted as part of a psychotherapy evaluation study (Sloane, Staples, Cristol, Yorkston, & Whipple, 1975) that Bergin and Lambert (1978) referred to as "probably the best comparative study of psychotherapy yet carried out" (p. 166). The clients served in a waiting-list control group and thus received *no additional treatment* between the intake and the outcome assessment *four months later*. Yet, at this later assessment, the control group had improved significantly on target symptoms. Consider. Clients freely chose to participate in a study designed to help them reach some goal. They then made a public and personal commitment to the study by devoting a full five and one half hours to an intake, or "initiation." The proper variables for dissonance arousal are all present. Thus it is not surprising from the standpoint of effort justification that the control clients improved. While the treatment groups (analytic- and behavior-oriented therapies) improved more, this, too, is consistent with effort justification, since these groups expended considerably more effort.

We see a glimpse, then, of how effort justification may apply in psychotherapy. In any of its many forms, therapy is almost always effortful. If the therapy is psychoanalytic, time, money, and emotional effort will be spent to learn the process of free association, then considerably more effort will go into delving into past memories and emotional traumata. As the therapy proceeds, emotional catharses occur in which difficult and formerly repressed impulses are brought into consciousness. It is a long and painful experience for most clients. In this vein, Freud noted early on how crucial it was for clients to exert themselves if therapy was to be successful. This began with the price of admission: "It is well known that the value of the treatment is not enhanced in the patient's eyes if a very low fee is asked" (1913/1963, p. 144). As to the therapy itself, Haak has stated, "The analysis must involve a sacrifice, otherwise it becomes a matter of indifference in the patient's life" (cited in Menninger, 1964, p. 35).

If the therapy is behavioral—desensitization, for instance—clients learn a technique of deep muscle relaxation and then engage in a procedure in which they imagine stimuli which make them anxious. These stimuli are ordered on an anxiety gradient such that patients begin with a stimulus of low anxiety and proceed toward stimuli of higher anxiety. The procedure is based upon the notion of classical conditioning. Stimuli which make patients anxious are paired with the newly learned relaxation response so that new conditioned reflexes are learned. If the therapy is successful, stimuli that were formerly anxiety-producing will come to produce the conditioned relaxed response. Here, too, note the effort. Rimm and Masters (1974) advise the therapist interested in desensitization to limit that portion of the session to 30 minutes or less because "while desensitization cannot be described as painful, it does require *considerable effort and concentration on the part of the client*" (p. 64; italics added).

From the standpoint of dissonance theory, desensitization is substantially similar to psychoanalysis in that a client voluntarily engages in an effortful procedure in order to attain a goal. *The precise form of this effort is of little importance as long as the participant is engaging in an activity which he or she finds difficult or unpleasant.*

In this regard, it is interesting that Wolosin and Raines (1966) found that desensitization procedures helped patients to improve in their ability to approach a feared object regardless of whether the participants' activity was based upon muscle relaxation or muscle tightening. And Marcia, Rubin, and Efran (1969) found that a bogus therapy was as effective as desensitization in improving participants' approach toward a feared object. The bogus therapy consisted of an effortful procedure in which subjects believed that they were viewing pictures of a feared object in a tachistoscope at a subliminal level and were shocked every time a picture of the feared object appeared. When choosing to undergo this procedure and believing it to be connected to their fear of snakes, subjects showed as much improvement as they did in desensitization treatments. While such results are inconsistent with the theoretical basis of desensitization therapy, they are consistent with a dissonance interpretation of the phenomenon.

In essence, we side with those theorists (Frank, 1961/1973; Strupp & Bergin, 1968) who feel that all forms of therapy, regardless of their surface differences, share a small core of essential features which contribute to their success. Our particular focus—effort justification—may be at the base of more parochial techniques.

From dissonance arousal to therapeutic outcome: Some thoughts on the process

There are at least three ways in which effort justification might lead to improvement in therapy. Most directly, the person's attitude about the goal object may change so that what was once disliked is now liked. For instance, a person who is phobic about snakes may come to reason, "Why am I putting myself through all this? Because I like to handle snakes." Or, consider someone who is unassertive. To overcome this, she or he may be asked to role play being assertive in some situation in which she or he would normally feel intimidated. Acting assertively is effortful and is counterattitudinal in that this person seldom behaves this way. To reduce the dissonance that arises, the client may conclude that she or he really does like being assertive and continues to behave in that way. This example is particularly close to social psychological demonstrations of the effects of cognitive dissonance on attitude change. The classic experiment by Festinger and Carlsmith (1959) involved subjects' role playing that they were interested in a boring task, and these subjects later described the task as more interesting than did subjects who performed the role playing for a large incentive (see also Wicklund & J. W. Brehm, 1976, for other examples of how role playing can lead to dissonance-induced attitude change). The reader may wonder how something the client is trying to achieve—being more assertive, liking snakes—can be considered initially counterattitudinal. It is true that some part of the person's attitude toward the goal may be positive, since he or she is in therapy to achieve this goal. But if the goal has yet to be achieved, we are assuming that other components of the attitude run counter to the goal, that part of the client wants to change and another part of him or her resists that change. Since the desired goal is not being realized, the resistant components of the attitude are taken to be stronger. Hence, even though the client may "want" to reach a certain goal, that goal can be considered initially counterattitudinal and subject to dissonance-induced change (S. S. Brehm, 1976).

A second way in which effort justification may lead to better therapy outcomes is by increasing the client's *motivation* to change. In this case, the client may justify the effort expended in therapy by concluding, "I'm putting myself through this because I *really* want to become more assertive." This is important since estimates are that the largest proportion of variance in therapy outcomes can be accounted for by client variables such as motivation for change (Bergin & Lambert, 1978).

A third possibility is that, through effort justification, the client may come to view the goal of therapy as more likely to be achieved. An experiment by Yaryan and Festinger (1961) is relevant there. Subjects were asked to prepare for an examination but were told that, for reasons beyond the subjects' control, the exam might not be given. In one condition, the preparation was highly effortful; in another, it was not. Those subjects who underwent the difficult preparation later considered it much more likely that the exam would actually be given. To have thought otherwise would have been highly dissonant, since the preparation would be going for naught. In psychotherapy, a client is likewise expending a great deal of effort toward a goal that may not be achieved. One way of reducing dissonance, then, may be to increase one's expectations about the likelihood of the therapy's success. The client may then behave in ways consistent with the expected success and thereby improve via a self-fulfilling prophecy.

Of course, there is no reason to assume that these therapy-enhancing processes are mutually exclusive. One can imagine the goal of therapy becoming more attractive, the motivation to reach that goal increasing, and the expectation of success rising all as a consequence of effort justification. Nor should these processes be considered exhaustive. Goldstein and his colleagues, for example, discuss the likelihood that effort justification will lead to increased attraction toward the *therapist* (Goldstein, Heller, & Sechrest, 1966; Goldstein & Simonson, 1971). Although this line of theorizing has been criticized as misdirected (S. S. Brehm, 1976; Strong, 1978), the point is that there may be other ways in which effort justification helps enhance therapy. Those mentioned above, however, seem to us most central.

The importance of personal responsibility

Now we would like to be more precise about the processes that may lead to dissonance arousal in psychotherapy. Until now, we have presented evidence that suggests that effort is related to outcomes. This is not equivalent to saying that effort *justification* is related to outcomes. The difference is subtle but important. There are many other explanations—most having little to do with dissonance theory—for why effort in and of itself might be related to outcomes. For example, perhaps more effort increases the perceived legitimacy of the therapy and therefore causes the therapy to be taken more seriously; expectations for success would be likely to rise also. To distinguish effort justification from "mere effort," it is first necessary to examine more closely exactly when effort justification is likely to occur.

Not all attitude-discrepant behavior will arouse dissonance. The inconsistency, for instance, must involve cognitions that the person considers important. But also—and this is crucial—*the person must feel a sense of personal responsibility for bringing about the inconsistency* (J. Cooper, 1971; Wicklund & J. W. Brehm, 1976). Personal responsibility has been taken by dissonance researchers to be composed of two central components: decision freedom to engage in the behavior and foreseeability of the aversive consequences.

Research has shown that a crucial consideration for effort justification to lead to dissonance arousal is the perception of freedom to engage in the effort. In their studies, Aronson and Mills (1959) and Zimbardo (1965) requested their participants to engage in the effortful task. Linder et al. (1968) showed that commitment to an effortful task leads to dissonance effects *only* if that commitment is undertaken with the perception of an informed choice. In the Linder et al. study, some subjects committed themselves to listening to a counterattitudinal communication with full knowledge that a difficult memorization task would precede the communication. Other subjects—the uninformed group—learned of the memorization task only *after* committing themselves to hear the communication. Only informed subjects showed the dissonance-induced attitude change toward the initially counterattitudinal communication. The perception of freedom is also incorporated into most psychotherapies. A client coming to psychotherapy is typically informed of the general procedure and cost of the therapy and makes a decision to proceed. This fact of psychotherapeutic work can be viewed from the standpoint of dissonance theory as enabling the effort justification sequence to lead to the tension state of dissonance.

The second crucial factor for dissonance to arise is that the aversive consequences stemming from an activity must be foreseeable by the person at the time he or she commits to the action (Collins & Hoyt, 1972; Goethals, Cooper, & Naficy, 1979). If the aversive consequences of an action are not foreseeable, then there is little inconsistency for the person undertaking the behavior. How could the person have known about the unpleasant consequences of the action? There is no inconsistency and therefore no dissonance.

Effort, then, should not inevitably lead to effort justification. The person must feel personally responsible for having undertaken the therapy. Two recent studies address this issue. In one, Mendonca (1980) manipulated whether overweight children could choose their own weight control program. These children were males and females between 8 and 15 years of age who were an average of 48 percent overweight. High-choice subjects were led to believe that they were choosing from among three different therapies. They were told that the three programs were similar, but that each had a different emphasis, leader, etc. To increase involvement and realism, the subjects were given a sheet containing comments by other children about each of the therapies. They then "chose" a therapy. Actually, all subjects received the same weight therapy. Low-choice subjects were made aware of the three programs and were shown the children's comments. They were told, however, that only one of the therapies was currently available and thus were assigned to the program. All subjects then completed the therapy—labeled the "Take Control" program—which was a comprehensive, eight-week group therapy run in groups of three or four children. The group leader was blind to the choice manipulations, and high- and low-choice subjects were mixed together, with appropriate precautions taken to assure that subjects would not reveal their choice assignment to one another. The therapy itself was quite involving, using restriction of food intake, exercise, daily self-recording of food intake, weekly self-recording of weight, appropriate parental rewards, and other behavior techniques.

What, then, might an hypothesis based solely on effort predict? If effort alone is crucial, then subjects in both conditions should perform equally well. After all, subjects received only one form of therapy, and high- and low-choice subjects were mixed together during the therapy sessions. One might argue that the burden of initially having to make a choice makes the high-choice condition more effortful, but this differential effort seems small against the backdrop of the overall experiment. Effort justification, in contrast, would predict a definite difference in outcome between the choice conditions, even though the two groups underwent similar amounts of effort. This is because low-choice subjects should feel less personal responsibility for their therapy. While this group probably should not be considered devoid of personal responsibility—they did answer an advertisement for the therapy—they should feel less responsible than the high-choice group. Pressures toward effort justification would be greater among high-choice subjects, who not only answered the advertisement but "chose" their own bitter medicine, so to speak. Consistent with an effort justification interpretation, high-choice subjects in fact lost significantly more weight (Table 11.1) both during the experimental period and during the four weeks following the termination of the experiment.

A study by Gordon (1976) makes a similar conceptual point. As in the Mendonca study, some subjects in this experiment were led to believe they were choosing one form of a relaxation therapy over another, and others were given no choice. Again, all subjects actually received the same therapy. This choice manipulation was crosscut by a second variation in personal responsibility: whether the subject had volunteered or was participating for extra class credit. On a measure of relaxation given after the session, only those who had volunteered *and* "chosen" their therapy, i.e., those for whom personal responsibility was presumably highest, reported significantly greater relaxation. Again, effort was roughly equal across the four conditions, and yet only where pressures toward effort justification existed was there evidence of therapeutic gain.

These studies are suggestive but, unfortunately, not definitive. They highlight the difference between predictions based on mere effort and those based on effort justification. But problems with each study leave their conclusions ambiguous. For example, the Mendonca study with overweight children lacked a no-treatment control group, and so the direction of reported differences is hard to interpret. Also, a premeasure of subject motivation revealed that those eventually assigned to the high-choice condition were more motivated to start with than their low-choice counterparts. Although analyses covarying away this initial motivation difference still revealed an effect for choice, the finding is left tainted. The Gordon study, although suggestive, is weakened by a lack of proper manipulation checks and by a failure to obtain anything beyond a self-reported measure of relaxation change (Gordon, 1978; Harris & Harvey, 1978).

Table 11.1. Weight Changes (in pounds) in Mendonca (1980) Weight Control Experiment

	Time of Measurement	
Choice Condition	At End of 8-Week Therapy Run	At Follow-Up[1]
High-choice	−6.43	−7.64
Low-choice	−4.06	−4.25

Note: Overall main effect for choice: $F(1,12) = 6.23$, $p < .05$.
[1] Four weeks after end of therapy run.

Effort therapy: Exercise your fears away

The effort justification hypothesis has little to say about what particular form the effort must take. As we noted above, effort has been conceptualized in diverse ways in social psychological experiments. The particular form of effort should make little difference, so long as the person finds the activity difficult or in some way aversive. Thus, we stated, psychoanalytic and behavior therapies are similar from the standpoint of effort justification. Developing this argument one step further, *any* form of effort theoretically could serve as the basis for a therapy, regardless of whether or not it is based on some preexisting theory of therapy. Such a therapy would appear bogus from a conventional perspective, but would be consistent with an effort justification analysis of psychotherapy. To illustrate this, we shall now describe several recent experiments we have conducted using "effort therapies" to produce therapeutic benefits.

J. Cooper (1980) reported two experiments similar in logic. He reasoned that if the ameliorative effects of psychotherapy were brought about by effort justification, then a therapy consisting solely of physical exercise should be as effective as a conventional psychotherapy, so long as the therapies were equated for amount of effort.

In the first experiment, the conventional therapy was a form of implosive therapy (Stampfl & Lewis, 1967). This therapy relies on the concept of extinction. It assumes that once one is punished, rejected, or deprived in childhood, one will begin to avoid those behaviors, situations, or phobic objects which initially caused the unpleasantness. Avoidance becomes rewarding because it reduces the anxiety associated with the presence of the noxious stimuli. To extinguish the avoidance behavior, according to Rimm and Masters (1974),

> the patient must be prevented from performing the avoidance behavior, if only in his imagination, and be forced to experience the intense anxiety in the absence of any real aversive consequences. When such anxiety is experienced without the occurrence of actual aversive consequences, such consequences will cease to be anticipated, and the anxiety will dissipate. The avoided behavior and stimuli will now be perceived without any attendant anxiety and the tendency for these behaviors and stimuli to evoke anxiety will undergo extinction. (p. 334)

A patient who is afraid of snakes may be asked to imagine himself or herself asleep at a campsite. He or she then may be asked to imagine the stimulation of a snake slithering and sliding up his or her leg. Therapists use their creativity to make the situation as lifelike and as anxiety-producing as possible.

The "effort therapy" was a concoction of physical exercises the subject performed, including running in place for ten minutes, jumping rope, and winding a stick which had a rope with a five-point weight attached. The rationale given to subjects was that the procedure was based upon the correlations that had been found between heightened physiological arousal and emotional sensitivity. It was then explained that a procedure that has the effect of increasing emotional sensitivity might have a positive effect on the reduction of fear, which was the focus of the study. This explanation was given to draw a connection between the effort and the therapy's goal.

Pretesting established that the two therapies were seen as approximately equal in degree of effort and degree of aversiveness. The rationales given the subjects for each therapy were also perceived as equally credible. Finally, both therapies lasted about the same length of time, roughly 40 minutes.

Again, dissonance theory would predict that each therapy would be equally effective, since they were equated for amount of effort. Implosive therapy, from a dissonance standpoint, creates a very high degree of unpleasant effort that should lead to a high degree of attitude or behavior change in order to justify the effort expended; hence, it is conceptually similar to the effort therapy. However, recall that effort does not inevitably lead to effort justification. If a dissonance explanation is truly tenable, then both therapies should be effective *only to the extent that variables crucial to dissonance arousal are present*, i.e., variables associated with personal responsibility. With this in mind, decision freedom to engage in the therapy was varied. Here, then, we have another point of contrast: From the standpoint of extinction, the variable of decision freedom is irrelevant. With or without perceived freedom, extinction would be expected to occur and lead to improved behavior or attitude to the goal. For dissonance theory, undergoing the effortful, anxiety-provoking procedure of implosive therapy would lead to improved attitudes toward the goal *only* if the participants perceived themselves to have freely undergone the procedure. A prediction based on implosive therapy would have type of therapy as the main effect: regardless of decision freedom, implosive therapy should work and effort therapy should not. A prediction based on dissonance would have decision freedom as the main effect: regardless of type of therapy, high-choice subjects should improve and low-choice subjects should not.

Subjects were 75 male snake phobics recruited from the Princeton University community through advertisements in the campus newspaper. Upon arriving at the laboratory, the subject was greeted by a female experimenter who unobtrusively measured how close he could approach a six-foot boa constrictor contained in a Plexiglas tank. The experimenter then introduced the choice variable. High-choice subjects were told, "I have been instructed to warn you that the next part of the procedure could be very effortful and anxiety-provoking. If you like, you can stop now and still be paid. Would you like to continue?" Only one subject in this condition excused himself at this point. Low-choice subjects were also warned that the procedure might be effortful or anxiety-producing. However, instead of offering the subject a choice, the experimenter merely stated, "Please come with me and I will introduce you to the person who will be conducting the procedure."

Subjects were then led to a different room where a second experimenter manipulated the therapy variable. Subjects underwent either the implosive therapy or the effort therapy. The first experimenter remained blind to the therapy condition, as did the second experimenter with regard to choice. After completing the therapy, subjects were returned to the first experimenter who again asked the subject to approach the boa. Subjects then completed a short questionnaire, were debriefed, and were paid two dollars for their participation. Fifteen subjects were randomly assigned to a control group. Between their two approach tests, these subjects merely waited comfortably with reading material in a nearby room. The rationale given for this wait was that the equipment and supplies had not yet arrived.

Changes in the subjects' ability to approach the boa can be seen in Table 11.2. Consistent with a dissonance-based effort justification hypothesis, a large and significant main effect emerged for choice ($F(1,69) = 7.11$, $p < .01$). When decision freedom to engage in the therapy was high, both therapies worked, irrespective of differences in their content; when decision freedom was low, neither therapy was effective. Subjects in the two choice conditions did not differ in their initial approach behavior (fear level). Furthermore, neither the therapy variable nor the therapy × choice interaction was significant. The re-

Table 11.2. Changes (in inches) in Approach Distance in Cooper (1980) Snake Phobia Experiment

	Therapy Condition	
Choice Condition	Effort Therapy Group	Impulsive Therapy Group
High	130	104
Low	16.3	12.1

Note: Test-retest control condition = 11.9. Per condition, n = 15 subjects.

sults appear to offer striking support for an effort justification explanation.

Still, several points should be considered. Most important, there is at least one alternative explanation for the choice effect. The first experimenter offered the opportunity to terminate only to some of the subjects. It is possible that high-choice subjects perceived the experimenter to be an especially fair and sympathetic person and thus tried harder on the second approach test in order to please her. Also, subjects' self-reported fear of snakes indicated no reliable differences between conditions at the experiment's conclusion. Although this lack of concordance between behavioral responses and self-report data is common both in therapy (Mylar & Clement, 1972) and in social psychology (Nisbett & Wilson, 1977), it nonetheless poses an interpretational problem. Finally, snake phobias are rather encapsulated fears and thus may not be typical of the sorts of problems for which psychotherapies are usually invoked (A. Cooper, Furst, & Bridger, 1969).

For these reasons, J. Cooper (1980) conducted a conceptual replication of the first experiment. The focus of the second study was nonassertiveness, a more pervasive and perhaps more debilitating problem. Again, two therapies were compared for their effectiveness in helping subjects become more assertive. One was an effort therapy similar to that used in the previous experiment; the other was modeled after a role-playing, or "behavior rehearsal," technique (e.g., Salter, 1949; Wolpe et al., 1964) frequently used to improve assertiveness. This therapy is based on learning theory and requires the client to participate in a series of behavior rehearsals. These rehearsals are considered anxiety-producing and effortful because they involve the client's acting assertively in situations in which he or she normally has extreme difficulty doing so. For instance, a person might be asked to imagine that he or she is asking someone out to dinner, but that the other person does not seem to be paying attention. By participating in a series of these behavior rehearsals, the client learns to become more assertive. The experiment also varied decision freedom to engage in the therapy. Thus, the design was similar to the first experiment, with two different therapies and two levels of choice. From the standpoint of learning theory, the behavior rehearsal therapy should work regardless of initial decision freedom—it is the therapy itself that matters. From this perspective the effort therapy is patent nonsense. An explanation based on effort justification however, would predict a successful outcome only with high initial decision freedom. Only then would the subject experience cognitive dissonance and be motivated to become more assertive as a way of justifying the effort.

Subjects in this study were males and females recruited through an advertisement in the campus paper. The advertisement noted that those who eventually took part in a one-hour session would be paid two dollars (the significance of the payment will be discussed below). As a further screening device, those offering to participate were contacted in their dormitory rooms and asked to complete an assertiveness questionnaire. It consisted of 20 forced-choice items such as "If I receive a grade that I feel is lower than I deserve, I would most likely (a) Talk to my instructor about it (b) Let the matter drop." The half of the subjects who scored lowest in assertiveness—a total of 50, 29 males and 21 females—then took part in the actual experiment. The subject was greeted by the first experimenter, who for this study played the role of the departmental receptionist. The experimenter manipulated the choice variable as in the first experiment, then escorted the subject to the second experimenter. The second experimenter conducted either the effort therapy or the behavior rehearsal therapy described above. The two therapies had been equated as to their perceived effortfulness and aversiveness by subjects who participated in a pretest. Both therapies lasted for approximately 40 minutes.

The crucial dependent measure of assertiveness was then collected. For this experiment, it was desired that the measurement be especially unobtrusive so that a desire to please the first experimenter would be less prominent. Toward this end, at the completion of therapy the subject was asked to complete a personality inventory. This inventory supposedly was to assess how successful the session had been in helping the subject to become assertive. In fact, it was the first few pages of the California Personality Inventory and was included only to cause the subject to believe that the assessment was completed. The subject then returned to the receptionist to receive the two-dollar payment. The receptionist first appeared to consult a list of names and then proceeded to pay the subject only one dollar. The subject's reaction to this situation constituted the main dependent measure.

Unbeknownst to the subject, two observers blind to the experimental manipulations were stationed behind a one-way mirror and recorded the subject's reaction. Responses were rated from zero to 4, with zero for subjects who accepted the dollar without question and 4 for subjects who, despite the receptionist's stating that there had been no error, expressed the intention of finding the therapist to correct the situation.[1] As the subject left the receptionist, he or she was stopped and invited back into the office. The receptionist explained that there was more to be revealed about the study, but first requested that the subject complete a brief questionnaire to help assess the results. The subject was then debriefed and paid the full two dollars originally promised.

The subjects' reactions to being underpaid were taken as the assessment of assertiveness. Table 11.3 shows the mean assertiveness score for each experimental condition. We see here, as in the first study, that the form of therapy had little impact. Whether the subject underwent behavior rehearsal or effort therapy, what mattered was decision freedom to engage in the therapy. When choice was high, both therapies were successful; when it was low, neither worked. The main effect for choice was statistically significant ($F(1,56) = 4.32, p < .05$).

These two studies, each addressing a different target problem, make the same conceptual points. The conventional therapies worked in both cases, but only to the extent that they were undertaken with high choice. Moreover,

Table 11.3. Assertiveness Scores in Cooper (1980) Experiment

	Therapy Condition	
Choice Condition	Effort Therapy Group	Behavior Rehearsal Group
High	3.2[1]	3.4
Low	1.9	2.1

Note: Per condition, $n = 15$.
[1]Rating was on a scale from zero to 4, with higher values indicating higher assertiveness levels.

these conventional therapies did no better than effort therapies based solely on the expenditure of physical effort. Both of these results are consistent with an explanation based on cognitive dissonance and effort justification.

The enduring nature of dissonance-produced therapy gains

Subjects in these studies were able to reduce their fear of snakes and to become more assertive, even when the therapy consisted purely of physical exercise. The reader may be wondering, Just how durable are these dissonance-induced improvements? Gains from psychotherapy ideally should be lasting. Yet each of the above studies assessed only immediate changes. One might expect that improvements brought about through effort justification would be relatively enduring if it is the goal of therapy that becomes more attractive. This goal should remain attractive beyond the therapy itself. Equally important is a second question: If effort therapies can, at least in some cases, bring about positive therapeutic gains, then will an effort therapy that requires much effort produce better outcomes than one that is easier? In this sense neither of J. Cooper's studies is a complete test of effort justification, since effort itself was not varied.

The following study (Axsom & Cooper, 1981) was designed to examine whether variations in the magnitude of effort in therapy produce variations in therapy outcome and to assess the enduring nature of dissonance-produced therapy changes. The focus of the study was weight control. In many ways, the problem of being overweight is an ideal one to study. It is pervasive in our culture and is something many people are trying to overcome. Because of this, the market is inundated with plans for shedding pounds, ranging from "fad" diets to all-out attacks such as Weight Watchers. An effort therapy may well capture what underlies the myriad of programs. The topic of weight control also offers a number of advantages for the researcher. Foremost, weight loss is an objective, unambiguous criterion of the therapy outcome; weight loss in and of itself thoroughly defines the criterion for a successful therapy (Wollersheim, 1970). An added advantage is that weight can be repeatedly measured in a relatively nonreactive manner. This makes weight loss a particularly good focus for a study examining outcomes over time.

The experiment employed a single effort therapy rather than comparing two seemingly different treatments. This effort therapy was divided into two versions, one involving a great deal of effort and the other being milder. Since weight loss was the goal, the effort therapy used previously, which relied on physical exertion, was abandoned. The physical exercise involved in that therapy could have been directly related to actual weight loss. Subjects would almost certainly have practiced the exercises outside the laboratory, making any attempt to distinguish high- from low-effort therapies impossible. The therapy that subjects undertook, therefore, consisted of various cognitive tasks that required much effort and concentration to master. For example, subjects were required to discriminate between almost imperceptibly different geometric figures presented at brief exposures through a tachistoscope. They also attempted recitation and oral reading comprehension tasks while speaking into a delayed auditory feedback machine (Zimbardo, 1965). These tasks were chosen not only for the effort they demanded but also because they could not be performed outside the laboratory. The high-effort group performed the cognitive tasks for about 50 minutes per session, more than 40 minutes longer than low-effort subjects. Also, the tasks were made difficult for the high-effort group. For example, the auditory delay was longer and was overdubbed with the voice of someone else working at material similar to what the subject was reciting or reading.

The effort therapy, then, seems sufficiently bogus with regard to weight loss to make it similar to the physical effort therapies used previously for snake phobias and nonassertiveness. There appear to be no preexisting theories of weight reduction which would predict such procedures to lead to weight loss.

But as we have emphasized, the particular form the therapy takes is less important for dissonance theory, so long as the procedures are effortful. Dissonance theory would predict greater weight loss among the high-effort subjects since, for them, pressures toward effort justification would be greater.

As a general overview, the experiment consisted of five experimental sessions and two follow-ups. The experimental sessions took place over a three-week period and ended with a thorough debriefing. Subjects were not, however, led to believe that they would be recontacted. Six months later they were contacted and asked to return for a weight measurement. A second follow-up was conducted six months later, i.e., one year after the initial experimental sessions.

Subjects were recruited through newspaper advertisements in the greater Princeton area. The response was overwhelmingly from females, and so they constituted the final subject population. Several additional criteria were adopted to enhance subject homogeneity. We selected only those age 18 and over, between 10 and 20 percent above desirable weight standards, living relatively nearby, and not already receiving weight-related therapy or medications. Fifty-two subjects who fulfilled these requirements made up the final subject pool. Each was paid one dollar per session.

Each subject participated in the experiment separately. Upon arriving at the first session, the subject was greeted and weighed by the first experimenter. A manipulation of choice to engage in the therapy was then attempted. This was similar to instructions given in the previous two studies. The subjects then were led to a second experimenter, who conducted the actual sessions. The experimenter explained how the procedures were allegedly related to weight loss in terms similar to those used previously, that is, heightened neurological arousal and emotional sensitivity leading to enhanced ability to lose weight. To enhance the credibility of the therapies, all subjects then completed a questionnaire assessing various weight-related behaviors; they were also given a small notebook in which to monitor their food intake during the three-week period. The therapy itself then began. To prevent the amount of effort that was required from being confounded with the length of each session, low-effort subjects spent 40 minutes relaxing and browsing through magazines between completion of the tachistoscopic task and the beginning of the delayed auditory feedback. The choice manipulation was attempted again by the first experimenter as the subject left the session. Remaining sessions were similar in format.

To provide a baseline indication of normal weight fluctuation among subjects in our sample, ten subjects from those who responded to the advertisement were randomly assigned to a control condition. When contacted to begin, they were told that they would be unable to participate as originally planned because of a change in the procedure that meant using fewer individuals. They were then asked to engage in an unrelated study concerning women's normal weight fluctuations over time. Those agreeing were merely weighed five times over the three-week period.

A dissonance prediction would be that only subjects in the high-effort, high-choice group should evidence improvement, i.e., should lose weight. If either effort or choice is low, there is little need to justify anything. In this experiment most subjects perceived themselves as having high choice. The attempt to induce in the low-choice group a perception of the lack of freedom to undergo the therapy was unsuccessful. This was probably because they returned for four additional sessions and thus knew full well that the choice to continue was indeed theirs. This being the case—that all experimental groups perceived a high degree of choice—the prediction based on effort justification is that high-effort subjects should lose more weight than either low-effort or control subjects. Over the three weeks of experimental sessions this began to occur (Table 11.4). Subjects in the high-effort group lost more weight than low-effort or control subjects, but only weakly ($p < .14$).

By the first follow-up, though, this difference had become striking and statistically sig-

Table 11.4. Weight Changes (in lbs.) in Axsom & Cooper (1981) Weight Control Experiment

Effort Condition	Time of Measurement		
	After 3 Weeks	After 6 Months	After 1 Year
High	−1.76	−8.55	−6.70
Low	−.82	−.07	−.34
Control	+.17	+.94	+1.86

nificant ($p < .001$). Low-effort subjects had actually gained slightly. This difference was maintained even when subjects were weighed one full year after the initial sessions: high-effort subjects had still lost more weight than either of the other groups ($p < .01$). Furthermore, the effect was consistent. By the first follow-up, 94 percent of high-effort subjects had lost weight versus 39 percent of low-effort subjects and 50 percent of control subjects. At one year, the percentages were still 90, 48, and 56, respectively.

In yet a third therapeutic setting, then, we see evidence consistent with the notion that effort justification induces positive therapy outcomes. Moreover, these changes were enduring, as might be expected from a dissonance analysis. Recall that it is the goal of weight loss that, as a consequence of effort justification, becomes more attractive. While this explanation is speculative on our part, it seems the most plausible account of the data.

There is no evidence that subjects in the high-effort conditions found that they could be successful at losing weight during the experimental sessions and continued their method over the long period of time prior to the follow-up measure. The data show little relationship between weight loss during the initial experimental sessions and weight loss until the first follow-up. Our initial statement of effort justification principles is consistent with this lack of relationship, for it is the goal that effort renders more attractive. Just as Aronson and Mills's (1959) subjects who underwent effort viewed the goal of belonging to the discussion group with greater attractiveness, so, too, did our subjects come to view the goal of losing weight with more zeal and fervor. As a result, subjects in the high-effort conditions pursued that goal *regardless* of how successful they might have been during the five experimental sessions. Subjects in the low-effort conditions, on the other hand, did not view the goal as being more attractive. Regardless of whether they had shown any weight loss during the five experimental sessions, they showed no consistent pattern of weight loss during the succeeding six months. Thus, the data are consistent with the notion that the goal of weight loss became more attractive.

The picture that emerges from the studies using effort therapies is of a relatively robust phenomenon. The target problems addressed were diverse: snake phobia, nonassertiveness, and weight control. The subjects were of both sexes and, in the weight study, were young and old, from the campus and the community. Effort was operationalized almost as diversely as one finds it expressed in psychotherapy—from running in place to reciting poems over delayed auditory feedback. Despite these variations, subjects in each case were able to improve when they underwent an effortful treatment under high initial choice. The therapies were successful regardless of the apparently vacuous nature of the tasks. While troublesome for conventional theories of psychotherapy, this is entirely consistent with an effort justification prediction.

There are other studies which also suggest that dissonance-based improvements are enduring. Recall the Mendonca (1980) study in which overweight children "chose" their therapy. These children not only lost more weight initially, they also maintained and even increased their weight loss over a four-week follow-up. Recall also the waiting-list control group in the Sloane et al. (1975) study mentioned earlier. These clients underwent a rigorous intake and then received no intervention for four months. Yet at the end of this period they had evidenced significant improvement. And finally, consider a study by Bogart, Loeb, and Rittman (1969). These researchers were concerned about attendance rates at group therapy sessions at a psychiatric rehabilitation center. They instituted a reward system which offered prizes for good monthly attendance. In one condition these rewards were high (a cash payment of eight dollars), which many dissonance studies (Festinger & Carlsmith, 1959) suggest will lead to little attitude change about the activity undertaken. In the other condition, the rewards were only 25 percent as much (two dollars), and here we might expect dissonance to arise since these subjects attended the sessions for so little money. If this were the case, attraction to the program should increase in this low-payment group and they should continue to attend after monetary rewards are withdrawn. The high-payment group, on the other hand, might be expected to increase their attendance under the inducement of payments, but to fall back again if financial incentives are withdrawn. In other words, attendance gains based on dissonance processes should endure. Bogart et al. found that both incentive groups increased their attendance initially but only the low-incentive group *maintained* the increase after rewards were withdrawn. All these studies suggest that dissonance-based changes may be relatively enduring.

Related explanations

There are at least two other theoretical approaches which might make predictions similar to those based on effort justification. One is Bem's (1972) notion of self-perception. Self-perception theory relies on attributional principles (Heider, 1958; Kelley, 1967) and makes no mention of aversive tension states, such as dissonance, that the person is motivated to reduce. Its basic tenet is that we infer our own attitudes in much the same way as someone else would—by observing our behavior in its situational context and inferring what our attitude should be. According to self-perception theory, a person in psychotherapy might reason, "I am working very hard to achieve this goal. I must really be attracted to it." Under conditions of low choice, of course, no such inference would be drawn. One distinction between this explanation and one based on dissonance is the notion of arousal. According to dissonance theory, when people are faced with the inconsistency of having engaged in an effortful task, they become aroused. Self-perception theory does not make this assumption. Future research, then, might distinguish these competing explanations by allowing subjects the opportunity to misattribute any negative arousal to some other source (Zanna & J. Cooper, 1976). The opportunity for misattribution is irrelevant if self-perception is at work. Not so for dissonance. If the negative arousal state of dissonance is misattributed to some other source, there should be little motivation for attitude change.

The experiments summarized here also may be relevant to the notion of self-efficacy. Bandura (1977) suggested that psychotherapies were successful because they increased the person's expectations of personal efficacy. In a similar vein, Frank (1974) proposed that the primary function of all psychotherapies was to restore a person's sense of mastery. These notions may be related to dissonance through the concept of *personal responsibility*. Personal responsibility is crucial for dissonance to occur, but its role in producing a sense of mastery, or personal efficacy, is less clear. In the experiments reported above, perhaps offering subjects high choice instilled in them a better sense of personal efficacy. In the experiment that varied effort but not choice, one might argue that completing more rigorous tasks likewise increased personal efficacy. The interrelationship between dissonance and self-efficacy is intriguing and demands future research. For now, we note that the concepts are not necessarily incompatible when applied to therapy. If, through effort justification, the therapy is successful, a greater sense of personal efficacy is likely to ensue. In this view, self-efficacy would come subsequent to successful dissonance reduction.

Future directions

There are a number of other issues that are important to address. Future research should begin to delineate more precisely how dissonance affects therapy outcomes. We mentioned several possibilities—chief among them that the goal of therapy becomes more attractive—but these should be assessed more directly.

Must the effort "make sense"? In each of the effort therapies described in this chapter, the effort was buttressed in some way by a rationale stating the mechanisms through which the therapy should work. This was done to ensure that expectations would be high and constant across conditions. Yet, to a certain extent, the less the therapy makes sense, the greater is the need to justify one's effort. The more patently absurd the therapy seems at first, the more effort justification may later ensue. The success of such therapies as primal scream comes immediately to mind. It is unclear whether the effort in therapy must be made contingent to *anything* short of one's personal responsibility for performing it.

And finally, the effort justification process must be studied *in vivo* during actual ongoing psychotherapy. The effort therapies employed until now are provocative because they are successful despite seeming devoid of therapeutic content. They are a way of isolating effort as a conceptual variable independent of any particular therapy technique, such as role playing or anxiety extinction. Furthermore, they enabled us to test the initial plausibility of a dissonance analysis in a highly controlled setting with as much "noise" as possible removed. However, only by research in ongoing therapy settings will the limits, if any, to a dissonance analysis of therapy become apparent. What are the boundary conditions of the phenomenon? At the conceptual level, personal responsibility is necessary for dissonance to be invoked. Are ongoing therapies less successful if they negate the person's feeling of personal responsibility for engaging in and continuing with them? It is even possible that the limiting conditions to a dissonance analysis are also the limiting condition to successful psychotherapy. These and other issues can be profitably studied within the context of ongoing therapy.

Some notes for clinical practice

A few words addressed specifically to the practice of clinical psychology might be appropriate to help clarify our position. First, we are not so brazen as to suggest that effort justification is the *only* factor in psychotherapy. Many things impinge on people both in and out of therapy, and these will affect how the therapy fares. However, we find the notion of effort justification a useful conceptual tool for thinking about the structure of psychotherapies. Therapies as diverse as psychoanalytic, behavioral, and existential can be seen to have a common core. The data show that effort justification can be an effective tool. To the extent that therapists take advantage of this process, they may enhance the efficacy of their treatments.

Some therapists may feel uneasy applying effort justification because the principles have become associated with the use of deception (S. S. Brehm, 1976). Such deception is not endemic to effort justification. In fact, effort justification could be relied upon by initially advising clients very truthfully of the effort and unpleasantness that lie ahead. As Freud (1966) stated, "When we take a neurotic patient into psychoanalytic treatment . . . we point out the difficulties of the method to him, the long duration, the efforts and sacrifices it calls for" (p. 15). Effort justification also stresses the client's personal responsibility for choosing to participate and remain in therapy. When viewed in this light, perhaps therapists will see the effort justification principle emanating from the social psychological laboratory as an attractive tool in the practice of psychotherapy.

Note

1. The raters received training beforehand with the coding system and for the experiment showed an interjudge reliability of $r = .87$.

References

Aronson, E., & Mills, J. The effects of severity of initiation on liking for a group. *Journal of Abnormal and Social Psychology*, 1959, *59*, 177-181.

Axsom, D., & Cooper, J. Reducing weight by reducing dissonance: The role of effort justification in inducing weight loss. In E. Aronson (Ed.), *Readings about the social animal* (3rd ed.). San Francisco: Freeman, 1981.

Bandura, A. Self-efficacy: Toward a unifying theory of behavioral change. *Psychological Review*, 1977, *84*, 191-215.

Bem, D. J. Self-perception theory. In L. Berkowitz (Ed.), *Advances in experimental social psychology* (Vol. 6). New York: Academic Press, 1972.

Bergin, A. E., & Lambert, M. J. The evaluation of therapeutic outcomes. In S. L. Garfield and A. E. Bergin (Eds.), *Handbook of psychotherapy and behavior change* (Vol. 2). New York: Wiley, 1978.

Bogart, K., Loeb, A., & Rittman, J. D. Behavioral consequences of cognitive dissonance. Paper presented at the meeting of the Eastern Psychological Association, April 1969.

Brehm, S. S. *The application of social psychology to clinical practice*. Washington, D.C.: Hemisphere, 1976.

Cohen, A. R. Communication discrepancy and attitude change: A dissonance theory approach. *Journal of Personality*, 1959, *58*, 383-387.

Collins, B. E., & Hoyt, M. G. Personal responsibility for consequences: An integration and extension of the "forced compliance" literature. *Journal of Experimental Social Psychology*, 1972, *8*, 558-593.

Cooper, A., Furst, J., & Bridger, W. A brief commentary on the usefulness of studying fears of snakes. *Journal of Abnormal Psychology*, 1969, *74*, 413.

Cooper, J. Personal responsibility and dissonance: The role of foreseen consequences. *Journal of Personality and Social Psychology*, 1971, *18*, 354-363.

Cooper, J. Reducing fears and increasing assertiveness: The role of dissonance reduction. *Journal of Experimental Social Psychology*, 1980, *16*, 199-213.

Festinger, L. *A theory of cognitive dissonance*. Stanford, Calif.: Stanford University Press, 1957.

Festinger, L. The psychological effects of insufficient reward. *American Psychologist*, 1961, *16*, 1-12.

Festinger, L., & Carlsmith, J. M. Cognitive consequences of forced compliance. *Journal of Abnormal and Social Psychology*, 1959, *58*, 203-210.

Frank, J. D. *Persuasion and healing*. Baltimore: Johns Hopkins Press, 1961/1973.

Frank, J. D. Psychotherapy: The restoration of morale. *American Journal of Psychiatry*, 1974, *131* (3), 271-274.

Freud, S. *Freud: Technique and therapy*. New York: Collier, 1963.

Freud, S. *Introductory lectures on psychoanalysis*. New York: Norton, 1966.

Gerard, H. B., & Mathewson, G. C. The effects of severity of initiation on liking for a group: A replication. *Journal of Experimental Social Psychology*, 1966, *2*, 278-287.

Goethals, G. R., Cooper, J., & Naficy, A. Role of foreseen, foreseeable, and unforeseeable behavioral consequences in the arousal of cognitive dissonance. *Journal of Personality and Social Psychology*, 1979, *37*, 1179-1185.

Goldstein, A. P., Heller, K., & Sechrest, L. B. *Psychotherapy and the psychology of behavior change*. New York: Wiley, 1966.

Goldstein, A. P., & Simonson, N. R. Social psychological approaches to psychotherapy research. In A. Bergin and S. Garfield (Eds.), *Handbook of psychotherapy and behavior change*. New York: Wiley, 1971.

Gordon, R. M. Effects of volunteering and responsibility on the perceived value and effectiveness of a clinical treatment. *Journal of Consulting and Clinical Psychology*, 1976, *44*, 799-801.

Gordon, R. M. Imprecision or dissonance? A reply to Harris and Harvey. *Journal of Consulting and Clinical Psychology*, 1978, *46*, 329-330.

Harris, B., & Harvey, J. H. Social psychological concepts applied to clinical processes: On the need for precision. *Journal of Consulting and Clinical Psychology*, 1978, *46*, 326-328.

Heider, F. *The psychology of interpersonal relations*. New York: Wiley, 1958.

Kelley, H. H. Attribution theory in social psychology. In D. Levine (Ed.), *Nebraska Sym-

posium on Motivation, 1967. Lincoln: University of Nebraska Press, 1967.

Linder, D. E., Cooper, J., & Wicklund, R. A. Pre-exposure persuasion as a result of commitment to pre-exposure effort. *Journal of Experimental Social Psychology*, 1968, *4*, 470–482.

Marcia, J. E., Rubin, B. M., & Efran, J. S. Systematic desensitization: Expectancy change or counter-conditioning? *Journal of Abnormal Psychology*, 1969, *74*, 382–386.

Mendonca, P. The effects of choice and client characteristics in the behavioral treatment of overweight children. Unpublished manuscript, University of Kansas, 1980.

Menninger, K. *Theory of psychoanalytic technique.* New York: Harper & Row, 1964.

Mylar, J. L., & Clement, P. W. Prediction and comparison of outcome in systematic desensitization and implosion. *Behavior Research and Therapy*, 1972, *10*, 235–246.

Nisbett, R. E., & Wilson, T. D. Telling more than we can know: Verbal reports on mental processes. *Psychological Review*, 1977, *84*, 231–259.

Rimm, D. C., & Masters, J. C. *Behavior therapy: Techniques and empirical findings.* New York: Academic Press, 1974.

Salter, A. *Conditioned reflex therapy: The direct approach to the reconstruction of personality.* New York: Creative Age Press, 1949.

Sloane, R. B., Staples, F. R., Cristol, A. H., Yorkston, N. J., & Whipple, K. *Short-term analytically oriented psychotherapy vs. behavior therapy.* Cambridge, Mass.: Harvard University Press, 1975.

Stampfl, T. & Levis, D. Essentials of implosive therapy: A learning theory based on psychodynamic behavioral therapy. *Journal of Abnormal Psychology*, 1967, *72*, 496.

Strong, S. R. Social psychological approach to psychotherapy research. In S. L. Garfield and A. E. Bergin (Eds.), *Handbook of psychotherapy and behavior change: An empirical analysis* (2nd ed.). New York: Wiley, 1978.

Strupp, H. H., & Bergin, A. E. Some empirical and conceptual bases for coordinated research in psychotherapy: A critical review of issues, trends, and evidence. *International Journal of Psychiatry*, 1969, *7*, 18–90.

Wicklund, R. A., & Brehm, J. W. *Perspectives on cognitive dissonance.* Hillsdale, N.J.: Erlbaum, 1976.

Wollersheim, J. Effectiveness of group therapy based upon learning principles on the treatment of overweight women. *Journal of Abnormal Psychology*, 1970, *76*, 462–474.

Wolosin, M., & Raines, J. Visual imagery, expected roles, and extinction as possible factors in reducing fear and avoidance behavior. *Behavior Research and Therapy*, 1966, *4*, 25.

Wolpe, J., Salter, A., & Reyna, L. J. (Eds.). *The conditioning therapies.* New York: Holt, Rinehart and Winston, 1964.

Yaryan, R. B., & Festinger, L. Preparatory action and belief in the probable occurrence of future events. *Journal of Abnormal Social Psychology*, 1961, *63*, 603–606.

Zanna, M. P., & Cooper, J. Attribution and the dissonance process. In J. Harvey, W. Ickes, and R. Kidd (Eds.), *New directions in attribution research* (Vol. 1). Hillsdale, N.J.: Erlbaum, 1976.

Zimbardo, P. G. The effect of effort and improvisation on self-persuasion produced by role playing. *Journal of Experimental Social Psychology*, 1965, *1*, 103–120.

12

A SOCIAL PSYCHOLOGICAL APPROACH TO HYPNOTIC BEHAVIOR

NICHOLAS P. SPANOS
CARLETON UNIVERSITY

Historically, hypnotic phenomena have been conceptualized as differing fundamentally from other types of social behavior (Spanos & Gottlieb, 1979). For instance, in the early 19th century these phenomena were thought to occur when subjects were placed in a "magnetic state" by certain stroking motions known as "passes" (e.g., Deleuze, 1879). In the mid-19th century, Braid (1960), misled by the lethargic appearance of his subjects, substituted the notion of "hypnosis" for that of "magnetic state." Today, many investigators continue to account for hypnotic behavior by positing special psychological processes such as "trance" and "dissociation" (Bowers, 1976; F. J. Evans, 1968; Gill & Brenman, 1959; E. R. Hilgard, 1977, 1979a; Kihlstrom, 1978; Weitzenhoffer, 1980).

Criticism of the notion that hypnosis involves special psychological processes also has a long history. Beginning with the French Commission of 1784 (Franklin et al., 1970) and continuing through the work of Faria (1906), Bertrand (1826), Hall (1845), and Hart (1898), this tradition criticized the notion that magnetic or hypnotic procedures produced extraordinary behavioral feats and instead attempted to account for the phenomena that did occur with more naturalistic concepts, such as attention, concentration, expectant desire, and imagination. This tradition has culminated in modern formulations that view hypnotic phenomena as similar to other forms of social behavior and that account for these phenomena without recourse to special psychological processes (Barber, 1964a, 1969, 1972; Barber, Spanos, & Chaves, 1974; Coe, 1978; Coe & Sarbin, 1977; Sarbin, 1950; Sarbin & Coe, 1972; Spanos, 1970, 1981). This paper is written from such a perspective. I argue throughout that hypnotic phenomena can best be understood by carefully examining (a) the interpersonal context in which they occur and (b) how hypnotic subjects construe and interpret that context. The fundamental tenets of this position were outlined by White (1941) more than a generation ago:

I thank H. L. Radtke and H. J. Stam for critically reading earlier versions of this paper.

Hypnotic behavior is meaningful goal-directed striving, its most general goal being to behave like a hypnotized person as this is continuously defined by the operator and understood by the subject.

In short, responsive hypnotic subjects are in no sense automata. They are active, cognizing individuals who are attuned to variations in social contexts and motivated to define themselves in a manner consistent with their interpretations of what constitutes "being hypnotized." Hypnotic situations typically consist of two components. The first is a hypnotic induction procedure that explicitly defines the situation as hypnotic and that bolsters this definition of the situation by unfolding in a manner consistent with most subjects' preconceptions about hypnosis (Spanos, Rivers, & Ross, 1977). For instance, standard induction procedures consist of interrelated suggestions that the subject is going to sleep, becoming relaxed, and entering a hypnotic state. Moreover, these suggestions are usually phrased to imply that these events are happening to the subject rather than being initiated by the subject.

The second component of the hypnotic situation involves the administration of test suggestions that call for specific phenomena traditionally associated with hypnosis, e.g., arm levitation, limb rigidity, age regression, analgesia, amnesia, hallucination. It is important to understand that the test suggestions used in hypnosis research do *not* directly instruct subjects to carry out overt behaviors. Instead, they typically invite them to construct a hypothetical (i.e., imaginary) situation that is consistent with the occurrence of some simple motor act (Sarbin & Coe, 1972; Spanos, 1971). For example, the arm levitation suggestion on the Barber (1969) Suggestibility Scale is worded as follows:

Imagine that the arm is becoming lighter and lighter, that it is moving up and up. . . . It's light as a feather, it's weightless and rising in the air. (pp. 243–244)

In short, test suggestions invite subjects to temporarily convince themselves, as well as the experimenter, that their arm is light, that a cat is in their lap, that they are unable to recall well-known facts, and so on. In effect, subjects are being asked to temporarily set aside the rules and assumptions usually employed to differentiate imagined situations from real events and in so doing to define the ongoing situation in terms of the hypothetical events described in the suggestions (Sarbin & Coe, 1972; Shor, 1959, 1970; Spanos, 1971).

One purpose of this paper is to apply these and related social psychological ideas to an understanding of hypnotic phenomena. Another is to critically examine traditional special-process formulations of hypnosis and the evidence on which these are based. Special-process views of hypnosis are firmly rooted in the cultural mythology of the past two centuries. The popular view of the hypnotic subject as a person in a trance who responds automatically to suggestions is not far removed from the position of numerous contemporary theorists and is taken for granted by many psychologists. Social psychological accounts of hypnosis sometimes appear unconvincing because they are inconsistent with implicit but erroneous beliefs about what hypnosis is "really like."

The first section of this paper briefly examines hypnotic susceptibility and its correlates. The second critically assesses evidence used to support special-process views of hypnosis, and the third provides detailed examinations of two phenomena considered central to hypnotic responding: hypnotic analgesia and hypnotic amnesia. While touched on from time to time, the burgeoning literature dealing with hypnotherapy is not reviewed systematically in this paper. The term "hypnotherapy" does not refer to a delimited set of procedures. In fact, any therapeutic intervention that is defined by the therapist as involving hypnosis can be considered hypnotherapy. As a result, procedures as diverse as psychoanalytically oriented age regression and "uncovering" therapies (Raginsky, 1967), direct suggestions for symptom removal (Gelder, Bancroft, Gath, Johnston, Mathews, & Shaw,

1973), variants of systematic desensitization (Gibbons, Kilbourne, Saunders, & Castles, 1970), and other behavior therapies (Kroger & Fezler, 1976) have all been considered hypnotherapy. The only thing tying these diverse practices together is the name "hypnosis" with its attendant mythology of altered states and wonderous feats. Most of the hypnotherapy literature consists of uncontrolled case reports. Some controlled studies have been conducted, but, in many of these, serious methodological problems preclude firm conclusions concerning the efficacy of hypnotic procedures (see partial reviews by Burrows & Dennerstein, 1980, and Weitzenhoffer, 1972). In short, there is little solid evidence available to be reviewed. In the last two decades, the literature on therapeutic hypnosis has played only a minor role in influencing theoretical developments in the field of hypnosis research. Most of these developments have stemmed from experimental studies aimed at understanding the basic nature of hypnotic phenomena. Consequently, this review will focus on experimental, rather than clinical, studies.

Hypnotic susceptibility and its correlates

A very large number of studies have been directed toward determining relationships between various psychological and physiological dimensions and hypnotic responsiveness. Typically, hypnotic responsiveness is assessed in these studies through the use of standardized scales of hypnotic susceptibility (Barber, 1965; Barber & Wilson, 1979; Weitzenhoffer & Hilgard, 1959, 1962). All of these scales involve a similar testing format. Subjects are administered a hypnotic induction procedure and a standardized series of test suggestions. On most scales, overt response to each suggestion is scored on a pass-fail basis and a single susceptibility score is obtained for each subject by summing the number of suggestions passed.[1] Correlations between the various commonly employed scales are substantial, and these scales are frequently used more or less interchangeably (see review by E. R. Hilgard, 1979b).

Psychological correlates of hypnotic susceptibility

Hypnotic susceptibility is a relatively stable attribute, and substantial test-retest reliabilities have been obtained even when testing periods were separated by ten years (E. R. Hilgard, 1979b; A. H. Morgan, Johnson, & Hilgard, 1974). Moreover, susceptibility does not appear to be greatly affected by such characteristics of the hypnotist as age, sex, friendliness, manner of dress, and ethnic background (Balaschak, Blocker, Rossiter, & Perin, 1972; Coe, 1976; Coe, Bailey, Hall, Howard, Janda, Kobayashi, & Parker, 1970; Cronin, Spanos, & Barber, 1971; D'Eon, Mah, Pawlak, & Spanos, 1979; Greenberg & Land, 1971; Weitzenhoffer & Weitzenhoffer, 1958).

On the other hand, it is becoming increasingly clear that susceptibility level can be influenced by a variety of social psychological variables (see reviews by Diamond, 1974, 1977). For instance, several studies (Cronin et al., 1971; Diamond, 1972; Gregory & Diamond, 1973; Katz, 1979; Kinney & Sachs, 1974; Sachs, 1971; Sachs & Anderson, 1967) indicate that the provision of positive information about hypnosis, special training in experiencing suggested effects, and exposure to models who verbalize the experiential aspects of their successful responding lead to significant enhancements in susceptibility. Conversely, negative information about hypnosis produces decrements in susceptibility (Barber & Calverley, 1964b, 1964c; Spanos & McPeake, 1975b). These findings may indicate that the usual stability found in test-retest studies of susceptibility in part reflects stability in situation-specific attitudes and expectations concerning hypnosis. Along these lines, it is notable that attitudes and expectations toward hypnosis are among the very few dimensions found to correlate consistently with hypnotic susceptibility (Barber & Calverley, 1966b; Derman & London, 1965; Diamond,

Gregory, Lenney, Steadman, & Talone, 1974; London, Cooper, & Johnson, 1962; Melei & Hilgard, 1964; Spanos & McPeake, 1975a; Spanos, Mah, et al., 1980).

Much effort has been expended assessing relationships between personality trait dimensions (e.g., introversion-extroversion, self-monitoring, masculinity-femininity, various measures of psychopathology) and hypnotic susceptibility. Nevertheless, stable findings have not emerged, and contradictory results are commonplace (see reviews by Barber, 1964b, 1969; E. R. Hilgard, 1965). Even in recent work, null findings and failures to replicate remain the order of the day (Kihlstrom, Diaz, McClellan, Ruskin, Pistole, & Shor, 1980; Spanos, Mah, et al., 1980). There are some indications that relationships between attribute variables and susceptibility may be moderated by factors such as subjects' sex, mood, and attitudes toward hypnosis, as well as by personality characteristics of hypnotists (Hedberg, 1974; Perry, Wilder, & Appignanesi, 1973; Silver, 1974; Spanos & McPeake, 1975b; Spanos, Stam, Radtke, & Nightingale, 1980). Nevertheless, more systematic work is necessary before firm conclusions concerning moderator variables can be proffered.

Attempts to relate susceptibility to performance measures (as opposed to questionnaire measures) of cognitive functioning have also produced inconsistent findings. For example, C. Graham and Evans (1977) reported a significant negative correlation between susceptibility and subjects' ability to generate numbers in random sequence (purportedly a measure of attentional ability). However, two recent studies (Morgan, 1979; Spanos, Mah, et al., 1980) were unable to replicate this effect. Similarly, a positive correlation between Gestalt closure performance and susceptibility reported by Crawford (1977) was not replicated by Spanos, Mah, et al.

In contradistinction to the work on personality and hypnosis, consistent relationships have been found between susceptibility and questionnaire measures of subjects' tendencies to become absorbed in such commonplace and imaginative pursuits as watching movies, daydreaming, and reading novels (As, 1962; Davis, Dawson, & Seay, 1978; J. R. Hilgard, 1974; O'Grady, 1980; Spanos & McPeake, 1975a; Spanos, Rivers, & Gottlieb, 1978; Spanos, Stam, Radtke, & Nightingale, 1980; Tellegen & Atkinson, 1974). Related work (reviewed by Spanos & Barber, 1974) which focused on cognitive activity during response to individual test suggestions may be summarized as follows. Degree of absorption in imaginings that are congruent with the events suggested has been found consistently to correlate with the experiencing of suggested effects.

In summary, consistent relationships between hypnotic susceptibility and traditional personality dimensions have not been demonstrated. On the other hand susceptibility has correlated consistently both with situation-specific attitudes and expectations and with subjects' proclivities for becoming absorbed in imaginative activities. From a social psychological perspective, these findings indicate that subjects are responsive to test suggestions when they are willing and able to define their behavior in a manner consistent with the events suggested. For most suggestions, such self-definition appears to involve the interrelated processes of elaborating imaginings that are consistent with the aim of the suggestion and disregarding information that is inconsistent with these imaginings (Spanos & Barber, 1974). Subjects who score high on absorption questionnaires are particularly proficient at engaging in the kinds of fantasy activities required by most suggestions. Therefore, given that they are willing to cooperate with the hypnotic procedures, they are particularly likely to generate the imaginings required for experiencing suggested effects.[2]

Physiological correlates of hypnotic susceptibility

Many investigators have attempted to relate hypnotic susceptibility to physiological activity occurring outside the hypnotic situation. For instance, one line of research has focused on EEG variables (e.g., EEG alpha density during a resting baseline) and their relation to susceptibility (Crosson, Meinz, Laur, Williams, & Andreychuk, 1977; Galbraith, London, Leibovitz, Cooper, & Hart, 1970; Hartnett, Nowlis, & Svorad, 1969; London, Hart, & Leibovitz, 1968; Paskewitz, 1977; Ulett, Akpinar, & Itil, 1972). Despite the volume of research conducted, consistent findings have not emerged (Dumas, 1977; F. J. Evans, 1972; Paskewitz, 1977). For instance, while a number of investigators have reported significant correlations between susceptibility and baseline EEG alpha density (Engstrom, 1970; London et al., 1968), as many others have failed to replicate these findings (Dumas, 1980; Dumas & Spitzer, 1978). Work by Dumas (1977) suggests that some of the conflicting EEG alpha findings may be related to differences in the subject populations sampled across studies. Other procedural differences that may be related to these inconsistent results include different electrode placements and recording techniques, differences in the condition of the subjects' eyes (open/closed), and differences in subjects' arousal level during baseline EEG testing (Barabasz, 1980; Paskewitz, 1977; Sarbin, 1973). In short, there is not as yet any consistent support for the notion that hypnotic susceptibility is related to waking EEG activity.

Recently, investigators have become intrigued with the idea that susceptibility may be related to functional asymmetry of the brain; more specifically, with a preference for processing information with the nondominant (i.e., usually the right) hemisphere (Bakan, 1969; K. R. Graham, 1977; R. C. Gur, 1978; R. C. Gur & Gur, 1974; J. R. Hilgard, 1979; Reyher, 1977). Bakan proposed that a subject's tendency to look to the left (i.e., leftmoving) when asked questions that required thought indexed a preference for processing information with the right hemisphere. In line with this notion, several investigators (Bakan, 1969; R. C. Gur & R. E. Gur, 1974; A. H. Morgan, McDonald, & Macdonald, 1971) reported positive correlations between leftmoving (particularly in right-handed males) and hypnotic susceptibility. Unfortunately, a number of studies (DeWitt & Averill, 1976; R. E. Gur & Reyher, 1973; Spanos, Pawlak, Mah, & D'Eon, 1980; Spanos, Rivers, & Gottlieb, 1978; Stam & Spanos, 1979) have failed to replicate these findings, and several studies have also failed to find significant relationships between left-moving and spatial abilities, imagery vividness, and other purported right-hemisphere activities (Ehrlichman, 1972; Hiscock, 1977; Spanos, Pawlak et al., 1980; Spanos, Rivers, & Gottlieb, 1978). Several studies (Foenander & Burrows, 1979; A. H. Morgan, Macdonald, & Hilgard, 1974; C. M. Morgan, 1979) have assessed EEG activity from the two cerebral hemispheres separately during performance on a variety of tasks (e.g., spatial vs. verbal tasks). While task characteristics have been shown to affect the ratio of EEG activity in the two hemispheres, differences in hemispheric activity as a function of subject susceptibility have not been consistently demonstrated. In short, the notion that hypnotic susceptibility is related to a stable preference for processing information in the right hemisphere has not been supported. Furthermore, the hypothesis that left-moving indexes hemispheric functioning has been viewed of late with increasing skepticism (Ehrlichman & Weinberger, 1978), as has the notion that the two hemispheres subserve unique cognitive styles (Corballis, 1980).[3]

Spiegel (1972, 1973, 1974) and Stern, Spiegel, and Nee (1979) reported a relationship between hypnotic susceptibility and the ability of subjects to roll their eyes up into their head while closing their eyelids. Although Spiegel (1974) contends that his "eye roll sign" is a "biological marker" of aptitude for hypnosis, at least five independent teams of investigators have failed to substantiate his findings (Eliseo, 1974; Orne, Hilgard, Spiegel, Spiegel, Crawford, Evans, Orne, & Frischholz, 1979; D. V. Sheehan, Latta, Regina, & Smith, 1979; Switras, 1974; Wheeler, Reis, Wolff, Grupsmith, & Mordkoff, 1974). F. J. Evans, Gustafson, O'Connell, and Orne (1969) reported that subjects' tendency to make specific motor responses during sleep to verbally presented cues was positively correlated with hypnotic susceptibility. However,

Perry, Evans, O'Connell, Orne, and Orne (1978) were unable to replicate these findings and suggested that the earlier results may have been "an artifact of differential rapport between subjects and the laboratory." Finally, A. H. Morgan (1973) reported that hypnotic susceptibility is more highly correlated in identical twins than in fraternal twins. Thorkelson (1973), however, was unable to replicate this finding.

In summary, the available evidence indicates that reliable physiological correlates of hypnotic susceptibility have not been demonstrated. Furthermore, the existence of such correlates would not in and of themselves provide evidence for a special-process view of hypnosis (Sarbin, 1973; Spanos & Barber, 1976). To obtain physiological evidence for hypnosis-specific processes, it must be demonstrated that (a) subjects having high hypnotic susceptibility (but not low susceptibles) undergo changes in one or more physiological variables when administered hypnotic procedures and (b) nonhypnotic procedures (e.g., progressive relaxation) do not elicit the same effects (Sarbin, 1973). Although a large number of physiological variables have been assessed during hypnotic testing (e.g., eye movements, electrodermal changes, heart rate, respiration rate, EEG alpha activity, oral temperature), there is no evidence to suggest physiological changes that are specific to hypnotic procedures (see reviews by Barber, 1970; Edmonston, 1979; and Sarbin & Slage, 1972). Edmonston (1979) has suggested that the physiological changes accompanying hypnotic testing can, by and large, be accounted for in terms of changes in level of relaxation.

The evidence for special processes

The notion that special psychological processes (e.g., a "trance state") are required to account for hypnotic behavior has been fostered by three persistent but erroneous propositions: (a) hypnotic subjects typically exhibit higher levels of responsiveness to suggestions than control subjects, (b) hypnotic subjects have unique experiences that are unavailable to control subjects, and (c) hypnotic behavior, at least in highly responsive subjects, occurs automatically. Evidence for the uniqueness of hypnotic phenomena has also been sought in demonstrations that hypnotic responsiveness is correlated with subjective reports of being "deeply hypnotized."

Heightened suggestibility

Throughout the 19th century, many investigators believed that "mesmerized" or "hypnotized" subjects could perform amazing feats that transcended normal volitional capacities (Dingwall, 1968; Spanos & Gottlieb, 1979). For instance, it was sometimes claimed that these subjects could enter a state of suspended animation, see with the back of their head, see through the skin to the internal organs of others, and communicate with the dead (Deleuze, 1879; Dodds, 1865; Haddock, 1865; Newman, 1865; Sextus, 1968). Most of these highly fanciful notions have, of course, disappeared from the hypnosis literature. Nevertheless, occasional reports of highly unusual, hypnosis-specific feats are still to be found. For instance, Barber (1969, 1970, 1972) critically examined the propositions that hypnotic suggestions could produce blindness and deafness that are indistinguishable from organic conditions, that suggested auditory and visual hallucinations give rise to the physiological changes that accompany perception, and that hypnotic age regression reinstates the cognitive and perceptual functioning of childhood. He concluded that none of the evidence used to support these propositions was convincing and that reliable evidence contradicted all of them.

More recent studies have contended that hypnotic age regression can reinstate lost perceptual abilities (Parrish, Lundy, & Leibowitz, 1969; Walker, Garrett, & Wallace, 1976) and that hypnotic anesthesia greatly reduces or eliminates proprioceptive feedback in the "anesthetized" limb (Wallace & Garrett, 1973; Wallace & Fisher, 1979). However, attempts to confirm these phenomena in independent laboratories have failed (Ascher, Barber, & Spanos, 1972; Porter, Woodward, Bisbee, & Fenker, 1972; Spanos, Ansari, & Stam, 1979;

Spanos, Gorassini, & Petrusic, 1981), and accounts of the unusual original findings in terms of social demands and other mundane factors have been provided.

The notion that hypnotic procedures are intrinsically more effective than control procedures at inducing heightened responsiveness to standard test suggestions persisted until relatively recently. However, an extensive series of studies (reviewed by Barber, 1969; Barber & Ham, 1974; Diamond, 1974) indicates that short instructions aimed at motivating subjects' performance (task-motivating instructions) usually produce increments in suggestibility that match (and sometimes exceed) those produced by hypnotic induction procedures. For example, in one extensive study Barber (1965) found that subjects who were administered either a standard hypnotic induction procedure or task-motivational instructions exhibited equally high levels of responsiveness on a susceptibility scale that assessed such behaviors as arm levitation, body immobility, and postsuggestion response. Equivalent levels of performance for hypnotic and task-motivated subjects have also been observed in studies that assessed responsiveness to suggestions for pain reduction (Barber & Hahn, 1962; M. B. Evans & Paul, 1970; Spanos, Barber, & Lang, 1974; Spanos, Radtke-Bodorik, Ferguson, & Jones, 1979), amnesia (Barber & Calverley, 1966a; Norris, 1973; Spanos & Ham, 1973), auditory and visual hallucinations (Barber & Calverley, 1964a; K. R. Graham, 1970; Ham & Spanos, 1974; Spanos & Barber, 1968; Spanos, Ham, & Barber, 1973; Spanos, Mullens, & Rivers, 1979), time distortion (Barber & Calverley, 1964d; Casey, 1966; Edmonston & Erbeck, 1967), and memory and abstract reasoning (Salzberg & DePiano, 1980).

Several recent studies (Spanos, Stam, D'Eon, Pawlak, & Radtke-Bodorik, 1980; Stam & Spanos, 1980) have manipulated the expectations conveyed to hypnotic and control subjects concerning their level of response to suggestions for pain reduction and amnesia. Depending on the direction of the expectancy manipulation, hypnotic subjects were induced to show either higher, lower, or equivalent levels of response to suggestion relative to controls. These findings are inconsistent with the notion that hypnotic procedures are intrinsically more effective than control instructions in facilitating response to suggestion. Other implications of these findings will be detailed later.

A different series of studies has compared unsuggestible subjects given explicit instructions to fake hypnosis with highly susceptible hypnotic subjects who are not asked to fake. By and large, these studies indicate that the faking subjects are as likely as the hypnotic subjects to give convincing demonstrations of age regression (O'Connell, Shor, & Orne, 1970), pain reduction (E. R. Hilgard, Macdonald, Morgan, & Johnson, 1978), optokinetic nystagmus (F. J. Evans, Reich, & Orne, 1972), and visual field narrowing (Leibowitz, Lundy, & Guez, 1980; Miller & Leibowitz, 1976). The faking subjects also are as likely to perform dangerous or "immoral" suggested behaviors (Coe, Kobayashi, & Howard, 1973; Levitt, Aronoff, Morgan, Toner, Overley, & Parrish, 1975; Orne & Evans, 1965). These findings do *not* mean that hypnotic subjects are simply faking. Nevertheless, they are consistent with the hypothesis that the overt behaviors of hypnotic subjects are well within normal limits.

A number of clinical investigators (Dengrove, 1973; Wolpe & Lazarus, 1966) combine hypnotic and behavior modification procedures because they believe that hypnotic techniques produce more profound levels of relaxation than do other procedures. The experimental evidence does not support this contention. On the contrary, Barber and Hahn (1963), Dunwoody and Edmonston (1974), Edmonston (1972), McAmmond, Davidson, and Kovitz (1971), Paul (1969b), and Spanos, Radtke-Bodorik, and Stam (1980) reported that hypnotic subjects and control subjects who were administered nonhypnotic relaxation procedures did not differ on electromyograph, electrodermal, electroocular, or verbal report indexes of relaxation. In a different study, Paul (1969a) found that progressive relaxation produced greater levels of tension reduction on several physiological indexes than did hypnotic procedures. In summary, the available evidence indicates that hypnotic procedures are no more effective than a variety of nonhypnotic control procedures in facilitating response to suggestion.

Unique subjective experiences

The history of hypnosis is characterized by reports of unusual subjective experiences that were thought to result from the properties of a special "state." For instance, some early investigators believed that religious visions were characteristic of magnetic somnambulism and that these visions provided evidence for the existence of God and the immortality of the soul (Deleuze, 1879; Grimes, 1845). Contemporary investigators have, of course, modified such outlandish notions. Nevertheless, some continue to argue that hypnosis is associated with unique subjective experiences. The best known position in this regard holds that hypnosis gives rise to a pattern of illogical thinking labeled "trance logic" and, more generally, to a tolerance for logical incongruity (F. J. Evans, 1968; E. R. Hilgard, 1965; Orne, 1959, 1966; Orne & Hammer, 1974; Perry & Walsh, 1978).

HYPNOSIS AND LOGICAL INCONGRUITIES. In what has become a classic study, Orne (1959) gave highly susceptible hypnotic subjects a suggestion to hallucinate a coexperimenter sitting in a chair. Subjects low in susceptibility were instructed to fake hypnosis (simulators) and were administered the same hallucination suggestion. The hypnotic subjects usually reported that they could simultaneously both see and see through the hallucinated coexperimenter (transparent hallucination), whereas the simulators usually stated that the hallucinated coexperimenter appeared opaque and solid. The hypnotic subjects also indicated that they could see both the hallucinated coexperimenter and the actual coexperimenter at the same time (double hallucination response). In contrast, the simulators indicated that they could see either the hallucinated coexperimenter or the actual coexperimenter, but could not see both simultaneously. On the basis of these observations, Orne concluded that subjects in a hypnotic state manifested a special type of logic that involved the "simultaneous perception and response to both hallucinations and reality without any apparent attempts to satisfy a need for logical consistency" (Orne, 1959). Trance logic, he argued, was part of the "essence" of hypnosis.

A number of experiments have consistently failed to replicate Orne's (1959) findings concerning the double hallucination response. Instead, these studies (Johnson, Maher, & Barber, 1972; McDonald & Smith, 1975; P. W. Sheehan, Obstoj, & McConkey, 1976) reported no significant differences in the frequency of the double hallucination response in hypnotic and simulating subjects. On the other hand, Johnson et al. and P. W. Sheehan et al. replicated Orne's (1959) findings concerning the transparency index: Hypnotic subjects were more likely than simulators to report transparent hallucinations. Johnson et al.'s study included nonhypnotic control subjects who were not instructed to simulate, but instead to simply imagine suggested effects. These imagination control subjects, like hypnotic subjects (but unlike simulators), tended to report transparent imagery. Similarly, Spanos, Ham, and Barber (1973) and Spanos, Mullens, and Rivers (1979) reported that hypnotic and task-motivated subjects given a visual hallucination suggestion were equally likely to rate their hallucinated images as transparent. In summary, when given a visual hallucination suggestion, hypnotic subjects and simulators perform similarly on the double hallucination index of trance logic. On the transparency index, hypnotic subjects perform differently from simulators but similarly to task-motivated and imagination control subjects.

The findings concerning transparency suggest the following account. Hypnotic and task-motivated subjects interpret a visual hallucination suggestion as an implicit request to imagine the suggested object with eyes open. When asked what they see, those who succeed in developing an image report honestly on their experience. Like most individuals asked to visually image with their eyes open, they are unable to conjure up images that have all the phenomenological properties of perception. Instead, such images tend to be described as less vivid than real objects, of short duration, unstable, and transparent (Drummond, 1926; Spanos & Stam, 1979). Thus, the reported transparency of suggested hallucinations probably has little to do with a special type of logic. It may simply reflect the fact that visual imagery generated with eyes open tends to be generally nonlifelike for most subjects.

According to this account, simulators do not interpret a hallucination suggestion as a request to imagine. Instead, they interpret it within the context of their faking instructions as a request to behave as if the suggested object were actually present and being seen by them. In effect, they do as they were instructed. They fake seeing and thereby describe the suggested object as though it were actually present, that is, as being stable, three-dimensional, solid, and so on.

Most simulator-control studies include only hypnotic and simulating groups. When differences in a dependent variable are found between these groups, there has been a tendency on the part of some investigators to attribute the difference to the unique effects of hypnosis. However, the fact that hypnotic and task-motivated subjects tend to perform similarly to one another but differently from simulators illustrates the danger in such interpretations. Differences between hypnotic subjects and simulators may be due to the special demands inherent in the faking attempt rather than to cognitive processes unique to hypnosis (Coe, 1973; P. W. Sheehan, 1970, 1971; Spanos & Barber, 1973).

A number of recent studies (McConkey & Sheehan, 1980; Obstoj & Sheehan, 1977; Perry & Walsh, 1978) have used dependent variables other than (or as well as) Orne's two indexes of trance logic to assess the notion that a tolerance for logical incongruity characterizes hypnotic responding. Obstoj and Sheehan assigned subjects who had previously scored high, medium, or low on a scale of hypnotic susceptibility to either an hypnotic or an imagination control group. All subjects were then tested on a series of tasks designed to assess a tolerance for logical incongruity. For instance, subjects were scored as making an incongruous response if they correctly spelled the word "psychological" while "regressed" to age 5. No differences were found between hypnotic and imagination control subjects. Nevertheless, the high susceptibles were more likely than the low susceptibles to make incongruous responses. The McConkey and Sheehan and Perry and Walsh studies compared hypnotic and simulating subjects and obtained mixed findings. Hypnotic subjects tended to show more incongruity than simulators on some tasks but not on others. Unfortunately, neither study included nonhypnotic, nonsimulating control subjects, and therefore conclusions concerning the relationship between incongruity and hypnosis are unwarranted. In summary, these studies, like the ones dealing with trance logic, indicate that hypnotic and nonsimulating control subjects perform similarly on indexes of incongruity. Comparisons between hypnotic and simulating subjects have yielded mixed results. Taken together, these findings offer no support for the contention that a tolerance for incongruity is unique to, or even facilitated by, hypnotic procedures.

HYPNOSIS AND IMAGERY VIVIDNESS. Many investigators have been less concerned with the issue of incongruities in hypnotic responding than with the notion that hypnotic procedures facilitate the vividness and subjective "reality" of subjects' imaginings. For instance, a number of clinicians (Astor, 1973; Dengrove, 1973; Fuchs, Hoch, Paldi, Abramovici, Brandes, Timor-Tritsch, & Kleinhaus, 1973; Kroger & Fezler, 1976) use hypnotic procedures as therapeutic adjuncts because they believe that such procedures heighten the vividness of imagery. Fuchs et al., for example, combine hypnosis and systematic desensitization "because imagery and visualization of suggested content under hypnosis are much more vivid and plastic." The available experimental evidence runs counter to this hypothesis. At least six studies (Barber

& Wilson, 1977; Coe, St. Jean, & Burger, 1980, Experiment 2; Ham & Spanos, 1974; Spanos, Ham, & Barber, 1973; Spanos, Mullens, & Rivers, 1979; Starker, 1974) have reported that ratings of imagery vividness following hypnotic procedures were not significantly higher (but were sometimes significantly lower) than ratings made under imagination control, task-motivation, or other control procedures.

The relationship between imagery vividness and hypnotic procedures is, however, more complex than indicated above. For instance, in an interesting study by Coe et al. (1980, Experiment 1), the same subjects rated the vividness of their imagery under imagination control and hypnotic conditions. Half the subjects were tested in the imagination control condition followed by hypnosis, and for the remaining half the order of testing was reversed. Subjects who received the imagination-hypnosis order rated their imagery as higher following hypnosis. Those who received the reverse order reported no differences in vividness between conditions. In a related study (Spanos, McPeake, & Carter, 1973), subjects in one group were tested on two equivalent visual hallucination suggestions: once before hypnosis (pretest) and again after (posttest). A second group was not pretested but was posttested following hypnosis. Pretested subjects reported a significant increment in the intensity of their hallucinations following the hypnotic procedure. However, nonpretested subjects rated their hypnotic hallucinations as less intense than did pretested subjects. In fact, the hypnotic hallucinations of the nonpretested subjects were not significantly different in rated intensity from the pretest hallucinations of the pretested subjects. A third group of subjects, who received pretest and posttest hallucination testing without an intervening hypnotic procedure, showed no pretest-to-posttest increment in hallucination intensity.

The findings of these two studies (Coe et al., 1980; Spanos, McPeake, & Carter, 1973) suggest that the assessment of imagery before and after hypnotic procedures provides subjects both with expectations for posttest improvement and an objective baseline (i.e., subjects' own nonhypnotic rating of vividness) against which to define improvement. Subjects who are administered hypnotic procedures without baseline testing are provided with expectations for high levels of performance, but have no standard against which to anchor their level of performance. Without a standard, subjects are unable to convert expectations for high levels of performance into a rating that will reflect improvement and, as a result, score no higher following hypnosis than they do before hypnosis. In summary, the available data suggest that hypnotic procedures may sometimes bias subjects' estimates of imagery vividness, but these data provide no support for the proposition that such procedures actually enhance imagery vividness. These findings, like those concerning tolerance for incongruity and the facilitation of overt response to suggestion, support the proposition that hypnotic responding can be understood only in terms of the interpretations and expectations conveyed to subjects by the social context in which such responding occurs. The findings provide no evidence for the notion that hypnotic responding is unique, or fundamentally different from nonhypnotic responding.

THE CREDIBILITY ASSIGNED TO IMAGININGS. As mentioned above, some investigators contend that hypnotic procedures facilitate not only the vividness but also the degree of "reality" that subjects attribute to their imaginings. Subjects sometimes describe their suggested imaginings with terms that are typically employed to refer to perceptual events (e.g., I really saw the [suggested] cat). However, the frequency of such descriptions varies greatly as a function of the options subjects are given for categorizing their experiences. For instance, McPeake and Spanos (1973) gave subjects a visual hallucination suggestion and then required them to rate their hallucinations on a unidimensional scale with alternatives ranging from "didn't see" to "clearly saw" the suggested object. Under these circumstances, 60 percent of the subjects chose a scale alternative that described their imaginings as "seen." An equivalent group of subjects was provided with the option of rating their suggested experiences either as having been "seen" or as having been "imagined." When given this choice, only 5 percent of the subjects rated their suggested hallucinations as "seen." These findings indicate that subjects who describe their suggested hallucinations as "seen" are, almost always, speaking metaphorically. They are using "see" as a synonym for "imagine," either because they have been implicitly or explicitly encouraged to do so and/or because they have not been given the option of describing these experiences as imagined (Barber, Spanos, & Chaves, 1974; Spanos, Ham, & Barber, 1973).

Inquiry procedures do not, of course, account completely for subjects' use of perceptual descriptors. In one study, for example, a very few subjects (about 2 percent of volunteers unselected for susceptibility) given a visual hallucination suggestion insisted postexperimentally that they "saw and really believed" (as opposed to imagined) that the suggested object had been present (Spanos, Ham, & Barber, 1973). Several studies (Ham & Spanos, 1974; Spanos, Ham, & Barber, 1973; Spanos, Mullens, & Rivers, 1979) have reported that this relatively rare response occurs with equal frequency in hypnotic and task-motivated subjects. Thus, whatever else might be said of this type of response, it is not unique to or greatly facilitated by hypnotic procedures.

As I implied when describing the trance logic studies, subjects who insist that they "really saw" a suggested object simultaneously describe it as waxing and waning in vividness, of short duration, fragmented, vague, transparent, and so on (P. W. Sheehan et al., 1976; Spanos, Ham & Barber, 1973; Spanos, Churchill, & McPeake, 1976). In short, when subjects insist that they "really saw" a suggested object, they do *not* mean that their suggested experience possessed all of the sensory qualities of perceptual experience. What reports of "really seeing" may instead reflect is that these subjects attended consistently to their imaginings and during this period were not concerned with the task of differentiating imaginings from external objects (Sarbin & Juhasz, 1978; Spanos, 1971; Spanos, Ham, & Barber, 1973; Spanos & Radtke, in press). Absorption in imaginings implies not only the generation and elaboration of fantasies but also a temporary failure to apply to those fantasies the implicit criteria typically employed for distinguishing imaginings from external events (Spanos & Barber, 1974). Thus, subjects who experience a suggested cat as "really there" do not employ the fact that their imagined cat is transparent or waxing and waning in vividness as evidence that it is not a real cat. Instead, by becoming absorbed in the process of imagining a cat, the "reality status" of their imaginings simply fails to arise as an issue. The empirical data available are consistent with this hypothesis. Two studies (Spanos & McPeake, 1974; Spanos & Stam, 1979) found that subjects' degree of rated absorption in their suggested imaginings correlated with the degree of credibility they assigned to their imaginings.

In summary, subjects given the option of describing their suggested hallucinations as either seen or imagined almost always describe them as imagined. Those few who do describe them as seen appear to be highly absorbed in their imaginings and thereby unconcerned with differentiating imaginings from external events. Responses of this type are not unique to hypnosis and occur with equal frequency in hypnotic and task-motivated subjects.

Automaticity of hypnotic responding

Responsive hypnotic subjects typically do not define their suggested behavior as occurring voluntarily. Instead, they define it as occurring effortlessly, automatically, or nonvolitionally (Spanos, Rivers, & Ross, 1977; Weitzenhoffer, 1978).

Traditionally, investigators have taken subjects at their word. Because hypnotic subjects report that their responses feel automatic, investigators have assumed that these responses are automatic. This conception of hypnotic responding extends back to 18th century notions of the "magnetized" subject as an automaton acted upon by forces emanating from the superior powers of the "magnetizer" (Deleuze, 1879; Spanos & Gottlieb, 1979). The notion of automatic responding was accepted by almost all 19th century investigators and survived the theoretical transition from "magnetism" to "hypnosis." Late 19th century antagonists like Charcot and Bernheim, despite their many differences, assumed that hypnotic behavior occurred automatically. For instance, Bernheim (1900) argued that suggested behavior bypassed the cortical processes involved in the execution of voluntary actions:

the idea suggested imposes itself with greater or less force upon the mind, and induces the corresponding action by means of a kind of cerebral automatism. (p. 28)

The notion that genuine hypnotic behavior is automatic and thereby fundamentally different from other types of social behavior is contained either implicitly or explicitly in the work of many contemporary investigators. Weitzenhoffer (1974, 1980), for example, is explicit in differentiating voluntary and nonvoluntary responses to suggestion and in accounting for the two in terms of different psychological mechanisms. Kihlstrom, Evans, Orne, and Orne (1980) make the same distinction in attempting to explain hypnotic amnesia. Similarly, E. R. Hilgard (1977, 1979a) argues that the occurrence of hypnotically suggested motor responses involves the operation of a "dissociated cognitive subsystem" and that hypnotic analgesia involves the automatic construction of an "amnesic barrier" that prevents "unconsciously experienced pain" from reaching conscious awareness. A major difficulty with formulations of this type is that hypnotic behavior is obviously strategic. While it may be experienced as nonvolitional, it clearly involves the kind of planning, attention to social contingencies, and coordinated decision making that characterizes the behavior we typically think of as goal-directed and voluntary (Barber, 1969; Coe & Sarbin, 1977; Haley, 1959; Spanos, 1981). This apparent paradox of hypnotic behavior—goal-directedness coupled with experienced nonvolition—was noted by White (1941) many years ago. However, he offered no real solution to the paradox and, instead, simply concluded that hypnosis was a state in which goal-directed behavior was experienced as nonvoluntary. Most contemporary theorists holding to a special-process perspective have dealt with this paradox simply by ignoring its implications or by deemphasizing the strategic nature of hypnotic responding.

From a social psychological perspective, this apparent paradox can be resolved without postulating special processes and without playing down the strategic nature of hypnotic responding. This resolution requires that a distinction be made between the variables that affect subjects' responses to suggestion and those that affect the attributions that they apply to their responses. For instance, a recent series of studies on hypnotic amnesia included postexperimental interviews designed to assess subjects' experiences (Radtke-Bodorik, Planas, & Spanos, 1980; Spanos & Bodorik, 1977; Spanos, Radtke-Bodorik, & Stam, 1980; Spanos, Stam, D'Eon, Pawlak, & Radtke-Bodorik, 1980). Some of the amnesic subjects in these studies indicated that their forgetting felt effortless, whereas others reported that forgetting required effort. The effortful forgetters reported that they forgot the words by purposefully shifting attention to other things. However, the effortless forgetters insisted that they did not do anything to forget: "the words just went away by themselves." Effortful and effortless forgetters did not differ either in the extent of amnesia or in the extent to which their recall was disorganized (Radtke-Bodorik et al., 1980; Spanos & Bodorik, 1977; Spanos, Radtke-Bodorik, & Stam, 1980).

Despite their insistence that they did nothing to forget, the testimony of effortless forgetters often indicated that they shifted attention away from the task of recalling during amnesia testing but failed to define their inattention as self-generated distraction. For instance, one subject stated explicitly that he did nothing to make himself forget but also reported "I just let myself think of things other than the words.... My mind wandered to other things." This subject obviously shifted his attention away from the task of recalling the target material. However, he defined this attentional shift as an effortless occurrence.

In short, the forgetting that occurs during hypnotic amnesia appears to be due to temporary, suggestion-generated inattention. However, subjects' reports of their forgetting occurring effortlessly or effortfully can be conceptualized as reflecting attributions that they make about the causes of their own behavior. Effortful forgetters attribute their recall deficit to their own voluntary self-generated activity ("I did it"), and effortless forgetters attribute it to events external to them ("It happened to me"). These differing attributions appear to be a function of such variables as preconceptions concerning hypnosis, expectations for effortless responding implicit in the wording of hypnotic procedures and test suggestions, and, in some cases, patterns of imaginal activity that are associated with response to many types of suggestion (Spanos, Rivers, & Ross, 1977). For instance Spanos, Stam, D'Eon, Pawlak, & Radtke-Bodorik (1980) reported that subjects instructed preexperimentally to interpret an amnesia suggestion as a request for effortful self-distraction were significantly less likely than uninstructed subjects to define their forgetting as effortless.

The wording of suggestions that call for specific motor acts implies that these acts are to be defined by the subject as involuntary occurrences (e.g., "your arm is rising" as opposed to "raise your arm"). Frequently these suggestions elicit imaginative activity as well as the overt act requested. Furthermore, some subjects imagine specific situations that are congruent with the idea that their overt behavior is occurring involuntarily. For example, a subject given a suggestion that her or his arm is rising might imagine that the arm is being pumped up with air or attached to a lever and being pulled upward. Imaginings of this type, which are congruent with the implicit expectations for involuntary responding contained in the suggestion, are labeled "goal-directed fantasies" (Spanos, 1971). When given identical suggestions, subjects who reported goal-directed fantasies were more likely than those who did not to define their overt responses as involuntary occurrences (Spanos & McPeake, 1977; Spanos, Rivers, & Ross, 1977; Spanos, Spillane, & McPeake, 1976). Furthermore, the degree of involuntariness that subjects attributed to their behavior was correlated significantly with the degree to which they became absorbed, or involved, in imaginings of this type (Spanos & McPeake, 1974). Spanos and Barber (1972) found that attributions of involuntariness were related to the wording of the suggestions administered to the subject. Hypnotic subjects were given a suggestion that instructed them either to imagine a balloon pulling their arm up or simply to raise their arm. Arm raising occurred with equal frequency for the two groups, but subjects asked to imagine were more likely than those asked simply to raise their arm to engage in goal-directed fantasy and also to rate their arm rising as feeling involuntary. These findings do not indicate that subjects' imaginings cause their overt response to suggestion. Instead, they suggest that concurrently occurring imaginative activity in part determines subjects' attributions of involuntariness.

The systematic assessment of variables that affect subjects' reports of effortlessness and automaticity has only just begun. Nevertheless, this preliminary work supports the utility of conceptualizing such reports as the outcome of an attribution process rather than as the reflection of unusual mental processes that produce automatic behavior.

Reports of having been hypnotized

It is common in hypnosis experiments to obtain ratings from subjects concerning the degree to which they believed themselves to have been hypnotized during the proceedings. Typically, subjects are simply asked to rate their experiences on a unidimensional continuum ranging from "not hypnotized" through various degrees (e.g., "lightly," "medium," "deeply") of being hypnotized (see Radtke & Spanos, 1981, and Tart, 1979, for reviews of depth scale construction and research). The results gathered with these scales indicate that (a) hypnotic subjects usually rate themselves as more deeply hypnotized than nonhypnotic control subjects (Connors & Sheehan, 1978; Gilbert & Barber, 1972; Ham & Spanos, 1974; Radtke-Bodorik, Spanos, & Haddad, 1979; Spanos & Barber, 1968; Spanos, Ham, & Barber, 1973; Spanos, Radtke-Bodorik, & Stam, 1980) and (b) among hypnotic subjects, depth ratings are positively correlated both with response on standardized scales of hypnotic susceptibility (Barber & Calverley, 1966b, 1969; Hatfield, 1961; E. R. Hilgard & Tart, 1966; Perry & Laurence, 1980; Tart, 1970) and with response to individual test suggestions (Ham & Spanos, 1974; Spanos & Barber, 1968; Spanos, Ham, & Barber, 1973).

Investigators who favor explanations of hypnotic phenomena in terms of special processes have interpreted these findings to mean that depth ratings accurately reflect degree of hypnosis, which in turn is related to degree of responsiveness to suggestions (E. R. Hilgard & Tart, 1966; Tart, 1970, 1979). In fact, a number of investigators have considered subjects' estimates of hypnotic depth to be a major source of validating evidence for the notion of a "hypnotic state" (Conn & Conn, 1967; E. R. Hilgard, 1965, 1979a; P. W. Sheehan, 1979c; P. W. Sheehan & Perry, 1980). For instance, Tart and Hilgard stated that "S's report that he feels hypnotized to some degree is primary data about the presence or absence of hypnosis, if not a criterion of hypnosis" (p. 253). Conn and Conn were even more emphatic: "the subject and only the subject can report whether or not he is 'in' or 'out' of hypnosis." A similar opinion was recently advanced by P. W. Sheehan and Perry: "The most appropriate basis for judging the presence of hypnosis appears to reside in the report of the subject that he finds a particular procedure results in the experience of his 'being hypnotized'" (p. 533).

The notion that subjects' depth ratings are valid indexes of a hypnotic state is based on the implicit assumption that hypnotic and nonhypnotic experiences are easily distinguishable. The available data do not support this hypothesis. The experiences most commonly reported following hypnotic induction procedures include relaxation, changes in body image, changes in time sense, and feelings of unreality (As & Ostvold, 1968; Barber & Calverley, 1969; Edmonston, 1977, 1979; Field, 1965; E. R. Hilgard, 1965). Reports very similar to, if not indistinguishable from, these are also associated with a wide variety of psychological procedures that involve minor sensory restriction, relaxation, and passive concentration on monotonous stimulation, e.g., progressive relaxation, EMG and EEG biofeedback training, and concentrative meditation techniques (Aaronson, 1973; Coleman, 1976; Deikman, 1963; Edmonston, 1979; Morse, Martin, Furst, & Dubin, 1977; Plotkin, 1979). Far from being distinctive and readily classifiable, the experiences associated with hypnotic procedures appear to be rather amorphous and ambiguous.

From a social psychological perspective, hypnotic depth ratings are seen not as direct reflections of an altered psychological state but, instead, as outcomes of an attributional process (Radtke & Spanos, 1981). Attribution formulations which are concerned with how individuals come to "know" their "internal state" are premised on the following hypothesis: When information from internal cues is ambiguous, individuals frequently label their experiences on the basis of observations of their own behavior and the context in which it occurs (Bem, 1972). Hypnotic situations are associated with a wide range of experiences that are potentially classifiable in many ways other than as "being hypnotized" (e.g., meditating, falling asleep, relaxing, imagining). As a result of this ambiguity, subjects use contextual information in classifying their experiences. From this perspective, hypnotic subjects are more likely than nonhypnotic subjects to rate themselves as hypnotized because only the hypnotic subjects are exposed to culturally meaningful rituals (the hypnotic induction procedures) that define the situation as hypnosis and that bolster that definition of the situation by conforming to popular stereotypes of what is involved in hypnosis (Barber,

1969; Sarbin & Coe, 1972; Radtke & Spanos, 1981). Similarly, the positive correlations found for hypnotic subjects between depth ratings and responsiveness to suggestions can be accounted for as follows. The defining of the situation as hypnosis encourages subjects to construe their successful responding as resulting from their being hypnotized and their unsuccessful responding as resulting from their not being sufficiently hypnotized. In other words, subjects' self-observations of their own responses to suggestion in a situation defined as hypnotic serve as potent determinants of the degree to which they consider themselves hypnotized (Barber, 1969; Radtke & Spanos, 1981).

An attributional formulation suggests that hypnotic subjects are often uncertain about how to rate their depth and, as a result, their ratings can be easily influenced by such contextual factors as expert opinion and the wording of the items used to assess depth. Both of these propositions are supported by the available data. For example, Barber, Dalal, and Calverley (1968) administered a hypnotic induction procedure and a standard set of test suggestions to three groups of subjects. Following these procedures, subjects were either (a) informed by the hypnotist that he thought them hypnotized, (b) informed that he thought them not hypnotized, or (c) given no opinion. The three groups did not differ in responsiveness to suggestion. Nevertheless, those told they were hypnotized rated themselves as more deeply hypnotized than those in the other two groups. Those told they were not hypnotized had lower depth ratings than those given no opinion. These findings are congruent with the hypothesis that hypnotic subjects cannot unambiguously classify their experiences and therefore rely on contextual information (e.g., expert opinion) to rate their depth of hypnosis. The findings are also consistent with studies in the attitude change literature which indicate that expert communications can produce potent changes in opinions and self-evaluations (Binderman, Fretz, Scott, & Abrams, 1972; McGuire, 1969; Webster & Sobieszek, 1974).

Psychological scales may do more than assess experiences; they may also affect the meanings that subjects attribute to their experiences. On the one hand, scales may suggest dimensions for defining experiences that subjects would not have otherwise used; on the other hand, they may restrict the range of categories subjects may use (Lunneborg, 1970; Whitley, 1979).

Recently, Radtke and Spanos (1980) assessed the effects of providing hypnotic subjects with alternative dimensions for classifying their experiences. Subjects in one group were asked to rate their hypnotic depth using a conventional unidimensional scale with alternatives ranging between "not hypnotized" and "deeply hypnotized." Those in another were asked to choose between two ratings: "hypnotized to varying degrees" and "absorbed in the suggestions to varying degrees but *not* hypnotized." Results were dramatic. When subjects were allowed to classify their experiences as either "absorbed" or "hypnotized," the large majority rejected hypnosis as a descriptor and chose to rate their experiences in terms of absorption. However, when subjects were given degrees of hypnosis on a continuum as the only dimension on which to classify their experiences, most rated themselves as hypnotized to some degree. These findings are inconsistent with the notion that hypnotic depth ratings are valid indexes of a hypnotic state. Instead, they indicate that depth scales force subjects to define their experiences in the experimenter's terms. As a result, many subjects indicate that they are hypnotized simply because they are not provided with alternative schemes for categorizing their experiences.

In summary, asking subjects to rate their hypnotic depth is not a straightforward request for easily available information about distinctive and unambiguous experiences. The experiences involved tend to be amorphous, and the requests themselves supply subjects with a frame of reference for organizing and categorizing their experiences. Responding to the requests necessitates a meaningful integration of contextual information, self-observation, and preconceptions concerning hypnosis. The traditional special-state view of hypnotic depth ratings simply fails to take complexities of this type into account.

Hypnotic analgesia and hypnotic amnesia

This section examines recent work on hypnotic analgesia and hypnotic amnesia in some detail. For each phenomenon, a social psychological account is contrasted with an account in terms of psychological dissociation. The notion that hypnotic phenomena involve the dissociation of cognitive functioning has become increasingly influential in recent years. These ideas have been explicated in most detail with reference to hypnotic analgesia. Therefore, I deal with this phenomenon first.

Hypnotic and waking analgesia

It is now abundantly clear that people's attitudes and cognitions play an important role in determining their responses to pain (Barber, 1959; Barber, Spanos, & Chaves, 1974; Meichenbaum, 1977; Melzack, 1973). For instance, a number of experimental studies (Blitz & Dinnerstein, 1968; Chaves & Barber, 1974; Rosenbaum, 1980; Scott & Barber, 1977; Scott & Leonard, 1978; Spanos, Brown, Jones, & Horner, in press; Spanos, Horton, & Chaves, 1975; Spanos, Stam, & Brazil, in press; Wothington, 1978) have demonstrated that subjects tend to show higher threshold and tolerance for painful stimuli and to report stimuli as significantly less painful after being given brief instructions or suggestions designed to help them cope with pain (e.g., instructions to imagine pleasant events during noxious stimulation). Moreover, the amount of pain subjects report before being given coping instructions, as well as the extent to which they reduce pain following such instructions, is related to their ongoing cognitive activity. Spanos, Stam, and Brazil (in press) used interviews and questionnaires to assess spontaneous coping and catastrophizing cognitions during the baseline immersion of a limb in ice water. Coping cognitions refer to such activities as imagining events inconsistent with the noxious stimulation, engaging in self-distraction, and making positive self-statements, such as "This isn't so bad" and "As long as I take it easy, this will be OK." Catastrophizing involves worrying about and exaggerating the noxious aspects of the situation and is indexed by such reports as "Oh, God, this is awful" and "If I don't take my arm out [of the ice water], I might get frostbite." Subjects' scores on indexes of coping and catastrophizing predicted 34 percent of the variance in their baseline pain ratings. Clearly, subjects did not experience noxious stimulation in a uniform manner. Some tried actively to cope with the situation, and others catastrophized. Moreover, their degree of involvement in these activities affected the degree of pain they reported.

In a related study Spanos, Brown, et al. (in press) divided subjects into those who had predominantly coped and those who had catastrophized during a baseline immersion. In a second session, both groups were given a coping suggestion instructing them to imagine their arm as numb and insensitive "like a piece of rubber." Following the suggestion, all subjects immersed their limb a second time. The suggestion was effective in reducing reported pain to the extent that it transformed catastrophizers (i.e., also called exaggerators) into copers. Subjects who coped before being given the suggestion reported no pain reduction following it. Similarly, those who catastrophized despite the suggestion reported the same high levels of pain on both immersions. In short, during noxious stimulation subjects' ongoing cognitive activity is related to their level of reported pain. Moreover, suggestions for analgesia appear to exert their effects by changing cognitive activity, by reducing subjects' tendencies to catastrophize, and/or by enhancing their tendencies to cope.

Earlier we noted that suggestions for analgesia produce equivalent reductions in reported pain for hypnotic and nonhypnotic subjects. Coupled with the findings concerning coping cognitions, these data suggest that the same cognitive variables mediate reported pain reductions in hypnotic and nonhypnotic situations, and that postulating of special processes to account for hypnotic analgesia is superfluous. Direct support for this hypothesis was obtained by Spanos, Radtke-Bodorik, Ferguson, and Jones (1979), who found that hypnotic and nonhypnotic subjects given an analgesia suggestion reported equivalent use of coping strategies as well as equivalent reductions in pain. Two studies (M. B. Evans & Paul, 1970; Spanos, Radtke-Bodorik, Ferguson, & Jones, 1979) reported that degree of pain reduction following analgesia suggestions was correlated with hypnotic susceptibility in both hypnotic and nonhypnotic subjects. Furthermore, Spanos, Radtke-Bodorik, Ferguson, & Jones (1979) found that highly susceptible subjects (both hypnotic and nonhypnotic) were more likely than low susceptibles to employ coping cognitions following analgesia suggestions. These data are consistent with the hypothesis that hypnotic susceptibility reflects subjects' proclivity for becoming absorbed in imaginative activity. Analgesia suggestions provide high susceptibles with the opportunity to exercise this proclivity for the purpose of moderating their pain.

EXPECTANCIES AND HYPNOTIC ANALGESIA. The hypnotic analgesia studies described thus far assigned different subjects to hypnotic and nonhypnotic treatments. However, a different group of experiments (E. R. Hilgard, Macdonald, et al., 1978; Stacher, Schuster, Bauer, Lahoda, & Schulze, 1975) gave the same subjects both waking analgesia and hypnotic analgesia at different times. For instance, E. R. Hilgard, Macdonald, et al. required highly susceptible subjects to immerse an arm in ice water three times. The first immersion was a baseline test, the second followed suggestion alone, and the third followed a hypnotic induction procedure plus suggestion. Subjects reported significantly more pain reduction during hypnotic analgesia than during waking analgesia. E. R. Hilgard (1977, 1979a) interpreted these results as meaning that hypnotic analgesia is intrinsically more effective than waking analgesia in reducing pain. He argued that hypnotic analgesia involves the dissociation of pain from conscious awareness whereas waking analgesia does not. According to this hypothesis, hypnotically analgesic subjects experience events simultaneously at two levels of consciousness. They continue to experience pain at an unconscious level, but the pain is somehow separated from conscious awareness by an amnesic barrier. Nonhypnotic subjects given an analgesia suggestion may be able to reduce their felt pain somewhat by employing conscious procedures like distraction, but they do not experience the more profound pain reduction that occurs when pain is dissociated from conscious awareness.

Hilgard's dissociation hypothesis cannot parsimoniously explain the equivalent reduction in reported pain found for hypnotic and waking analgesia treatments in studies that assigned different subjects to these two treatments (Barber & Hahn, 1962; M. B. Evans & Paul, 1970; Spanos, Barber, & Lang, 1974; Spanos, Radtke-Bodorik, Ferguson, & Jones, 1979). On the other hand, E. R. Hilgard, Macdonald, et al.'s findings can be accounted for parsimoniously and without recourse to the notion of dissociation if consideration is given to the social context in which experiments on hypnotic analgesia are performed. Highly susceptible subjects have a strong investment in validating their role performance as *good hypnotic* subjects (Dolby & Sheehan, 1977; Sarbin & Coe, 1972; P. W. Sheehan, 1979a; Spanos, Stam, D'Eon, Pawlak, & Radtke-Bodorik, 1980). When they are given both waking analgesia and hypnotic analgesia, they are aware that these two treatments are being compared. Therefore, they may perform less than optimally when given a suggestion alone so that they can improve significantly with hypnosis (Coe et al., 1980; Spanos, McPeake, & Carter, 1973; Zamansky, Scharf, & Brightbill, 1964).

In a recent study that examined these ideas, Stam and Spanos (1980) tested four groups of highly susceptible subjects, all of whom immersed their arm in ice water for 60 seconds on three different trials. For each immersion, subjects rated their degree of pain at 60 seconds. Subjects in one group received the order of treatments used by E. R. Hilgard, Macdonald, et al. (1978): baseline, suggestion alone, hypnosis and suggestion (B/S/H&S). As in the E. R. Hilgard, Macdonald, et al. study, this treatment order led to significantly more pain reduction for hypnotic analgesia than for waking analgesia. Subjects in the second group were not given a hypnotic procedure. Instead, they received a baseline test and then two immersions following suggestion alone (B/S/S). These subjects showed as much pain reduction on their two waking analgesia immersions as those in the B/S/H&S group showed with hypnotic analgesia. In short, subjects who received waking analgesia while knowing that hypnotic analgesia was to follow seem to have performed less than optimally during the suggestion alone so that they could later show an improvement with hypnosis.

Following baseline testing, a third group was given hypnotic analgesia followed by waking analgesia (B/H&S/S). Before receiving the hypnotic analgesia treatment, they were told that they would later receive waking analgesia and that they would probably experience less pain reduction with hypnosis than with suggestion alone. This expectancy manipulation reduced response to both hypnotic and waking analgesia. It seems that these subjects were not certain how to respond and, therefore, chose the conservative option of responding minimally to both treatments. Subjects in the fourth group simply underwent the baseline procedure on all three immersions (B/B/B). Practice at ice water immersion did not in and of itself lead to reductions in reported pain.

Following the pain testing sequence, subjects estimated the percentage of time during their third immersion that they imagined events inconsistent with pain. Subjects' imagining scores closely paralleled their third immersion pain ratings. Subjects in the B/S/H&S and B/S/S groups had the lowest third-immersion pain ratings and the highest percentage of time imagining ratings. Those in the B/H&S/S and B/B/B groups had the highest third-immersion pain ratings and the lowest percentage of time imagining ratings. When treatments were combined, the correlation between pain ratings on the third immersion and percentage time of imagining estimates was a substantial $r = .70, p < .01$.

Stam and Spanos' (1980) findings contradict the hypothesis that hypnotic analgesia is intrinsically more effective than waking analgesia. Indeed, hypnotic analgesia was equally effective, more effective, or less effective than waking analgesia depending upon the expectations conveyed to subjects. It is important to note that subjects moderated their response to suggestions in terms of expectations that were *not* explicitly included in the test suggestions. Moreover, they seemed to meet these implicit expectations by selectively employing coping strategies that led to the desired results. When expectations called for high levels of pain reduction, subjects spent a good deal of time engaged in imaginings that were inconsistent with the noxious situation. When implicit expectations did not call for pain reduction (despite the explicit requests of an analgesia suggestion), they engaged only minimally in coping imagery and reported relatively high degrees of pain. These findings portray the highly susceptible hypnotic subject as an actively cognizing individual who is attuned to subtle social expectations and who modifies his or her imaginative activities to meet these expectations. All of this is quite different from the automatic responding envisioned by a dissociation hypothesis of hypnosis.

HYPNOTIC ANALGESIA AND THE HIDDEN OBSERVER. The findings most frequently cited in support of the hypnosis-as-dissociation hypothesis come from a series of "hidden observer" studies conducted by E. R. Hilgard and his colleagues (Knox, Morgan, & Hilgard, 1974; E. R. Hilgard, Morgan, & Macdonald, 1975; E. R. Hilgard, Hilgard, Macdonald, Morgan, & Johnson, 1978). Hilgard (1977, 1979a) contends that intense pain continues to be felt at an unconscious level during hypnotic analgesia. However, this "dissociated" pain is hidden from conscious awareness behind an amnesic barrier. Hilgard further contends that the experimenter can contact this "hidden part" of the hypnotically analgesic subject and obtain pain intensity estimates from the hidden part (i.e., hidden pain estimates). At the same time, the conscious part of the hypnotically analgesic subject can estimate the degree of pain that *it* feels (i.e., overt pain estimates).

In a typical hidden observer experiment (E. R. Hilgard et al., 1975), highly susceptible subjects are given a baseline limb immersion during which they verbally estimate their pain intensity every five seconds. Later, subjects are administered a hypnotic induction procedure and instructed that there is a hidden part of them that is aware of experiences that their hypnotized part is unaware of. These hidden observer instructions are quite explicit. For instance:

When I place my hand on your shoulder, I shall be able to talk to a hidden part of you that knows things that are going on in your body, things that are unknown to the part of you to which I am now talking. The part of you to which I am now talking will not know what you are telling me. (Knox et al., 1974)

Subjects are also given practice at performing two tasks simultaneously while supposedly maintaining one of the tasks out of awareness. For example, on one task subjects name colors verbally while "unconsciously" tapping out a pattern on a key-pressing device. Later, during hypnotic analgesia, subjects are instructed to give two types of pain reports every five seconds; overt (verbal) reports that index the pain felt by their "hypnotized part" and hidden reports (numbers tapped out in a key-pressing code) that reflect the pain experienced by their "hidden part."

Hilgard and his associates (E. R. Hilgard et al., 1975; Hilgard, Hilgard, et al., 1978; Knox et al., 1974) have consistently found that (a) overt pain reports from subjects' "hypnotized part" indicate reduced pain relative to waking control pain reports and (b) hidden reports indicate more pain than overt reports and about the same degree of pain as waking control reports. According to Hilgard (1977, 1979a), hidden reports do not result from suggestion. He does not view the experimental instructions employed in his studies as communications that teach subjects to behave as though they had hidden parts. Instead, he sees hidden reports as reflecting the intrinsic characteristics of a dissociated state and the experimental instructions as creating a structured setting in which these intrinsic characteristics can come to light (E. R. Hilgard, 1979a).

Recently, Spanos and Hewitt (1980) proposed an account for the hidden observer effect that does not revolve around the notion of dissociation. They argued that hidden reports were engendered and shaped by the interpersonal communications contained in hidden observer experiments. From this perspective, hidden reports more closely approximate experimental creations than the discovery of a novel psychological phenomenon. Spanos and Hewitt assessed this hypothesis by testing a group of highly susceptible subjects under Hilgard et al.'s (1975) procedures for eliciting hypnotic analgesia and overt and hidden pain reports. High susceptibles in a second group received similar instructions but with one important difference. They were informed that their hidden part was so deeply hidden that it would be even *less* aware of what was being experienced than their hypnotized part. In short, these two groups were provided with opposite expectations concerning the experiences that would be felt by their hidden parts. Those in the "more aware" hidden observer group were implicitly informed that their hidden part would experience more pain than their hypnotized part, and those in the "less aware" hidden observer group were informed that their hidden part would experience less pain than their hypnotized part. Figure 12.1 plots the results. The graph on the left displays the data from the "more aware" subjects and clearly replicates the pattern of results observed by Hilgard et al. (1975): more hidden pain than overt pain. Comparison of the graphs for the two groups supports the social expectancy hypothesis. "More aware" and "less aware" subjects showed hidden observers with opposite characteristics: high reported sensitivity to pain in one case and greatly reduced sensitivity to pain in the other.

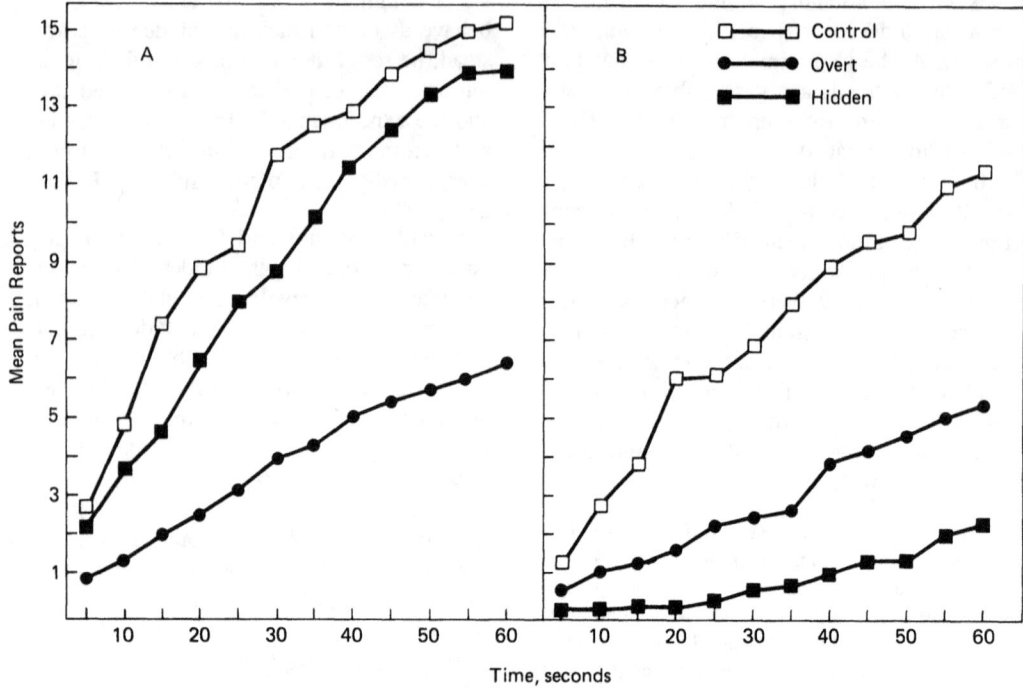

Figure 12.1. Mean pain reports for the awareness level × control/overt/hidden × 12 durations interaction (A = more aware treatment; B = less aware treatment).

These data indicate that the experimental procedures used in hidden observer studies do not simply provide a context that allows the intrinsic characteristics of a dissociated subsystem to become manifest. Instead, they provide willing subjects with information that encourages them to construe and describe their experiences in terms of dissociated parts that have particular characteristics.

Taken together, the findings discussed above are inconsistent with the notion that hypnotic analgesia results automatically from a dissociative process. They indicate instead that hypnotic analgesia is something that subjects actively bring about by gearing their cognitive activity in terms of the expectations and coping strategies contained in the procedures administered to them.

WHAT GETS "REDUCED" DURING SUGGESTED ANALGESIA? Thus far, I have referred to "reported pain reductions" and have thereby avoided the hoary issue of what these reports index. This issue, however, is as important as it is controversial and therefore deserves some comment.

Experiments on suggested/hypnotic analgesia almost always assess pain magnitude through the use of category rating scales. For example, subjects who immerse an arm in ice water might be asked to periodically rate their level of pain on a 10-point scale where 0 means "no pain" and 10 means "excruciating pain" (e.g., Spanos, Radtke-Bodorik, Ferguson, & Jones, 1979). Frequently, such ratings are made both before and after some treatment manipulation designed to reduce pain. There are at least two ways of interpreting the reported pain reductions that occur in such experiments. The first hypothesis holds that suggestion-induced cognitive activity effects changes in pain sensitivity. According to this hypothesis, category ratings accurately reflect the fact that analgesia suggestions and coping strategies lower subjects' sensitivity to painful stimulation whereas catastrophizing enhances such sensitivity. There is, in fact, little evidence to support this hypothesis. Category rating procedures are subject to a number of systematic biases (e.g., Poulton, 1979) that preclude their use as accurate indexes of pain sensitivity. Alternative scaling procedures also provide no support for the reduced sensitivity hypothesis. Thus, neither analgesia suggestions nor coping strategies appear to be consistently related to pain reduction when painfulness is measured with signal detection procedures (Clark, 1974; Clark & Goodman, 1974), functional measurement procedures (Jones & Spanos, 1980), or magnitude estimation procedures (Spanos, Jones, Brown, & Horner, 1980; Stam, Petrusic, & Spanos, 1981).[4] In short, there is little support for the hypothesis that reductions in category ratings of pain reflect reduced perceptual sensitivity to noxious stimulation.

An alternative hypothesis for the results of category rating experiments holds that cognitive variables affect the manner in which subjects interpret and report their sensory experiences but leave the sensory aspects of pain unchanged (Clark & Goodman, 1974; Spanos, Brown, et al., in press). This hypothesis does not necessarily imply that subjects are lying when they rate their pain as reduced following suggestion. Instead, it may indicate that the intensity of sensory events remains unchanged but the manner in which these events are defined to the self (i.e., the pain level assigned to them) has changed. For example, sensory events previously labeled "painful" may now be categorized in some alternative way, e.g., "intense but not painful," "numb," "very cold," "prickly sensation" (Rollman, 1977; Spanos, Brown, et al., in press; Stam & Spanos, 1980). This hypothesis implies that subjects who report pain reductions revaluate their experiences and in this sense feel less pain. However, this hypothesis does not imply that they are less able to discriminate between different intensities of noxious stimulation, i.e., they are not necessarily less sensitive to pain. With respect to the typical ice water immersion experiments used to assess hypnotic analgesia, this hypothesis suggests the following account.[5]

The experiences of subjects who immerse a limb in ice water are ambiguous. Such experiences involve a complex of diverse and changing sensations (e.g., cold, ache, throbbing, prickliness) that subjects are forced to periodically categorize along a unitary "painfulness" dimension with a restricted range of numbers. Changes in painfulness ratings, may, in part, reflect attentional shifts to different facets of the sensory complex. These ratings involve the integration of diverse and changing sensory events and the expression of the integration as a single number (or successive set of numbers). However, this integration may involve the weighting of various facets of the sensory complex differently under different circumstances. For example, changes in the relative weightings given to "cold" and "ache" sensations before and after an analgesia suggestion may be one factor leading a subject to conclude that the water is cold, "but doesn't really hurt as much as before."

Category ratings of pain are likely to be influenced by nonsensory (as well as sensory) information. Two of the most salient pieces of nonsensory information available to subjects in hypnotic analgesia experiments are expectations of pain reduction created by the suggestions and self-observations of reacting to the noxious stimulation either by coping or by catastrophizing. Thus, subjects' category ratings of pain intensity may involve an attribution process. Because their sensory experiences are ambiguous and not easily classifiable in terms of the available category units, subjects' pain ratings may be influenced by their observations of their own responses to the noxious situation. According to this hypothesis, those who observe themselves behaving in a manner inconsistent with high levels of pain (e.g., remaining calm, engaging in coping cognitions) infer (and rate themselves as feeling) relatively little pain. Those who observe themselves catastrophizing infer relatively high levels of pain, and those who observed themselves catastrophizing on the baseline test but coping after the suggestion infer that their posttest pain has been reduced by the suggestion (Spanos, Brown, et al., in press).

Studies that have used category ratings of pain intensity are consistent with these ideas (Bandler, Madaras, & Bem, 1968; Lanzetta, Cartwright-Smith, & Kleck, 1976; Nisbett & Schachter, 1966). For example, Lanzetta et al. induced subjects to display behavioral expressions of either suffering (e.g., wincing) or calmness during electric shock. Despite being exposed to the same shock levels, those who displayed suffering reported greater pain than those who displayed calmness. In a related study, Nisbett and Schachter gave subjects a placebo followed by a series of mild electric shocks. Subjects who attributed signs of autonomic arousal (e.g., flushing, increased heart rate) to the placebo rated the shock as less painful than those who attributed their arousal to the effects of shock. In short, category ratings of painfulness appear to be determined at least in part by attributions based on subjects' observations of their own behavior as well as by the magnitude and complexity of the sensory effects produced by the noxious stimulation.

Recall that for E. R. Hilgard (1977, 1979a) pain reduction following a waking suggestion involves distraction and other attention deployment procedures, whereas hypnotic analgesia involves the automatic construction of an amnesic barrier that separates the pain experience from conscious awareness. Implicit in this is the notion that hypnotic amnesia involves automatic dissociative processes that differ fundamentally from such attention deployment procedures as self-distraction. As we shall see, the available evidence runs contrary to this notion.

Hypnotic amnesia

Hypnotic amnesia is a temporary, suggestion-induced decrease in recall (Nace, Orne, & Hammer, 1974; Spanos & Radtke-Bodorik, 1980). The temporary nature of hypnotic amnesia is demonstrated by its reversibility. Amnesic subjects are able to recall the forgotten material without practice or relearning when they are provided with a prearranged cue that cancels their amnesia (Spanos & Bodorik, 1977). Traditionally, investigators have explained this phenomenon by positing processes like repression and dissociation that supposedly interfere automatically with recall (Clemes, 1964; E. R. Hilgard, 1977; Kihlstrom, 1978). Kihlstrom and Shor (1978), for example, have argued that hypnotically amnesic subjects are unable to generate the retrieval cues that will reinstate recall and have described such amnesia as "a dissociation of memories from conscious control."

Some of the investigators who favor special-process theories, however, are acutely aware that these formulations have severe shortcomings. Cooper (1979), for example, stated that "there appears to be no strong support at the present time for a process of repression in posthypnotic amnesia" (p. 345). Similarly, Kihlstrom (1978), in agreement with those who favor a social psychological perspective, noted that his own dissociation hypothesis is unable to account for the two most important aspects of hypnotic amnesia: why amnesia suggestions lead to forgetting and why the cancellation cue restores recall. Addressing these points, he asks:

What is it about hypnosis, and the administration of the amnesia suggestion, that allows posthypnotic amnesia to occur? And how does the reversibility cue function to restore access to the critical memories? It is premature to offer any detailed speculations in this regard: we simply do not know enough yet about memory, amnesia and hypnosis. (Kihlstrom, 1978)

From a social psychological perspective, this dead end in Kihlstrom's theorizing stems not from a lack of information about hypnosis or memory but from the misleading questions that theorists are forced to ask when they adopt a dissociation perspective. For example, from this perspective, questions such as the following are considered central: How can brief verbal instructions (i.e., an amnesia suggestion) instigate an automatic dissociation of target material from conscious control? and, How can a cancellation signal (which must be understood as such to be effective) suddenly terminate an automatic process? A social psychological perspective toward hypnotic amnesia holds that questions of this type are both irrelevant and misleading. Hypnotic amnesia can begin and terminate as a function of verbal cues precisely because it is *not* an automatic process. More specifically, amnesia can be conceptualized in terms of attention deployment, with its occurrence being determined by what subjects attend to and ignore during designated aspects of a standardized testing sequence (Spanos & Radtke-Bodorik, 1980; Spanos, Radtke-Bodorik, & Stam, 1980; Spanos, Stam, D'Eon, Pawlak, & Radtke-Bodorik, 1980; Stam, Radtke-Bodorik, & Spanos, 1980). Typically, however, the amnesia testing situation is ambiguous. Therefore, the events that subjects attend to are largely determined by how they construe the conflicting demands inherent in this situation.

THE AMNESIA TESTING SITUATION. The ambiguous nature of the amnesia testing situation can be illustrated by describing the testing sequence employed in a recent series of amnesia studies (Radtke-Bodorik et al., 1979; Radtke-Bodorik, et al., 1980; Spanos & Bodorik, 1977; Spanos, D'Eon, Pawlak, & Radtke-Bodorik, 1980; Spanos, Radtke-Bodorik, & Shabinsky, 1980; Spanos, Radtke-Bodorik, & Stam, 1980). Following an hypnotic induction procedure or task motivation instruction, subjects typically learned a short word list to a stringent criterion and were then exposed to the following amnesia testing sequence: A suggestion informed them that they would be unable to recall the list until given an explicit signal that canceled their amnesia. Before receiving the cancellation signal, they were challenged to try to recall the list and given an opportunity to do so. Finally, the cancellation signal was presented and subjects were again asked to recall all of the words. Subjects were considered to be amnesic if they recalled fewer words after the challenge than after presentation of the cancellation signal and if they reported postexperimentally that they actually forgot (as opposed to remembered but withheld) the words that they failed to recall following the challenge.

One source of ambiguity in this testing sequence involves the wording of amnesia suggestions. Frequently, these suggestions imply both that subjects are to actively participate in forgetting ("I want you to forget . . . ") and also that forgetting will occur automatically ("The words will be gone from your mind"). Thus, some subjects may interpret these suggestions as requests to direct attention away from recall of the target material, and others may interpret them as requests to continue attending to this material and to wait for amnesia to happen.

A second source of ambiguity is found in the "challenge to remember" that occurs before the cancellation signal. Subjects can interpret this challenge either as a serious request to refocus attention on the task of recalling the words (active recall interpretation) or as a request to recall words that "happen to come to mind" while attention is maintained elsewhere (passive recall interpretation).

Spanos, Stam, D'Eon, Pawlak, & Radtke-Bodorik (1980, Experiment 2) attempted to eliminate these sources of ambiguity by preexperimentally instructing hypnotic and task-motivated subjects to interpret the amnesia suggestion as a request to direct and maintain attention away from the target material until they received the cancellation signal. They were instructed to interpret the remember challenge in terms of passive recall, that is, to say whatever words "came to mind" but not to interfere with forgetting. Under these conditions, both hypnotic and task-motivated subjects showed substantially more amnesia than corresponding subjects who did not receive preexperimental instructions. When hypnotic and task-motivated treatments were combined, 75 percent of the preexperimental-instruction subjects showed amnesia as compared with only 36 percent of the no-instruction subjects. In a related study (Spanos, Stam, D'Eon, Pawlak, & Radtke-Bodorik, 1980, Experiment 1), hypnotic and task-motivated subjects were preexperimentally instructed to interpret the remember challenge in terms of active recall, that is, to treat the challenge as a serious request to refocus attention on the recall task. Under these circumstances, amnesia was practically eliminated in both the hypnotic and task-motivated subjects. Taken together, these findings support the hypothesis of amnesia as inattention. Moreover, they suggest that the wide individual differences typically found in amnesia studies occur *not* because some subjects become dissociated and others do not but because the amnesia testing situation is ambiguous and thereby subject to alternative interpretations.

"BREACHING" AMNESIA. Recall that Spanos, Stam, D'Eon, Pawlak, & Radtke-Bodorik (1980, Experiment 1) virtually eliminated amnesia when subjects were instructed to interpret the remember challenge as a request to actively refocus attention on the recall task. This finding was obtained using subjects who were unselected with respect to hypnotic susceptibility. In other words, relatively few of the subjects in that experiment obtained high scores on hypnotic susceptibility. On the other hand, three studies (Howard & Coe, 1980; Kihlstrom, Evans, Orne, & Orne, 1980; Schuyler & Coe, 1981) have found that some highly susceptible amnesics continued to show forgetting despite various instructions aimed at "breaching" their amnesia. For instance, Kihlstrom et al. (1980) challenged subjects to recall target material twice before presenting the cancellation signal. Before the second challenge, however, subjects were treated in various ways. Some were told to try their best to remember, some were told simply to be honest, some were told to employ an organizational retrieval strategy to aid recall, and some were given no special (control) instructions. High and medium susceptibles given breaching instructions continued to show as much amnesia as uninstructed control subjects. Kihlstrom, Evans, Orne and Orne (1980) did not present data concerning subjects' experiences during amnesia. Nevertheless, in discussing these data, Kihlstrom (1975) argued that "the hypnotized amnesia subject appears to be trying about as hard as he can [to recall the forgotten material]. . . . There is some impediment in retrieval that prevents him from easily and efficiently recollecting any more of the available memories" (p. 75).

An alternative interpretation of these findings emphasizes that highly susceptible subjects are particularly intent on successfully fulfilling the requirements of the role of the good hypnotic subject. As was pointed out earlier, these subjects respond in terms of what they believe these requirements to be even when the requirements are explicitly contradicted by other aspects of the experimental situation (Dolby & Sheehan, 1977; Orne, 1971; P. W. Sheehan & Dolby, 1975). In an amnesia testing situation, responding to the remember challenge by actively refocusing attention on the task of recalling the target material (even when explicitly instructed to do so) conflicts with maintaining the role of a good hypnotic subject. If highly susceptible subjects refocus attention on retrieval cues and try to recall the target material, they will remember it. However, if they remember it, they violate the role requirements for being good hypnotic subjects.

Spanos, Stam, D'Eon, Pawlak, & Radtke-Bodorik (1980, Experiment 3) compared highly susceptible hypnotic subjects given preliminary instructions to actively attend to target recall when given the remember challenge with corresponding highly susceptible hypnotic subjects given no instructions about the challenge. As anticipated, the preliminary active recall instructions failed to induce breaching. Subjects in the two treatments showed equivalent degrees of amnesia. More important, however, rating scale data and interview testimony indicated that the active recall subjects failed to follow their explicit preliminary instructions. Instead of refocusing their attention on the recall task as instructed, these subjects reported experiences such as the following during their amnesia: "I concentrated on driving very fast down an open highway repeating 'I cannot remember' and just concentrating on moving ahead quickly . . . " or "I went over and over in my mind saying 'forget' over and over . . . " (Spanos, Stam, D'Eon, Pawlak, & Radtke-Bodorik, 1980, Experiment 3). In short, high susceptibles faced with the choice of either following preliminary instructions that would lead to role violation or ignoring those instructions in order to meet role requirements tended to choose the latter course of action. They ignored their preliminary instructions and thereby maintained their status as good hypnotic subjects.

These findings are not consistent with formulations that view amnesia as the result of an automatic process that prevents recall (E. R. Hilgard, 1977; Kihlstrom, 1975, 1978; Kihlstrom, Evans, Orne, & Orne, 1980). Notions such as dissociation imply an inability to recall despite sustained attention and effort directed toward the recall task. The findings of Spanos, Stam, D'Eon, Pawlak, & Radtke-Bodorik (1980) suggest, instead, that subjects remain amnesic to the extent that they maintain attention away from rather than toward the recall task. Moreover, these findings indicate that the responding of hypnotic subjects is determined by their interpretations of the experimental situation. For the highly susceptible individual, performing as a good hypnotic subject is an important consideration. It is therefore not surprising that such a person tends to ignore or reinterpret instructions that conflict with good hypnotic performance.

EPISODIC AND SEMANTIC MEMORY IN HYPNOTIC AMNESIA. Tulving (1972) has distinguished between episodic and semantic components of memory. Episodic memories are tied to specific temporal and spatial contexts. They are memories of specific events, or episodes, such as recalling your last birthday party, the time a horse stepped on your foot, or the word list you learned as part of an introductory psychology experiment. Semantic memories represent knowledge that is independent of specific context. Knowing the dictionary meanings of common words or the fact that 2 + 2 = 4 without recalling the situation in which these facts were learned are examples of semantic memories. Kihlstrom (1980) hypothesized that hypnotic amnesia involved a dissociation between episodic and semantic components of memory. Such amnesia, he contended, impairs performance on episodic memory tasks but not on semantic memory tasks.

Kihlstrom taught subjects a list of words and then gave them a posthypnotic suggestion to forget the words. When challenged to recall (episodic memory task), highly susceptible subjects showed substantial amnesia (i.e., poor recall). Following the recall trial, subjects were administered a word-association test (WAT, semantic memory task). Half of the WAT stimulus words elicited as primary associates the list words covered by the amnesia suggestion (i.e., critical words). For example, if "light" was a list (critical) word, "dark" was the WAT stimulus word used to elicit "light." The remaining WAT stimulus words elicited nonlist (i.e., neutral) words as primary associates. Subjects who showed recall amnesia for the critical words did not show impairments on the WAT. In fact, they generated more critical than neutral words as associates and showed no response latency differences in generating critical and neutral words. Following the WAT, subjects were given a second challenge to recall the list. Despite having generated the critical words on the WAT, highly susceptible subjects continued to show recall amnesia for these words. In short, Kihlstrom's subjects showed memory impairments on episodic but not on semantic tasks.

Spanos, Radtke, and Dubreuil (in press) suggested that Kihlstrom's (1980) findings could be accounted for without recourse to the notion of dissociation. The amnesia suggestion used by Kihlstrom explicitly informed subjects that they would be unable to recall the critical words, but it did not imply that they would be unable to generate these words in a context other than list recall. Thus, Kihlstrom's failure to find semantic impairments during amnesia testing may have occurred simply because subjects did not construe the semantic task as relevant to their amnesia performance.

Spanos, Radtke, and Dubreuil tested two groups of subjects in Kihlstrom's paradigm. One group was given the verbatim amnesia suggestion used by Kihlstrom. The suggestion given to the second group also provided explicit expectations for recall amnesia but, in addition, subtly implied that amnesia would be shown on other tasks as well. High susceptibles given Kihlstrom's suggestion showed recall amnesia but no impairments on the WAT—the same pattern of results as in Kihlstrom's study. On the other hand, high susceptibles given the modified suggestion showed impairments both on the recall task and on the WAT. In short, subtle changes in the experimental context determined whether hypnotic subjects showed episodic impairments but no semantic impairments or both episodic and semantic impairments. These findings are inconsistent with the notion that an automatically occurring dissociation between episodic and semantic components of memory is an intrinsic characteristic of hypnotic amnesia. On the other hand, these findings offer strong support for the contention that amnesia is a strategic social enactment. Subjects' interpretations of, and motivations to comply with, the task requirements of the test situation play a central role in determining the characteristics of hypnotic amnesia.

RECALL ORGANIZATION AND HYPNOTIC AMNESIA. Modern information-processing approaches to memory frequently emphasize the notion of recall organization (Puff, 1979; Sternberg & Tulving, 1977). Suppose, for example, that subjects learn a list of words that fall into several taxonomic categories (e.g., birds, flowers). The words are presented in a different random order on each trial, and subjects are told that they can recall the words in any order they like. Under these circumstances, subjects usually recall together words from the same category (Murphy, 1979; Shuell, 1969). This tendency is called "clustering," and many investigators interpret it as a strategy that aids recall (Murphy, 1979). Thus, organizing list words into clusters may be one way to enhance their accessibility. If this is the case, then subjects who temporarily fail to organize their recall might be expected to experience a temporary difficulty in obtaining access to the list words.

A recent series of studies indicates that suggested amnesia for a categorized word list is associated with a temporary "breakdown" in the clustering of recall (Radtke-Bodorik et al., 1979; Radtke-Bodorik et al., 1980; Spanos & Bodorik, 1977; Spanos, Radtke-Bodorik, & Stam, 1980). In these studies, clustering was measured at three different points: (a) immediately before the amnesia suggestion (on the last learning trial), (b) following the remember challenge, and (c) after the cancellation signal. Partial amnesics clustered significantly less following the remember challenge than they did either before the suggestion or after the cancellation signal. (Clustering cannot be measured in total amnesics because there is no recall to measure.) On the other hand, full recallers continued to cluster to the same high degree before the suggestion, following the challenge, and after the cancellation signal (Spanos & Bodorik, 1977; Spanos, Radtke-Bodorik, & Stam, 1980). The tendency for partial amnesics to cluster less during amnesia than either before or after is labeled "disorganized recall." Hypnotic and task-motivated partial amnesics showed equivalent degrees of disorganized recall, and highly susceptible partial amnesics were more likely than low susceptible to show such disorganization (Spanos, Radtke-Bodorik, & Stam, 1980). Among hypnotic partial amnesics, a clustering breakdown occurred even when the word list was long and incompletely learned (Radtke-Bodorik et al., 1980) and when recall was written rather than spoken (Radtke-Bodorik et al., 1979). Spanos, Radtke-Bodorik, and Stam (1980) demonstrated that the disorganized recall associated with partial amnesia was *not* a statistical artifact produced by reduced recall and that such disorganization did not occur when nonamnesic subjects were simply instructed to withhold (rather than forget) part of their recall. In short, disorganized recall is a robust phenomenon reliably associated with suggested amnesia. How is it to be explained?[6]

According to F. J. Evans and Kihlstrom (1973), disorganized recall is a defining characteristic of hypnotic amnesia. Spanos and Radtke-Bodorik (1980) suggested instead that neither a hypnotic procedure nor amnesia suggestions nor high susceptibility is a necessary condition for producing disorganized recall. They contended that any procedure that temporarily diverts subjects' attention from the recall task should lead to both reduced recall and disorganization. Spanos and D'Eon (1980) tested these ideas in an experiment that involved three groups of subjects. Those in the first group were high susceptibles administered a hypnotic induction procedure and tested in a standard list-learning–amnesia-suggestion paradigm. A second group of high susceptibles did not receive a hypnotic induction procedure and carried out an attention diversion task in place of the amnesia suggestion. These subjects learned the same word list as those in the first group. In place of the amnesia suggestion, they counted backwards by three in writing while simultaneously trying to recall the words orally. They were instructed preexperimentally to focus on counting efficiently but to say any words that "came to mind" as they counted. A third group consisted of low susceptibles given the same attention diversion treatment as those in the second group. Within each group, subjects were divided into partial recallers and full recallers. The partial recallers in all three groups showed an equivalent breakdown in clustering following the remember challenge. The full recallers in all three groups failed to show a clustering breakdown. Thus, diverting attention from the task of recall reduced recall and produced the same degree of disorganization as an amnesia suggestion given to highly susceptible hypnotic subjects. These findings are consistent with the hypothesis that suggested amnesia results from inattention to the task of recall. They also indicate that disorganized recall cannot be used as an unambiguous index of the type of automatic, nonconscious blocking of retrieval functions implied by concepts such as dissociation.[7]

Taken together, findings concerning suggested analgesia and suggested amnesia argue strongly against the notion that hypnotic responding occurs automatically. Subjects' interpretations and expectations do not simply provide a readiness that allows the automatic emergence of dissociative processes. Instead, these variables determine the attentional shifts, imaginings, and other cognitive processes that subjects selectively carry out in order to meet the implicit and explicit demands of the test situation. In short, hypnotic analgesia and hypnotic amnesia are not events that happen to subjects. They are experiences that subjects must strategically bring about (Barber, Spanos, & Chaves, 1974; Coe & Sarbin, 1977; Spanos et al., 1980; Stam & Spanos, 1980).

Implications

For over 200 years, hypnosis (or previously, mesmerism) has been considered a special condition, or state, of the person. Depending on their theoretical orientation, investigators have attempted to induce this state by passing their hands along the subject's body (thereby transmitting "magnetic fluid"), by having the subject visually fixate on a shiny object (thereby inducing "neural inhibition"), by administering repeated suggestions for sleep and relaxation (thereby inducing a "sleeplike" state), and so on. The behaviors enacted by subjects "susceptible" to these various influences have varied as a function of the theoretical formulations held by investigators and at one time or another have included convulsions, purported communication with spirits, spontaneous amnesia, and, most recently, communication with dissociated "hidden observers." Thus, investigators have often agreed upon the necessity of positing a hypnotic state but have been unable to agree upon or demonstrate the characteristics of this purported state, the variables responsible for inducing it, or the behaviors that uniquely reflect its presence. Furthermore, the wide variability in procedures and types of responses historically associated with this topic seems rather inconsistent with the notion of special processes that possess unique or invariant properties.

When viewed from a social psychological perspective, a common thread becomes evident in the various procedures traditionally labeled as hypnotic. These procedures invite subjects (a) to define themselves as being altered in some fundamental way and (b) to behave in a manner consistent with the specific alterations implied by the structure of the situation. "Good" hypnotic subjects are those who accept the definition of the situation provided and whose enactments reflect this acceptance.

A social psychological formulation does not imply that subjects are necessarily faking. On the contrary, one of the most interesting aspects of the enactments associated with hypnosis is that subjects, to varying degrees, succeed in temporarily convincing themselves that their arm cannot bend, that a cat is in their lap, that they can no longer remember well-learned material, and so on. Nor does this perspective imply that subjects' responses are necessarily a direct reflection of experimental demands. For instance, visual hallucination suggestions do not imply transparent imagery, and amnesia suggestions do not imply incomplete but disorganized recall. Instead, these responses appear to result from subjects' honest but only partially successful attempts to meet the demands of suggestions. Thus, transparent imagery appears to result when subjects who have their eyes open attempt unsuccessfully to construct visual images that have all the phenomenological properties of perception. Similarly, disorganized recall appears to reflect their failure to disattend completely from retrieval cues during amnesia testing.

What a social psychological formulation does imply is that hypnotic behavior is, first and foremost, social behavior. It can be understood only by taking into consideration (a) subjects' motivations to respond in terms of the role requirements specified by the hypnotic context and (b) the understandings they develop concerning those requirements. Subjects' understanding of these requirements vary because test suggestions and other aspects of the hypnotic situation are ambiguous and therefore open to alternative interpretations.

Recently, Kihlstrom, Evans, Orne, & Orne (1980) sought to distinguish social psychological and cognitive approaches toward hypnotic responding. Any such distinction is, however, misleading. Social psychological accounts of hypnotic responding are not alternatives to cognitive accounts; they *are* cognitive accounts. More specifically, social psychological accounts construe hypnotic subjects as continuously modifying their cognitive activities and behavior in terms of the changing social context that constitutes the ongoing hypnotic situation. From this perspective, cognitive activities may result either directly, as attempts to meet specific demands (e.g., imagery generated by a visual hallucination suggestion), or indirectly, as unrequested consequences of attempting to fulfill role requirements (e.g., nonsuggested feelings of warmth and changes in body image that sometimes accompany becoming relaxed during hypnotic induction procedures). Thus, social psychological accounts differ from those special-process formulations that construe experiential and behavioral changes as the automatic accompaniments of unique or unusual mental processes (e.g., "amnesic barriers" that prevent "dissociated" pain from reaching consciousness in hypnotically analgesic subjects). Social psychological accounts stress the intimate and continuous interplay of context and cognition. Special-process approaches tend to downplay contextual variables and view "genuine" hypnotic responding as occurring more or less independently of subjects' construals. This approach, of course, contains a potential danger. Behavioral effects assumed to occur automatically may, on closer examination, be found to result from the contextually generated expectations that special-process approaches sometimes ignore (Spanos & Hewitt, 1980; Spanos, Radtke, & Dubreuil, in press; Stam & Spanos, 1980).

Many aspects of hypnotic responding remain incompletely understood. For instance, delineation of the variables that affect subjects' attributions of nonvolition remains an important incompleted task. Similarly, a satisfactory account of "pain reduction" during suggested analgesia has yet to be fully developed. This review suggests that these and other questions relevant to the topic of hypnosis will best be answered within a framework that views hypnotic responding as goal-directed social behavior.

Notes

1. Factor-analytic studies of susceptibility scales usually result in several orthogonal factors (E. R. Hilgard, 1965; Sarbin & Coe, 1972; Spanos, Mah, Pawlak, D'Eon, & Ritchie, 1980). Interpretation of the multiple factors is controversial. One position contends that these factors are artifacts of the differential difficulty level of hypnotic test suggestions (Coe & Sarbin, 1971), and the other holds that they reflect distinct psychological dimensions. The empirical data relating to this issue remain inconclusive (Spanos, Mah, et al., 1980).

2. Attempts to relate hypnotic susceptibility to other paper and pencil indexes of imaginal ability (e.g., imagery vividness, control of imagery) have yielded inconsistent findings (see P. W. Sheehan, 1979b, for a thorough review of this research).

3. Recently, Sackeim, Paulhus & Weiman (1979) contended that classroom seating preference (i.e., the left or right side of the room) indexed hemispherisity, and reported that seating preference was related to hypnotic susceptibility. The appropriateness of the statistical procedures employed by Sackeim et al. is debatable. Stam, Spanos, Radtke, and Jones (1981) reported several failures to replicate their findings.

4. The measurement of painfulness, and the conclusions that may be legitimately drawn from the results of signal detection and magnitude estimation procedures, remain controversial issues (see Jones, 1979; Poulton, 1968, 1979; Rollman, 1977, 1979).

5. When noxious stimulation is presented under baseline (no hypnosis, no suggestion) conditions, verbal reports of pain intensity correlate to a moderate degree with such involuntary physiological responses as heart rate and blood pressure changes. However, suggestion-induced reductions in reported pain are not accompanied by corresponding reductions in these physiological indexes in either hypnotic or nonhypnotic subjects (Barber & Hahn, 1962; M. B. Evans & Paul, 1970; E. R. Hilgard & Morgan, 1975; Shor, 1967). The meaning of these findings is, however, unclear. For example, subjects simply asked to imagine pain, and also subjects anticipating a forthcoming pain, often show physiological changes that are indistinguishable from those that accompany actual noxious stimulation. Thus, increments in blood pressure, heart rate, and so on are a function of many variables other than pain (e.g., anticipatory stress). For this reason, the occurrence of these increments during suggested analgesia need not mean that subjects who report pain reductions are simply lying about the amount of pain they feel.

6. F. J. Evans and Kihlstrom (1973) and Kihlstrom and Evans (1979) investigated temporal organization (as opposed to catagorical organization) in the recall of unrelated material during amnesia testing. Although their findings suggested a correlation between temporal disorganization and hypnotic amnesia, methodological difficulties with their paradigm (detailed by Radtke & Spanos, 1981) preclude firm conclusions. Three recent studies by independent investigators (Radtke & Spanos, 1981; St. Jean & Coe, 1981) have failed to replicate their most important results.

7. Spanos and Radtke-Bodorik (1980) indicated that the inattention hypothesis is consistent with Tulving's (1974) notion of encoding specificity. This idea holds that recall will be successful to the extent that retrieval cues present during recall match those that were associated with the target material at the time of its encoding. Thus, the recall of list words is likely to be successful only to the extent that the "cognitive environment" present during recall matches the cognitive environment that was present during initial learning (Tulving, 1974). By shifting attention away from the recall task following the amnesia suggestion, subjects are, in effect, altering that cognitive environment. To the extent that inattention is maintained, the retrieval cues that were present at encoding will not be present at recall. Therefore, recall will occur less efficiently than usual (i.e., subjects will show amnesia). Among the important cues used to learn a categorized list are the category labels inferred from the list. Because partial amnesics are paying relatively little attention to these or other retrieval cues, category labels are less likely than usual to provide a structure for the organization of their recall. Therefore, the inefficient recall of these subjects tends to be disorganized.

References

Aaronson, B. ASCID trance, hypnotic trance, just trance. *American Journal of Clinical Hypnosis*, 1973, *16*, 110–117.

As, A. Non-hypnotic experiences related to hypnotizability in male and female college students. *Scandinavian Journal of Psychology*, 1962, *3*, 112–121.

As, A., & Ostvold, S. Hypnosis as subjective experience. *Scandanavian Journal of Psychology, 1968, 9,* 33-38.

Ascher, L. M., Barber, T. X., & Spanos, N. P. Two attempts to replicate the Parrish–Lundy–Leibowitz experiment on hypnotic age regression. *American Journal of Clinical Hypnosis,* 1972, *14,* 178-185.

Astor, M. H. Hypnosis and behaviour modification combined with psychoanalytic psychotherapy. *International Journal of Clinical and Experimental Hypnosis,* 1973, *21,* 18-24.

Bakan, P. Hypnotizabilty, laterality of eye movement and functional brain asymmetry. *Perceptual and Motor Skills,* 1969, *28,* 927-932.

Balaschak, B., Blocker, K., Rossiter, T., & Perin, C. T. The influence of race and expressed experience of the hypnotist on hypnotic susceptibility. *International Journal of Clinical and Experimental Hypnosis,* 1972, *20,* 38-45.

Bandler, R. J., Madaras, G. R., & Bem, D. J. Self-observation as a source of pain perception. *Journal of Personality and Social Psychology,* 1968, *9,* 205-209.

Barabasz, A. F. EEG alpha, skin conductance and hypnotizability in Antarctica. *International Journal of Clinical and Experimental Hypnosis,* 1980, *28,* 63-74

Barber, T. X. Toward a theory of pain: Relief of chronic pain by prefrontal leucotomy, opiates, placebos, and hypnosis. *Psychological Bulletin,* 1959, *56,* 430-460

Barber, T. X. "Hypnosis" as a causal variable in present-day psychology: A critical analysis. *Psychological Reports,* 1964, *14,* 839-842. (a)

Barber, T. X. Hypnotizability, suggestibility, and personality: V. A critical review of research findings. *Psychological Reports,* 1964, *14,* 299-320. (b)

Barber, T. X. Measuring "hypnotic-like" suggestibility with and without "hypnotic induction"; psychometric properties, norms, and variables influencing response to the Barber Suggestibility Scale (BSS). *Psychological Reports,* 1965, *16,* 809-844.

Barber, T. X. *Hypnosis: A scientific approach.* New York: Van Nostrand Reinhold, 1969.

Barber, T. X. *LSD, marijuana, yoga and hypnosis.* Chicago: Aldine, 1970.

Barber, T. X. Suggested ("hypnotic") behavior: The trance paradigm versus an alternative paradigm. In E. Fromm & R. E. Shor (Eds.) *Hypnosis: Research developments and perspectives.* Chicago: Aldine-Atherton, 1972.

Barber, T. X., & Calverley, D. S. An experimental study of "hypnotic" (auditory and visual) hallucinations. *Journal of Abnormal and Social Psychology,* 1964, *63,* 13-20. (a)

Barber, T. X., & Calverley, D. S. Empirical evidence for a theory of "hypnotic" behavior: Effects of pretest instructions on response to primary suggestions. *Psychological Record,* 1964, *15,* 139-144. (b)

Barber, T. X., & Calverley, D. S. The definiton of the situation as a variable effecting "hypnotic-like" suggestibility. *Journal of Clinical Psychology,* 1964, *20,* 438-440. (c)

Barber, T. X., & Calverley, D. S. Toward a theory of "hypnotic" behavior: An experimental study of "hypnotic time distortion." *Archives of General Psychiatry,* 1964, *10,* 209-216. (d)

Barber, T. X., & Calverley, D. S. Toward a theory of "hypnotic" behavior: Experimental analysis of suggested amnesia. *Journal of Abnormal Psychology,* 1966, *71,* 95-107. (a)

Barber, T. X., & Calverley, D. S. Toward a theory of hypnotic behavior: Experimental evaluation of Hull's postulate that hypnotic susceptibility is a habit phenomenon. *Journal of Personality,* 1966, *34,* 416-433. (b)

Barber, T. X., & Calverley, D. S. Multidimensional analysis of "hypnotic" behavior. *Journal of Abnormal Psychology,* 1969, *74,* 209-220.

Barber, T. X., Dalal, A. S., & Calverley, D. S. The subjective reports of hypnotic subjects. *American Journal of Clinical Hypnosis,* 1968, *11,* 74-88.

Barber, T. X., & Hahn, K. W. Jr. Physiological and subjective responses to pain producing stimulation under hypnotically-suggested and waking-imagined "analgesia." *Journal of Abnormal and Social Psychology,* 1962, *65,* 411-418.

Barber, T. X., & Hahn, K. W. Jr. Hypnotic induction and "relaxation": An experimental study. *Archives of General Psychology,* 1963, *8,* 295-300.

Barber, T. X., & Hahn, K. W. Jr. Experimental studies in "hypnotic" behavior: Physiological and subjective effects of imagined pain. *Journal of Nervous and Mental Disease,* 1964, *139,* 416-425.

Barber, T. X., & Ham, M. W. *Hypnotic phenomena.* Morristown, N.J.: General Learning Press, 1974.

Barber, T. X., Spanos, N. P., & Chaves, J. F. *Hypnosis, imagination and human potentiali-*

ties. New York: Pergamon, 1974.
Barber, T. X., & Wilson, S. C. Hypnosis, suggestions, and altered states of consciousness: Experimental evaluation of the new cognitive-behavioural theory and the traditional trance-state theory of "hypnosis." *Annals of the New York Academy of Sciences*, 1977, *296*, 34–47.
Barber, T. X., & Wilson, S. C. The Barber Suggestibility Scale and the Creative Imagination Scale: Experimental and clinical applications. *American Journal of Clinical Hypnosis*, 1979, *21*, 68–83.
Bem, D. J. Self-perception theory. In L. Berkowitz (Ed.), *Advances in experimental social psychology*. New York: Academic Press, 1972.
Bernheim, H. *Suggestive therapeutics*. New York: Putnam, 1900. (Originally published 1886)
Bertrand, A. J. F. *Du magnetisme animal en France*. Paris: Balliere et Fils, 1826.
Binderman, R. M., Fretz, B. R., Scott, N. A., & Abrams, M. H. Effects of interpreter credibility and discrepancy level of results on response to test results. *Journal of Counseling Psychology*, 1972, *19*, 399–403.
Blitz, B., & Dinnerstein, A. Effects of different types of instructions on pain parameters. *Journal of Abnormal Psychology*, 1968, *73*, 276–280.
Bowers, K. S. *Hypnosis for the seriously curious*. Monterey, Calif.: Brooks Cole, 1976.
Braid, J. *Neurypnology*. Reprinted as *Braid on hypnotism*, with an introduction by A. E. Waite. New York: Julian, 1960. (Originally published 1843)
Burrows, G. D., & Dennerstein, L. (Eds.). *Handbook of hypnosis and psychosomatic medicine*. Amsterdam: Elsevier/North-Holland Biomedical Press, 1980.
Casey, G. A. *Hypnotic time distortion and learning*. Unpublished Ph.D. dissertation, Michigan State University, 1966.
Chaves, J. F., & Barber, T. X. Cognitive strategies, experimenter modeling and expectation in the attenuation of pain. *Journal of Abnormal Psychology*, 1974, *83*, 356–363.
Clark, W. C. Pain sensitivity and the report of pain: An introduction to sensory decision theory. *Anesthesiology*, 1974, *40*, 272–287.
Clark, W. C., & Goodman, J. S. Effects of suggestion on dp and Cx for pain detection and pain tolerance. *Journal of Abnormal Psychology*, 1974, *83*, 364–372.
Clemes, S. R. Repression and hypnotic amnesia. *Journal of Abnormal and Social Psychology*, 1964, *69*, 62–69.
Coe, W. C. Experimental designs and the state-nonstate issue in hypnosis. *American Journal of Clinical Hypnosis*, 1973, *16*, 118–128.
Coe, W. C. Effects of hypnotist susceptibility and sex on the administration of standard hypnotic susceptibility scales. *International Journal of Clinical and Experimental Hypnosis*, 1976, *24*, 281-286
Coe, W. C. The credibility of posthypnotic amnesia: A contextualist's view. *International Journal of Clinical and Experimental Hypnosis*, 1978, *26*, 281-286.
Coe, W. C., Bailey, J. R., Hall, J. C., Howard, M. L., Janda, R. L., Kobayashi, K., & Parker, M. D. Hypnosis as role enactment: The role location variable. *Proceedings of the 78th Annual Convention of the American Psychological Association*, 1970, 839–840.
Coe, W. C., Kobayashi, K., & Howard, M. L. Experimental and ethical problems of evaluating the influence of hypnosis in antisocial conduct. *Journal of Abnormal Psychology*, 1973, *82*, 476-482.
Coe, W. C., & Sarbin, T. R. An alternative interpretation of the multiple composition of hypnotic scales: A single role relevant skill. *Journal of Personality and Social Psychology*, 1971, *18*, 1–8.
Coe, W. C., & Sarbin, T. R. Hypnosis from the standpoint of a contextualist. *Annals of the New York Academy of Sciences*, 1977, *296*, 2–13.
Coe, W. C., St. Jean, R. L., & Burger, J. M. Hypnosis and the enhancement of visual imagery. *International Journal of Clinical and Experimental Hypnosis*, 1980, *28*, 225–243.
Coleman, T. R. A comparative study of certain behavioural, physiological and phenomenological effects of hypnotic induction and two progressive relaxation procedures (doctoral dissertation, Brigham Young University, 1976). *Dissertation Abstracts International*, 1976, *36*, 4147B.
Conn, J. H., & Conn, R. N. Discussion of T. X. Barber's "hypnosis as a causal variable in present day psychology: A critical analysis." *International Journal of Clinical and Experimental Hypnosis*, 1967, *15*, 106–110
Connors, J., & Sheehan, P. W. The influence of control comparison tasks and between-versus-within subject effects in hypnotic responsivity. *International Journal of Clinical and Experimental Hypnosis*, 1978, *26*, 104–122.

Cooper, L. M. Hypnotic amnesia. In E. Fromm & R. E. Shor (Eds.), *Hypnosis: Developments in research and new perspectives* (2nd ed.). New York: Aldine, 1979.

Corballis, M. C. Laterality and myth. *American Psychologist*, 1980, *35*, 284-295.

Crawford, H. J. *Hypnotic susceptibility and "right hemisphere" functioning: Gestalt closure ability correlates*. Paper presented at the annual meeting of the American Psychological Association, San Francisco, August 1977.

Cronin, D. M., Spanos, N. P., & Barber, T. X. Augmenting hypnotic suggestibility by providing favourable information about hypnosis. *American Journal of Clinical Hypnosis*, 1971, *13*, 259-264.

Crosson, B., Meinz, R., Laur, E., Williams, D., & Andreychuk, T. EEG alpha training, hypnotic susceptibility, and baseline techniques. *International Journal of Clinical and Experimental Hypnosis*, 1977, *25*, 348-360.

Davis, S., Dawson, J. G., & Seay, B. Prediction of hypnotic susceptibility from imaginative involvement. *American Journal of Clinical Hypnosis*, 1978, *20*, 194-198.

Deikman, A. J. Experimental meditation. *Journal of Nervous and Mental Disease*, 1963, *236*, 329-343.

Deleuze, J. P. F. *Animal Magnetism*. New York: Wills, 1879. (Originally published 1825)

Dengrove, E. The uses of hypnosis in behaviour therapy. *International Journal of Clinical and Experimental Hypnosis*, 1973, *21*, 13-17.

D'Eon, J. L., Mah, C. D., Pawlak, A. E., & Spanos, N. P. Effects of hypnotists' and subjects' sex on hypnotic susceptibility. *Perceptual and Motor Skills*, 1979, *48*, 1232-1234.

Derman, D., & London, P. Correlates of hypnotic susceptibility. *Journal of Consulting Psychology*, 1965, *29*, 537-545.

DeWitt, G. W., & Averill, J. R. Lateral eye movements, hypnotic susceptibility and field-dependence. *Perceptual and Motor Skills*, 1976, *43*, 1179-1184.

Diamond, M. J. The use of observationally presented information to modify hypnotic susceptibility. *Journal of Abnormal Psychology*, 1972, *79*, 174-180.

Diamond, M. J. Modification of hypnotizability: A review. *Psychological Bulletin*, 1974, *81*, 180-198.

Diamond, M. J. Hypnotizability is modifiable: An alternative approach. *International Journal of Clinical and Experimental Hypnosis*, 1977, *25*, 147-166.

Diamond, M. J., Gregory, J., Lenney, E., Steadman, C., & Talone, J. M. An alternative approach to personality correlates of hypnotizability: Hypnosis-specific mediational attitudes. *International Journal of Clinical and Experimental Hypnosis*, 1974, *22*, 346-353.

Dingwall, E. J. *Abnormal hypnotic phenomena* (Vol. 1). New York: Barnes & Noble, 1968.

Dodds, J. B. *Philosophy of mesmerism*. New York: Fowler & Wells, 1865.

Dolby, R. M. & Sheehan, P. W. Cognitive processing and expectancy behavior in hypnosis. *Journal of Abnormal Psychology*, 1977, *86*, 334-345.

Drummond, M. The nature of images. *British Journal of Psychology*, 1926, *17*, 10-19.

Dumas, R. EEG alpha-hypnotizability correlations: A review. *Psychophysiology*, 1977, *14*, 431-438.

Dumas, R. A. Cognitive control in hypnosis and biofeedback. *International Journal of Clinical and Experimental Hypnosis*, 1980, *28*, 53-62.

Dumas, R. A. & Spitzer, S. E. Influences of subject self-selection on the EEG alpha-hypnotizability correlation. *Psychophysiology*, 1978, *15*, 606-608.

Dunwoody, R. C., & Edmonston, W. E. Jr. Hypnosis and slow eye movements. *American Journal of Clinical Hypnosis*, 1974, *16*, 270-274.

Edmonston, W. E. Jr. Relaxation as an appropriate experimental control in hypnosis studies. *American Journal of Clinical Hypnosis*, 1972, *14*, 218-228.

Edmonston, W. E. Jr. Neutral hypnosis as relaxation. *American Journal of Clinical Hypnosis*, 1977, *20*, 69-75.

Edmonston, W. E. Jr. The effects of neutral hypnosis on conditioned responses: Implications for hypnosis as relaxation. In E. Fromm & R. E. Shor (Eds.) *Hypnosis: Developments in research and new perspectives* (2nd ed.). New York: Aldine, 1979.

Edmonston, W. E.Jr., & Erbeck, J. R. Hypnotic time distortion: A note. *American Journal of Clinical Hypnosis*, 1967, *10*, 79-80.

Ehrlichman, H. Hemispheric functioning and individual differences in cognitive abilities (doctoral dissertation, New School for Social Research, 1971). *Dissertation Abstracts International*, 1972, *33*, 2319B. (University Microfilms No. 72-27, 869)

Ehrlichman, H., & Weinberger, A. Lateral eye movements and hemispheric asymmetry: A critical review. *Psychological Bulletin*, 1978,

85, 1080-1101.

Eliseo, T. S. The hypnotic induction profile and hypnotic susceptibility. *International Journal of Clinical and Experimental Hypnosis*, 1974, *22*, 320-326.

Engstrom, D. R. The enhancement of EEG alpha production and its effects on hypnotic susceptibility. Unpublished doctoral dissertation, University of Southern California, 1970.

Evans, F. J. Recent trends in experimental hypnosis. *Behavioral Science*, 1968, *13*, 477-487.

Evans, F. J. Hypnosis and sleep: Techniques for exploring cognitive activity during sleep. In E. Fromm & R. E. Shor (Eds.), *Hypnosis: Research developments and perspectives*. Chicago: Aldine-Atherton, 1972.

Evans, F. J., Gustafson, L. A., O'Connell, D. N., Orne, M. T., & Shor, R. E. Sleep-induced behavioral response: Relationship to susceptibility to hypnosis and laboratory sleep patterns. *Journal of Nervous and Mental Disease*, 1969, *148*, 467-476.

Evans, F. J., & Kihlstrom, J. F. Posthypnotic amnesia as disrupted retrieval. *Journal of Abnormal Psychology*, 1973, *82*, 317-323.

Evans, F. J., Reich, L. H., & Orne, M. T. Optokinetic nystagmus, eye movements, and hypnotically induced hallucinations. *Journal of Nervous and Mental Disease*, 1972, *152*, 419-431.

Evans, M. B., & Paul, G. L. Effects of hypnotically suggested analgesia on physiological and subjective response to cold stress. *Journal of Consulting and Clinical Psychology*, 1970, *35*, 362-371.

Faria, J. C. *De la cause du sommeil lucide, ou étude sur la nature de l'homme* (2nd ed.). Paris: Henri Sauve, 1906. (Originally published 1819)

Field, P. B. An inventory scale of hypnotic depth. *International Journal of Clinical and Experimental Hypnosis*, 1965, *13*, 238-249.

Foenander, G., & Burrows, G. D. Bilateral EEG alpha activity in hypnosis. In G. D. Burrows, D. R. Collison, & L. Dennerstein (Eds.), *Hypnosis 1979*. Amsterdam: Elsevier/North-Holland Biomedical Press, 1979.

Franklin, B., et al. [Report of Dr. Benjamin Franklin and the other commissioners, charged by the king of France, with the examination of the animal magnetism now practiced at Paris.] W. Godwin, Trans. In M. Tinterow (Ed.), *Foundations of hypnosis*. Springfield, Ill.: C. C. Thomas, 1970. (Originally published 1785)

Fuchs, K., Hoch, A., Paldi, E., Abramovici, H., Brandes, J. M., Timor-Tritsch, I., & Kleinhaus, M. Hypno-desensitization therapy of vaginismus: Part I: "In vitro" method. *International Journal of Clinical and Experimental Hypnosis*, 1973, *21*, 144–156.

Galbraith, G. C., London, P., Leibovitz, M. P., Cooper, L. M., & Hart, J. T. EEG and hypnotic susceptibility. *Journal of Comparative and Physiological Psychology*, 1970, *72*, 125–131.

Gelder, M. G., Bancroft, J. H., Gath, D. H., Johnston, D. W., Mathews, A. M., & Shaw, P. M. Specific and non-specific factors in behavior therapy. *British Journal of Psychiatry*, 1973, *123*, 445–462.

Gibbons, D., Kilbourne, L., Saunders, A., & Castles, C. The cognitive control of behavior: A comparison of systematic desensitization and hypnotically induced "directed experience" techniques. *American Journal of Clinical Hypnosis*, 1970, *12*, 141–145.

Gilbert, J. E., & Barber, T. X. Effects of hypnotic induction, motivational suggestions, and level of suggestibility on cognitive performance. *International Journal of Clinical and Experimental Hypnosis*, 1972, *20*, 156–158.

Gill, M. M., & Brenman, M. *Hypnosis and related states*. New York: International Universities Press, 1959.

Graham, K. R. Optokinetic nystagmus as a criterion of visual imagery. *Journal of Nervous and Mental Disease*, 1970, *151*, 411–414.

Graham, K. R. Perceptual processes and hypnosis: Support for a cognitive-state theory based on laterality. *Annals of the New York Academy of Sciences*, 1977, *296*, 274–283.

Graham, C., & Evans, F. J. Hypnotizability and the deployment of waking attention. *Journal of Abnormal Psychology*, 1977, *86*, 631–638.

Greenberg, R. P., & Land, J. M. Influence of some hypnotist and subject variables on hypnotic susceptibility. *Journal of Consulting and Clinical Psychology*, 1971, *37*, 111-115.

Gregory, J., & Diamond, M. J. Increasing hypnotic susceptibility by means of positive expectancies and written instructions. *Journal of Abnormal Psychology*, 1973, *82*, 363-367.

Grimes, J. S. *Eterology: Or the philosophy of mesmerism and phrenology: Including a new philosophy of sleep and of consciousness, with a review of pretensions of neurology and phrenomagnetism*. New York: Saxon & Miles, 1845.

Gur, R. C. Imagery, absorption, and the tendency toward "mind exploration" as correlates of hypnotic susceptibility in males and females. In F. H. Frankel & H. S. Zamansky (Eds.), *Hypnosis at its bicentennial*. New York: Plenum, 1978.

Gur, R. C., & Gur, R. E. Handedness, sex, and eyedness and moderating variables in the relation between hypnotic susceptibility and functional brain asymmetry. *Journal of Abnormal Psychology*, 1974, *83*, 635–643.

Gur, R. E., & Reyher, J. Relationship between style of hypnotic induction and direction of lateral eye movements. *Journal of Abnormal Psychology*, 1973, *82*, 499-505.

Haddock, J. Psychology: Or the science of the soul, considered physiologically and philosophically. Reprinted in *Library of Mesmerism* (Vol. 2). New York: Fowler & Wells, 1865.

Haley, J. An interactional explanation of hypnosis. *American Journal of Clinical Hypnosis*, 1959, *1*, 41–57.

Hall, C. R. *Mesmerism: Its rise, progress and mysteries*. London: Burgess, Stringer, 1845.

Ham, M. W., & Spanos, N. P. Suggested auditory and visual hallucinations in task-motivated and hypnotic subjects. *American Journal of Clinical Hypnosis*, 1974, *17*, 94–101.

Hart, E. *Hypnotism, mesmerism and the new witchcraft*. New York: Appleton, 1898.

Hartnett, J., Nowlis, D., & Svorad, D. Hypnotic susceptibility and EEG alpha: Three correlations. Hawthorn House Res. Memo. No. 97, Stanford University, Stanford, Calif., 1969.

Hatfield, E. C. The validity of the LeCron method of evaluating hypnotic depth. *International Journal of Clinical and Experimental Hypnosis*, 1961, *9*, 15–22.

Hedberg, A. G. The effects of certain examiner and subject characteristics on responsiveness to suggestion. *International Journal of Clinical and Experimental Hypnosis*, 1974, *22*, 354–364.

Hilgard, E. R. *Hypnotic susceptibility*. New York: Harcourt, 1965.

Hilgard, E. R. *Divided consciousness*. New York: Wiley, 1977.

Hilgard, E. R. Divided consciousness in hypnosis: The implications of the hidden observer. In E. Fromm & R. E. Shor (Eds.), *Hypnosis: Developments in research and new perspectives* (2nd ed.). New York: Aldine, 1979. (a)

Hilgard, E. R. The Stanford Hypnotic Susceptibility Scales as related to other measures of hypnotic responsiveness. *American Journal of Clinical Hypnosis*, 1979, *21*, 68–83. (b)

Hilgard, E. R., Hilgard, J. R., Macdonald, H., Morgan, A. H., & Johnson, L. S. Covert pain in hypnotic analgesia: Its reality as tested by the real-simulator. *Journal of Abnormal Psychology*, 1978, *87*, 655–663.

Hilgard, E. R., Macdonald, H., Marshall, G. D., & Morgan, A. H. The anticipation of pain and pain control under hypnosis: Heart rate and blood pressure responses in the cold pressor test. *Journal of Abnormal Psychology*, 1974, *83*, 561–568.

Hilgard, E. R., Macdonald, H., Morgan, A. H., & Johnson, L. S. The reality of hypnotic analgesia: A comparison of highly hypnotizables with simulators. *Journal of Abnormal Psychology*, 1978, *87*, 239–246.

Hilgard, E. R., & Morgan, A. H. Heart rate and blood pressure in the study of laboratory pain in man under normal conditions and as influenced by hypnosis. *Neurobiologiae Experimentalis*, 1975, *35*, 741–759.

Hilgard, E. R., Morgan, A. H., & Macdonald, H. Pain and dissociation in the cold pressor test: A study of hypnotic analgesia with "hidden reports" through automatic key-pressing and automatic talking. *Journal of Abnormal Psychology*, 1975, *84*, 280–289.

Hilgard, E. R., & Tart, C. T. Responsiveness to suggestions following waking and imagination instructions and following induction of hypnosis. *Journal of Abnormal Psychology*, 1966, *71*, 196–208.

Hilgard, J. R. Imaginative involvement: Some characteristics of the highly hypnotizable and the non-hypnotizable. *International Journal of Clinical and Experimental Hypnosis*, 1974, *22*, 138–156.

Hilgard, J. R. Imaginative and sensory-affective involvements in everyday life and in hypnosis. In E. Fromm & R. E. Shor (Eds.), *Hypnosis: Developments in research and new perspectives*. New York: Aldine, 1979.

Hiscock, M. Eye-movement symmetry and hemisperic function: An examination of individual differences. *Journal of Psychology*, 1977, *97*, 49–52.

Howard, M. L., & Coe, W. C. The effects of context and subjects' perceived control in breaching posthypnotic amnesia. *Journal of Personality*, 1980, *48*, 342–359.

Johnson, R. F. Q., Maher, B. A., & Barber, T. X. Artifact in the "essence of hypnosis": An evaluation of trance logic. *Journal of Abnormal Psychology*, 1972, *79*, 234–238.

Jones, B. Signal detection theory and pain research. *Pain*, 1979, *7*, 305–312.

Jones, B., & Spanos, N. P. Functional measurement analysis of hypnotic analgesia. Paper presented at the APA annual convention, Montreal, August 1980.

Katz, N. W. Comparative efficacy of behavioral training, training plus relaxation and a sleep/trance hypnotic induction in increasing hypnotic susceptibility. *Journal of Consulting and Clinical Psychology*, 1979, *43*, 119–127.

Kihlstrom, J. F. The effects of organization and motivation on recall during posthypnotic amnesia (doctoral dissertation, University of Pennsylvania, 1975). *Dissertation Abstracts International*, 1975, *36*, 2473B-247b. (University Microfilms No. 75-24082)

Kihlstrom, J. F. Context and cognition in posthypnotic amnesia. *International Journal of Clinical and Experimental Hypnosis*, 1978, *26*, 246–267.

Kihlstrom, J. F. Posthypnotic amnesia for recently learned material: Interactions with "episodic" and "semantic" memory. *Cognitive Psychology*, 1980, *12*, 227-251.

Kihlstrom, J. F., Diaz, W. A., McClellan, G. E., Ruskin, P. M., Pistole, D. D., & Shor, R. E. Personality correlates of hypnotic susceptibility: Needs for achievement and autonomy, self-monitoring and masculinity-femininity. *American Journal of Clinical Hypnosis*, 1980, *22*, 225–230.

Kihlstrom, J. F., & Evans, F. J. Memory retrieval processes during posthypnotic amnesia. In J. F. Kihlstrom & F. J. Evans (Eds.), *Functional disorders of memory*. Hillsdale, N.J.: Erlbaum, 1979.

Kihlstrom, J. F., Evans, F. J., Orne, M. T., & Orne, E. C. Attempting to breach posthypnotic amnesia. *Journal of Abnormal Psychology*, 1980, *89*, 603-616.

Kihlstrom, J. F., & Shor, R. E. Recall and recognition during posthypnotic amnesia. *International Journal of Clinical and Experimental Hypnosis*, 1978, *26*, 330-349.

Kinney, J. M., & Sachs, L. B. Increasing hypnotic susceptibility. *Journal of Abnormal Psychology*, 1974, *83*, 145-150.

Knox, V. J., Morgan, A. H., & Hilgard, E. R. Pain and suffering in ischemia: The paradox of hypnotically suggested anesthesia as contradicted by reports from the "hidden observer." *Archives of General Psychiatry*, 1974, *30*, 840-847.

Kroger, W. S., & Fezler, W. D. *Hypnosis and behavior modification: Imagery conditioning*. Philadelphia: Lippincott, 1976.

Lanzetta, J. T., Cartwright-Smith, J., & Kleck, R. E. Effects of non-verbal dissimulation on emotional experience and autonomic arousal. *Journal of Personality and Social Psychology*, 1976, *33*, 354–370.

Leibowitz, H. W., Lundy, R. M., & Guez, J. R. The effects of testing distance on suggestion-induced visual field narrowing. *International Journal of Clinical and Experimental Hypnosis*, 1980, *28*, 409–420.

Levitt, E. E., Arnoff, G., Morgan, C. D., Toner, M., Overley, M., & Parrish, M. Testing the coercive power of hypnosis: Committing objectionable acts. *International Journal of Clinical and Experimental Hypnosis*, 1975, *23*, 59–67.

London, P., Cooper, L. M., & Johnson, H. J. Subject characteristics in hypnosis research. II: Attitudes toward hypnosis, volunteer status, and personality measures. III: Some correlates of hypnotic susceptibility. *International Journal of Clinical and Experimental Hypnosis*, 1962, *10*, 13–21.

London, P., Hart, J. T., & Leibovitz, M. P. EEG alpha rhythms and susceptibility to hypnosis. *Nature* (London), 1968, *219*, 71–72.

Lunneborg, P. W. Stereotypic aspects in masculinity-femininity measurement. *Journal of Consulting and Clinical Psychology*, 1970, *34*, 113–118.

McAmmond, D. M., Davidson, P. O., & Kovitz, D. M. A comparison of the effects of hypnosis and relaxation training on stress reactions in a dental situation. *American Journal of Clinical Hypnosis*, 1971, *13*, 233–242.

McConkey, K. M., & Sheehan, P. W. Inconsistency in hypnotic age regression and cue structure as applied by the hypnotist. *International Journal of Clinical and Experimental Hypnosis*, 1980, *28*, 409–420.

McDonald, R. D., & Smith, J. R. Trance logic in tranceable and simulating subjects. *International Journal of Clinical and Experimental Hypnosis*, 1975, *23*, 80–89.

McGuire, W. J. The nature of attitudes and attitude change. In G. Lindzey & E. Aronson (Eds.), *The handbook of social psychology* (2nd ed., Vol. 3). Reading, Mass.: Addison-Wesley, 1969.

McPeake, J. D., & Spanos, N. P. The effects of the wording of rating scales on hypnotic subjects: Descriptions of visual hallucinations. *American Journal of Clinical Hypnosis*, 1973, *15*, 239–244.

Meichenbaum, D. *Cognitive-behavior modifica-

Melei, J., & Hilgard, E. R. Attitudes toward hypnosis, self-predictions and hypnotic susceptibility. *International Journal of Clinical and Experimental Hypnosis*, 1964, *12*, 99–108.

Melzack, R. *The puzzle of pain*. Middlesex, England: Penguin, 1973.

Miller, R. J., & Leibowitz, H. W. A signal detection analysis of hypnotically induced narrowing of the peripheral visual field. *Journal of Abnormal Psychology*, 1976, *85*, 446-454.

Morgan, A. H. The heritability of hypnotic susceptibility in twins. *Journal of Abnormal Psychology*, 1973, *82*, 55-61.

Morgan, A. H., Johnson, D. L., & Hilgard, E. R. The stability of hypnotic susceptibility: A longitudinal study. *International Journal of Clinical and Experimental Hypnosis*, 1974, *22*, 249-257.

Morgan, A. H., Macdonald, H., & Hilgard, E. R. EEG alpha: Lateral asymmetry related to task and hypnotizability. *Psychophysiology*, 1974, *11*, 275-282.

Morgan, A. H., McDonald, P. J., & Macdonald, H. Differences in bilateral alpha activity as a function of experimental task, with a note on lateral eye movements. *Neuropsychologia*, 1971, *9*, 459–469.

Morgan, C. M. Hypnotic susceptibility, EEG theta and alpha waves and hemispheric specificity. In G. D. Burrows, D. R. Collison, & L. Dennerstein (Eds.), *Hypnosis 1979*. Amsterdam: Elsevier/North Holland Biomedical Press, 1979.

Morse, D. R., Martin, J. S., Furst, M. L., & Dubin, T. T. A physiological and subjective evaluation of meditation, hypnosis and relaxation. *Psychosomatic Medicine*, 1977, *39*, 304–324.

Murphy, M. D. Measurement of category clustering in free recall. In C. R. Puff (Ed.), *Memory organization and structure*. New York: Academic Press, 1979.

Nace, E. P., Orne, M. T., & Hammer, A. G. Posthypnotic amnesia as an active psychic process: The reversability amnesia. *Archives of General Psychiatry*, 1974, *31*, 257–260.

Newman, J. B. Fascination, or the philosophy of charming illustrating the principles of life in connection with spirit and matter. In *Library of Mesmerism* (Vol. I). New York: Fowler & Wells, 1865.

Nisbett, R. E., & Schachter, S. Cognitive manipulation of pain. *Journal of Experimental Social Psychology*, 1966, *2*, 227–236.

Norris, D. L. Barber's task-motivational theory and post-hypnotic amnesia. *American Journal of Clinical Hypnosis*, 1973, *15*, 181–236.

Obstoj, I., & Sheehan, P. W. Aptitude for trance, task generalizability, and incongruity response in hypnosis. *Journal of Abnormal Psychology*, 1977, *86*, 543–552.

O'Connell, D. N., Shor, R. E., & Orne, M. T. Hypnotic age regression: An empirical and methodological analysis. *Journal of Abnormal Psychology*, 1970, *76* (3, Pt. 2).

O'Grady, K. E. The absorption scale: A factor-analytic assessment. *International Journal of Clinical and Experimental Hypnosis*, 1980, *28*, 281–288.

Orne, M. T. The nature of hypnosis: Artifact and essence. *Journal of Abnormal and Social Psychology*, 1959, *58*, 277–299.

Orne, M. T. Hypnosis, motivation and compliance. *American Journal of Psychiatry*, 1966, *122*, 721–726.

Orne, M. T. The simulation of hypnosis: Why, how, and what it means. *International Journal of Clinical and Experimental Hypnosis*, 1971, *19*, 183–210.

Orne, M. T., & Evans, F. J. Social control in the psychological experiment: Antisocial behavior and hypnosis. *Journal of Personality and Social Psychology*, 1965, *1*, 189–200.

Orne, M. T., & Hammer, A. G. Hypnosis. In *Encyclopedia Britannica* (15th ed.). Chicago: Benton, 1974.

Orne, M. T., Hilgard, E. R., Spiegel, H., Spiegel, D., Crawford, H. J., Evans, F. J., Orne, E. C., & Frischholz, E. J. The relation between the hypnotic induction profile and the Stanford hypnotic susceptibility scales. *International Journal of Clinical and Experimental Hypnosis*, 1979, *27*, 85–102.

Parrish, M., Lundy, R. M., & Leibowitz, H. W. Effect of hypnotic age regression on the magnitude of the Ponzo and Poggendorff illusions. *Journal of Abnormal Psychology*, 1969, *74*, 693–698.

Paskewitz, D. A. EEG alpha activity and its relationship to altered states of consciousness. *Annals of the New York Academy of Sciences*, 1977, *296*, 154–161.

Paul, G. L. Inhibition of physiological response to stressful imagery by relaxation training and hypnotically suggested relaxation. *Behavior Research and Therapy*, 1969, 7, 249–256. (a)

Paul, G. L. Physiological effects of relaxation training and hypnotic suggestion. *Journal of Abnormal Psychology*, 1969, *74*, 425–437. (b)

Perry, C. W., Evans, F. J., O'Connell, D. N., Orne, E. C., & Orne, M. T. Behavioral response to verbal stimuli administered and tested during REM sleep: A further investigation. *Waking and Sleeping*, 1978, *2*, 35–42.

Perry, C. W., & Laurence, J. Hypnotic depth and hypnotic susceptibility: A replicated finding. *International Journal of Clinical and Experimental Hypnosis*, 1980, *28*, 272–280.

Perry, C. W., & Walsh, B. Inconsistencies and anomalies of response as a defining characteristic of hypnosis. *Journal of Abnormal Psychology*, 1978, *87*, 574–577.

Perry, C. W., Wilder, S., & Appignanesi, A. Hypnotic susceptibility and performance in a battery of creative measures. *American Journal of Clinical Hypnosis*, 1973, *15*, 170–180.

Plotkin, W. B. The alpha experience revisited: Biofeedback in the transformation of a psychological state. *Psychological Bulletin*, 1979, *86*, 1132–1148.

Porter, J. W., Woodward, J. A., Bisbee, T. C., & Fenker, R. M. Jr. Effects of hypnotic age regression on the magnitude of the Ponzo illusion. *Journal of Abnormal Psychology*, 1972, *79*, 189–194.

Poulton, E. C. The new psychophysics: Six models for magnitude estimation. *Psychological Bulletin*, 1968, *69*, 1–19.

Poulton, E. C. Models for biases in judging sensory magnitude. *Psychological Bulletin*, 1979, *86*, 777–803.

Puff, C. R. (Ed.). *Memory organization and structure*. New York: Academic Press, 1979.

Radtke, H. L., & Spanos, N. P. Temporal sequencing during posthypnotic amnesia: A methodological critique. *Journal of Abnormal Psychology*, 1981, *90*, 476–485.

Radtke, H. L., & Spanos, N. P. The effect of wording of hypnotic depth scales on reports of hypnotic depth. Unpublished manuscript, Carleton University, 1980.

Radtke, H. L., & Spanos, N. P. Was I hypnotized? A social psychological analysis of hypnotic depth reports. *Psychiatry*, 1981, *44*, 359–376.

Radtke-Bodorik, H. L., Planas, M., & Spanos, N. P. Suggested amnesia, verbal inhibition, and disorganized recall for a long word list. *Canadian Journal of Behavioral Science*, 1980, *12*, 87–97.

Radtke-Bodorik, H. L., Spanos, N. P., & Haddad, M. G. The effects of spoken versus written recall on suggested amnesia in hypnotic and task-motivated subjects. *American Journal of Clinical Hypnosis*, 1979, *22*, 8–16.

Raginsky, B. B. Rapid regression to the oral and anal levels through sensory hypnoplasty. *International Journal of Clinical and Experimental Hypnosis*, 1967, *15*, 19–30.

Reyher, J. Clinical and experimental hypnosis: Implications for theory and methodology. *Annals of the New York Academy of Sciences*, 1977, *296*, 69–85.

Rollman, G. B. Signal detection theory assessment of pain: A review and critique. *Pain*, 1977, *4*, 187–211.

Rollman, G. B. Signal detection theory pain measures: Empirical validation studies and adaptation level effects. *Pain*, 1979, *6*, 9–21.

Rosenbaum, M. Individual differences in self-control behaviors and tolerance of painful stimulation. *Journal of Abnormal Psychology*, 1980, *89*, 581–590.

Sachs, L. B. Construing hypnosis as modifiable behavior. In A. Jacobs & L. B. Sachs (Eds.), *The psychology of private events*. New York: Academic Press, 1971.

Sachs, L. B., & Anderson, W. L. Modification of hypnotic susceptibility. *International Journal of Clinical and Experimental Hypnosis*, 1967, *15*, 172–180.

Sackeim, H. A., Paulhus, D., & Weiman, A. L. Classroom seating and hypnotic susceptibility. *Journal of Abnormal Psychology*, 1979, *88*, 81–84.

Salzberg, H. C., & DePiano, F. A. Hypnotizability and task motivating suggestions: A further look. *International Journal of Clinical and Experimental Hypnosis*, 1980, *28*, 261–271.

Sarbin, T. R. Contributions to role-taking theory: I. Hypnotic behavior. *Psychological Review*, 1950, *57*, 255–270.

Sarbin, T. R. The concept of hallucination. *Journal of Personality*, 1967, *35*, 359–380.

Sarbin, T. R. On the recently reported physiological and pharmacological reality of the hypnotic state. *Psychological Record*, 1973, *23*, 505–511.

Sarbin, T. R., & Coe, W. C. *Hypnotic behavior: The psychology of influence communication*. New York: Holt, 1972.

Sarbin, T. R., & Juhasz, J. B. The social psychology of hallucinations. *Journal of Mental Imagery*, 1978, *2*, 117–144.

Sarbin, T. R., & Slage, R. W. Hypnosis and psychophysiological outcomes. In E. Fromm & R. E. Shor (Eds.), *Hypnosis: Research developments and perspectives*. Chicago: Aldine-Atherton, 1972.

Schuyler, B. A., & Coe, W. C. A physiological

investigation of volition and nonvolition experience during posthypnotic amnesia. *Journal of Personality and Social Psychology*, 1981, *40*, 1160–1169.

Scott, D. S., & Barber, T. X. Cognitive control of pain: Effects of multiple cognitive strategies. *Psychological Record*, 1977, *27*, 373–383.

Scott, D. S., & Leonard, C. F. Jr. Modification of pain threshold by the covert reinforcement procedure and a cognitive strategy. *Psychological Record*, 1978, *28*, 49–57.

Sextus, C. *Hypnotism*. Hollywood, Calif.: Wilshire Books, 1968. (Originally published 1893)

Sheehan, D. V., Latta, W. D., Regina, E. G., & Smith, G. M. Empirical assessment of Spiegel's hypnotic induction profile and eye-roll hypothesis. *International Journal of Clinical and Experimental Hypnosis*, 1979, *27*, 103–110.

Sheehan, P. W. Analysis of the treatment effects of simulation instructions in the application of the real-simulating model of hypnosis. *Journal of Abnormal Psychology*, 1970, *75*, 98–103.

Sheehan, P. W. A methodological analysis of the simulating technique. *International Journal of Clinical and Experimental Hypnosis*, 1971, *19*, 83–99.

Sheehan, P. W. Expectancy reactions in hypnosis. In G. D. Burrows, D. R. Collison, & L. Dennerstein (Eds.), *Hypnosis 1979*. Amsterdam: Elsevier/North Holland Biomedical Press, 1979. (a)

Sheehan, P. W. Hypnosis and the processes of imagination. In E. Fromm & R. E. Shor (Eds.), *Hypnosis: Developments in research and new perspectives* (2nd ed.). New York: Aldine, 1979. (b)

Sheehan, P. W. Hypnosis considered as altered state of consciousness. In G. Underwood & R. Stevens (Eds.), *Aspects of consciousness*. New York: Academic Press, 1979. (c)

Sheehan, P. W., & Dolby, R. M. Hypnosis and the influence of most recently perceived events. *Journal of Abnormal Psychology*, 1975, *84*, 331–345.

Sheehan, P. W., Obstoj, I., & McConkey, K. Trance logic and cue structure as supplied by the hypnotist. *Journal of Abnormal Psychology*, 1976, *85*, 459–472.

Sheehan, P. W., & Perry, C. W. Research in hypnosis: An overview of current methods. In G. D. Burrows & L. Dennerstein (Eds.), *Handbook of hypnosis and psychosomatic medicine*. Amsterdam: Elsevier/North Holland Biomedical Press, 1980.

Shor, R. E. Hypnosis and the concept of the generalized reality orientation. *American Journal of Psychotherapy*, 1959, *13*, 582–602.

Shor, R. E. Physiological effects of painful stimulation during hypnotic analgesia. In J. E. Gordon (Ed.), *Handbook of clinical and experimental hypnosis*. New York: Macmillan, 1967.

Shor, R. E. The three factor theory of hypnosis as applied to the book reading fantasy. *International Journal of Clinical and Experimental Hypnosis*, 1970, *18*, 89–98.

Shuell, T. J. Clustering and organization in free recall. *Psychological Bulletin*, 1969, *72*, 353–374.

Silver, M. J. Hypnotizability as a function of repression, adaptive regression and mood. *Journal of Consulting and Clinical Psychology*, 1974, *42*, 41–46.

Spanos, N. P. Barber's reconceptualization of hypnosis: An evaluation of criticisms. *Journal of Experimental Research in Personality*, 1970, *4*, 241–258.

Spanos, N. P. Goal-directed fantasy and the performance of hypnotic test suggestions. *Psychiatry*, 1971, *34*, 86–96.

Spanos, N. P. Hypnotic responding: Automatic dissociation or situation relevant cognizing? In E. Klinger (Ed.), *Imagery: Concepts, results and applications*. New York: Plenum, 1981.

Spanos, N. P., Ansari, F., & Stam, H. J. Hypnotic age regression and eidetic imagery: A failure to replicate. *Journal of Abnormal Psychology*, 1979, *88*, 88–91.

Spanos, N. P., & Barber, T. X. "Hypnotic" experiences as inferred from subjective reports: Auditory and visual hallucinations. *Journal of Experimental Research in Personality*, 1968, *3*, 136–150.

Spanos, N. P., & Barber, T. X. Cognitive activity during hypnotic suggestion: Goal-directed fantasy and the experience of non-volition. *Journal of Personality*, 1972, *40*, 510–524.

Spanos, N. P. & Barber, T. X. A review of Orne's "Hypnosis, motivation and the ecological validity of the psychological experiment." *American Journal of Clinical Hypnosis*, 1973, *16*, 138–141.

Spanos, N. P., & Barber, T. X. Toward a convergence in hypnosis research. *American Psychologist*, 1974, *29*, 500–511.

Spanos, N. P., & Barber, T. X. Behavior modification and hypnosis. In M. Hersen, R. M. Eisler, & P. Miller (Eds.), *Progress in behavior modification* (Vol. 3). New York: Academic

Spanos, N. P., Barber, T. X., & Lang, G. Cognition and self-control: Cognitive control of painful sensory input. In H. London & R. E. Nisbett (Eds.), *Thought and feeling: Cognitive alteration of feeling states*. Chicago: Aldine, 1974.

Spanos, N. P., & Bodorik, H. L. Suggested amnesia and disorganized recall in hypnotic and task-motivated subjects. *Journal of Abnormal Psychology*, 1977, *86*, 295–305.

Spanos, N. P., Brown, J. M., Jones, B., & Horner, D. Cognitive activity and suggestions for analgesia in the reduction of reported pain. *Journal of Abnormal Psychology*, in press.

Spanos, N. P., Churchill, N., & McPeake, J. D. Experiential response to auditory and visual hallucination suggestions in hypnotic subjects. *Journal of Consulting and Clinical Psychology*, 1976, *44*, 729–783.

Spanos, N. P., & D'Eon, J. L. Hypnotic amnesia, disorganized recall and inattention. *Journal of Abnormal Psychology*, 1980, *89*, 744–750.

Spanos, N. P., Gorassini, D., & Petrusic, W. Hypnotically induced limb anesthesia and adaptation to displacing prisms: A failure to replicate. *Journal of Abnormal Psychology*, 1981, *90*, 329–333.

Spanos, N. P., & Gottlieb, J. Demonic possession, mesmerism and hysteria: A social psychological perspective on their historical interrelations. *Journal of Abnormal Psychology*, 1979, *88*, 527–546.

Spanos, N. P., & Ham, M. L. Cognitive activity in response to hypnotic suggestion: Goal-directed fantasy and selective amnesia. *American Journal of Clinical Hypnosis*, 1973, *15*, 191–198.

Spanos, N. P., Ham, M. W., & Barber, T. X. Suggested ("hypnotic") visual hallucinations: Experimental and phenomenological data. *Journal of Abnormal Psychology*, 1973, *81*, 96–106.

Spanos, N. P., & Hewitt, E. C. The hidden observer in hypnotic analgesia: Discovery or experimental creation? *Journal of Personality and Social Psychology*, 1980, *39*, 1201–1214.

Spanos, N. P., Horton, C., & Chaves, J. F. The effects of two cognitive strategies on pain threshold. *Journal of Abnormal Psychology*, 1975, *84*, 677–681.

Spanos, N. P., Jones, B., Brown, J. M., & Horner, D. Magnitude estimates of cold pressor pain: Effects of suggestion, cognitive strategy and tolerance. Unpublished manuscript, Carleton University, 1980.

Spanos, N. P., Mah, C. D., Pawlak, A. E., D'Eon, J. L., & Ritchie, G. A multi-variate and factor analytic study of hypnotic susceptibility. Unpublished manuscript, Carleton University, 1980.

Spanos, N. P., & McPeake, J. D. Involvement in suggestion related imaginings, experienced involuntariness and credibility assigned to imaginings in hypnotic subjects. *Journal of Abnormal Psychology*, 1974, *83*, 687–690.

Spanos, N. P., & McPeake, J. D. Involvement in everyday imaginative activities, attitudes toward hypnosis, and hypnotic susceptibility. *Journal of Personality and Social Psychology*, 1975, *31*, 594–598. (a)

Spanos, N. P., & McPeake, J. D. The interaction of attitudes toward hypnosis and involvement in everyday imaginative activities on hypnotic suggestibility. *American Journal of Clinical Hypnosis*, 1975, *17*, 247–252. (b)

Spanos, N. P., & McPeake, J. D. Cognitive strategies, goal-directed fantasy and response to suggestion in hypnotic subjects. *American Journal of Clinical Hypnosis*, 1977, *20*, 114–123.

Spanos, N. P., McPeake, J. D., & Carter, W. The effects of pretesting on response to a visual hallucination suggestion in hypnotic subjects. *Journal of Personality and Social Psychology*, 1973, *28*, 293–297.

Spanos, N. P., Mullens, D., & Rivers, S. M. The effects of suggestion structure and hypnotic vs. task-motivation instructions on response to hallucination suggestions. *Journal of Research in Personality*, 1979, *13*, 59–70.

Spanos, N. P., Pawlak, A. E., Mah, C. D., & D'Eon, J. L. Lateral eye movements, hypnotic susceptibility and imaginal ability in right-handers. *Perceptual and Motor Skills*, 1980, *50*, 287–294.

Spanos, N. P., & Radtke, H. L. Hypnotic visual hallucinations as imaginings: A cognitive-social psychological perspective. *Cognition, Imagination and Personality*, in press.

Spanos, N. P., Radtke, H. L., & Dubreuil, D. L. "Episodic" and "semantic" memory in posthypnotic amnesia: A reevaluation. *Journal of Personality and Social Psychology*, in press.

Spanos, N. P., & Radtke-Bodorik, H. L. Integrating hypnotic phenomena with cognitive psychology: An illustration using suggested amnesia. *Bulletin of the British Society of Experimental and Clinical Hypnosis*, 1980, *3*, 4–7.

Spanos, N. P., Radtke-Bodorik, H. L., Ferguson, J. D., & Jones, B. The effects of hypnotic susceptibility, suggestions for analgesia and the utilization of cognitive strategies on the reduction of pain. *Journal of Abnormal Psychology*, 1979, *88*, 282–292.

Spanos, N. P., Radtke-Bodorik, H. L., & Shabinsky, M. A. Amnesia subjective organization and learning of a list of unrelated words in hypnotic and task-motivated subjects. *International Journal of Clinical and Experimental Hypnosis*, 1980, *28*, 126–139.

Spanos, N. P., Radtke-Bodorik, H. L., & Stam, H. J. Disorganized recall during suggested amnesia: Fact not artifact. *Journal of Abnormal Psychology*, 1980, *89*, 1–19.

Spanos, N. P., Rivers, S. M., & Gottlieb, J. Hypnotic responsivity, meditation and laterality of eye movements. *Journal of Abnormal Psychology*, 1978, *87*, 566–569.

Spanos, N. P., Rivers, S. M., & Ross, S. Experienced involuntariness and response to hypnotic suggestions. *Annals of the New York Academy of Sciences*, 1977, *296*, 208–221.

Spanos, N. P., Spillane, J., & McPeake, J. D. Cognitive strategies and response to suggestion in hypnotic and task-motivated subjects. *American Journal of Clinical Hypnosis*, 1976, *18*, 252–262.

Spanos, N. P., & Stam, H. J. The elicitation of visual hallucinations via brief instructions in a normal sample. *Journal of Nervous and Mental Disease*, 1979, *167*, 488–494.

Spanos, N. P., Stam, H. J., & Brazil, K. The effects of suggestion and distraction on coping ideation and reported pain. *Journal of Mental Imagery*, in press.

Spanos, N. P., Stam, H. J., D'Eon, J. L., Pawlak, A. E., & Radtke-Bodorik, H. L. The effects of social psychological variables on hypnotic amnesia. *Journal of Personality and Social Psychology*, 1980, *39*, 737–750.

Spanos, N. P., Stam, H. J., Radtke-Bodorik, H. L., & Nightingale, M. E. Absorption in imaginings, sex role orientation and recall of dreams by males and females. *Journal of Personality Assessment*, 1980, *44*, 277–282.

Spiegel, H. An eye roll test for hypnotizability. *American Journal of Clinical Hypnosis*, 1972, *15*, 25–27.

Spiegel, H. *Manual for hypnotic induction profile: Eye roll levitation method* (Rev. ed.). New York: Sonj Medica, 1973.

Spiegel, H. The grade 5 syndrome and the highly hypnotizable person. *International Journal of Clinical and Experimental Hypnosis*, 1974, *22*, 303–319.

Stacher, G., Schuster, P., Bauer, P., Lahoda, R., & Schulze, D. Effects of relaxation or analgesia on pain threshold and pain tolerance in the waking and in hypnotic state. *Journal of Psychosomatic Research*, 1975, *19*, 259–265.

Stam, H. J., Petrusic, W. M., & Spanos, N. P. Magnitude scales for cold pressor pain. *Perception and Psychophysics*, 1981, *29*, 612–617.

Stam, H. J., Radtke-Bodorik, H. L., & Spanos, N. P. Repression and hypnotic amnesia: A failure to replicate and an alternative formulation. *Journal of Abnormal Psychology*, 1980, *89*, 551–559.

Stam, H. J., & Spanos, N. P. Lateral eye movements and indices of nonanalytic attending in right-handed females. *Perceptual and Motor Skills*, 1979, *48*, 123–127.

Stam, H. J., & Spanos, N. P. Experimental designs, expectancy effects and hypnotic analgesia. *Journal of Abnormal Psychology*, 1980, *89*, 751–762.

Stam, H. J., Spanos, N. P., Radtke, H. L., & Jones, B. A further investigation of the relationship between hypnotic susceptibility and classroom seating. *Perceptual and Motor Skills*, 1981, *52*, 831–836.

Starker, S. Effects of hypnotic induction upon visual imagery. *Journal of Nervous and Mental Disease*, 1974, *159*, 433–437.

Stern, D. B., Spiegel, H., & Nee, J.C.M. The hypnotic induction profile: Normative observations, reliability and validity. *American Journal of Clinical Hypnosis*, 1979, *21*, 109–133.

Sternberg, R. J., & Tulving, E. The measurement of subjective organization in free recall. *Psychological Bulletin*, 1977, *84*, 539–556.

St. Jean, R., & Coe, W. C. Recall and recognition memory during posthypnotic amnesia: A failure to confirm the disrupted retrieval hypothesis and the memory disorganization hypothesis. *Journal of Abnormal Psychology*, 1981, *90*, 231–241.

Switras, J. E. A comparison of the eye-roll test for hypnotizability and the Stanford Hypnotic Susceptibility Scale: Form A. *American Journal of Clinical Hypnosis*, 1974, *17*, 54–55.

Tart, C. T. Self-report scales of hypnotic depth. *International Journal of Clinical and Experimental Hypnosis*, 1970, *18*, 105–125.

Tart, C. T. Quick and convenient assessment of hypnotic depth: Self-report scales. *American*

Journal of Clinical Hypnosis, 1979, 21, 186–207.

Tart, C. T., & Hilgard, E. R. Responsiveness to suggestions under "hypnosis" and "waking-imagination" conditions: A methodological observation. International Journal of Clinical and Experimental Hypnosis, 1966, 14, 247–256.

Tellegen, A., & Atkinson, G. Openness to absorbing and self-altering experiences ("absorption"), a trait related to hypnotic susceptibility. Journal of Abnormal Psychology, 1974, 83, 268–277.

Tellegen, A., & Atkinson, G. Complexity and measurement of hypnotic susceptibility: A comment on Coe and Sarbin's alternative interpretation. Journal of Personality and Social Psychology, 1976, 33, 142–148.

Thorkelson, K. E. The relationship between hypnotic susceptibility and certain personality, physiological and electroencephalographic variables in monozygotic and dizygotic twin pairs. Unpublished doctoral dissertation, University of Minnesota, 1973.

Tulving, E. Episodic and semantic memory. In E. Tulving & W. Donaldson (Eds.), *Organization of memory*. New York: Academic Press, 1972.

Tulving, E. Cue dependent forgetting. American Scientist, 1974, 62, 74–82.

Ulett, G. A., Akpinar, S., & Itil, T. M. Hypnosis: Physiological pharmacological reality. American Journal of Psychiatry, 1972, 128, 799–805.

Walker, N. S., Garrett, J. B., & Wallace, B. Restoration of eidetic imagery via hypnotic age regression: A preliminary report. Journal of Abnormal Psychology, 1976, 85, 335–337.

Wallace, B., & Fisher, L. E. Proprioception and the production of adaptation and intermural transfer to prismatic displacement. Perception and Psychophysics, 1979, 26, 113–117.

Wallace, B., & Garrett, J. B. Reduced felt arm sensation effects on visual adaptation. Perception and Psychophysics, 1973, 14, 597–600.

Wallace, B., & Garrett, J. B. Perceptual adaptation with selective reductions of felt sensation. Perception, 1975, 4, 437–445.

Webster, M., & Sobieszek, B. I. *Sources of self-evaluation: A formal theory of significant others and social influence*. New York: Wiley, 1974.

Weitzenhoffer, A. M. Behavior therapeutic techniques and hypnotherapeutic methods. American Journal of Clinical Hypnosis, 1972, 15, 71–82.

Weitzenhoffer, A. M. When is an "instruction" an "instruction"? International Journal of Clinical and Experimental Hypnosis, 1974, 22, 258–269.

Weitzenhoffer, A. M. What did he (Bernheim) say? In F. H. Frankel & H. S. Zamansky (Eds.), *Hypnosis at its bicentennial*. New York: Plenum, 1978.

Weitzenhoffer, A. M. Hypnotic susceptibility revisited. American Journal of Clinical Hypnosis, 1980, 22, 130–146.

Weitzenhoffer, A. M., & Hilgard, E. R. *Stanford Hypnotic Susceptibility Scale, Forms A and B*. Palo Alto, Calif.: Consulting Psychologists Press, 1959.

Weitzenhoffer, A. M., & Hilgard, E. R. *Stanford Hypnotic Susceptibility Scale, Form C*. Palo Alto, Calif.: Consulting Psychologists Press, 1962.

Weitzenhoffer, A. M., & Weitzenhoffer, G. B. Sex, transference, and susceptibility to hypnosis. American Journal of Clinical Hypnosis, 1958, 1, 15–24.

Wheeler, L., Reis, H. T., Wolff, E., Grupsmith, E., & Mordkoff, A. M. Eye-roll and hypnotic susceptibility. International Journal of Clinical and Experimental Hypnosis, 1974, 22, 327–334.

White, R. W. A preface toward a theory of hypnotism. Journal of Abnormal and Social Psychology, 1941, 36, 477–505.

Whitley, B. E. Jr. Sex roles and psychotherapy: A current approach. Psychological Bulletin, 1979, 86, 1309–1321.

Wolpe, J., & Lazarus, A. A. *Behavior therapy techniques*. Oxford, England: Pergamon, 1966.

Wothington, E. L. The effects of imagery content, choice of imagery context and self-verbalization on the self-control of pain. Cognitive Therapy and Research, 1978, 2, 225–240.

Zamansky, H. S., Scharf, B., & Brightbill, R. The effect of expectancy for hypnosis on prehypnotic performance. Journal of Personality, 1964, 32, 236–248.

13

SOCIAL SUPPORT, ADJUSTMENT, AND THE ELDERLY SPINAL CORD INJURED: A SOCIAL PSYCHOLOGICAL ANALYSIS

RICHARD SCHULZ
PORTLAND STATE UNIVERSITY

SUSAN DECKER
UNIVERSITY OF PORTLAND

Each year in the United States between 6,000 and 11,000 persons suffer traumatic spinal cord injuries which result in varying degrees of permanent paralysis (Bachman, 1978; Roessler & Bolton, 1978). It is estimated that the total number of persons in America disabled as a result of spinal cord injury varies between 125,000 and 250,000 (Bachman). The majority of the injuries occur in males between the ages of 15 and 30, with the leading causes being automobile accidents, falls, diving accidents, industrial accidents, gunshot wounds, and sports accidents (Statistical Report, 1975).

Although the population at highest risk for sustaining spinal injury is the teen/young adult male, the long-term survival rate of persons with this injury has greatly increased because of advances in antibiotic therapy and rehabilitation medicine. Before the widespread use of antibiotics, many people with spinal cord injury died from urinary tract or respiratory infections, or from septicemia generated from decubitus ulcers (Abramson, 1967). Fine (1979–80) points out that many of the advances responsible for the improved prognosis of the spinal cord injured person occurred during World War II:

The short and long term prognosis for the cord-injured patient did not improve until the Second World War when the British pioneered far-reaching medical achievements in the care of their patients. The efforts and achievements of Guttman and others have markedly increased life expectancy of the spinal cord injured patient and have enabled practitioners to consider sequelae of cord injuries much as their predecessors considered the progression of infections and non-chronic disorders.

The increased longevity of spinal cord injured persons is illustrated in Table 13.1. The individual who incurs a spinal cord lesion at age 30 can expect to live from 16 to 45 years or more, depending on the level of the lesion, whether it was complete or incomplete, and the gender of the individual. Thus, a quadriplegic male with an incomplete lesion injured at age 30 can expect to live into his sixties, and a similar female into her seventies.

In addition to the increased long-term survival of cord injured persons, the incidence of

---

Preparation of this manuscript was supported by a grant from the NRTA/AARP ANDRUS Foundation.

Table 13.1. Life Expectancies for Spinal Cord Injury Victims by Age at Time of Injury and Impairment Category

Age at Hospital Discharge	Gender	General Population	Life Expectancy (Remaining Years)			
			Paraplegia		Quadriplegia	
			Incomplete	Complete	Incomplete	Complete
10	Male	59.09	57.22	42.20	49.88	28.60
	Female	65.59	64.09	50.94	58.05	37.81
20	Male	49.65	47.85	33.73	40.88	21.57
	Female	55.85	54.41	41.75	48.75	29.56
30	Male	40.61	38.95	26.29	32.57	16.15
	Female	46.24	44.82	32.85	39.24	21.83
40	Male	31.53	29.98	18.55	24.13	10.49
	Female	36.80	35.47	24.40	30.27	14.77
50	Male	23.08	21.70	11.96	16.61	5.90
	Female	27.84	26.64	17.03	22.06	9.29
60	Male	15.75	24.65	7.08	10.61	2.97
	Female	19.50	18.52	10.94	14.86	5.37
70	Male	9.72	9.00	3.93	6.29	1.50
	Female	11.84	11.15	6.02	8.68	2.55

Source: National Spinal Cord Injury Data Research Center, Phoenix.

cord injuries among the aged has been and continues to be substantial and may be on the increase. Data collected in 1971 (National Center for Health Statistics) showed that the age at onset for more than 32 percent of all spinal cord injuries in the United States was 50 years of age and older. More recent but unpublished data from the National Health Interview Survey (National Center for Health Statistics) showed that of the 9,365 persons suffering cord injury impairments in 1977, 16 percent were aged 65 and older. This represents a rate of 6.7 per 100,000 population. The rate for the general population is 4.4 per 100,000.

Similarly, a study at a large spinal injury unit serving central England revealed that between 1955 and 1974, about 11 percent (99 patients) of all admissions were aged 60 and over. When admissions were analyzed in five-year periods, the data showed that the percentage of elderly spinal cord injured patients regularly increased from 6 to 18 percent in a 19-year period (Watson, 1976).

Together, these data suggest that we can expect both an increase in the number of newly acquired spinal cord injuries among the elderly and an increase in the number of young spinal cord injured persons living to old age. In view of the many coping problems associated with being old, along with the additional demands of being severely disabled, it becomes important to ask what factors contribute to the quality of life of the elderly in general and to the quality of life of the spinal cord injured elderly in particular.

Quality of life among the elderly

Forty years of research on older Americans reveals that those who are ill or physically disabled are much less likely than others to report contentment with their lives (Edwards & Klemmack, 1973; George, 1978; Palmore & Kivett, 1977; Palmore & Luikart, 1972; Spreitzer & Snyder, 1974; Thompson, 1973). In view of this, one would expect that elderly persons experiencing mobility-limiting disabilities such as spinal cord injury, amputation, or rheumatoid arthritis would express less contentment about their lives than would nondisabled persons. However, the question still remains as to what factors in addition to health status are associated with better coping and adjustment within the disabled elderly population. Why do some elderly disabled persons report more life satisfaction than others?

Based on a comprehensive review of the literature, Larson (1978) reported that aside from health status, socioeconomic factors and social interaction were the variables most strongly related to the life satisfaction, morale, and adjustment of the elderly. The role of health and socioeconomic status in facilitating life satisfaction is relatively well understood, but debate still exists regarding the relationship between social interaction and life satisfaction. Lohmann (1980) reports that although many studies demonstrate a positive relationship between social interaction and life satisfaction (Graney, 1975; Lawton, 1972; Palmore & Luikart, 1972; Pihlblad & Adams, 1972; Seymour, 1972), others show that this relationship disappears when other variables are controlled (Bull & AuCoin, 1975; Edwards & Klemmack, 1973; Lemon, Bengtson, & Peterson, 1972) and still others report no relationship between social interaction and life satisfaction (Cumming & Henry, 1961; Thompson, 1973).

It seems likely that much of the confusion regarding the relationship between social interaction and life satisfaction is due to variations in measurement, a lack of conceptual clarity regarding the nature of social interaction, and an emphasis on correlational as opposed to experimental research. What is it about social interaction that facilitates coping with stress and promotes life satisfaction? One of the goals of this chapter is to answer this question by examining those mechanisms through which interpersonal relationships promote positive outcomes.

Coping problems associated with spinal cord injury

Persons sustaining a severe spinal cord injury face numerous adaptation demands. In addition to problems associated with loss of mobility and sensation, the spinal cord injured person undergoes tremendous psychological stresses. Spinal cord injury represents a threat to life, self-identity, social position, job, and love relationships. Persons who become severely disabled frequently exhibit a grieving process similar to that of persons responding to the death of a loved one. Indeed, several authors (Milhouse, 1979; Weller & Miller, 1977) characterize the spinal cord injured person as passing through several stages identified as shock, denial, depression, anger, and reconstruction, although little systematically collected data exist verifying these stages. According to these authors, the individual ideally should move through the grieving process to acceptance of the disability and then commence a productive and meaningful life. However, problems associated with the psychological adjustment to a severe injury of this type may hinder the achievement of this desired outcome. For example, Tucker (1980) suggests that the mourning for lost physical capacity is never completed but is repeatedly reworked as the individual encounters situations which trigger awareness of the disability.

The spinal cord injured person faces difficult psychological tasks related to self-acceptance. In a society where disability is accorded a negative status, Vargo (1978) states that in order to truly adapt, individuals must combat misconceptions (Wright, 1960) which devalue them as human beings. These include:

1. My disability is a punishment.
2. It is important to conform, not to be different.
3. Most people are physically normal.
4. Normal physique is one of the most important values.
5. Physique is important for personal evaluation.
6. A deformed body leads to a deformed mind.
7. No one will marry me.
8. I will be a burden on my family.
9. My deformity is revolting.
10. I am less valuable because I cannot get around as others do.

Gunther (1969) suggests that spinal cord injured individuals experience fragmentation of the cohesive adult self. In order to adjust to the disability, they must undergo a painful reintegration process which includes dealing with feelings of self-blame, self-hatred, depression, dependency, and an altered body image (Geis, 1972; Tucker, 1980). Such individuals must develop a value system that allows them to feel good about themselves.

As the spinal cord injured person grows older, there may be additional problems in coping as a result of stressors associated with old age, such as loss of friends and family. Particularly for the individual who has relied upon relatives (e.g., parents) for psychological and physical support, the loss of this support system through death creates a new set of adaptation demands. The list of potential stressors becomes even longer when we consider the increased probability of additional health problems and/or the aggravation of existing ones with increasing age.

Social support system as a facilitator of coping with spinal cord injury

For the past three decades, much of the research in social gerontology has been aimed at finding ways for maximizing levels of wellness in older persons. Frequently, researchers and practitioners have sought ways of facilitating the individual's ability to cope with major life stressors. Successful coping is typically characterized by (1) the absence of psychological distress and the presence of a self-perception of well-being and (2) the maintenance of functioning in interpersonal societal roles. Frequently, one of the important contributors to successful coping has been the availability of a social support system for an individual.

Literature from various sources supports the idea that social support is a facilitator of coping with stressful life events (Caplan, 1974; Cassel, 1975; Cobb, 1976; Heller, 1979; Litwak, 1979). For example, Aguilera and Messick (1974, p. 64) consider social supports (i.e., persons in the environment who can be depended upon to help solve a problem) as a crucial factor in determining whether or not an individual will experience a stressful event as a crisis. They suggest that the persons who provide social support facilitate coping by alleviating feelings of loss and reinforcing feelings of ego-integrity through their appraisals of the individual. Similarly, Veroff, Douvan, and Kulka (in press) concluded that turning to informal support systems is one of the critical ways Americans deal with their life problems.

A recent longitudinal study by Berkman and Syme (1979) further illustrates the importance of social support in the general population. They assessed the relationship between social and community ties and mortality in a random sample of 6,928 adults in Alameda County, California. An analysis of mortality rates within this population nine years later revealed that people who lacked social and community ties were more likely to die in the follow-up period than those with more extensive contacts. The association between social ties and mortality was found to be independent of self-reported physical health status, socio-economic status, and health practices at the time of the original survey. The most important sources of social contact seemed to be marriage and contact with close friends and relatives, followed by church membership and informal and formal group associations. In every age category, people who reported having few friends and relatives and/or who saw them infrequently had higher mortality rates than those with many friends and relatives whom they saw frequently. These differences in mortality rates were found for both men and women.

These are only a few of the many studies indicating a relationship between social support and coping. Indeed, there are studies identifying social support as a mediator of individual well-being when confronted with any one of a large number of life stressors, including rape (Burgess & Holmstrom, 1978), open heart surgery (Kimball, 1969), chronic kidney disease (MacElveen & Smith-DiJulio, 1978), cancer (Jamison, Wellisch, & Pasnau, 1978; Vachon, 1979; Weisman, 1976; Weisman & Worden, 1975), terminal illness (Carey,

1974), job termination (Cobb & Kasl, 1977), and bereavement (Clayton, Halikas, & Maurice, 1972; Maddison & Walker, 1967; Walker, MacBride, & Vachon, 1977).

Of particular interest to this discussion are studies showing a relationship between family support and coping with physical disability. For example, Kemp and Vash (1971) compared productive and less productive spinal cord injured persons and identified interpersonal support as a decisive variable fostering a constructive orientation. Productivity was defined as including employment, avocational pursuits, group participation, and family responsibilities. Persons with quadriplegia were less productive than those with paraplegia in the absence of high emotional support. However, in the presence of high support, no difference in productivity between those with paraplegia and those with quadriplegia was noted. In a study of 145 spinal cord injured veterans (70 percent paraplegic and 30 percent quadriplegic), Frielich (1977) found that rehabilitation success as measured by vocational and avocational adjustment was significantly correlated with being married and maintaining interpersonal relationships. In another study of 35 quadriplegics, 1.5 to 4.5 years postdischarge from a rehabilitation program, Rogers and Figone (1979) concluded that the affiliative network was crucial in facilitating adaptation. These researchers asked subjects the primary ways in which subjects' support network was influential in helping them adapt to their disability. The greatest number of responses, 78 percent, indicated that others helped them adapt by giving psychological support and encouragement, both passive and active. Passive psychological support included such things as standing by, being available, listening and understanding; active support included behaviors such as giving encouragement, pushing subject to go on, telling subject not to give up, and "standing up for me."

Finally, Peterson, King, and Davis (1978) studied a population of older (50 years +), noninstitutionalized amputees and concluded through field interviews that the existence of a strong family support network is a key factor in the older person's readjustment after amputation. Their study indicated that a strong family support network does exist for this group and that interaction with family and friends increased markedly after the amputation. Friends were found to play an increasingly important role as the older amputee aged. This theme is repeated several times in other studies. Stable, supportive relationships between a disabled person and his or her family are repeatedly found to be important facilitators of adjustment (Guttman, 1976; Kerr & Thompson, 1972; Petrus & Balaban, 1953; Thorn, Von Salzer, & Fromme, 1946).

Mechanisms of social support

The literature described thus far is correlational, but suggestive of a causal relationship between social support and successful coping with life stressors in general and with severe physical disability in particular. The task remaining is to identify what processes operate, within the context of what we collectively call social support, that might account for the observed relationships. In the next sections, three types of explanations are examined. First, we examine explanations that emphasize the possibility that the correlational data in fact do not reflect a causal relationship between social support and successful coping. Second are explanations that assume causality and identify mechanisms through which social support may operate to improve well-being. Third, we examine these same mechanisms through the lenses of three social psychological theoretical perspectives.

Social support as a correlate or consequence of coping

Because of the correlational nature of most of the research in this area, several investigators have raised questions concerning the causal relationships between social support and better coping (Heller, 1979; Silver & Wortman, 1980). A prospective longitudinal study in which different levels and types of social support at one time are shown to predict coping at a later time has not been carried out (Silver

& Wortman, 1980a). In the absence of such a study, observed relationships between social support and coping are open to several alternative explanations.

UNDERESTIMATION OF SUPPORT. Individuals who are poor copers, badly adjusted, or ill may underestimate the amount of support available. This explanation suggests that persons who are coping poorly have a distorted view of their world. They may underestimate the availability of support because of factors such as low self-esteem or anxiety.

COPING AS A DETERMINANT. How well one copes may determine the level of social support one receives. Persons who do not cope well may alienate their support system because of social incompetencies or because of their prognosis. Poor copers may be more likely to behave in socially inappropriate ways, or the nature of their condition may make others feel vulnerable, awkward, or inadequate (Coates, Wortman, & Abbey, 1979; Wortman & Dunkel-Schetter, 1979). An example of this phenomenon is provided in an experimental study by Coyne (1976), who found that depressed individuals induced depression, anxiety, and hostility in nondepressed persons conversing with them by telephone. Through nonreciprocal high levels of disclosure of intimate problems, the depressed individuals seemed to arouse guilt in others while inhibiting any direct expression of annoyance or hostility.

Social support as a mediator of coping

Notwithstanding the explanations discussed above, it is generally believed that social support plays an important ameliorative role by tempering the impact of highly stressful events on human beings. The mechanisms through which social support might operate is the focus of our discussion here.

PROVISION OF TANGIBLE AID. A very important but frequently neglected possibility is that social support groups provide valuable tangible aid, whether it be financial support, transportation, or help in carrying out bodily functions. Individuals in one's support system may become extensions through which one is able to indirectly control outcomes which were previously under one's direct control.

PROVISION OF INFORMATION. Support persons may also provide a large variety of information that enhances the individual's capacity to negotiate her or his world. The information provided may range from the very specific "how to" variety to more subtle types concerning how the individual should feel as well as the appropriateness of certain feelings and goals. For example, support persons may help the individual to realistically appraise the threat of a situation and his or her ability to deal with the stressors involved. This may take the form of acknowledging the appropriateness of the individual's beliefs and feelings or of assisting him or her in modifying perceptions. Such information should be critical to the development of feelings of autonomy, the elimination of counterproductive defense mechanisms, and the establishment of realistic goals.

EXPRESSION OF POSITIVE REGARD. Finally, social support likely has an effect on the recipient by communicating direct positive affect. The individual is given feedback that he or she is loved and respected and "belongs." Such support is likely to foster positive self-esteem and a sense of self-efficacy.

Undoubtedly, these three mechanisms are highly interactive in mediating the effects of environmental stress. In addition, it is important to note that the perceived availability of these benefits may be as valuable as the actual receiving of them. Thus, the individual who feels that tangible aid, information, or positive regard is available should she or he need it may benefit as much as the individual who actually receives these benefits. Similarly, individuals may benefit from the perceptions that they are receiving positive regard, for example, even though, by others' standards, they are not receiving such feedback. In sum, the three types of benefits a support system may provide can, for a given individual, exert their positive impact simply by being perceived as either present or potentially available. The social psychological theoretical perspectives that follow should further clarify how these mechanisms facilitate coping and satisfaction with life.

Social psychological theoretical perspectives

To the previous explanations of social support, we can add perspectives gained from three social psychological theories: learned helplessness, social comparison, and exchange. By examining these perspectives jointly, it should be possible to identify with greater clarity and confidence the specific mechanisms involved.

LEARNED HELPLESSNESS THEORY. Seligman first proposed learned helplessness theory as a model to explain depression in humans. According to this theory (Abramson, Seligman, & Teasdale, 1978; Seligman, 1975), when individuals are exposed to uncontrollable outcomes they develop expectations that future outcomes will also be uncontrollable. This in turn leads to the motivational, cognitive, and emotional deficits associated with helplessness and depression.

In a reformulation of the learned helplessness theory, Abramson et al. proposed that the degree of helplessness and depression will vary as a function of the type of *attribution* the individual makes about the cause of the noncontingency. Attributions about the cause can be classified along three orthogonal dimensions: (a) internal/external—internal causes stem from the individual and external causes from the environment; (b) stable/unstable—stable factors are long-lived and recurrent, whereas unstable factors are short-lived and intermittent; and (c) global/specific—global factors occur across situations, whereas specific factors are unique to a particular context. Each type of attribution has specific consequences for the individual: attributions to internal/external factors should affect self-esteem, attributions to stable/unstable factors should determine the long-term consequences of a particular experience, and attributions to global/specific factors should determine the extent to which individuals will generalize a particular experience to other situations. In general, the most damaging effects are expected when an individual makes internal, stable, global attributions concerning the cause of an undesirable event. As an example, consider a man who loses his spouse, blames himself, and believes that the death was largely due to his uncaring and negligent nature (internal, global, stable attribution). Compared with another man who is convinced that he lost his wife because of a rare, incurable disease (external, unstable, specific attribution), the former should suffer greater self-esteem deficits, the experience should generalize to a larger variety of events and situations, and the negative impact of the loss should be longer lasting. In trying to understand the elderly spinal cord injured individual's adjustment to his or her disability, this perspective suggests that one must examine not only the individual's perception of control over her or his present daily life, but also the degree to which the individual feels she or he had control over the situation which led to the disabling event.

Although this model has not been rigorously tested with an aged population, it has stimulated considerable research on aging in general and on the impact of institutionalization on aged individuals in particular. Several researchers (Langer & Rodin, 1976; Schulz, 1976, 1978) have suggested that aging is a process characterized by large decreases in the individual's ability to control important outcomes as a result of shrinking financial resources, decreased physical ability, loss of work role, etc. According to this view of aging, then, the withdrawal and high rates of depression observed among the aged are attributable in part to the shrinking sphere of personal control over the environment. Several studies have been carried out to test derivations from this model. In particular, data are now available demonstrating the positive impact of control-enhancing interventions on the institutionalized aged (Langer & Rodin, 1976; Schulz, 1976), the long-term effects of these interventions (Rodin & Langer, 1977; Schulz & Hanusa, 1978), the relationship between these interventions and individual differences (Schulz & Hanusa, 1980), and the relationship between competence and control in promoting health-related outcomes among the institutionalized aged (Schulz & Hanusa, 1979).

Lending further support to the theoretical soundness of the learned helplessness perspective as applied to psychological adjustment of the elderly is a new instrument designed by Reid and Ziegler (1980) to measure the desire for, and expectancy of, control over various aspects of daily life. When the contributions of expected and desired control subscores on the instrument were compared with various measures of adjustment, it was always the expectancy of control score that received the greater weight. Those results support the view that it is not so much the desire for control over particular aspects of life that affects the sense of well-being among the elderly, but rather the *expectancy* of whether or not one can attain desired outcomes. Reid and Ziegler state that the results of their study support the proposition that personal control is an important factor in psychological adjustment among the elderly.

With respect to spinal cord injured persons, Silver and Wortman (1980b) found that although most persons with newly acquired injuries had unrealistically positive expectations about their prognosis, they did differ in how they expected this improvement to occur. As learned helplessness theory would predict, those who believed their improvement depended on their own efforts were more likely to cope well than those who felt improvement was out of their hands. However, this relationship between expectation of control and coping effectiveness has been demonstrated only in the immediate postinjury period and, the stability of the relationship over time remains to be validated.

Viewed through the lens of learned helplessness theory, social support may facilitate coping with a severe physical disability because it fosters the perception of control and thereby promotes feelings of competency and an active, coping orientation toward life. The issue of control is likely to be a very important one for the person faced with paraplegia or quadriplegia, since this person has lost so much control over his or her own body and physical environment. Accompanying these losses is the additional threat to control over the psychological and social environment in that this person's sense of self and role identity may be greatly disrupted. For example, Rogers and Figone (1979) found that less than one half of their sample of quadriplegics were committed to goal-directed activity, defined as the initiation of concrete activity to accomplish self-defined life goals in any number of life arenas, such as occupation, education, leisure, and self-maintenance. This lack of goal-directed activity could be interpreted as a learned helplessness response, i.e., a belief that they are incapable of effecting desired outcomes.

Significant others in the environment can help the individual regain or increase his or her perception of control over the psychosocial and physical environment. These support persons may do this simply by assuring the individual that they are available as a stable part of the environment that the individual can count on and, in a more active way, by fostering positive internal self-attributions and encouraging direct action through statements such as "I know you can do it," "You've never been a quitter," or "Keep on trying, you're doing a little more every day." Support may also operate by encouraging the individual to focus on more positive aspects of a difficult situation, thus leading the individual to appraise the situation as less threatening and as one that he or she can cope with. Providing accurate information may also be viewed as increasing the actual and perceived control of the individual, since reality-based information provides the basis for a problem-solving approach to the many physical and emotional difficulties associated with paraplegia and quadriplegia.

SOCIAL COMPARISON THEORY. Over two decades ago, Festinger (1954) proposed his theory of social comparison processes. The underlying assumption of the theory is that there exists in humans a basic drive to evaluate their opinions and abilities. In the absence of objective evidence (e.g., physical reality), persons will compare themselves with others to assess the validity of their views. In Festinger's words, "An opinion, belief, and attitude is 'correct,' 'valid,' and 'proper' to the extent that it is anchored in a group of people with similar beliefs, opinions, and attitudes" (1950). Sociological counterparts to social comparison theory can be found in the work of Cooley (1956) and Mead (1934).

The relevance of social comparison processes to an understanding of adjustment to late life is evident once we recognize that there is no physical reality that readily provides an answer to questions such as How should I feel about my life? and, How happy am I? With the possible exception of extreme cases, how we respond to or feel about a wide array of circumstances and outcomes depends on the opinions, beliefs, abilities, and attributes of relevant others. Who are the relevant others for the aged or, more precisely, for the physically disabled aged? This is a recurrent and pivotal question for several theories such as learned helplessness and, indeed, for several sociological theories traditionally identified with social gerontology. Social comparison theory, and a recent derivation, temporal comparison theory (Albert, 1977), suggest two possible answers to this question. One option is to identify similar others in the environment and use them as reference persons. This is reflected in corollary III(A) of social comparison theory, which states that, given a range of possible persons for comparisons, one will choose someone close to one's own ability or opinion (Festinger, 1954).

A second option is to make historical, or temporal, comparisons. This is an intraindividual comparison in which present circumstances, outcomes, abilities, etc., are compared with past circumstances, outcomes, abilities, etc. (Albert, 1977; Schulz, in press, a and b).

To the extent that any comparison yields personally unfavorable discrepancies, individuals are likely to feel badly about themselves or their situation. Thus, for example, old persons who perceive relevant others to be considerably better off than themselves or who find the past to be better than the present are likely to experience negative affect. Positive affect should result when comparisons yield personally favorable discrepancies or perceived equality.

Which of the two processes dominates should have important consequences for adjustment to late life. Given the many real declines associated with old age (e.g., physical and cognitive ability, economic resources) in addition to those associated with a spinal cord injury, comparisons based on the past (particularly the preinjury period) are likely to yield personally unfavorable discrepancies and hence negative affective states. Alternatively, the aged individual who uses her or his contemporaries as comparison others should be less likely to experience personally unfavorable discrepancies.

As an example, consider the spinal cord injured person and the types of events he or she is likely to encounter. Clearly, if such an individual compares preinjury leisure activities, physical mobility, and daily events in general with present conditions, he or she is likely to experience negative affect. However, if the same individual uses as a basis for comparison the circumstances and outcomes of similar individuals in the immediate environment (other spinal cord injured older persons), there is less likelihood of experiencing personally unfavorable discrepancies and hence negative affect. This analysis is supported, at least anecdotally, by observations of King (personal communication) who reports that to the extent that spinal cord injured persons associate with others with the same condition, adaptation to the disability is facilitated. Rohrer, Adelman, Puckett, Toomey, Talbert and Johnson (1980) report that group meetings for spinal cord injured individuals and their families are beneficial in decreasing feelings of anxiety, helplessness, and isolation; in increasing knowledge and understanding of spinal cord injury; and in facilitating mutual support between family members. Mann, Godfrey, and Dowd (1973) also report the beneficial effect of peer group counseling in the psychological rehabilitation of spinal cord injured persons.

The type of comparison processes older persons engage in can be inferred from some recent data reported by Zemore and Eames (1979). In their study, residents of old-age homes reported no more symptoms of depression than either a group of waiting-list controls or a noninstitutionalized young group. This would be expected *if* individuals engage in contemporary rather than historical comparison processes. A similar inference can be derived from the large number of studies on morale and well-being in the aged (for a review of this literature, see Larson, 1978). Despite large differences in objective conditions of young, middle-age, and aged individuals, few studies report any age-related differences in self-report of well-being and morale. One interpretation of these data is that different age groups adjust their expectancies in line with the prevailing conditions for that group. Such strategies are adaptive in that they minimize disappointment, although they also tend to promote the status quo.

Further support for the view that persons may tend to make predominantly contemporary comparisons is found in data reported by Rogers and Figone (1979) showing that quadriplegic clients desired more contact with peer models or similar successful rehabilitants. There are a number of reasons why severely disabled persons may desire interaction with other disabled individuals. Contact with similar others who are coping successfully with paralysis may foster the belief and hope that one will be able to do the same; this contact may enable the individual, in attributional terms, to make positive internal attributions about his or her ability to achieve similar goals. Contact with successful models may also assist the individual in accepting that he or she is different, but equal, by deemphasizing physique as a value and emphasizing other attributes, such as personality, intellect, and interpersonal skills, as focal points of comparison with others. Finally, contact with similar others may increase perceived control by providing information about future problems and possible solutions, thus enabling the individual to rehearse for coping with future potential problems. In general, a successful model can convey that one can feel good even though one is old and handicapped. This discussion illustrates the complementary nature of learned helplessness and social comparison theories. By engaging in comparisons with others that yield personally favorable discrepancies or perceived equality, the individual is able to make attributions about herself or himself that foster a sense of personal control.

McKay (1980) states that despite a disproportionately high percentage of rehabilitation counselors who are themselves disabled, the effect of counselors' physical disability on similarly disabled clients' perceptions of the counselors' social influence (attractiveness, expertness, and trustworthiness) and empathy is not understood. McKay conducted an experiment in which 48 wheelchair-using persons (75 percent male, 87 percent spinal injured) viewed videotapes of two counselors, one disabled (wheelchaired) and one nondisabled, who had been coached to be alternately high and low in social influence and empathy. Each subject evaluated the counselors under the four experimental conditions and selected a preferred counselor from the disabled/nondisabled and high/low social influence counselors. High-influence/disabled counselors were rated significantly more desirable than high-influence/nondisabled counselors. No such preference, however, was shown for low-influence/disabled counselors, whose ineffectual behavior made them less desirable. These results are consistent with the view that contact with similar others who are coping successfully with paralysis is much desired, in that such contact facilitates positive internal attribution and an increased perception of control.

EXCHANGE THEORY. Exchange theory (Dowd, 1975) is a more recent entry into the social gerontology theory pool. Broadly speaking, it attempts to explain the decreased social interaction of the aged in terms of economic exchanges à la Blau (1964), Emerson (1962, 1972), and Homans (1961). The basic assumption of all exchange theories is that interactions between individuals occur and are sustained because the rewards (e.g., money, esteem, compliance, novelty) are greater than the costs (e.g., time, boredom, anxiety). An interaction is imbalanced when one of the partners in a social exchange is unable to reciprocate the rewarding behavior of the other. According to Dowd, the aged become increasingly unable to enter into balanced exchange relationships with other groups because of the decline in power resources associated with old age. The imbalanced exchange ratio ultimately forces the aged to exchange compliance—a costly generalized reinforcer—for their continued sustenance. Disengagement occurs when the costs of compliance and self-respect reach a point "beyond which additional costs become prohibitive" (Dowd, 1975).

Dowd cautiously describes the aging exchange model as a "preface" to theory. This seems wise since many questions are left unanswered (Schulz, in press a). However, the basic idea of exchange theory, that social exchanges must be reasonably reciprocal in order to be maintained, is relevant to an understanding of the workings of a social support sytem.

Froland's (1978) research suggests that an important, necessary characteristic of the support system for the severely disabled is that the exchanges be mutual. Without some form of reciprocity, the door is left open for maladaptive relationships in which the quadriplegic or paraplegic fears alienating anyone on whom he or she must depend for the simplest functions (Mann et al., 1973). Working with cancer patients, Weisman and Worden (1975) also noted that survival was better among patients who maintained active and "mutually responsive relationships, provided that the intensity of demands was not so extreme as to alienate people responsible for the patient's care." As exchange theory would predict, these studies illustrate the need of the disabled person to contribute something to an interaction despite her or his reduced capacity to do so.

Conclusion

Social scientists and policy makers rarely have the luxury of anticipating a potential problem. More often than not, their efforts are focused on problems that have already reached catastrophic proportion and require immediate solutions. Our concern for the elderly spinal cord injured person is an exception to this scenario in that we are anticipating rather than identifying a problem. As the absolute number and proportion of elderly persons increase in the next few decades, the number of elderly spinal cord injured will increase as well, and probably at a higher rate than that of the elderly population as a whole. As is the case with other frail elderly persons, it is likely that the survival of this group in community settings is largely dependent on the availability of a support system. If residing in the community is to remain an option for this group, it is important that we understand the characteristics and functions of the support network that serves them.

We have identified three complementary social psychological theoretical perspectives which may help us understand the processes through which social support facilitates effective coping. Learned helplessness, social comparison, and exchange theories all point to specific and frequently different characteristics and functions of a support system that might account for the positive impact of what we collectively call social support.

For the researcher, these theories can serve as valuable guides in constructing questions for studying the severely disabled elderly. For the policy maker and clinician, they provide an essential context within which social programs and individual interventions can be evaluated.

Unfortunately, the validity of this analysis remains to be tested. There are no existing studies that directly support the conceptual scheme presented here. Although costly, the most appropriate type of study for the ideas discussed in this chapter would be a prospective longitudinal study, one that followed a group of elderly, community-residing spinal cord injured persons through old age until they died. Such a study would not only identify those characteristics of the support system which facilitate community survival but would also allow us to assess the impact of a changing support system (e.g., as a result of deaths) on the elderly disabled individual. Data from such a study could very well contribute to the development of programs that would reduce the likelihood that problems of the disabled aged will reach catastrophic proportions.

References

Abramson, A. J. Modern concepts of management of the patient with spinal cord injury. *Archives of Physical Medicine and Rehabilitation*, 1967, *48*, 113–121.

Abramson, L. Y., Seligman, M. E. P., & Teasdale, J. D. Learned helplessness in humans: Critique and reformulation. *Journal of Abnormal Psychology*, 1978, *87*, 49–74.

Aguilera, D., & Messick, J. *Crisis intervention—theory and methodology*. St. Louis: C. V. Mosby, 1974.

Albert, S. Temporal comparison theory. *Psychological Review*, 1977, *84*, 485–503.

Bachman, L. Spinal cord injury committee. *Pennsylvania Medicine*, 1978, *31*, 31–54.

Berkman, L., & Syme, S. Social networks, host resistance, and mortality: A nine year followup study of Alameda County residents. *American Journal of Epidemiology*, 1979, *109*(2), 186–204.

Blau, P. M. *Exchange and power in social life*. New York: Wiley, 1964.

Bull, C., & AuCoin, J. Voluntary association participation and life satisfaction: A replication note. *Journal of Gerontology*, 1975, *30*(1), 73–76.

Burgess, A. W., & Holmstrom, L. L. Recovery from rape and prior life stress. *Research in Nursing and Health*, 1978, *1*, 165–174.

Caplan, G. *Support systems and community mental health*. New York: Behavioral Publications, 1974.

Carey, R. Emotional adjustment in terminal patients: A quantitative approach. *Journal of Counseling Psychology*, 1974, *21*, 433–439.

Cassel, J. Social science in epidemiology: Psychosocial processes and "stress" theoretical formulation. In E. L. Struening and M. Guttentag (Eds.), *Handbook of evaluation research* (Vol. I). Beverly Hills, Calif.: Sage Publications, 1975.

Clayton, P. M., Halikas, J. A., & Maurice, W. L. The depression of widowhood. *British Journal of Psychiatry*, 1972, *120*, 71–78.

Coates, D., Wortman, C., & Abbey, A. Reactions to victims. In I. Frieze, D. Bar-Tal, and J. Carroll (Eds.), *New approaches to social problems*. San Francisco: Jossey-Bass, 1979.

Cobb, S. Social support as a moderator of life stress. *Psychosomatic Medicine*, 1976, *38*, 300–314.

Cobb, S., & Kasl, S. Termination: The consequences of job loss. (Publication LR 77–224). Washington, D.C.: DHEW (NIOSH), 1977.

Cooley, C. H. *Human nature and the social order*. Glencoe, Ill.: Free Press, 1956.

Coyne, J. Depression and the response of others. *Journal of Abnormal Psychology*, 1976, *85*(2), 186–193.

Cumming, E., & Henry, W. *Growing old*. New York: Basic Books, 1961.

Dowd, J. Aging as exchange: A preface to theory. *Journal of Gerontology*, 1975, *30*, 584–594.

Edwards, J., & Klemmack, D. Correlates of life satisfaction: A reexamination. *Journal of Gerontology*, 1973, *28*, 497–502.

Emerson, R. M. Power-dependence relations. *American Sociological Review*, 1962, *27*, 31–41.

Emerson, R. M. Exchange theory, Parts 1 & 2. In J. Berger, and M. Zelditch (Eds.), *Sociological theories in progress, Vol. II*. Boston: Houghton-Mifflin, 1972.

Festinger, L. Informal social communication. *Psychological Review*, 1950, *57*, 271–282.

Festinger, L. A theory of social comparison processes. *Human Relations*, 1954, *7*, 117–140.

Fine, P. Spinal cord injury: An epidemiological perspective. *Paraplegia*, 1979–80, *17*, 237–250.

Frielich, M. Vocational and avocational adjustment: A followup study of discharged paraplegic and quadriplegic veterans. *Dissertation Abstracts International*, 1977, *37*(12), Pt. 1-A, 7682.

Froland, C. Improving the social adjustment of mental health clients: The case for social support networks. Unpublished doctoral dissertation, University of California, Berkeley, 1978.

Geis, H. The problem of personal worth in the physically disabled patient. *Rehabilitation Literature*, 1972, *33*(2), 34–39.

George, L. The impact of personality and social status factors upon activity level and psychological well-being. *Journal of Gerontology*, 1978, *33*(6), 840–847.

Graney, M. Happiness and social participation in aging. *Journal of Gerontology*, 1975, *30*, 701–706.

Gunther, M. S. Emotional aspects. In D. Ruge (Ed.), *Spinal cord injuries*. Springfield, Mass.: Charles C. Thomas, 1969.

Guttman, L. *Spinal cord injuries—comprehensive management and research*. Oxford, England: Blackwell Scientific Publications, 1976.

Heller, K. The effects of social support: Prevention and treatment implications. In A. P. Goldstein and F. H. Kanfer (Eds.), *Maximizing treatment gains: Transfer enhancement in psychotherapy*. New York: Academic Press, 1979.

Homans, G. C. *Social behavior: Its elementary forms*. New York: Harcourt, Brace & World, 1961.

Jamison, K. R., Wellisch, D. K., & Pasnau, R. O. Psychosocial aspects of mastectomy: The woman's perspective. *American Journal of Psychiatry*, 1978, *135*, 432–436.

Kemp, B., & Vash, C. Productivity after injury in a sample of spinal cord injured persons: A pilot study. *Journal of Chronic Disease*, 1971, *24*, 259–275.

Kerr, W., & Thompson, M. Acceptance of disability at sudden onset in paraplegia. *Paraplegia*, 1972, *10*, 94–102.

Kimball, C. P. Psychological responses to the experience of open-heart surgery. *American Journal of Psychiatry*, 1969, *126*, 96–107.

Langer, E., & Rodin, J. The effects of choice and enhanced personal responsibility for the aged: A field experiment in an institutional setting. *Journal of Personality and Social Psychology*, 1976, *34*, 191–198.

Larson, R. Thirty years of research on the subjective well-being of older Americans. *Journal of Gerontology*, 1978, *33*, 109–125.

Lawton, M. The dimensions of morale. In D. Kent, R. Kastenbaum, and S. Sherwood (Eds.), *Research, planning, and action for the elderly*. New York: Behavioral Publications, 1972.

Lemon, B., Bengtson, V., & Peterson, J. An exploration of the activity theory of aging: Activity types and life satisfaction among in-movers to a retirement community. *Journal of Gerontology*, 1972, *27*, 511–523.

Litwak, E. Research patterns in the health of the elderly: The community mental health center. In E. .F. Borgatta and N. G. McCluskey (Eds.), *Aging and Society*. Beverly Hills, Calif.: Sage Publications, 1979.

Lohmann, N. Life satisfaction research in aging: Implications for policy development. In N. Datan and N. Lohmann (Eds.), *Transitions of Aging*. New York: Academic Press, 1980.

MacElveen-Hoehn, P., & Smith-DiJulio, K. Social network behavior in long term illness: Preliminary analysis. In *Networks for helping, Proceedings of the Conference on Networks*, Portland State University, Portland, Oregon, Nov. 1–2, 1978.

Maddison, D., & Walker, W. L. Factors affecting the outcome of conjugal bereavement. *British Journal of Psychiatry*, 1967, *113*, 1057–1067.

Mann, W., Godfrey, M., & Dowd, E. The use of group counselling procedures in the rehabilitation of spinal cord injured patients. *The American Journal of Occupational Therapy*, 1973, *27*(2), 73–77.

McKay, J. The effect of rehabilitation counselor disability status on similarly disabled clients' perceptions of counselor social influence and empathy. *Dissertation Abstracts International*, 1980, *40*(9), 11-A, 4898.

Mead, G. H. *Mind, self, and society*. Chicago: University of Chicago Press, 1934.

Milhouse, R. Emotional adjustments to spinal cord injury. In *National resource directory*. Newton Upper Falls, Mass.: National Spinal Cord Injury Foundation, 1979.

Palmore, E., & Kivett, V. Change in life satisfaction: A longitudinal study of persons aged 46–70. *Journal of Gerontology*, 1977, *32*(3), 311–316.

Palmore, E., & Luikart, C. Jr. Health and social factors related to life satisfaction. *Health and Social Behavior*, 1972, *13*, 68–80.

Peterson, D., King, P., & Davis, K. Age and lifestyle adjustment as a result of amputation. Paper presented at the annual meeting of the Gerontological Society, Dallas, Nov. 16–20, 1978.

Petrus, J., & Balaban, A. Special psychiatric problems of the paraplegic. *American Journal of Psychiatry*, 1953, *109*, 693–695.

Pihlblad, C., & Adams, D. Widowhood, social participation, and life satisfaction. *Aging and Human Development*, 1972, *3*, 323–330.

Reid, D., & Ziegler, M. Validity and stability of a new desired control measure pertaining to psychological adjustment of the elderly. *Journal of Gerontology*, 1980, *35*(3), 395–402.

Rodin, J., & Langer, E. Long-term effects of a

control-relevant intervention with the institutionalized aged. *Journal of Personality and Social Psychology*, 1977, *35*, 897–902.

Roessler, R., & Bolton, B. *Psychosocial adjustment to disability*. Baltimore: University Park Press, 1978.

Rogers, J., & Figone, J. Psychosocial parameters in treating the person with quadriplegia. *The American Journal of Occupational Therapy*, 1979, *33*(7), 432–439.

Rohrer, K., Adelman, B., Puckett, J., Toomey, B., Talbert, D., & Johnson, E. W., Rehabilitation in spinal cord injury: Use of a patient-family group. *Archives of Physical Medicine and Rehabilitation*, 1980, *61*, 225–229.

Schulz, R. The effects of control and predictability on the psychological and physical well-being of the institutionalized aged. *Journal of Personality and Social Psychology*, 1976, *33*, 563–573.

Schulz, R. *Psychology of death, dying and bereavement*. Reading, Mass.: Addison-Wesley, 1978.

Schulz, R. Aging, health and theoretical social gerontology: Where are we and where should we go? In M. R. Eiser (Ed.), *Social psychology and behavioral medicine*. New York: Wiley, in press. (a)

Schulz, R. Emotionality and aging. In K. Blankenstein and J. Polivy (Eds.), *Communication and affect* (Vol. IX). New York: Plenum Press, in press. (b)

Schulz, R., & Hanusa, B. Long-term effects of predictability and control enhancing interventions: Findings and ethical issues. *Journal of Personality and Social Psychology*, 1978, *36*, 1194–1201.

Schulz, R., & Hanusa, B. Environmental influences on the effectiveness of control and competence enhancing interventions. In L. C. Perlmutter and R. A. Monty (Eds.), *Choice and perceived control*. Hillsdale, N.J.: Erlbaum, 1979.

Schulz, R., & Hanusa, B. Experimental social gerontology: A social psychological perspective. *Journal of Social Issues*, 1980, *36*, 30–47.

Seligman, M. *Helplessness: On depression, development and death*. San Francisco: W. H. Freeman, 1975.

Seymour, G. Activity level, the sense of personal autonomy and life satisfaction in old age (doctoral dissertation, Boston University Graduate School, 1972). *Dissertation Abstracts International*, 1972, *33*(5B), 2331–2332.

Silver, R., & Wortman, C. Coping with undesirable life events. In J. Garber and M.E.P. Seligman (Eds.), *Human helplessness*. New York: Academic Press, 1980. (a)

Silver, R., & Wortman, C. Expectations of control and coping with permanent paralysis. Paper presented at "Issues of Control in Health" symposium, APA Convention, Montreal, September 1980. (b)

Spreitzer, E., & Snyder, E. Correlates of life satisfaction. *Journal of Gerontology*, 1974, *29*(4), 454–458.

Statistical Report. Phoenix: Southwest Regional System for Treatment of Spinal Injury, 1975.

Thompson, G. Work versus leisure roles: An investigation of morale among employed and retired men. *Journal of Gerontology*, 1973, *18*(3), 339–344.

Thorn, I., Von Salzer, C., & Fromme, A. Psychological aspects of the paraplegic patient. *Medical Clinics of North America*, 1946, *30*, 473.

Tucker, S. J. The psychology of spinal cord injury: Patient-staff interaction. *Rehabilitation Literature*, 1980, *41*(5–6), 114–121, 160.

Vachon, M.L.S., Lyall, W. A., Rogers, J., Formo, A., Freedman, K., Cochrane, J., & Freeman, S. The use of group meetings with cancer patients and their families. In J. Tache, H. Selye, and S. B. Day (Eds.), *Cancer, stress and death*. New York: Plenum, 1979.

Vargo, J. Some psychological effects of physical disability. *American Journal of Occupational Therapy*, 1978, *32*, 31–34.

Veroff, J., Douvan, E., & Kulka, R. *The American experience: A self-portrait over two decades*. New York: Basic Books, in press.

Walker, K. N., MacBride, A., & Vachon, M.L.S. Social support networks and the crisis of bereavement. *Social Science and Medicine*, 1977, *11*, 35–41.

Watson, N. Pattern of spinal cord injury in the elderly. *Paraplegia*, 1976, *14*, 36–40.

Weisman, A. D. Early diagnosis of vulnerability in cancer patients. *American Journal of the Medical Sciences*, 1976, *271*, 187–196.

Weisman, A. D., & Worden, J. W. Psychological analysis of cancer deaths. *Omega*, 1975, *6*, 61–75.

Weller, D., & Miller, P. Emotional reactions of patient, family and staff in acute-care period of spinal cord injury, Pt. I. *Social Work in Health Care*, Summer, 1977, 367–379.

Wortman, C. B., & Dunkel-Schetter, C. Interpersonal relationships and cancer: A theoretical analysis. *Journal of Social Issues*, 1979, *35*, 120–155.

Wright, B. A. *Physical disability: A psychological approach*. New York: Harper and Row, 1960.

Zemore, R., & Eames, N. Psychic and somatic symptoms of depression among young adults, institutionalized aged, and noninstitutionalized aged. *Journal of Gerontology*, 1979, *34*, 716–722.

14

COMMENTARY:
THE SOCIAL PSYCHOLOGY OF CLINICAL INTERVENTION: APPLIED PRECISION OR USEFUL PERSPECTIVES?

PHILIP R. COSTANZO
DUKE UNIVERSITY

The therapeutic intervention of a trained clinician in the life distresses of another human being has probably constituted psychology's major applied challenge. Can a science of human behavior discern explicit principles of human functioning which allow for the remediation, redirection, and/or amelioration of problems in living? The answer to this question is difficult, and data pertaining to such an answer are woefully incomplete. Nevertheless, appealing to the wisdom of my Italian ancestry, I would offer the answer *mezza-mezza*—literally, half and half. That is, while it is unlikely that any branch of scientific psychology might provide clear *technological* solutions to clinical problems, the practice of psychotherapy can certainly be advanced by invoking *perspectives* on human functioning which grow out of the theories and data of scientific psychology.

Much of what clinical psychologists do to help effect changes in their clients is dependent upon how they, the psychologists, view human beings and how they view the processes accompanying human behavioral, emotional, and cognitive change. This fact is amply illustrated through retrospective consideration of the history of psychotherapeutic intervention. For example, no less a figure than Sigmund Freud changed the face of psychotherapeutic practice by his laborious deduction that human behavior is largely determined by unseen and unacknowledged developmentally acquired motives. This "principle" spawned a still-prominent therapeutic approach which relegates overt behavior to the status of symptom and has clients encounter their underlying motives through free verbal association. Presumably, through such processes of association (guided by the symbolic interpretations of a therapist), a client forms self-relevant insights which eventuate in "corrective" emotional experiences. While this abbreviated portrayal of analytic therapy does it little justice, it does illustrate the impact that a particular view of human functioning has upon the process of clinical intervention. Similar illustrations could easily be framed from client-centered therapy, behavior therapy, role-construct therapy, and the like. In each case, a view of human nature that suggests a set of interrelated principles of human behavior and human change processes is appealed to as a source of psychotherapeutic change strategies.

From the vantage point of this commentator, the four preceding chapters in this section nicely explore the applied possibilities of some perspectives on human behavior evident in contemporary social psychology. In my opinion, if the reader is to fully appreciate the possibilities of a social psychology of clinical intervention, he or she must discard the view that might represent clinical practices as direct *technological* sequelae of social psychological data and theory. One can hardly frame an exacting technology from competing hypotheses and principles for which the evidence is qualified, incomplete, and, at times, contradictory. Instead, for the clinician, the corpus of social psychology represents a rich set of perspectives for viewing interpersonal and intrapersonal functioning. These perspectives allow for the creative introduction of intervention strategies which incorporate a social psychology of attitude and behavior change. In the next several paragraphs, we shall view the critical directions for clinical intervention suggested by the four papers in this section.

The search for effective models of intervention

Strong's effortful attempts to discern the clinical implications of social psychology represent an admirable career odyssey for the reader to follow. His ambition to construct effective and active strategies of clinical intervention had its origins in this discontentment with the "passive" intervention approach suggested by Rogerian thought. From Strong's perspective, it is hardly deniable that therapy is a powerful process and that therapists (whether they wish it or not) possess and exercise great power over their clients. Such a construal of therapeutic intervention led Strong to reason that the effective reagent bringing about therapeutic change should inhere in the systematic deployment of therapist power on behalf of client behavior change.

Given the available psychological models of the early 1960's, Strong began his examination of "power-assertive" therapies with an eye toward Skinner's model of operant behavior control. Yet, it became clear that therapy was not simply a process of influence but an interactive structure best described as a naturalistic occasion for *social influence* processes. Influenced by the thought of dissonance theorists and researchers, Strong chose to view therapy as an attitude change process. Therapists would realize their curative power by confronting clients with sufficiently discrepant communications to bring about motivational pressures to change. In pursuing the analogic relationship of dissonance processes to clinical change processes, Strong, to his credit, empirically examined the role of attitude change variables in clinical circumstances. While he found some support for a social influence construal of the psychotherapy relationship, the outcomes of his clinical research were sufficiently discrepant from dissonance implications to lead him to continue his search for a model more descriptive of the psychotherapy process. The remainder of Strong's chapter details this search.

From the perspective of this commentator, several implications of the remainder of Strong's work are pivotal for social psychology–clinical process integrations:

1. *While the clinical client might be analogically compared with the experimental recipient of persuasive communications, she or he is far from an exact counterpart.* It is quite difficult to construe the client as the "victim" of manipulations of situation variables (e.g., communicator credibility). Given the importance of the influence topic (i.e., the client's life problems), any social psychological model of therapy must keep track of the client's active phenomenology.
2. *Strong, in his search for therapy applications, locates two very important elements in this phenomenology:* (1) the attributions—self as well as environmental—which mediate between the receipt of therapeutic influence and actual change and (2) the related factor of the client's need to

establish the sources of control both in her or his life space outside the clinic confines and in the clinical situation.

3. *The clinical dyad is a "real-life" interaction unit which is similar to other real units in the client's life* (e.g., marital relationships, friendships, employment relationships). Such units need to be understood through the consideration of processes involved in the mutual control of interaction and communication. Thus, from Strong's current vantage point, both the clinical interaction itself and the construal of the client's problems in the outside world can be effectively managed only by conceptually embedding processes of social influence, attribution, and mutual control within an interaction model. The fact that Strong has arrived at an interaction model that incorporates the implications of the several single process models he earlier invoked in clinical contexts points to the complexity of a social-behavioral analysis of clinical problems and processes. While the social psychology researcher and theorist have the luxury of empirically isolating single processes (e.g., dissonance or causal attribution), the clinician must in fact simultaneously consider the conjoint operation of several processes. Strong's terminus in a general interaction model constitutes a recognition of this last point.

The Spanos paper constitutes a quite comprehensive and thoughtful review of the literature on the nature of hypnotic processes. While it does not in and of itself suggest ready bridges between social psychology and clinical process, it is rich with implications for such bridging efforts. While the study of hypnosis has typically been directed at examining the boundaries of conscious functioning and/or the role of susceptibility and suggestion in human behavior, it has also been employed as an ameliorative tool for a wide variety of human difficulties. As such, an examination of hypnotic suggestibility provides some interesting implications for clinical process.

As the reader will note, Spanos comprehensively documents that hypnosis is best conceptualized in terms of "ordinary" cognitive processes. Against a backdrop of past perspectives which have represented hypnotic states as unusual transformations of mental process, Spanos's work is quite informative. Aside from the role that Spanos's paper might serve in disabusing the field of a special-process view of hypnosis, the terms in which Spanos empirically demystifies hypnosis are useful ones for a social psychology of clinical process. It appears from Spanos's analysis that the success of hypnotic interventions and the nature of hypnosis are dependent upon two large categories of variables:

1. *The subjects' attributional mediation of hypnotic suggestion.* From Spanos's perspective, the imaginative activity which follows upon hypnotic suggestion is a product of several attributional phenomena induced in the subjects. These phenomena range from the subjects' attribution that their behavior under hypnosis is involuntary (despite empirical evidence which represents such behavior as nonautomatic) to attributions involved in self-perception/self-persuasion processes and self-distraction processes.

2. *The degree to which the hypnotic subject responds to the demand characteristics of hypnosis.* In short, hypnotic suggestions meet with greater success when individuals adopt the expected role of a hypnotic subject.

Both of these classes of phenomena are viewed by Spanos as pivotal variables in individual differences in hypnotic suggestibility. More important, this empirically documented portrayal of hypnosis represents it as a mundane process continuous with other waking processes of consciousness rather than a rarified state of trancelike, transformed consciousness. As such, it seems likely that the data from the study of hypnosis are quite applicable to the study of other contexts in which human suggestibility is a critical factor. Indeed, clinical intervention is one such context for which the suggestibility of the client and the suggestive nature of change interventions are important. Like Strong's more explicit analysis of clinical-social phenomena, Spanos's work suggests the overriding importance of client, or subject, phenomenology (around issues of causal attribution, control and voluntariness attributions, and the defintion of the social situation) in the success of intervention processes. It is clear that the general explorations of laboratory social psychology serve to provide avenues for understanding such processes in their clinical context.

The Strong paper, in the end, attempts to frame analyses which provide for a comprehensive portrayal of social psychological process models of clinical intervention. In contrast, Cooper and Axsom examine, in depth, the clinical applicability of a single principle derived from a single model in social psychology. More explicitly, Cooper and Axsom explore the potential uses of an effort justification model based on cognitive dissonance for processes of clinically relevant change. The work they report upon is quite convincing and serves to establish the plausibility of the careful application of an effort justification procedure in psychotherapy. They are careful to note that their interest in exploring this process is to portray effort justification not as a comprehensive, all-defining model of *the* change agent in psychotherapy, but rather as a tool which might be usefully employed by clinicians. Cooper and Axsom's work empirically demonstrates that the manipulation of client effort in the interest of various goals (e.g., weight loss, assertiveness, fear reduction) enhances the probability that clients will change in the direction of those goals. These authors nicely note that clinicians of various stripes may have unsystematically and unwittingly applied effort justification notions in their therapeutic regimens in the past. The burdens of fee expenditure, painful self-disclosure, and the like have been frequently noted in clinical accounts as factors which serve to enhance the motivations of the client to encounter difficult behavior changes and reconstructions of self. What Cooper and Axsom's analysis suggests is that clinical intervention outcomes might benefit from a self-conscious application of an effort justification principle.

While Cooper and Axsom carefully suggest three bases for the success of an applied effort justification model in clinical settings, these three bases conceptually reduce to one overarching perspective on human nature: *People prefer to think of themselves as rational beings.* Rational beings do not exert heavy effort in the interest of trivial or hopeless goals. As a consequence, those who exert high effort on behalf of behavior change goals are seen as tending either to change their attitudes toward the goal object (or behavior domain) in a positive direction, to increase their motivation to change in the direction of the desired goal, or to view the desired goal as more attainable than those who exert minimal effort. Any one of these psychological alterations in internal perspective or motive renders the expenditure of effort a sensible and rational act. Indeed, the clients' eventual change in the direction of the goal (e.g., weight reduction) *empirically* justifies the expenditure of effort.

The major boundary condition on the success of an effort justification intervention is one of the primary boundary conditions specified by Festinger in his original treatment of cognitive dissonance processes. That is, the client or subject must feel *responsible* for engaging in the effortful behavior. Cooper and Axsom, inducing felt responsibility in their subjects/clients through the manipulation of perceived choice, empirically validate the overriding importance of this boundary condition on the applied value of dissonance processes. This responsibility qualifier on the Cooper and Axsom intervention approach is quite congruent with most clinical perspectives on therapeutic change. Nearly every form of therapy proposes that therapeutic success is moderated by client perception of choice. For example, therapists involved in inducing change through client insight arrange the conditions for eliciting insights so that clients *own* the insight arrived at. Such therapists would view the practice of handing interpretations to clients as counterproductive. In short, the lion's share of therapies adopt one or another strategy for enhancing the clients' felt responsibility for engaging the change process. The fact that subject/client responsibility is such an integral part of a theory of dissonance-induced changes enhances the potential applied value of procedures such as Cooper and Axsom's.

I would like to end my commentary on the Cooper and Axsom work with an ironic observation. It may well be that dissonance theory propositions are more applicable to the clinic circumstance than they ever were to the laboratory circumstance. It must be remembered that a prime boundary condition on the arousal of dissonance proposed by Festinger was represented by the *importance* of the cognitive or behavior domain to the person. In the laboratory situation, there exist ethical and/or procedural limitations on the manipulation or use of life issues of true importance to subjects. No such limits exist in the naturalistic circumstance of the clinic, where clients present themselves for help with problems of clear and overriding personal importance. In short, the clinic is a seemingly ideal arena for the application of cognitive dissonance theory.

Schulz and Decker provide a very useful analysis of the factors involved in *psychosocial* recovery from an extremely debilitating trauma: spinal cord injury. Their analysis of the issues involved in psychosocial recovery processes is potentially applicable to a wide variety of natural (e.g., aging) and traumatic (e.g., bodily injury) conditions encountered by humans. A shorthand way of expressing the general applied sweep of the Schulz and Decker proposals is to note that they apply to *any decline in function to a level drastically below a previous level of function*. Such debilitating physical difficulties have the potential for realigning a person's perception of his or her social attractiveness and general effectiveness. While some realignment of personal perspective is congruent with the reality of the individual's newly acquired physical condition, psychological difficulties arise when the individual pervasively overgeneralizes decrement in function to domains in which effectiveness and social attractiveness are realistically unaffected.

In offering their analysis, Schulz and Decker examine the sources of this form of overgeneralization from the vantage point of several social psychological models. In doing so, they provide a useful contribution to the *social psychology of health intervention*. As distinguished from the circumstance of clinical intervention, applied social psychology in health settings requires as much of a focus on the client's general *life situation* as on the *person*. Schulz and Decker make this point quite clearly when they discuss the ameliorative possibilities of social support systems on the adjustment of persons affected with spinal cord injury. According to these authors, social support can serve to facilitate the coping of an individual with spinal cord injury (and by extension the coping of persons with any clearly debilitating condition) by offering the individual tangible supports, realistic information concerning the process of coping, and/or positive social regard. While individuals suffering the aftermath of spinal cord injury are particularly dependent on the support of others in their social network, the needs defining their dependence correspond to the needs that each of us have in the social environment. As Jones and Gerard (1967) have noted, social dependency originates from two conditions of need—one defined by *information dependence*, the other by *effect dependence*. From the Schulz and Decker analysis, one could reasonably surmise that those with spinal cord injuries have an enhanced need for both information from the social environment and positive material and psychological resources from others in that environment. By extension, any process of intervention aimed at ameliorating the distress of injured individuals must devise methods for the delivery of such supports.

While Schulz and Decker consider three nonexclusive theoretical frameworks that help to explain the psychological plight of traumatically injured individuals, the amelioration proposed in the case of each model inheres in some variant of social support. Whether the psychological effects of spinal cord injury are best explained by reference to a generalized perception of loss of control (à la learned helplessness), a decrease in perceived relative capability (à la social comparison theory), or a decrease in the impaired person's perception of the resources available for social interaction (à la exchange theory), one form or another of social support would seem to constitute the prime intervention approach.

While social psychological research has frequently examined the parameters defining social support functions in the laboratory, Schulz and Decker's work provides a challenge of applying this work to the real life circumstances occasioned by health related difficulties.

A derivation of some common beginning "principles"

The above discussion of the four papers in this section would not provide a reasonably complete commentary without some consideration of the common perspectives invoked by the various authors. Taken together, these works offer a rather comprehensive portrayal of the potential usefulness of a social psychology of clinical intervention. While each of the papers is idiosyncratic in its focus and domain of concern, they all share the same orienting influence—social psychology. By considering those ideas and provisional principles commonly suggested by the four papers, one can discern a beginning set of propositions to guide the integration of social psychology and clinical intervention. Below I shall briefly note four propositions which appear to pervade the intervention scenarios of Strong, Cooper and Axsom, Spanos, and Schulz and Decker.

1. *The perception of client choice and volition is directly related to the magnitude and stability of change following intervention.* As noted earlier, while such a proposition is not new to experienced clinicians, social psychology provides a variety of perspectives which account for the dynamic relationships between perceived volition and client change. These perspectives include the several propositions of attribution theory, dissonance theory, and self-perception theory. Each of these theories accords considerable importance to choice as a variable that affects a wide variety of self-perceptual and behavioral processes. It is also the case that each theory suggests those conditions which give rise to the perception of choice and those factors which govern the behavior changes following upon the exercise of volition. In doing so, they serve as potent bases for the construction of clinical intervention strategies.

2. *Individuals seek to perceive themselves as controlling the outcome they achieve in the environment.* While this proposition relates closely to the choice proposition, it deals with a slightly different clinically relevant phenomena. More explicitly, while the choice proposition deals with the consequences of the perception of choice, the control proposition refers to the motive force provided by individuals' desires to behave effectively in the environment. In the clinical arena, many clients who present themselves for treatment perceive themselves as victimized by environmental forces and incapable of changing that state of affairs. Social psychology's data and theories provide for methods of altering the internality of control perception. In applying such methods, clinicians have as an ally the natural motive tendencies of individuals to seek control. Each of the foregoing papers addresses this issue in one form or another, and its repetitiveness defines its convergent reliability as an item for clinical intervention. It should be parenthetically noted that, in clinical context, the control proposition might operate bidirectionally. That is, individuals might seek intervention in their life problems under conditions of excessive perceptions of control (e.g., in problems of guilt) as well as under conditions of lower perceived control. The theoretical base of social psychology should provide useful perspectives on intervention in either instance.

3. *Changes contingent on intervention can be enhanced and stabilized by social support*

processes. While the Schulz and Decker paper provides the clearest exemplar of this proposition, each of the other papers alludes explicitly or implicitly to the influential nature of the social system surrounding the client. Since social psychology had its beginnings in the study of social influence and social reference, there is a long history of inquiry to support the development of intervention strategies based upon this proposition. Furthermore, the potency of social support as a factor in human change suggests that the efforts of an applied social psychology should be at least partially invested in the understanding of approaches to social system intervention.

4. *Subjects/clients are inclined to cognitively integrate myriad influences extant in any intervention circumstance.* This final proposition is best exemplified in the work of Strong, who, as he sought a comprehensive social psychological model of psychotherapy, found that many factors simultaneously penetrate the phenomenology of the client. In the social psychology laboratory one can focus upon the parameters governing a single process domain. In the clinic or applied arena no such control is possible, nor is it desirable. Hence, the future usefulness of social psychological paradigms of intervention is dependent upon inquiry into the manner by which clients apprehend and respond to the influence of several co-acting factors extant in the clinical circumstance.

While the above propositions are quite general derivatives of the four papers in this section, they do suggest the issues in the corpus of social psychology that seem most likely to contribute to advances in intervention.

Conclusion

It is my belief that the work presented in this book represents a promising beginning for promoting the effective application of the thought and data of social psychology to the domain of "real-life" problems. It is also the case that in beginning such an integrative effort, social psychology will be moved in new and interesting directions. A "true" social psychology of clinical intervention will eventually need to grapple with issues of both individual differences and human development. In the clinic individuals are *not* a source of error variance, they are *the* object of study and change. Their idiosyncratic proclivities and histories will indeed alter social psychology's perspective on the generality of its principles and theories. While this is an altogether healthy development, it may indeed be the most difficult problem in forging an integration of social and clinical psychology. Using the very fine papers that appear in this section as a base, this commentator is impressed that social psychologists have made considerable headway in resolving this problem.

five

CONCLUSION

15

THE INTEGRATION OF CLINICAL AND SOCIAL PSYCHOLOGY: CURRENT STATUS AND FUTURE DIRECTIONS

GIFFORD WEARY
HERBERT L. MIRELS
JOHN S. JORDAN
OHIO STATE UNIVERSITY

In preceding chapters, we have had an opportunity to consider the potential importance of applying social psychological perspectives to understanding the development, assessment, and treatment of maladaptive behavior patterns. Despite the diversity of phenomena considered and theoretical perspectives represented in these chapters, it is possible to discern an underlying philosophy shared by our contributors. Because the philosophy underlying integrative clinical-social approaches provides a common thread and because it influences the way problems are defined and the types of methodologies employed, our concluding chapter attempts to delineate aspects of this general philosophy. In addition, the chapter considers the importance and likely future directions of integrative clinical-social research.

General philosophy underlying clinical-social research

The question often boils down to whether clinical psychology is an art or a science and whether the "basic science" of pyschology has anything to contribute to the art of the clinical practice. (Strupp, 1976)

If this question were posed to the contributors of this volume, they undoubtedly would agree that the hallmark of clinical psychology is its scientific foundation and that the "basic science" of psychology has much to offer clinical practice. Indeed, this volume clearly focuses directly on employing the science of psychology (in particular, social psychology) to enhance our understanding of personality and of clinical assessment and treatment processes.

What does such a view of clinical psychology imply? First, it indicates a strong commitment to the advancement of knowledge through a systematic, empirical search for general principles of behavior and experience, principles that generally are extracted and examined within the context of the experimental-laboratory model. Despite general agreement concerning the power of this model, there recently has been vigorous debate as to its limitations and abuses in all areas of psychology (Kazdin, 1978; Petrinovich, 1979; Proshansky, 1981). Much of this controversy turns on the relative importance of internal versus external validity. As Gibbs (1979) has noted, critics of the experimental method have bemoaned the lopsided emphasis on method over meaning (Koch, 1959), manipulation over understanding (Kaplan, 1964), and rigor over sensitivity to human subtlety (Sanford, 1965). It is important to note, however, that "there is nothing intrinsic in the experimental-laboratory model that hinders the development of cumulative knowledge in psychology. . . . But the question is when it should be used, for what problems, and at what stages in the development of a field of inquiry" (Proshansky, 1981, p. 112). Surely the recent history of clinical psychology argues forcefully that both theoretical and applied advances require a knowledge base developed from ecologically oriented experimental inquiry.

As illustrated in several chapters of this volume (see, for example, Chapter 1 by Brehm and Smith and Chapter 8 by Coates and Peterson), the essential components of experimental research have been adapted to investigations of the relatively complex issues, exigencies, and constraints typical of field settings. Advances in the application of the experimental approach to social behavior outside the laboratory will require the development of conceptual schemes for characterizing or "dimensionalizing" environments in terms coordinate with psychological theory. Important efforts along these lines that exemplify the integration of clinical and social psychological perspectives have been initiated by Frederiksen (1972), Moos (1973, 1974), Sells (1976), and others. Moos (1974), in studies of clinical populations, for example, has demonstrated that reliably measured dimensions of the social environment are related to such indexes of treatment outcome as dropout rate, release rate, and tenure in the community. Work of this type encourages the anticipation that our knowledge about the ways in which characteristics of the natural environment influence important behavioral outcomes will extend beyond clinical hunches and intuitive surmise.

The philosophy shared by workers attempting to integrate clinical and social psychology also implies a belief that the principles governing behavior assessment and behavior change processes are not unique to psychodiagnosis and psychotherapy (Goldstein, Heller, & Sechrest, 1966; McLemore & Benjamin, 1979), but rather that these principles are implicated in accounts of all personally and socially important behaviors (Goldstein, 1971; Harvey & Weary, 1979). In particular, the clinical-social approach posits that the individual and his or her social context are crucial in the determination of personality and behavior and, accordingly, that systematic attention to social psychological principles is essential to any understanding of the definition, development, maintenance, and modification of maladaptive behavior patterns. Carson (1969) has noted that "personality disorder . . . is a matter of how one *behaves* (including what one *says*) in the presence of others; its definition is public and social in nature" (p. 225). Similarly, McLemore and Benjamin (1979) have argued "that the selection of a traditional diagnosis for a particular individual is frequently based on reports or observations of social performance" (p. 32). Accordingly, these authors further suggest that a focus on interpersonal activities can be expected to enhance our understanding of the etiology of psychological difficulties and lead to the development of procedures for their treatment and prevention.

The integrative orientation advocated and exemplified in this volume can be expected to provoke systematic conceptual consideration of the types of assessment and intervention procedures appropriate to various problematic behaviors. More generally, it seeks to encourage our development as interdisciplinary workers and will extend and deepen our understanding of the relationships between concepts, theories, and data at the interface of clinical and social psychology.

The promise of integrative clinical-social research

A rapidly accelerating interest of psychologists in interdisciplinary work is reflected in the recent emergence and popularity of such specialities as medical psychology, bioclinical psychology, pediatric psychology, clinical psychophysiology, and neuropsychology. In general, these specialities concern themselves with the interplay of psychological and biological perspectives. In contrast, the integration of clinical and social psychology promises important advantages at a level of analysis that is likely to be compatible with the social science orientation of workers in both domains and that is distinctively psychological. Indeed, as Petrinovich (1979) has argued, "since all behavior takes place in some medium with which the organism must interact, all psychological analysis is, in essence, at the level of social psychology" (p. 378). Attention to the social context of human behavior and experience appears likely to eventuate in conceptualizations of personality, psychological disorders, and change processes that rely less heavily on intrapsychic causal determinants than do traditional approaches. Moreover, as the clinical-social approach tends to generate relatively precise conceptualizations, it offers a promising alternative to traditional clinical formulations that often are very tenuously tied to operational descriptions of specific behavior disorders and intervention techniques. Concerning the latter, Proshansky has noted that

These [approaches] were and are far more general theoretical approaches or orientations than "working" theoretical formulations. The theory was more a pronouncement of faith in one or more general assumptions, and was therefore so broad and general that its direct connection to the conceptualization of particular problems and issues was tenuous, to say the least. (1981, p. 10)

In a similar vein, Strupp has suggested that

There were various theories to account more or less adequately for the patient's suffering and turmoil. Articulated to these theories, there was a body of psychological techniques that were brought to bear on the amelioration, modification or cure of the difficulties that brought the patient to the psychotherapist. [Questions have been raised, however] concerning the degree to which techniques are congruent with or articulated to a theory of psychotherapy. (1976, p. 568)

It may be reasonable to anticipate that theories of social behavior that have successfully suffered the test of empirical research may provide "working" suggestions for clinical practice.

A recent study by Mirels and McPeek (1977) may serve as an illustration. Within an attitudinal advocacy paradigm, some subjects in that study were induced to write self-laudatory essays concerning a number of personality attributes. These subjects were instructed to "present the strongest case you can—with one restriction . . . that whatever you write must be true." After completing the essays, subjects were invited to participate in a survey dealing with students' attitudes about participation in psychological experiments. The survey was conducted in another room by a person allegedly unaffiliated with the experimenter. The final section of the survey, introduced on the pretext that it was designed to ascertain the characteristics of participants in psychological studies, contained the major dependent measures: bipolar scales which the subjects used to characterize their degree of agreeableness, conscientiousness, and emotional stability. Analyses revealed that subjects instructed to write the self-laudatory essays rated themselves more favorably with respect to each of these characteristics than did subjects who had been instructed to write essays on a current social issue (federal funds for the space program).

Although the findings of this study provide no evidence regarding the durability of the enhanced self-descriptions, they suggest that important aspects of one's self-concept are vulnerable to the kinds of influence procedures derived from social psychological theory. This, of course, is not meant to imply that such procedures be directly transplanted into the kinds of interventions appropriate for given clients and problems. In this connection, Mirels and McPeek note that

From a clinical perspective the durability of the effect would need to obtain over a much longer period. At the same time it should be noted that the effect was achieved with a relatively "light" and brief manipulation. Therapeutic effects of self-advocacy might best be evaluated with repeated self-persuasion exercises in conjunction with feedback from the therapist. (1977, p. 1131)

Future directions of integrative clinical-social research

One of the most significant recent developments in the field of psychotherapy research is the growing interest in identifying principles and strategies of behavior change that are common to all psychotherapeutic endeavors. For example, Strupp and Bergin (1969) have suggested that there are a specifiable number of social influence factors that are implicated in all of the major psychotherapies. Among these, Strupp and Bergin included imitation, identification, persuasion, empathy, warmth, interpretation, counterconditioning, extinction, discrimination learning, reward, and punishment. More recently, Goldfried (1980) has argued that

> Although commonalities across approaches may be found in the realm of specific techniques (e.g., role playing, relaxation training), it is unlikely that such comparisons would reveal much more than trivial points of similarity. I would suggest, however, that the possibility of finding meaningful consensus exists at a level of abstraction somewhere between theory and technique which, for want of a better term, we might call clinical strategies. . . . In essence, such strategies function as clinical heuristics that implicitly guide our efforts during the course of therapy. (p. 994)

Goldfried suggests two such clinical strategies that may be common to all therapeutic approaches: (a) providing the client with new, corrective experiences and (b) giving the client direct feedback.

To the extent that such a set of common strategies, or principles, can be identified, an integrated clinical-social perspective would seem to be not only a viable future direction for psychotherapy research but also essential to an understanding of the mechanisms and processes underlying these strategies. For illustrative purposes, let us assume that the strategy of providing clients with direct feedback is found to be common across therapeutic approaches. In general, this strategy would entail inducing clients to become aware of what they are (or are not) doing, feeling, and thinking in a variety of situations. More concretely, this strategy would require that we examine those aspects of the source (e.g., credibility, number, trustworthiness, perceived intentions, motives, and similarity to client), the message (e.g., discrepancy between position espoused in the feedback and client's position about her or his behavior, thoughts, and feelings; emotional arousal engendered by the feedback), and the client (e.g., self-esteem, intelligence, social isolation, distraction) that would be expected to determine the effects of direct feedback. We also would need to investigate the process or processes (e.g., cognitive dissonance, affect, self-perception) that would be expected to mediate the effects of direct feedback on changes in clients' attitudes and behaviors. It would seem obvious that three decades of social psychological research attention to attitude development and change could provide an extensive empirical foundation for the investigation of direct feedback as a clinical strategy. Indeed, to ignore the considerable social psychological research on models of social influence would seem counterproductive. By the same token, it would be equally ill-advised for social psychology to overlook clinical situations as a source of data about important human concerns and motivations, a source unlikely to have its equivalent in public discourse or behavior. The revelations of patients in psychotherapy and the experience-born insights of gifted clinicians, when examined from a social psychological perspective, might well inspire methods for the development and enhancement of intervention procedures and might provoke important theoretical advances in clinical and social psychological theory.

In discussing likely future directions of integrative clinical-social research, we have focused on the psychotherapeutic endeavor. Specifically, we have emphasized that as principles of behavior change common to the major approaches to psychotherapy are identified, it will become increasingly difficult for scholars to escape the fact that clinical and social psychologists often are concerned with similar psychological processes. This emphasis is not meant to imply that the advantages of clinical-social research are limited to the psychotherapy domain. As illustrated in many chapters of this volume, basic research on the attribution, development, and maintenance of maladaptive behavior patterns is also resulting in the specification of social psychological processes that are relevant to a variety of clinical and mental health issues. Indeed, Brehm and Smith (Chapter 1 of this volume) have noted that the most active area of integrative work currently is that concerning the development and maintenance of maladaptive behaviors.

Whatever the reasons for or benefits that may derive from the integration of clinical and social psychology, it must be recognized that such an approach will not be met with ready acceptance. The reasons for this are several. To begin with, an integrative approach necessarily requires an extensive knowledge base. Specifically, it demands a refined knowledge of clinical and social psychological theories and the detailed conceptualization and research obtaining in these areas (Harvey & Weary, 1979). Second, many social and clinical psychologists may believe that the kinds of behaviors and attitudes of concern to the two domains differ widely with respect to such characteristics as affective intensity, generality, and resistance to change. Clinicians familiar with traditional laboratory research in social psychology are likely to view the kinds of attitudes and behaviors targeted for change as "easy pickings" compared with the entrenched, tenacious, complex, and emotionally charged problems seen in the consulting room, clinic, and hospital. Certainly from most conventional perspectives, students' attitudes toward the legal drinking age and depressed persons' derogatory self-characterizations are sufficiently discrepant in terms of "depth" and embeddedness in the personality to all but preclude consideration of their possible generic similarities. Moreover, conventional perspectives would be unlikely to foster an appreciation of the commonalities between laboratory manipulations and therapeutic interventions. When confronting the kinds of anguished concerns that prompt the search for professional help, clinicians are likely to regard procedures such as counterattitudinal advocacy or effort justification as having the force of a toy pistol when compared with the presumed potency of dream interpretation, aversive conditioning, implosion, and unconditional positive regard. Third, for social psychologists, serious attention to clinical problems may entail some obvious short-term drawbacks. Research with clinical as opposed to student populations typically requires more time for the recruitment and scheduling of subjects, greater ingenuity in dealing with matters of control and standardization of procedures, and greater tolerance for delays and interruptions necessitated by various crises and clinical exigencies.

In addition to the obstacles mentioned above, Sanford (1976) has noted a problem encountered in most integrative endeavors. Specifically, he has argued that "the academic man or woman is less often taken up with satisfying curiosity than with gaining recognition in his or her professional field, less concerned with deepening human understanding than with enhancing the status and power of a chosen discipline." We firmly believe, however, that if psychology is to contribute to the solution of complex human behavior problems, it will be necessary for psychologists to forge links between heretofore disparate lines of inquiry and to work against the continued domination of disciplinary parochialism.

References

Carson, R. C. *Interaction concepts of personality.* Chicago: Aldine, 1969.

Frederiksen, N. Toward a taxonomy of situations. *American Psychologist*, 1972, *27*, 114–123.

Gibbs, J. C. The meaning of ecologically oriented inquiry in contemporary psychology. *American Psychologist*, 1979, *34*, 127–140.

Goldfried, M. R. Toward the delineation of therapeutic change principles. *American Psychologist*, 1980, *35*, 991–999.

Goldstein, A. P. *Psychotherapeutic attraction.* New York: Pergamon Press, 1971.

Goldstein, A. P., Heller, K., & Sechrest, L. B. *Psychotherapy and the psychology of behavior change*. New York: Wiley, 1966.

Harvey, J. H., & Weary, G. The integration of social and clinical psychology training programs. *Personality and Social Psychology Bulletin*, 1979, *5*, 511–515.

Kaplan, A. *The conduct of inquiry: Methodology for behavioral science*. San Francisco: Chandler, 1964.

Kazdin, A. E. Evaluating the generality of findings in analogue therapy research. *Journal of Consulting and Clinical Psychology*, 1978, *46*, 673–686.

Koch, S. Epilogue. Some trends of study I. In S. Koch (Ed.), *Psychology: A study of a science* (Vol. 3). New York: McGraw-Hill, 1959.

McLemore, C. W., & Benjamin, L. S. Whatever happened to interpersonal diagnosis? A psychosocial alternative to DSM-III. *American Psychologist*, 1979, *34*, 17–34.

Mirels, H. L., & McPeek, R. W. Self-advocacy and self-esteem. *Journal of Consulting and Clinical Psychology*, 1977, *45*, 1132–1138.

Moos, R. H. Conceptualizations of human environments. *American Psychologist*, 1973, *28*, 652–665.

Moos, R. H. *Evaluating treatment environments: A social ecological approach*. New York: Wiley, 1974.

Petrinovich, L. Probabilistic functionalism: A conception of research method. *American Psychologist*, 1979, *34*, 373–390.

Proshansky, H. M. An environmental psychologist's perspective on the interdisciplinary approach in psychology. In J. H. Harvey (Ed.), *Cognition, social behavior and the environment*. Hillsdale, N.J.: Erlbaum, 1981.

Sanford, N. Will psychologists study human problems? *American Psychologist*, 1965, *20*, 192–202.

Sanford, N. Graduate education then and now. *American Psychologist*, 1976, *31*, 756–764.

Sells, S. B. Dimensions of stimulus situations which account for behavior variance. In N. S. Endler and D. Magnusson (Eds.), *Interactional psychology and personality*. New York: Wiley, 1976.

Strupp, H. H. Clinical psychology, irrationalism, and the erosion of excellence. *American Psychologist*, 1976, *31*, 561–571.

Strupp, H. H., & Bergin, A. E. Some empirical and conceptual bases for coordinated research in psychotherapy. *International Journal of Psychiatry*, 1969, *7*, 18–90.

AUTHOR INDEX

Aaronson, B., 244, 259
Abbey, A, 156, 157, 160, 162, 167, 277, 283
Abelson, R.P., 38, 47, 62, 70, 72, 76
Abramovici, H., 239, 263
Abrams, M.H., 245, 261
Abramson, A.J., 278, 283
Abramson, L.Y., 22, 24, 149, 159, 167, 272, 283
Adams, D., 274, 284
Adams, H.E., 169
Adams, N.E., 131, 149
Adelman, B., 280, 285
Adler, A., 104, 106–13, 123, 124
Aguilera, D., 275, 283
Akpinar, S., 235, 271
Albee, G.W., 199, 209
Albert, S., 209, 280, 283
Allison, A.S., 158, 168
Allison, M.G., 20–22
Alloy, L.B., 149, 159, 167
Allport, G.W., 174, 177
Altman, J.H., 91, 101
Anchin, J.C., 194, 209, 211
Anderson, W.L., 233, 267
Andreasen, A.R., 156, 167
Andrews, F.M., 156, 167
Andreychuk, T., 235, 262
Ansari, F., 236, 268
Ansbacher, H.L., 105, 124
Ansbacher, R.R., 105, 124
Antze, P., 164, 167
Appignanesi, A. 234, 267
Aries, P., 155, 167
Arkes, H.R., 75, 76
Arkin, R.M., 123, 127
Arkowitz, H., 131, 149, 150, 172, 174, 176–78
Arnoff, G., 237, 265
Aronson, E., 182, 192, 198, 209, 214–15, 226, 229, 265
Artiss, K., 106, 124
As, A., 234, 244, 259

Asch, S.E., 154, 167
Ascher, L.M., 236, 260
Astor, M.H., 239, 260
Atkinson, G., 234, 271
AuCoin, J., 274, 283
Austin, A.W., 182, 210
Austin, G., 30, 46
Averill, J.R., 118, 124, 235, 262
Axsom, D., 224–27, 229
Ayllon, T., 20–22

Bachman, L., 272, 283
Bailey, J.R., 233, 261
Bakan, D., 235, 260
Balaban, A., 276, 284
Balaschak, B. 233, 260
Baldridge, B. 37, 47
Bancroft, J.H., 232, 263
Bandler, R.J., 197, 210, 252, 260
Bandura, A., 37, 46, 128, 131, 136, 149, 171, 177, 200, 210, 227, 229
Bank, S., 208, 210
Barabasz, A. 235, 260
Barber, T.X., 231–34, 236–47, 257; 259–63, 268, 269
Bart, P.B., 154, 157, 167
Bar-Tal, D., 167, 169, 283
Barton, R., 90, 92, 96, 102, 148, 151, 159, 169
Bateson, G., 194, 208, 210
Batson, C.D., 21, 22, 24, 117, 119, 124
Bauer, P., 247, 270
Baum, A., 167
Beavin, J., 192, 213
Beck, A.T., 79, 81–83, 86, 88, 91, 92, 101–3, 128, 138, 141, 149, 158, 159, 163, 167, 171, 177
Beck, J.T., 203, 205, 210
Becker, E., 56–57, 70
Becker, R.E., 51, 63, 71

Beckman, L., 51, 69
Beier, E.G., 195, 202, 210
Belknap, I., 106, 124
Bem, D.J., 172, 177, 185, 210, 229, 244, 252, 260, 261
Bender, E.I., 164, 168
Bengtson, V., 274, 284
Benjamin, L.S., 298, 302
Bennett, D.H., 120, 124
Berger, J., 283
Bergin, A.E., 22, 198, 210, 212, 215–17, 229, 230, 300, 302
Berglas, S., 106–11, 114, 121, 122, 124, 126
Berkman, L., 275, 283
Berkowitz, L., 46, 101, 153, 169, 177, 212, 229, 261
Berne, E., 106, 124
Bernheim, H., 242, 261
Bernstein, A., 207, 211
Berscheid, E., 134, 151
Bertrand, A.J.F., 231, 261
Best, A., 156, 167
Beyer, J., 131, 149
Bieber, M.R., 209, 210
Biggs, D.A., 131, 150
Binder, D.M., 131, 150
Binderman, R.M., 245, 261
Bisbee, T.C., 236, 267
Blake, J.B., 51, 70
Blau, P.M., 281, 283
Blitz, B., 246, 261
Blorker, K., 233, 260
Blumberg, H.H., 134, 150
Blumberg, S.R., 22, 23
Bodoric, H.L., 252, 253, 269
Bogart, K., 229
Bolen, D., 200, 211
Bolton, B., 272, 284
Bonoma, T.V., 194, 213
Bordin, E.S., 197, 210
Borgatta, E.F., 284
Borgida, E., 157, 159, 160, 163, 164, 166, 169
Borkman, T., 164, 167
Borkovec, T.D., 131, 150, 173, 178
Bower, G.H., 128, 150
Bowers, K.S., 231, 261
Borman, L.D., 164, 169
Boscolo, L., 194, 202, 212
Bowerman, W.R., 109, 124
Bradley, G.W., 109, 119, 123, 124, 127, 129, 150, 298, 301, 302
Braginski, B., 21, 22, 106, 113, 117, 124
Braginski, D., 21, 22, 106, 113, 117, 124
Braid, J., 231, 261
Brandes, J.M., 239, 263

Brandt, D., 208, 211
Braun, J.R., 210
Braver, S.L., 199, 210
Brazil, K., 246, 270
Brehm, J.W., 11, 15, 19, 22, 217, 218, 230
Brehm, S.S., 9–11, 15–19, 21–24, 217, 218, 228, 229
Brenman, M., 231, 263
Brewer, D., 82, 101
Brickman, P., 67–69, 131, 151, 200, 211
Bridger, W., 222, 229
Brightbill, R., 247, 271
Brockner, J., 133, 138, 150, 152
Brown, J.M., 246, 251, 269
Bruner, J.S., 30, 46
Buchwald, A.M., 92, 101, 141, 149, 150
Bull, C., 274, 283
Burger, J.M., 240, 261
Burgess, A.W., 275, 283
Burgess, E.P., 156, 157, 167
Burish, T.G., 107, 120, 124, 125
Burnam, M., 111, 125
Burrows, G.D., 233, 235, 261, 263, 268
Bushell, J.D., 59, 71
Butler, D., 195–97, 212
Butler, R., 66, 69
Byrne, D., 163, 167

Cacioppo, J.T., 143, 150
Calhoun, K.S., 169
Calverly, D.S., 233, 237, 244, 245, 260
Campbell, D.T., 173, 178
Cantor, N., 29–31, 33–35, 37–39, 42–44, 46, 47, 80, 98, 101
Caplan, G., 275, 283
Carey, R. 275, 283
Carkhuff, R.R., 117, 125, 183, 210
Carlsmith, J.M., 195, 198, 210, 217, 229
Carroll, J.S., 167, 169, 283
Carson, R.C., 9, 22, 73, 76, 298, 301
Carter, W., 240, 247, 269
Cartwright-Smith, J., 252, 265
Carver, C.J., 16, 18, 22, 24, 111, 125
Casey, G.A., 237, 261
Cassel, J., 275, 283
Castles, C., 233, 263
Cecchin, G., 194, 202, 212
Ceely, S.G., 128, 151
Chan, D.W., 79, 90, 102
Chaplin, W., 90, 92, 96, 102, 148, 151, 159, 169
Chapman, J.P., 18, 22
Chapman, L.J., 18, 22
Chaves, J.F., 231, 241, 246, 257, 260, 261, 269
Churchill, N., 241, 269

AUTHOR INDEX

Cialdini, R.B., 196, 199, 210
Claiborn, C.D., 191–93, 198, 209, 210, 212
Clark, G.M., 21, 24
Clark, W.C., 251, 261
Clayton, P.M., 276, 283
Clement, P.W., 222, 230
Clemes, S.R., 252, 261
Cleveland, S.E., 55, 71
Coates, D., 67–69, 155–57, 160–64, 167, 277, 283
Cobb, S., 275, 276, 283
Cochrane, J., 285
Cochrane, R., 15, 22
Coe, W.C., 231–33, 237, 239, 240, 242, 245, 247, 254, 257, 259, 261, 264, 267
Cofer, D.H., 91, 102
Cohen, A.R., 133, 152, 215, 229
Cohen, J., 37, 47, 69
Cohn, E., 62, 67–69
Colby, K.M., 105, 125
Coleman, A., 111, 125
Coleman, R.E., 143, 150
Coleman, T.R., 244, 261
Colleti, G., 65, 66, 69, 70
Collins, B.E., 195, 201, 211, 218, 229
Collison, D.R., 263, 268
Colson, S.E., 57, 70
Conn, J.H., 244, 261
Conn, R.N., 244, 261
Connors, J., 244, 261
Cooley, C.H., 133, 150, 280, 283
Cooper, A., 222, 229
Cooper, J., 215, 218, 220–23, 224–27, 229, 230
Cooper, L.M., 234, 235, 252, 261, 263, 265
Cooper, R.K., 189–91, 213
Corballis, M.C., 235, 262
Corrigan, J.B., 184, 210
Corwin, T.T., 199, 210
Costin, F., 51, 70
Cottrell, N.B., 155, 162, 167
Cox, M.G., 95, 102
Coyne, J.C., 98, 102, 115–16, 124, 125, 156, 157, 160, 162, 163, 168, 277, 283
Craighead, L., 15, 22
Craighead, W.E., 15, 22, 81, 91, 92, 102, 103, 141, 144, 149, 150, 151
Craik, F.I.M., 80, 85, 87, 102
Crowder, J.E., 207, 210
Crandall, R., 157, 159, 163, 164, 166, 169
Crary, W.G., 140, 150
Crawford, H.J., 234, 235, 262, 266
Creaser, J., 147, 152
Cristol, A.H., 10, 24, 215, 227, 230
Cronin, D.M., 233, 262
Crosson, B., 235, 262

Cumming, E. 274, 283
Cummings, N., 69, 70

Dalal, A.S., 245, 260
Danieli, Y., 164, 168
Danser, D.A., 185–86, 213
Darley, J.M., 95, 98, 102, 118, 125
Davidson, P.O., 237, 265
Davis, D.E., 121, 125
Davis, F., 157, 168
Davis, H., 83, 85, 86, 88, 99, 101, 102
Davis, K.E., 109, 114, 126, 185, 211, 276, 284
Davis, S., 234, 262
Davis, W.L., 121, 125
Davison, G.C., 15, 23, 60, 65, 70, 119, 125
Dawson, J.G., 234, 262
Decenteceo, E.T., 15, 23, 120, 125
Deikman, A.J., 244, 262
Deleuze, J.P.F., 231, 236, 238, 242, 262
Dell, D.M., 184, 210
Dembroski, T., 16, 23
DeMonbreun, B.G., 81, 91, 102, 141, 144, 149, 150
Dengrove, E., 237, 239, 262
Denner, B., 71
Dennerstein, L., 233, 261, 263, 268
Denney, D.R., 159, 169
D'Eon, J.L., 234, 235, 237, 242, 243, 247, 253–55, 257, 259, 262, 269, 270
DePaulo, B.M., 67, 70
DePiano, F.A., 237, 267
Depue, R.A., 100, 102, 144, 150
Derman, D., 233, 262
Derry, P.A., 38, 47, 79, 83–91, 98–99, 102
Detre, T., 51, 70
Deutsch, A., 50, 70
Devine, D.A., 19, 23
DeWitt, G.W., 118, 124, 235, 262
Diamond, M.J., 233, 237, 262, 263
Diaz, W.A., 234, 265
Diggory, J., 102
Dingwall, E.J., 236, 262
Dinnerstein, A., 246, 261
Dixon, D.N., 184, 198, 212
Dodds, J.B., 262
Dolby, R.M., 247, 254, 262, 268
Donnelly, E.F., 18, 23
Doughtie, E.B., 82, 101
Douvan, E., 275, 285
Dowd, E., 280, 281, 284
Dowd, J., 282, 283
Doyle, C., 143, 151
Drummond, M., 239, 262
Dubin, T.T., 244, 266

Dubreuil, D.L., 255, 258, 269
Dubrey, R.J., 157, 168
Duffey, R.F., 51, 60, 71
Dumas, R.A., 235, 262
Duncan, D.B., 147, 152
Dunham, H.W., 106, 125
Dunkel-Schetter, C., 155, 156, 163, 164, 170, 277, 285
Dunwoody, R.C., 237, 262
Duval, S., 18, 23, 129, 145, 150, 208, 210
Dweck, C.S., 187, 210

Eames, N., 281, 286
Eastman, C. 156, 168
Ebbesen, E.B., 137, 148, 151
Ebner, E., 51, 70
Edmonston, W.E., Jr., 236, 237, 244, 262
Edwards, J., 273, 274, 283
Efran, J.S., 216, 230
Ehrlichman, H., 235, 262
Einhorn, H.J., 37, 39, 41, 47
Eiser, M.R., 285
Eisler, R.M., 268
Ekeland, T.J., 55, 71
Eliseo, T.S., 235, 263
Ellis, A., 16, 23, 108, 120, 125, 129, 147, 150, 166, 168, 197, 210
Ellsworth, R., 62, 70
Emerson, R.M., 281, 283
Emery, G., 79, 81–82, 101, 138, 150
Engstrom, D.R., 235, 263
Epley, S.W., 155, 162, 167
Epstein, S., 128, 136, 150
Erbaugh, J., 86, 101
Erbeck, J.R., 237, 262
Eshbaugh, R.N., 202, 210
Evans, F.J., 231, 234, 235, 237, 238, 242, 254–57, 259, 263, 265, 266
Evans, M.B., 237, 247, 259, 263
Evenbeck, C., 196, 210

Faria, J.C., 231, 263
Farina, A., 49–52, 54–56, 59, 60, 67, 68, 70, 71, 166, 168
Fazio, R.H., 18, 23, 95, 98, 102, 118, 125, 208, 212
Feather, N.T., 133, 150
Federoff, N., 18, 23
Feld, S. 53, 70
Fenker, R.M., 236, 267
Fentiman, J.R., 59, 71
Ferguson, J.D., 237, 247, 250, 269
Fernald, P.S., 19, 23

Festinger, L., 106, 125, 181–82, 195, 210, 211, 214, 217, 229, 230, 279–80, 283
Fezler, W.D., 233, 239, 265
Field, P.B., 244, 263
Figone, J., 276, 279, 281, 285
Fine, P., 272, 283
Fisch, R., 157, 162, 170, 192–94, 213
Fischer, E.H., 51, 55–56, 60, 67, 68, 70, 166, 168
Fischhoff, B., 28, 41, 47
Fishbein, M., 47, 70, 212
Fisher, J.D., 51, 52, 55–56, 60, 67, 68, 70, 166, 168
Fisher, L.E, 236, 271
Fiske, S.T., 95, 102
Foa, E.B., 73, 76
Foa, V.G., 73, 76
Foenander, G., 235, 263
Fontana, A.F., 106, 113, 125
Formo, A., 285
Forsyth, D.R., 195, 212
Fox, D.A., 51, 70
Francis, W.N., 102
Frank, J.D., 9, 23, 37, 47, 182, 183, 210, 216, 227, 229
Frankel, F.H., 264
Franklin, B., 231, 263
Franks, C.D., 167, 169
Frederiksen, N., 298, 301
Freedman, K., 285
Freeman, S., 285
French, R., 29–31, 33–35, 47
Fretz, B.R., 245, 261
Freud, A., 105, 125
Freud, S., 105, 125, 216, 228, 229
Friedman, M., 111, 125
Friedman, R.J., 167
Frielich, M., 276, 283
Frieze, I.H., 167, 169, 283
Frischholz, E.J., 235, 266
Froland, C., 282, 283
Fromme, A., 276, 285
Fromm, E., 260, 263, 264, 267, 268
Frost, M., 158, 168
Fuchs, K., 239, 263
Fuhriman, A.J., 209, 210
Furst, J., 222, 229
Furst, M.L., 244, 266

Gaes, G.G., 196, 201, 210
Garber, J., 61, 70, 169, 285
Galbraith, G.C., 235, 263
Garfield, S.L., 22, 23, 212, 229
Garrett, J.B., 236, 271
Gastorf, J., 111, 125

AUTHOR INDEX

Gath, D.H., 232, 263
Geis, H., 275, 283
Gelder, M.G., 232, 263
Gelfand, J., 51, 70
George, L., 273, 284
Gerard, H.B., 215, 229
Gergen, K.J., 156, 157, 160, 162, 168
Gessner, T., 106, 125
Getter, H., 51, 55–56, 60, 67, 68, 70, 166, 168
Gewitz, H., 51, 70
Gibbons, D., 233, 263
Gibbons, F.X., 18, 22–24
Gibbs, J.C., 298, 301
Gilbert, J.E., 244, 263
Gill, M.M., 231, 263
Gilligan, S.G., 128, 150
Glaros, A.G., 60, 65, 70
Glaser, K., 164, 168
Glasgow, R., 131, 150, 173, 178
Glass, C.R., 143, 150
Glass, D.C., 16, 23, 111, 125
Glasser, W., 197, 210
Glick, I.O., 157, 168
Glucksberg, S., 35, 47
Godfrey, M., 280, 282, 284
Goethals, G.R., 158, 168, 218, 229
Golding, S.L., 56–57, 70
Golin, S., 160, 163, 164, 168
Goffman, E., 21, 23, 105, 125, 134, 150, 194, 208, 210
Goffman, J., 210
Goldfried, M.R., 15, 23, 120, 125, 300, 301
Goldstein, A.P., 9, 23, 147, 150, 184, 211, 217, 229, 284, 298, 301, 302
Goodman, J.S., 251, 261
Goodnow, J.J., 30, 46
Goodwin, F.K., 18, 23
Gorassini, D., 237, 269
Gordon, J.E., 268
Gordon, R.M., 19, 23, 219, 229
Gordon, S.B., 171, 174, 178
Gorer, G., 156, 168
Gottlieb, J., 231, 234–36, 242, 269, 270
Gould, R., 208, 211
Graham, C., 234, 263
Graham, K.R., 235, 237, 263
Graney, M., 274, 284
Gray, B.L., 185, 212
Green, D., 155, 157–59, 169
Greenberg, R.P., 233, 263
Greenspoon, J., 181, 211
Greenwald, A.G., 128, 150
Gregory, J., 233, 234, 262, 263
Grimes, J.S., 238, 263
Grimm, L.G., 19, 23, 69, 70

Grinder, J. 197, 210
Grosse, K., 106, 113, 125
Grupsmith, E., 235, 271
Guetzkow, H., 167
Guez, J.R., 237, 265
Gunther, M.S., 275, 284
Gur, R.C., 18, 23, 123, 125, 235, 264
Gur, R.E., 235, 264
Gurin, G., 53, 70
Gussow, Z., 164, 168, 169
Gustafson, L.A., 235, 263
Guttentag, M., 283
Guttman, L., 276, 284

Haas, H.I., 132, 150
Habenstein, R.W., 156, 168
Haddad, M.G., 244, 256, 267
Haddock, J., 236, 264
Hahn, K.W., 237, 247, 259, 260
Haley, J., 14, 23, 106, 125, 194, 202, 207, 208, 210, 242, 264
Halikas, J.A., 276, 283
Hall, C.R., 233, 264
Hall, J.C., 231, 261
Halperin, K., 134, 146, 150
Ham, M.W., 237, 238, 240, 241, 244, 260, 264, 269
Hamilton, M., 85–86, 102
Hammen, C.L., 160, 168
Hammer, A.G., 238, 252, 266
Handelsman, M.M., 111–12, 126, 172, 178
Hanson, G.D., 55, 71
Hanson, P.G., 59, 71
Hanusa, B.H., 20, 24, 279, 285
Harris, B., 19, 23, 219, 229
Harris, L., 121, 125
Harrow, M., 51, 70
Hart, E. 264
Hart, J.T., 231, 235, 263, 265
Hartman, S.A., 160, 163, 164, 168
Hartnett, J., 235, 264
Harvey, J.H., 18, 19, 23, 119, 124, 126, 127, 212, 219, 229, 298, 301, 302
Hastorf, A.H., 157, 168
Hatfield, E.C., 244, 264
Hatcher, C., 210
Hays, D., 164, 168
Hechler, P.D., 132, 151
Hedberg, A.G., 234, 264
Heider, F., 106, 125, 172, 178, 211, 229
Heim, M., 157, 169
Heller, K., 9, 23, 184, 211, 217, 229, 275, 276, 284, 298, 302
Henig, R.M., 69

Henley, M.D., 195, 201, 211
Henry, G.W., 50, 71
Henry, W., 274, 283
Herman, C.P., 47
Herman, C.R., 196, 210
Hersen, M., 268
Hewitt, E.C., 249, 258, 269
Higgins, E.T., 47
Higgins, R., 111, 125
Hilgard, E.R., 231, 233–35, 237, 238, 242, 244, 247–49, 252, 255, 259, 264–66, 271
Hilgard, J.R., 234, 235, 249, 264, 265
Hill, C.E., 145, 151
Himelstein, P., 210
Hinchliffe, M.K., 157, 168
Hines, P., 131, 149
Hiscock, M., 235, 264
Hoch, A., 239, 263
Hodges, K.K., 208, 211
Hogarth, R.M., 37, 39, 40, 42, 47
Hogg, E., 131, 151
Hokanson, J.E., 22, 23, 157, 168
Holdridge-Crane, S., 59, 71
Holland, J.L., 131, 151
Hollander, E.P., 154, 168
Hollen, S.I., 102
Hollon, S.D., 138, 151
Holmes, C., 131, 151
Holmes, D.S., 120, 124
Holmstrom, L.L., 275, 283
Holzberg, J.D., 51, 70, 106, 125
Homans, G.C., 281, 284
Hood, R., 18, 23
Hooper, D., 157, 168
Horner, D., 251, 252, 269
Horowitz, L.M., 74, 76
Horton, C., 246, 269
House, P., 155, 157–59, 169
Houston, B.K., 107, 120, 124, 125, 134, 146, 150
Houts, P.S., 51, 70
Howard, L., 147, 152
Howard, M.L., 233, 237, 254, 261, 264
Howes, M.J., 157, 168
Hoyt, M.F., 195, 201, 211
Hoyt, M.G., 218, 229
Hulton, A.J.B., 133, 150
Hurvitz, N., 164, 168

Ickes, W.J., 127, 212
Itil, T.M., 235, 271

Jacklin, C.N., 121, 126
Jackson, D.A., 156, 166, 169, 192, 194, 213

Jackson, D.D., 202, 208, 210
Jackson, D.N., 74, 76, 79, 83, 90, 102
Jacobs, L., 134, 151
Jacobson, L., 118, 126
Jamison, K.R., 275, 284
Janda, R.L., 233, 261
Jenni, M., 17, 23
Joe, V.C., 121, 125
Johnson, D.L., 55, 71, 233, 266
Johnson, E.W., 280, 285
Johnson, H.J., 234, 265
Johnson, L.S., 237, 247–48, 264
Johnson, R.F.Q., 238, 264
Johnston, D.W., 232, 263
Johnston, W.A., 149, 151
Jones, B., 237, 246, 247, 250, 251, 252, 259, 264, 269, 270
Jones, E.E., 106–11, 114, 121, 122, 124, 126, 146, 151, 185, 195, 199, 208, 210
Jones, J.G., 131, 150
Jones, R.G., 16, 23
Jones, S.C., 136, 151
Jourard, S.M., 166, 168
Juhasz, J.B., 241, 267

Kahneman, D., 28, 37, 39, 42, 45, 47, 75, 76
Kalle, R.J., 196, 201, 210
Kallman, F.J., 48, 70
Kaloupek, D., 131, 150
Kandel, H.J., 20–21, 22
Kanfer, F.H., 19, 23, 171, 178, 284
Kanter, N., 120, 126
Kaplan, A., 298, 302
Kaplan, H.B., 107, 126
Karoly, P. 22
Karst, T., 120, 127
Karuza, J., 67–69
Kasl, S., 276, 283
Kastenbaum, R.J., 155, 168, 284
Katz, A.H., 164, 168
Katz, M.M., 167
Katz, N.W., 233, 265
Kazdin, A.E., 9–10, 15, 23, 297, 302
Keefe, F.J., 171, 174, 178
Keefer, K.E., 131, 151
Kelley, H.H., 28, 47, 106, 114, 126, 172, 178, 185, 192, 195–97, 208, 211, 212, 229
Kelly, G.A., 73, 76
Kelly, R.J., 139–40, 152
Kemp, B., 276, 284
Kendall, P.C., 102, 138, 151
Kendell, R.E., 155, 168
Kent, D., 284
Kent, R.N., 173, 178

AUTHOR INDEX

Kerr, W.D., 51, 70, 276, 284
Kessler, S., 209
Kidd, R., 127, 212
Kidder, L., 67–68, 69
Kiesler, D.J., 193–195, 199, 207, 209, 211
Kihlstrom, J.F., 47, 83, 88, 100, 102, 231, 234, 242, 252, 254–57, 259, 263, 265
Kilbourne, L., 233, 263
Kimball, 275
King, P., 276, 284
Kinney, J.M., 233, 265
Kirker, W.S., 80, 83, 85, 87, 92, 98, 100, 103, 128, 151
Kivett, V., 273, 284
Klatt, E.N., 160, 163, 164, 168
Kleck, R.E., 157, 168, 252, 265
Klein, E.B., 106, 113, 125
Klein, Z.E., 14, 23
Kleinhaus, M., 239, 263
Klemmack, D., 273, 274, 283
Kligfield, B., 156, 168
Klinger, E. 268
Klir, G.J., 187, 211
Klyver, N.W., 121, 126
Knox, V.J., 248, 249, 265
Kobayashi, K., 233, 237, 261
Koch, S., 298, 302
Koenig, K.P., 173, 178
Koocher, G.P., 132, 151
Kopel, S.A., 65, 66, 69, 171, 172, 174, 176–78
Korman, A.K., 139, 151
Kovacs, M., 82, 102
Kovitz, D.M., 237, 265
Kramer, M., 37, 47
Krane, R.V., 143, 153
Krantz, S., 160, 168
Krasner, L., 171, 178
Kroger, W.S., 233, 239, 265
Krupp, G.R., 156, 168
Kucera, H., 102
Kuhn, T.S., 29, 47
Kuiper, N.A., 38, 47, 79, 80, 82–100, 102, 103, 128, 151
Kukla, A., 187, 213
Kukla, R., 275, 285

L'Abate, L., 202, 211
Lahoda, R., 247, 270
Lambert, M.J., 215, 217, 229
Lamers, W.M., 156, 168
Lamiell, J.T., 121, 126
Land, J.M., 233, 263
Landrum, G.C., 22, 23
Lang, G., 237, 247, 268

Langer, E.J., 19–20, 23, 24, 38, 47, 62, 66, 70–72, 76, 278, 279, 284
Lanzetta, J.T., 252, 265
Larson, R.W., 208, 211, 274, 281, 284
Latta, W.D., 235, 268
Laur, E., 235, 262
Laurence, J., 244, 267
Lawrence, D.H., 181, 211
Lawton, M., 274, 284
Laxer, R.M., 81, 91, 102
Lazarus, A.A., 237, 271
Leary, M.R., 196, 212
Leary, T., 73, 74, 76
Lefcourt, H.M., 121, 126, 131, 151
Leibovitz, M.P., 235, 263
Leibowitz, H.W., 236, 237, 265, 266
Lemon, B., 274, 284
Lennard, H.L., 207, 211
Lenney, E., 234, 262
Leonard, C.F., 246, 268
Lerner, M.J., 69, 71, 162, 168
Leutgert, M.J., 147, 152
Levine, D., 178, 211, 229
Levine, L., 106, 113, 125
Levitt, E.E., 237, 265
Levy, A., 196, 210
Levy, L.H., 164, 166, 169
Lewin, K., 9, 187, 211
Lewis, K.N., 184, 210
Lewinsohn, P.M., 90, 92, 96, 98, 102, 103, 148, 151, 155, 157, 159, 168
Lewis, D., 220, 230
Lewis, E., 106, 113, 125
Liberman, R.P., 156, 164, 169
Lichtenstein, E., 131, 149
Lichtenstein, S., 28, 41, 47
Lieberman, M.A., 169
Lindemann, E., 166, 169
Linder, D.E., 215, 218, 230
Linehan, M., 120, 125
Linder, D.E., 199, 210
Lindsley, O.R., 181, 211
Lindzey, G., 265
Linsenmeier, J.A.W., 131, 151
Lipsher, D.H. 37, 46
Lishman, W.A., 81, 88, 92, 93, 99, 102
Little, B.R., 73, 76
Litwak, E., 275, 284
Lloyd, B.B., 76
Lloyd, C.G., 88, 92, 93, 99, 102
Lloyd, D.L., 160–64, 167
Lloyds, B.B., 47
Lobitz, W.C., 82, 96, 102
Loeb, A., 102, 229
Loevinger, J., 74, 76

Lohmann, N., 274, 284
London, H.S., 178
London, P., 233–35, 262, 263, 265
Lopez, F.G., 189–92, 203–4, 211, 213
Lorge, I., 131, 151
Lowe, C.M., 199, 211
Lowery, C.R., 139, 152, 159, 169
Lubin, B., 82, 83, 101, 103
Luikart, C., 273, 274, 284
Lundy, R.M., 236, 237, 265, 266
Lunghi, M.E., 81, 91, 92, 96, 103
Lunneborg, P.W., 245, 265
Lyall, W.A., 285

MacBride, A., 276, 285
Macdonald, H., 235, 237, 247–48, 249, 264, 266
Mac Elveen-Hoehn, P., 275, 284
Madaras, G.R., 252, 260
Maddison, D., 276, 284
Maehr, M.L., 132, 150, 151
Maccoby, E.E., 121, 126
MacDonald, M.R., 90–98, 102
MacDougall, J., 16, 23
MacIntosh, S., 207, 211
Madrazo-Peterson, R., 63, 71
Mah, C.D., 234, 235, 259, 262, 269
Maher, B.A., 238, 264
Mancuso, J.C., 128, 151
Mandel, N.M., 131, 151
Manis, M., 51, 70
Mann, W., 280, 282, 284
Marcia, J.E., 216, 230
Markman, H., 208, 210
Markus, H., 38, 47, 80, 92, 98, 101, 103, 128, 151
Marlatt, A., 111, 125
Marris, R., 157, 169
Marshall, G.D., 264
Martin, J.S., 244, 266
Martin, P.J., 147, 151
Marz, B., 119, 124
Masters, J.C., 216, 220, 230
Mathews, A.M., 232, 263
Mathewson, G.C., 215, 229
Mathios, A.D., 136–37, 141–42, 152
Mathison, J., 156, 169
Matross, R.P., 184, 185–86, 212
Maurice, W.L., 276, 283
McAllister, D.A., 19, 22
McAmmond, D.M., 237, 265
McCaul, K.D., 119, 127
McClellan, G.E., 234, 265
McCloskey, M.E., 35, 47
McCluskey, N.G., 284

McConkey, K.M., 238, 239, 241, 265, 268
McDonald, P.J., 235, 266
McDonald, R.D., 238, 265
McGovern, K., 131, 149
McGuire, W.J., 245, 265
McInnis, T.L., 51, 71
McKaul, K.D., 159, 169
McKay, J., 281, 284
McLemore, C.W., 298, 302
McPeake, J.D., 233, 234, 240, 241, 243, 247, 265, 269, 270
McPeek, R., 299, 302
McTavish, D.G., 121, 126
Mead, G.H., 133, 151, 280, 284
Medin, D., 30, 32, 47
Meehl, P.E., 72, 76
Meichenbaum, D., 17, 23, 171, 178, 246, 265
Meinz, R., 235, 262
Melei, J., 234, 265
Melzack, R., 246, 266
Mendelson, M., 86, 101
Mendonca, P., 218–20, 226, 230
Menninger, K., 216, 230
Mensing, J., 132, 151
Merluzzi, T.V., 143, 150
Messi, L.A., 208, 211
Messick, J., 275, 283
Mezzich, J., 29–31, 33–35, 47
Michaels, G.Y., 208, 211
Michela, J.L., 208, 212
Milgram, S., 59, 70
Milhouse, R., 274, 284
Miller, A.G., 70
Miller, G., 29, 47
Miller, D.T., 123, 126
Miller, P.E., 37, 44, 46, 268, 274, 285
Miller, R.J., 237, 266
Miller, R.L., 167, 200, 211
Miller, R.S., 196, 212
Millon, T., 74, 76
Mills, J., 214–15, 218, 226, 229
Minton, H.L., 121, 126
Minuchin, S., 202, 211
Mirels, H.L., 199, 210, 299, 302
Mischel, W., 30–31, 35, 46, 80, 90, 92, 96, 98, 101, 102, 137, 148, 151, 159, 169
Mitchell, K.M., 169
Mock, J., 86, 101
Monroe, S.M., 100, 102, 144, 150
Monty, R.A., 285
Moos, R.H., 207, 211, 298, 302
Mordkoff, A.M., 235, 271
Morgan, A.H., 247–48, 249, 259, 264, 265, 266
Morgan, C.D., 237, 265
Morgan, C.M., 233, 234, 236, 237, 266

AUTHOR INDEX

Morrison, J.K., 51, 59, 63, 71
Morse, D.R., 244, 266
Mullens, D., 237, 238, 240, 241, 269
Munroe, R.L., 105, 126
Munz, K., 160, 163, 164, 168
Murphy, D.L., 18, 23
Murphy, M.D., 256, 266
Musante, L., 16, 23
Myers, J., 101, 103
Mylar, J.L., 222, 230

Nace, E.P., 252, 266
Nadler, A., 67, 70
Naficy, A., 218, 229
Nash, D.L., 135, 152
Nashby, W., 83, 88, 100, 102
Natzger, S., 132, 151
Naun, R., 207, 212
Nee, J.C.M., 235, 270
Neisser, U., 73, 76
Nelson, R.E., 81, 92, 103, 141, 144, 151, 173, 178
Nevid, J.S., 51, 71
Newman, J.B., 236, 266
Nichols, J.G., 123, 126
Nichols, R.C., 131, 151
Nightingale, M.E., 234, 270
Nisbett, R.E., 28, 37, 39, 41, 43, 45, 47, 73, 75, 76, 119, 127, 146, 151, 157, 159, 160, 163, 164, 166, 169, 172, 173, 178, 195, 208, 211, 222, 230, 252, 266
Norris, D.L., 237, 266
Northcroft, G.B., 157, 168
Notarius, C., 210
Novaco, R., 17, 23
Novak, D.W., 69, 71
Nowlis, D., 235, 264
Nunnally, J.C., 49, 51, 58, 59, 71

O'Brien, G., 131, 150
Obstoj, I., 238, 239, 241, 266, 268
O'Connell, D.N., 235, 237, 263, 266
O'Grady, K.E., 234, 266
Ommundsen, R., 55, 71
Ono, H., 157, 168
Orne, E.C., 235, 242, 254, 255, 257, 265
Orne, M.T., 235, 237, 238, 242, 252, 254, 255, 257, 265, 266
Ortmeyer, D., 37, 47
Orvis, B.T., 195–97, 212
Osberg, T.M., 132, 142, 152
Osborne, D., 140, 152
Oskamp, S., 37, 47

Ostvold, S., 244, 259
Overly, M., 237, 265

Page, W., 140, 152
Paivio, A.V., 83, 103
Palazzoli, M.S., 194, 202, 212
Paldi, E., 239, 263
Palmore, E., 273, 274, 284
Parker, M.D., 233, 261
Parkes, C.M., 157, 168
Parrish, M., 236, 237, 265, 266
Paskewitz, D.A., 235, 266
Pasnau, R.O., 275, 284
Passer, M.W., 208, 212
Patton, M.J., 209, 210
Paul, G.L., 51, 71, 237, 247, 259, 266
Paulhus, D., 259, 267
Pawlak, A.E., 234, 235, 237, 242, 243, 247, 253–55, 259, 262, 269, 270
Payne, J.W., 169
Pennebaker, J., 111, 125
Peplau, L.A., 157, 169
Perkins, S., 112, 122, 126
Perlmutter, L.C., 285
Perin, C.T., 233, 260
Perry, C.W., 234, 235, 238, 239, 244, 266–68
Peterson, D., 276, 284
Peterson, J., 274, 284
Petrinovich, L., 297, 299, 302
Petrus, J., 276, 284
Petrusic, W., 237, 251, 269, 270
Phares, E.J., 121, 126
Phillips, J.S., 171, 178
Phillips, L., 45, 47
Pittman, T.S., 187, 212
Picciotto, S.R., 157, 168
Pihlblad, C., 274, 284
Pistole, D.D., 234, 265
Planas, M., 242, 256, 267
Platman, S.R., 74, 76
Plotkin, W.B., 244, 267
Plutchik, R., 74, 76
Polwy, J., 143, 151
Porter, J.W., 236, 267
Post, R.D., 82, 96, 102
Poulton, E.C., 251, 259, 267
Prata, G., 194, 202, 212
Press, S., 14, 24
Price, R.H., 71
Proshansky, H., 298, 299, 302
Pryor, J.B., 18, 23
Puckett, J., 280, 285
Puff, C.R., 256, 267
Purkey, W.W., 132, 151

Rabinowitz, V.C., 67–69
Rabkin, J.G., 49, 71
Radtke, H.L. (Radtke-Bodorik, H.L.), 234, 237, 241–245, 247, 250, 252, 253–56, 258, 259, 267, 269, 270
Raginsky, B.B., 232, 267
Raines, J., 216, 230
Rappaport, J., 56–57, 70
Raskin, D.E., 14, 23, 156, 169
Raven, B.H., 183, 212
Ray, A., 173, 178
Read, S.J., 137, 148, 152
Reed, H., 157, 159, 163, 164, 166, 169
Regina, E.G., 235, 268
Rehm, L.P., 138, 139, 141, 149, 151, 152
Reich, L.H., 237, 263
Reid, D., 279, 284
Reid, J., 173, 178
Reinehr, R.C., 145, 151
Reis, H.T., 235, 271
Regan, D.T., 208, 212
Reyher, J., 235, 264, 267
Reyna, L.J., 222, 230
Ridley, 106, 125
Riggs, J., 38–39, 47
Rimm, D.C., 216, 220, 230
Ring, K., 21, 22, 59, 71, 106, 113, 125
Ritchie, G., 234, 259, 269
Rittman, J.D., 229
Rivers, S.M., 232, 234, 235, 237, 238, 240, 241, 243, 269, 270
Rizley, R.C., 82, 103
Roberts, J.F., 157, 168
Rodin, J., 19–20, 23, 24, 66, 70, 71, 278–79, 284
Roessler, R., 272, 285
Rogers, C.R., 197, 209, 212
Rogers, J., 276, 279, 281, 285
Rogers, P.J., 103
Rogers, T.B., 80, 83, 85, 87–89, 92, 98, 100, 102, 103, 128, 151
Rohrbaugh, M., 14, 24
Rohrer, K., 280, 285
Rollman, G.B., 251, 259, 267
Roman, P., 167
Rosch, E., 28, 30, 45, 47, 73, 76
Rosen, E., 173, 178
Rosen, G.M., 173, 178
Rosen, J., 14, 24
Rosenbaum, M., 168, 246, 267
Rosenberg, S.E., 132, 139, 152
Rosenblatt, P.C., 156, 166, 169
Rosenfield, D., 109, 123, 124, 126
Rosenman, R., 111, 125
Rosenthal, R., 118, 126

Ross, L., 28, 37, 39, 41, 43, 45, 47, 73, 75, 76, 155, 157–59, 169, 192, 212
Ross, M., 128, 151
Ross, S., 232, 241, 243, 270
Rossiter, T., 233, 260
Roth, C.H., 147, 152
Roth, D., 138, 139, 144, 151
Rothaus, P., 55, 71
Rotter, J.B., 67, 71, 121, 126
Rubin, B.M., 216, 230
Rubin, D.B., 118, 126
Rubin, M.E., 210
Rubin, R.D., 167, 169
Ruge, D., 284
Rush, A.J., 79, 81–82, 101, 138, 150
Rushton, J.P., 70
Ruskin, P.M., 234, 265
Russell, D., 157, 169
Ruzicka, M.R., 207, 212

Sacco, W.P., 22, 23
Sachs, L.B., 233, 265, 267
Sackeim, H.A., 18, 23, 123, 125, 259, 267
Salter, A. 222, 230
Salzberg, H.C., 237, 267
Saltzman, C., 147, 152
Sanford, N., 298, 301, 302
Sarason, D., 124
Sarbin, T.R., 231, 232, 235, 236, 241, 242, 245, 247, 257, 259, 261, 267
Satir, V., 197, 210
Saunders, A., 233, 263
Sawyer, J., 74, 76
Schacht, S., 41, 47
Schachter, S., 155, 160, 162, 169, 172, 173, 178, 252, 266
Schaefer, E.S., 74, 76
Schaffer, M., 157, 169
Schalon, C.L., 133, 152
Scharf, B., 247, 271
Scheff, T.J., 54, 71, 166, 169
Scheier, M.F., 18, 24
Schlenker, B.R., 194, 195, 212, 213
Schmidt, A., 21, 24, 117, 119, 126
Schmidt, L.D., 183–85, 212, 213
Schneider, F.W., 121, 126
Schoeneman, T.J., 133, 135, 152
Schofield, W., 182, 183, 212
Schroeder, D.J., 18, 22, 23
Shuell, T.J., 256, 268
Schultz, R., 19–20, 24, 164, 169
Schulz, D., 247, 270
Schulz, R., 278–80, 282, 285

AUTHOR INDEX

Schur, E.M., 126
Schuster, P., 247, 270
Schuyler, B.A., 254, 267
Schwartz, J., 31, 46
Scott, D.S., 245, 246, 268
Scott, N.A., 261
Seay, B., 234, 262
Sechrest, L.B., 9, 23, 184, 211, 217, 229, 298, 302
Segal, R.M., 91, 92, 103
Seligman, M.E.P., 22, 24, 61, 66, 67, 70, 71, 169, 278, 283, 285
Sells, S.B., 298, 302
Semmel, A., 22, 24
Sextus, C., 236, 268
Seymour, G., 274, 285
Shabinsky, M.A., 253, 270
Shakow, D., 18, 24, 113, 126
Shaw, B.F., 79, 81–82, 101, 103, 138, 150
Shaw, D.A., 157, 169
Shaw, M., 29, 42, 43, 45, 47
Shaw, P.M., 232, 263
Sheehan, D.V., 235, 268
Sheehan, P.W., 238, 239, 241, 244, 247, 254, 259, 261, 262, 265, 266, 268
Sheldon, D.M., 164, 169
Shenkel, R.J., 21, 24, 117, 119, 126, 134, 139, 146, 150, 152, 158, 169
Sheras, P.L., 9, 24
Sherif, M.A., 154, 169
Sherman, S., 56–57, 70
Sherwood, S., 284
Shipman, W.B., 147, 150
Shor, R.E., 232, 234, 237, 252, 259, 260, 263–68
Shrauger, J.S., 128, 129, 131–33, 136–42, 149, 151, 152
Sicoly, F., 128, 151
Sigall, H., 208, 211
Silver, M.J., 234, 268
Silver, R.L., 156, 157, 166, 169, 276, 279, 285
Silverman, I., 140, 152
Simmons, C.H., 162, 168
Simon, H.A., 29, 47
Simon, P., 104
Simons, P., 71
Simonson, N.R., 217, 229
Singer, J.E., 167, 173, 178
Skinner, B.F., 181–82
Slage, R.W., 236, 267
Sloane, R.B., 10, 24, 215, 227, 230
Slovic, P., 28, 41, 47
Smith, E., 29–35, 47
Smith, G.M., 235, 268
Smith, J., 38, 47, 51, 71, 101, 103, 120, 125

Smith, J.R., 238, 265
Smith, T.W., 15–18, 22–24, 111–12, 122, 126, 172, 178
Smith-DiJulio, K., 275, 284
Snadowsky, A., 168
Snyder, C.R., 15, 21, 24, 111–12, 117, 119, 122, 126, 134, 138, 139, 146, 150, 152, 158, 169, 172, 178
Snyder, E., 273, 285
Snyder, Mark, 28, 37–39, 45, 47, 118, 126
Snyder, Melvin L., 106, 109, 123, 126, 192, 212
Sobel, D., 30
Sobieszek, B.I., 245, 271
Sobol, M.P., 15, 22
Solomon, H., 131, 151
Sorman, P.B., 133, 152
Sorrentino, R.M., 70
Spanos, N.P., 231–60, 262, 264–70
Spiegel, D., 266
Spiegel, H., 235, 266, 270
Spielberger, C.D., 124
Spillane, J., 243, 270
Spitzer, S.E., 235, 262
Spreitzer, E., 273, 285
Stacher, G., 247, 270
Stainbrook, E., 154, 169
Stam, H.J., 234, 236, 237, 239, 241–44, 246, 248, 251, 253–59, 268, 270
Stampfl, T., 220, 230
Stanley, J.C., 173, 178
Stannard, D.E., 167
Staples, F.R., 10, 24, 215, 227, 230
Starker, S., 240, 270
Steadman, C., 234, 262
Steffen, J.J., 22
Steiner, I., 70
Steiner, J.D., 212
Steinman, R., 164, 169
Stern, D.B., 235, 270
Stern, L., 65, 66, 70
Sternberg, R.J., 256, 270
Sterne, A.L., 147, 151
Stephan, W.G., 109, 123, 124, 126
Stevens, R., 268
St. Jean, R.L., 240, 259, 261
Stone, N., 131, 150, 173, 178
Stivers, M., 11–15, 21, 24
Stollak, G.E., 208, 211
Storms, M.D., 119, 127, 159, 169, 173, 178
Stotland, E., 133, 152
Straus, E., 208, 212
Strong, S.R., 181, 183–89, 197, 198, 203–5, 209, 210, 212, 213, 218, 230
Strowig, R.W., 131, 150

Struening, E.L., 62, 69, 283
Strupp, H.H., 216, 230, 297, 299, 300, 302
Struthers, S., 131, 151
Suinn, R.M., 140, 152
Sullivan, H.S., 73, 194, 213
Suls, J.M., 167
Svorad, D., 235, 264
Swann, W.B., 38, 47, 118, 126, 137, 138, 140, 148, 152
Switras, J.E., 235, 270
Syme, S., 275, 283
Szasz, T., 106, 127

Tabor, L.E., 135, 152
Talbert, D., 280, 285
Talone, J.M., 234, 262
Tart, C.T., 243, 244, 264, 270, 271
Teasdale, J.D., 278, 283
Tedeschi, J.T., 194, 196, 201, 210, 213
Teevan, R., 111, 125
Tellegen, A., 234, 271
Tennen, H., 14, 24
Terbovic, M.L., 128, 132, 138, 149, 152
Terrill, L.A., 157, 168
Terry, S., 53, 71
Teta, D.C., 51, 71
Thomas, E., 133, 152
Thompson, G., 273, 274, 285
Thompson, M., 276, 284
Thorkelson, K.E., 271
Thorley, S., 133, 152
Thorn, I., 276, 285
Timor-Tritsch, I. 239, 263
Tinsley, D.J., 131, 150
Toner, M., 237, 265
Toomey, B., 280, 285
Tracy, G.S., 164, 168, 169
Traunstein, D.M., 164, 169
Trexler, L., 120, 127
Trice, H., 167
Tsujimoto, R.N., 60, 65, 70
Tucker, S.J., 274, 275, 285
Tulving, E., 80, 85, 87, 102, 255, 256, 259, 271
Turner, J., 198, 210
Turner, L., 129, 152
Tversky, A., 28, 37, 39, 42, 45, 47, 75, 76

Uhlenhuth, E.H., 147, 152
Ulett, G.A., 235, 271
Ullmann, L.P., 51, 70, 171, 178
Underwood, G., 268
Unruh, W.R., 101, 102

Vachon, M.L.S., 275, 285
Valach, M., 187, 211
Valins, S., 60, 65, 70, 119, 127, 172, 173, 178
VanDerVeen, F., 207, 213
Varela, J.A., 20–21, 24
Vargo, J., 274, 285
Vash, C., 276, 284
Vasta, R., 138, 152
Velten, E., 143, 152
Verhaeghe, H., 196, 213
Veroff, J., 53, 70, 275, 285
vonBaeyer, C., 22, 24
Von Bertalanffy, 187, 192, 213
Von Salzer, C., 276, 285
Vygotsky, L.S., 30, 47

Wainer, H., 75, 76
Waldman, I.N., 18, 23
Walker, K.N., 276, 285
Walker, N.S., 236, 271
Walker, W.L., 276, 284
Wall, R.L., 173, 178
Wallace, B., 236, 271
Walsh, B., 238, 239, 267
Walsh, R.P., 156, 166, 169
Walster, E., 134, 151
Wambach, C.A., 189–91, 203–4, 211, 213
Ward, C.H., 86, 101
Ward, S.R., 191, 210
Watson, N., 273, 285
Watzlawick, P., 157, 162, 170, 192–94, 202, 213
Weakland, J., 157, 162, 170, 192–94, 210, 213
Weary, G., 109, 119, 123, 124, 127, 129, 150, 298, 301, 302
Webster, M., 245, 271
Weeks, G., 202, 211
Wehler, R., 69, 71
Weick, K.E., 182, 213
Weidner, G., 111, 127
Weiman, A.L., 259, 267
Weinberg, L., 15, 23
Weinberg, S.K., 106, 210, 125
Weinberger, A., 235, 262
Weiner, B., 187, 213
Weiner, Y., 132, 151
Weinstein, M.S., 157, 169
Weinstein, N.D., 149, 152
Weintraub, M., 91, 92, 103
Weisman, A.D., 275, 282, 285
Weiss, R.S., 157, 168
Weitzenhoffer, A.M., 231, 233, 241, 242, 271
Weitzenhoffer, G.B., 233, 271
Welkowitz, J., 37, 47

AUTHOR INDEX

Weller, D., 274, 285
Wellisch, D.K., 275, 284
Wener, A., 141, 149, 152
Wexler, P., 164, 170
Wheeler, L., 235, 271
Whipple, K., 10, 24, 215, 227, 230
Whitcher, S.T., 67, 70
White, G.M., 74, 76
White, M.D., 14, 24
White, R.W., 136, 152, 231, 242, 271
Whitley, B.E., 245, 271
Whitman, J.R., 51, 71
Whitman, R.M., 37, 47
Wicklund, R.A., 18, 23, 106, 127, 129, 145, 150, 152, 210, 213, 215, 217, 218, 229, 230
Wilder, S., 234, 267
Williams, D., 235, 262
Willis, R.H., 154, 168
Wills, T.A., 145, 146, 153
Wilson, A.R., 143, 153
Wilson, G.T., 173, 178
Wilson, K.G., 121, 126
Wilson, S.C., 233, 240, 261
Wilson, T.D., 222, 230
Winett, R.A., 9, 24
Wishnov, B., 156, 157, 160, 162, 168
Withey, S.B., 156, 167
Wittenborn, J.R., 91, 101, 102
Wolff, E., 235, 271
Wolfgang, G.L., 160, 163, 164, 168
Wollersheim, J., 17, 23, 224, 230
Wolosin, M., 216, 230
Wolpe, J., 222, 230, 237, 271

Woodward, J.A., 236, 267
Worchel, S., 9, 24
Worden, J.W., 275, 282, 285
Wortman, C.B., 155–57, 160, 162, 163, 164, 166, 167, 169, 170, 276, 277, 279, 283, 285
Wothington, E.L., 246, 271
Wright, B.A., 274, 286
Wright, R.M., 203–6, 213
Wrightsman, L.S., 155, 170
Wyatt, R.J., 18, 23
Wylie, R.C., 80, 103, 109, 127

Yaryan, R.B., 217, 230
Yoppi, B., 208, 210
Yorkston, N.J., 9, 24, 215, 227, 230
Youngren, M.A., 90, 98, 103

Zamansky, 247, 264, 271
Zander, A., 133, 152
Zanna, M., 47, 227, 230
Zeiss, A.M., 137, 148, 151
Zelditch, M., 283
Zenmore, R., 281, 286
Ziegler, M., 279, 284
Zigler, E., 45, 47
Zilboorg, S., 50, 71
Zimbardo, P.G., 215, 218, 224, 230
Zimmer, M., 118, 124
Zuckerman, M., 124
Zung, W.W.K., 165, 170

SUBJECT INDEX

Analogue research, 9–10, 143–45
Attributions
  and compliance, 200
  as control strategies, 195
  as defense mechanisms, 196
  in learned helplessness, 278, 281
  manipulation of, 172
  misattribution, 173, 187, 252
  process in hypnosis, 242–45, 252
  and self-handicapping, 109, 119
  therapy, role of, 185–88, 197, 201, 208, 288–90

Behavior modification, 237

Categorization
  descriptive, 28
  prescriptive, 28
  in psychiatric diagnosis, 29–36, 45
Clinical populations
  in laboratory research, 18
  precursor, 15
  use of nonclinical populations in research, 143–45
  use of self-handicapping strategies, 112–14, 117
Cognitive behavior therapy, 147
Cognitive dissonance
  in effort justification, 214
  and implosive therapy, 221
  in therapy, 182, 215–18, 221, 223–27, 288, 290–91

Defense mechanisms
  attributions as, 196
  and hypnosis, 252
  self-handicapping as, 106–9
  symptoms as, 104–5
Depression
  cognitive model of, 81
  and false consensus bias, 157–59

  importance of social validation in, 154–57, 162
  and information processes, 138, 141
  learned helplessness model of, 278–79
  and perception of others, 96
  self-handicapping, use of, 116
  self-schemas in, 83, 98–100

Exchange theory, 281–82

Freedom
  client, 11
  therapist, 12

Gestalt therapy, 202

Implosive therapy, 220–21
Impression management, 105–6, 194
Interaction theory of behavior change
  attributions, role of, 195
  and communication theory, 194–95
  and forced compliance, 195–97, 201
  relationship with other psychological theories, 192
  and therapeutic change, 197, 200

Learned helplessness
  and adjustment, 281
  attribution processes in, 278, 281
  disease beliefs, 67
  theory of, 278–79
Locus of control
  and expectations of control, 67
  in self-handicapping, 121

Medical model. *See also* Mental disorders
  consequences for field of mental health, 57–59
  for patient, 59–61
  for public, 55–57
Mental disorders

history of beliefs about, 49–51
medical model of, 52–54
social learning model of, 52

Objective self-awareness
role of in therapy, 18–19, 145, 208

Paradoxical therapy, 202, 204–5, 207–9
Prototypes, 29
in psychiatric diagnosis, 30–36, 45
of self, 80
Psychological reactance, 12, 14–15

Rational emotive therapy, 120
Role-playing
in analogue research, 10–15
in therapy, 217

Schemas. *See also* Prototypes
definition of, 80, 82
in depression, 82, 83, 91, 98–100
of self, 80, 83
Self-efficacy
and adjustment, 277
role of in therapy, 227
Self-esteem
and adjustment, 277
and competence, 132
following feedback, 139
maintenance in mental patients, 112–14
perceived threat to, 115
and self-evaluation, 138–39
and self-handicapping, 106–9, 111–14
and task performance, 132–33
and Type-A behavior, 111
Self-perception
of competence, 131
and recall of information, 140
role of others in, 133–35
and selective attention, 135–36, 138
in therapy, 145, 227
Self-perception theory
in therapy, 227
Social comparison theory, 106, 279–81
Social learning model. *See also* Mental disorders
consequences of for field of mental health, 27–59
consequences of for patient, 59–61
consequences of for public, 55–57
view of psychopathology, 174
Symbolic interactionism, 133
Systematic desensitization, 216, 239

Therapy. *See also* Behavior modification, Cognitive behavior therapy, Gestalt therapy, Implosive therapy, Paradoxical therapy, Rational emotive therapy
attributions, role of, 185–88, 197, 201, 208, 288–90
choice, role of, 219, 223, 292
cognitive dissonance, role of in, 182, 215–18, 221, 224–27, 288, 290–91
common principles across therapies, 300–301
evaluating effectiveness of, 19, 122, 200
expectations, role of in, 148
misattribution, use of, 159, 187
personal responsibility, role of, 218
problem-solving approach, 175–77
self-focus in, 145
and self-handicapping, 119, 122
self-help groups, use of, 164–65
use of selective information, 143, 147–49
as a social influence process, 182–84
therapist's role, 145–47, 183–84, 198–99, 206, 287
Trait model of personality, 174–75
Type A behavior, 16–18, 111

www.ingramcontent.com/pod-product-compliance
Lightning Source LLC
LaVergne TN
LVHW010337260326
834688LV00036B/743